THE HANDBOOK OF EMPLOYEE BENEFITS

DESIGN, FUNDING, AND ADMINISTRATION

Third Edition

VOLUME II

Edited by Jerry S. Rosenbloom

IRWIN
Professional Publishing
Burr Ridge, Illinois
New York, New York

This symbol indicates that the paper in this book is made from recycled paper. Its fiber content exceeds the recommended minimum of 50% waste paper fibers as specified by the EPA.

Sponsoring editor: Amy Hollands
Project editor: Jane Lightell
Production manager: Ann Cassady
Designer: Heidi J. Baughman
Compositor: Carlisle Communications, Ltd.
Typeface: 11/13 Times Roman
Printer: R. R. Donnelley & Sons Company

Library of Congress Cataloging-in-Publication Data

Rosenbloom, Jerry S.
    The handbook of employee benefits : design, funding, and administration / Jerry S. Rosenbloom.—3rd ed.
        p.   cm.
    Includes index.
    ISBN Vol. 1, 1-55623-483-X   Vol. 2, 1-55623-884-3 (Hardback)
           Vol. 1, 1-55623-503-8   Vol. 2, 1-55623-886-X (Paperback)
           1-55623-887-8 (2 volume set, paperback)
    1. Employee fringe benefits—United States. 2. Employee fringe benefits—Law and legislation—United States. 3. Employee fringe benefits—Taxation—Law and legislation—Unites States. I. Title.
HD4928.N62U6353   1992
331.25'5'0973—dc20   91–40776

Printed in the United States of America

3 4 5 6 7 8 9 0 DOC 9 8 7 6 5 4

PREFACE

Much has taken place in the employee benefits field since the publication of the second edition of *The Handbook of Employee Benefits* in 1988. Dramatic changes have been caused by major new pieces of legislation, and many new employee benefit concepts have been developed and implemented. Moreover, the last several years have witnessed an ever-increasing emphasis on cost containment in all forms of employee benefits. This third edition of *The Handbook* recognizes these fundamental changes with revisions of many of the chapters in the second edition and the addition of chapters covering new and emerging areas in employee benefits. These changes emphasize the basic premise that employee benefits can no longer be considered "fringe benefits" but must be regarded as an integral and extremely important component of an individual's financial security. The most recent U.S. Chamber of Commerce study on employee benefits indicates that, on average, employee benefits account for nearly 40 percent of a worker's total compensation. In light of the ever-increasing importance of benefit plans, those dealing with them must be well versed in the objectives, design, costing, funding, implementation, and administration of such plans.

While *The Handbook of Employee Benefits* is intended for students in the benefits field and for professionals as a handy reference, it can serve as a valuable tool for anyone with an interest in the field in general or in a specific employee benefit topic. *The Handbook* can be used as a reference work for benefit professionals or as a textbook for college courses, professional education, and company training programs. Each chapter of *The Handbook* stands alone and is complete in itself. While this produces some overlap in certain areas, in many cases it eliminates the need to refer to other chapters and provides important reinforcement of difficult concepts.

The chapters of *The Handbook* are structured into 13 parts, each covering a major component of the employee benefit planning process. These are: Part One, The Environment of Employee Benefit Plans; Part Two, Social Insurance Programs; Part Three, Death Benefits; Part Four, Medical and Other Health Benefits; Part Five, Disability Income Plans; Part Six, Other Welfare Benefit Plans; Part Seven, Flexible Benefit Plans; Part Eight, Retirement and Capital Accumulation Plans; Part Nine, Accounting, Funding, and Taxation of Employee Benefit Plans; Part Ten, Employee Benefit Plan Administration; Part Eleven, Employee Benefit Plan Communication; Part Twelve, Employee Benefit Plans for Small Business; and Part Thirteen, Employee Benefit Plan Issues.

The Handbook consists of 63 chapters written by distinguished experts—academics, actuaries, attorneys, consultants, and other benefit professionals—covering all areas of the employee benefits field. Their practical experience and breadth of knowledge provide insightful coverage of the employee benefits mechanism, and the examples presented throughout *The Handbook* illustrate the concepts presented.

The chapters that remain from the second edition have been updated to incorporate legislative and other changes in the field, and several of the chapters from the second edition have been expanded to include related topics such as eldercare. The coverage of certain subjects has been amplified with additional chapters on disability income, flexible benefits, and communication. New chapters have been added on: Risk Concepts and Employee Benefit Planning; Workers' Compensation; Fundamentals of Unemployment Compensation Programs; Health Maintenance Organizations; Preferred Provider Organizations; Managed Care; Long-term Care; Family Leave Programs; Payments for Nonproduction Time, Time Not Worked and Miscellaneous Benefits; Cash Balance Plans; Retirement Plans for Not-for-Profit Organizations; Section 457 Deferred Compensation Plans; Accounting and Financial Reporting for Health and Welfare Plans; Federal Taxation Environment for Welfare Benefit Plans; ERISA Fiduciary Liability Issues and Multiemployer Plans.

In such a massive project, many people provided invaluable assistance, and it would be impossible to mention them all here. Thanks must be extended, however, to the authors of the individual chapters for the outstanding coverage of their subject areas in a comprehensive and readable manner. Special thanks are due to Mr. Everett T. Allen, Jr., a long-time friend who read the entire manuscript and made many constructive comments and suggestions. I would like to thank Dr. Davis

W. Gregg, the former president of The American College, for his encouragement over the years to undertake such a project. Appreciation also must go to my most able assistant Diana Krigelman, who spent many hours on all aspects of the manuscript and handled her duties in her usual totally professional manner.

In a work of this magnitude, it is almost inevitable that some mistakes may have escaped the eyes of the many readers of the manuscript. For these oversights I accept full responsibility and ask the reader's indulgence.

Jerry S. Rosenbloom

CONTRIBUTORS

Bradley J. Allen, Partner, Coopers & Lybrand

Everett T. Allen, Jr., Vice President and Principal, Towers, Perrin, Forster & Crosby, Retired

Mark S. Allen, Consultant, Hewitt Associates

Dwight K. Bartlett III, Visiting Executive Professor, Wharton School, University of Pennsylvania

Burton T. Beam, Jr., CLU, CPCU, Associate Professor of Insurance, The American College

John M. Bernard, Esq., Partner, Ballard Spahr, Andrews & Ingersoll

Melvin W. Borleis, CEBS, Managing Director, William M. Mercer, Incorporated

Sarah H. Bourne, Consultant, Hewitt Associates

Lawrence T. Brennan, FSA, Partner, Kwasha Lipton

Henry Bright, FSA, Vice President, The Wyatt Company

Gregory K. Brown, Esq., Attorney, Keck, Mahin & Cate

Eugene B. Burroughs, CFA, Senior Advisor, The Prudential Asset Management Company, Inc.

Mary A. Carroll, CPCU, CEBS, ARM, Benefits Consultant

Joseph Casey, University of Central Florida

Alan P. Cleveland, Esq., Partner, Sheehan, Phinney, Bass & Green

William M. Cobourn, Jr., Manager, Coopers & Lybrand

Dennis Coleman, Esq., Partner, Kwasha Lipton

Ann Costello, Ph.D., Associate Professor of Insurance, School of Business and Public Administration, University of Hartford

William E. Decker, Partner, Coopers & Lybrand

Douglas R. Divelbiss, Senior Manager, National Office, Ernst & Young

Donald J. Doudna, Ph.D., CLU, CPCU, Director of Insurance Education, State of Iowa, and Executive Vice President, Bryton Management Corporation

Cynthia J. Drinkwater, J.D., Director of Research, International Foundation of Employee Benefit Plans

James C. Fee, Associate Professor of Accountancy, College of Commerce and Finance, Villanova University

Edmund W. Fitzpatrick, Ph.D, CFP, Vice President and Professor of Financial Planning, The American College

Anthony J. Gajda, Principal, William M. Mercer, Incorporated

Susan Garrahan, Market Research Analyst, Merck & Company, Inc.

Sharon S. Graham, D.B.A., CFA, Assistant Professor of Finance, University of Central Florida

Linda Grosso, Director, Pensions-Communications Services, Metropolitan Life Insurance Company

Donald S. Grubbs, Jr., J.D., FSA, President, Grubbs and Company, Incorporated

Charles P. Hall, Jr., Ph.D., Professor of Health, Administration, Insurance and Risk, Department of Risk Management and Insurance, Temple University

G. Victor Hallman III, Ph.D., J.D., CPCU, CLU, Lecturer in Financial and Estate Planning, Wharton School, University of Pennsylvania

Carlton Harker, FSA, EA, CLU, President, ACS Group, a North Carolina Actuarial/Benefit Consulting/TPA

Waldo L. Hayes, Director, LTD Products/Markets, EB Disability Development, UNUM Life Insurance Company

Charles E. Hughes, D.B.A., CLU, CPCU, Associate Professor of Insurance, The American College

Ronald L. Huling, Principal, Williams, Thacher & Rand

David R. Klock, Ph.D., CLU, Professor of Insurance, University of Central Florida

Harry V. Lamon, Jr., Esq., Partner, Hurt, Richardson, Garner, Todd & Cadenhead

Robert T. LeClair, Ph.D., Associate Professor, Finance-Marketing Department, College of Commerce and Finance, Villanova University

Howard Lichtenstein, Executive Vice President, Mutual of America Life Insurance Company

Claude C. Lilly III, Ph.D., CLU, CPCU, Professor of Risk Management and Insurance, Florida State University

Zelda Lipton, Vice President of Marketing, Blue Cross/Blue Shield of Maryland

Ernest L. Martin, Ph.D., FLMI, Director, Examinations Department, Life Office Management Association (LOMA)

Thomas Martinez, Assistant Professor, Villanova University

Harry McBrierty, Vice President, The Wyatt Company

Dan M. McGill, Ph.D., Professor Emeritus, Insurance and Risk Management Department, Wharton School, University of Pennsylvania

Alfred F. Meyer, President, Delaware Valley HMO

Ronald J. Murray, Director, Accounting, Auditing and SEC Consulting, Coopers & Lybrand

Robert J. Myers, L.L.D., FSA, Professor Emeritus, Temple University, Chief Actuary, Social Security Administration, 1947–70; Deputy Commissioner, Social Security Administration, 1981–82; and Executive Director, National Commission on Social Security Reform, 1982–83

Robert V. Nally, J.D., CLU, Associate Professor, Villanova University

Richard Ostuw, FSA, Vice President, Towers, Perrin, Forster & Crosby, Inc.

Bruce A. Palmer, Ph.D., CLU, Professor of Risk Management and Insurance, Georgia State University

Phillip D. Pierce, Assistant Vice President, Aetna Life Insurance Company

William H. Rabel, Ph.D., FLMI, CLU, Senior Vice President, Life Management Institute, Life Office Management Association (LOMA)

George E. Rejda, Ph.D., CLU, V.J. Skutt Distinguished Professor of Insurance, University of Nebraska

Jerry S. Rosenbloom, Ph.D., CLU, CPCU, Chairman and Frederick H. Ecker Professor of Life Insurance, Department of Insurance and Risk Management, and Academic Director, Certified Employee Benefit Specialist (CEBS) Program, The Wharton School, University of Pennsylvania

Daniel J. Ryterband, Associate, Legal and Research Services, A. Foster Higgins & Co., Inc.

Dallas L. Salisbury, President, Employee Benefit Research Institute

Bernard E. Schaeffer, Senior Vice President, Research Group, Hay/Huggins Company, Inc.

Clifford J. Schoner, Esq., Associate Tax Counsel, Sun Company, Incorporated

Kathleen Hunter Sloan, Ph.D., Associate Professor and Chairman, Department of Public Administration, Barney School of Business and Public Administration, University of Hartford

Robert W. Smiley, Jr., L.L.B., Chairman and Chief Executive Officer, Benefit Capital, Incorporated

Gary K. Stone, Ph.D., Vice President-Academics, The American College

Garry N. Teesdale, Vice President, Hay Group

Richard L. Tewksbury, Jr., Vice President, Vice President and Director, Consulting and Marketing Services, Miller, Mason & Dickenson

Richard H. Towers, Director, National Office, Ernst & Young

Jack L. VanDerhei, Ph.D., CEBS, Associate Professor, Department of Risk Management and Insurance, Temple University

Bernard L. Webb, CPCU, FCAS, MAAA, Professor, Georgia State University

Joel Wells, Esq., Attorney

William G. Williams, Director, Health Care Relations, Provident Mutual Insurance Company of Philadelphia, Retired

Jack D. Worrall, Ph.D., Professor of Economics, Rutgers University

Eugene J. Ziurys, Jr., Product Manager, Managed Care and Employee Benefit Operations, Marketing and Product Development, The Travelers Companies

CONTENTS

VOLUME I

PART 8
RETIREMENT AND CAPITAL ACCUMULATION PLANS   657

CONTENTS

VOLUME II

PART 13
EMPLOYEE BENEFIT PLAN ISSUES   453

PART 9

ACCOUNTING, FUNDING, AND TAXATION OF EMPLOYEE BENEFIT PLANS

Part nine covers the crucial areas of accounting, funding and taxation of employee benefit plans. Chapters 42 and 43 review accounting and reporting by employee benefit plans and accounting for employer's pension costs respectively. Chapter 44 focuses specifically on accounting and financial reporting for health and welfare plans.

Utilizing the appropriate actuarial cost methods to determine the cost of retirement plans is essential so that appropriate funding decisions can be made and is covered in the first part of Chapter 45. The balance of the chapter reviews the different funding vehicles that can be used to set aside assets to meet retirement plan obligations.

Chapter 46 continues the discussion of the investment process for retirement plans by concentrating on investment objectives which must be the starting point in appropriately designing the correct investment strategy.

While several of the previous chapters in this part covered retirement plan funding approaches, Chapter 47 reviews the alternative methods available through insurance companies to fund health and welfare plans from full insurance to administrative services-only type arrangements. Chapter 48 completes the funding possibilities for health and welfare plans by examining self-funding techniques.

Chapters 49 and 50 cover the crucial issues involved in the taxation of employee benefit plans. The tax treatment of qualified plan distributions forms the basis of Chapter 49, and Chapter 50 brings together the federal tax environment for all forms of welfare benefits.

CHAPTER 42

EMPLOYERS' ACCOUNTING FOR PENSION COSTS

William E. Decker
Ronald J. Murray

The Financial Accounting Standards Board (FASB) believes that the current pension accounting standards contained in *Statements of Financial Accounting Standards (SFAS) No. 87, Employers' Accounting for Pensions,* and *No. 88, Employers' Accounting for Settlements and Curtailments of Defined Benefit Pension Plans and for Termination Benefits,* represent an important step toward a more meaningful and useful approach to pension accounting. The FASB also points out, however, in an appendix to *SFAS No. 87,* that these standards are not likely to be the final step in the evolution of employers' accounting for pensions.

In *SFAS No. 87,* the FASB expresses the view that it would be conceptually appropriate and preferable to recognize a net pension liability or asset measured as the difference between the projected benefit obligation and plan assets, either with no delay in the recognition of gains and losses, or perhaps with gains and losses reported currently in comprehensive income but not in earnings. Under this approach, if there were no delay in the recognition of gains and losses, pension cost would be the difference between what the FASB considers to be the conceptually appropriate balance-sheet amounts at the beginning and end of any period. However, the FASB decided that this approach would represent too great a change from past practice to be viable at this time. Therefore, the statement allows for gains and losses, the cost of plan amendments that give credit for past service, and the effects of adopting *SFAS No. 87* to be recognized in pension cost over future periods. Many of the complex aspects of *SFAS*

No. 87 result from the provisions developed to accomplish the delayed recognition of these off-balance-sheet amounts.

This chapter deals primarily with the pension accounting standards contained in *SFAS Nos. 87* and *88.*

HISTORICAL BACKGROUND

Statements of the American Institute of Certified Public Accounts (AICPA)

The AICPA's first pronouncement on accounting for pension plan costs was issued by the Committee on Accounting Procedure, in *Accounting Research Bulletin (ARB) No. 36, Pension Plans: Accounting for Annuity Costs Based on Past Services,* published in 1948. In this bulletin the committee expressed the belief that costs of annuities based on past service were generally incurred in contemplation of present and future services, not necessarily of the individual affected, but of the organization as a whole. Thus, the AICPA took the position that such costs should be allocated to current and future services and not charged to retained earnings. It did not, however, specify how pension costs should be recognized in the accounts.

In 1956, *ARB No. 47, Accounting for Costs of Pension Plans,* was issued. In this bulletin the committee specified how past service cost should be accounted for and also recognized the concept of vested benefits. The bulletin reflected the AICPA's preference for full accrual of pension costs over the remaining service lives of employees covered by a plan, generally on the basis of actuarial calculations. However, it regarded as acceptable (''for the present'') minimum accruals whereby ''the accounts and financial statements should reflect the accruals which equal the present worth, actuarially calculated, of pension commitments to employees to the extent that pension rights have vested in the employees. . . .'' The committee stated that these accruals should not necessarily depend on funding arrangements, or on strict legal interpretations of a plan, and suggested that past service cost should be charged off over a reasonable period on a systematic and rational basis that would not distort the operating results of any one year.

Divergent accounting practices nevertheless continued. In 1958, several companies that had previously accrued the full amount of current service costs (which coincided with contributions to the funds) either eliminated or drastically reduced pension costs charged to income. The supporters of these actions justified them on the grounds that funds provided in the past were sufficient to afford reasonable assurance that pension payments could be continued, and were more than sufficient to meet the company's obligation for the then-vested rights of employees. Thus, they believed that the minimum requirements of *ARB No. 47* were satisfied.

Against this background, the Accounting Principles Board (APB), which succeeded the Committee on Accounting Procedure, decided that the subject needed further study and authorized an accounting research study. This study, published in 1965, detailed the accounting complexities of pension plans. In 1966, after lengthy consideration, the APB promulgated its *Opinion No. 8, Accounting for the Cost of Pension Plans,* primarily to eliminate inappropriate fluctuations in the amount of annual provisions for pension costs.

APB Opinion No. 8

Under *APB Opinion No. 8,* the provision for pension cost was based on an actuarial cost method that gave effect, in a consistent manner, to pension benefits, pension fund earnings, investment gains or losses (including unrealized gains and losses), and other assumptions regarding future events, and resulted in a systematic and rational allocation of the total cost of pensions.

Limits on the annual provision for pension cost were narrowed when *APB Opinion No. 8:*

- Required the minimum annual provision for pension cost to be the sum of (1) normal cost, (2) interest on unfunded prior service cost, and (3) a provision for vested benefits, if applicable.
- Required that actuarial gains and losses and unrealized appreciation and depreciation be recognized in the computation of the annual provision for pension cost in a consistent manner that reflected the long-range nature of pension cost and avoided giving undue weight to short-term market fluctuations.
- Eliminated pay-as-you-go and terminal funding as acceptable methods of computing the annual provision for pension cost, except in the rare instances in which their application did not result in amounts differing materially from those obtained by the application of acceptable actuarial cost methods.

The APB concluded that all employees who could reasonably be expected to receive benefits under a pension plan should be included in the pension cost determination. It also concluded that any change made in the method of accounting for pension cost should not be applied retroactively. The opinion set forth disclosure requirements for accounting method changes as well as for other pertinent pension cost data.

APB Opinion No. 8 applied "both to written plans and to plans whose existence may be implied from a well-defined, although perhaps unwritten, company policy." If a company had been providing its retired employees with benefits that could be determined or estimated in advance, there was generally a presumption that a pension plan existed within the meaning contemplated by the opinion.

FASB Statement No. 36

The FASB, which replaced the APB, issued *SFAS No. 36, Disclosure of Pension Information,* in 1980, amending the disclosure requirements of *APB Opinion No. 8*. This statement addressed the lack of comparable disclosures in employers' financial statements concerning the financial status of their pension plans and prescribed new disclosures to help correct this deficiency. It did not, however, modify any of the other provisions of *APB Opinion No. 8*.

FASB Statement No. 87

After several more years of deliberating the complex and controversial issues related to pension accounting, the FASB issued *SFAS No. 87, Employers' Accounting for Pensions,* in 1985. This statement supersedes *APB Opinion No. 8, SFAS No. 36,* and *FASB Interpretation No. 3, Accounting for the Cost of Pension Plans Subject to the Employee Retirement Income Security Act of 1974.*

SFAS No. 87 establishes financial reporting and accounting standards for employers that offer pension benefits to their employees. Such benefits are ordinarily periodic pension payments to retired employees, but may also include lump-sum payments and other types of benefits (such as death and disability benefits) provided through a pension plan. While the provisions of *SFAS No. 87* apply to *any* arrangement that is similar in substance to a pension plan, regardless of the form or means of financing,[1] they have the most significant impact on defined benefit plans. *SFAS No. 87:*

- Requires that a single attribution (or actuarial cost) method be used to calculate pension cost and obligations.[2]
- Provides specific guidance on how to select (actuarial) assumptions.
- Requires amortization of (actuarial) gains and losses in excess of a prescribed amount.
- Limits the acceptable methods and time periods for amortizing prior service cost.
- Requires that a transition amount be computed when *SFAS No. 87* is adopted and that it be amortized to expense on a straight-line basis over future periods.
- Specifies that an employer's balance sheet reflect a liability for any unfunded accumulated pension benefits (without considering salary progression), generally offset by an intangible asset.
- Requires that a significant amount of additional pension information be disclosed in a company's financial statements.

Figure 42–1 highlights some of the key terms used in *SFAS No. 87.*

FIGURE 42–1
Glossary of Terms

---

accumulated benefit obligation (ABO)   Actuarial present value of benefits as of a specified date, determined according to the terms of a pension plan and based on employees' compensation and service to that date. (Salary progression is not considered in making this computation.)

actuarial gains and losses   Same as gains or losses.

adjusted plan assets   Fair value of plan assets *plus* previously recognized unfunded accrued pension cost *or less* previously recognized prepaid pension cost on the employer's balance sheet.

---

[1]*SFAS No. 87* does not apply to a plan that provides only life and/or health insurance benefits to retirees. Employers also are not required to apply *SFAS No. 87* to a plan that provides postretirement health care benefits, although they are permitted to do so. In December 1990, the FASB issued *SFAS No. 106, Employers' Accounting for Postretirement Benefits Other Than Pensions,* which addresses plans of this nature.

[2]*SFAS No. 87* avoids using the adjective *actuarial* whenever possible and introduces terminology that is different from that used previously. In certain instances, the term *actuarial* is included parenthetically as an aid in the transition to the revised language.

FIGURE 42-1 (*continued*)

benefit approaches Group of basic approaches for allocating or attributing benefits or the cost of benefits to service periods (heretofore referred to as *actuarial* methods). These approaches assign a unit of retirement benefit to each year of credited service. The actuarial present value of that unit of benefit is computed separately and determines the cost assigned to that year. The projected unit credit method and the unit credit method are benefit approaches.

career average pay plan Pension plan that provides benefits based on a benefit formula using the amount of compensation over an employee's entire service life.

corridor approach Method of accounting for amortizing gains and losses whereby employer amortizes only the portion of the accumulated net gain or loss that exceeds a prescribed limit—10 percent of the greater of the market-related value of plan assets or the projected benefit obligation.

cost approaches Group of basic approaches for allocating or attributing benefits or the cost of benefits to service periods (heretofore referred to as *actuarial* methods). These approaches assign pension cost to periods so that the same amount of cost or the same percentage of compensation is allocated to each period. The entry age normal, attained age normal, individual level premium, and aggregate methods are cost approaches.

curtailment Event that significantly reduces the expected years of future service of present employees or eliminates for a significant number of employees the accrual of defined benefits for some or all of their future services.

defined benefit pension plan Pension plan that specifies a determinable pension benefit, usually based on factors such as age, years of service, and compensation. Under *SFAS No. 87* any plan that is not a defined contribution pension plan is considered a defined benefit pension plan.

defined contribution pension plan Pension plan that provides an individual account for each participant and specifies how contributions to the individual's account are to be determined, instead of specifying the amount of benefits the individual is to receive. Under a defined contribution pension plan, the benefits a participant will receive depend solely on the amount contributed to the participant's account, plus any income, expense, gains or losses, and forfeitures of other participants' benefits that may be allocated to such participant's account.

discount rate Assumed interest rate at which the pension obligation could be effectively settled or eliminated, used to adjust for the time value of money between a specified date and the expected dates of payment. Also referred to as the *settlement rate.*

earnings rate Average long-term rate of return expected to be earned on pension fund assets.

final pay plan Pension plan that provides retirement benefits based on a benefit formula using the amount of employee compensation over a specified period near the end of the employee's service life.

FIGURE 42–1   (*continued*)

---

flat benefit plan   Pension plan that provides retirement benefits based on a fixed amount for each year of employee service.

gains or losses   Changes in the value of either the projected benefit obligation or plan assets resulting from experience different from that assumed and from changes in assumptions.

market-related asset value   Either the fair market value of an asset or a calculated value derived by systematic and rational adjustments to fair market value over a period of not more than five years.

multiemployer plan   Pension plan to which two or more unrelated employers contribute, usually pursuant to one or more collective bargaining agreements.

participating annuity contract   Annuity contract that provides for the purchaser to participate in the investment performance and possibly other experience, both favorable and unfavorable (e.g., mortality), of the insurance company.

prior service cost   Cost of retroactive benefits granted in a plan amendment (or a new plan).

projected benefit obligation (PBO)   Actuarial present value of all benefits attributed to employee service up to a specific date, based on the terms of the plan. A salary progression factor is included for final pay and career average pay plans.

projected unit credit method   Benefit/years-of-service actuarial approach generally required to be used for final pay and career average pay plans. Under

this method, an equal portion of the total estimated benefit (including a salary progression factor) is attributed to each year of service. The cost of that benefit is then computed, with appropriate consideration to reflect the time value of money (discounting) and the probability of payment (e.g., mortality and turnover). Accordingly, this method results in progressively higher benefit costs each successive year for each participant, since the probability of survival to normal retirement increases and the discount period decreases.

salary progression   Projection of the assumed rate of salaries to be earned in future years based on all components of future compensation levels (i.e., merit, productivity, and inflation).

service cost   Portion of benefits attributed to employee service for the period.

settlement rate   *See* discount rate.

settlement   Transaction that is an irrevocable action, relieves the employer (or the plan) of primary responsibility for a pension benefit obligation, and eliminates significant risks related to the obligation and the assets used to effect the settlement.

transition amount   Difference between the projected benefit obligation and the fair value of adjusted plan assets at the date *SFAS No. 87* is adopted. If the projected benefit obligation exceeds adjusted plan assets, there is an unrecognized net obligation and loss (or transition debit). Conversely, if adjusted plan assets exceed the projected

FIGURE 42–1   *(concluded)*

benefit obligation, there is an unrecognized net asset and gain (or transition credit).

unit credit method   Accumulated benefits approach generally required to be used for flat benefit plans. Under this method, benefits earned to date are based on the plan formula and employees' history of pay, service, and other factors.

volatility   Changes in pension cost from period to period.

FASB Statement No. 88

In conjunction with *SFAS No. 87*, the FASB also issued *SFAS No. 88, Employers' Accounting for Settlements and Curtailments of Defined Benefit Pension Plans and for Termination Benefits*. This statement defines an event (a settlement) that requires, among other things, immediate recognition of previously unrecognized gains and losses and another event (a curtailment) that requires immediate recognition of previously unrecognized prior service cost.

FASB Staff Special Reports

The FASB does not attempt to anticipate all of the implementation questions that may arise in connection with a particular accounting pronouncement, nor to provide answers to those questions when the pronouncement is issued. Accordingly, many implementation issues are addressed orally by the FASB staff. Because of the unusually high number of questions raised and the inherent complexities of pension accounting, the FASB staff published two special reports, one entitled *A Guide to Implementation of Statement 87 on Employers' Accounting for Pensions*, and the other titled *A Guide to Implementation of Statement 88 on Employers' Accounting for Settlements and Curtailments of Defined Benefit Pension Plans and for Termination Benefits*. The special reports contain the FASB staff members' views on a wide range of issues relating to the implementation of *SFAS Nos. 87 and 88*.

The publications clearly state that the opinions expressed are those of its authors and should not be considered the official positions of the FASB. However, the SEC staff has taken the position that companies subject to SEC reporting requirements should be prepared to justify any significant deviations from the guidance set forth in the special reports.

DEFINED BENEFIT PENSION PLANS: ANNUAL PROVISION FOR PENSION COST

The FASB recognizes that under *SFAS No. 87,* pension cost is likely to be more volatile (that is, pension cost may change by a significant amount from year to year) than it was under prior pronouncements as a result of:

- Changing from a discount rate based on the expected long-term earnings on plan assets (a rate that fluctuated infrequently and moderately) to discount (settlement) rate assumptions based on point-in-time interest rates.
- Changing from a method of amortizing prior service cost that provided a level amount of prior service cost and interest to a method that generally accelerates amortization over a shorter period.

Companies are permitted some latitude in the mechanics of applying the standards, the objective being to control pension cost volatility to some extent. Whether this objective will be achieved over time is still an open question. Under the rules set forth in the statement:

- Some forms of smoothed asset values are allowed, and asset gains and losses not reflected in these values need not be amortized.
- Only the portion of accumulated gains and losses that exceeds a prescribed amount is required to be amortized.

Components of Pension Cost

Under *SFAS No. 87,* an employer is required to select a consistent date on which to measure plan assets and obligations (and thus determine pension cost) from year to year. This "measurement date" is defined as either the employer's year-end or a date not more than three months before the year-end date. The FASB staff's special report, *A Guide to Implementation of Statement 87 on Employers' Accounting for Pensions,* indicates that:

- Although the pension obligation (and thus pension cost) must be based on census data and actuarial assumptions as of the measurement date, a full actuarial valuation is not required if a company is satisfied that the amount of the pension obligation determined by rolling forward data based on a valuation prior to the measurement date is substantially the same as the amount that would be determined by an actuarial valuation as of that date.

- If an employer remeasures plan assets and obligations or performs a full actuarial valuation as of an interim date other than the established measurement date, pension cost for the period prior to the remeasurement should not be restated. However, pension cost for the remainder of the year should be based on the revised measurements.

SFAS No. 87 requires that an employer's pension cost consist of several components, computed as follows:

- **Service cost**   The increase in the projected benefit obligation attributable to employee service for the period calculated using the beginning-of-the-year discount rate and the required cost method.[3]
- **Interest cost**   The increase in the projected benefit obligation attributable to the accrual of interest on the beginning-of-the-year balance of the obligation calculated using the beginning-of-the-year discount rate. Anticipated changes in the projected benefit obligation for employee services rendered and benefit payments made during the year needs to be considered in determining interest cost.
- **Return on plan assets**   The expected earnings on plan assets calculated using the assumed long-term earnings rate and the market-related value of plan assets (both at the beginning of the year) taking into consideration anticipated contributions and benefit payments made during the year. Although paragraph 20 of *SFAS No. 87* specifies the "actual" return on plan assets as a component of pension cost, paragraph 34(a) states that the difference between the actual and expected return on plan assets must be accounted for as part of the gain or loss component of pension cost. The net result of these paragraphs is that the expected return on plan assets is used to calculate pension cost for the period.

  The market-related value of plan assets is defined as fair value or a calculated value that recognizes changes in fair value in a

---

[3]The projected benefit obligation is the actuarial present value as of a specified date of all benefits attributed by the pension benefit formula to employee service rendered prior to that date. It is measured using assumptions regarding future compensation levels if the pension benefit formula is based on those future compensation levels (e.g., final pay or career average pay plans).

systematic or rational manner over not more than five years. Employers may use different methods of calculating the market-related value for different classes of assets (for example, an employer might use fair value for bonds and a five-year moving average value for equities), provided that the methodologies are applied consistently from year to year. Some employers find that the use of a market-related value other than fair value reduces pension cost volatility somewhat, since the expected return component is based on a smoothed asset value.

* **Prior service cost**   The amortization of prior service cost resulting from plan amendments.
* **Gains and losses**   The amortization of the beginning-of-the-year net gain or loss.
* **Transition amount**   The amortization of the transition amount.

An illustrative example of the manner in which pension cost is calculated under *SFAS No. 87* is included in Figure 42–2.

Attribution Method

Companies are required to use a single attribution method based on the plan's terms to determine pension cost (a benefits approach). For final pay and career average pay plans, this is equivalent to the projected unit credit method. For flat benefit plans, the unit credit method is required. Companies may not use cost approaches (for example, entry age normal or aggregate method) for accounting purposes, although they may do so for funding purposes.

Substantive Commitments

Paragraph 41 of *SFAS No. 87* states that in some situations, a history of regular amendments that improve benefits in flat benefit or career average plans (in addition to other evidence) may indicate that a company has a present commitment to make future amendments and that the substance of the plan is to provide benefits greater than the benefits defined by its written terms. In these situations, the "substantive commitment" is required to be taken into consideration in determining pension cost and obligations.

This provision has created confusion with respect to what constitutes a substantive commitment. The FASB staff's special report indicates that determining whether a substantive commitment exists requires careful consideration of the facts and circumstances surrounding the pension plan and points out that the company's past actions, including communications to employees, may embody a commitment to have a benefit formula that provides benefits beyond those specified by the written terms of the plan. The special report also indicates, however, that it is not the intent of paragraph 41 to permit the anticipation of an individual plan amendment (that is, one that is not part of a series).

In the authors' experience, most companies have concluded that they do not have a substantive commitment to make future plan amendments. Consequently, they do not include the cost of anticipated amendments in the calculation of pension cost and obligations until they have been contractually agreed to. However, some companies have concluded that they have such a commitment and make their pension calculations accordingly; in these cases, paragraph 41 requires footnote disclosure of the existence and nature of the commitment.

Selecting Assumptions

Explicit Assumptions
Each significant assumption is required to reflect the best estimate solely with respect to that individual assumption (referred to as an *explicit* approach).

Two Interest Rates
Companies are required to select two interest rates: (1) an assumed discount (or settlement) rate based on the rate at which the pension obligation could be effectively settled or eliminated and (2) an expected long-term rate of return on plan assets (earnings rate).

The discount rate is used to measure the projected, accumulated, and vested benefit obligations and the service and interest cost components of pension cost. A certain degree of latitude is permissible in selecting this rate. In this connection, paragraph 44 of *SFAS No. 87* states:

> Assumed discount rates shall reflect the rates at which the pension benefits could be effectively settled. It is appropriate in estimating those rates to look to available information about rates implicit in current prices of annuity contracts that could be used to effect settlement of the obligation (including information about available annuity rates currently published by

the Pension Benefit Guaranty Corporation). In making those estimates, employers may also look to rates of return on high-quality fixed-income investments currently available and expected to be available during the period to maturity of the pension benefits.

This rather broad guidance has given rise to a number of questions with respect to the appropriate methodology for determining the discount rate. The FASB staff's special report indicates that selecting the discount rate is not a mechanical process based on a standard formula. It states that the primary objective of selecting the discount rate is to select the *best* estimate of the interest rates inherent in the price at which the pension obligation could be settled, given the pension plan's particular facts and circumstances and current market conditions, and that the methodology used in the selection process is subordinate to that primary objective.

The following specific guidance on selecting the discount rate is provided in the special report:

- A methodology for determining the discount rate, once selected, should be followed consistently. If the facts and circumstances surrounding the pension plan do not change from year to year, it would be inappropriate to change the methodology, particularly if the intent in changing it is to avoid a change in the discount rate.
- A change in facts and circumstances may, however, warrant the use of a different approach for determining the discount rate. This change in methodology—which, in the authors' view, would occur infrequently—would be a change in accounting estimate, not a change in accounting method.
- The discount rate should be reevaluated each year to determine whether it reflects current market conditions. The discount rate is *expected* to change as interest rates generally decline or rise.
- It would be inappropriate to use a range of rates (for example, from PBGC rates at one end to high-quality bond rates at the other) and to
  —Arbitrarily select any rate within the range or
  —Use the same rate each year provided it falls within the range.
- If the pension plan has a "dedicated" bond portfolio, that yield should not be used as the discount rate, since it is the current rates of return on those investments (not historical rates of return as of the dedication date) that are relevant.

Based on the foregoing, it is apparent that the authors of the special report expect pension cost to be more volatile under *SFAS No. 87* and that any attempt to manage the discount rate to avoid such volatility would be inappropriate. While there is some latitude regarding the methodology a particular company may select to determine the discount rate, it is clear that whatever approach is selected should be followed consistently (unless circumstances change).

The earnings rate is used in connection with the market-related value of plan assets to compute the return-on-assets component of pension cost. In estimating that rate, consideration needs to be given to current returns being earned and returns expected to be available for reinvestment.

As a general rule, the expected long-term rate of return on plan assets is less volatile than the actual rate of return on assets, since the expected rate contemplates not only current rates of return, but also expected reinvestment rates. The expected long-term rate of return is *not* the equivalent of the discount rate used to measure interest cost related to the projected benefit obligation, since the discount rate is intended to be the current rate at which the obligation could be settled immediately. *SFAS No. 87* does not preclude the selection of different rates of return for different classes of plan assets (for example, one rate for bonds and another for equity securities).

Salary Progression Rate

In determining the salary progression assumption, employers are required to consider all salary-increase components (merit, productivity, promotion, and inflation). All assumptions are required to be consistent to the extent that each reflects expectations of the same future economic conditions, such as rates of inflation. For example, if an employer uses a 5 percent inflation factor for purposes of determining the earnings rate, that same factor is required to be used to determine the inflation component of the salary progression rate.

Amortization of Prior Service Cost

Historically, the costs related to plan changes—or to new plans—that give credit for past service have been recognized over future periods, using a variety of acceptable methods that generally produced a level amount representing the sum of prior service cost and interest on the unamortized balance. *SFAS No. 87* prescribes a method of amortization that separates these two elements and uses an accelerated method to amortize the prior service cost, generally over fewer years. As a result, prior service cost is generally amortized to expense at a faster rate than under previous practice, which in some cases contributes to the volatility of pension cost.

Amortization Period

SFAS No. 87 requires that pension cost include amortization of prior service cost, generally over the future service period of employees active as of the date of amendment who are expected to receive benefits under the plan. The FASB staff's special report indicates that once an amortization period has been established, it may be revised only if a curtailment (as defined in *SFAS No. 88*) occurs or if events indicate that (1) the period benefited is shorter than originally estimated or (2) the future economic benefits of the plan amendment have been impaired. The special report also indicates that the amortization period would not necessarily be revised because of ordinary variances in the expected future service period of employees.

Amortization Method

Prior service cost and the related interest on the unrecognized amount are required to be accounted for separately. The interest component of pension cost includes the interest on the unamortized prior service cost, while the principal is amortized to expense using an accelerated method that results in a declining amortization pattern. This method assigns an equal amount of prior service cost to each future period of service of each employee active at the date of the plan amendment who is expected to receive benefits under the plan. In other words, the method (similar to sum-of-the-years' digits) is based on the relationship between the total expected employee years of service and the service years expected to expire in a period.

 SFAS No. 87, however, also indicates that methods that result in amortization that is more rapid than the method described above can be used—including straight-line amortization over the average remaining service period of employees expected to receive benefits.

 Using the amortization method set forth in the statement results in accelerated principal amortization of prior service cost. If an alternative method (such as straight-line) is selected, the amortization period must be reduced to no more than the average remaining service period to achieve the more rapid amortization called for by the statement. In either case, under *SFAS No. 87,* prior service cost is generally amortized to expense at a faster rate than under previous practice.

Some employers have expressed the view that immediate recognition of prior service cost resulting from *all* plan amendments (present and future) is an acceptable alternative amortization method. The special report indicates that immediate recognition is appropriate only if, after assessing the facts and circumstances surrounding the particular plan amendment, the employer does not expect to realize any future economic benefits from that plan amendment. Accordingly, an employer may not adopt an accounting policy to immediately recognize prior service cost, since such a policy would preclude the employer from making this assessment for future plan amendments *as they occur.*

Plans with a History of Regular Amendments
The statement also indicates that a shorter amortization period for certain plans may be warranted. Paragraph 27 states that if a company has a history of regular plan amendments (for example, when flat benefit plans are amended with each renegotiation of a union contract), that practice, along with other evidence, may indicate a shortening of the period during which the company expects economic benefits from each amendment. When a situation of this nature is deemed to exist, amortization is required over the period benefited. In its deliberations, the Board considered, and rejected, recommendations that the final statement specify that the ''period benefited'' (and thus the prior service cost amortization period) is the period between contract renegotiations.

The language in paragraph 27 has created confusion with respect to what constitutes a history of regular plan amendments and what amortization period should be used if such a situation exists. While it addresses these issues, the special report provides little additional guidance, essentially indicating that the assessment of whether such a situation exists and, if so, what amortization period should be used is fact specific. It therefore appears that the appropriate amortization period in a situation of this nature is not necessarily the contract period. The authors are aware of a number of companies that, based on an assessment of the particular facts and circumstances involved, have been able to support an amortization period in such a situation that is longer than the contract period but not longer than the future service period of active employees expected to receive benefits under the plan.

Paragraph 27 is not limited to pension plans that are subject to collective bargaining agreements. An employer with a non-union shop that regularly grants cost-of-living increases must also consider the provisions of paragraph 27.

If a plan amendment eliminates the accrual of defined benefits for future services, it is considered a curtailment under *SFAS No. 88,* and all prior service cost related to years of service no longer expected to be rendered is eliminated in computing the gain or loss on curtailment.

In certain instances, an employer may be able to reduce pension benefits because of economic conditions (for example, a union "give-back"). In such instances, the reduced benefits are offset against existing unrecognized prior service cost. When a company has unrecognized prior service cost relating to several plan amendments that have differing amortization periods, the issue arises as to which plan amendment should first be offset by the benefit from a subsequent plan amendment that reduces the projected benefit obligation. The FASB staff's special report indicates that unless the retroactive plan amendment that reduces benefits can be specifically related to a prior amendment, any systematic and rational method (for example, LIFO, FIFO, or pro rata), applied on a consistent basis, is acceptable. If an employer terminates a defined benefit pension plan and establishes a successor plan that provides reduced benefits for employees' future service, the transaction is required to be accounted for as a negative plan amendment, not as a curtailment.

Gains and Losses

Gains and losses are defined as changes in either the projected benefit obligation *or* plan assets resulting from experience different from that assumed *and* from changes in assumptions. All gains and losses, including those arising from changes in the discount rate, are accounted for on a combined basis. Companies are permitted to apply consistently any systematic and rational amortization method, as long as it results in the amortization of the net gain or loss in an amount greater than the minimum based on the so-called corridor approach. The FASB staff's special report indicates that companies may immediately recognize gains and losses (instead of delaying their recognition) provided that (1) this approach is applied consistently, (2) the method is applied to *both* gains and losses (on plan assets *and* obligations), and (3) the method used is disclosed.

Under the corridor approach, only the portion of the net gain or loss that exceeds a prescribed amount (10 percent of the greater of the market-related value of plan assets or the projected benefit obligation, both as of the beginning of the year) must be amortized. The excess is required to be amortized on a straight-line basis over the average remaining service period of active employees expected to receive benefits. Asset gains and losses not yet reflected in the market-related value of plan assets (the difference between the fair value and the market-related value of plan assets) are not, however, required to be included in the computation.

Controlling Volatility

As noted above, the FASB developed the corridor approach and the market-related value of plan assets concept in an attempt to reduce the volatility of pension cost as follows:

- First, only the asset gains or losses reflected in the market-related value of plan assets must be considered for amortization (as little as 20 percent per year).
- Second, all gains and losses may be offset; amortization is required only if the net gain or loss is in excess of the corridor.
- Third, the excess may be spread over the average remaining service period of active employees expected to receive benefits.

Balance Sheet Recognition

Under previous accounting rules, a pension liability was recorded only if the employer's contributions to the plan were less than cumulative pension cost determined under an acceptable actuarial cost method. Conversely, a pension asset was recorded only if the contributions were more than the recorded cost. While *SFAS No. 87* retains those practices, it also requires that an additional liability be recognized when the unfunded accumulated benefit obligation (the excess of the accumulated benefit obligation over the fair value of plan assets) exceeds the balance-sheet liability for accrued pension cost. Under this approach, when an additional liability is recorded, an intangible asset is also recognized to the extent that unamortized prior service cost and/or an unamortized transition debit (discussed in the following section) exists. If the additional liability exceeds the total of these two items, the excess (on a net of tax basis) is recorded as a separate component (that is, a reduction) of stockholders' equity. Under no circumstances does the recording of the additional liability affect earnings. The FASB staff's special report points out that because prior service cost and the transition debit are amortized as part of pension expense, the intangible asset is not subject to separate amortization, since that would result in double-counting of expense.

For companies with more than one plan, liability recognition is determined on a plan-by-plan basis. For example, unless an employer clearly has a right to use the assets of one plan to pay the benefits of another, the excess assets of an overfunded plan cannot offset the additional liability for unfunded accumulated benefits of another plan sponsored by the same company. Thus, as a general rule, companies that previously disclosed plan assets in excess of accumulated benefits are now required to recognize a liability under *SFAS No. 87* if they sponsor any underfunded plans.

SFAS No. 87 does not allow companies with overfunded plans to reflect surplus plan assets as an asset on their balance sheets.

With respect to the appropriate balance-sheet classification of the additional liability and intangible asset required to be recognized, the FASB staff's special report indicates that the criteria for current and noncurrent classification of the additional liability are the same as for any other liability. Thus, the classification of any additional liability should be based on the company's intent to fund the amount involved. However, the special report states that the intangible asset should be classified as noncurrent, since it represents either unrecognized prior service cost or the remaining unamortized portion of the transition debit.

Transition

SFAS No. 87 requires a "transition amount" to have been computed as of the measurement date for the beginning of the fiscal year in which the statement was first applied. This transition amount is the difference between:

- The projected benefit obligation, including a salary progression factor and computed using the attribution method and the assumption guidance set forth in *SFAS No. 87*.
- Adjusted plan assets, an amount representing the fair value of plan assets plus the pension liability or less the pension asset on the employer's balance sheet at the measurement date.

To the extent the projected benefit obligation exceeded adjusted plan assets, a transition debit resulted; if adjusted plan assets exceeded the projected benefit obligation, a transition credit resulted. In either case, the transition amount (which is not recorded in the financial statements) is required to be amortized on a straight-line basis over the average remaining service period of active employees expected to receive benefits under the plan except that (1) the employer may elect to use a 15-year period if this average remaining period is less than 15 years, and (2) if all or almost all of the plan's participants are inactive, the employer must use the average remaining life expectancy of the inactive participants.

Figure 42–2 provides an illustrative example of the pension cost calculation for a company with a single defined benefit pension plan.

DEFINED CONTRIBUTION PENSION PLANS

The periodic cost of a defined contribution plan is measured by the required contribution amount determined using the plan formula, since, in a defined contribution plan, the pension benefits that participants will receive depend only on the amount contributed to the participants' accounts, the returns earned on investments of these contributions, and forfeitures of other participants' benefits that may be reallocated. If a plan requires contributions to continue after participants retire or terminate, the cost of these benefits also should be accrued during the participants' service periods.

When a plan has both a formula for plan contributions and a scale for plan benefits, a careful analysis is required to determine whether the substance of the plan is to provide a defined contribution or a defined benefit. If the plan history indicates that the scale of benefits is adjusted to reflect the amount actually contributed, as a general rule the plan should be treated as a defined contribution plan. If, however, a company's liability for pension benefits is not limited by the amount of the pension fund or if the plan history indicates (and/or the current employer policy contemplates) the maintenance of benefit levels regardless of the amount of defined contribution or legal limitation of the employer's liability for such benefits, as a general rule the plan is required to be treated as a defined benefit plan. The accounting and disclosure requirements are determined by the applicable provisions of *SFAS No. 87*.

FIGURE 42-2
Illustrative Example of the Pension Cost Calculation

XYZ Company has a defined benefit pension plan covering substantially all of its employees. The company adopted *SFAS No. 87* as of January 1, 1989.

Plan Data and Key (Actuarial) Assumptions

Benefit formula	Career average	
Accounting policies		
Amortization of gains and losses	Corridor approach	
Amortization of transition amount	Average future service period of employees	
Market-related value of plan assets	Equal to fair value	

	1989	1990
Assumed discount rate	11.5%	10%
Assumed salary progression rate	6	6
Assumed earnings rate	11	9

	1989	1990
Plan assets and obligations (as of beginning of year)		
Vested benefit obligation (VBO)	$ 8,500,000	$11,700,000
Accumulated benefit obligation (ABO)	10,000,000	13,800,000
Projected benefit obligation (PBO)	11,500,000	14,653,000
Fair value of plan assets	12,000,000	$15,000,000

Prepaid pension cost as of January 1, 1989	$ 1,000,000

For the year ended December 31, 1989	
Service cost	$ 300,000
Benefit payments made	360,000*
Contributions made	500,000†
Actual return on plan assets	$ 2,860,000

XYZ Company's pension cost for the year ended December 31, 1989, was $338,215, computed as follows:

Service cost		$ 300,000
Interest Cost‡		
PBO at 1/1/89	$11,500,000	
Discount rate at 1/1/89	× 11½%	$ 1,322,500

FIGURE 42–2   (*concluded*)

Expected return on plan assets		
Market-related value at 1/1/89	12,000,000	
Earnings rate at 1/1/89	× 11%	(1,320,000)
Amortization of prior service cost		— §
Amortization of gains and losses		— ‖
Amortization of transition amount		
Fair value of plan assets at 1/1/89	12,000,000	
Less prepaid pension cost at 1/1/89	(1,000,000)	
Less PBO at 1/1/89	(11,500,000)	
Transition debit	500,000	
Average future service period		
of employees at 1/1/89	÷ 14 years	35,715
Pension cost for the year ended		
December 31, 1989		$ 338,215

The company's additional liability at December 31, 1989, was $0, computed as follows:

Fair value of plan assets at 12/31/89		$15,000,000
Less prepaid pension cost at 12/31/89		
Prepaid pension cost at 1/1/89	$ 1,000,000	
Contribution on 12/31/89	500,000	
Pension cost for the year		
ended 12/31/89	(338,215)	(1,161,785)
Less ABO at 12/31/89		(13,800,000)
		$ 38,215
Amount of additional liability		$ 0#

*Benefits payments are made ratably during the year.
†Contributions are made on December 31.
‡The calculation of the interest cost component should take into consideration anticipated benefit payments; however, they were not considered for purposes of this illustrative example.
§There were no plan amendments in 1989.
‖ The corridor approach requires amortization of the beginning-of-the-year unrecognized net gain or loss. At January 1, 1989, this amount was $0.
#Since adjusted plan assets exceed the ABO at December 31, 1989, no additional liability is required to be recorded. Note that *SFAS No. 87* does not permit companies to record a pension asset in a situation of this nature.

MULTIEMPLOYER PENSION PLANS

A multiemployer plan is a pension plan to which two or more unrelated employers contribute, usually pursuant to one or more collective bargaining agreements. A characteristic of multiemployer plans is that assets contributed by one participating employer may be used to provide benefits to employees of other participating employers, since assets contributed by an employer are not segregated in a separate account or restricted to provide benefits only to employees of that employer.

An employer participating in a multiemployer plan is required to recognize as pension cost the required contribution for the period and recognize as a liability any contributions due and unpaid. In other words, even though a multiemployer plan may be a defined benefit plan, the employer is able to account for its participation as though it were a defined contribution plan. This would be the case even though the employer, as part of entering a multiemployer pension plan or amending the benefits under the plan, unconditionally promises to pay certain future contributions to the plan (calculated based on the plan's prior service cost associated with the participant's entering the plan or the improved benefits), and executes an agreement that specifies the amounts of those future contributions.

DISCLOSURE

A significant amount of information must be disclosed by all sponsors of defined benefit plans, including descriptive information about plan provisions, funding policy, plan assets, and employee groups covered; the components of pension cost; the interest rate and salary progression assumptions; and a reconciliation of the projected benefit obligation to the asset or liability recorded on the company's balance sheet. Disclosures regarding defined contribution and multiemployer plans are also required. Figure 42–3 summarizes these disclosure requirements.

The reconciliation of the projected benefit obligation to the balance-sheet amounts recorded by sponsors of defined benefit plans provides users of financial statements with information that is consistent with the FASB's theoretical preference regarding the asset or liability that should be recorded—the difference between the projected benefit obligation and the fair value of plan assets. The remaining items in the reconciliation reflect the delayed recognition of prior service cost, gains and losses, and the transition provisions of *SFAS No. 87*. Companies may not aggregate plans with pension assets (that is, plan assets in excess of accumulated benefits) with plans that have pension liabilities (that is, accumulated

FIGURE 42-3
Required Pension Disclosures Under SFAS No. 87

Defined Benefit Plans
A description of the plan, including employee groups covered, type of benefit formula, funding policy, types of assets held, and significant nonbenefit liabilities, as well as the nature and effect of significant matters affecting comparability of information for all periods presented.

Net pension cost for the period, showing separately service cost, interest cost, actual return on plan assets for the period, and the net total of other components.

A schedule reconciling the funded status of the plan with amounts reported in the employer's balance sheet, showing separately:

1. The fair value of plan assets.
2. The projected benefit obligation, identifying:
   a. The accumulated benefit obligation.
   b. The vested benefit obligation.
3. The amount of unrecognized prior service cost.
4. The amount of unrecognized net gain or loss (including asset gains and losses not yet reflected in the market-related value of assets).
5. The balance of the unrecognized transition amount.
6. The amount of any additional liability recognized.
7. The amount of net pension asset or liability recognized in the balance sheet (the net result of combining the preceding six items).

The weighted-average assumed discount and earnings' rates and the salary progression rate used.

The amounts and types of securities of the employer and related parties included in plan assets and the amount of annual benefits of employees and retirees covered by annuity contracts issued by the employer and related parties.

A description of any alternative methods used to amortize prior service cost and gains or losses and the existence and nature of commitments beyond the written terms of the plan.

Defined Contribution Plans
A description of the plan, including employee groups covered, the basis for determining contributions, and the nature and effect of significant matters affecting comparability of information for all periods presented.

The amount of cost recognized during the period.

Multiemployer Plans
A general description of the multiemployer plan, including employee groups covered, the type of benefits (defined benefit or defined contribution), and the nature and effect of significant matters affecting comparability of information for all periods presented.

The amount of cost recognized during the period.

If withdrawal from a multiemployer plan is reasonably possible, the amount (if reasonably estimable) of obligation the employer would have on withdrawal from the plan. If the amount is not reasonably estimable, the best reasonably available general information about the extent of the obligation the employer would have on withdrawal from the plan.

benefits in excess of plan assets) for purposes of complying with this disclosure requirement. Furthermore, companies may not aggregate foreign and domestic plans for purposes of this disclosure requirement unless the foreign plans use similar assumptions.

Figure 42–4 provides an illustrative example of the financial statement disclosures of the XYZ Company (based on the same hypothetical facts used in the illustrative example in Figure 42–2). The format presented and the wording of the footnote are consistent with Illustration 6 in *SFAS No. 87.*

FUNDING AND PLAN ADMINISTRATION

As previously noted, prior to *SFAS No. 87* a substantial number of companies funded the amount of pension cost that was accrued for financial statement purposes. This may now not be possible for some companies, because pension cost determined pursuant to *SFAS No. 87* is greater than the maximum deductible amount permitted under the Internal Revenue Code or less than the minimum required contribution under ERISA. Some companies have therefore elected to modify their funding policies in an attempt to attain some level of consistency with the methodology under *SFAS No. 87.*

In some cases, however, this consistency is difficult to achieve. Certainly, companies that historically have used a different actuarial cost method from the one required by the statement may switch to the new method for funding purposes as well. However, the new methods and periods for amortizing prior service cost and gains and losses, and certain other requirements of the statement, are not permissible for purposes of computing the maximum allowable income-tax deduction. Furthermore, actuarial assumptions may sometimes differ because the discount rate assumption required by *SFAS No. 87* may be too high to use for funding purposes. Accordingly, many companies are finding it necessary to perform separate actuarial calculations for funding and accounting purposes.

Moreover, companies are being confronted with another problem:

- If funding levels are reduced to reflect lower pension cost, appropriate explanations and communications are needed to explain the reduced funding levels to plan participants and other interested parties.

FIGURE 42–4
Illustrative Example of Financial Statement Disclosures

NOTE P: The company has a defined benefit pension plan covering substantially all of its employees. The benefits are based on years of service and the employee's average compensation during employment. The company's funding policy is to contribute annually the maximum amount that can be deducted for federal income tax purposes. Contributions are intended to provide not only for benefits attributed to service to date but also for those expected to be earned in the future.

The following table sets forth the plan's funded status and amounts recognized in the company's statement of financial position at December 31, 1989 (in thousands):

Actuarial present value of benefit obligations:	
Accumulated benefit obligation, including vested benefits of $11,700	$13,800
Projected benefit obligation for service rendered to date	($14,653)
Plan assets at fair value, primarily listed stocks and U.S. bonds	15,000
Plan assets in excess of projected benefit obligation	347
Unrecognized net loss from past experience different from that assumed and effects of changes in assumptions	351*
Unrecognized net transition debit at January 1, 1989, being recognized over 14 years	464
Prepaid pension cost included in other assets	$ 1,162

Net pension cost for 1989 included the following components (in thousands):

Service cost—benefits earned during the period	$ 300
Interest cost on the projected benefit obligation	1,322
Actual return on plan assets	(2,860)
Net amortization and deferral	1,576†
Net pension cost	$ 338

The weighted average discount rate and rate of increase in future compensation levels used in determining the actuarial present value of the projected benefit obligation were 10 percent and 6 percent, respectively. The expected long-term rate of return on assets was 11 percent.

*The sum of (1) a loss ($1,891) equal to the difference between the expected PBO at 12/31/89 ($11,500 + 300 + 1,322 − 360) and the actual PBO at 12/31/89 ($14,653) and (2) a gain ($1,540) equal to the difference between the actual return on plan assets ($2,860) and the expected return on plan assets ($1,320).

†The sum of (1) the reversal of the deferred gain for the period ($1,540) that should not be reflected in pension cost but that is required to be included in the actual return on plan assets and (2) the amortization of the transition debit ($36).

- If funding levels are not reduced even though pension cost is lower, management needs to explain the difference between these levels and the reduced pension cost, as well as the potentially large assets included on the company's balance sheet based on the excess of amounts funded over amounts expensed, to stockholders, the board of directors, plan participants, and other interested parties.

ACCOUNTING FOR SETTLEMENTS AND CURTAILMENTS OF DEFINED BENEFIT PLANS AND TERMINATION BENEFITS

SFAS No. 88 defines an event—a settlement—that requires, among other things, immediate recognition of previously unrecognized gains and losses but no accelerated recognition of prior service cost, and another event—a curtailment—that requires immediate recognition of previously unrecognized prior service cost, but no accelerated recognition of previously unrecognized gains and losses.

SFAS No. 88 also requires all companies to accelerate the recognition of prior service cost when it is probable a curtailment will occur, thus providing more consistent accounting among companies for the same types of transactions.

Accounting for Settlements

SFAS No. 88 defines a settlement as a transaction that:

- Is an irrevocable action.
- Relieves the employer (or the plan) of primary responsibility for a pension benefit obligation.
- Eliminates significant risks related to the obligation and the assets used to effect the settlement.

The statement indicates that purchasing annuity contracts or making lump-sum cash payments to plan participants in exchange for their rights to receive specified pension benefits constitutes a settlement, since all three criteria are met. However, a decision to invest in a portfolio of high-quality, fixed-income securities with principal and interest payment dates similar to the estimated payment dates of benefits does not constitute a settlement, since such a decision (1) may be reversed, (2) does not relieve the employer of primary responsibility for the obligation, and (3) does not eliminate mortality risk.

The FASB staff's special report confirms that a settlement has generally not occurred until an exchange has been accomplished (that is, cash has been disbursed to participants or annuities have been purchased). Other actions, including the intent to complete the exchange, the probability of completion of the irrevocable action, the completion of negotiations, or the establishment of a commitment to purchase annuities, are not sufficient to effect a settlement.

SFAS No. 88 requires that companies accelerate the recognition of previously unrecognized gains and losses when a settlement occurs, since the possibility of future gains or losses related to the obligation and to the assets used to effect the transaction is eliminated in such a situation. Specifically, the new rules require companies to immediately recognize a percentage of (1) the previously unrecognized net gain or loss, (2) the gain or loss arising from the settlement (that is, the difference between the expected value of the pension obligation and plan assets and their actual (remeasured) value at the time of the settlement), and (3) the unamortized transition credit (as defined on pages 14 and 15) based on the percentage of the projected benefit obligation eliminated by the settlement. The amortization of prior service cost and/or transition debit (if any) is not, however, accelerated unless a curtailment also takes place, since the benefits derived from the future services of employees (which is one of the bases for delayed recognition of prior service cost) have not been affected by the settlement. Figure 42–5 illustrates how a settlement gain would be calculated.

Whenever a defined benefit plan is terminated (and a settlement occurs) and a replacement defined benefit plan is established, the gain (or loss in rare cases) recognized is to be determined not by the amount of assets that revert to the company, but by the settlement computation discussed in the preceding paragraph. The difference between the recognized gain (or loss) and the reverted assets is accounted for as an asset or liability on the company's balance sheet. In theory this asset or liability will be eliminated by differences between funding and expense over future years.

SFAS No. 88 specifies that routine annuity purchases (for retiring employees, for example) result in a settlement. However, employers may elect to adopt a consistently applied policy of not recognizing a gain or loss if the cost of all settlements in a year is less than or equal to the sum of the service cost and the interest cost components of pension cost for the year.

FIGURE 42–5
Illustrative Example of a Settlement Gain Calculation

ABC Company sponsors a final pay, defined benefit pension plan. On July 15, 1990, the plan settled its accumulated benefit obligation through the purchase of nonparticipating annuity contracts for $18 million. In order to determine the settlement gain of $5,148,000, the company remeasured its plan assets and obligations as of the settlement date, July 15, 1990.

	Revaluation (in thousands)		
	Expected Values at 7/15/90	*Revaluation**	*Actual Values at 7/15/90*
Accumulated benefit obligation (ABO)	($16,000)	($ 2,000)	($18,000)
Projected benefit obligation (PBO)	($23,700)	($ 3,600)	($27,300)
Fair value of plan assets	31,300	2,700	34,000
Funded status	7,600	(900)	6,700
Unamortized transition (credit)	(8,700)		(8,700)
Unrecognized net loss	-0-	900	900
(Accrued) pension cost	($ 1,100)	$ -0-	($ 1,100)

Settlement Gain Calculation (in thousands)

Maximum gain
    Unrecognized net gain/loss before the revaluation $ -0-
    Loss arising from the settlement   900
    Unamortized transition credit   (8,700) $ 7,800

Percentage of the PBO settled
    ABO after the revaluation $ 18,000
    PBO after the revaluation   ÷ 27,300   × 66%

Settlement gain $ 5,148

*The revaluation is necessary in this situation because the discount rate at 7/15/90 (9 percent) is lower than the assumed discount rate (10 percent) at 1/1/90, and the actual return on plan assets is greater than the expected return.

Figure 42–6 discusses how settlement accounting is applied in some common situations.

Accounting for Curtailments

SFAS No. 88 defines a curtailment as an event that significantly reduces the expected years of future service of present employees or eliminates,

FIGURE 42–6
Settlement Accounting in Common Situations

A defined benefit plan is terminated and replaced with a defined contribution plan.

This type of transaction is both a curtailment (because pension benefits cease to accumulate) and a settlement (because annuities are purchased to eliminate the obligation). As a result, the unrecognized prior service cost, the unrecognized net gain or loss, and the remaining transition amount are recognized immediately, with the amount of the gain generally being equal to the excess assets that revert to the company. The FASB staff's special report confirms that the gain should not be recorded as an extraordinary item.

A defined benefit plan is terminated and replaced with another defined benefit plan.

Since employees continue to earn benefits under the successor plan, this transaction is not considered a curtailment, and unrecognized prior service cost continues to be amortized as before the termination. It is considered to be a settlement, however, since annuities must be purchased under IRS/Department of Labor/PBGC [Pension Benefit Guaranty Corporation] guidelines. The gain is to be computed as follows:

- **Flat benefit plans:** Because 100 percent of the PBO (before termination) is settled by purchasing annuities—salary progression is not considered in actuarial calculations for flat benefit plans—the entire unrecognized gain (including any gain or loss arising directly from the annuity purchase and any remaining unamortized transition credit) is recognized immediately.

- **Final pay or career average plans:** Because to the best of our knowledge insurance companies do not sell annuities for the salary progression component of the PBO, it is impossible to settle 100 percent of the PBO for such plans. Pro rata recognition is required when less than 100 percent of the PBO is settled. The immediate gain or loss recognized is computed:

  Recognized amount = Percentage reduction of the PBO
  $$\times \text{ Maximum gain or loss}$$

  The maximum gain or loss equals the unrecognized net gain or loss (including asset gains and losses not yet reflected in the market-related value of plan assets as discussed in paragraphs 30 and 31 of *SFAS No. 87*) plus or minus the gain or loss first measured at the time of the annuity purchase plus any remaining unamortized transition credit (see paragraph 77 of *SFAS No. 87*).

- The FASB staff's special report indicates that both plan assets and obligations are required to be remeasured as of the date of settlement in order to compute the maximum gain or loss and the percentage reduction in the PBO.

FIGURE 42–6   (*continued*)

Annuities are purchased without plan termination or asset reversion.

Under the new rules, if a company purchases annuities in order to settle all or part of the vested benefits portion of the PBO, a pro rata portion of the maximum gain or loss is recognized immediately. It is, therefore, not necessary to terminate the plan and recover the assets in order to recognize a gain. Thus, companies in an overfunded situation can trigger gain recognition by purchasing annuities at any particular time.

- **Negative contributions:** Presently, an employer in the United States is precluded from withdrawing excess plan assets from a pension plan without settling the obligation by making lump-sum payments or by purchasing annuities, except in the case in which the excess assets are transferred to an employee stock ownership plan (ESOP). The FASB staff's special report indicates that an ESOP transfer situation not involving the purchase of annuities does not constitute a settlement. The withdrawal of assets should be recorded as a "negative contribution" by increasing cash and reducing prepaid pension cost or increasing accrued pension liability.

- **Annuities purchased from an affiliate:** Annuities purchased from an insurance company controlled by the employer do not constitute a settlement, since the risk has not been eliminated but merely transferred within the group. The FASB staff's special report indicates that when a subsidiary purchases annuities from an insurance company that is a subsidiary of the same parent company, settlement accounting should be reflected in the separate company financial statements of the subsidiary purchasing the annuities; however, for consolidated financial statement purposes, no settlement is deemed to have occurred.

If the insurance company is less-than-majority-owned and not controlled by the employer, the special report states that the entire settlement gain may be recognized by the employer. (For example, if the insurer is a 40 percent-owned investee, 100 percent of the settlement gain should be reflected in the employer's financial statements.) The special report acknowledges that this conclusion is a departure from traditional accounting under the equity method and is not intended to be a precedent for nonpension intercompany transactions.

The critical factor in determining whether settlement has occurred in situations of this nature is whether risk has been transferred. As discussed in footnote 1 of *SFAS No. 88* and in the FASB staff's special report, transfer of risk within a controlled group does not constitute settlement; risk transferred outside the group does. Risk has also not been transferred if there is reasonable doubt that the insurer will meet its obligations under an annuity contract, and, therefore, the purchase of the contract from such an insurer does not constitute settlement.

The pension obligation is settled using participating annuity contracts.

SFAS No. 88 describes some contracts with insurance companies (referred to as *participating annuities*) that allow a company or the plan to receive dividends

FIGURE 42–6   *(concluded)*

---

if the insurance company has favorable experience. *SFAS No. 88* indicates that if the substance of a participating annuity contract is such that the employer remains subject to all or most of the risks and rewards associated with the benefit obligation covered or the assets transferred to the insurance company, the purchase of the contract does not constitute a settlement. In interpreting this provision, however, the prevailing view appears to be that if an employer transfers the risks associated with the benefit obligation and plan assets but retains some potential rewards, the transaction should be considered a settlement.

If a participating annuity contract does constitute a settlement of the pension benefit obligation, a gain or loss should be recognized. Although the wording in *SFAS No. 88* is somewhat complex, the gain is generally measured by reducing the amount to be recognized by the cost of the participation feature. (While footnote 3 states that the gain or loss first measured at the time of the annuity purchase is computed by excluding the cost of the participating feature, paragraph 10 states that the maximum gain must be reduced by the cost of the participating feature. These two provisions normally cancel each other.)

---

for a significant number of employees, the accrual of defined benefits for some or all of their future services. Curtailments include:

- Termination of employees' service earlier than had been expected, which may or may not involve closing a facility or discontinuing a segment of a business.
- Termination or suspension of a plan so that employees do not earn additional defined benefits for future services.

When it is probable a curtailment will occur *and* its impact (dollar effect) can be reasonably estimated, an employer is required to compute a net gain or loss that includes accelerated recognition of previously unrecognized prior service cost. Unless an employer also settles the pension obligation, accelerated recognition of previously unrecognized gains or losses is not permitted, since the employer has not been relieved of the primary responsibility for the pension obligation and remains subject to the risks associated with it as well as the related plan assets. If the result of this computation is a net loss, an employer must recognize the amount involved immediately. However, if the result is a net gain, an employer may recognize this amount only when realized (that is, when the related employees terminate or the plan suspension or amendment is adopted). *SFAS No. 88* sets forth the specific computational requirements to be followed when determining the net gain or loss in a curtailment situation. In very basic terms, the net gain or loss represents the sum of two items:

- A loss computed as the portion of unrecognized prior service cost that relates to years of service no longer expected to be rendered.
- A gain or loss computed as the net change in the projected benefit obligation resulting from the event. If the net change is a gain, it must first be offset against any existing unrecognized net loss. If the net change is a loss, it must first be offset against any existing unrecognized net gain.

For purposes of these computations, any remaining unamortized transition credit is considered to be an unrecognized net gain; any remaining transition debit is considered to be an unrecognized prior service cost.

Termination Benefits

The accounting provisions of *SFAS No. 88* also deal with "special termination benefits offered 'only for a short period of time' to employees in connection with their termination of employment." In situations of this nature, an employer is required to recognize a liability and a loss when the employees accept the offer and the amount can be reasonably estimated. The FASB staff's special report indicates that an employer may not recognize a loss at the date the offer is made based on the estimated acceptance rate. In the authors' opinion, however, this interpretation would not apply to a situation in which a company has reached the decision to terminate a specified number of employees irrespective of how many will accept the special termination benefit offer.

SFAS No. 88 also addresses "contractual termination benefits" provided by the existing terms of a plan but payable only if a specified event (such as a plant closing) occurs. An employer that provides such benefits is required to recognize a liability and a loss when it is probable that employees will be entitled to benefits and the amount can be reasonably estimated. The FASB staff's special report indicates that supplemental early retirement benefits should not be considered contractual termination benefits, because they are not based on the occurrence of a specific event that causes employees' services to be involuntarily terminated. However, termination indemnities paid only in the case of involuntary termination of employment due to a specific event should qualify as contractual termination benefits.

A situation involving termination benefits would generally also involve a curtailment that must be accounted for under *SFAS No. 88.*

Recognition, Classification, and Disclosure

SFAS No. 88 contains the following provisions regarding financial-statement recognition, classification, and disclosure:

• A description of the event and the amount of gain or loss resulting from settlement, curtailment, or termination benefits are required to be disclosed.

• Extraordinary item treatment is not permitted unless the requirements of *APB Opinion No. 30, Reporting the Results of Operations—Reporting the Effects of Disposal of a Segment of a Business, and Extraordinary, Unusual, and Infrequently Occurring Events and Transactions,* are met. (Note that the event must be both unusual and infrequent.) However, Appendix A (paragraph 48) of *SFAS No. 88* and the FASB staff's special report indicate that the gains or losses resulting from settlements, curtailments, or termination benefits generally do not result from the type of unusual and infrequent event required by *APB Opinion No. 30* to be reported as an extraordinary item. The authors agree with this interpretation.

• The effect of a settlement and/or curtailment and/or the offer of termination benefits directly related to a disposal of a segment of a business is required to be recognized as part of the gain or loss associated with the disposal, not as part of pension cost. The gain or loss on disposal of a segment of a business is computed and recognized in accordance with *APB Opinion No. 30.*

• Unless the settlement or curtailment or the offer of termination benefits is directly related to a disposal of a segment (see the preceding paragraph), *SFAS No. 88* appears to call for the recognition criteria of each event to be followed, even if a single management decision results in recognizing gains or losses in different reporting periods. A settlement gain or loss is recognized when the transaction is completed; a curtailment loss is recognized when it is probable a curtailment will occur and the amount can be estimated; a curtailment gain is recognized when realized; a special termination benefits loss is recognized when the employees accept the offer; and a contractual termination benefits loss is recognized when it is probable that employees will be entitled to benefits and the amount can be estimated. Therefore, a situation could arise in which a plan is terminated and a curtailment loss and the loss relating to contractual termination benefits granted to the employees are recognized in one period (when it is probable that the events will occur and the amounts can be estimated), the loss relating to special termination benefits offered in the same period is recognized in a later period (when the offer is accepted), and the gain on settlement is recognized in still another later period (when the annuities are purchased).

• A gain or loss from settlement or curtailment may occur after the pension plan's measurement date but prior to the employer's fiscal year-end. The FASB staff's special report indicates that the employer should generally not include that gain or loss in determining that fiscal year's results of operations. The gain or loss should be recognized in the financial statements for the subsequent fiscal year. However, if the gain or loss results from the employer terminating the pension plan and not establishing a successor pension plan, the effect of the settlement and curtailment should be recognized in the current fiscal year. If the gain or loss is directly related to another event of the current fiscal year (for example, a disposal of a segment of a business or the sale of a division requiring that a portion of the pension obligation be settled), the gain or loss should be recognized in the current fiscal year.

The special report also notes that if the gain or loss is not recognized in the current fiscal year and the employer's financial position or results of operations would have been materially affected had it been recognized, disclosure of the event, its consequences, and when recognition will occur should be made in the financial statements for the current fiscal year.

OTHER ISSUES

Business Combinations

In a business combination accounted for under the purchase method prescribed in *APB Opinion No. 16, Business Combinations,* the acquiring company is required to recognize a liability (or asset) if the acquired company has a defined benefit pension plan with projected benefit obligation in excess of (or less than) fair value of plan assets. For purposes of this calculation, the projected benefit obligation and the fair value of plan assets at the date of the acquisition should reflect current interest rates and assumptions and the effects of intended plan restructuring. For a multi-employer plan, the estimated withdrawal liability should be recorded only when it is probable that the acquiring company will withdraw from the plan.

The pension asset or liability thus recorded eliminates any previously unrecognized gain or loss, unrecognized prior service cost, and transition debit or credit. To the extent that the pension asset or liability is considered in determining the level of funding, the difference between the acquirer's net pension cost and contributions will reduce the liability or asset recognized at the date of acquisition.

Interest on the acquired pension liability or asset is included in the interest cost or return-on-assets component of net periodic pension cost as it arises subsequent to the acquisition. Because the interest is included in accounting for the pension plan (that is, through the pension cost computation), it is inappropriate to accrue additional interest on the acquired pension obligation or asset.

Some companies have questioned the appropriate accounting when the acquiring company includes in its pension plan employees of an acquired company that did not have a pension plan of its own and grants them credit for prior service. The FASB staff's special report indicates that careful consideration of the facts and circumstances surrounding the acquisition is required to determine the appropriate accounting. If the granting of credit by the acquiring company for prior service is required by the terms of the acquisition agreement, such amount should be considered as part of the cost of the acquisition to be accounted for pursuant to *APB Opinion No. 16, Business Combinations.* Otherwise, the credit for prior service should be accounted for as a plan amendment.

Rate-Regulated Enterprises

SFAS Nos. 87 and *88* do not contain special provisions relating to employers subject to certain types of regulation. In this connection, paragraph 210 of *SFAS No. 87* states:

> For rate-regulated enterprises, *FASB Statement No. 71, Accounting for the Effects of Certain Types of Regulation,* may require that the difference between net periodic pension cost as defined in this *Statement* and amounts of pension cost considered for rate-making purposes be recognized as an asset [if the criteria in paragraph 9 of *SFAS No. 71* are met] or a liability [if

the situation is as described in paragraph 11(b) of *SFAS No. 71*] created by the actions of the regulator. Those actions of the regulator change the timing of recognition of net pension cost as an expense; they do not otherwise affect the requirements of this *Statement*.

Paragraph 9 of *SFAS No. 71* states:

Rate actions of a regulator can provide reasonable assurance of the existence of an asset. An enterprise shall capitalize all or part of an incurred cost that would otherwise be charged to expense if both of the following criteria are met:

a. It is probable that future revenue in an amount at least equal to the capitalized cost will result from inclusion of that cost in allowable costs for rate-making purposes.

b. Based on available evidence, the future revenue will be provided to permit recovery of the previously incurred cost rather than to provide for expected levels of similar future costs. If the revenue will be provided through an automatic rate-adjustment clause, this criterion requires that the regulator's intent clearly be to permit recovery of the previously incurred cost.

Paragraph 11(b) of *SFAS No. 71* states:

Rate actions of a regulator can impose a liability on a regulated enterprise. Such liabilities are usually obligations to the enterprise's customers. The following are the usual ways in which liabilities can be imposed and the resulting accounting:

* * * * *

b. A regulator can provide current rates intended to recover costs that are expected to be incurred in the future with the understanding that if those costs are not incurred future rates will be reduced by corresponding amounts. If current rates are intended to recover such costs and the regulator requires the enterprise to remain accountable for any amounts charged pursuant to such rates and not yet expended for the intended purpose, the enterprise shall not recognize as revenues amounts charged pursuant to such rates. Those amounts shall be recognized as liabilities and taken to income only when the associated costs are incurred.

The FASB staff's special report indicates that continued use of different methods of determining pension cost for rate-making purposes and financial accounting purposes would result in the criteria in paragraph 9 of *SFAS No. 71* being met, in which case an asset would be recorded due to the actions of the regulators. However, the special report also indicates that the criteria in paragraph 9 of *SFAS No. 71* would *not* be met, and thus an asset could not be recorded, if:

> (a) it is probable that the regulator soon will accept a change for rate-making purposes so that pension cost is determined in accordance with *Statement 87* and (b) it is not probable that the regulator will provide revenue to recover the excess cost that results from the use of *Statement 87* for financial reporting purposes during the period between the date that the employer adopts *Statement 87* and the rate case implementing the change.

Similarly, the special report indicates that the situation would not be as described in paragraph 11(b) of *SFAS No. 71,* and a liability due to the actions of the regulator would not be required to be recorded, if it is probable that:

> (a) the regulator soon will accept a change for rate-making purposes so that pension cost is determined in accordance with *Statement 87,* (b) the regulator will not hold the employer responsible for the costs that were intended to be recovered by the current rates and that have been deferred by the change in method, and (c) the regulator will provide revenue to recover those same costs when they are eventually recognized under the method required by *Statement 87.*

The special report indicates that rate-regulated enterprises may record an asset only if it is probable that the "excess" costs will be recovered from the ratepayers in the future.

State and Local Governments

In September 1986, the Governmental Accounting Standards Board (GASB) issued its *Statement No. 4, Applicability of FASB Statement No. 87, "Employers' Accounting for Pensions," to State and Local Governmental Employers.* Paragraph 10 of *GASB Statement No. 4* states:

> State and local governmental employers, including proprietary and similar trust funds, should not change their accounting and reporting of pension activities as a result of the issuance of *FASB Statement No. 87.*

The statement also indicates, however, that employers may change to any attribution (actuarial cost) method, provided the method (1) is in conformity with *APB Opinion No. 8,* National Council on Government Accounting *(NCGA) Statement 1, Governmental Accounting and Financial Reporting Principles,* and *NCGA Statement 6, Pension Accounting and Financial Reporting: Public Employee Retirement Systems and State and Local Government Employers,* and (2) is considered preferable for purposes of making an accounting change in accordance with *APB Opinion No. 20, Accounting Changes.*

On January 31, 1990, the GASB issued an Exposure Draft of a proposed statement entitled *Accounting for Pensions by State and Local Governmental Employers.* The proposed statement would require accrual-basis recognition of pension expenditure/expense in all fund types used to account for a state or local governmental employer's commitment to provide pension benefits to its employees. At present the GASB's deliberations are still in process. As proposed, the statement would be effective for periods beginning after June 15, 1994.

Government Contracts

Some companies perform work for the U.S. federal government under contracts that are subject to price adjustment pursuant to the rules of the Cost Accounting Standards Board (CASB). Certain of the standards issued by the CASB have provisions that are at variance with *SFAS Nos. 87* and *88.* For example:

- *SFAS No. 87* prescribes specific methodologies for determining pension cost and emphasizes that pension cost is *not* necessarily determined by the amount the employer decides to contribute to the plan. For cost accounting purposes the CASB rules limit the pension provision to amounts the employer is legally "compelled" to fund (for example, under ERISA) or to amounts actually funded up to the amount of the provision for financial accounting purposes.
- *SFAS No. 87* requires employers to amortize (actuarial) gains and losses over the expected future service period of employees using the corridor approach. CASB rules generally require these gains and losses to be amortized over a 15-year period.

The above examples represent only two of the existing variances. Auditors engaged in an examination of financial statements of a company subject to CASB standards should be aware of these and other differences that may exist between *SFAS Nos. 87* and *88* and the CASB standards. Auditors should also be aware that adjustments may be needed when financial statements prepared in accordance with generally accepted accounting principles are to be used for CASB purposes, as such differences may affect the company's position in the determination or redetermination of prices under its government contracts.

Plan Compliance with ERISA

SFAS No. 87 requires companies to compute pension cost in accordance with the plan's requirements. If the plan is not in compliance with ERISA, the provision for pension cost may be based on plan provisions that do not comply with ERISA. This may result in a loss contingency that may need to be reflected in the financial statements, depending on the likelihood of incurring and reasonably estimating the amount of a liability. In this connection, the guidance in *SFAS No. 5, Accounting for Contingencies,* although not directly applicable, may be helpful. To illustrate, if a plan instrument does not conform to ERISA's participation requirements, the provision for pension cost would be computed excluding certain legally eligible participants, and the pension accrual will be inadequate. Thus, a determination would need to be made as to the likelihood (as defined by *SFAS No. 5*) that a liability will be incurred for the additional benefits, and for any fines and penalties that may be imposed for lack of compliance.[4]

---

[4]ERISA specifies that certain penalties are levied against the plan or against the plan administrator. However, the employer may ultimately become liable for such penalties even if it is not the plan administrator.

CHAPTER 43

EMPLOYEE BENEFIT PLAN ACCOUNTING AND REPORTING

Bradley J. Allen
William M. Cobourn

Since the enactment of Employee Retirement Income Security Act of 1974 (ERISA), there has been a more pronounced focus on plan sponsors' financial management of assets held in trust for the benefit of plan participants. As a result, the role of plan financial statements has increased in importance, causing the Financial Accounting Standards Board (FASB) to address the needs of the users of the plan financial statements and the objectives of those statements.

The most important objective of the plan financial statements is to assist the user in assessing the ability of the plan to pay benefits when due. Who is the user? Obviously, the plan is for the benefit of the participants, and the ability of the plan to pay benefits when due is of critical importance to the participant. However, "the 'typical' plan participant would be uninterested in or unable to properly assimilate the information presented in plan financial statements and thus would be confused and possibly misled."[1] The FASB concluded that, even if some participants might need to be educated regarding the plan financial statements, those financial statements should nonetheless focus on their needs. Thus, the primary users are deemed to be the participants, or those who advise or represent them.

---

[1] *Statement of Financial Accounting Standards No. 35*, Paragraph 48.

This chapter presents an overview of the general financial reporting and accounting requirements of employee benefit plans. Employers' accounting for pension plans is discussed in Chapter 42.

FINANCIAL STATEMENT REQUIREMENTS

ERISA requires that many different reports be prepared and filed with the Internal Revenue Service (IRS) and furnished to participants, beneficiaries, the Department of Labor (DOL), and others. ERISA requires that most plans file an annual report with the IRS, which provides a copy to the DOL.

While it is ERISA that requires the plans to file an annual report, it is IRS and DOL regulations that specify the filing requirements for plan financial statements. Principally, the requirements are that each plan must file an annual report containing IRS Form 5500 plus certain attachments. The attachments include, among other things, financial statements, notes thereto, supporting schedules, and an accountant's report. Pursuant to DOL regulations, the following plans are not required to file financial statements:

- Small plans (fewer than 100 participants at the beginning of the plan year or plans with more than 100 participants but fewer than 120 that file Form 5500 C/R under the 80–120 rule of DOL Reg. 2520.103-1(d)).
- Insured plans funded exclusively through allocated insurance contracts and whose benefits are fully guaranteed by the insurance carrier.
- Unfunded plans.

DOL regulations generally provide that a plan required to file an annual report has the option of either reporting the information prescribed by "Section 103 of the Act, or in accordance with a limited exemption or alternative method of compliance (LEAM)."[2] The LEAM permits plans to fulfill annual reporting requirements by filing an annual report containing IRS Form 5500 (including required schedules), financial

---

[2]ERISA, Section 2520.103-1.

statements and notes, separate financial schedules, and an accountant's report. Since the rules for filing under the LEAM are more definitive, most plans now elect that method. In contrast to plans filing under the Act, the LEAM does not require the financial statements to be prepared in accordance with generally accepted accounting principles (GAAP). However, the LEAM regulations require disclosure of variations from GAAP.

Prior to 1980, there were no published guidelines on the application of GAAP to employee benefit plans. Consequently, there was great diversity in the accounting principles adopted and the methods of disclosure used in plan financial statements. For example, where one plan may have reported its assets at their cost basis, another plan may have adjusted the cost basis of the assets to reflect market appreciation or depreciation.

In March 1980 the FASB issued *Statement of Financial Accounting Standards (SFAS) No. 35, Accounting and Reporting by Defined Benefit Pension Plans*. Since *SFAS No. 35* addressed only defined benefit plans, the American Institute of Certified Public Accountants (AICPA), when it issued its *Audit and Accounting Guide: Audits of Employee Benefit Plans* (the Guide) in 1983, incorporated accounting and reporting guidelines for defined contribution and health and welfare plans.

The remainder of this section is devoted to a discussion of the accounting records needed by, and the generally accepted accounting principles applicable to, defined benefit, defined contribution, and health and welfare employee benefit plans.

ACCOUNTING RECORDS

As with any entity, certain records are needed to produce information necessary for effective management of the entity and for preparing its financial statements. Such records for employee benefit plans usually are maintained at a number of locations, such as with the employer, trustee, and/or administrator. Depending on the plan, typical records include (but are not limited to):

- Investment asset records—Such records should include a portfolio listing of all investments and investment transactions.
- Participant records—Demographic records are needed to determine eligibility for participation and benefit payments.

- Contribution records—Records of contributions received and due are particularly important for plans having more than one contributor.
- Claim records—Records of claims for health and welfare plans are not only important for establishing claims history, but also for determining when benefit limits have been reached.
- Distribution records—These records, including entitlement, commencement data, forfeitures, terminations, etc., are necessary to support all distributions from the plan.
- Separate participants' accounts—Defined contribution plans require separate accounts to be maintained for each participant reflecting his or her share of the net assets of the plan.

EMPLOYEE BENEFIT PLAN FINANCIAL STATEMENTS

The general requirements for financial statements prescribed by the FASB and AICPA for defined benefit, defined contribution, and health and welfare plans are similar in many aspects. This section of the chapter is organized into a discussion of the general requirements equally applicable to all types of plans followed by some of the particular requirements applicable to the specific types of plans. Sample financial statements of a defined benefit pension plan are included in the chapter appendix. Financial accounting and reporting standards for defined contribution plans are in conformity with those of defined benefit plans to the extent that this is appropriate. For example, under a defined contribution plan, information regarding the actuarial present value of accumulated plan benefits would not be applicable, because the amount of benefits a participant receives is not determinable until time of payment. In other respects the financial statements of defined contribution plans are substantially the same as those of defined benefit plans.

Overview of General Requirements

SFAS No. 35 requires that every plan issuing financial statements present a statement of net assets available for plan benefits as of the end of the plan year, a statement of changes in net assets for the year then ended, and the related notes to the financial statements.

All plans filing under ERISA must present the financial statements in comparative form; that is, statements for the current year must be presented alongside statements for the previous year. Plans filing under the LEAM may present a statement of net assets available for plan benefits for two years, while presenting the statement of changes in net assets available for plan benefits for one year.

Under GAAP, the financial statements must be presented using the accrual basis of accounting whereby financial recognition is given to an event when it occurs, regardless of whether cash was paid or received. The accrual basis also contemplates that, generally, purchases and sales of securities must be recognized on a "trade-date" basis, as opposed to a "settlement-date" basis. Under the LEAM, the modified accrual, modified cash, and cash basis methods are also acceptable.

Statement of Net Assets Available for Plan Benefits

The statement of net assets available for plan benefits shall present information regarding net assets in such reasonable detail as is necessary to identify the plan's resources available to pay plan benefits.

Plan resources typically include investments, contributions receivable, cash, and operating assets less any liabilities of the plan.

Investments

Since investments are usually a pension plan's largest asset, their valuation is particularly important. All plan investments except contracts with insurance companies, which are discussed below, are required to be stated at fair value as of the date of the financial statements.

Determining Fair Value
The fair value of an investment is the amount a pension plan could realistically expect to receive in a transaction between a willing buyer and a willing seller. Fair value is often difficult to determine because of the nature of the investment. For securities traded on an active market, the determination is relatively easy—fair value is the quoted market price. For securities for which there is no quoted market price, the determination of fair value becomes more difficult. Securities of closely held companies or investments in real estate generally will not have an active market. In

these cases, market price must be determined using alternative means, such as discounted cash flow or valuations performed by independent experts.

Contracts with Insurance Companies

Contracts with insurance companies must be presented in the same manner required by ERISA. The presentation will generally depend on whether the payment to the insurance company is allocated to purchase insurance or annuities for the individual participants or whether the payments are accumulated in an unallocated fund to be used to pay retirement benefits. These are referred to as *allocated* and *unallocated* arrangements, respectively.

Allocated funding arrangements include contracts in which the insurer has a legally enforceable obligation to make the benefit payments. The obligations of the plan have been removed to the insurer, and the investment in the allocated insurance contract should be excluded from plan assets. Conversely, unallocated funding instruments apply to any arrangement under which contributions are held in an undivided fund until they are used to pay retirement benefits.

Unallocated funds are, therefore, included in plan assets. Examples of allocated contracts include individual insurance, annuity contracts, group permanent insurance contracts, and conventional deferred group annuity contracts. Unallocated arrangements include deposit administration contracts and immediate participation guarantee contracts.

With respect to determining the value of the insurance contracts, generally accepted accounting principles require that the contracts be measured in the same manner as required by ERISA. The instructions to Form 5500 call for investments in separate accounts to be carried at fair value, but permit other insurance contracts to be valued at either fair value or amounts determined by the insurance company. Contract value is almost universally used to value insurance contracts because insurance companies generally do not report fair value.

Other investment vehicles exist that are similar in substance but not held with insurance companies (for example, guaranteed investment contracts offered by banks). The FASB's Emerging Issues Task Force (EITF) considered the accounting for these investments in EITF Issue 89-1. It did not reach a consensus on the need to change accounting for insurance contracts or to adopt similar accounting for these other investment vehicles offered by noninsurance institutions. In April 1990, the FASB added a project to its agenda to address the accounting for these contracts.

Commingled and Master Trust Funds

Common or commingled trust funds, pooled separate accounts of insurance companies, and master trust funds generally contain the assets of two or more plans that are pooled for investment purposes. Common or commingled funds and insurance company pooled separate accounts generally contain plans sponsored by two or more employers. Master trusts hold the assets of plans sponsored by a single employer or by members of a controlled group. In a common or commingled fund or pooled separate account, the plan generally requires units of participation in the fund. The value of these investments is based on the unit value of the funds, but must be stated at fair value.

The accounting and reporting requirements for master trusts present certain additional considerations. Plans generally have two options as to how they account for such investments:

- A plan may present its interest in the master trust as one line—that is, as "Investment in master trust"—or
- A plan may present its allocable share of each master trust line item.

While either method is acceptable under GAAP, the "one-line" method is required by IRS Form 5500. Plans that use the one-line method should also disclose their percentage interest in the master trust. Summarized financial information of the master trust should be presented in a footnote along with the information mentioned above regarding the method of determining fair value and general types of investments.

Disclosure

Disclosure must be provided, usually in the footnotes, of whether fair value was measured using quoted market prices in an active market or was otherwise determined. Contracts with insurance companies, as noted, are presented in the same manner required by ERISA. The method of valuation of insurance contracts must be disclosed. Detail of the investments must be provided either on the face of the statement of net assets available for plan benefits or in a footnote. Investments must be segregated, where material, by general types such as corporate stocks, bonds, and the like. In addition, individual investments representing 5 percent or more of net assets available for plan benefits must be separately disclosed.

Receivables

Receivables must be stated separately, if material, for the following:

- Employer contributions.
- Participant contributions.
- Amounts due from brokers for securities sold.
- Accrued interest and dividends.
- Other.

Contributions receivable may only include amounts due as of the reporting date. Participant contributions receivable, generally, are those amounts withheld from participants' pay and not yet remitted to the plan. Employer contributions can be evidenced by the following:

1. A legal or contractual obligation.
2. A formal commitment evidenced by:
   a. A resolution by the employer's governing body.
   b. A consistent pattern of making payments after the plan's year-end pursuant to an established funding policy.
   c. A deduction for federal income taxes by the employer.
   d. The employer's recognition of a liability (although recognition of a liability by the employer in and of itself may not be sufficient to justify recording a receivable).

Advance employer contributions that relate to future years but are made to obtain a current tax deduction should be deferred on the plan's financial statements and described in a footnote. Conversely, if a deficiency in the plan's funding standard account exists at year-end, consideration should be given to establishing a receivable from the employer.

All of the foregoing should be tempered by the need to establish an appropriate allowance for estimated uncollectable receivables and, if material, disclose such allowance. For example, assume an employer has a contractual obligation to make a contribution to the plan. If the employer is a financially troubled company there may be some uncertainty that the full amount of the contribution will be received. In this situation, the amount of the contribution receivable should be reduced by the amount estimated to be uncollectable and this fact should be disclosed in the footnotes.

Other Assets

Typically, most plans do not have significant assets other than investments and contributions receivable. However, other types of assets that may exist are residual cash that has not yet been invested and operating assets such as buildings and equipment.

Cash and cash equivalents are recorded at face value but should be segregated between interest-bearing and noninterest-bearing deposits.

GAAP requires that operating assets be recorded at cost less depreciation and amortization. ERISA requires these assets be recorded at fair value. This should rarely present a significant difference.

Liabilities

Liabilities, such as those for the purchase of investments, should be stated at the amount owed by the plan.

Statement of Changes in Net Assets Available for Plan Benefits

The effects of significant changes in net assets available for plan benefits must be disclosed. At a minimum, this disclosure should include:

- The net appreciation or depreciation in fair value for each significant class of investment, segregated between investments whose fair values have been measured by quoted market prices and those whose fair values have been otherwise determined. The net appreciation or depreciation includes realized gains or losses from sales of investments and unrealized gains or losses from market appreciation or depreciation. Separate disclosure of realized gains or losses is not required by GAAP but is required for IRS Form 5500.

    Prior to 1988, many plans utilized historical cost as the basis to calculate and report realized and unrealized investment gains and losses in Form 5500. The DOL recently revised its instructions to Form 5500 to require that realized and unrealized gains and losses be determined using the value of the asset as of the beginning of the plan year ("current value method") rather than the historical cost basis. Filings for plan years beginning on or after January 1, 1990, must comply with the revised instructions. The adoption of the current value method may require significant record-keeping changes.

- Investment income exclusive of amount included in net appreciation of investments.
- Contributions from employer(s), participants, and others.
- Benefits paid to participants.
- Payments to insurance companies to purchase contracts that are excluded from plan assets.
- Administrative expenses.

Statement of Cash Flows

FASB Statement No. 102, Statement of Cash Flows—Exemption of Certain Enterprises and Classification of Cash Flows from Certain Securities Acquired for Resale, exempts employee benefit plans that present financial information required by *SFAS No. 35* from the requirement to present a statement of cash flows. However, benefit plans are encouraged to include a statement of cash flows with their annual financial statements when that statement would provide relevant information about the ability of the plan to meet future obligations.

Additional Financial Statement Disclosures

Disclosure of the plan's accounting policies should include a description of the methods and significant assumptions used to determine the fair value of investments and the reported value of contracts with insurance companies. The accounting policy footnote should also disclose any variances from GAAP. This could be an important disclosure since, as already mentioned, the LEAM does not require plans to follow GAAP, and plans using the LEAM may have significant variations from GAAP.

The notes to financial statements shall include the following additional information:

1. Description of the plan.
   a. A brief, general description of the plan agreement including, but not limited to, vesting, benefit, and allocation provisions. Reference to a plan agreement or a description thereof may be made in lieu of this disclosure provided that the information is otherwise published and made available.
   b. A description of significant plan amendments adopted during the year.
   c. A brief general description of (1) the priority order of participants' claims to the assets of the plan upon plan termination and (2) benefits guaranteed by the Pension Benefit Guaranty Corporation (PBGC).
2. Funding policy.
   a. A description of the funding policy and any changes in the funding policy during the year.
   b. A description, in general terms and in layman's language, of how contributions are determined.
   c. For contributory plans, the method of determining participants' contributions.
   d. For plans subject to ERISA, whether or not the minimum funding requirements have been met.
   e. The amount of significant administrative costs borne by the employer, if any.
3. The policy regarding the purchase of contracts with insurance companies that are excluded from plan assets.
4. The tax status of the plan if a favorable determination letter has not been obtained is required by GAAP. DOL regulations require disclosure of whether or not a tax ruling or determination letter has been obtained.
5. Significant real-estate or other transactions in which the plan and any of the following parties participated:
   a. Sponsor.
   b. Employer(s).
   c. Employee organizations.
6. Unusual or infrequent events or transactions occurring before issuance of the financial statements.
7. Information principally regarding financial instruments with off-balance-sheet risk of accounting loss and significant concentrations of credit risk.

Supplemental Schedules

In addition to the requirements of *SFAS No. 35* and the Guide, ERISA and DOL regulations specify separate schedules of:

- Investment assets (one schedule of assets held at the plan year-end and another showing plan assets acquired or disposed of during the plan year) showing both cost and fair value or sales proceeds.
- Transactions with parties in interest.
- Loans on fixed-income obligations in default or uncollectable.
- Leases in default or uncollectable.
- Reportable transactions.

DEFINED BENEFIT PLANS

A defined benefit plan is one that promises to pay participants' benefits that are determinable based on such factors as age, years of service, and compensation.

In addition to the general financial statement requirements, defined benefit plans must also disclose information regarding the actuarial present value of accumulated plan benefits (PVAB) as of either the beginning or end of the plan year and changes in the PVAB from year to year.

It is important to understand that the PVAB will generally not be the same amount as the actuarially determined liability pursuant to the cost method in the plan. This actuarial liability represents the present value of the estimated benefits that will be payable to participants upon retirement. The PVAB represents only those benefits that have accumulated as of a specific date, as opposed to estimated benefits at retirement. There is no requirement that the assumptions used to calculate the PVAB (for example, discount rates, investment rates, and the like) be the same as for the actuarial liability. Consequently, significant differences could exist.

Statement of Accumulated Plan Benefits

Information regarding the PVAB may be presented in the financial statements (on the same page as the statement of net assets available for plan benefits or as a separate statement) or in the footnotes and must be segmented into the following categories:

- Vested benefits of participants currently receiving benefits (including benefits due and payable as of the benefit information date).
- Other vested benefits.
- Nonvested benefits.

A description of the method and significant assumptions (for example, assumed rate of return, inflation rates, and retirement ages) used to determine the PVAB must be disclosed in the footnotes. The benefit information should exclude benefits to be paid by insurance companies pursuant to contracts that are excluded from plan assets.

Note that *SFAS No. 35* requires a statement of net assets available for plan benefits only as of the end of the plan year. However, when the accumulated benefit information is presented as of the beginning of the plan year, a statement of net assets available for plan benefits must be included as of the preceding plan year-end. The reason is to give the reader the ability to make a comparison between plan assets available to pay benefits with the related accumulated benefits as of the same date. If the plan assets are as of the end of the year and the benefit information is as of the beginning of the year, such comparability does not exist. By including plan assets as of the preceding year-end, there is comparability with the beginning-of-the-year benefit information. For plans complying with ERISA, this will not pose any problems because, as mentioned, ERISA requires comparative financial statements.

Statement of Changes in Accumulated Plan Benefits

Information regarding changes in the PVAB from the preceding to the current benefit-information dates can be presented as a separate financial statement or in the footnotes and in either a narrative or reconciliation format. The effects of any changes in accumulated plan benefits should be accounted for in the year of the change, not by restating amounts previously reported.

If significant, either individually or in the aggregate, the effects of certain factors affecting the change in the PVAB from the preceding to the current benefit-information dates shall be identified. Minimum disclosure shall include the following:

- Plan amendments.
- Changes in the nature of the plan (for example, a plan spin-off or merger).
- Changes in actuarial assumptions.

Any significant changes in methods or assumptions shall be described in the footnotes.

The significant effects of other factors may also be identified, including, for example, benefits accumulated (including actuarial gains or losses), the increase (for interest) as a result of the decrease in the discount period, benefits paid, and the like.

If the minimum required information is presented in other than a reconciliation format, the PVAB as of the preceding benefit-information date shall also be presented.

DEFINED CONTRIBUTION PLANS

A defined contribution plan is one that provides individual accounts for each participant's benefits based on amounts contributed to the participants' accounts, investment experience, and if applicable, forfeitures allocated to the account.

The additional key financial statement issue to address is the allocation of the plan assets to the participants' accounts. Required financial statement disclosures include:

- Amount of unallocated assets.
- The basis used to allocate asset values to participants' accounts when that basis differs from the one used to record assets in the financial statements.
- Amount of net assets and changes in net assets allocated to separate investment funds, if the plan provides for separate investment programs.
- The number of units of participation and net asset value per unit, if applicable.
- Amounts allocated to participants who have withdrawn from the plan.

Some defined contribution plans, such as employee stock purchase plans, are required to register and report to the Securities and Exchange

Commission (SEC). The form and content of the financial statements that must be filed with the SEC are prescribed in Regulation S-X.

The general requirements are included in Articles 1, 2, 3, and 4 of Regulation S-X. Article 6A of Regulation S-X includes the specific requirements applicable to employee stock purchase, savings, and similar plans.

Article 6A requires that plans present their net assets available for plan benefits in statements of financial condition for the two most recent years. Plan assets to be disclosed in this statement include:

1. Investments in securities of participating employer(s), stated separately for each employer.
2. Investments in securities of unaffiliated issuers, segregated between U.S. government obligations and other. Other securities must be segregated between marketable securities and other.
3. Investments other than securities.
4. Dividends and interest receivable.
5. Cash.
6. Other assets, stating separately amounts due from participating employers, directors, officers or principal shareholders, trustees or managers of the plan, and other.

Liabilities and equity that must be disclosed include:

1. Liabilities, stating separately any payables to employers, employees, and other.
2. Reserves and other credits.
3. Plan equity, which is equivalent to the net assets available for plan benefits.

In addition, statements of income and changes in plan equity are required for the three most recent years. These statements must include:

1. Net investment income, stating separately:
   a. Income, stating separately cash dividends, interest, and other. Income from investments in or indebtedness of participating employers shall be segregated.
   b. Expenses.
   c. Net investment income.
2. Realized gain or loss on investments, stating separately gains or losses from investments in securities of participating employer(s), other investments in securities, and other investments.

3. Unrealized appreciation or depreciation of investments. In addition, in a footnote, the unrealized appreciation or depreciation as of the beginning and end of the period must be disclosed.
4. Contributions and deposits, separated between employer(s) and employees.
5. Withdrawals, lapses, and forfeitures, stating separately the balances of the employees' accounts, the amounts disbursed in settlement of the accounts, and the disposition of the remaining balance.
6. Plan equity at the beginning of the period and at the end of the period.

In addition, Article 6A requires certain schedules to be filed if the information is not readily apparent from the financial statements. These are

Schedule I—Investments.

Schedule II—Allocation of plan assets and liabilities to investment programs.

Schedule III—Allocation of plan income and changes in plan equity to investment programs.

The form and content of these schedules are specified in Rule 6A–05.

HEALTH AND WELFARE PLANS

Employee health and welfare plans are those plans providing benefits, such as medical, dental, scholarship, and the like to employees of a single employer or group of employers. Such benefits may be provided by the plan or transferred to an insurance company. Whether a premium paid to an insurance company represents a deposit (that is, an investment) or a transfer of risk depends upon the exact nature of the contract.

Payment of a premium where the risk is transferred to the insurance company represents a reduction in the net assets of the plan. Premiums paid that represent deposits should be reflected as plan assets until such time as the deposit is refunded or applied against claims.

In an insured plan, claims reported and claims incurred but not reported will be paid by the insurance company. Such claims should not appear in the plan's financial statements. Self-insured plans should report those amounts. The footnotes should describe the significant assumptions and changes in assumptions used to determine such liabilities.

Certain group insurance contracts provide for experience rating adjustments that could result in a refund (premiums exceed claims) or deficit (claims exceed premiums). If the amount of a refund can be reasonably estimated, then a receivable should be recorded. If the amount of a deficit can be reasonably estimated and if it will be applied against future premiums, then a payable should be recorded. If a payable for a deficit is not recorded because one of the two conditions has not been met, disclosure should be made.

Some plans provide for payment of insurance benefits for a period of time subsequent to the financial statement date for participants who have accumulated a certain number of eligibility credits. Such credits will permit payment of benefits during times of unemployment and represent a liability of the plan as they have arisen from prior employee service. The liability should be calculated as follows:

- Insured plans—current insurance premium rates should be applied to the accumulated credits.
- Self-insured plans—the average cost per person of the benefits should be applied to the accumulated credits.

More detailed coverage of accounting and reporting for health and welfare benefit plans is presented in Chapter 44.

AUDITOR'S REPORT

The purpose of an audit is to attest to management's representations in financial statements. An auditor's report on employee benefit plan financial statements is generally included as part of the annual report required by ERISA standards. *AICPA Statement of Position (SOP) 88–2, Illustrative Auditor's Reports on Financial Statements of Employee Benefit Plans Comporting with Statement on Auditing Standards No. 58, Reports on Audited Financial Statements (SAS 58),* provides illustrative auditor's reports on financial statements of employee benefit plans that comply with *SAS 58*. Illustrative examples of standard reports and certain departures therefrom are provided in the appendix at the end of the chapter. The general form of the illustrative examples are in accordance with the SOP.

Standard Report

A standard auditor's report provides users with a reasonable assurance that the plan's financial statements have been presented fairly, in all material respects, in conformity with generally accepted accounting principles. The chapter appendix contains illustrative examples of standard audit reports for a defined benefit, a defined contribution, and a health and welfare benefit plan. The exact wording of each report in practice will depend upon the relevant circumstances involved. For example, although the illustrative reports included here are for financial statements covering one year, two-year comparative statements are frequently presented.

Supplemental Schedules

As indicated earlier in this chapter, in addition to the requirements of *SFAS No. 35* and the Guide, ERISA and DOL regulations require certain supplemental schedules. These schedules must be covered by the auditor's report, which requires a modification to the standard report. When the auditor's report covers this additional information and the auditor has applied auditing procedures, an illustrative separate paragraph of the report is as follows:

> Our audit was made for the purpose of forming an opinion on the basic financial statements taken as a whole. The supplemental schedules of (identify) are presented for purposes of complying with the Department of Labor's Rules and Regulations for Reporting and Disclosure under the Employee Retirement Income Security Act of 1974 and are not a required part of the basic financial statements. The supplemental schedules have been subjected to the auditing procedures applied in the audit of the basic financial statements and, in our opinion, are fairly stated in all material respects in relation to the basic financial statements taken as a whole.

Nonstandard Reports

The standard auditor's report will not always be appropriate. Some of the more common circumstances in which the auditor might use nonstandard wording include the preparation of financial statements on a non-GAAP basis (for example, on a cash or modified cash basis), scope limitations imposed by the plan administrator pursuant to DOL regulations, and inadequacies related to investment valuation or internal control.

As mentioned earlier, the DOL permits alternative methods of filing that allow modified cash and cash basis methods for preparation of financial statements. As these methods are not in accordance with GAAP, the standard report is not appropriate. An illustrative example of a report on the financial statements of a defined benefit plan prepared on a modified cash basis is provided in the chapter appendix.

Plan administrators commonly limit the scope of the auditor's examination to exclude information provided by a bank or insurance company subject to certain stipulations. This limitation restricts the scope of the auditor. Due to the significance that this information generally carries, the restriction prevents the auditor from reaching an opinion on the financial statements taken as a whole. An illustrative example of a report that might be issued in this situation also is provided in the appendix.

At times, benefit plans may hold material investments that do not have a readily determinable market value. This may cause a standard report to be inappropriate. An illustrative report when the plan's procedures to determine the fair value of investments are not adequate appears in the appendix.

When the auditor concludes that departures from generally accepted accounting principles are so material that the financial statements of the plan do not fairly present the plan's financial position and results, the auditor issues an adverse opinion.

SUMMARY

This chapter serves as a general explanation of the financial reporting and accounting requirements of employee benefit plans. It does not replace authoritative accounting and auditing literature or ERISA or other official instructions or published regulations of the DOL or IRS. Readers of this chapter should refer to those specific sources for more detailed information.

The importance of employee benefit plans in the economy has continued to grow over the past several years. There are approximately 66 million participants and beneficiaries of employee benefit plans in the United States, and the assets of these plans total approximately $2 trillion. Accompanying this growth, the various regulatory authorities governing these plans have increased their focus on a number of areas.

Congress has amended ERISA to tighten the plan sponsor's responsibility to fund pension plans and to pay taxes on excess contributions for which those sponsors receive large tax deductions. Additionally, the Tax Reform Act of 1986 created penalties to discourage the tax-free accumulation of assets in pension funds. Form 5500 filings have also undergone revisions and are being subjected to more detailed and comprehensive review by the IRS and DOL. This increased focus will most likely continue in the future and add to the complexity of accounting and reporting by employee benefit plans.

APPENDIX TO CHAPTER 43

SAMPLE PENSION PLAN FINANCIAL STATEMENTS

SAMPLE COMPANY
PENSION PLAN

**Statements of Net Assets Available for Plan Benefits
and of Accumulated Plan Benefits**

December 31, 19X2 and 19X1

	19X2	*19X1*
Net assets available for plan benefits		
Any Insurance Company immediate participation guarantee contract, at contract value	$2,278,000	$1,934,000
U.S. government securities, at fair value	250,000	150,000
Employer contribution receivable	41,000	141,000
Total net assets available for plan benefits	$2,569,000	$2,225,000
Accumulated plan benefits as of January 1, 19X2		
Actuarial present value of accumulated plan benefits:		
Vested benefits		
Participants currently receiving payments		$1,980,000
Other participants		177,000
		2,157,000
Nonvested benefits		264,000
Total actuarial present value of accumulated plan benefits		$2,421,000

**Statement of Changes in Net Assets
Available for Plan Benefits**

For the Years Ended December 31, 19X2 and 19X1

	19X2	*19X1*
Additions		
Contributions from employer	$ 183,000	$ 141,000
Net appreciation of U.S. government securities	20,000	10,000
Interest income	250,000	201,000
	453,000	352,000
Deductions		
Benefits paid	101,000	80,000
Administrative expenses	8,000	8,000
	109,000	88,000
Net additions	344,000	264,000
Net assets available for plan benefits, beginning of year	2,225,000	1,961,000
Net assets available for plan benefits, end of year	$2,569,000	$2,225,000

Notes to Financial Statements

General Description of the Plan

The Sample Company Pension Plan (Plan) is a noncontributory defined benefit plan covering all employees of Sample Company who have at least one year of service. Participants should refer to the Plan agreement for more complete information regarding benefit, vesting, and termination provisions.

Summary of Significant Accounting Policies

The underlying assets of the immediate participation guarantee contract (Contract) are invested in the unallocated general assets of an insurance company. The Contract is valued at fair value as determined by the insurance company. The Contract provides, among other matters, that the investment account is to be credited with the contributions received during the contract period plus its share of the insurance company's actual investment income. Annuities purchased in prior years to provide benefits are excluded from Plan assets.

Sample Company makes contributions, as are necessary, on an actuarial basis, to provide the Plan with assets sufficient to meet the benefits to be paid to Plan members. Contributions by Sample Company are designed to fund the Plan's normal cost on a current basis and to amortize the Plan's prior service cost (plus interest) over a period of twenty years. For the years ended December 31, 19X2 and 19X1, Sample Company has met the minimum funding requirements.

While Sample Company has not expressed any intent to discontinue its contributions, it is free to do so at any time, subject to penalties set forth in the Employee Retirement Income Security Act of 1974 (ERISA). In the event such discontinuance should result in the termination of the Plan, its net assets generally will not be available on a pro rata basis to provide a particular participant's benefits. Whether a particular participant's accumulated Plan benefits will be paid depends on both the priority of those benefits and the level of benefits guaranteed by the Pension Benefit Guaranty Corporation (PBGC) at that time. Some benefits may be fully or partially provided for by the then-existing assets and the PBGC guaranty, while other benefits may not be provided for at all.

Significant Actuarial Information

Accumulated plan benefits are those future periodic payments, including lump-sum distributions, that are attributable under the Plan's provisions to the service employees have rendered. Accumulated plan benefits include benefits expected to be paid to (a) retired or terminated employees or their beneficiaries, (b) beneficiaries of employees who have died, and (c) present employees or their beneficiaries. Benefits under the Plan are based on employees' compensation during their last full 60 months of service. The accumulated plan benefits as of January 1, 19X2, for active employees are based on their service rendered and history of compensation as of December 31, 19X1.

Benefits payable under all circumstances (retirement, death, disability, and termination of employment) are included to the extent they are deemed attributable to employee service rendered to the valuation date. Benefits to be provided via annuity contracts excluded from Plan assets are excluded from accumulated plan benefits.

The actuarial present value of accumulated plan benefits is that amount that results from applying actuarial assumptions to adjust the accumulated plan benefits to reflect the time value of money (through discounts for interest) and the probability of payment (by means of decrements such as for death, disability, withdrawal, or retirement) between the valuation date and the expected date of payment. The significant assumptions used in the actuarial valuation and/or the computation of the present value of accumulated plan benefits as of January 1, 19X2, are as follows:

Actuarial Factor	Assumption
Funding purposes	Entry age normal.
Accumulated benefits	Projected unit credit.
Rate of return on investments	7.5 percent per annum compounded annually.
Mortality basis	1971 Group Annuity Table.
Expenses	4.0 percent of estimated plan costs.
Retirement age	Normal, attained age 65; Early, attained age 55.
Salary increase	6.5 percent increase each year until retirement.
Social Security projection	Benefits expected to be available at retirement based on a 6.0 percent increase in the Social Security average earnings and a 5.5 percent increase in the Consumer Price Index.
Asset valuation method	Fixed-income assets are valued on a contract basis.
Withdrawal rates	Table 6 of *The Actuary's Pension Handbook*.

The total actuarial present value of accumulated plan benefits as of January 1, 19X1, was $2,075,000. In September 19X1, the Plan was amended to increase benefit levels. The effect of the changes was to increase the actuarial present value of accumulated plan benefits by approximately $285,000 as of January 1, 19X2.

Tax Status

The United States Treasury Department has advised the plan trustees that the Plan constitutes a qualified trust under Section 401(a) of the Internal Revenue Code and is, therefore, exempt from federal income taxes under provisions of Section 501(a).

ILLUSTRATIONS OF AUDITOR'S REPORTS ON FINANCIAL STATEMENTS

Standard Auditor's Reports

A Defined Benefit Plan

INDEPENDENT AUDITOR'S REPORT

Addressee:

We have audited the accompanying statements of net assets available for benefits and of accumulated plan benefits of XYZ Pension Plan as of December 31, 19X2, and the related statements of changes in net assets available for benefits and of changes in accumulated plan benefits for the year then ended. These financial statements are the responsibility of the Plan's management. Our responsibility is to express an opinion on these financial statements based on our audit.

We conducted our audit in accordance with generally accepted auditing standards. Those standards require that we plan and perform the audit to obtain reasonable assurance about whether the financial statements are free of material misstatement. An audit includes examining, on a test basis, evidence supporting the amounts and disclosures in the financial statements. An audit also includes assessing the accounting principles used and significant estimates made by management, as well as evaluating the overall financial statement presentation. We believe that our audit provides a reasonable basis for our opinion.

In our opinion, the financial statements referred to above present fairly, in all material respects, the financial status of the Plan as of December 31, 19X2, and the changes in its financial status for the year then ended in conformity with generally accepted accounting principles.

[City and State]   [Signature of Firm]
[Date]

A Defined Contribution Plan

INDEPENDENT AUDITOR'S REPORT

Addressee:

We have audited the accompanying statement of net assets available for plan benefits of XYZ Company Profit-Sharing Plan as of December 31, 19X1, and the related statement of changes in net assets available for plan benefits for the year then ended. These financial statements are the responsibility of the Plan's management. Our responsibility is to express an opinion on these financial statements based on our audit.

We conducted our audit in accordance with generally accepted auditing standards. Those standards require that we plan and perform the audit to obtain reasonable assurance about whether the financial statements are free of material misstatement. An audit includes examining, on a test basis, evidence supporting the amounts and disclosures in the financial statements. An audit also includes assessing the accounting principles used and significant estimates made by management, as well as evaluating the overall financial statement presentation. We believe that our audit provides a reasonable basis for our opinion.

In our opinion, the financial statements referred to above present fairly, in all material respects, the net assets available for plan benefits of the Plan as of December 31, 19X1, and the changes in net assets available for plan benefits for the year then ended in conformity with generally accepted accounting principles.

[City and State]   [Signature of Firm]
[Date]

A Health and Welfare Benefit Plan

INDEPENDENT AUDITOR'S REPORT

Addressee:

We have audited the accompanying statement of net assets of Bizco Corporation Employee Health and Welfare Benefit Plan as of December 31, 19X1, and the related statement of changes in net assets for the year then ended. These financial statements are the responsibility of the Plan's management. Our responsibility is to express an opinion on these financial statements based on our audit.

We conducted our audit in accordance with generally accepted auditing standards. Those standards require that we plan and perform the audit to obtain reasonable assurance about whether the financial statements are free of material misstatement. An audit includes examining, on a test basis, evidence supporting the amounts and disclosures in the financial statements. An audit also includes assessing the accounting principles used and significant estimates made by management, as well as evaluating the overall financial statement presentation. We believe that our audit provides a reasonable basis for our opinion.

In our opinion, the financial statements referred to above present fairly, in all material respects, the net assets of the Plan as of December 31, 19X1, and the changes in net assets for the year then ended in conformity with generally accepted accounting principles.

[City and State]   [Signature of Firm]
[Date]

Nonstandard Auditor's Reports

A Non-GAAP-Basis Financial Statement

INDEPENDENT AUDITOR'S REPORT

Addressee:

We have audited the accompanying statements of net assets available for plan benefits (modified cash basis) of XYZ Pension Plan as of December 31, 19X2 and 19X1, and the related statement of changes in the net assets available for plan benefits (modified cash basis) for the year ended December 31, 19X2. These financial statements are the responsibility of the Plan's management. Our responsibility is to express an opinion on these financial statements based on our audits.

We conducted our audits in accordance with generally accepted auditing standards. Those standards require that we plan and perform the audit to obtain reasonable assurance about whether the financial statements are free of material misstatement. An audit includes examining, on a test basis, evidence supporting the amounts and disclosures in the financial statements. An audit also includes assessing the accounting principles used and significant estimates made by management, as well as evaluating the overall financial statement presentation. We believe that our audits provide a reasonable basis for our opinion.

As described in Note X, the Plan's policy is to prepare its financial statements and supplemental schedules on a modified cash basis of accounting, which differs from generally accepted accounting principles. Accordingly, the accompanying financial statements and schedules are not intended to be presented in conformity with generally accepted accounting principles.

In our opinion, the financial statements referred to above present fairly, in all material respects, the financial status of XYZ Pension Plan as of December 31, 19X2 and 19X1, and the changes in its financial status for the year ended December 19X2, on the basis of accounting described in Note X.

(continued)

A Non-GAAP-Basis Financial Statement   (concluded)

Our audits were made for the purpose of forming an opinion on the financial statements taken as a whole. The supplemental schedules (modified cash basis) of (1) assets held for investment, (2) transactions in excess of x percent of the current value of plan assets, and (3) investments in loans and fixed-income obligations in default or classified as uncollectable as of or for the year ended December 31, 19X2, are presented for purposes of complying with the Department of Labor's Rules and Regulations for Reporting and Disclosure under the Employee Retirement Income Security Act of 1974 and are not a required part of the basic financial statements. The supplemental schedules have been subjected to the auditing procedures applied in the audits of the basic financial statements and, in our opinion, are fairly stated in all material respects in relation to the basic financial statements taken as a whole.

[City and State]	[Signature of Firm]
[Date]	

A Limited-Scope Audit under DOL Regulations

INDEPENDENT AUDITOR'S REPORT

Addressee:

We were engaged to audit the financial statements and schedules of XYZ Pension Plan as of December 31, 19X1, and for the year then ended, as listed in the accompanying index. These financial statements and schedules are the responsibility of the Plan's management.

As permitted by Section 2520.103-8 of the Department of Labor's Rules and Regulations for Reporting and Disclosure under the Employee Retirement Income Security Act of 1974, the Plan administrator instructed us not to perform, and we did not perform, any auditing procedures with respect to the information summarized in Note X, which was certified by ABC Bank, the trustee of the Plan, except for comparing the information with the related information included in the 19X1 financial statements and supplemental schedules. We have been informed by the Plan administrator that the trustee holds the Plan's investment assets and executes investment transactions. The Plan administrator has obtained a certification from the trustee as of and for the year ended December 31, 19X1, that the information provided to the plan administrator by the trustee is complete and accurate.

Because of the significance of the information that we did not audit, we are unable to, and do not, express an opinion on the accompanying financial statements and schedules taken as a whole. The form and content of the information included in the financial statements and schedules, other than that derived from the information certified by the trustee, have been audited by us in accordance with generally accepted auditing standards and, in our opinion, are presented in compliance with the Department of Labor's Rules and Regulations for Reporting and Disclosure under the Employee Retirement Income Security Act of 1974.

[City and State]   [Signature of Firm]
[Date]

A Defined Benefit Plan Audit Assuming Inadequate Procedures to Value Investments

---

INDEPENDENT AUDITOR'S REPORT

Addressee:

We have audited the accompanying statements of net assets available for benefits and of accumulated plan benefits of XYZ Pension Plan as of December 31, 19X2, and the related statements of changes in net assets available for benefits and of changes in accumulated Plan benefits for the year then ended. These financial statements are the responsibility of the Plan's management. Our responsibility is to express an opinion on these financial statements based on our audit.

We conducted our audit in accordance with generally accepted auditing standards. Those standards require that we plan and perform the audit to obtain reasonable assurance about whether the financial statements are free of material misstatement. An audit includes examining, on a test basis, evidence supporting the amounts and disclosures in the financial statements. An audit also includes assessing the accounting principles used and significant estimates made by management, as well as evaluating the overall financial statement presentation. We believe that our audit provides a reasonable basis for our opinion.

As discussed in Note X, investments amounting to $_____ (__ percent of net assets available for benefits) as of December 31, 19X2, have been valued at estimated fair value as determined by the Board of Trustees. We have reviewed the procedures applied by the trustees in valuing the securities and have inspected the underlying documentation. In our opinion, those procedures are not adequate to determine the fair value of the investments in conformity with generally accepted accounting principles. The effect on the financial statements and supplemental schedules of not applying adequate procedures to determine the fair value of the securities is not determinable.

(continued)

A Defined Benefit Plan Audit Assuming Inadequate Procedures to Value Investments (concluded)

In our opinion, except for the effects of the procedures used by the Board of Trustees to determine the valuation of investments as described in the preceding paragraph, the financial statements referred to above present fairly, in all material respects, the financialstatus of XYZ Pension Plan as of December 31, 19X2, and the changes in its financial status for the year then ended in conformity with generally accepted accounting principles.

Our audit was made for the purpose of forming an opinion on the financial statements taken as a whole. The additional information presented in supplemental schedules of (1) assets held for investment, (2) transactions in excess of *x* percent of the current value of Plan assets, and (3) investments in loans and fixed-income obligations in default or classified as uncollectable as of or for the year ended December 31, 19X2, are presented for purposes of complying with the Department of Labor's Rules and Regulations for Reporting and Disclosure under the Employee Retirement Income Security Act of 1974 and is not a required part of the basic financial statements. That additional information has been subjected to the auditing procedures applied in the audit of the basic financial statements for the year ended December 31, 19X2; and in our opinion, except for the effects of the valuation of investments, as described above, the additional information is fairly stated in all material respects in relation to the basic financial statements taken as a whole.

[City and State]   _____
[Date]   [Signature of Firm]

CHAPTER 44

ACCOUNTING AND FINANCIAL REPORTING FOR HEALTH AND WELFARE BENEFIT PLANS

Richard H. Towers
Douglas R. Divelbiss

NATURE OF THE PLANS

Health and welfare benefit plans can be either defined benefit or defined contribution plans and they share a number of characteristics with pension plans. Whereas pension plans primarily provide for income benefits during retirement,[1] health and welfare benefit plans provide a wide variety of benefits primarily to active employees, although certain types of benefits are commonly provided to retirees as well. The range of benefits offered by these plans includes:

- Medical, dental, vision, hearing, prescription drug, dependent care, psychiatric, and long-term care benefits.
- Life insurance benefits.
- Accidental death or dismemberment benefits.
- Unemployment, severance, or disability pay.
- Vacation or holiday pay.

---

[1]Some pension plans provide ancillary benefits of the same nature as some of those provided by health and welfare plans.

- Other miscellaneous benefits, such as legal services, day care, tuition assistance, apprenticeships, and housing allowances.

Like pension plans, health and welfare benefit plans can exist as single-employer or multiemployer plans, may require actuarial valuations, and, in most cases, are subject to the Employee Retirement Income Security Act of 1974 (ERISA). The form of most plans is governed by tax law, such as for a voluntary employees' beneficiary association (VEBA) trust under Internal Revenue Code Section 501(c)(9). Contributions may be voluntary or through a collective bargaining agreement and may be paid by the plan sponsor, plan participants, or both.

In recent years, companies have focused increasing attention on the health and welfare benefit plans they sponsor, primarily because the health care benefits provided by many of these plans have been subjected to significant inflationary cost increases. One result of this increased attention on health care benefits is that many plan sponsors are modifying their plans in an effort to better manage the escalating costs. These cost increases also have emphasized the importance of developing a standard for *employer* accounting for retiree benefits of this nature, titled *Financial Accounting Standards Board Statement No. 106 (SFAS No. 106), Employers' Accounting for Postretirement Benefits Other than Pensions*.

PLAN ACCOUNTING AND REPORTING

Present requirements for accounting and reporting by health and welfare benefit plans are prescribed in Chapter 4 of the AICPA's audit and accounting guide, *Audits of Employee Benefit Plans* (the Guide).[2] Those rules are similar in many respects to those prescribed by *SFAS No. 35* for defined benefit pension plans. Health and welfare benefit plans reporting under generally accepted accounting principles are required to use the accrual basis of accounting, although modified cash basis financial statements are sometimes prepared (in accordance with rules governing reporting under a basis of accounting other than generally accepted accounting principles).

---

[2]To the degree that the nature of a plan's benefits are defined contribution, rather than defined benefit, Chapter 3 of the Guide applies.

For defined benefit health and welfare plans, it is especially important to understand the nature of the plan benefits and any related insurance arrangements before determining the appropriate accounting. Specifically, it must be determined who is at risk for the benefit obligations. The insurance company may assume all or a portion of the financial risk or it may provide only administrative, benefit payment, or investment management services. In a situation that is considered to be "fully insured," the plan generally has no obligation for the covered benefits (other than for payment of premiums to the insurance company), and accordingly, the benefit obligation is not reported in the plan's financial statements.

The financial statements of a health and welfare benefit plan consist of a Statement of Net Assets and a Statement of Changes in Net Assets. These statement titles differ from those for a defined benefit pension plan (which include the phrase . . . *Available for Plan Benefits*), because the benefit obligations of health-and-welfare plans are recorded on the face of the financial statements as liabilities, instead of as disclosures in the footnotes. Health and welfare plan benefit obligations commonly reported as liabilities in the Statement of Net Assets include:

1. Insurance premiums payable (premium-deposit assets may also exist).
2. Insurance premium deficits—"Experience rating adjustments" that arise under some insurance contracts and represent a degree of risk-sharing with the insurer. Deficits are liabilities, and refunds due are assets.
3. Claims payable—For plans that are at least partly self-insured, claims that are reported but unpaid are liabilities and are determined by the records of the plan.
4. Estimated claims incurred but not reported—For plans that are at least partly self-insured, these liabilities generally are determined by a specialist such as the plan's actuary.
5. Estimated future death benefits—For plans that are at least partly self-insured and provide death benefits, an estimate of the death-benefit liability is accrued, based on determinations made by the plan's actuary.
6. Estimated future benefits for accumulated eligibility credits— Some plans provide insurance payments or direct benefit amounts for a period of time after year-end for participants who have

accumulated sufficient "eligibility credits." Such credits permit eligible participants to receive benefits during periods of subsequent unemployment. This liability generally is estimated by applying current insurance premium rates or the average benefit cost (for self-insured plans) to the accumulated eligibility credits.

The Statement of Changes in Net Assets also is much like its *SFAS No. 35* pension counterpart, except that it also must account for changes in the above benefit-related liabilities unique to health and welfare benefit plans.

Footnote disclosures for health and welfare benefit plans generally are similar to those of pension plans but differ somewhat in their requirements for descriptions of:

- The nature of the benefits provided and the accounting policy regarding purchase of insurance contracts excluded from plan assets.
- Significant actuarial assumptions used in estimating certain plan benefit liabilities and the effects of significant changes therein.
- The plan's funding policy, including, if applicable, the method of funding a deficit in net assets.
- Certain information as to insurance premium deposits and experience rating adjustments.

PROPOSED FUTURE CHANGES IN PLAN ACCOUNTING AND REPORTING

The AICPA presently is considering an amendment to the health and welfare plan accounting prescribed in Chapter 4 of the Guide. The proposed changes, which at the date of this writing have not received final approval, are significant and would make the accounting and reporting more consistent with that of defined benefit pension plans (as governed by *SFAS No. 35*) and employer accounting for "postretirement benefits other than pensions" (as governed by *SFAS No. 106*). The proposed changes would have two primary effects:

1. For the first time, plans would report an obligation for postretirement benefits that participants have earned to date under the terms of the plan. This postretirement benefit obligation would be determined using the measurement principles of *SFAS No. 106*. For many plans, this previously unreported postretirement obligation is material and would significantly affect the funded status reported in the plans' financial statements.

2. Plans would report benefit-related obligations (including the postretirement benefit obligation) either in the footnotes or in a financial statement separate from the Statement of Net Assets. This proposed change, to remove benefit-related obligations from the face of the Statement of Net Assets, is consistent with the reporting rules for pension plans under *SFAS No. 35*.

SUMMARY

While health and welfare benefit plans share a number of characteristics with pension plans, they also have unique distinguishing features and thus have their own important place in the overall structure of an employer's benefits program.

As pointed out in this chapter, these plans, their increasing costs, and their accounting and financial reporting are receiving more attention. This additional focus is likely to continue for some time, especially because the presently proposed major changes to plan accounting and reporting are in process and the new employer accounting under *SFAS No. 106* for such benefits paid to retirees is in the implementation period.

The sample financial statements in the appendix that follows illustrate the financial reporting for a health care plan under the present requirements.

APPENDIX TO CHAPTER 44

HEALTH CARE PLAN FINANCIAL STATEMENTS

SAMPLE COMPANY
HEALTH CARE PLAN

Statement of Net Assets

December 31, 19X2 and 19X1

	19X2	19X1
Assets		
Investments at fair value		
U.S. government securities	$217,000	$142,000
Corporate bonds	200,000	103,000
Common stock	289,000	394,000
	706,000	639,000
Receivables		
Contributions of Sample Company	111,000	101,000
Contributions of employees	64,000	54,000
Accrued interest and dividends	13,000	9,000
	188,000	164,000
Cash	70,000	90,000
Total assets	964,000	893,000
Liabilities		
Claims payable	261,000	189,000
Estimated claims incurred but not reported	364,000	407,000
Estimated future benefits for accumulated		
eligibility credits	282,000	268,000
Other liabilities	16,000	16,000
Total liabilities	923,000	880,000
Net Assets	$ 41,000	$ 13,000

Statement of Changes in Net Assets

For the Years Ended December 31, 19X2 and 19X1

	19X2	19X1
Additions		
Investment income		
Net realized and unrealized appreciation (depreciation) in fair value of investments	$ 73,000	$ (4,000)
Interest	39,000	20,000
Dividends	11,000	16,000
	123,000	32,000
Less investment expenses	(8,000)	(6,000)
	115,000	26,000
Contributions		
Sample Company	659,000	654,000
Employees	214,000	197,000
	873,000	851,000
Total additions	988,000	877,000
Deductions		
Payments for health claims	884,000	801,000
Additions to liabilities for:		
Health claims	29,000	3,000
Participants' accumulated eligibility	14,000	39,000
	43,000	42,000
Administrative expenses	33,000	29,000
Total deductions	960,000	872,000
Net increase	28,000	5,000
Net assets at beginning of year	13,000	8,000
Net assets at end of year	$ 41,000	$ 13,000

Notes to Financial Statements

General Description of the Plan

The Sample Company Health Care Plan (Plan) provides health care benefits covering substantially all employees of the Company. The following description provides only general information; participants should refer to the Plan agreement for more complete information regarding operation of the Plan.

The Plan provides health benefits (hospital, surgical, and major medical) covering full-time Company employees with 1,000 service hours annually. The Plan also provides certain future health benefits to employees who accumulate excess eligibility credits. Benefits are presently self-insured, although claim processing is handled by an insurance company.

The Plan agreement provides that the Company is to make bimonthly contributions to the Plan, as determined annually by the Plan's actuary, of a specified amount for each hour worked (approximately 10¢ and 9¢ in 19X2 and 19X1, respectively). Employee contributions are required, relative to the coverage received, as determined annually by the Plan Committee. Certain dependent coverage may be elected at extra cost to the employee.

Administrative expenses are paid by the Plan, except that certain professional fees and administrative overhead costs are borne by the Company.

The Plan is subject to the provisions of the Employee Retirement Income Security Act of 1974 (ERISA). Although it has not expressed any intent to do so, the Company has the right to discontinue its contributions at any time and to terminate the Plan subject to the provisions of ERISA.

Summary of Significant Accounting Policies

Investments of the Plan are reported at fair value. Quoted market prices were available to value virtually all investments during 19X2 and 19X1.

Plan liabilities for claims incurred but not reported and for future benefits for accumulated eligibility credits are estimated by the Plan's actuary in accordance with accepted actuarial principles.

Investments

Investments of the Plan are held in a bank trust fund. No individual investments represent 5 percent or more of total plan assets. Net appreciation (depreciation) in fair value of Plan investments during 19X2 and 19X1 (as determined by quoted market prices) was as follows:

	19X2	19X1
U.S. government securities	(2,000)	6,000
Corporate bonds	(3,000)	4,000
Common stocks	78,000	(14,000)
	$73,000	$ (4,000)

Income Tax Status

A September 27, 19X2, Internal Revenue Service ruling states that the Plan and its trust qualify under Section 501(c)(9) of the Internal Revenue Code and are thus not subject to tax under the present income tax law.*

---

*None of the schedules that may be required under ERISA nor certain other ERISA disclosures are provided in this appendix.

CHAPTER 45

COSTING AND FUNDING RETIREMENT BENEFITS

Donald S. Grubbs, Jr.

Funding retirement benefits includes setting aside contributions, investing them in a funding medium, and making benefit payments from the amounts set aside. It involves administrative and accounting functions and important tax considerations.

This chapter discusses funding retirement programs that are qualified plans under the Internal Revenue Code (IRC). Special considerations, not discussed here, apply to plans covering employees of governmental bodies and of churches.

FUNDING MEDIA

The funding medium is the vehicle containing the plan's assets, from which the benefits are paid. All pension plan assets must be held by one or more trusts, custodial accounts, annuity contracts, or insurance contracts.[1]

Trusts

Trusts are the investment medium for about two thirds of all pension plan assets. Governed by state law, a trust is a legal entity under which a trustee holds assets for the benefit of another. Whereas the Internal

---

[1]Employee Retirement Income Security Act of 1974 (ERISA) Sec. 403; IRC of 1986 Secs. 401(a),(f), 403(a), 404(a)(2).

83

Revenue Service (IRS) deems a trust to exist even before it has a corpus (assets), most state laws require a corpus for a trust to exist.[2] A trust agreement is entered into between the employer or other plan sponsor and the trustee(s).

The trust instrument states the purpose of the trust and defines the authority and the responsibilities of the trustee. It includes provisions for terminating the trust and for replacing the trustee. A trust must provide that plan assets are to be used for the exclusive benefit of participants and beneficiaries.[3]

Trustees

Generally, trustees may be either individuals or institutions with trust powers such as banks or trust companies. A bank usually is designated as trustee. Some large plans divide plan assets among two or more banks serving as trustees.

Some plans have a board of trustees consisting of a group of individuals. Collectively bargained multiemployer plans usually follow this approach. In such a case, the board of trustees usually enters a second trust agreement with a bank, delegating responsibility for holding and investing plan assets. Sometimes the trustee is a single individual, but many individuals are reluctant to assume the fiduciary responsibilities of trustees.

The duties of trustees differ from plan to plan. In every case the trustee must hold the plan assets and account for them. Some trustees have complete responsibility for determining investment policy and making investment decisions. Under other trust agreements the trustee is required to follow investment decisions made by the employer or investment manager. For many plans the trustee's authority lies between these two extremes; for example, the trustee may make individual investments in accordance with investment policies or limitations established by the employer, an investment manager, or trust agreement.

Trustees usually pay the plan's benefits to participants and often assume other administrative responsibilities as well. Sometimes the trustee is designated plan administrator with full responsibility for administering

---

[2]Rev. Rul. 57-419, 1957-2 CB 264.
[3]IRC Sec. 401(a)(2).

the plan. The trustee is a fiduciary of the plan and subject to ERISA's fiduciary responsibilities.

Trust Investments

Many banks maintain one or more collective trust funds to pool the assets of a number of plans for investment purposes. These commingled trust funds are very similar to mutual funds. They may provide more diversification, better investment management, and reduced investment expense—particularly for small plans—compared to a single trust investing in individual securities. Many banks have several separate commingled funds for particular types of investments; for example, common stocks or bonds. For the same reasons that some trusts invest in commingled funds, others invest in mutual funds as an intermediary. Most larger trusts acquire individual securities rather than use commingled funds or mutual funds.

Many trusts invest only in securities listed on a major stock exchange to assure marketability, avoid valuation problems, and reduce fiduciary problems. Common stocks and corporate bonds are the most common investments. Trusts also often invest in preferred stocks, certificates of deposit, commercial and government notes, government bonds, mortgages, and real estate. Occasionally, they invest in art, precious metals, and other collectibles, but this is, in effect, prohibited if individuals direct the investment of their own accounts in a defined contribution plan.

A plan may invest in securities of the employer only if they are "qualifying employer securities." A qualifying employer security is either a stock or a marketable security of the employer that meets several criteria of ERISA. A defined benefit plan generally may not invest more than 10 percent of its assets in securities of the employer, but stock bonus plans, profit-sharing plans, and some money purchase pension plans are not so limited.

Insured Plans

Approximately one third of pension plan assets are held by insurance companies. Many different kinds of contracts are used. These include group contracts covering a group of participants and individual contracts covering each participant.

Annuity contracts and insurance contracts are used, and both generally provide annuity income after retirement. Life insurance contracts generally guarantee to pay death benefits exceeding the reserve for the individual participant, while annuity contracts generally do not. The extent to which the contracts guarantee the payment of benefits or the employer's costs varies greatly among contract types.

Deposit Administration (DA) Group Annuity Contract

A deposit administration (DA) contract has a deposit fund into which all contributions to the plan are deposited. For defined benefit plans the fund is not allocated among participants. The insurance company credits the fund with interest at a guaranteed rate and may assess the fund with a stipulated expense charge. When a participant becomes eligible for a pension, a withdrawal is made from the deposit fund to purchase an annuity. Sometimes lump-sum distributions, disability payments, or other benefits are paid directly from the deposit fund without the purchase of an annuity.

The DA contract specifies the guaranteed rate of interest to be credited to the deposit fund, the expense charge to be subtracted from the deposit fund, and the rates that will be used to purchase annuities when individuals retire. There generally is no expense charge for larger plans. The insurer guarantees payment of the pensions after annuities have been purchased but does not guarantee that the deposit fund will be sufficient to purchase the annuities.

The guaranteed interest rates and annuity purchase rates generally are quite conservative. When actual experience is more favorable than the guaranteed assumptions, the difference may be recognized by adding dividends or experience credits to the deposit fund. Consulting, administrative, and actuarial services for the plan may be provided by the insurance company, independent consultants, or the employer.

If the contract is discontinued, it may allow the employer either to apply the balance of the deposit fund to purchase annuities or to transfer it to a trust or another insurance company. If the fund is transferred in a lump sum, the insurance company may deduct a surrender charge or a market value adjustment or, alternatively, the insurer may require that the transfer be made in installments over a period of years.

The assets of the deposit fund represent a contractual obligation of the insurer but do not represent any particular assets of the insurer. The insurer invests the monies received as part of the total assets of the insurance company, usually primarily in bonds and mortgages. The insurer usually reflects the investment earnings of its entire portfolio in determining the amount of interest to credit in dividends or experience credits. In determining the interest to credit, most insurers use the "investment year" or "new money" method, which determines the rate of investment earnings on investments made by the insurance company in each year deposits were added to the deposit fund.

Many deposit administration contracts provide that part or all of the employer contributions to the plan may be invested in separate accounts rather than the deposit fund. Separate accounts operate similarly to mutual funds and are invested in common stocks or other forms of investment. The employer may direct transfers from the deposit account into the separate account. As in a mutual fund, deposits to the fund are converted to units by dividing by the current unit value of the separate account. The unit value equals the total market value of the fund divided by the number of units held by all of the contracts that invest in the separate account. Withdrawals also are based upon the current unit value. Many insurance companies maintain separate accounts for common stocks, bonds, mortgages, and other classes of investment.

Immediate Participation Guarantee (IPG) Contract

An immediate participation guarantee (IPG) contract, like a deposit administration contract, has a deposit account into which employer contributions are paid. The insurance company generally agrees to credit to the deposit account the actual rate of investment earnings it earns on its general portfolio using the investment-year method and to deduct an allocation of expenses for the particular contract based upon accounting records for that contract. Pensions are paid from the deposit account monthly as they become due, rather than from a purchased annuity. Thus the contract immediately participates in its actual experience for mortality, expenses, and investment income. Annuity purchase rates are guaranteed under the contract, but annuities are not usually purchased unless the contract is discontinued. Some companies use an accounting device that appears to purchase annuities, but ordinarily no annuities are actually purchased. Some insurers call such contracts *pension administration* or *investment only* contracts, rather than *IPG* contracts. Separate accounts generally are used with IPG contracts, just as they are with DA contracts.

Guaranteed Investment Contract (GIC)

A guaranteed investment contract (GIC) guarantees the rate of interest to be credited to the deposit account for a limited period, usually from 30 days to 20 years. Most GICs guarantee that the full principal will be paid out with no surrender charge or adjustment at the end of that period. It may provide only for an initial deposit or may provide for continuing deposits during a "window" period. It may allow benefits to be paid from the deposit account during that period. These characteristics can be particularly valuable for a thrift plan or a regular profit-sharing plan where the entire fund balance is allocated to individual participants; many participants want a guarantee of principal and interest.

The GIC may include all the plan's assets, or it may be only one of several investments held by the plan's trust. At the end of the guarantee period, the entire balance of the GIC will be paid out to the trust or other funding medium of the plan, or it may be left on deposit and a new guarantee period established. The GIC may have annuity purchase options, but in practice annuities usually are not purchased.

Group Deferred Annuity Contracts

A deferred annuity contract is one under which the insurance company promises to pay a monthly annuity beginning at a future date. Under a group deferred annuity contract, the employer purchases a deferred annuity for each participant each year to fund the amount of pension earned in that year. The insurance company guarantees payment of the pension purchased to date, beginning at the normal retirement date, or payment of a reduced pension beginning at an early retirement date.

For example, assume a pension plan provides a pension at age 65 equal to $10 monthly for each year of participation in the plan. Each year the employer pays a premium for each participant to purchase a deferred annuity of $10 monthly to begin at age 65. Premium rates are based on the participant's age and sex. Since a small deferred annuity is purchased and guaranteed each year, by the time a participant reaches age 65 his or her entire pension will be purchased.

Before deposit administration contracts became popular, group deferred annuities were the most common type of group annuity. In recent years, however, very few new deferred annuity contracts have been issued, except to purchase annuities under terminated plans. Most plans that formerly used deferred annuities have changed to other methods of funding pensions earned after the date of change, but deferred annuities purchased before the change remain in force.

Individual Level Premium Annuities

Under some plans, usually small ones, an individual level premium annuity contract is purchased to fund the projected pension of each participant. The insurance company deducts an expense charge from each premium and accumulates the balance at a guaranteed rate of interest. At retirement the balance of the account is converted into a monthly annuity, applying guaranteed purchase rates. The insurance company actually may use interest credits and annuity purchase rates more favorable than the conservative rates guaranteed in the contract.

The annual premium is the level annual amount determined so that the accumulation at normal retirement age is sufficient to purchase the promised pension. If the participant receives a salary increase that causes the originally projected pension to increase, a second level premium annuity is purchased to fund the increase. Further salary increases may require purchase of a third level, fourth level, and so on.

Upon termination of employment before retirement, the accumulated balance (cash value) of each policy is available to provide a benefit for the employee if he or she is vested or a credit for the employer if the employee is not vested. Upon death before retirement, the death benefit usually equals the greater of the cash value or the sum of the premiums paid.

Individual Retirement Income Insurance Contracts

An individual retirement income insurance contract (sometimes called *income endowment*) is similar to an individual level premium annuity, except the death benefit equals the greater of the cash value or 100 times the projected monthly pension. The retirement income contract also has level annual premiums, but these must be larger than under the level-premium annuity to provide the larger death benefit.

Split-Funded Plans—Individual Life Insurance and an Auxiliary Fund

Many plans are funded by a combination of individual life-insurance policies plus an auxiliary fund ("side fund"). The type of policy used is most frequently an ordinary life ("whole life") policy or a universal life policy. In many defined benefit plans, the amount of life insurance equals 100 times the projected pension, as in the retirement income contracts. The life insurance contract builds up a cash value sufficient to provide part of the pension. Deposits are made to the auxiliary fund to provide the balance. The auxiliary fund may be held by the insurance company or may be in a trust.

At retirement, two alternatives are available to provide a pension. Some plans surrender the insurance contract at retirement, deposit the cash value in the trust, and pay pensions monthly out of the trust. Other plans make a transfer from the trust to the insurance company at the time of retirement; the amount transferred is the amount required, together with the policy cash value, to purchase an annuity from the insurer to guarantee payment of the pension.

Many plans originally funded with retirement income insurance contracts have been converted to a split funded basis to reduce the cost of funding the plan and to allow part of the plan's assets to be invested in common stocks. In turn, many split funded plans have been converted to fund the pensions with a trust or group annuity contract and to provide the death benefits outside the pension plan under group term insurance in order to reduce the employer's cost. Because individual policies generally have a higher cost than group policies, the purchase of individual policies may constitute a breach of fiduciary responsibility.

When death benefits are funded with individual insurance under a qualified plan, the employee has current taxable income equal to the cost of the insurance ("P.S. 58" cost). On the other hand, if death benefits are funded outside the plan with group term life insurance, the cost of providing the first $50,000 of insurance paid by employer contributions is tax-free to the employee, and the cost of insurance on amounts over $50,000 is computed on a less expensive basis than under individual contracts. Thus, employees pay less income tax if death benefits are funded outside the plan with group term insurance.

Group Permanent Contracts

Group permanent insurance contracts are designed to preserve the characteristics of individual insurance contracts while achieving some of the economy of group insurance. Whole life, universal life, and other types of contracts are available. All participants are covered under a single contract that has cash values, death benefits, and other characteristics similar to a collection of individual contracts. Because the group contract pays lower commissions and has lower administrative expense than individual contracts, the premiums are lower. Such contracts are termed *permanent* insurance to distinguish them from group term insurance.

FACTORS AFFECTING FUNDING

Many factors affect the amount an employer contributes to the pension plan. Different considerations affect different plans.

Type of Plan

The type of plan and its provisions often completely or partially determine the amount of the employer contribution. A thrift plan, for example, may require the employer to match employee contributions up to 6 percent of pay. A profit-sharing plan may require the employer to contribute 20 percent of profits but not more than 15 percent of pay. A money purchase pension plan may require contributions of 10 percent of pay. Such plans leave no discretion in the amount of contribution. But most profit-sharing plans provide the employer complete discretion in determining what, if anything, to contribute, and most defined benefit pension plans allow substantial discretion in determining how much to contribute each year. Details on the factors affecting the funding of specific retirement plans are contained in the respective chapters of this *Handbook*.

Laws and Regulations

An employer may want to contribute more in a year when it is in a higher tax bracket and less in a year when it is in a low tax bracket or has no taxable income at all. Minimum funding requirements under ERISA set an absolute minimum on the contributions for most pension plans. These are described later.

If the employer is a taxpayer, it is subject to limits on the amount of pension contribution that may be claimed as a deduction for income tax purposes. Employers are subject to a 10 percent excise tax on any contributions greater than can be deducted currently.[4]

Other governmental requirements affect the amount of contributions of some employers. Federal Procurement Regulations and Defense Acquisition Regulations control pension costs assessed under federal contracts. The Department of Housing and Urban Development has rules

---

[4]IRC Sec. 4972.

applicable to reimbursement of pension costs for local housing authorities. Public utilities commissions regulate the amount of pension contributions that may be recognized for rate-making purposes by utilities.

Collective Bargaining

Collective bargaining agreements affect the funding of many plans. Some collective bargaining agreements set the amount of employer contributions specifically in cents per hour, as a percent of pay, or as, for example, cents per ton of coal produced. Many other collective bargaining agreements, however, specify what benefits the plan provides but do not specify the amount of employer contributions.

Funding Media

Under most plans funded with group annuity contracts or with trusts, the funding medium does not usually limit the amount of contributions. Under a traditional deposit-administration group annuity contract, the deposit fund must be sufficient to purchase annuities for individuals currently retiring. Usually, the deposit fund is far more than sufficient for this purpose, so this requirement has no impact. But occasionally the deposit fund is not sufficient, particularly if a number of employees with large pensions retire shortly after the plan is established; this may require additional employer contributions to purchase annuities. To solve this problem, deposit administration contracts often are modified to allow annuities to be purchased in installments after retirement.

Accounting

Generally accepted accounting principles (GAAP) establish the charge for pension expense in the employer's profit and loss statement. This does not directly control the amount actually contributed, but some employers prefer the amount contributed to equal the charge to expense.

Financial Considerations

An employer often considers its cash position in determining the amount of contribution to the plan. Cash shortages may stem from lack of profits or from a need to reinvest earnings in the business or to reduce indebtedness. Reducing pension contributions helps solve cash shortages. But an employer in a strong cash position may want to increase its pension contributions, since an additional dollar paid this year reduces the required contributions in future years and earns tax-free income in the pension trust. For an employer with lots of cash, larger pension contributions may help in avoiding the accumulated earnings tax on accumulated earnings in excess of the greater of $250,000 or the amount required for the reasonable needs of the business.[5] Larger contributions also reduce the cash available for dividends.

Interest rates often are considered. Increasing the pension contribution may require increased borrowing by the employer or may prevent reducing debts. The rate of interest on debt may be compared with the rate of investment earnings of the pension fund, but taxes also should be considered. Similarly, an employer with no indebtedness may consider how much could be earned by additional investments in the business, using amounts that would otherwise be contributed to the pension fund.

Employers may establish a funding policy based on many other considerations. Most employers want the plan to be soundly funded so as to assure that it will be able to pay promised benefits. Some employers want pension costs to be stable as a percent of pay over future years. The employer may decide to fund the unfunded liabilities over a fixed period, such as 20 years. Future trends in pension costs may be projected, based upon projected increases or decreases in the number of future participants, changes in work pattern histories, investment earnings, future salary increases, anticipated plan amendments, or possible plan termination or merger.

Statutory Requirement for Funding Policy

ERISA requires every employee benefit plan to "provide a procedure for establishing and carrying out a funding policy and method."[6] Many plan documents merely state the employer will contribute to the trust each year the minimum amount required by ERISA's minimum funding standards and such additional amounts as the employer determines at its discretion. This retains the maximum discretion to change the funding policy without a plan amendment.

---

[5]IRC Sec. 531–537.
[6]ERISA Sec. 402(b)(1).

ACTUARIAL COSTS

Fundamental concepts of actuarial science are used in the costing of retirement benefits. The following illustrate the factors involved in the actuarial costing of such benefits.

Probability

When rolling an honest die, the probability of getting a 3 is 1/6 (or .16667). This statement does not tell us what the outcome of the next roll will be, but it does tell us something about the average experience that might be expected if many dice were rolled.

Mortality tables show the probability of dying at each particular age of life. This probability is determined by examining the experience of many thousands of lives. For example, according to one mortality table the probability of a man's dying at age 30 is .000991. This means if there were 1 million men aged 30, it might be expected that 991 of them would die before reaching age 31. It does not tell us which ones might die and which ones might live and hence tells us nothing about the expected lifetime of any one individual. But it does give us information about the average experiences to be expected in a large group of men aged 30.

Interest Discount

If someone deposits $100.00 in a savings account at 5 percent interest, one year later it will have grown to $105.00 (1.05 × $100.00). If the individual leaves the funds on deposit for a second year they will grow to $110.25 (1.05 × 105.00). Thus, if an individual wants to obtain $110.25 two years from now (assuming 5 percent interest), $100.00 must be deposited today. The $100.00 is the "present value" of $110.25 payable two years from now.

Viewed another way, the present value of an amount payable two years from now is .907029 times that amount (determined by dividing $100.00 by $110.25). At 5 percent interest, .907029 is the present value factor, or *interest discount factor,* for two years. To know the present value of any amount due two years from now (assuming 5 percent interest), simply multiply it by .907029.

There is a discount factor for any number of years for any interest rate. Sample discount factors for zero years to five years at 5 percent interest and 6 percent interest are shown in Table 45–1.

Present Value of Future Amounts

Suppose a woman agrees that two years from now 600 dice will be rolled and that she will pay $1.00 for each 3 that results. Further suppose that she wants to know the present value—the amount that she can set aside in a savings account today—that can be expected to be sufficient, together with interest, to pay the amounts when they become due. The total expected payments are $100.00 (1/6 × 600 × $1.00). Assuming 5 percent interest, the present value of that is $90.70 (the two-year discount factor or .907029 × $100.00). Thus, if she deposits $90.70 today it will have grown to $100.00 two years from now, which will be sufficient to make the expected payments if exactly one sixth of the 600 dice turn up a 3. Thus, $90.70 is the present value of the expected future payments. Of course, it might turn out to be more or less than needed, if the account earns more or less than the 5 percent assumed or if more or less than exactly one sixth of the dice turn up a 3. *The present value of any future event is the number of exposures* (600 dice) *times the probability of occurrence* (1/6) *times the amount of payment on each occurrence* ($1.00) *times the interest discount factor* (.907029).

Suppose, in addition to the obligation related to the 600 dice to be rolled two years from now, the woman has an obligation to pay $3.00 for each head that results from flipping 1,000 coins five years from now. The present value of the coin-flipping could be determined similarly to that for

TABLE 45–1
Sample Discount Factors

Number of Years	Interest Discount Factor	
	5 Percent	6 Percent
0	1.000000	1.000000
1	.952381	.943396
2	.907029	.889996
3	.863838	.839619
4	.822702	.792094
5	.783526	.747258

the dice-throwing. Then the two present values for dice-rolling and coin-flipping could be added to get the total present value of both obligations combined. Similarly, total present value can be determined for combinations of many possible future events, each with its own exposure, probability of occurrence, amount of payment, and time of occurrence.

Actuarial Cost Methods

Underlying actuarial concepts of pension funding are the actuarial cost methods that establish the level of pension contributions needed to fund promised pension benefits.

When a pension plan is first established, it may give past service credit to provide benefits related to employment before the effective date. Employees then covered under the plan will work for various amounts of time in the future. When employees terminate employment, some of them will be eligible to receive benefits, either beginning immediately or deferred into the future. After pension benefits begin, they usually continue for the retiree's lifetime, and sometimes payments are made after death to beneficiaries.

Actuarial cost methods are merely methods for assigning the cost of the benefit payments to particular years. Ultimately, the cost of a pension plan equals the sum of all the benefits and expenses paid from the plan, less any employee contributions and less the plan's investment return. If the employer contributes an additional dollar in any year, that dollar together with the interest it earns reduces the amount the employer needs to contribute in future years. Actuarial cost methods do not affect these ultimate costs, although they indirectly may influence the amount of investment income by influencing the size of the fund or the timing of contributions.

To the extent that any insurance or annuity contracts guarantee the costs of the plan, the employer's cost equals the premiums paid to the insurance company reduced by any dividends or credits, rather than the plan's own experience of benefits and expenses paid and investment return.

Basic Categories of Actuarial Cost Methods

All actuarial cost methods for pensions fall into three categories: current disbursement, terminal funding, and advance funding. All are in current use, although advance funding is most commonly used and is required for plans subject to ERISA's minimum funding requirements.

Under the *current disbursement* method, also called *pay-as-you-go,* each year the employer contributes the current year's benefit payments. This is not really an actuarial cost method at all. However, actuarial techniques can be used to project payments in future years, which may assist those responsible for the plan's operation. If a plan is funded precisely under the current disbursement method, the plan will have no assets whatsoever available to pay future benefits; next month's benefits will depend on next month's contributions.

Under *terminal funding,* as under current disbursement, no cost is recognized for a participant while he or she continues employment. The entire cost of the participant's future benefits is recognized, however, at the moment the participant retires and benefits begin. If a participant terminates and is entitled to a deferred pension beginning at a later date, the cost of the pension may be recognized either at the time of termination of employment or at the time payments begin, under two variations of the terminal funding method. If a plan is funded under the terminal funding method, the assets are expected to be sufficient to pay all the future benefits for those already retired (and terminated vested participants, if they also have been funded); no assets would be available to provide benefits for those not yet retired.

With *advance funding,* the cost of a participant's pension is spread over his or her working lifetime. It recognizes the cost of a worker's pension as a cost of employment. If all the costs attributable to the past have been funded, the plan assets usually are larger than under the terminal funding method and usually are expected to be sufficient to provide all future benefits for those already retired and terminated and to have some additional assets available to provide benefits for those still employed. Advance funding usually results in more rapid funding than terminal funding, but that is not always the case.

Except as otherwise noted herein, all actuarial cost methods are assumed to be advance funding methods.

Present Value of Future Benefits

For any group of individuals, the present value of their future benefits is the amount expected to be sufficient to pay those future benefits. If the present value of the future benefits were invested in a fund today, it would be sufficient, together with the investment income, to pay all such future benefits as they become due; no additional contributions would be needed, but the fund would be exactly exhausted when the last individual dies.

A participant or beneficiary may become eligible to receive future benefits if he or she retires (before or after normal retirement date), becomes disabled, dies, or otherwise terminates employment. The present value of future benefits is determined by the same principles as described earlier.

Consider a new employee just hired at age 25 under a pension plan that provides normal retirement benefits at age 65, assuming all payments are made annually at the beginning of the year. The present value of the single payment he may receive at age 65 is determined by multiplying the number of exposures (one person) times the probability of occurrence (the probability he will not die or terminate employment before age 65 and will then retire) times the amount of payment (the annual pension) times the interest discount factor (for 40 years from age 25 to 65). The present value of the payments to be received at 66, and each later age, could be similarly calculated. In each case the probability would need to consider not only the employee's chance of receiving the first payment, but of continuing to survive to receive subsequent payments, and the interest discount factor would be smaller as the years become more distant. By adding the present value of each future normal retirement payment, the present value of all normal retirement payments can be determined. By similar techniques the present value of the payments that may be paid for this worker in the event of early retirement, disability, death, or vested termination can be determined. Adding all these together, the present value of all future benefits that may become payable to the individual or his beneficiary is ascertained.

For this individual, the present value may be meaningless. He may quit before becoming vested and never receive a cent. Or he may collect a pension until age 99, with costs greater than anticipated. But if the plan has a large number of participants, the sum of their present values will accurately reflect the amount needed to pay all future benefits, *if* the assumptions are correct concerning the various probabilities, the interest rate, and the amount of each future payment that might become payable. This concept is key to all actuarial cost methods.

Components of Present Value of Future Benefits

Actuarial cost methods generally divide the present value of future benefits into two portions, the part attributable to the past and the part attributable to the future. The part attributable to the past is called the *accrued liability*. It also has sometimes been called *past service liability, prior service liability, actuarial liability, supplemental present value,* and the like. The part of the present value of future benefits attributable to the future is called *the present value of future normal costs*. This present value of future normal costs is the portion of the present value expected to be paid in the future by "normal costs," the cost attributable to each of the future years.

If the same assumptions are used, all actuarial cost methods have the same present value of future benefits (although under one of the methods it is not required to calculate the present value of future benefits). The methods differ in how they divide this present value between the accrued liability and the present value of future normal costs. Obviously, a method that produces a larger accrued liability has a smaller present value of future normal costs and vice versa. Under some methods, when a plan is first established no accrued liability exists at all, even though benefits are actually credited for past service. In this case, the present value of future normal costs equals the entire present value of future benefits.

Except when a plan is first established, it usually will have assets equal to part of the accrued liability. Any excess of the total accrued liability over the assets is the "unfunded accrued liability," or the "unfunded past service liability."[7]

If the assets exactly equal the accrued liability, there is no unfunded accrued liability, and the plan is "fully funded." Under some actuarial cost methods, the assets always exactly equal the accrued liability and there never is an unfunded liability.

Each actuarial method determines the normal cost for the current year.[8] The normal cost usually is calculated for the year beginning on the valuation date, but under one method it is sometimes calculated for the year ending on the valuation date. The normal cost may be calculated in

---

[7]ERISA Sec. 3(30), 302(b)(2)(B), IRC Sec. 412(b)(2)(B).
[8]ERISA Sec. 3(28).

dollars or it may be calculated in a number of other ways, including as a percent of payroll, cost per employee, per hour, or per shift. If not originally expressed in dollars, it is converted to dollars by multiplying by the actual or expected payroll, number of employees, hours, shifts, and so on. The normal cost for the coming year is, of course, part of the present value of future normal costs.

Gain or Loss

As part of the actuarial valuation, the actuary can calculate what the present unfunded liability would have been expected to be currently if the experience since the date of the last actuarial valuation had exactly followed the actuarial assumptions. This expected unfunded liability can then be compared with the actual unfunded liability calculated in the current valuation. The difference between the expected unfunded liability and the actual unfunded liability is the gain or loss since the last valuation. This gain or loss shows the extent to which the actual experience was better or worse than would have been expected by the actuarial assumptions.

Under some actuarial cost methods (''spread gain'' methods) the actual unfunded liability is assumed to equal the expected unfunded liability and thus there is no gain or loss. Under these methods deviations between expected and actual experience are spread over the future working lifetimes of participants as increases or decreases in the normal cost.

Summary of Valuation Results

Under every actuarial cost method, the valuation produces the following results:

1. Normal cost for the current year.
2. Accrued liability.
3. Assets.
4. Unfunded accrued liability (the accrued liability less the assets, assumed $0 under one method).
5. Gain or loss (assumed $0 under spread gain methods).

ACTUARIAL COST METHODS

Statutory Requirements for Actuarial Cost Methods

ERISA states,

> The term *advance funding actuarial cost method* or *actuarial cost method* means a recognized actuarial technique utilized for establishing the amount and incidence of the annual actuarial cost of pension plan benefits and expenses. Acceptable actuarial cost methods shall include the accrued benefit cost method (unit credit method), the entry age normal cost method, the individual level premium cost method, the aggregate cost method, the attained age normal cost method, and the frozen liability cost method. The terminal funding cost method and the current funding (pay-as-you-go) cost method are not acceptable actuarial cost methods. The Secretary of the Treasury shall issue regulations to further define acceptable actuarial cost methods.[9]

Under the statute, the Internal Revenue Service may recognize other methods as "acceptable" for determining ERISA's minimum funding requirements. They have so far recognized one additional method, the shortfall method. The same actuarial cost method and the same assumptions must be used for determining deductible limits as are used for minimum funding purposes.[10] The actuarial cost method and actuarial assumptions must be reasonable in the aggregate and must offer the actuary's best estimate of anticipated experience under the plan.[11]

Classification of Actuarial Cost Methods

There are a variety of ways in which actuarial cost methods may be classified. Only advance funding methods are considered in the following classifications.

1. Methods may be divided between (*a*) those that allocate the *benefits* of the plan to particular plan years and then determine the actuarial present value associated with the benefits assigned, and (*b*) those that

---

[9] ERISA Sec. 3(31).

[10] IRC Sec. 404(a)(1)(A).

[11] ERISA Sec. 302(c)(3), IRC Sec. 412(c)(3).

allocate the actuarial present *value* of all future benefits to particular plan years without allocating the benefits themselves. Those methods that allocate the benefits to particular plan years may be further divided between those that allocate the benefits according to the plan's provisions describing the accrued benefit and those that allocate the projected benefits as a level dollar benefit for each year of service.

2. A second way of classifying actuarial cost methods is between accrued benefit methods and projected benefit methods. An accrued benefit method is based upon the amount of benefit earned to date, while a projected benefit method is instead based upon the projected amounts of benefits expected to be paid from the plan upon retirement or other termination of employment. This is similar to the first classification above, since all *accrued* benefit methods allocate the *benefits* to particular years, while *projected* benefit methods generally allocate the actuarial present *value* to particular years.

3. A third way of classifying divides actuarial cost methods between those that directly determine the actuarial gain or loss and those that do not. Actuarial cost methods that do not directly determine the actuarial gain or loss have the effect of automatically spreading the gain or loss over the future working lifetimes of all active participants as part of the normal cost; such methods are called *spread gain methods*.

4. A fourth way of classifying divides actuarial cost methods between individual methods and aggregate methods. Under an individual method, the normal cost and the accrued liability may be calculated for each individual participant; the normal cost and the accrued liability for the entire plan are the sums of these respective items for all of the participants. Under an aggregate method, the costs are determined for the group as a whole in such a way that they cannot be determined separately for individuals.

5. A fifth way of classifying is between methods that result in an initial accrued liability when the plan is established or amended (usually related to past service benefits or plan amendments that increase accrued benefits) and those that do not. If a method does not produce an initial accrued liability, the cost of all benefits (including past service benefits) must be funded through normal costs.

6. A sixth way of classifying is between methods that use an entry age basis and those that use an attained age basis. Under an attained age basis, the normal cost is determined on the basis of the participants' current attained ages, without reference to their ages at entry.

Under an entry age basis, age at entry is a key element in determining normal cost.

7. A seventh way of classifying is between open group methods and closed group methods. A closed group method considers only the group of present plan participants, while an open group method considers employees expected to be hired in the future as well.[12] Except as otherwise specifically noted, this chapter only considers closed group methods. All six methods listed in ERISA are this type.

The above classifications are each presented as dichotomies. A number of methods exist that combine elements of the dichotomies.

Accrued Benefit Cost Method

The plan document usually defines the ''accrued benefit,'' the annual amount of benefit earned to date that is payable at normal retirement age. If a participant is 100 percent vested, his vested benefit equals his accrued benefit.[13]

The accrued benefit cost method, also called the *unit credit cost method,* defines the accrued liability as the present value of the plan's accrued benefits. The normal cost equals the present value of the benefit accrued during the current year.

The traditional accrued benefit cost method is based upon the accrued benefit defined in the plan. This does not recognize future salary increases. If a plan's benefits are based upon final average pay, salary increases will cause the benefit credited for past years to increase from year to year as salaries increase, causing liabilities to increase and creating actuarial losses. For this reason, the IRS will not allow a final average pay plan to use the traditional accrued benefit cost method.

A modified accrued benefit cost method may be used for final average pay plans and other plans. Under this method, the projected benefit at normal retirement age is first calculated based upon projected service to normal retirement age and future salary increases. A modified accrued benefit is then calculated, equal to the projected benefit multiplied by the ratio of the participant's actual years of service to date to his

---

[12]For a discussion of an open group method, see Donald R. Fleischer, ''The Forecast Valuation Method for Pension Plans,'' *Transactions 27* (1975), pp. 93–154, Society of Actuaries.

[13]ERISA Sec. 3(23), 204, IRC Sec. 411(b).

or her projected years of service at normal retirement age. This modified accrued benefit cost method, sometimes called the *projected unit credit method,* does not have the problems of increasing liabilities and actuarial losses because of salary increases that are part of the traditional method.

Entry Age Normal Cost Method

The entry age normal cost method is a type of projected benefit cost method. This means the cost is based upon the projected amount of pension expected to be payable at retirement, rather than the accrued benefit earned to date.

The entry age normal cost equals the level annual amount of contribution (level in dollars or as a percent of pay) from an employee's date of hire (or other entry age) to retirement date, calculated as sufficient to fund the projected benefit. The accrued liability equals the present value of all future benefits for retired and present employees and their beneficiaries, less the portion of that value expected to be funded by future normal costs.

Under the entry age normal cost method, unlike the accrued benefit cost method, the normal cost of each individual is expected to remain level each year. For plans with benefits not related to pay, the normal cost is calculated to remain level in dollars; for a plan with benefits expressed as a percentage of pay, the normal cost is calculated to remain level as a percentage of pay. The average normal cost for the entire group can also usually be expected to remain fairly level per employee or as a percentage of pay, even if the average attained age increases, unless there is a change in the average *entry* age.

Under the entry age normal cost method, when the plan is first established an initial accrued liability exists that equals the accumulation of the normal costs for members for years prior to the effective date. Similarly, if an amendment increases benefits, there is an increase in the accrued liability equal to the accumulation of prior normal costs for the increase in projected benefits.

Individual Level Premium Cost Method

The individual level premium cost method determines the level annual cost to fund each participant's projected pension from the date participation begins to normal retirement date. When participation begins, the plan has no accrued liability, even if the participant has substantial benefits credited for past service. Usually no salary increase assumption is used in projecting the benefit at retirement. If a participant's projected benefit increases during a year, this increase in the projected benefit will be separately funded by an additional level annual cost from the participant's then-attained age to normal retirement age. If a plan amendment increases benefits, the increase in the projected benefit for each individual is funded by a level premium from his or her then-attained age to retirement age, with no immediate increase in the accrued liability.

Under the individual level premium cost method, the accrued liability for each individual equals the present value of future benefits less the present value of future normal costs. The accrued liability for the entire plan, less the plan assets, equals the unfunded accrued liability.

An allowable variation of this method is the "individual aggregate method." Under this variation, the normal cost for the first year is the same as previously described. To determine the normal cost in subsequent years, it is first necessary to allocate the plan's assets. The assets attributable to retired or terminated vested employees are assumed to equal the present value of their benefits; those assets attributable to retired and terminated employees are subtracted from the total actual assets to determine the portion of the actual assets attributable to active employees. Several methods are used to allocate assets among active employees. Each individual's allocated assets are subtracted from the present value of future benefits to obtain the remaining unfunded cost of his benefits. This unfunded cost is spread as a level premium (level in dollars or as a percentage of pay) from attained age to the participant's retirement age.

Aggregate Cost Method

The aggregate cost method is another projected benefit cost method. Under this method, there is no unfunded liability. The accrued liability is, in effect, assumed to equal the assets. Thus, all costs are funded through the future normal costs, determined as a level percent of pay (or level in dollars) during the future working lifetimes of all current employees from their current attained ages.

The excess of the present value of future benefits over the value of any plan assets is the portion of that present value that must be funded by normal costs in the future. This excess is the present value of future normal costs. The actuary then determines the present value of all future compensation for all employees. By dividing the present value of future normal costs by the present value of future compensation, the actuary determines the ratio of future normal costs to future compensation. The actuary multiplies this ratio by the current year's compensation to determine the current year's normal cost. A similar procedure is used to determine the normal cost per employee, rather than as a percent of compensation, if benefits are not related to compensation.

Costs are determined in the aggregate and cannot be determined individually. Thus, the normal cost is calculated as a percentage of the total payroll, or a cost per employee for the entire group. The aggregate cost method automatically spreads gains and losses through the future normal costs and has no separately identifiable gains or losses.

Attained Age Normal Cost Method

The attained age normal method combines the unit credit cost method with either the aggregate cost method or the individual level premium cost method. The accrued liability at the plan's effective date is calculated using the accrued benefit cost method. The cost of the excess of the projected benefit over the accrued benefit on the effective date is funded by level costs over the future working lifetimes of participants, using either the individual level premium cost method or the aggregate cost method. Both individual and aggregate variations have long been recognized as the attained age normal cost method, but some use the name only to apply to one or the other variation.

If the individual variation is used, each individual's original past-service benefit is valued every year using the unit credit cost method to determine the accrued liability. The difference between the employee's total projected benefit and this frozen past-service benefit is valued as under the individual level premium cost method, without spreading gains. This method funds any increase in projected benefits because of salary increases from the then-attained age to retirement age.

If the aggregate variation is chosen after the first year, the frozen initial liability technique, described below, is used. In that event, gains and losses are spread over the future working lifetimes of employees.

Frozen Initial Liability Cost Method

ERISA lists the frozen initial liability method. Many actuaries do not regard this as an actuarial cost method at all but rather a method for spreading gains under other methods. This latter group might describe a method as "entry age normal cost method with frozen initial liability" or as "attained age normal cost method with frozen liability." But this difference of viewpoint does not reflect an actual difference in how the method operates.

The frozen initial liability method is not a method for determining the plan's initial accrued liability. The entry age normal cost method usually is used to determine the initial accrued liability and the first year's normal cost, but sometimes the attained age normal cost method is used instead. In subsequent years the unfunded liability is "frozen" and does not reflect actuarial gains and losses. This method has no gain or loss. What would be a gain or loss is spread over the future working lifetimes of all participants through increases or decreases in future normal costs.

To accomplish this, the unfunded accrued liability on the valuation date is set equal to the expected unfunded liability; that is, what the unfunded liability would be if the actuarial assumptions had been exactly realized during the prior year. This unfunded liability plus the plan assets equals the total accrued liability. The excess of the present value of all future benefits over the accrued liability is the portion of that present value that must be funded by future normal costs and is designated as the present value of future normal costs. From this present value of future normal costs, the current year's normal cost is determined in the same manner as for the aggregate cost method.

Shortfall Method

The shortfall method was created to solve a problem created by ERISA's minimum funding requirements. It applies only to collectively bargained plans. The shortfall method is not really an actuarial cost method but a way of adapting other actuarial methods to ERISA's funding requirements.[14]

Retired and Terminated Participants and Beneficiaries

Under the traditional accrued benefit cost method, the accrued liability equals the value of accrued benefits. This is true for retired participants,

---

[14]Treasury Reg. 1.412(c)(1)-2.

terminated participants with vested rights, and beneficiaries of deceased participants, as well as for active employees.

This same approach is used for retired and terminated members and beneficiaries under all actuarial cost methods that determine the accrued liability on an individual basis. Thus, the accrued liability for retired and terminated members and beneficiaries is the same under the entry age normal cost method as under the accrued benefit cost method.

For aggregate methods, this same value for retired and terminated members and beneficiaries is part of the present value of future benefits.

Table 45–2 summarizes the actuarial cost methods.

TABLE 45–2
Summary of Actuarial Cost Methods (excluding shortfall)

	Accrued Benefit or Projected Benefit	Calculates Gain or Loss	Individual or Aggregate	Initial Accrued Liability	Age Used for Computation of Normal Cost
1. Accrued benefit cost	Accrued	Yes	Individual	Yes	Attained
2. Entry age normal cost					
a. Individual ages	Projected	Yes	Individual	Yes	Entry
b. Average entry age	Projected	Yes	Aggregate	Yes	Entry (average)
3. Individual level premium cost					
a. No spread	Projected	Yes	Individual	No	Attained
b. Spread gain	Projected	No	Individual	No	Attained
4. Aggregate cost	Projected	No	Aggregate	No	Attained
5. Attained age normal cost					
a. Individual	Mixed	Yes	Individual	Yes	Attained
b. Aggregate	Mixed	No	Aggregate	Yes	Attained
6. Frozen initial liability cost	Projected	No	Aggregate	Yes	Attained

Note: For a more detailed presentation of actuarial cost methods, see C. L. Trowbridge and C. E. Farr, *The Theory and Practice of Pension Funding* (Homewood, Ill.: Richard D. Irwin, 1976); and B. N. Berin, *The Fundamentals of Pension Mathematics* (Schaumburg, Ill.: Society of Actuaries, 1989).

Actuarial Assumptions

Purpose of Assumptions

Determining the present value of future benefits is basic to all actuarial cost methods. *The present value of any future benefit is the amount of the future benefit times the probability it will be paid, discounted to present value at interest.* For example, a plan may provide a disability benefit equal to 50 percent of pay to workers who become disabled after 15 years of service. The amount of future benefits depends upon the probability each worker will survive in the group to become eligible; that is, that he or she will not die, retire, become disabled, or otherwise terminate employment before becoming eligible for such benefits. The amount of future benefits also depends upon the probabilities of becoming disabled, as well as the period of disability before either death or recovery. It also depends on future salary increases. Actuarial assumptions are used to predict these matters.

The present value of future benefits is calculated using an interest discount. It may not be apparent why an assumption concerning the assets is used to determine the present value of future benefits. The present value of a future benefit is the amount of assets that would need to be invested today to assure that the assets plus the interest they would earn would be sufficient to provide the expected benefits in the future. The interest to be earned is key to determining what amount of present assets are needed.

The actuarial valuation allocates the present value of benefits to various periods of the past and future. Frequently, that allocation is made in proportion to periods of employment or to compensation. For example, actuarial assumptions are used to estimate those periods of employment or amount of compensation. Thus, the selection of the assumptions affects the allocation of present values between periods of the past and future.

Long-Range Nature of Assumptions

For an employee now aged 25, the actuarial assumptions are used to estimate whether he or she will be eligible for a pension 40 years in the future, what the employee's salary will be after 40 years, how long the employee will live to receive a pension, and what the fund will earn over the entire period.

Thus, the actuarial assumptions are extremely long range in nature. The more distant any event is, the less likely it can be predicted accurately. Mortality rates for next year are fairly predictable (barring a war), but mortality rates 50 years hence may depend upon events that cannot possibly be predicted, such as remarkable medical discoveries or a disastrous deterioration of the environment. Assumptions other than mortality are even less predictable for long periods. The experience of last year, or the expected experience of next year, is relevant to the process of establishing assumptions only to the extent that it may indicate long-term trends.

Most experts will not even conjecture for such long periods. When economists talk of long-range projections, they often mean five years. Yet such long-range assumptions are essential to actuarial valuations. The actuary, faced with this difficult task, usually assumes the future will be generally similar to the present, often with some element of conservatism (conservative in the direction of producing higher costs).

ERISA Requirements for Assumptions

ERISA requires the actuary to use reasonable actuarial assumptions and methods (taking into account the experience of the plan and reasonable expectations), which, in combination, offer the actuary's best estimate of anticipated experience under the plan.[15] The statutory language provides more questions than answers. What is the meaning of *reasonable?* How can the assumptions be reasonably related to the plan's experience when the large majority of plans are so small that their experience is not statistically valid? Is the "best estimate" one that has a 50 percent chance of being on the high side and a 50 percent chance of being on the low side? Detailed discussion of the individual assumptions can be found in the actuarial literature.[16]

In addition to the above requirements, which apply to all of the actuarial assumptions in the aggregate, additional requirements apply to the interest assumption.

---

[15]ERISA Sec. 302(c)(3), IRC Sec. 412(c)(3).

[16]Study notes of the Society of Actuaries and articles and discussions in numerous volumes of the *Transactions* and *Record* of the Society of Actuaries, and the *Proceedings* of the Conference of Actuaries in Public Practice.

Asset Valuation Methods

Under some actuarial cost methods, the value of plan assets affects the unfunded liability, which must be funded by amortization payments. Under other actuarial cost methods, the value of plan assets affects the normal cost. Under either approach, the method used to determine the value of plan assets determines the required employer contributions for a particular year and the fluctuation in contributions from year to year.

Some plans use the market value of assets for the actuarial valuation. It is argued this is the real value of the plan's assets and therefore makes the valuation more realistic. The disadvantage of this method is that fluctuations in market value may result in substantial fluctuation in the required employer contributions from year to year, which is generally undesirable.

Some plans use cost or book value of assets for the actuarial valuation. This can avoid the problems of fluctuation in plan costs. However, if the asset value used differs substantially from market value, it may present an unrealistic picture of the true costs and liabilities.

A variety of actuarial methods of asset valuation are used to avoid these problems. Some plans use the cost or book value so long as it lies within a stated corridor around market value; for example, not less than 80 percent or more than 120 percent of market value. Some plans use a formula or method to gradually recognize asset appreciation; for example, five-year-average market value. A wide variety of methods are used to gradually recognize appreciation but avoid extreme asset value fluctuation. ERISA requires plans to use "any reasonable actuarial method of valuation which takes into account fair market value and which is permitted under regulations." Regulations require that the asset value used be either between 80 percent and 120 percent of market value or between 85 percent and 115 percent of the average market value for a period of five years or less.

MINIMUM FUNDING REQUIREMENTS

General Requirements

ERISA established minimum funding requirements to provide greater assurance that pension plans will be able to pay the promised benefits.

Applicability

The minimum funding requirements appear twice in ERISA in duplicate language, in Title I and Title II.[17] The IRS issues regulations that apply to both Title I and Title II.

Under Title II the minimum funding requirements apply to almost all qualified pension plans (excluding profit-sharing and stock bonus plans) except government plans, church plans, and "insurance contract plans."

Under Title I, the minimum funding requirements apply to non-qualified plans as well as qualified plans. The exemptions described above for Title II also apply under Title I, along with a few other exemptions. Plans exempt from the funding requirements include "a plan which is unfunded and is maintained by an employer primarily for the purpose of providing deferred compensation for a select group of management or highly compensated employees" and "excess benefit plans." The broad definition of *pension plan* under ERISA makes the funding requirements apply to many deferred-compensation arrangements, previously unfunded plans, and other arrangements not previously thought of as pension plans.

Basic Requirements

Employers are required to contribute at least the normal cost plus amounts calculated to amortize any unfunded liabilities over a period of years. The required amortization period ranges from 5 years to 40 years, depending on when it arose and its source. Additional requirements apply to certain plans with a low level of funding. If contributions in any year exceed the minimum required, the excess reduces the minimum required in subsequent years.

Penalties and Enforcement

If contributions are less than required, the shortfall is an "accumulated funding deficiency." If an accumulated funding deficiency exists at the end of the plan year, a 5 percent excise tax is assessed on the deficiency. If the funding deficiency is not corrected within 90 days after the IRS mails a notice of deficiency, an additional tax is imposed equal to 100 percent of any uncorrected deficiency. In addition to paying these non-

---

[17]ERISA Sec. 301–306, IRC Sec. 412.

deductible taxes, the employer must also correct the accumulated funding deficiency itself. These taxes apply only to qualified plans. Whether or not the plan is qualified, the Secretary of Labor, participants, beneficiaries, and fiduciaries may bring civil actions to enforce the minimum funding requirements.

Funding Standard Account

A "funding standard account" is an accounting device used to keep track of the funding requirements. Amounts that increase the funding obligation for the year are charges to the funding standard account. These include the normal cost and annual payments needed to amortize any unfunded liabilities. Amounts that decrease the employer's obligation are credits to the funding standard account. These include employer contributions and annual amounts that may be used to amortize any decrease in the unfunded liability.

If the credits exceed the charges for a year, the excess is carried over as a credit balance to decrease the contributions required for the following year. Similarly, if the credits are less than the charges, the resulting accumulated funding deficiency is carried forward to increase the contributions required in the following year.

Reporting

For defined benefit pension plans, the plan administrator must engage an enrolled actuary "on behalf of all plan participants." Satisfaction of the minimum funding requirements is demonstrated on Schedule B "Actuarial Information," which must be certified by an enrolled actuary and attached to Form 5500. For defined contribution pension plans, satisfaction of the requirements is shown on Form 5500 itself.

Timing of Contributions

The entire contribution required for a plan year must be paid no later than 8½ months after the end of the year. In addition, a portion of the required contribution must be paid no later than each of four quarterly contribution dates.

Minimum Contribution Requirement

Additional funding requirements apply to any plan with more than 100 participants if its "current liability" (the liability for accrued benefits) exceeds the value of its assets. If the "deficit reduction contribution" needed to amortize the unfunded current liability exceeds the amortization amounts included in the regular funding requirement, the excess must be added to the regular funding requirement.

Full Funding Limitation

No employer is required or allowed to contribute more than the amount needed to fully fund the accrued liability or the amount needed to fund 150 percent of the current liability. This full funding limitation may reduce or eliminate the minimum contribution otherwise required. Special rules govern the determination of the amounts of assets and liabilities for this purpose.

Alternative Minimum Funding Standard

Some plans are allowed to use the alternative minimum funding standard to determine their minimum funding requirement. If a plan uses the alternative minimum funding standard, it must nonetheless also maintain records for the regular funding standard account. A plan may not use the alternative minimum funding standard unless it uses the entry age normal cost method under its regular funding standard account. If an alternative minimum funding standard account is maintained, it is charged with (1) the lesser of the normal cost under the actuarial cost method used under the plan or the normal cost determined under the unit credit cost method, (2) the excess, if any, of the present value of accrued benefits over the fair market value of assets, and (3) any credit balance in the account as of the beginning of the year. The alternative minimum funding standard account is credited with employer contributions for the year.

The alternative minimum funding standard is based upon a plan discontinuance concept. It is not a sound basis for funding an ongoing plan, and very few plans use it.

Extension of Amortization Period

Another form of relief from the minimum funding requirement is an extension of the amortization periods. The Internal Revenue Service may extend the time required to amortize any unfunded liability by up to 10 years. Extending an amortization period reduces slightly the required employer contribution. No employer is known to have ever applied for such an extension.

Waiver

The IRS may grant a waiver of part or all of the minimum funding requirement. A waiver will be approved only if the employer faces ''substantial business hardship'' and if failure to approve the waiver would be ''adverse to the interests of plan participants in the aggregate.''

Multiemployer Plan Requirements

ERISA contained slightly different funding requirements for collectively bargained multiemployer plans than for other plans. The Multiemployer Pension Plans Amendment Act of 1980 (MEPPA) made further changes for multiemployer plans. The most significant difference is that an employer that withdraws from a multiemployer plan may be assessed ''withdrawal liability,'' requiring significant contributions after the withdrawal.

TAX DEDUCTION OF EMPLOYER CONTRIBUTIONS

Purposes

Like most other business expenses, contributions to qualified pension plans must be deducted as ordinary and necessary business expenses. In addition, Section 404 of the Internal Revenue Code sets maximum limits on the amount that may be deducted in each year. Section 404 reflects two concerns of Congress.

First, Congress wanted to encourage employers to establish qualified plans for their employees. Congress also wanted to encourage employers to soundly fund the plans to assure that promised benefits would be paid. Thus Congress wanted to allow tax deductions for the amounts needed to soundly fund the plans.

Second, Congress wanted to limit the deduction for a particular year to expense attributable to that year. This would serve to prevent an employer from prepaying future expenses in order to evade taxes. It is not clear how much of the payments for past service costs and actuarial gains and losses should be considered attributable to a particular year, however.

Timing of Deductible Contributions

To be deductible, contributions to pension and profit-sharing plans for a year must be paid no later than the tax filing date for the year, including extensions. No deduction may be claimed for the contribution of a promissory note of the employer, even if secured.

If the employer contributes more than the deductible limit for a year, the excess is carried over to be deducted in future years, subject to the deductible limit in future years. However, a 10 percent excise tax is assessed on any contributions that exceed the maximum deductible amount for the year.[18]

Maximum Deductible Limit for Pension Plans

Section 404 has three alternative ways to determine the maximum limit on deductible employer contributions for a pension plan. Usually, the maximum deductible limit equals the normal cost plus the amount needed to amortize any past service liability over 10 years. If a plan has no unfunded liability, its deductible limit does not include a past service amount.

The amount of past service cost to be amortized is called a *10-year amortization base*. For a new plan, the 10-year amortization base equals the initial unfunded accrued liability base. If the unfunded accrued liability is changed by a plan amendment, change in the actuarial method or assumptions, or actuarial gains or losses, the amount of change in the unfunded accrued liability becomes an additional 10-year amortization base. The old base continues until it is fully amortized. Any event that increases the unfunded liability creates a new positive base. Any event that decreases the unfunded liability creates a new negative base. A plan may have many bases.

The amount required to amortize each 10-year amortization base over 10 years is the "limit adjustment." Each 10-year amortization base has its own limit adjustment. The limit adjustment is positive if its base is positive and negative if its base is negative. All of a plan's limit adjust-

---

[18]IRC Sec. 4972.

ments are added to determine the plan's maximum deductible limit for past service contributions. Detailed regulations provide rules for determining the amount of bases and limit adjustments.[19]

The second method of determining the maximum deductible limit is the individual aggregate method. The maximum deductible limit for each participant is the amount necessary to provide the remaining unfunded cost of the projected benefit distributed as a level amount, or a level percentage of compensation, over the participant's remaining future service. But if the remaining unfunded cost for any three individuals exceeds 50 percent of the unfunded cost for the entire plan, then the unfunded cost for each such individual must be distributed over at least five years.

The third alternative for determining the deductible limit equals the amount required to satisfy the plan's minimum funding requirement. The full-funding limitation determined under the minimum funding requirements is an overriding maximum limit on the amount that may be deducted for a year.

Maximum Deductible Limits for Profit-Sharing and Stock Bonus Plans

The maximum deductible limit for a profit-sharing plan or stock bonus plan is 15 percent of the compensation paid or accrued for all participants during the tax year. The limitation is on the aggregate contributions for all participants, not the contribution for each. Thus, more than 15 percent may be contributed and deducted for a particular participant if the aggregate limit is not exceeded.

Maximum Deductible for Combined Plans

If an employer maintains more than one profit-sharing or stock bonus plan, they are treated as a single plan for purposes of determining the deductible limit. If an employer maintains both a defined benefit plan and a defined contribution plan that have one or more participants in common, there is an additional limitation on deductible contributions. Deductible contributions to the combined plans are limited to 25 percent of

---

[19] Treasury Reg. Sec. 1.404(a).

compensation of all of the participants in either plan or, if greater, the pension plan contribution required by the minimum funding requirements. This is so even though an employer that has no defined contribution plan may deduct more than 25 percent of pay under a defined benefit plan. If contributions to combined defined benefit and defined contribution plans exceed the combined 25 percent limit, they may be carried over for deduction in a later year, but the 10 percent excise tax on nondeductible contributions applies.

DEDUCTION OF EMPLOYEE CONTRIBUTIONS

Some plans require employees to contribute to the plan as a condition for participation or for receiving certain employer-provided benefits. Some plans allow employees to make voluntary contributions to increase the benefits otherwise provided under the plan. Neither mandatory nor voluntary employee contributions are deductible by employees.

Under a 401(k) plan an employee may elect to defer receipt of part of his or her compensation and have the employer contribute it to the plan. Subject to limits, the amount deferred is excluded from the employee's taxable income and is treated as an employer contribution.

ACCOUNTING FOR PENSION PLAN LIABILITIES AND COSTS

There are two parts to pension plan accounting: accounting for the plan itself and accounting for the employer. A brief description of each follows. For a more detailed discussion of plan accounting, see Chapter 43. *Employer* accounting for pension plans is covered in Chapter 42.

Accounting for the Plan

Form 5500 or a related form must be filed each year with the Internal Revenue Service. Form 5500 includes a statement of plan assets and liabilities, a statement of income and expenses, and certain other financial information. For plans with 100 or more participants the plan administrator is required to engage an independent qualified public accountant. A statement from the accountant, prepared in accordance with generally accepted accounting principles, must be attached to Form 5500. *Statement of Financial Accounting Standards No. 35* of the Financial Accounting Standards Board (FASB) established generally accepted accounting principles for pension plans.

For defined benefit plans with 100 or more participants Schedule B of Form 5500 requires reporting the value of accrued benefits. This same item is required in accounting statements under *Statement No. 35*. It ordinarily bears no relation to the plan's funding, is misleading as an indication of funding for an ongoing plan, and does not purport to represent the plan's liabilities if the plan should be discontinued.

Both Form 5500 and *Statement No. 35* also require a statement of assets and liabilities (other than actuarial liabilities), a statement of changes in fund balances, and additional information.

Accounting for the Employer

An employer's accounting for a defined contribution plan usually is simple. Contributions paid for the employer's fiscal year are treated as an expense. An employer's accounting for a defined benefit plan is more complex. It requires certain disclosures in addition to determining the charge to expense and possible balance sheet entries.

For a defined benefit plan an employer's charge to expense for pension cost is the subject of *Statements No. 87* and *No. 88* of the Financial Accounting Standards Board. *Statement No. 87* requires the profit and loss statement to include a charge for pension expense that represents the pension cost properly attributable to the current year, regardless of the amount contributed for the year.

The employer's pension expense is the "net periodic pension cost." It must be determined using the projected unit credit cost method.

The net periodic pension cost consists of six components:

1. Service cost.
2. Interest cost.
3. Actual return on plan assets.
4. Amortization of any prior service cost.
5. Gain or loss (including the effect of changes in actuarial assumptions).
6. Amortization of unrecognized obligation at the date of initial application of *Statement No. 87*.

The service cost is the plan's normal cost. The interest cost equals one year's interest at the valuation interest rate ("discount rate") on the plan's accrued liability ("projected benefit obligation"). The "actual return on plan assets," which reduces the net periodic pension cost, equals the investment income earned plus realized and unrealized appreciation and depreciation of the fair value of plan assets. The initial projected benefit obligation for a new plan, or the increase in the projected benefit obligation resulting from a plan amendment, generally must be amortized over the expected future period of service of participants expected to receive benefits; this forms the annual amortization of any prior service cost. In order to smooth fluctuations in pension cost from year to year, *Statement No. 87* includes rules for delaying and spreading the recognition of actuarial gains and losses, so that only a portion of the gain or loss is included in the net periodic pension cost for any year. However, any difference between the actual return on plan assets and the expected return on plan assets in the year is recognized currently, immediately offsetting any investment return greater or smaller than expected. The difference between the projected benefit obligation and the fair value of plan assets on the effective date of *Statement No. 87,* adjusted for an accrued or prepaid pension cost at that date, is the plan's unrecognized net obligation or asset at that date. This amount is to be amortized over the expected future period of service of participants expected to receive benefits, although the employer may elect to use a 15-year amortization period if that is longer.

Negative components of the net periodic pension cost may exceed positive components, resulting in a negative net periodic pension cost.

Differences between the net periodic pension cost and the amount of contribution to the plan result in a balance sheet asset or liability for prepaid or accrued pension cost. In addition, any excess of the value of accrued benefits ("accumulated benefit obligation") over the fair value of plan assets will require recognition on the balance sheet as a liability. In this case an offsetting intangible asset is usually allowed on the balance sheet.

Statement No. 87 also requires certain disclosures in the employer's financial statements. It contains accounting rules related to termination or curtailment of plans, purchase of annuities, and payment of lump-sum distributions under plans.

Relationship of Accounting and Funding

Accounting for the pension plan itself and accounting for the employer do not directly control the plan's funding. However, there may be an important indirect effect, since the manner in which accountants report funding influences some employers' decisions concerning funding.

CHAPTER 46

FUNDING RETIREMENT PLANS—INVESTMENT OBJECTIVES

Eugene B. Burroughs

The successful funding of the future pension-benefit-payment promise through investment operations is made possible through the exercise of prudence, the application of time-proven principles, the dedication of people conducting themselves in a professional manner, and the resultant efficacy of the adopted policy and practices. The growth in real asset value over time through successful investment funding activities will require fewer contributions and will allow greater potential for enhancing retirement benefit payments.

Representatives of sponsors of employee benefit plans play a significant role in the benefit payments funding process, for if they collectively address the asset management part of their responsibilities in an objective and professional manner, their stewardship may produce the major portion of the benefit-payments stream from the pension plan. The power of compounded interest, reinvested earnings, redeployed rents, and realized capital appreciation are powerful elements in the wealth-enhancement process. To the degree the supervising fiduciaries are successful in systematically adding value over time from investment operations, less of a need exists to increase employer, or employee, contributions to the plan.

It, therefore, behooves the supervising group to endeavor through knowledge and insight into the workings of the financial markets to propitiously allocate plan assets. Unfortunately, many plan sponsors miss their opportunities to add value to the plan by:

- The frequent hiring of "winning" managers and firing of "losing" managers.
- Excessive turnover in the portfolio.
- Inordinate emphasis on stock-picking activities as opposed to the more productive asset-allocation decisions.
- Assuming unrealizable return expectations based upon the most recent market experience and ignoring the long-term risk/return relationships in the securities markets.

Since asset stewardship activities so significantly impact the net bottom line, choosing among funding vehicles is extremely important. This chapter's discussion of funding pensions through asset management activities provides the elements basic to the process. The discussion is necessarily limited to investing alternatives. The important point of this discussion is to grasp the principles and process to achieve a plan's funding goals through investment operations.

The discussion includes:

1. *Four elements fundamental to successful investing* of employee benefit plan monies.
2. Attributes of the *prudent fiduciary.*
3. Characteristics of the *three favored classes of investments.*
4. Identification of appropriate *investment objectives.*
5. Evaluation and selection of the *investment facility.*
6. Development and documentation of *investment policy.*
7. Exercising the option to engage in *strategic asset deployment* activities.
8. *Monitoring, reevaluation, and modification* of policy and strategy.

FOUR FUNDAMENTAL ELEMENTS OF SUCCESSFUL INVESTING

Before proceeding with the discussion of investment planning as it relates to achieving funding objectives, it is necessary to review four principles fundamental to the investment process:

1. The level of risk assumed by a fund determines the level of return achieved (Figure 46–1).

FIGURE 46–1
Risk versus Return

Level of Risk Assumed Determines Level of Return Achieved

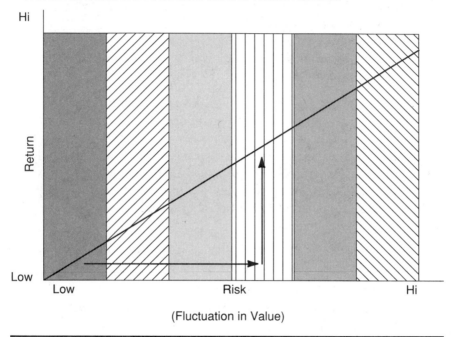

(Fluctuation in Value)

2. Returns normally attributed to variable assets (common stock, long-duration bonds, and real estate) are assured only as the holding period is extended (Figure 46–2).
3. The time permitted to lapse before converting an investment position to cash determines the level of return.
4. Market studies have confirmed the orderliness that exists between risk and reward in the financial markets (Figure 46–3).

THE PRUDENT FIDUCIARY

Since successful investment programs are a product of human judgment, it is also important to consider briefly the attributes of a prudent fiduciary. ERISA, Sec. 404(a)(1)(B), stipulates that a fiduciary shall discharge his

FIGURE 46–2
Return Expectations versus Realized Variable Assets (Stocks, Long Bonds, Real Estate)

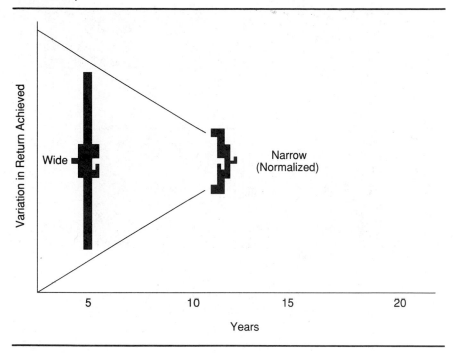

or her duties with respect to a plan solely in the interest of the participants and beneficiaries, and "with the care, skill, prudence, and diligence under the circumstances then prevailing that a prudent man acting in a like capacity and familiar with such matters would use in the conduct of an enterprise of a like character and with like aims."

To qualify as prudent, in retrospect, fiduciaries of plans must have conducted themselves as *prudent experts*, having set up an administrative approach to facilitate the decision-making process, considered internal factors of the fund, hired and listened to investment experts and qualified legal counsel, obtained independent studies when advisable, considered the financial variables of the prospective course of action, and set up an arm's-length mechanism to negotiate with any parties-in-interest. Such a documented sequence of activities probably should be sufficient to stand the test of prudence required by the law.

FIGURE 46–3
Orderliness in Financial Markets (Types of Mutual Funds)

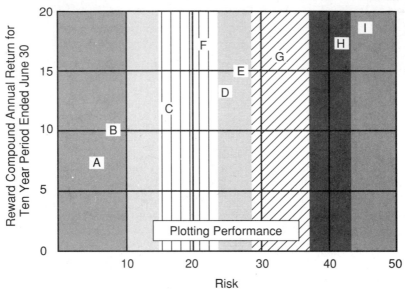

Maximum Fluctuation, in Percentage Points,
Between Best and Worst Quarters Over the Past Ten Years

Categories of Funds
1. 91 Day U.S. Treasury Bills (Short Term Instruments)
2. Money Market Funds (Short Term Fixed Income Pool)
3. Fixed Income Funds (More than 75% in Fixed Income Assets)
4. Balanced Funds (Conserves Principal; Mix of Stocks and Bonds)
5. Growth and Income Funds (Stock Mix Aimed for Short and Long Term)
6. Equity Income Funds (Mostly Stocks with High Current Value)
7. Growth Funds (Stocks with Higher Growth than Market Average)
8. Capital Appreciation Funds (Diverse Means to Build Capital)
9. Small Company Growth Funds

Source: Lipper Advisory Services, Inc., Milwaukee.

In any technically demanding investment course of action, there should be an effective blending of the judgment of those charged to be the overseers of a trust fund with the opinions of the experts who provide counsel and research in support of a defensible conclusion. If done properly, this team approach will most likely be judged sufficient to support a sound decision. There also should be a careful preservation of the lines of demarcation among cofiduciaries. Plans go afoul with the counsel of too few. Sufficient counsel increases the likelihood of success. This is not a carte blanche vote in favor of multimanagement investment systems, but recognition that just as the diversification requirement calls for balance in assembling the components of the portfolio, prudence calls for balance and effectiveness in the selection of people and how they perform their varied assignments.

There is no substitute for the fiduciary's exercise of informed and reasoned judgment. The fiduciary must pursue each alternative until he or she gets to the heart of the matter, examining all the facts available prior to making the decision. In addition to exercising resourceful due diligence, there appears to be unanimous agreement among legal counselors on the necessity for the preparation of resourceful documentation on the part of all fiduciaries party to the process.

Put succinctly, the "prudent" fiduciary possesses the following characteristics:

1. Determination.
2. Knowledge that leads to insightful decisions.
3. Organization.
4. Openmindedness.
5. Objectivity.
6. Realistic expectations.
7. Patience.

There are myriad investment vehicles available as funding vehicles—insured, noninsured; pooled separate accounts; aggregated pools of individual securities; privately placed and publicly traded. The characteristics of the investment medium chosen should be conducive to the attainment of the investment objectives sought. To recognize which vehicles are most appropriate, a fiduciary needs to understand the differing characteristics of the various classes of investments.

CHARACTERISTICS OF THE THREE FAVORED CLASSES OF INVESTMENTS

To understand why fiduciaries choose to blend equity and fixed income securities in portfolios, the characteristics of common stock, fixed income securities and real estate are reviewed. In order of preference, common stock is the preferred investment medium, with bonds, cash equivalents and real estate vehicles following.

Common Stock

The characteristic that most attracts the employee-benefit-plan investor to common stock is its ability to add real value to a portfolio. According to Salomon Brothers, the Standard & Poor's 500 achieved + 12.5 percent per year in real return over the ten years ending June 1, 1990. If, during this time, a plan manager was able to constructively exploit this class of investment, the fund was able to compete effectively with, and substantially outdistance, inflation's impact on portfolio values. Since one of the long-range goals for many employee benefit plans is to pay benefits in inflation-adjusted dollars, then the choice of common stock as the preferred asset class has proven to be a productive funding facility.

The driving forces behind stock prices are *earnings, return on equity,* and the issuing firm's *dividend policy.* Increased earnings influence the company's board of directors to increase dividend payouts, which in turn influences stock analysts to pay a higher price for the shares. As demand for the shares increases, at some point the stock becomes fully valued, or overvalued, which should lead the investment manager to take the plan's profits and reinvest the proceeds in a stock that is still passing through the undervalued part of its pricing cycle. Such portfolio management should produce the historical 6 percent real return expected from common-stock ownership. The astute manager picks up additional return from his or her superior information-processing ability.

The rewards of stock ownership, resulting from a combination of an increasing dividend stream and appreciation in the value of the shares, can be unlimited. These rewards accrue from investors' willingness to pay a higher multiple for the increased earnings and the ability of the firm to "manage its store" successfully. The increases in the price/earnings (p/e) multiple and dividend-payout stream flow in part from the firm's ability to capitalize on its research and development activity. This in turn fosters consumer acceptance of its products or services and eventually leads to increased sales. If costs are efficiently controlled, increasing sales should lead to growing earning power, profitable reinvestment opportunities for the earnings, and ultimately increased confidence shown by the investment community in the firm's ability to manage its affairs successfully in the future. Investors, reflecting their increased confidence in the future fortunes of the firm, will increase their activity in accumulating the stock, which in turn will bid up the price/earnings multiple. Thus, the p/e multiple becomes a measure of the attractiveness of a particular security versus all other available securities as determined by the investing public.

Even though common stock as a class has proven to be an attractive funding facility, plan sponsors need to identify stock managers who have developed and can apply superior selection techniques. Unless the manager can consistently buy stock with a present price at or below its intrinsic value, the sponsor may have to forsake active management and opt for dollar-cost averaging into a passively managed index fund. The sponsor in turn must exercise patience permitting the long-term investment trends to overcome the shorter-term cyclical influences in the determination of share value. Actively managing a portfolio of common stock can achieve superior results, but the results do not come automatically. It takes superior stock selection, or insightful market timing, or a combination of both, to outperform the passive "market" portfolio.

Charles Ellis of Greenwich Research Associates sums this up well when he says that the "keys to successful common-stock management are: (1) adopt a policy (style) and apply it consistently; (2) strive for excellence in a few areas; (3) concentrate on when to sell; and (4) maintain modest expectations."

Many plan sponsors have adopted passive stock management (a style of management that seeks to obtain average, risk-adjusted performance), because the *net* returns achieved from active management have not compared to the *net* returns achieved by index funds. To justify its use, the return from active management must exceed the return from a comparable market index plus a recoupment return for the higher relative transaction costs. Plan sponsors are also adopting passive strategies to implement asset redeployment moves to complement their existing active managers and as a temporary parking place for equity-destined monies while undertaking a management search.

Common stock has evolved over time to become the favored investment medium of the funds because it offers the possibility of providing the most attractive real rate of return. However, before that possibility becomes a reality, a plan sponsor has two options. The sponsor can find a manager who can recognize change early, select those stocks whose emerging positive attributes will be discovered by other analysts, and pays attention to the price paid for stocks as a class, and for his or her stocks in particular. Or, in the absence of finding such a manager, the sponsor can participate in a passively supervised stock portfolio for that portion of the total portfolio dedicated to long-term common-stock ownership.

Fixed-Income Securities

Fixed-income securities have traditionally been the bellwether asset in employee-benefit-plan portfolios. However, the turbulence created in interest rates several years ago by unanticipated and volatile inflation rates, has shaken confidence in the traditionally passive approach to bond management. Because of the resultant concern for volatility, bond managers have developed a number of strategies and products to more effectively compete with the challenging environment.

There are many alternatives to choose from in the fixed income area. Within the money market area alone, one can choose from a broad spectrum of securities. The advent of money-market deposit accounts and short-term investment fund (STIF) accounts offered by banks in the deregulation environment has increased both the options and relative yields for monies limited to short-term maturities. For a plan willing to embrace a higher degree of credit risk, Eurodollar CD's, corporate master notes, and repurchase agreements are available. CARS (Consumer Auto Receivables), CATS (Certificates of Accrual on Treasury Securities), and TIGRS (Treasury Investment Growth Receipts) are examples of the many new fixed-income products available in the bond markets.

With the proliferation of products has come an increase in the number of ways of increasing wealth in a portfolio through the use of fixed-income securities. Whether a plan's supervising fiduciaries accomplish their goals through a high- or low-turnover approach, there is no substitute for the adoption of and adherence to a reasoned, disciplined strategy. To the degree possible, a plan should exploit its longer-term planning horizon and forsake the extreme comfort of money-market instruments by extending the duration of its fixed-income portfolio. Here again there are a number of alternatives and strategies—active/active, passive/active, passive/passive. You can make active bets on interest-rate movements while also engaging in sector swaps, etc.; you can forgo (or limit) your interest-rate-anticipation moves while still actively trading the portfolio with arbitrage moves; or you can immunize or dedicate the portfolio and forgo shorter-term upside potential (or limit downside risk) through a wholly passive approach. These strategies can be implemented using governments, corporates, and utilities or the more recent market entrants—mortgage-backed securities and derivative instruments. The newest entrant is the "accounts receivable–backed bond," which securitizes credit-card and automobile purchases.

Why would a fiduciary include bonds as a part of a plan's funding mechanism? First, the plan (the lender) has a preferred claim on the income and assets of the issuer (the borrower). The lender has a contractual right to the return of stated principal and a contractual right to receive the periodic stated interest payments. From this right springs a plan's expectation of receiving and cultivating an income stream. It is the periodic reinvestment of this income stream that permits a plan to exploit the principle of the "power of compounding interest." In just 20 years, $100 growing at 7 percent (that is, 4 percent inflation + 3 percent "rent" for loaning money) results in an accumulation of $386. The tax-exempt status of the plan increases all the more the efficacy of compounding interest.

The success of a bond investment depends upon whether the financial accumulation from ownership compares favorably with the original expectations at purchase. If a plan's objective is to produce a real rate of return, the income stream from the bond should exceed the loss due to inflation in purchasing power of the principal. Unfortunately, this is only one of the risks faced in bond investment. Others are credit (default) risk (if the issuer goes bankrupt), interest-rate risk (if bonds must be sold below the price paid), call risk (if the issuer calls in the bond in a lower interest-rate environment), and reinvestment risk (if comparable, creditworthy bonds are paying a lower rate of interest when principal or coupons are being reinvested).

Bond risk can be controlled. In addition to the use of interest-rate futures (not in the scope of this discussion), there are many portfolio-management techniques that can provide comfort to the plan sponsor. Inflation risk can be reduced by buying bonds only when the real spread (interest rates minus probable inflation) is at a historical premium. Correctly assessing when a premium spread is available takes a combination of astute historical perspective, forecasting ability, and luck! The phenomenon of lagging return premiums probably exists because bond buyers, having previously erred in their forecasting of inflation's rise, demand high rates long after inflation has subsided in intensity. (Although inflation peaked in March 1980, wider than usual spreads have been available for quite some time now.) Credit risk can be controlled through the exercise of superior credit analysis and adequate quality-threshold guidelines. Interest-rate risk can be reduced by keeping maturities short, dollar-cost-averaging purchases, and adopting the various immunization and dedication strategies.

Partitioning out the retired lives and purchasing bonds dedicated to meet these benefit payments as they fall due has become a popular planning technique. In some cases, the potential this technique offers for withdrawal-liabilities reduction (or elimination) to the multiemployer plans has been sufficient to justify the trustees' implementing such a risk-reduction strategy. Single-sponsor plans also have chosen such techniques to control the fluctuation in plan surplus, or the rate at which contributions are required. To manage call risk, one must simply "read the fine print." Reinvestment risk can be eliminated by purchasing zero-coupon bonds or laddering the bond maturities.

Real Estate

A third, less popular funding facility is the fee ownership of real properties. The class of equity real estate is added to a portfolio within the context of a pension plan's objectives *(a)* to exploit its long-term time horizon, *(b)* to defend against the possibility that higher inflationary periods may reappear (repeat of the 1976–1981 environment), *(c)* to add a third asset class that offers the potential to produce real rates of return in all price environments, and *(d)* because of its noncovariance characteristics when combined with stocks and bonds in a portfolio.

Like common stock, equity real estate has the potential to add significant real value over time. Its hybrid nature as both financial (leases) and tangible (bricks and mortar) enables its owner to hedge effectively against either low or high inflation. Overage rents, net net leases, expense-escalation clauses, equity-equivalent loans, and so on, all result in the investor being assured that his or her principal will stay competitive with inflation. The hybrid nature of convertible participating mortgages enables the pension fund sponsor to hedge against an unknown future.

Successful real-estate investing requires attention to *location, product,* and *management.* Therefore, a fund must retain a real-estate manager with a resourceful research staff. Since real estate is a relatively inefficient market, a real-estate-management organization should, by processing information in an effective manner, ultimately acquire those properties whose configurations of attributes will assure relatively high demand. Building on a firm base of research capability, the manager(s) must have developed a strategic approach compatible with the plan and have demonstrated the ability to acquire properties astutely through analytical talent and negotiating skills. An underrated resource of a manager is his or her property (asset) management capability, whether developed in-house or successfully retained and monitored. It also is important to determine that the principals of the firm have formed a team that enjoys industry-peer-group respect. It takes time and effort to develop marketing packages for complex properties. Those management teams who *(a)* have attracted a sufficient client base to provide continuing cash flow availability, *(b)* have available the diverse disciplines to evaluate a deal effectively, and *(c)* can quickly respond to the offer to capitalize on a market opportunity, will be afforded priority in being shown the more desirable properties.

Other caveats that must be considered are that: (1) the properties acquired must be well conceived, well located, and well managed; (2) the sponsor must be willing to undergo "income only" years in anticipation of the slower-emerging capital-appreciation years; (3) the manager must purchase the properties using the current effective rents as the basis for determining value; (4) a plan just beginning in real estate may be well advised to dollar-cost-average into the market over several years; and (5) if a plan is going into open-ended funds that use net-asset valuations supported by yearly appraisals of the portfolio properties, due diligence should be performed by the plan sponsor to assure that the net-asset valuation used reflects the realities of the current marketplace. One would not want to place new dollars indirectly into real-estate assets at inflated valuations resulting from a lagging recognition of deteriorating portfolio values.

Asset Allocation

Although collectively the classes of common stock, bonds, and equity real estate represent the preponderance of allocations in employee-benefit-plan portfolios, other vehicles used in the funding process include guaranteed-investment contracts, mortgages, venture capital, and oil and gas investments. To protect a fund's future valuations from being overly vulnerable to the fortunes of any one class, supervising fiduciaries construct diversified portfolios. An employee-benefit-plan portfolio's value is the sum of its component parts. If the plan is to reach its ultimate performance objectives, these component parts must, each in its own way, make a contribution to the whole fund. No class of assets exists in isolation. Such an orderly blending of related units is not happenstance, but must be carefully orchestrated to produce a harmonious conclusion. Thus, a cardinal rule in plan investing is "diversify, diversify, diversify."

Someone, or some group, usually serves in the role of "investment coordinator" for a plan. The following list describes the coordinator's duties and responsibilities.

1. Lead the plan's professional team in the identification of the investment and noninvestment constraints of the plan and the subsequent development of the appropriate portfolio performance objectives, policies, and strategies.

2. Continually examine and evaluate all acceptable investment alternatives, and recognize and value the strengths that each team member can bring to the task.

3. Watch for early warning signs of weaknesses evidenced by people, policies, or practices of the program, and foster the reasonable expectations of investment performance, recognizing the inherent limitations in the investment-management process.

4. Recognize the importance of establishing an appropriate risk posture for the fund predicated on a thorough examination of the risk/reward trade-offs.

5. Set targets in ranges rather than in absolutes.

6. Recognize and be responsive to change, and be knowledgeable of techniques on the cutting edge of contemporary investment management.

7. Respect the opinions of gray-haired peers, realizing that to ignore the past may cause the fund to repeat it.

8. Foster a spirit of meaningful review, evaluation, and modification of previous policy decisions.

Since numerous studies have confirmed that the single most significant decision in terms of its potential to add value to the portfolio is the asset allocation decision, it is important that the plan's portfolio be effectively supervised in the aggregate. Because one is always dealing with an uncertain future, portfolios must be broadly diversified, and thus hedged against the possibilities of higher inflation, continuing stable inflation, or the onset of deflation. Having diversified the bulk of the portfolio's assets, strategic moves can be made from cycle to cycle with a smaller portion of the assets in the quest to achieve rates of return above the rates of return the longer-term policy portfolio produces. Any strategic moves made will be the result of an assessment of changes in the general prices within the economy, the profits of the companies in which assets are invested, and ultimately, the valuation of the asset classes themselves, both now and projected into the future. All this activity is for the purpose of tilting the portfolio toward investment success. Producing real gains in value is the ultimate goal of asset management, since such gains will be used to replace the lost wages of the deserving retirees and to pay benefits to the beneficiaries of the plans.

The extent of permitted flexibility in asset allocation and asset shifting depends upon the volatility constraint that logically evolves from the investment objectives and goals adopted by the benefit plan's representatives. Before a discussion can proceed to conclusion on what would appear to be the "best" allocation of the assets from time to time, a constraints analysis must be performed. Such analysis coordinates the portfolio-building activities of the investment manager with the objectives and goals as perceived and articulated by the plan sponsor.

The place to begin in the asset allocation process is with the plan sponsor representative(s). As previously mentioned, this could be the investment coordinator. An ideal plan sponsor representative:

1. Has researched and properly analyzed the demographics of the plan.
2. Can speak for the intentions of the principals of the contributing source as to their attitudes toward funding and risk-taking policies.
3. Understands the risk/reward dimensions of the investment markets.
4. Has thorough knowledge, insight, and experience, and is emotionally capable of handling investment fluctuations without abandoning the adopted long-term policy.

Asset allocation decisions are policy and strategy decisions that are separate and distinct from objective setting. Objective setting has to do with the sponsor targeting a desired result, or range of results. The characteristics of the plan are the driving force in objective setting. Policy and strategy are implementation phases, which evolve logically in the quest to attain the objectives. Thus, the ideal fiduciary sets out initially to articulate, as succinctly as possible, the appropriate objectives for the investment program and then adopts the appropriate policy and strategy methodology.

IDENTIFICATION OF APPROPRIATE INVESTMENT OBJECTIVES

Setting portfolio guidelines should not be confused with *setting investment objectives*. Guidelines are adopted to facilitate the attainment of the objectives and, thus, form the building blocks of policy and strategy. Not only do some fiduciaries confuse objectives with guidelines, but they adopt guidelines that impede the attainment of their stated objectives!

Investment objective setting by employee-benefit-plan representatives is a delicate balancing act. The supervising fiduciaries find their loyalties pulled in different directions due to the natural tendencies that exist among the economic players in the process. These understandable tendencies create tensions among fiduciaries when adopting policy. The contributing sponsor wants to pay the highest level of benefits for the least cost. The participant wants the assurance that the pension promise will be fulfilled at an acceptable cost-of-living standard. The regulators want ''prudent management,'' resulting in principal protection and growth in assets to assure that private plans in the aggregate will fulfill the socially redeeming goal of providing financial security during retirement. The plans' fiduciaries themselves often have their own agendas; in addition to embracing worthy and constructive goals, they often desire personal fulfillment and respect from their peer group, reelection to office, promotion in a job, and so on. Since it is impossible to satisfy all these conflicting aspirations and influences simultaneously, investment objective setting in many instances becomes a process of negotiation and compromise. The goals of the various constituencies are weighted according to importance, and in the process, policy and strategy evolve. To the extent that the process can remain professionally objective, the probability increases that the objectives ultimately adopted will be the most appropriate given the long-term needs of the plan.

Investment objectives should be set in tandem with the overall funding policy of the plan. Conservative funding—that is, accelerated reduction in the unfunded liabilities—can be accompanied by an aggressive investment posture. Conversely, a sponsor who chooses to fund the liabilities as minimally as possible out of current resources, may be obligated to the participants to manage those fewer accumulated assets in a conservative manner. However, sponsors' attitudes toward risk may very well reverse these relationships. In any event, an important principle to apply in objective setting is funding coordination.

What are some of the specific elements in objective setting? Foremost, the objectives adopted should be in conformance with the plan's documents and with the fiduciary standards of ERISA and related regulations. Also, an objective fundamental to all plans is that cash be available to make benefit payments in a timely manner. No investment course of action is complete until cash has been returned to the fund. To facilitate the setting of this objective, the consulting actuary should develop a financial profile of the fund that projects the immediate, short-term, and long-term cash-flow requirements. In such an analysis the present value of assets, investment return expectations, anticipated contributions, and liabilities are considered, and the fiscal integrity of the sponsoring entity is projected.

After the cash-flow needs are identified and targeted, the planning process turns to risk/reward considerations. To what degree can the fund sustain volatility in values in the quest for higher returns? How important is it to the sponsors that the future flow of contributions be stabilized and controlled? Is there a limit on the level of contributions that can be expected? Must principal value be preserved or enhanced? Does it seem wise, in the case of a plan with a relatively young work force, to place added importance on seeking growth in value in *real* terms? Conversely, in the case of a mature plan, should the manager seek cash flow from income-producing investments to augment dwindling contributions? How willing is the control group to exercise patience and accept short-term disappointment as a "contrarian investor" in the search for long-term positive results? The answers to these questions become the portfolio constraints. The aggregation of constraints influence policy and strategy decisions, including asset allocation. Portfolio guidelines, beta, quality, diversification, and so on, also emanate from the constraints analysis.

Part and parcel with establishing the investment-return objectives is the selection of the performance measurement period and the comparative benchmarks to be used in the monitoring process. The performance objectives can be set in nominal terms, or *real* terms, and several performance objectives can be adopted for the same fund. For instance, it may be deemed appropriate to compare the *aggregate* portfolio on a *real* basis—that is, compare the total return to a cost-of-living index—while comparing *segments* of the fund to referenced benchmarks on a nominal basis—that is, comparing the growth-stock component to an index of growth-stock portfolios and the bond component to the Shearson Lehman Government Corporate Bond Index. A set of performance objectives, both nominal and real, spanning differing time frames, may be more insightful to the stewards of the fund than relying on a single measurement statistic.

Very few sponsors still express their performance objectives using a single absolute number. Since most fiduciaries are aware that the investment-earnings assumption used by the actuary for planning purposes is an inappropriate performance target (it should follow, not lead, the investment experience), any other single absolute number chosen is even more of an arbitrary target. An 8 percent absolute target return would seem reasonable and attainable in a disinflationary environment; it would be less meaningful and attainable in higher-inflation periods. More funds seem to be favoring the adoption of relative return objectives—returns relative to the CPI, returns relative to chosen referenced benchmarks, and the like. The acceptance of relative return objectives recognizes the inherent environmental limitations that exist in the management of institutional portfolios.

Producing a real rate of return can be a formidable, and rewarding, task for an employee benefit plan. There is obviously no single way to accomplish this quest, but careful attention to detail and skillful consideration of many alternatives just may add sufficient basis points to a fund's bottom line to enable it to compete effectively with the problem of purchasing-power erosion. Certainly, with a modicum of success from the management process, real value may very well be added to the plan's portfolio if the responsible fiduciaries:

- Assume responsibility for allocating the portfolio's assets in the aggregate.
- Develop a resourceful information system resulting in group conviction as to which direction the general prices in the nation are heading.
- Understand historically the attractiveness of various investment media in different price environments.

- Consistently diversify a majority of the portfolio to hedge against the occurrence of general price-level extremes in either direction.
- Preserve flexibility in the management of a minority of the portfolio to exploit the evolving price-environment scenario.

The following objectives excerpted from a plan's statement of investment policy exemplify the use of relative *and* real rate-of-return objectives:

> The long-term investment objective of the Trust is to produce a total rate of return of three percent (3 percent) in excess of the rate of inflation as measured by the Department of Labor, Bureau of Labor Statistics Consumer Price Index, All Cities Average, 1967 = 100. Since the duration, direction, and intensity of inflation cycles vary from cycle to cycle, it is recognized that the return experienced by the Trust over any one cycle may vary from this objective; but it is deemed reasonable to expect a three percent (3 percent) real rate of return over succeeding cycles. A complementary investment objective of the Trust is that the total rate of return achieved by the Trust competes favorably, when compared over comparable periods, to other trust funds having similar objectives and constraints and using similar investment media.

Other examples of portfolio performance objectives, stated or implied, include the following:

1. To achieve the rate of return of a published index, including income, plus x percent.
2. To achieve the rate of return of a special benchmark index reflecting a chosen risk/reward preference.
3. To achieve performance comparability to other accounts having similar objectives.
4. To achieve a minimum of x percent.
5. To preserve portfolio value sufficient to eliminate the potential for withdrawal liability (Taft-Hartley funds).
6. To achieve total return sufficient to stabilize contributions at x percent of payroll.
7. To maintain a specified level of plan surplus.

Performance objectives expressed in risk-adjusted returns are preferred. Returns expressed in risk-adjusted terms are the most precise in objective setting, since they take into account volatility as well as return.

Unfortunately risk-adjusted return analysis has not been broadly practiced, and thus, statistics are not readily available for comparative purposes.

It has been said that the application of portfolio management operations is both an art and a science. Engineering the portfolio to attain the stated objectives would seem to be more scientific in nature, particularly since the advent of computer technology to assist in modeling and portfolio-control activities. The fact finding and related analysis so vital to the objective-setting process also requires resourceful analytical activities. The "artful" part of the process would seem, in the present environment, to be at the plan sponsor level. The supervising fiduciaries must examine the facts, balance what appear to be opposing agendas of the various constituencies, fend off any potentially inhibiting subjective influences, objectively adopt the most appropriate set of investment objectives, and carefully articulate them to the managers of the assets. Choosing appropriate objectives points the manager of the assets in the proper direction in the quest to assist in fulfilling the benefit-payment promise.

EVALUATION AND SELECTION OF THE INVESTMENT FACILITY

Having identified appropriate investment objectives, the supervising group can next turn to evaluating and selecting the investment facility. If the sponsor decides to invest passively, then an organization is sought that can administratively replicate the return of the chosen benchmark portfolios. If, however, the sponsor chooses value-added management, the structure of the organization is not nearly as important as is its demonstrated ability to add value to the portfolio. Success in investment decision making is indifferent to the structure of the organization as well as to its size and location. Whether the firm is organized as a bank, insurance company, mutual fund organization, or independent counsel firm, the keys to success are its people and program. To the degree any one of these four organizational classes becomes more successful in attracting, compensating, and motivating the best and brightest professionals, this group as a class should eventually produce superior performance.

To be successful, an investment management firm should possess certain characteristics. It should have an approach to investing that has proven successful in the past. It should consistently apply that approach and articulate it clearly. The firm should have highly intelligent, insightful, well-trained, experienced people and motivate them with performance incentives. It should cultivate an environment conducive to creativity and innovation. It should target investment-management activities that will attain the client's objectives and goals. It should have resourceful, quantitative support systems. It should maintain high internal quality-control systems in the delivery of investment services and communicate effectively with the client's representatives.

Funding the benefit-payment promise through asset-enhancement activities requires systematic planning and execution. Having identified the objectives and with the manager in place, the supervising fiduciaries, together with a consultant, can address themselves collectively to finalizing an investment policy statement. Before proceeding with a discussion of the elements of a written policy statement, let us review the relevant issues covered thus far.

DEVELOPMENT AND DOCUMENTATION OF INVESTMENT POLICY

To produce a cohesive, well-organized, investment policy statement, fiduciaries of an employee benefit plan, assisted by the plan's legal counsel, actuary, administrator, investment manager, and other consultants (as deemed appropriate) must identify, debate, and define the relevant issues and identify the investment objectives that will complement and augment the overall funding process.

The policy development process includes the identification and analysis of various internal compelling forces:

- Characteristics of the plan's sponsors that produce a certain attitude toward risk taking.
- Trends within the sponsors' industries.
- The current funding level of the plan's obligations.
- The cash-flow projection from a financial profile analysis.

Thus, the sponsors' attitude toward risk, the industry and company trends, the plan's status (underfunding, full funding, or overfunding), and the prospective cash-flow needs all impact investment-policy choices because they impact funding requirements. Funding policies necessarily influence investment policies, since the return from investments over the life of the plan plays such an important part in the benefit payment delivery process.

After examining the internal plan factors and other noninvestment criteria embraced by the group, one can move next to the external factors, an examination of the capital markets themselves. Risk and reward trade-offs are considered. Will the fiduciaries be satisfied with achieving the markets' rates of return, or do they want to attempt to achieve returns, with the accompanying volatility, above the markets' returns? This decision has an impact on the investment management structure that is adopted. The range of choices includes:

1. Using only accounts that replicate the markets' returns (*passive* approach).
2. Using accounts that replicate the return of a chosen referenced (benchmark) portfolio (*passive-plus* approach).
3. Using accounts that are supervised within the discretion of the investment management organization (*active* approach).
4. Using a weighted combination of the above (*passive/active* approach).

As mentioned previously, a supervising group's *attitude* toward risk will affect the degree of flexibility in policy. Is the group willing to achieve slower growth in value in exchange for less volatile returns, or does it seek faster growth in value accompanied by higher volatility? The former would constrain the system to include, at the riskiest level, balanced growth and income stocks and real estate vehicles; the latter would permit moving out further on the risk spectrum and include the use of growth and capital-appreciation stocks and small-company growth stocks.

How much management risk is the group willing to embrace? The answer to this question indicates how much of the portfolio can be deployed to value-adding active managers. Fiduciaries desiring to eliminate investment-management risk completely must content themselves with the markets' rates of return and suffer the accompanying short-term volatility. The group in reality trades off investment-manager vulnerability for market vulnerability; it accepts prices set by the masses in lieu of a value assessment by a professional.

Part and parcel of finalizing the investment policy statement is an articulation of the investment performance objectives, as previously reviewed. Choices of objectives are influenced by the somewhat conflict-ing goals of preserving principal value, producing current income, enhancing principal value, preserving purchasing power, producing capital gains, and enhancing purchasing power. To the degree one emphasizes the performance objective of value enhancement over value preservation, one must be willing to move out on the risk/reward spectrum. The wider the range of alternatives granted the investment managers, the less control the supervising group maintains over portfolio values. Objectives to preserve and enhance principal value, produce current income, and preserve purchasing power would most probably encourage the use of money-market accounts, fixed-income accounts, equity-income accounts, and real-estate accounts. Performance objectives to enhance purchasing power and produce capital gains would most probably encourage the use of real-estate accounts, balanced (stocks and bonds) accounts, growth and income accounts, growth-stock accounts, capital-appreciation accounts, and small-company-growth-stocks ac-counts, and even venture capital.

Once the objectives are articulated, a decision must be made whether to adopt a *fixed* asset mix, a *flexible* posture, or some *combina-tion* of both. A fixed posture is constrained to accept the long-term risk/reward trade-offs in the markets. A flexible posture assumes that a management system can periodically exploit the occasional undervalua-tions that exist and do it consistently enough to add value over and above what a passive fixed policy would have achieved. Because of the difficulty in correctly and consistently timing the markets, many funds prefer a combination of the two approaches. An example would be the decision to allocate 80 percent of the assets to be fully invested at all times, weighted among the classes in accordance with long-term histor-ical returns and attendant volatility, and then to grant discretion to an investment manager to strategically redeploy the remaining 20 percent of the fund based upon an assessment of the short-term cyclical pricing outlook.

If the supervising group has the confidence in its manager to grant the use of either a flexible policy or a fixed/flexible posture, it needs to adopt procedures that can be accomplished in a timely enough fashion to opportunistically exploit market turns. In most cases, boards and com-mittees function poorly with such time constraints. This is the reason that the majority of funds embracing such a market approach use an in-house coordinator, an investment consultant, and/or an investment manager(s), or some combination of these professionals. Timely market awareness to capitalize on market turns is generally only available through a full-time information-gathering and analysis process. Thus supervising fiduciaries who attempt cyclical redeployment activities must realize they are competing with highly trained professionals who work full time in their search for value. And, for all their effort and expertise, the record reveals that a majority of the professionals attempting to fortuitously time the markets fail to add value to the portfolios. Part-time fiduciaries, to be successful in this highly competitive game, must either be unusually prescient or lucky, or both.

Prior to implementing any strategic portfolio moves permitted within the plan's overall policy constraints, a methodology must be adopted to assess the levels of investment risk. Financial (business) risk, market (interest-rate) risk, inflation (purchasing-power) risk, political (confiscation) risk, and social-change risk should be evaluated. Within the context of such an analysis, an assessment is next made as to whether a class or subclass of investments is undervalued, fully valued, or overvalued. If sufficient belief in the evaluation system exists, the supervising group may comfortably grant full discretion to the professional(s) to implement such periodic asset shifts. The degree to which discretion is granted is influenced by the willingness of the group to embrace timing risk, the group's confidence in the manager to whom full discretion is delegated, and the previous experience of the fiduciaries in asset-shift activities.

Needless to say, those boards or committees who have seen portfolio values squandered due to poor timing decisions generally are inclined to constrain such activities in the future. Also, it is better to learn from observation or through published studies than from disappointing first-hand experience.

Even when an employee benefit fund permits strategic asset-mix shifts, it generally permits only a small shift at any one time. Portfolio repositioning phased in over time profits from *the principle of time diversification*. Significant asset shifts implemented all at once place at risk the long-term value enhancement objective of most funds. Contrariness is wonderful when it's right, but the opportunity costs (or real losses) can be very expensive if proven wrong.

Both the approach to policy adoption and the approach to strategy implementation should be systematic. A step-by-step "seek and search" mission should coalesce into both policy decisions, which enable the fund to attain its long-term investment objective, and strategic decisions that add value over time above that which the policy alone would have achieved. Resourceful documentation accumulated during the dialogue when policy and strategy constraints were considered can be very helpful when finalizing the investment policy statement.

In investing, the way one approaches the process is just as important as the choice of the particular vehicles. Thus, the policy statement becomes the necessary road map to successful funding. The absence of a cohesive written statement results in an investment context composed of a loose aggregation of ideas, which usually results in a fuzzy understanding of the objectives. The investment manager may be seeking objectives incompatible with the needs of the plan, or the investment vehicles selected for the plan may be inappropriate, given its needs. If a policy is not in writing, it cannot be mutually understood, and the absence of understanding between the supervising groups and professionals is the most significant cause of poor investment results.

The investment policy statement becomes the overall "game plan" from which all substrategies and implementation of those strategies evolve. Investment decisions will then be in concert with the needs of the plan, and the group's stewardship role will have been fulfilled as the "management of risk" directives have been effectively articulated. Cohesive investment policy fosters good understanding among all participants in the process. Lines of demarcation are carefully drawn, permitting appropriate accountability and adjustments in the review, reevaluation, and modification process. Diverse areas—the requirements of ERISA, fiduciary liability, acceptable performance, diversification, the discretion delegated to managers, and any attitudes toward social investing—need to be addressed. Without the development of policy and its subsequent reduction to a written statement, the plan, like a ship without a rudder, may flounder in a dynamic economic environment.

Such an empirical process is an ongoing effort. The policy and evolving strategies of the plan must respond to its dynamic political, social, and economic environment. The policy statement for the plan in the aggregate then becomes the stepping stone for the individual policy statements for the particular investment manager.

Reducing a plan's investment policy to a written statement provides legal protection, improves communication, and supplies instructions to investment managers. The statement prepared for the fund in the aggregate generally includes at least the following elements:

1. Background information on the fund.
2. Identification of fiduciaries.
3. Organizational structure.
4. Cash-flow requirements.
5. Lines of authority and delegation.
6. Diversification of the portfolio.
7. Active/passive strategies.
8. Definition of assets.
9. Performance objectives.
10. Guidelines.
11. Brokerage.
12. Voting of proxies.
13. Trusteeship/custodianship.

The statement related to each investment manager would include background information; future fund and cash-flow projection; investment objectives; policies related to the voting of proxies; portfolio guidelines; reporting requirements; and review, evaluation, and modification methods.

Monitoring, reevaluation, and modification of the investment funding process is an unending task because of the dynamic spheres of influence affecting policy selection. Characteristics of the plan sponsor change, plan demographics change, markets change, and investing facilities change. Thus an ongoing ability to effectively monitor and modify, if necessary, is important to long-term success. Independent performance measurement services assist in objective evaluation. Plan liability studies assist in achieving objective-setting precision. Analysis of expected rates of return helps in portfolio-tilting activities. The exercise of patience on the part of the plan fiduciaries is important to assure that counterproductive changes do not unnecessarily squander portfolio values.

Quality control in management procedures is important in order to attain maximum productiveness from the accumulated assets. In summary, the ultimate result of this procedural quest for successful funding techniques through successful stewardship of accumulated assets is to adopt an appropriate long-term investment policy, and, if one is so inclined, to periodically implement successful investment strategy moves permitted within the overall policy constraints.

The investment funding process begins with those fiduciaries charged with the stewardship responsibility. Determined to ask the right questions and resourcefully armed with knowledge of basic investment principles, the fiduciaries can add significant value to a plan's portfolio. With such determination, knowledge, and insight, the supervising fiduciaries need to examine the internal factors to adopt investment objectives appropriate to the plan's requirements. They must next examine the long-term historical risk/reward characteristics of the various investment classes. Then, with the objectives in mind, and with an awareness of which classes and subclasses of securities can best facilitate the attainment of those objectives, they can next turn to the selection of the funding vehicles. The most appropriate investment-management structure is identified, evaluated, and selected. Part and parcel with the adoption of these policy decisions is the asset-mix policy decision—whether it will over time be fixed, flexible, or a combination of both.

If an element of flexibility is permitted in the asset-mix policy, then an additional set of procedures must be adopted that provides the context within which strategy moves are implemented. It is in the strategy area that most groups supervising employee benefit plans choose to retain either an in-house coordinator or an independent investment consultant, and/or to engage investment manager(s). And finally, the process of monitoring, reevaluation, and modification must be accomplished with thoroughness and insight.

CHAPTER 47

ALTERNATIVE INSURED FUNDING ARRANGEMENTS

Richard L. Tewksbury, Jr.

The cost of employee group insurance plans has become a significant part of the corporate budget, and as these plans have grown in size, employers have taken steps to control plan assets and liabilities. These factors have caused the conventional insurance arrangement to be considered as much a corporate financing tool as an insurance arrangement.

In response, insurance companies have designed a number of alternative arrangements for insuring group insurance programs. This chapter highlights the development of alternative insured funding arrangements and describes each in detail.

CONVENTIONAL INSURANCE ARRANGEMENT

Alternative insured funding arrangements provide ways to potentially reduce the normal costs of a conventional insurance arrangement. It is important to first define a conventional insurance arrangement and its various cost factors so that the purpose and advantages of alternative insurance arrangements become apparent.

Definition

In a conventional insurance arrangement, an employer purchases a group insurance contract and agrees to pay premiums to an insurance company. In return, the insurance company agrees to pay specific benefit amounts for such events as death, medical care expenses, or disability. The employer's annual premium cost is based on the financial experience of employers of similar size and characteristics and the actuarial statistics and administrative expenses of the insurance company.

The insurance company uses the premiums paid by all employers to pay the claims incurred under the group insurance plans. Employers whose actual claims costs are less than their premium payments subsidize employers whose claims costs exceed their premium payments. In a conventional insurance arrangement, there is no reconciliation of an employer's premium payments to its actual claims costs. Instead, any adjustment of premium charges reflects the overall loss experience of all employers.

Premium Cost Factors

The insurance company considers a number of factors in determining the total cost of insuring a risk.

Paid Claims
This is the total benefits paid to insured employees or their dependents during the policy period.

Reserves
This cost reflects the insurance company's liability to pay benefits in the future for a loss incurred during the policy year. The most common reserve is the incurred but unreported claim reserve established to pay losses incurred during the policy year but not reported for payment until after the policy year has ended. Reserves also are established for special benefit payment liabilities. The most common special reserves are the life insurance waiver of premium reserve and the reserve for future disability benefit payments.

Other Claim Charges
Several additional costs are assumed by the insurance company for providing special benefit coverages such as extended liability coverage and conversion to an individual insurance policy when a participant terminates employment.

Administrative Charges
Although the terminology and allocation of administrative expenses vary by insurance company, there are six main cost categories:

1. *Commissions.*   This is the payment to a licensed insurance agent or broker for helping the employer obtain the insurance coverage and administer the plan. The commission amount normally is determined as a percentage of the premium paid with the percentage either remaining level or declining as the premium increases.

2. *Premium Taxes.*   A state tax is levied on the premiums received by insurance companies in the resident states of insured employees. This tax expense is passed directly to the employer, normally as a percentage of premium paid. The current tax rate averages about 2 percent of premium but varies from state to state.

3. *Risk Charge.*   Each insured employer contributes to the insurance company's contingency reserve for unexpected, catastrophic claims. The risk charge normally is determined by a formula based on the premium amount.

4. *Claims Administration Expenses.*   These are the expenses incurred by the insurance company to investigate claims and calculate and pay the appropriate benefits. These expenses normally are fixed per claim, with the per claim cost varying by the type of benefits paid. For example, life insurance benefits are relatively simple and quick to administer and have a low administrative cost per claim compared to disability and medical claims, which often require medical review and more difficult benefit calculations.

5. *Other Administrative Expenses.*   Charges for actuarial, legal, accounting, and other such services plus overhead expenses are shared by all contract holders. These expenses are determined either as a percentage of the premium amount, a fixed charge, or a variable charge based on the insurance company's actual services provided to the employer.

6. *Insurance Company Profit (Stock Company) or Contribution to Surplus (Mutual Company).*

ALTERNATIVE INSURED FUNDING ARRANGEMENTS

Definition

An alternative insured funding arrangement in some way *defers* or *reduces* the premium paid by the employer to the insurance company to transfer risk. Essentially, this is accomplished in various ways that affect the normal reserves, claim charges, and administrative costs of the insurance company.

The deferral or reduction of the premium provides the employer *direct* and *indirect* savings. Direct savings result from the reduction or elimination of specific insurance company charges. Indirect savings are gained through the more profitable corporate use of monies that normally are held and invested by the insurance company.

The trade-off for these employer savings is the employer's assumption of insurance company functions or risk. For example, the employer might assume all or part of the financial liability—that is, benefit payments to employees—and therefore reduce the necessary premium paid to the insurance company to pay benefit claims. Similarly, the employer might agree to administer all or part of the plan to reduce the insurance company's administrative charges.

Reasons for Alternative Arrangements

Premium Charges

The employer's main reason for purchasing group insurance is to transfer a personnel risk that has unpredictable occurrence and potential costs greater than the insurance company's premium charge. If a substantial loss occurs, the insurance is a valuable investment. But if losses over a period of time are less than the premium charges, employers analyze the insured risk and the value of the conventional insurance arrangement.

Employers with large insured employee groups have more predictable loss experience. They can reasonably project the expected claims costs of their employee groups over time and determine the *expected* annual cost to provide the group insurance benefits. The value of the conventional insurance arrangement becomes protecting against unexpected catastrophic losses.

Because large employers can reasonably project their future benefit costs, they can determine the financial advantages and trade-offs of participating in the financing and assumption of the risk. This participation reduces the premium paid to the insurer and potentially reduces the overall cost to the employer through reduced claims charges, premium tax, risk charge, and other administrative charges. These financial advantages have been the impetus to such alternative insured arrangements as participating and experience-rated contracts. Many variations of self insurance also have been adapted by employers to reduce premium charges and otherwise effect cost savings in their benefit programs. Self-insurance is mentioned in this chapter when its use is germane to a topic under discussion and is covered in detail in Chapter 48.

Corporate Value of Money

The significance of corporate value of money increases with rising premium costs and interest rates. Under the conventional insurance arrangement, the insurance company invests the excess premiums when paid premium exceeds plan costs. The insurance company also invests the various claim reserves it maintains for each group insurance plan.

Some of this investment income is credited to the employer. However, if the employer can earn more than this interest credit, it is advantageous to minimize the transfer of funds to the insurer. This factor has encouraged the development of deferred premium arrangements, reduction or waiver of accumulated reserves, and various self-insurance arrangements.

Competition

There is intense competition among insurance companies for insuring "good" risks. As already mentioned, under the conventional insurance arrangement, employers have similar premium charges, which means that employers with favorable loss experience (premiums exceed plan costs) subsidize employers with unfavorable loss experience (plan costs exceed premiums). Employers with favorable loss experience—the "good" risks—will look for funding alternatives that better reflect their actual costs. The financial advantages and administrative flexibility of alternative insured funding arrangements are often the key factors in an employer selecting and continuing with an insurance company.

Also, many employers with favorable loss experience have changed to, or at least considered, self-insurance of all or part of their group insurance program, thereby minimizing or even eliminating the need for an insurance company. For instance, a recent study found that 59 percent of surveyed employers self-insured their medical-expense plans in some form in 1990, compared to 29 percent in 1980.[1]

To attract and maintain insured group insurance plans and stop the movement toward self-insurance, insurance companies have introduced

---

[1]Foster Higgins 1990 Corporate Health Care Benefits Survey.

alternative insurance arrangements that meet the employer's financial needs and offer essentially the same advantages as self-insurance.

BASIC ALTERNATIVE INSURED FUNDING ARRANGEMENTS

Participating Arrangement

In a *participating insurance arrangement* the employer shares in its favorable or unfavorable financial experience during the policy period. If the financial experience is favorable—that is, the claims and administrative costs are less than the premium paid during the policy period—the employer receives the surplus premium from the insurance company at the end of the policy year. If the financial experience is unfavorable—if the claims and administrative costs are greater than the premium paid during the policy period—the plan is considered to be in a deficit balance equal to the difference between total plan costs and paid premium. In most instances, this deficit balance is carried forward by the insurance company to be recovered in future years of favorable experience.

Therefore, in a participating insurance arrangement the true cost, or *net cost,* of a group insurance plan is the premium paid during the policy year adjusted for the balance remaining at year-end.

Underwriting Factors

Because the insurance company shares with each employer in the actual financial experience of the group insurance plans, several underwriting factors are included in a participating insurance arrangement that are unnecessary in a conventional insurance arrangement.

Employer Participation
An insurance company will vary the *percentage of employer participation* in the actual financial experience depending on two key factors: the "spread" of risk and the predictability of losses.

Spread of risk refers to the ability of the employer's benefit plan to absorb a major, catastrophic loss relative to its paid premium base. The larger the employee group, the easier it becomes to incur a major loss without substantially affecting the year-end actual financial experience. This is because the total annual premium is large enough to pay the infrequent major losses as well as the normal benefit costs. The risk is effectively "spread" across the premium base of the insured employee group. Employee groups of more than 50 employees typically are considered large enough for a participating insurance arrangement, although competition among insurance companies is encouraging participating arrangements for employee groups as small as 20 employees.

Predictability of losses is the key factor in determining the percentage of participation. Essentially, the more predictable the total losses for each year, the greater the percentage of employer participation. Plans such as medical care, dental care, and short-term disability cover risks in which losses normally occur frequently and at relatively low benefit costs per occurrence. The predictability of loss experience for these plans is much better than for life insurance and long-term disability plans that cover risks with less frequent losses and normally much higher total benefit costs per loss. For this reason, participating insurance arrangements are more common in medical care, dental, and short-term disability plans.

To control the employer's percentage of participation in the plan's actual financial experience, the insurance company sets *pooling points*. A pooling point is an annual dollar limit of individual benefit costs that will be included in the actual financial experience of the participating insurance arrangement. Any individual benefit costs in excess of the pooling point will not be included in the plan's financial experience. Instead, this excess amount is included in the insurance company's "pool" of conventional insurance arrangements for the same risk. For example, a group life insurance plan could insure employees with potential benefits of $100,000 or more but have a pooling point of $50,000. This means an individual's benefit claim up to $50,000 is reflected in the plan's actual financial experience, and any benefit amounts in excess of $50,000 are assumed by the insurance company.

The employer pays an additional premium charge, called a *pooling charge,* for the exclusion of benefits in excess of the pooling point. This charge is based on the "pool's" loss experience and reflects the type of risk and expected average benefit costs that each employer will have in excess of the pooling point. For instance, a life-insurance-plan pooling charge normally equals the volume of life insurance in excess of the pooling point, multiplied by the insurance company's conventional arrangement premium charge. The medical-care-plan pooling charge normally is determined as a percentage of annual premium or paid claims.

Table 47–1 illustrates a typical schedule of pooling–point levels for medical care and life insurance plans, which are the most common participating insurance arrangements requiring pooling points.

Underwriting Margin

The premium paid under a participating insurance arrangement includes a charge for the possible fluctuation of actual costs in excess of the expected claims and administrative costs during the policy year. This charge commonly is called the insurance company's *underwriting margin*.

Underwriting margin reflects the normal range of deviation of the plan's actual loss experience in any year to the expected loss experience. The underwriting margin is determined from actuarial studies on the fluctuation of actual claims experience relative to insurance company norms for similar employee groups and types of insurance coverage. In

TABLE 47–1
Pooling Points

Life Insurance Plan

Volume of Insurance	Pooling Point
$ 1 million	$ 20,000
2.5 million	25,000
5 million	35,000
10 million	60,000
25 million	85,000
50 million	135,000

Medical Care Insurance Plan

Annual Claims (000s)	Annual Benefit Pooling Point
Less than $200	$ 25,000
$ 200–300	30,000
300–400	35,000
400–500	40,000
500–600	45,000
600–750	50,000
750–1,500	75,000
1,500–2,000	100,000
Over 2,000	None

general, the underwriting margin decreases as the predictability of the plan's expected claims experience increases.

The underwriting margin for a basic group life insurance plan varies between 10 percent and 20 percent of premium depending on the size of the employee group and volume of life insurance. Table 47–2 illustrates the typical level of underwriting margins for medical care plans.

Determining the Year-End Balance

The key principle in a participating insurance arrangement is the employer's final or net cost equals paid premiums adjusted for the year-end balance (surplus or deficit). The year-end balance is determined by the *actual* plan costs in relation to the paid premium.

Basic Formula
The determination of a surplus or deficit year-end balance for group insurance plans is straightforward:

Paid premium − Claims costs − Administrative costs = Balance

Paid premium refers to the employer's total payments to the insurance company during the plan year.

The *claims costs* factor is made up of various charges:

1. *Paid claims*—the actual benefit payments during the policy year.
2. *Reserve charge*—the establishment of or adjustment to claims reserves held for incurred but unreported claims and any other specific pending liabilities, such as waiver of premium life insurance claims and unsettled claims payments at year-end.

TABLE 47–2
Medical Care Insurance Plan

Number of Covered Employees	Percent of Premium
Fewer than 250	10–15%
250 to 1,000	7–10
Over 1,000	5–7

3. *Pooling charge*—the additional cost for having large individual claims "pooled" in excess of a specific pooling point.

4. *Other claim charges*—the most common charge is a penalty charge levied against the employer when a terminated employee converts from a group to an individual insurance policy.

The *administrative costs* essentially are the same six expense categories mentioned previously for a conventional insurance arrangement.

Surplus Balance

If the year-end balance is positive, there will be surplus premiums available to be returned to the employer. The following example illustrates how a surplus year-end balance is determined.

Example: During the policy year the employer pays $500,000 of group insurance premiums to the insurance company. Claims paid during the year are $375,000, reserve charges are $10,000, pooling charges are $20,000 and other claim charges $5,000, for a total of $410,000 in claims costs. Total administrative costs equal $60,000. These total costs related to the paid premium result in a year-end balance of $30,000 surplus premium.

Paid premium		$500,000
Less: Claims costs		$410,000
Paid claims	$375,000	
Reserve charges	10,000	
Pooling charges	20,000	
Other charges	5,000	
Less: Administrative costs		$ 60,000
Year-end balance		$ 30,000

Surplus premium that accumulates with the insurance company during the plan year normally is credited with interest earnings that are used to reduce the insurance company's administrative costs. The interest rate credited is based on the investment performance of the insurance company's general assets.

The insurance company can return the surplus balance by issuing a *dividend* check equal to the surplus amount. This dividend reduces the year-end employer-paid premium total that is tax-deductible as an ordinary business expense under Section 162 of the Internal Revenue Code.

Alternatively, the insurance company deposits the surplus balance in a special reserve, normally called a *premium stabilization reserve*. The major advantages of a premium stabilization reserve are to:

- Avoid a reduction in the tax-deductible paid premium amount at year-end.
- Help stabilize the future budget and cash flow requirements of the plan by supplementing premium rate increases with funds from the special reserve.
- Receive tax-free investment earnings on the reserve balance.

A disadvantage of a premium stabilization reserve is the low interest rate credited by the insurance company on the reserve amount. Also, an insurance company may be able to retain and use these funds to pay unexpected plan costs after contract termination.

Another disadvantage of premium stabilization reserves is the potential tax implications if the reserve amount does not meet specific definitions of a "welfare benefit fund." The "fund" definitions were established in the 1984 Deficit Reduction Act (DEFRA) tax reform legislation under Section 419 of the Internal Revenue Code. The principal purpose of this legislation is to prevent employers from taking premature deductions for expenses that have not yet been incurred. In essence, a premium stabilization reserve is considered reasonable, and deposits to the reserve tax-deductible, if there is no guarantee of renewal of the insurance contract and the reserve amount is subject to "significant current risk of economic loss."

Deficit Balance

A negative year-end balance, or *deficit balance,* occurs when the employer's premium paid during the policy year is insufficient to pay the plan's total costs during the year. Such a situation is illustrated in the following example.

Example: The premium and plan costs are the same as in the previous example, except paid claims during the year are $425,000 and the total administrative costs are $70,000. The total plan costs now result in a year-end deficit balance of ($30,000) premium.

Paid premium		$500,000
Less: Claims costs		$460,000
Paid claims	$425,000	
Reserve charges	10,000	
Pooling charges	20,000	
Other charges	5,000	
Less: Administrative costs		$ 70,000
Year-end balance		$(30,000)

The deficit balance is offset during the policy year from the insurance company's corporate surplus to pay all claims and other immediate costs of the plan. In a sense, these insurance company funds act as a "loan" to the employer. In most instances, an employer's deficit balance will be carried forward and will be repaid through surplus premium balances that may result in future policy years. However, the employer normally is not *contractually* required to repay this insurance company "loan" and can switch insurance companies while a plan deficit is outstanding. This is a risk assumed by the insurance company and is reflected in the risk charge and the underwriting margins of the insurer. While a plan deficit exists, the outstanding balance is charged with an interest expense similar to the interest credited on surplus premiums of other policyholders.

Instead of repaying the deficit balance through future surplus premium, the employer can negotiate with the insurance company to repay the "loan" in a lump sum or in installments over a specified period. However, the insurance company interest charge on the outstanding deficit balance often is less than the interest charge if the employer were to borrow monies from another financial institution. In these instances, it is more cost-effective to repay the outstanding deficit balance through future surplus premiums.

In some participating insurance arrangements, the insurance company contractually *cannot* recover deficit balances from future employer surplus balances but still shares annual surplus balances with the employer. This type of arrangement reduces the insurance company's risk of an employer to switching insurance companies before repaying a deficit balance. Also, this type of participating insurance arrangement may be more favorable for the employer because it participates only in years of positive financial results. The trade-off will be a higher annual risk charge or underwriting margin compared to an arrangement that participates in both year-end surplus and deficit-balance situations.

Employer Advantages

The advantage of a participating insurance arrangement is that the employer pays its "actual" insurance cost and is rewarded for favorable financial experience by the return of year-end surplus premium. During a policy year of favorable experience, cost savings can be gained in several additional ways:

1. *Premium tax* is reduced because it is based on the *net* premium received by an insurance company; that is, the employer's premium paid during the policy year less the surplus balance returned at year-end.

2. *Administrative costs* are reduced by lower general overhead charges based on net premium paid and by interest income earned on the surplus premium during the policy year.

The financial trade-off to the employer of a participating insurance arrangement is a higher risk charge and underwriting margin in comparison with a conventional insurance arrangement. Also, the carryover of deficit balances will increase the future years' plan costs due to interest charges on the outstanding deficit balance and possibly additional underwriting margins required by the insurance company.

Experience-Rating Arrangement

Whereas a participating insurance arrangement lets the employer share in year-end surplus or deficit balances, an *experience-rating insurance arrangement* enables the actual financial experience of previous policy years to affect the employer's future premium charges. If the employer's actual financial experience has been favorable in the past, the future premium rates will be less than the conventional premium rate of other similar employers. Similarly, if the loss experience has been unfavorable, future premium rates will be increased more than the rates of conventionally insured employers.

An experience-rating arrangement can be included with either a participating or a conventional, nonparticipating insurance arrangement. In either case, the actual previous financial experience of the employer's plan is the basis for determining the future plan year's premium rates.

Underwriting Factors

If an employer's actual loss experience has fluctuated significantly in the past, substantial changes can occur in the experience-rated premium charges from year to year. For example, a plan year with favorable loss experience could substantially reduce the next year's premium charges. If unfavorable experience actually occurred during that next year, subsequent premium charges likewise would increase substantially to reflect this unfavorable year. Such yearly swings in premium costs usually disturb employers and hinder their ability to budget future costs and control cash flow needs. Similarly, the insurance company usually finds it more difficult to maintain the loyalty and understanding of the employer when the required premium charges vary significantly from year to year.

To minimize this problem, the insurance company controls the significance of an employer's actual loss experience in determining premium charges. This is done through underwriting factors based on the statistical credibility of the actual paid claims experience and the type of risk.

Statistical Credibility

Statistical credibility refers to the validity of an employee group's actual paid claims experience representing the normal, expected loss experience of such a group. The greater the statistical credibility, the greater the significance given the plan's year-end financial results in determining future premium rates.

Statistical credibility is based on the applicability of the *law of large numbers,* which states that:

> The larger the number of separate risks of a like nature combined into one group, the less uncertainty there will be as to the relative amount of loss that will be incurred within a given period.[2]

In addition to employee group size, statistical credibility is determined by the number of years of actual-paid-claims experience that can be analyzed. The statistical credibility of cumulative years of actual experience for a smaller employee group will be similar to that of a much

---

[2]S. S. Huebner and K. Black, *Life Insurance*, 10th ed. (Englewood Cliffs, N.J.: Prentice-Hall, 1982), p. 3.

larger employee group for a one-year period. For example, the cumulative five-year life insurance experience of a 350- to 400-employee group has similar statistical credibility to the one-year experience of a 1,750- to 2,000-employee group.

The importance of the *type of risk* is similar to the underwriting of a participating insurance arrangement. Statistical credibility of actual loss experience is greater for risks that occur more frequently and have a lesser average cost per occurrence, such as medical care and short-term disability. Therefore, greater significance can be given to the actual-paid-claims experience for these types of risks. For instance, one to three years of loss experience normally are necessary to determine the experience-rated premium charges of medical care, dental, and short-term disability coverages.

On the other hand, the insurance company applies statistical credibility to the employer's life insurance and long-term disability loss experience only if three to five years of paid claims experience are available for review. This is due to the volatility of loss experience from year to year for these coverages. By analyzing three to five years' loss experience, individual years of unusually favorable or unfavorable loss experience are melded into a more common overall trend of claims costs.

Credibility Factors

There are several ways an insurance company measures the statistical credibility of actual loss experience in an experience-rated insurance arrangement. The most common method is to use a weighted average of the employer's actual claims experience and the insurance company's normal loss factors for a similar conventional insurance arrangement. The percentage factor applied to the employer's actual paid claims experience is called the *credibility factor.* The greater the statistical credibility of the risk, the closer the credibility factor is to 100 percent—which would imply that the employer's prior loss experience is wholly representative of future loss experience.

Table 47–3 shows the common credibility factors applied to life insurance and medical care plans. The life insurance factors are determined by the number of covered employees and the number of available years of actual claims experience. The factors for a medical plan normally are based on the number of employees covered by the plan.

For example, if an employer's medical plan covers 200 employees and incurred $400,000 of paid claims last year, a 75 percent credibility

TABLE 47–3
Credibility Factors

Life Insurance Plan

Number of Covered Employees	Number of Years of Experience		
	1	3	5
250–500	10%	25%	35%
500–1,000	20	55	75
1,000–2,500	40	65	85
2,500–5,000	65	85	100
5,000–10,000	80	100	100
Over 10,000	100	100	100

Medical Care Insurance Plan

Number of Covered Employees	Credibility Factors
50–100	30–50%
100–150	50–65
150–250	65–97
Over 250	100

factor is applied to this loss experience. If the insurance company's expected losses for a similar size and type of employee group is $500,000, the expected paid claims for this employee group would be $425,000.

$$\underset{\$400,000}{\underset{\text{year's actual claims}}{\text{Employer's past}}} \times \frac{\text{Credibility factor}}{.75} = \$300,000$$

Plus

$$\underset{\$500,000}{\underset{\text{losses}}{\text{Insurer's expected}}} \times \frac{\underset{\text{factor}}{\text{Noncredible}}}{.25} = \$125,000$$

Expected claims cost $= \underline{\$425,000}$

Pooling Points

A second method of controlling loss-experience volatility is to establish *pooling points,* as described previously in the section on participating insurance arrangements. By placing dollar maximums on the individual and total plan claim costs that will be included in each plan year's actual financial experience, the volatility of losses in any year is substantially limited. For providing this limitation on the employer's "experience-rated" losses, the insurance company levies a fixed annual charge, or pooling charge.

With a life insurance plan, the pooling charge is added to the average of the prior years' experience-rated paid claims to determine the expected claims costs for the next policy year. For example, if the average experience-rated claims cost over the last five plan years is $100,000, the life insurance volume in excess of the pooling point is $2,500,000, and the monthly pooling charge is $.60 per $1,000 of life insurance, the expected claims costs for the next policy year are $118,000, as calculated here:

Pooling cost	
Excess life insurance volume	$2,500,000
Monthly premium charge	.00060
Monthly cost	$ 1,500
	×12
Annual pooling cost	$ 18,000
Experience-rated claims cost	$100,000
Next year's expected claims cost	$118,000

The medical-insurance pooling charge normally is stated as a percentage of annual premium or paid claims. For instance, if the paid premium is $500,000, the pooling point is $45,000 per individual, and the pooling charge is 4 percent of premium, a charge of $20,000 would be included in determining the necessary premium charges for the next year.

Premium-Stabilization Reserve
Another alternative for controlling the effect of annual loss fluctuation on premium charges is a *premium-stabilization reserve,* previously discussed in the section on participating insurance arrangements. If additional premium is required in the coming plan year to reflect previous years of unfavorable loss experience, a part or all of the necessary premium rate

increase is supplemented by premium-stabilization-reserve funds. For example, assume a premium-stabilization reserve of $45,000 exists and additional premium of $40,000 is necessary to equal expected losses for the coming plan year. All or part of this additional premium could come from the premium-stabilization reserve.

Determining the Experience-Rated Premium

The exact method for determining the experience-rated premium charges varies by the type of insurance coverage and the insurance company. The explanation here describes the common principles for life insurance and medical care coverages.

Life Insurance
The life-insurance-premium charge is based on the expected paid claims, underwriting margin, reserve adjustment, pooling charge, and administrative costs.

Expected Paid Claims.   Determining the next year's expected paid claims depends on the credibility factor given to the employer's previous actual loss experience. The credibility factor is applied to the average actual-paid-claims total for a three- to five-year period. This average actual-paid-claims total should reflect annual changes in the volume of life insurance to provide a meaningful comparison of year-to-year claims experience.

Reserve Adjustment.   The incurred but unreported reserve initially is established as a percentage of premium or paid claims and is adjusted each year thereafter to reflect changes in these factors. An estimate of the next year's adjustment is included in the premium-charge calculation based on expected paid claims or premium.

Underwriting Margin.   This charge normally is stated as a percentage of expected paid claims and reserve adjustments or of total premium. If a participating insurance arrangement is included with the experience-rated arrangement, additional underwriting margin is added.

Pooling Charge.   An annual charge is included based on the volume of "pooled" life insurance and premium rate for the employee group.

Administrative Costs.   These normally are determined as a percentage of the experience-rated premium charges.

The sum of these factors determines the experience-rated life-insurance-premium charge for the next policy year. An example of calculating a required premium rate is illustrated in Figure 47–1.

Medical Insurance

The medical-insurance-premium charge is based on expected paid claims, inflation/utilization trend, underwriting margin, reserve adjustments, pooling charge, and administrative costs. These factors are determined in the same manner as for life insurance premium charges, *except* for the following.

Expected Paid Claims.   Much greater credibility is given to the loss experience of the prior plan year, such that developing average loss history over several years normally is unnecessary.

Inflation/Utilization Trend.   Rising medical costs (inflation) and plan utilization are distinct economic factors that will increase the next

FIGURE 47–1
Life Insurance Experience-Rating Calculation

Assumptions: Five-year average actual paid claims	$100,000
Expected annual losses*	80,000
Credibility factor	.60
Underwriting margin	10% of incurred claims
Reserve adjustment	2,000
Pooling charges	6,600
Administrative costs	10,000
Example:	
1. Expected paid claims: ($100,000 × .6) + ($80,000 × .4)	$ 92,000
2. Reserve adjustment	2,000
3. Incurred claims	94,000
4. Margin: 10% of incurred claims	9,400
5. Pooling charges	6,600
6. Administrative costs	10,000
Required premium	$120,000

*Based on insurance company's actuarial statistics.

year's paid claims; therefore, the expected paid claims are increased by a trend factor projected for the next policy year.

Pooling Charge. This charge normally is a percentage of paid claims or premium.

The sum of these factors determines the experience-rated medical premium charge, as illustrated in Figure 47–2.

Employer Advantage

An experience-rated insurance arrangement is much more a financing method for the employer's actual plan costs than a true insurance arrangement in which employers share in the loss experience and have a common premium rate. With the experience-rating arrangement, the primary insurance protection is against the unexpected catastrophic losses in one plan year that might severely affect the ongoing financial condition of the plan. To the employer with favorable and predictable claims

FIGURE 47–2
Medical Care Experience-Rating Calculation

Assumptions:	Prior year's paid claims	$250,000		
	Expected annual losses*	300,000		
	Credibility factor	.75		
	Pooling charge	6% of paid claims		
	Inflation/utilization trend	16% of expected claims costs		
	Underwriting margin	10% of trended losses		
	Reserve adjustment	10,000		
	Administrative costs	37,000		

Calculation:

1. Expected paid claims			$262,500
Actual experience factor	($250,000 × .75)	$187,500	
Insurance company factor	($300,000 × .25)	75,000	
2. Pooling charge			15,750
3. Inflation/utilization trend: (1) + (2) × 16%			44,520
4. Trended loses: (1) + (2) + (3)			322,770
5. Underwriting margin: (4) × 10%			32,277
6. Reserve adjustment			10,000
7. Administrative costs			37,000
Required premium: (4) + (5) + (6) + (7)			$402,047

*Based on insurance company's actuarial statistics.

experience, this arrangement is a very cost effective way to share the plan's financial gains without assuming significant financial risks.

ADVANCED ALTERNATIVE INSURED FUNDING ARRANGEMENTS

Advanced alternative insurance arrangements are variations of the basic alternative arrangements. They increase the financial and administrative flexibility of employer-sponsored group insurance programs.

Realizing the initial savings gained through the basic alternative insurance arrangements, large employers have become more aware of their own personnel risks and the predictability and severity of losses. With this increased understanding, the decision to purchase insurance is based on the same cost-benefit analysis as other major investments.

The employer's goal is to pay only the actual claims costs incurred during the plan year and reasonable administrative costs, without losing the budget stability of a maximum expected plan cost per policy year. To attain this goal, many of the insurance company's specific claim and administrative charges have been reduced or eliminated by the employer's assuming the financial liability or administrative function. This reduction, or at least deferral, of premium payments to the insurance company has maximized the cash flow and direct cost savings to the employer.

Financial Alternatives for the Total Plan

Deferred Premium Arrangement
One to three months' premium payments to the insurance company can be deferred and used more advantageously by the employer. If and when the insurance contract terminates, the deferred premium must be paid to the insurance company.

In essence, this arrangement allows the employer to retain an amount similar to the plan's incurred but unreported reserves until it is actually needed by the insurance company at contract termination. The necessary amount of reserve varies by the type of coverage, with life insurance plan reserves equaling one to two months' premium, and disability and medical plan reserves being three to four months' premium. These reserves are part of the insurance company's total corporate assets and normally earn investment income that reduces the employer's administrative charges or are used to reduce the necessary reserve amount held by the insurer. The interest credit is related to the insurance company's after-tax investment return on its general assets, which often is significantly less than an employer's after-tax rate of return earned on assets.

In this situation, the deferred premium arrangement allows an employer to invest the incurred but unreported reserves more effectively and thus enhance its cash flow and year-end earnings level.

To illustrate this advantage, assume an employer normally pays monthly premiums of $50,000 and has an after-tax corporate value of money of 14 percent. The insurance company currently credits 7 percent interest on incurred but unreported reserves. If the employer and insurer agree to a three-month deferred premium arrangement, the financial advantage is the annual *additional* investment earnings the employer earns on the three-month deferred premium amount. In this case, the employer would earn an additional 7 percent return on each of the $50,000 monthly premium deferrals for the remainder of the policy year, which provides an annual cash flow advantage of $9,625. This is shown in Table 47–4.

The loss of the interest credits from the insurance company is reflected in higher annual administrative or reserve charges. However, these increases should be offset by the additional employer investment earnings.

Annual Retrospective Premium Arrangement

An annual retrospective premium arrangement reduces the employer's monthly premium payments by a specified percentage with the understanding this percentage of premium will be paid to the insurance com-

TABLE 47–4
Example of Savings to Employer under a Three-Month Deferred Premium Arrangement

Month	Deferred Premium		Additional Interest Credit		Duration of Policy Year		Savings
1	$50,000	×	7%	×	1 year	=	$3,500
2	50,000	×	7%	×	11/12 year	=	3,208
3	50,000	×	7%	×	10/12 year	=	2,917
					Total	=	$9,625

pany at year-end if the plan's actual claim and administrative costs exceed the paid premium to date. The specific percentage reduction of premium normally relates to the insurance company's underwriting margin. The employer gains a cash flow advantage through the corporate use of this premium amount during the plan year if the corporate value of money exceeds the insurance company's interest credit on surplus premium.

Underwriting margin provides the insurer with premium in excess of the premium necessary to pay expected claims and administrative charges, as illustrated here. During the plan year, any surplus premiums held by the insurance company are credited with interest based on the investment return of the insurance company's general corporate assets. In a participating insurance arrangement, this surplus premium is returned to the employer at the end of the plan year.

Total premium payable to insurance company	Underwriting margin	Retrospective premium
	Administrative charges	Premium paid during plan year
	Expected claim charges	

If the insurance company's interest credit is less than the corporate value of money, an annual retrospective premium arrangement is advantageous. By investing during the plan year the premium amount otherwise held by the insurer as underwriting margin, the employer can improve its current cash flow and its year-end earnings level through the additional investment income earned.

For example, assume an employer's annual premium cost is $3 million, or $250,000 per month, and the plan's underwriting margin is 10 percent of premium. A 10 percent annual retrospective premium arrangement would reduce the premium payments to $2,700,000 per year and provide $300,000 premium to be invested by the employer during the plan year. The financial advantage is the *additional* investment earnings the employer can earn on the $300,000 reduced premium amount. If the corporate after-tax value of money is 14 percent and the insurance company interest credit is 7 percent, the additional investment income to the employer is approximately $10,500. (This value assumes premiums are paid monthly and that the additional investment earnings equal the monthly interest rate multiplied by the remaining months of the plan year.)

As part of the annual retrospective premium arrangement, the employer agrees to pay a part or all of the reduced premium amount to the insurance company at the end of the policy year if the actual claims and administrative charges exceed the actual premium paid during the plan year. The insurance company pays charges in excess of paid premium during the year from its capital or surplus accounts. An interest charge is applied to these excess charges that represents the insurance company's lost investment earnings.

Terminal Retrospective Premium Arrangement

With a terminal retrospective premium arrangement, the employer agrees to pay the outstanding deficit that may exist at the time the insurance contract is terminated with the insurance company. The agreement usually specifies a maximum percentage of premium or dollar amount up to which the employer will indemnify the insurance company at contract termination.

In this arrangement the insurance company substantially reduces the annual risk charge and the underwriting margin, which are additional, contingency premium to be used in case of unexpected, catastrophic claim costs. The terminal retrospective premium arrangement transfers some of this catastrophic risk to the employer; therefore, these charges can be reduced. This reduction is reflected in lower monthly premium costs and gives the employer use of this reduced premium amount for potentially more profitable corporate investment.

Also, this arrangement offers more underwriting flexibility for insuring high benefit limits and special plan design features that pose a potentially greater financial risk to the insurance company. Because some of the risk of underestimating the losses from these special benefit arrangements is transferred to the employer, the insurance company is more apt to underwrite the coverage to satisfy the employer's needs.

Both annual and terminal retrospective premium arrangements can be included to maximize the reduction of the risk charge and underwriting margin and the potential cash flow savings. However, the terminal retrospective premium arrangement is less common than the annual arrangement. Insurance companies are less apt to offer a terminal retrospective premium arrangement, because its long-term nature makes it difficult to determine a reasonable value to the insurer. Secondly, its attractiveness is limited to the very large employer that is willing to assume a potential long-term liability and that is considered a good, long-term credit risk by the insurance company. Therefore, the applicability and current use of this alternative insurance arrangement is rather incidental.

Extended Plan Year Accounting

Some insurance companies extend the plan year's accounting of claims paid as a means of reducing or eliminating the necessary incurred but unreported claims reserves. These insurers record the claims *incurred before* the end of the plan year but *paid after* the plan year as actual paid claims during that plan year. This extended accounting period, which normally is an additional one- or two-month period, allows the actual incurred but unreported claims to be more accurately accounted to the appropriate plan year and substantially reduces or even eliminates the incurred but unreported claims reserves maintained by the insurance company.

For example, if the accounting period for a life insurance plan is extended an additional month, the incurred but unreported reserve, which normally is about 10 percent of premium, often is reduced to 2 to 3 percent of premium. Similarly, extending by two months the plan-year accounting for a medical care plan may reduce the incurred but unreported reserve by 50 percent or more.

This financial alternative normally is available only to large employers with predictable monthly claims experience. For such employers, this arrangement provides an accurate accounting of incurred but unreported claims. To the extent these actual claims are less than the insurance company's normal reserve factors, the employer gains a direct savings and cash flow advantage.

ADMINISTRATIVE ALTERNATIVES
FOR THE TOTAL PLAN

In addition to considering financial alternatives, many employers have implemented administrative options that can provide substantial savings for their group insurance plans. Computers have made repetitive administrative functions of a group insurance plan relatively easy and inexpensive for an employer to assume. Also, the growing interest in self-insuring group insurance plans has created a substantial market of plan administration firms, called *third-party administrators (TPAs)*. A recent survey found that 29 percent of all employers use a TPA and an additional 6 percent of employers self-administer their medical plans.[3] Such firms mainly offer computerized claims payment and database services of varying sophistication. These services often can be adapted to the employer's needs and are offered at a cost significantly less than the normal administrative costs of a conventional or basic alternative insurance arrangement. In response to this competition, insurance companies offer several administrative alternatives to an employer.

Administrative Services Only Contract

If an employer self-insures all or part of its group insurance plans, the insurance company may provide only the administrative services for these plans through an administrative services only (ASO) contract. This contract is in direct response to the competition of TPAs and the employers' move to self-insured plans. *No* risk is assumed by the insurance company, and therefore, its administrative charges for this contract differ in several significant ways from an insured arrangement:

1. No premium tax liability is incurred by the insurance company on this type of contract; therefore, no premium taxes are transferred to it and paid by the employer.
2. There is no risk charge because the insurance company assumes no financial liability for the payment of benefits.
3. Normally no commission payments are made through an ASO contract.

---

[3]Foster Higgins 1990 Corporate Health Care Benefits Survey.

4. General administrative and underwriting activities normally are much less in an ASO contract, which significantly reduces the costs for these activities in comparison to an insured arrangement.

An ASO contract is more effective for self-insured group insurance plans with high claim utilization and greater complexity in the payment of claims. Specifically, self-insured medical care, dental, and short-term disability plans are most often administered through an ASO contract.

There are a number of reasons why an employer might purchase an ASO contract instead of administering the plan itself:

1. The investment in and dedication of computer hardware and storage capacity is quite substantial.

2. Normally, the computer software for a claims payment system must be purchased because the details of such a system are complex and unfamiliar to the employer's computer programmers.

3. The hiring and training of employees to administer the plans can be costly and time-consuming to the employer.

4. There are economies of scale in standard operations performed by the insurance company for all customers that cannot be attained by the employer.

5. The insurance company is staffed with legal, medical, and other technical expertise necessary to administer the group insurance plans, especially the complex and unique claims that may be disputed or denied or that require extensive professional consultation.

6. The employer maintains a third-party "buffer" in disputing or denying benefit payments.

The insurance company administers the plan and determines the benefit payments under an ASO contract in the same manner as a conventional insurance arrangement. By performing these services, the insurance company accepts the fiduciary responsibilities and powers necessary to administer the plan. However, the insurance company assumes no financial responsibility under this contract. The benefit payment checks are drawn against the employer's cash balances, and the insurance company normally is not identified on these checks.

The services generally provided by the insurance company in an ASO contract include:

Claims processing.

Financial and administrative reports.

Plan descriptions for employees.

Banking arrangements.

Government reporting requirements.

Underwriting services.

Individual conversion policies.

Legal, medical, and other professional services needed to administer the plans.

Selected Administrative Services Arrangement

Many large employers are interested in assuming some but not all of the group insurance plan administration in order to reduce an insurer's administrative charges as well as to gain more control over plan administration. An example is maintaining specific data about plan utilization and costs in order to analyze financial trends and identify additional ways of controlling medical care and other plan costs. To meet these needs, some insurance companies are providing selected administrative services through their ASO contracts.

In most cases, the insurance company offers this arrangement only if some group insurance coverage, most often life insurance, is insured with the insurance company.

The selected administrative services arrangement is rather new and just beginning to be provided to employers that specifically request it. However, as employers become increasingly involved in the financing and administration of their group insurance plans, this type of arrangement should become more common.

ALTERNATIVES FOR LIFE INSURANCE PLANS

Exclusion of the Waiver of Premium Provision

The waiver-of-premium provision is common in a group life insurance program. It continues coverage for a totally and permanently disabled employee without continued premium payments by the employer for the employee's coverage. Although such a provision sounds attractive, the additional cost to include it in the life insurance plan often is greater than its actual value, especially for large employers.

It is common for the monthly premium costs to increase 10 to 15 percent due to the increase in incurred but unreported claims reserves and the additional risk of the waiver of premium provision. The additional monthly cost of this provision can be avoided in large part by the employer merely continuing to pay monthly premiums for the disabled employees. In most cases, the total cost of these continued premium payments after the disability date will be substantially less than the additional 10 to 15 percent monthly premium charge for *all* employees.

A disadvantage to excluding the waiver of premium provision potentially can exist if the employer changes insurance companies. There can be a problem continuing life insurance coverage for previously disabled employees with the new insurer, because most contracts only insure employees *actively at work* as of the effective date of the new life insurance coverage. Insurance companies often waive this provision for large employers, but they may hesitate to do so for smaller employers if the inclusion of disabled employees' coverage could adversely distort the expected loss experience. Therefore, excluding the waiver of premium provision often is suggested only for larger employers.

Claims-Plus Premium Arrangement

A claims-plus premium arrangement bases the employer's monthly life insurance premium on the *actual* loss experience of previous months *plus* fixed monthly administrative and reserve charges. To the extent actual monthly loss experience is *less* than the level monthly premium payments normally paid during the plan year, this difference can remain with the employer as additional cash flow. If the employer's corporate value of money is greater than the insurer's interest credit on surplus premium, the employer gains additional investment income on this difference during the plan year.

To limit the risk of the employer having a cash flow loss by incurring benefit claim payments in one or more months in excess of the level monthly premium amount, many insurance companies set the maximum monthly employer cost at the level monthly premium amount plus any "surplus" accumulated from prior months. Also, the maximum annual employer cost is limited to the annual premium cost based on the level monthly premium amount. In this way, the employer still is fully insured against unexpected or catastrophic loss experience that may occur during any policy year.

To illustrate how this claims-plus premium arrangement works, assume the employer's normal annual life insurance premium cost is $360,000, or a level monthly premium payment of $30,000. This $30,000 monthly premium payment is based on $27,000 of expected losses per month and a standard monthly administrative and reserve charge of $3,000. Table 47–5 shows the actual monthly premium costs under a claims-plus arrangement given the above assumptions and assumed actual loss experience during the plan year.

The normal administration of the claims-plus arrangement is for the first month's premium payment to equal the level monthly premium payment amount and thereafter to equal the actual loss experience of the previous month plus the standard administrative and reserve charge. In the example illustrated in Table 47–5, the employer pays the normal monthly premium payment of $30,000 in month 1 and from then on pays the actual losses of the previous month plus the standard monthly administrative and reserve charge of $3,000. For instance, the premium payment for month 2 is $23,000; that is, $20,000 of actual losses in month 1 plus the $3,000 administrative charge. The cumulative balance for month 2 and thereafter equals the cumulative difference between actual monthly payments and the normal monthly premium payments. In months 5, 9, and 11, the employer pays substantially more than the normal premium payment, reflecting the previous months' high actual losses. This can occur under this arrangement as long as any monthly premium amount does not exceed the normal premium payment plus the cumulative balance as of that date.

Insurance companies have various trade names for this arrangement, the most common being *flexible funding* and *minimum premium* arrangement. Normally, such an arrangement is offered only to large employers that have substantial monthly life insurance premiums. Normally, for employers with less than a $15,000 monthly life insurance premium, this arrangement is not advantageous because of the increased internal administration and administrative costs, the volatile fluctuation in monthly claims, and limited potential financial gain.

TABLE 47-5
Life Insurance Claims-Plus Arrangement ($ thousands)

	Months												
	1	2	3	4	5	6	7	8	9	10	11	12	Total
Normal premium	$30	$30	$30	$30	$30	$30	$30	$30	$30	$30	$30	$30	$360
Actual losses	20	0	20	50	10	0	0	70	20	50	30	20	290
Administrative/reserve	3	3	3	3	3	3	3	3	3	3	3	3	36
Actual monthly payment	30	23	3	23	53	13	3	3	73	23	53	26	326
Cumulative balance	—	7	34	41	18	35	62	89	46	53	30	34	34

ALTERNATIVES FOR LONG-TERM DISABILITY PLANS

Long-term disability insurance promises to pay a significant percentage of an employee's income for the duration of his or her total and permanent disability. Typically the number of claims incurred by an employer is few, but the total cost per claim is quite large because of the duration of benefit payments. In the plan year that a long-term disability claim is incurred, a reserve is charged to that year's financial experience equal to the expected cost of all future benefit payments. Often, the reserve charge is greater than the annual paid premium. However, the limited number of claims over a three- to five-year period allows the insurance company to set the premium rate at the expected average annual cost over this time period, thereby keeping it relatively stable and affordable for the employer.

Partial Self-Insurance

The employer can partially self-insure its group long-term disability plan by assuming the financial liability of any claim for a specific duration and transferring the remaining liability to the insurance company. This arrangement reduces the monthly premium payments to the insurance company, provides potential cash flow savings through increased investment earnings on the premium difference, and still provides the employer significant insurance protection against a catastrophic claim situation. Two other financial advantages to a partially self-insured arrangement are that (1) the incurred but unreported reserve requirement normally is reduced, and (2) the premium tax liability is reduced.

There are two ways this arrangement can be designed. The more common method is for the insurer to assume the benefit payment liability for the first two to five years and the employer to continue benefit payments beyond this specific time period. The advantages of this plan design are several:

1. The average duration for a long-term disability claim is less than two years, so the long-term financial liability and administration assumed by the employer is limited.

2. The insurance company does not establish large reserves for future benefit payments in comparison to a fully insured arrangement, which reduces the required premium payment and offers cash flow savings to the employer.

3. Because an extended period exists before the employer assumes financial liability and begins periodic benefit payments, the employer typically prefunds its liability only when the disability actually occurs.

The second plan design option is for the employer to pay the long-term disability benefits for the initial two to five years and the insurance company to assume the risk thereafter. The main employer advantage is that premiums are substantially reduced because the employer is assuming the full liability of most long-term disability claims.

As a general rule, this alternative insurance arrangement is offered only to employers with at least 1,500 to 2,000 employees. For smaller plans, the claim occurrence is too volatile and the potential long-term financial liability normally too large for the employer to effectively self-insure the risk.

ALTERNATIVES FOR MEDICAL AND SHORT-TERM DISABILITY PLANS

Minimum Premium Arrangement

In a minimum premium arrangement, the employer pays the medical care and/or short-term disability benefits directly from a corporate cash account instead of transferring the money to pay benefits through premium payments to the insurance company. The employer essentially self-insures the payment of benefits up to the expected loss level for the plan year, with the insurance company assuming the financial liability for any claims costs in excess of the expected loss level. The only premium paid to the insurer is for the normal administrative, risk, and reserve charges.

A minimum premium arrangement in large part simulates and provides the advantages of a self-insured/ASO arrangement without the employer assuming the financial risk of benefit payments in excess of the annual expected loss level.

The primary advantages of this arrangement are twofold: reduced premium tax liability and potential cash flow savings. The payment of benefits from a corporate cash account is not considered an insurance arrangement in most states;[4] therefore, no premium tax liability is incurred. This offers a direct annual savings on the average equal to 2 percent of the normal premium amount used to pay benefits. Normally, a minimum premium arrangement is suggested only for employers with at least $250,000 premiums. At this minimum level of premium, approximately 85 percent of premium, or $212,500, is used to pay benefits. This implies the annual savings from reduced-premium tax liability is approximately $4,250 (2 percent of $212,500). As the premium size increases, the percentage of premium used to pay benefits similarly increases, and the premium tax savings becomes more significant. For instance, an employer paying $5 million in annual medical premium may use 93 percent of the normal premium to pay benefits, or $4,650,000. At this level, the annual premium tax savings would be $93,000.

The second advantage is potential cash flow savings gained by the employer having the corporate use of "surplus" funds during the plan year. Minimum premium arrangements are generally designed so the employer pays benefit claims during the plan year up to the annual expected loss level determined by the insurance company. This limit often is called *the employer maximum liability.* The employer pays benefits periodically from a separate cash account[5] to meet the plan's claims liability. If the actual claims paid during the initial months of the plan year are less than the proportionate monthly level of expected claims costs, a "surplus" develops in the cash account. To the extent the investment return earned by the corporation on this "surplus" is greater than the insurance company's interest credit on surplus premium, the employer gains additional investment earnings and a cash flow advantage compared to a basic alternative insurance arrangement.

By paying benefit claims as they are reported during the plan year, the employer also could have a cash flow *loss* if claims in the initial months are greater than the proportionate level of expected claims costs. To avoid this possibility, a minimum premium arrangement can be designed such that the maximum monthly payment of claims from the cash account equals the proportionate monthly level of expected claims

---

[4]Connecticut, Texas, and California assess a premium tax on minimum premium arrangements.

[5]This corporate cash account typically is either a direct-deposit account of a bank or savings institution or a 501(c)(9) trust.

costs *plus* any "surplus" funds accumulated during the plan year. If the actual claims costs in a month do exceed this limit, the insurance company pays all excess benefit claims from its funds. If "surplus" funds develop in future months, the insurer immediately uses these "surplus" funds to recoup its payment amount of prior months. The insurance company normally increases its administrative and risk charges to reflect the potential additional monthly liability it assumes in this specific case.

In a minimum premium arrangement, the insurance company administers all claims payments and assumes the risk of claims costs in excess of the annual expected loss level, just as in a conventional or basic alternative insurance arrangement. Figure 47–3 illustrates the flow of a benefit claim from its initial receipt, review, and benefit determination by the insurance company to the issuing and clearing of a corporate check through the corporate account.

The insurance company normally has similar administrative, risk, and reserve charges as in a basic alternative insurance arrangement. The employer pays a monthly premium to the insurer equal to the expected annual cost of these charges. Premium taxes must be paid by the employer on these monthly premium amounts. In the previous examples where 85 percent and 93 percent of normal premium are deposited into

FIGURE 47–3
Claim Flow of Minimum Premium Arrangement

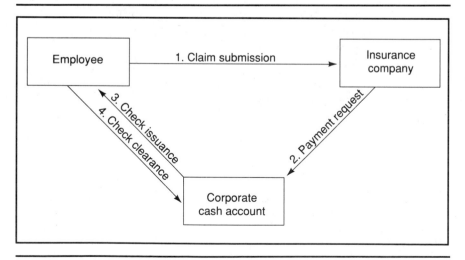

the corporate cash account, the remaining 15 percent and 7 percent of normal premium, respectively, reflect the monthly premium charge for administrative, risk, and reserve costs.

Minimum Premium–No Reserve Arrangement

A significant difference between a minimum premium and self-insured/ ASO arrangement is that in the minimum premium arrangement the insurance company still maintains a substantial reserve for incurred but unreported claims. As in other alternative insurance arrangements, the employer potentially can gain a cash flow savings by gaining the corporate use of the reserves. To meet this employer demand, the insurance companies offer a minimum premium–no reserve arrangement.

The employer gains the use of these reserves by the insurance company returning the incurred but unreported reserves it has been holding and reducing the future premium charges paid to the insurance company. This arrangement allows the corporation to use the reserve funds until they are required to pay incurred but unreported claims at the time of plan or contract termination. Because of state insurance regulations, it is generally agreed by insurance companies that they cannot fully release to the employer the financial liability for incurred but unreported claims at termination of its insurance contract with the employer. Therefore, the employer must either repay the reserve amount to the insurer at time of termination or specifically pay the incurred but unreported claims up to the insurer's normal reserve amount for a similar medical and/or short-term disability plan.

The minimum premium–no reserve arrangement essentially offers all the financial advantages of a self-insured/ASO arrangement, with the additional advantage of limiting the employer's liability for benefit payments in excess of the expected annual loss level. The liability for these possible unexpected costs is still assumed by the insurance company. A disadvantage to the minimum premium–no reserve arrangement is that administrative costs will be higher than a normal minimum-premium arrangement, because the interest credited by the insurance company on reserves—which is applied to reduce the administrative charges—no longer exists. However, the additional investment income gained through the corporate use of these funds significantly offsets this disadvantage.

Multi-Option Arrangements

Employers are moving to alternative medical delivery systems such as health maintenance organizations (HMOs) and preferred provider organizations (PPOs) to control their medical expense plan claim costs. These arrangements are designed to control costs by steering patients to hospitals and physicians that have agreed to a reduced payment and by managing utilization of all services. Employees typically choose between an existing indemnity medical-benefits plan and these new "managed" options, and employers establish separate benefit, funding, administrative, and insurance arrangements to govern these additional plans.

While a multi-option benefit program helps control total claim costs, the additional plan administration and separate funding arrangements can cause problems. Plan administration is more complex due to the additional reporting, employee communication and tracking of eligibility, payments, and expenses. This complexity increases internal and third-party administration costs. When employee participation is spread among several plans, the previously discussed alternative insured arrangements may have less impact or even be inappropriate. For instance, the employer's credibility factor may be substantially less in an experience-rating arrangement if the number of participants in the indemnity plan significantly decreases. And, if this insured group becomes too small, cash flow arrangements such as minimum premium may not be feasible.

In addition, the separate financial arrangements can limit the employer's ability to share in the overall claims cost savings. HMO coverage typically is provided through a fully insured arrangement, with premium rates based on the average costs of all HMO participants and the employer unable to participate in the year-end financial settlement. If the actual claims costs of the employer's HMO participants are less than the overall community costs, the employer is subsidizing the plan and not gaining the total savings of the HMO option.

In response, insurance companies are combining the indemnity, HMO, and PPO options under one funding, administrative, and insurance arrangement. The insurance company provides the various plan options offered to the employees. After the employees make their plan choices, a multi-option arrangement essentially works as if it is one plan. The enrollment, reporting, and communications activities are consolidated, typically reducing both internal and third-party administrative expenses. The financial results of each plan option are combined to determine the year-end balance, which enables the employer to fully share in any plan savings. And, the insurance companies typically offer the basic- and advanced-funding arrangements previously discussed in this chapter.

Table 47–6 illustrates the potential financial advantages of a multi-option arrangement. Assume there are three plans—indemnity, PPO, and HMO—with 1,000 employees covered in each plan. The indemnity and PPO plans are separate, participating insurance arrangements, whereas the HMO is conventionally insured, which means the employer doesn't participate in a year-end surplus balance. The premiums and total expenses for each plan are different, resulting in a $200,000 deficit balance for the indemnity plan, a $50,000 surplus balance for the PPO, and a $350,000 surplus balance for the HMO. The balance in the Separate Plan Totals column is a $150,000 deficit balance, because the employer doesn't receive the $350,000 surplus balance from the HMO plan. However, with a multi-option funding arrangement, the employer has a $300,000 surplus balance total at year-end. This favorable result is due to the HMO surplus balance being included in the total balance and a $100,000 reduction in administration expenses under the multi-option arrangement.

The multi-option arrangement is relatively new and still being developed by many insurance companies. The arrangement is available primarily to large employers—typically those with at least 500 employees—whose employee locations match the locations of the insurance company's alternative delivery systems. Some states limit the scope of this arrangement by restricting the consolidation of actual HMO financial results with the other employer-sponsored plans.

TABLE 47–6
Multi-option Arrangement Financial Advantages ($000)

	Indemnity	PPO	HMO	Separate Plan Totals	Multi-Option Plan Total
Employees	1,000	1,000	1,000	3,000	3,000
Premiums	$3,100	$2,700	$2,500	$8,300	$8,300
Expenses					
Claims	$3,000	$2,250	$1,700	$6,950	$6,950
Administration	300	400	450	1,150	1,050
Total	$3,300	$2,650	$2,150	$8,100	$8,000
Balance	($ 200)	$ 50	$ 350	($ 150)	$ 300

CHAPTER 48

SELF-FUNDING OF HEALTH AND WELFARE BENEFITS*

Carlton Harker

This chapter reviews briefly some of the more significant aspects of the self-funding of health and welfare benefits by employers.[1] The most common health care benefits currently being self-funded are medical, dental, disability, and related benefits. Death benefits generally are not self-funded because noninsured benefits of this type in excess of $5,000 are taxable to the beneficiary.[2] (Workers' compensation benefits are excluded because they are not ERISA-covered benefits[3] and also may not be funded by a tax-exempt trust.[4])

The term *employer,* as it is used in this chapter, includes both governmental employers and joint boards of trustees as defined by the Labor Management Relations Act of 1947 (Taft-Hartley Act).[5]

---

*Carlton Harker, *Self-Funding of Health Care Benefits* (Brookfield, Wis.: International Foundation of Employee Benefits Plans, 1988) treats self-funding of health care benefits in a substantially expanded form. This chapter is a condensation of portions of that book.

[1]Employee Retirement Income Security Act of 1974 (ERISA), Sec. 3(1).

[2]Internal Revenue Code, Sec. 101. See also *Ross* v. *Odom,* 401 F. 2d 464 5th Cir. (1968), and Internal Revenue Service Technical Advice Memorandum, E.B.P.R. Research Reports, 341.3-21 (1979).

[3]ERISA Sec. 4(b)(3).

[4]Rev. Rul. 74-18, 1974-1 C.B. 139.

[5]Ibid., codified at 29 U.S.C., Sec. 141-187 (1976).

GENERAL BACKGROUND

Definitions

Self-funding, as used in this chapter, is limited to those arrangements where the total and ultimate responsibility for providing all plan benefits remains with the employer. Since this is the case with excess loss agreements, they are treated as part of self-funding. Where insurers administer self-funded plans under "administrative services only" (ASO) agreements, such arrangements are self-funded. Traditional fully experienced-rated group contracts are deemed to have no substantive element of self-funding because of the "upside limit" of risk to the employer and therefore are not covered here. Modified insured arrangements, such as minimum premium, claims-plus, retrospective premium agreements, and others that modify conventional group insurance by amendatory agreements are not considered. These and other "alternative insured funding arrangements" are discussed in detail in Chapter 47.

Dual-Funding

Considerable interest has been shown in recent years in *dual-funding,* in which the plan is split into two separate free-standing plans. (With self-funding, the plan is undivided and wholly the responsibility of the employer; excess loss coverage, outside the plan, protects the employer from shock losses.)

With dual-funding the employer assumes the responsibility for the portion of the risk up to the attachment point and finances such risk by self-funding. The insurer assumes the responsibility for the portion of the risk over the attachment point and finances such risk by means of high-deductible group plans. The advantages of dual-funding include:

- The employer is relieved of the "reimbursement" problem. In self-funding, the employer must pay first and then seek reimbursement with a cancelled check for the excess-loss carrier. Dual-funded is indemnity; the insurer must assume responsibility when the attachment point is reached.
- The employer is comforted that the larger claims are controlled by a contract filed with the insurance department, under the jurisdic-

tion of the commissioner and subject to the policy provisions requirements of the state.

- The benefits, provisions, and so forth, of the self-funded and the fully insured plan documents need not be, nor are they generally, the same.

Current Interest in Self-Funding

Meaningful data on the nature and extent of self-funding are unavailable, but if we consider only the plans of the larger multistate and government employers and jointly administered (Taft-Hartley) trusts, a substantial percentage of welfare plans are self-funded. Because insurers offer administrative services only agreements and excess-loss coverages to small and medium-size companies, interest in self-funding has been increasing among such employers.

Some of the reasons for the current interest in self-funding are explained here.

Economic Considerations.   The rapidly increasing cost of providing welfare benefits and high interest rates have encouraged employers to consider self-funding in an attempt to control costs. Some employers wish to control, or reduce, reserves because of the current high value of money, and some believe cash flow is more easily managed with a self-funded program. In addition, certain expenses such as insurer risk charges and state premium taxes may be avoided with a self-funded program.

Avoidance of State-Mandated Benefit Requirements.   Since the Employee Retirement Income Security Act of 1974 (ERISA) exempts employee benefit plans from state regulation, the self-funding multistate employer need not meet the requirements of state-mandated benefits or deal with the effects of the increasing aggressiveness of both the courts and regulators in applying these mandated benefits extraterritorially.

Acceptance by Insurers.   Many insurers facilitate self-funding by offering ASO agreements by which they provide only administrative services and do not assume any obligation for claims developing under the contract except at contract termination and for excess-loss coverages, under which an employer is covered for claims that exceed a specified amount.

Judicial Clarification.   In *Farmer* v. *Monsanto* it was held that self-funding should not be construed as *doing an insurance business* if the self-funding is limited to the employees and dependents of the employer and affiliates and the profit motive is absent.[6]

ERISA Preemption.   State laws attempting to regulate employee benefit plans generally were preempted by ERISA.[7] This preemption clause of ERISA has been subject to much discussion and litigation and is discussed in more detail later in this chapter.

Elimination of the 85 Percent Income Restriction.   The Tax Reform Act of 1969 eliminated the 85 percent income restriction, which required that at least 85 percent of the income to a 501(c)(9) trust be made from employer or employee contributions. The restriction had existed because the interest earnings on asset accumulations were not tax-exempt.

Increasing Popularity of Risk Management.   The increase in the practice of risk-management techniques by employers with other programs (for example, state-required disability and workers' compensation) has contributed to employer interest in self-funding of welfare benefits and has facilitated the adoption of such programs.

Potential Limitations of Self-Funding

Many employers carefully consider self-funding and reject the option. There are several reasons why employers may not wish to self-fund. An employer may have a concern over the administrative and financial responsibilities involved, fear an unfavorable employee or union reaction, want to have a third-party benefit-buffer, or want to retain the protection of the traditional arrangements—for example, state insurance department protection, ease of providing conversion, or extended coverages. Then, too, some employers look to their insurers as a source of credit or as a carrier for their casualty policies.

---

[6]State ex. rel. *Farmer* v. *Monsanto Co.*, 517 SW. 2d 129 (Mo. Sup. Ct. 1974).
[7]ERISA Sec. 514.

When Self-Funding Is Appropriate

A welfare plan may be fully insured, fully self-funded, or partially self-funded. When an employer has considered the advantages and disadvantages of each, it may decide to take a middle course and adopt partial self-funding in order to obtain some advantages of both extremes. In all cases, an employer's individual circumstances should be taken into consideration and a feasibility study done to determine the best approach for each employer.

Legal Issues

A number of legal issues relative to self-funding of welfare benefits should be reviewed. Most of the issues discussed here have been settled.

Doing an Insurance Business
As mentioned earlier, it was held in *Farmer* v. *Monsanto* that self-funding by an employer would not necessarily be deemed *doing an insurance business*. A survey of the 50 state insurance departments conducted by this writer indicated that no state, of the 29 that responded, would question the *Farmer* v. *Monsanto* decision.

ERISA Preemption
While Congress intended that ERISA would preempt those state laws attempting to regulate employee benefit plans, it worded the preemption very cautiously.[8] First, the preemption did not apply to insurance, banking, or securities laws.[9] Second, the Committee of Conference expected the Task Force provided by ERISA to consult closely with the states in its study and report to Congress.[10] Third, the preemption was limited to fiduciary and reporting and disclosure responsibilities.[11] Court decisions and law journal articles resulting from the preemption provi-

---

[8]ERISA Sec. 514(a).

[9]ERISA Sec. 514(b)(2)(A).

[10]ERISA Sec. 3022(a)(4), and *II Legislative History of ERISA* (Washington, D.C.: U.S. Government Printing Office, 1974), p. 4650.

[11]See note 1.

sions are too numerous to be cited here, but some observations relating to the preemption provisions are that:

1. The preemption issue is far from settled; there is a possibility of future clarifying ERISA amendments.
2. Preemption already has had an impact on several state laws; particularly significant is the preemption of self-funded plans by state laws mandating benefits.
3. Preemption does not apply to providers of health care or to insurers; the question of indirect state regulation of self-funded plans has remained unanswered.
4. Significant state regulation of Taft-Hartley welfare funds has been preempted; this preemption may have been both an unanticipated and undesired result of the preemption provision.

State-Mandated Benefits

Nearly half of the states currently have some state-mandated benefits such as required coverage for physical therapy, convalescent home care, and surviving-spouse medical expenses. The primary reason for the existence of such benefits is the political influence of special interest groups, which is brought about in two ways. First, the groups lobby for special legislation, and second, the groups encourage the regulatory and judicial authorities to administer the laws extraterritorially. By self-funding, state-mandated benefits generally are preempted from state law.[12] Some observers have noted that state-mandated benefits will further encourage self-funding and weaken even more the states' ability to regulate.[13]

Multiple-Employer Trusts

Shortly after the enactment of ERISA, a number of multiple-employer trusts claimed status as employee benefit plans in order to achieve preemption from state regulation.

---

[12]ERISA Sec. 514; *Wadsworth* v. *Whaland*, 562 F. 2d 70 (1st Cir.), *cert. denied*, 435 U.S. 980 (1978).

[13]R. E. Younger, "Mandated Insurance Coverage—The Achilles Heel of State Regulation?", *Proceedings of the Association of Life Insurance Counsel*, 1978, p. 769.

Several significant court decisions held that entrepreneur-sponsored multiple-employer trusts were not employee benefit plans and therefore were subject to regulation by the state.[14] The courts held that the trusts were not employee benefit plans in cases in which a commonality of employment was lacking and there existed a profit motive by the entrepreneur.

The Department of Labor, in various opinion letters, has ruled that a multiple-employer trust is not an employee benefit plan unless it is established and maintained by the employer.[15]

Multiple-Employer Welfare Arrangements (MEWA)
Congress enacted legislation in 1982[16] providing that self-funded multiple-employer trusts were not employee benefit plans automatically eligible for ERISA preemption. MEWAs were to be subject to state regulations regarding financial considerations (reserves, for example) but not regarding state-mandated benefits.

Discrimination Issues
The Revenue Act of 1978 and proposed regulations require that self-insured medical reimbursement plans must meet certain nondiscrimination standards in order for the prohibited group to receive favorable tax treatment.[17] The current federal laws and clarifying regulations required that self-funded plans must not discriminate in favor of the prohibited group as to benefits or eligibility thereto. Insured plans, however, were unaffected and continued to provide fully insured discriminatory plans—often with only a tinge of actual risk shift. The 1986 Tax Reform Act (TRA '86)[18] permits both the fully insured and the self-insured plan to discriminate in favor of the prohibited group—*but* only to a very minor extent.

---

[14]*Bell* v. *Employee Security Benefit Ass'n*, 437 F Supp. 382 (D. Ken. 1977); *Hamberlin* v. *VIP Ins. Trust*, 434 F. Supp. 1196 (D. Ariz. 1977); *Nat'l Bus. Conf.* v. *Anderson*, 451 Supp. 458 (S.D. Ia. 1977); *Wayne Chem. Inc.* v. *Columbus Agc'y Serv. Corp.*, 426 F. Supp. 316 (N.D. Ind.), *aff'd as modified*, 567 F. 2d 692 (7th Cir. 1977).

[15]Dept. of Labor Op. Ltrs. 79-41A, June 29, 1979; 79-46A, July 19, 1979; 79-49A, July 31, 1979; 79-54A, Aug. 5, 1979; and 79-61A, August 29, 1979.

[16]Miscellaneous Tax and ERISA Provisions, PL 97-473, *codified* at 96 STAT 2611.

[17]Pub. L. 95-600, Sec. 366, *codified at* IRC, Sec. 105(h), and Treas. Reg., Sec. 1.105-7 (1981).

[18]Pub. L. 99-514.

Self-Funding and Collective Bargaining

Since the National Labor Relations Board ruled in 1973 that the selection of an insurer for welfare plans is a mandatory subject for collective bargaining, collective-bargaining negotiations may have a significant impact on self-funding.[19]

FUNDING

So far as the funding of plan benefits is concerned, self-funded plans may be classified in one of four ways:

1. *General Asset Plan:* This method uses no trust.
2. *Tax-Exempt Trusteed Plan:* This method uses a tax-exempt trust that generally is qualified under Internal Revenue Code Section 501(c)(9).
3. *Non-Tax-Exempt Trusteed Plan:* This method would use a non-tax-exempt trust and is rarely seen because of the lack of tax advantages.
4. *Captive Insurer:* By this method the employer uses its own insurer to fund the plan benefits.

General Asset Plan

With a general asset plan, any plan assets are commingled with the general assets of the employer. There usually are no plan assets other than withheld employee contributions, because ERISA requires plan assets to be under a trust, and contributions to general-asset-plan liabilities usually are not tax deductible by the employer.[20]

Several administrative advantages are gained with a general asset plan. Certain filing requirements are avoided (filing for the tax-exemption of a trust)[21] or simplified (a modified Form 5500 without financial statements or an independent auditor's opinion).[22] Furthermore, no

---

[19]Connecticut Light & Power Co., 196 N.L.R.B. No. 149 (1972).

[20]See note 18; Rev. Rul. 79-338, 1979-2 C.B. 212.

[21]IRS Forms 1024 (1980) and 990 (1980).

[22]Instructions to the Annual Return/Report, Form 5500.

fidelity bond is required, and plan restrictions of the Treasury regulations on the 501(c)(9) trust are avoided.[23]

Tax-Exempt Trusteed Plan

501(a) Trust
An employer may self-fund medical benefits for certain retired lives as part of a qualified retirement plan.[24] In such circumstances, a pension or profit-sharing trust qualified under Internal Revenue Code Section 501(a) would be used. More commonly seen is a situation where the tax-exempt trust qualifies under Internal Revenue Code Section 501(c)(9).

501(c)(9) Trust
A special tax-exempt trust is provided by the Internal Revenue Code and Treasury Regulations for a voluntary employees' beneficiary association.[25] When used herein, a 501(c)(9) trust means a vehicle used for self-funding. A 501(c)(9) trust also may be used as a conduit into which employer contributions may flow and out of which insurance premiums may flow, but the term is not used in that sense in this chapter.

The regulations (*a*) set forth the conditions a voluntary employees' beneficiary association must meet in order to be a qualifying organization, (*b*) specify the membership requirements, (*c*) enumerate the permitted benefits, (*d*) provide certain guidelines relative to discrimination, and (*e*) set forth other requirements relative to dissolution and record keeping.

Several significant Revenue Rulings have clarified the operation of the 501(c)(9) trust:

1. A 1958 Revenue Ruling determined that the plan and trust are interdependent agreements, which together create a voluntary employees' beneficiary association within the contemplation of that term.[26]

---

[23]Treas. Reg. Sec. 1.501(c)(9) (1981).

[24]IRC Sec. 401(h); Treas. Reg. Sec. 1.401-14 (1964).

[25]IRC Sec. 501(c)(9); Treas. Reg. Sec. 1.501(c)(9) (1980).

[26]Rev. Rul. 58-442, 1958-2 C.B. 194.

2. A 1959 Revenue Ruling determined that membership in a 501(c)(9) trust would exclude such persons as individuals, proprietors, partners, self-employed persons, or trustees designated to administer the funds.[27] This position of the Internal Revenue Service was upheld by the court.[28]

3. A 1969 Revenue Ruling determined that a nonforfeitable contribution to a 501(c)(9) trust with retired lives benefits is deductible as an ordinary and necessary business expense and not as a contribution to a plan of deferred compensation.[29]

4. A 1973 Revenue Ruling determined that a contribution to a 501(c)(9) trust is deductible if it is actuarially determined and legal.[30]

5. A 1974 Revenue Ruling determined that workers' compensation benefits are not acceptable benefits for a 501(c)(9) program.[31]

Recent changes to the Internal Revenue Code[32] gave an employer a "safe-harbor" basis for determining deductible 501(c)(9) reserves; that is, unless reserves in excess of the statutory limit are claimed. No actuarial certification is required. Safe-harbor reserves for group health plans are 35 percent of annual paid benefits.

Non-Tax-Exempt Trusteed Plan

While it is possible to meet the trust requirements of ERISA by using a non-tax-exempt trust, there are no tax advantages in doing so. Therefore, such a trust would likely never be used.

Captive Insurer

A captive insurer is formed by a firm for the primary purpose of underwriting some or all of the sponsoring company's risk.[33] ERISA views insuring with a captive insurer as a form of self-dealing but

---

[27]Rev. Rul. 59-28, 1959-1 C.B. 120.

[28]*Milwaukee Sign Painters Welfare Fund* v. *U.S.*, 17 A.F.T.R. 2d 264 (E.D. Wisc. 1965).

[29]Rev. Rul. 69-478, 1969-2 C.B. 29; IRC Sec. 162; IRC Sec. 404(a).

[30]Rev. Rul. 73-599, 1973-2 C.B. 40.

[31]Rev. Rul. 74-18, 1974-C.B. 139.

[32]1984 DEFRA, P.L. 98-369, *codified* at 98 STAT 854.

[33]See note 18.

provides an exemption if less than 5 percent of the insurer's premiums are those of the sponsor.[34] This statutory 5 percent limitation was increased to 50 percent by the Department of Labor in 1979.[35]

ADMINISTRATION

When an employer self-funds, the administrative services to the plan may be provided by the employer, by a third-party administrator under a benefit services agreement, or by an insurer under an administrative services only agreement. The three most important services from the viewpoint of the employer usually are benefit administration, accounting, and actuarial services.

Benefit Administration

Benefit administration probably is the single most important administrative consideration in a self-funding arrangement. Some aspects of benefit administration are:

1. Benefit complaint, denial, and litigation.
2. Benefit control activities, such as peer review.
3. Monitoring for duplicate coverage and abuse.
4. Statistical reports.
5. Coverage interpretation.
6. Determining and processing benefit payments.
7. Cash flow planning.

A third-party buffer to help protect the employer from potential employee relations problems associated with benefit payment difficulties may be desirable in a self-funding arrangement.

Accounting

The three accounting considerations connected with a self-funded welfare plan are deduction accounting, plan accounting, and employer accounting.

---

[34]ERISA Sec. 406; ERISA Sec. 408(b)(5).

[35]Prohibited Transaction Exemption 79-41, 44 Fed. Reg. 46,365 (1979).

Deduction Accounting

General Asset Plan.   A basic theme supported by statutory, regulatory, and judicial law is that an employer payment to a self-funded reserve maintained in a general asset plan is deductible only when the events establishing the liability have all occurred and the liability is reasonably ascertainable.[36] Deduction for such reserve contribution has not been easily obtained.

Trusteed Tax-Exempt Plan.   Contributions to a 501(c)(9) trust generally are deductible as ordinary and necessary business expenses if they are irrevocable, reasonable, and actuarially supportable.[37]

Plan Accounting

Plan accounting is the process by which the plan and trust are reflected in the required government reporting and disclosure forms. Table 48–1 summarizes the government reporting and disclosure requirements for self-funded plans.

The Internal Revenue Code requires that an annual return be filed for a tax-exempt trust.[38] ERISA requires that an annual return be filed for a welfare plan unless an exemption is provided.[39] A trust return is due 4½ months after the end of a trust year, and a plan return is due seven months after the end of a plan year.[40] A general-asset welfare plan with fewer than 100 participants need not file an annual return.[41] A general-asset welfare plan with 100 or more participants need only file a modified

---

[36]IRC Sec. 461(a); Treas. Reg. Sec. 1.461-1 (1960); Rev. Rul. 79-338, 1979-2 C.B. 212; Rev. Rul. 70-262, 1970-1 C.B. 122; Rev. Rul. 69-512, 1969-2 C.B. 24; Rev. Rul. 57-485, 1957-2 C.B. 117; *Wien Consol. Airlines* v. *Comm'r of Int. Rev.*, 528 F.2d 753 (9th Cir. 1976); *Crescent Wharf & Warehouse Co.* v. *Comm'r of Int. Rev.*, 518 F.2d 772 (9th Cir. 1975); *Thriftmart, Inc.* v. *Comm'r of Int. Rev.*, 59 T.C. 598 (1973).

[37]IRC Sec. 162(s)(i); Treas. Reg. Sec. 1.162-10 (1958); Rev. Rul. 56-102 1956-1 C.B. 90; Rev. Rul. 58-128, 1958-1 C.B. 89; Rev. Rul. 69-478, 1969-2 C.B. 29; Rev. Rul. 73-599, 1973-2 C.B. 41; Ltr. Rul. 7828030, April 12, 1978; Ltr. Rul. 7839040, June 28, 1978.

[38]IRC Sec. 6033; Treas. Reg. Sec. 1.6033 (1972).

[39]ERISA Sec. 103.

[40]Instructions to Internal Revenue Service Form 990; Instructions to Annual Return/Report Form 5500.

[41]29 C.F.R. Sec. 2550.104-20 (1975).

TABLE 48-1
Government Reporting and Disclosure Regulations for Self-Funded Plans

Method of Funding	Number of Participants	Annual Plan Return	Annual Trust Return
General asset	Fewer than 100	No	No
	100 or more	Yes; Mod. Form 5500	No
501(c)(9) trust	Fewer than 100	Yes; Form 5500–C	Yes; Form 990
	100 or more	Yes; Form 5500	Yes; Form 990

annual return that has no financial data and need not have an independent auditor's opinion.[42] Late-filing penalties accrue with the trust return.[43]

Employer Accounting
Employer accounting is the process by which the plan is reflected in the employer's accounts and in any footnote disclosure. Presently there is a lack of clear authority in the employer accounting of self-funded welfare plans. The recent attention has been directed primarily to accounting for postretirement benefits as reflected in *Financial Accounting Standards Board Statement No. 106*. There is, however, a study in progress on proposed major changes in accounting for these plans.

The most significant current accounting guides are the *American Institute of Certified Public Accountants Audit Guide* and the various guides provided by the federal government.[44] For a more detailed discussion of accounting and financial reporting for health and welfare-benefit plans, see Chapter 44 of this *Handbook*.

Actuarial Considerations

Regardless of how the benefits are funded, there usually are certain matters to which actuarial attention is, or should be, directed. A feasibility study of self-funding should be made, as should a cash-flow

---

[42]Ibid. Sec. 2550.104-44 (1975).

[43]IRC Sec. 6033.

[44]*Audits of Employee Health and Welfare Funds* (N.Y.: A.I.C.P.A., 1972); *Medicare Provider Reimbursement Manual* (1980); *Armed Services Procurement Regulation*, 32 C.F.R. Sec. X. Par. 502 (1976); *Cost Accounting Standards Board Regulations*, 4 C.F.R. Sec. 416.50 to 416.80 (1978).

study. Levels of contributions and reserves should be reasonable and adequate, management benefit or control-type statistical reports should be prepared, and attachment points with related excess-loss coverage should be reasonable. It may be either legally required or prudent to have an actuary provide the following to the plan:

- Certification of 501(c)(9) reserves.
- Certification of COBRA[45] Continuation Premiums.
- Estimate of future funding levels.
- Estimate of economic values on plan benefits for purposes of meeting discrimination tests.

RECENT DEVELOPMENTS

Cost-Containment

Because of the statutes and regulatory inflexibility of fully insured plans, self-funded plans tend to be selected by employers wishing to adapt cost-containment programs. Examples of cases in which self-funded plans would be more serviceable include:

- Triple funding, whereby providers assume some of the upside risk in exchange for being treated as preferred providers.
- Benefit formula reductions for ''teaching hospitals'' unless such case was medically necessary.
- Subrogation and coordination with automobile medical benefits.
- When minimum plan benefit extension is desired in order to shift the risk from the plan to a COBRA Continuation Trust as soon as possible.

COBRA Continuation Requirements

As is discussed elsewhere with regard to employer-sponsored plans, the COBRA legislation mandates the assumption of coverage on certain former participants. Some self-funders have been alarmed at the increase

---

[45]Consolidated Omnibus Budget Reconciliation Act of 1983, Pub. L. 99-272.

in their potential liability and the endangerment by COBRA to their excess-loss arrangements.

Other self-funders reason that their added administrative and cost-containment programs give them sufficient control to overcome any dangers. There are also several risk-transfer devices, by which self-funders can arrange to have COBRA risks transferred, in large part, from their plan to a fully insured plan.

CHAPTER 49

TAX TREATMENT OF QUALIFIED PLAN DISTRIBUTIONS AFTER THE TAX REFORM ACT OF 1986

John M. Bernard
Clifford J. Schoner

The Tax Reform Act of 1986 (TRA) made numerous changes in the taxation of amounts received from plans qualified under Section 401(a) of the Internal Revenue Code of 1986 (IRC or Code). In general, these changes reflect a congressional desire to discourage use of qualified plans to accumulate capital rather than to provide retirement income. This policy is particularly apparent in the way the TRA restricts or penalizes payments that begin before age 59½, or after age 70½, while continuing the tax preference for benefits payable on a lifetime basis during what are commonly considered retirement years. With these aspects of the TRA as an organizing principle, this chapter will survey the changes made by the TRA in the treatment of amounts received from qualified plans.[1]

AMOUNTS RECEIVED FROM QUALIFIED PLANS DURING EMPLOYMENT

Limiting access to amounts held in qualified plans during employment is a major theme of the TRA. The TRA discourages access to these

---

[1]This article reflects the law as in effect and interpreted by the government through August 8, 1991. Interpretations of the TRA subsequent to that date are not reflected herein.

amounts by fundamentally changing the way income is computed for in-service withdrawals, by imposing a 10 percent additional tax on the taxable portion of most distributions before age 59½, by reducing the availability and attractiveness of loans, and by drastically restricting the scope of hardship withdrawals under plans described in Section 401(k). As the discussion that follows demonstrates, however, reducing the availability of the money does not reduce the complexity of the rules.

Basis Recovery Rules

Prior to the TRA, an interest in a qualified plan was almost always treated as a single contract for the purposes of applying the basis recovery rules of Section 72.[2] Thus, any amount withdrawn before the annuity starting date was treated first as a nontaxable return of the participant's basis in the plan.[3] A participant's basis in a qualified plan generally reflects amounts held by the plan on which the participant has already paid federal income tax (that is, primarily after-tax contributions, but also P.S. 58 costs, repayments of taxable loans, and employer contributions made during a period when the plan was not qualified). Thus, in a profit-sharing plan with after-tax contributions or in a thrift plan (even a plan in which contributions attributable to each year were accounted for separately), any amount withdrawn from the plan before separation from service (and thus before the annuity starting date) would have been nontaxable to the extent of any unwithdrawn participant after-tax contributions.[4]

Sheltered by this rule, a participant could make aftertax contributions throughout his period of participation, withdrawing nontaxable money from time to time and leaving the earnings on such contributions behind for further tax-deferred accumulation. This feature contributed

---

[2]E.g., PLR 7951156, PLR 8125071, PLR 8639065; Treas. Reg. Sec. 1.72–2(a)(3). However, at an earlier time, the government took a position that sometimes resulted in a conclusion that a single plan consisted of multiple contracts. Treas. Reg. Sec. 1.72–2(a)(3)(iv), Ex. (3). More recent PLRs, including those cited above, appear to reflect a modification of the IRS's position.

[3]Internal Revenue Code of 1954, Sec. 72(e); Treas Reg. Sec. 1.72–1(d).

[4]Ibid.

greatly to the popularity of after-tax thrift plans, which operated as tax-free investment funds with the added bonus of an employer-matched contribution.[5]

After the TRA, however, the general rule is that amounts received before the annuity starting date from a qualified plan will be treated as partially taxable.[6] For qualified plans that did not permit in-service withdrawals of aftertax contributions on May 5, 1986, the new rule is effective for preannuity starting date payments made after July 1, 1986.[7] For qualified plans that did permit such in-service withdrawals on May 5, 1986, the new rule is effective for preannuity starting date payments made after December 31, 1986.[8] However, participants in qualified plans that did permit in-service withdrawals of aftertax contributions on May 5, 1986, benefit from a grandfathering provision that permits them to make nontaxable withdrawals under the pre-TRA rules until they exhaust their basis in the qualified plan as of December 31, 1986.[9]

Preannuity starting date distributions from a qualified plan subject to the TRA are treated as returning to a participant a pro rata portion of his basis in the qualified plan.[10] The portion of a distribution that is to be treated as a nontaxable return of the employee's basis in the qualified plan is calculated by multiplying the distribution by the ratio of the participant's basis in the qualified plan to the vested portion of the participant's

---

[5]Prior to the Tax Reform Act of 1984, the favorable tax treatment given preannuity starting date withdrawals was available even if no employer contributions were being made to the qualified plan. A plan of this type permitted a participant to enjoy tax-deferred earnings on his after-tax contributions and still have virtually unfettered access to his after-tax contributions on a tax-free basis. The Tax Reform Act of 1984 legislated against these plans by adding Sec. 72(e)(7), which treats the first amounts withdrawn before the annuity starting date as a return of earnings when 85 percent or more of contributions to the qualified plan during a "representative period" are after-tax contributions. This prevents such qualified plans from being used to provide tax-deferred savings accounts. The Technical and Miscellaneous Revenue Act of 1988 (P.L. 100-647, hereinafter cited as "TAMRA") repealed Sec. 72(e)(7) effective for preannuity starting date payments made after December 31, 1986. TAMRA Sec. 1011A(b)(9)(A).

[6]Internal Revenue Code of 1986 (hereinafter cited as "IRC") Sec. 72(e)(8)(A); IRC Sec. 72(e)(2)(B).

[7]TRA Sec. 1122(h)(2)(C).

[8]TRA Sec. 1122(h)(1).

[9]IRC Sec. 72(e)(8)(D).

[10]IRC Sec. 72(e)(2)(B).

interest in the qualified plan.[11] The remainder of the distribution is taxable income to the participant.[12]

In a significant departure from prior law, the TRA permits defined contribution and certain defined benefit plans to categorize the portion of a participant's interest in the qualified plan attributable to after-tax

---

[11]IRC Sec. 72(e)(8)(B); Internal Revenue Service Advance Notice 87–13, I.R.B. No. 1987–4, p. 14 (hereinafter cited as "Notice 87–13"), Q&A–11. The participant's basis in the qualified plan and the value of the vested portion of the total account balance or accrued benefit generally are to be determined as of the date of distribution. As an alternative, the taxpayer's basis in the qualified plan may be determined as of December 31 of the calendar year immediately preceding the year of distribution, and the total value of the vested account balance may be determined as of the last valuation date in that preceding calendar year if this date is used on a reasonable and consistent basis for all preannuity starting date distributions. Instead of being based on the vested account balance as of the last valuation date in the preceding calendar year, the value of the account balance may be determined as of any valuation date during the preceding calendar year which is not more than one hundred days before the end of such calendar year. If the vested account balance is valued other than on the date of distribution, the value of the account balance as of the valuation date in the preceding calendar year must be reduced by the value of any distribution after the valuation date but before the end of the preceding calendar year, increased by the value of any contributions or forfeitures between the valuation date and the end of the preceding calendar year and also increased by the value of any portion of the account balance which became vested after the valuation date but before the end of the preceding calendar year. Although these complicated rules are to be used uniformly, the qualified plan is not required to contain provisions identifying the method and valuation dates. See Notice 87–13, Q&A–12.

The value of the total account balance in a defined contribution plan generally is the fair market value of the assets attributable to such account including, for example, net unrealized appreciation on employer securities. If the account includes employer securities attributable to employee contributions with net unrealized appreciation that would be excluded from a distributee's gross income under IRC Sec. 402(a)(1), the value of the vested portion of the account balance is reduced by the amount of the net unrealized appreciation (whether or not all of such securities are distributed) for the purpose of determining how much of the taxable portion of the distribution is to be treated as a return of the participant's basis in the qualified plan. Internal Revenue Service Notice 89–25, I.R.B. No. 1989–8, p. 25 (hereinafter cited as "Notice 89–25").

In the case of a defined benefit plan, the present value of the vested portion of the accrued benefit is treated as the vested portion of the account balance. Present value is determined with reference to the factors set forth in the qualified plan for calculating single-sum distributions. Notice 87–13, Q&A–11.

[12]IRC Sec. 72(e)(8)(B). Apparently to prevent circumvention of the new TRA basis proration rules, rollovers of partial distributions are now limited to instances in which a separation from service has occurred. IRC Sec. 402(a)(5)(D). See text at fns. 85 through 91. This prevents a participant from receiving a distribution during employment and rolling over all but the portion of such distribution that represents a return of his basis.

contributions and earnings thereon as a separate contract for Section 72 purposes.[13] A qualified plan that can take advantage of the ability to create a separate contract for amounts attributable to after-tax contributions provides a significant tax benefit to its participants. Preannuity starting date distributions from this contract can be prorated with respect to the ratio of the participant's basis in this contract to the separate account balance attributable to such contract.[14] In most instances a preannuity starting date distribution from this separate contract will return a higher proportion of nontaxable amounts to a participant than a distribution prorated with respect to a qualified plan as a whole.

To be given effect as a separate contract, employee contributions and earnings thereon must be accounted for on an acceptable basis by the qualified plan, and the plan document (or plan procedure) must either specify the contract from which each distribution is deemed made or permit the participant to select the contract from which the distribution is made.[15]

A qualified plan maintains adequate separate accounts if a separate record of after-tax contributions (and earnings) is kept and the allocation of earnings, gains, losses, and other credits between this account and the remainder of the interests in the qualified plan is done on a reasonable and consistent basis.[16] Most defined contribution plans that permit aftertax contributions will already maintain adequate separate accounts; however,

---

[13]IRC Sec. 72(d). A defined benefit plan is to be treated as a defined contribution plan for purposes of applying Section 72(d) to the extent that a separate account is maintained for employee contributions to which is credited actual earnings and losses. Crediting employee contributions with a specified rate of earnings will not be sufficient to create a separate account. Notice 87–13, Q&A–14. Except for plans permitting unmatched voluntary contributions allocated to a separate account, most employee-contributory defined benefit plans will probably not involve an adequate separate accounting for employee contributions. When the separate accounting requirement is not met, a nonannuity distribution will be nontaxable to the extent calculated on the basis of the participant's entire interest in the plan.

[14]IRC Sec. 72(d). The participant's basis in the qualified plan is not necessarily allocable in its entirety to the separate contract created for aftertax contributions and earnings thereon. Bases attributable to PS-58 costs or repayment of a taxable loan, for example, is allocated to the contract under the qualified plan to which such costs or repayments relate. Notice 87–13, Q&A–16.

[15]Notice 87–13, Q&A–14.

[16]Ibid.

a qualified plan that has not met the accounting requirement may begin to maintain acceptable records prospectively at any time.[17]

The discretion to treat after-tax contributions and earnings thereon as a separate contract on a prospective basis gives rise to a planning opportunity for qualified plans that provided for after-tax contributions before December 31, 1986, and that continue to provide for such contributions after that date. According to the Internal Revenue Service, these plans can treat post-1986 after-tax contributions and earnings thereon as a separate contract for section 72 purposes, thereby allocating pre-1987 after-tax contributions and earnings on such contributions (including earnings actually occurring after 1986) to the plan's other contract. Under this approach, preannuity starting date distributions will first be offset by the pre-1987 grandfathered employee after-tax contributions[18] (if the qualified plan making the distribution qualifies)[19] and then be prorated by looking solely to post-1986 after-tax contributions and earnings thereon.[20]

In effect, the Internal Revenue Service has granted qualified plans the opportunity to give their participants a fresh start in calculating the after-tax contributions and earnings that will make up the separate contract. This fresh start will be particularly beneficial to participants in qualified plans that permitted preannuity starting date distributions before December 31, 1986. Because of frequent withdrawals, it is not unusual for participants in such plans to have earnings on pre-1987 after-tax contributions far in excess of the unwithdrawn amount of after-tax contributions. The ability to ignore the impact of pre-1987 earnings in calculating the taxable portion of withdrawals from post-1986 employee contributions will minimize taxability in such instances. Moreover, the operation of the grandfather rule will result in the participant's earnings on pre-1987 after-tax con-

---

[17]Ibid.

[18]IRC Sec. 72(e)(8)(D).

[19]*See* text at fn. 9.

[20]Notice 87–13, Q&A–15. A qualified plan can also begin treating after-tax contributions and earnings thereon as a separate contract on a prospective basis at any time, regardless of when it began complying with the record–keeping requirements necessary to create the separate contract. Notice 87–13, Q&A–14.

tributions continuing to compound on a tax-deferred basis even after all of the pre-1987 after-tax contributions have been withdrawn.

An Example

The impact of the TRA's rules can be illustrated by comparing the tax consequences of a participant's in-service withdrawal from a profit-sharing plan in 1990 to those that would have arisen if prior law had continued to apply. Since the participant's tax consequences depend in part on the features of the profit-sharing plan, this illustration also highlights the somewhat surprising fact that participants with identical profit-sharing plan account balances can have different tax consequences (depending on the recordkeeping procedures applied) when making in-service withdrawals.

For purposes of the illustration, assume that X Company established a profit-sharing plan in 1975. The profit-sharing plan is funded with company contributions and voluntary aftertax employee contributions of up to 10 percent of compensation. On December 31, 1986, employee A's company account has a value of $20,000, and his separate voluntary account consists of $10,000 of contributions and $5,000 of earnings thereon. On December 31, 1989, A's company account has a value of $32,000. His voluntary account has a value of $31,000, consisting of

$10,000 of pre-1987 contributions,

$11,000 of earnings on these contributions,

$ 7,000 of post-1986 voluntary contributions, and

$ 3,000 of earnings on these contributions.

A's accounts are fully vested, and he has made no withdrawals from the plan since December 31, 1986. A wishes to make a withdrawal of $12,000 on January 1, 1990, while employed. The profit-sharing plan specifies that withdrawals (after use of the grandfathered amount, if applicable) are first charged against the contract maintained for aftertax contributions and earnings thereon, if any, and then against the other contract maintained under the profit-sharing plan. The table presents A's potential tax consequences.

Distribution from Profit-Sharing Plan

Alternative	Nontaxable	Taxable
1. Pre-TRA.	$12,000	$ 0
2. Post-TRA; plan is treated as single contract; grandfather rule is not applicable.	3,238[21]	8,762
3. Post-TRA; plan is treated as single contract; grandfather rule applies.	10,264[22]	1,736
4. Post-TRA; plan is treated as two contracts (all after-tax contributions and earnings allocated to one contract); grandfather rule not applicable.	6,581[23]	5,419
5. Post-TRA; plan is treated as two contracts (post-1986 after-tax contributions and earnings allocated to one contract); grandfather rule not applicable.	7,377[24]	4,623
6. Post-TRA; plan is treated as two contracts (all after-tax contributions and earnings allocated to one contract); grandfather rule applies.	10,667[25]	1,333
7. Post-TRA; plan is treated as two contracts; (post-1986 after-tax contributions and earnings allocated to one contract; grandfather rule applies.	11,400[26]	600

In addition to the results shown in the table, even under a plan established in 1987, there are a number of alternatives.[27]

---

[21] $12,000 \times \dfrac{\$17,000}{\$63,000}.$

[22] $10,000 grandfathered plus $2,000 \times \dfrac{\$7,000}{\$53,000}.$

[23] $12,000 \times \dfrac{\$17,000}{\$31,000}.$

[24] $7,000 nontaxable out of the post-1986 after-tax contract, plus $377 derived by:

$2,000 \times \dfrac{\$10,000}{\$53,000}$

[25] $10,000 grandfathered plus $2,000 \times \dfrac{\$7,000}{\$21,000}.$

[26] $10,000 grandfathered plus $2,000 \times \dfrac{\$7,000}{\$10,000}.$

[27] Assume that an employer establishes a class-year savings plan that is treated as one contract under Section 72. The plan accounts for employee contributions (and earnings) separately from employer contributions (and earnings) on a class-year basis. The employee contributions and related earnings are such as may be treated as a separate Section 72(d) contract. The participant makes the following contributions and receives the following employer matching contributions for the first three class years:

Ten Percent Additional Tax on Early Distributions

In addition to distributed amounts no longer being treated simply as nontaxable to the extent not in excess of basis, a further impediment to distributions before the annuity starting date is the 10 percent *additional* tax on the taxable portion of early distributions.[28] Consistent with the congressional desire to have qualified plans used as vehicles to provide

Class Year	Employee Contributions	Earnings	Employer Contributions	Earnings	Total
1987	$1,000	$ 750	$ 500	$375	$2,625
1988	1,000	500	500	250	2,250
1989	1,000	250	500	125	1,875
Totals	$3,000	$1,500	$1,500	$750	$6,750

On January 1, 1990, the participant receives a distribution of $2,625. If the plan treats this distribution as a complete distribution of the 1987 class-year balance, $1,750 will be treated as coming from the separate section 72(d) contract and $875 will be treated as coming from the remaining contract. On these facts, the $1,750 employee contributory withdrawal is treated as nontaxable to the extent of $3,000 over $4,500, or $1,166.67. The remaining $583.33 of the $1,750 portion of the distribution is included in the participant's income. The entire $875 from the employer-contribution contract is fully taxable.

If, however, the plan treats the entire $2,625 distribution as coming from the separate section 72(d) contract (even though the amount of the distribution is determined by reference to the 1987 class-year balance), the full $2,625 is subject to proration on the basis of $3,000 of employee after-tax contributions divided by a $4,500 employee contributory account. Thus, $1,750 of that distribution will be nontaxable, with the remaining $875 being included in income as a result of the proration. In this latter instance, because of the plan record-keeping method, the entire distribution was deemed subject to proration on the basis of the separate contract derived from employee contributions.

If, as a third alternative, the plan treated the entire $2,625 as coming from the portion of the plan comprising employer contributions, the full amount of the distribution could be taxable. Notice 87-13, Q&A–14, Ex. 2.

While tax consequences do not have to follow the manner in which the amount of the distribution is calculated (*i.e.*, a distribution of $2,625 in the above example can be treated as entirely out of the separate Section 72(d) contract), plan record-keeping may become excessively complicated if the plans and tax consequences do not correspond.

[28]The 10 percent tax applies to distributions from qualified plans, tax-sheltered annuities, and individual retirement accounts (but not to Section 457 plans) after December 31, 1986. Two types of distributions are exempted from the 10 percent tax. First, distributions made to an employee who, as of March 1, 1986, had separated from service with the employer maintaining the qualified plan, commenced receiving benefits, and elected in writing a specific distribution schedule for the payments he is receiving from the qualified plan are exempted from the 10 percent tax. A change in the distribution schedule subjects subsequent payments to the 10 percent tax. TRA Sec. 1123(e)(3). Second, under a transition rule, distributions for which the employee elects special treatment are viewed as if received by the employee when he separated from service in 1986, and thus are exempt from the 10 percent tax. TRA Sec. 1124(a).

retirement income, the major category of distributions excepted from the 10 percent additional tax are those that have retirement-type attributes. Another category of distributions (for example those needed for unusually heavy medical expenses) has also been excluded from the tax for no purpose other than a congressional determination to grant such distributions favored status.

The age and status of the participant are two of the major criteria used by the TRA to exempt retirement-type distributions from the 10 percent additional tax. Thus, distributions (whether before or after the annuity starting date) from a qualified plan to a person who has attained age 59½ are not subject to the 10 percent additional tax.[29] Similarly, the 10 percent additional tax does not apply to payments on account of an employee's death or disability of a severe and anticipated long-term nature.[30]

To qualify for the exception from the additional tax granted for distributions after separation from service, the separation from service must occur after attainment of age 55.[31] Although Section 72(t)(2)(v) had originally indicated that the separation must also have occurred "on account of early retirement under the plan," the Technical and Miscellaneous Revenue Act of 1988 (TAMRA) amended Section 72(t)(2)(v) to delete that requirement.[32] The 10 percent tax will apply, however, to an employee who separates from service before the calendar year in which he attains age 55 with benefits not commencing until after age 55 (but before age 59½).[33]

---

[29]IRC Sec. 72(t)(2)(A)(i).

[30]IRC Sec. 72(t)(2)(A)(ii) and (iii). An individual is considered disabled under this provision:

> if he is unable to engage in any substantial gainful activity by reason of any medically determinable physical or mental impairment which can be expected to result in death or to be of long-continued and indefinite duration. IRC Sec.72(m)(7).

Even a disability of a sort sufficient to result in payments under many long-term disability plans might not be sufficient to exempt corresponding distributions from a qualified plan from the 10 percent additional tax.

[31]IRC Sec. 72(t)(2)(v). It is not clear whether a "separation from service" under Sec. 72(t) means (1) a "separation from service" as that term has been interpreted for purposes of Sec. 402(e) or (2) a "severance of employment" as that term has been interpreted for purposes of Section 401(a).

Generally speaking, the Internal Revenue Service will not recognize a "separation from service" to have occurred in the former situation when an employee continues performing the same services after a sale of his employer, but may treat such a sale as resulting in a "severance of employment" in the latter situation. *Compare* Rev. Rul. 81–141, 1981–1 C.B. 204 and Rev. Rul. 79–336, 1979–2 C.B. 1987 *with* G.C.M. 39824 (August 15, 1990).

[32]TAMRA Sec. 1011A(c)(1).

[33]H.R. Rept. 99–841, 99th Cong., 2d Sess., p. II–457 (hereinafter cited as "Conference Report").

The other factor identified by the statute as indicative of a retirement-type distribution is a payout duration tied to life or life expectancy. Thus, any payment, even one commencing before age 55, is exempt from the additional tax if it is part of a series of substantially equal periodic payments (at least annual in frequency) for the life or life expectancy of the employee or for the joint lives or joint life expectancies of the employee and his designated beneficiary.[34] However, to qualify for this exception, periodic payments from a qualified plan must begin after separation from service.[35]

So as to avoid manipulation, if substantially equal payments begin for life or a period measured with respect to life expectancy, and the series is modified (other than because of death or disability) before the employee attains age 59½ or after the employee attains 59½ but before five full years of payments have been made, the 10 percent tax is triggered in the year in which the modification occurs.[36] The 10 percent tax, plus interest, is then owed on all payments previously received.[37]

Although not having any retirement-type attributes, the TRA exception for distributions to an employee to the extent of the deduction allowable under Section 213 for medical expenses[38] is relatively easy to understand from a policy perspective. Limiting this exclusion to an amount equal to the portion of an employee's deductible medical expenses that exceed 7.5 percent of his adjusted gross income appears consistent with the congressional policy underlying Section 213. Further, not conditioning the exception on the employee's actually claiming the deduction on an itemized return ensures its uniform availability.

Payments under qualified domestic relations orders (QDROs) are also exempt from the 10 percent additional tax.[39] This exemption encourages the use of QDROs and is consistent with the congressional policy behind their creation in the Retirement Equity Act.

Distributions exempted from the 10 percent additional tax include dividends distributed to participants under Section 404(k).[40] Certain

---

[34]IRC Sec. 72(t)(2)(A)(iv).

[35]IRC Sec. 72(t)(3)(B).

[36]IRC Sec. 72(t)(4)(A).

[37]IRC Sec. 72(t)(4)(B).

[38]IRC Sec. 72(t)(2)(B).

[39]IRC Sec. 72(t)(2)(D).

[40]IRC Sec. 72(t)(2)(A)(vi).

distributions from employee stock ownership plans (ESOPs) made before January 1, 1990, were also excepted from the additional tax.[41]

Although numerous types of distributions are exempted from the 10 percent additional tax, most in-service distributions are not of these types. Thus, the 10 percent additional tax is best viewed as a penalty designed to discourage in-service withdrawals. It is open to question whether the 10 percent additional tax when combined with reduced tax rates for many employees will act as an effective deterrent.

Loans

Loans have long been a popular means of providing participants in qualified plans with access to plan assets during employment. The tax-free use of the funds borrowed, combined with an interest deduction for federal income tax purposes and often the crediting of the interest payment to the debtor participant's own account balance in a defined contribution plan, made loans very attractive to participants. Loan provisions have been particularly useful in encouraging employees to participate in Section 401(k) plans notwithstanding the in-service withdrawal restrictions applicable to such plans.

The availability of loans was first curtailed by the Tax Equity and Fiscal Responsibility Act of 1982 (TEFRA).[42] For the most part, the TRA refines the limitations introduced by TEFRA.

The maximum amount that can be borrowed from all employer plans without the borrower being deemed to have received a taxable distribution is limited to the lesser of $50,000 or one half the present value of the participant's nonforfeitable account (or $10,000 if greater). The $50,000 figure, however, now must be reduced not only by any other outstanding loans from plans of the employer (applying subsections 414(b), (c), and (m)),[43] but also by the excess, if any, of the highest outstanding loan balance during the one-year period before the date on which a loan was made over the outstanding balance of loans from the plan on the date on which such loan was made.[44] Thus, an employee who borrowed $25,000

---

[41]IRC Sec. 72(t)(2)(C).

[42]P.L. 97–248, Sec. 236(a). Of course, loan provisions must also comply with Section 408(b)(1) of the Employee Retirement Income Security Act of 1974 and the regulations promulgated thereunder at 29 C.F.R. Section 2550.408b–1.

[43]IRC Sec. 72(p)(2)(D).

[44]IRC Sec. 72(p)(2)(A).

on January 1, 1988, and who repays $5,000 of the balance by August 1, 1988, cannot borrow on August 2, 1988, more than $25,000—that is, $50,000 reduced by the $20,000 outstanding balance on that date and reduced as well by the $5,000 excess of $25,000, the highest outstanding balance during the preceding one-year period, over the $20,000 outstanding balance.

Whereas under TEFRA the term of any loan used to "acquire, construct, reconstruct, or substantially rehabilitate" any dwelling unit to be a principal residence of the participant or a member of the participant's family could have extended for more than five years, only loans used to "acquire" a dwelling that is to be the "principal residence of the participant" can now be for a period longer than five years.[45] From a policy perspective it seems that the construction of a new residence should come within the definition of *acquire;* the wording of the TRA, however, seems to indicate a contrary conclusion.

Moreover, all loans must be amortized on a substantially level basis requiring payments no less frequently than quarterly.[46] This rule eliminates balloon loans and, combined with the offsets to the $50,000 maximum, prevents the maintenance of a large permanent loan balance.

The new loan provisions are effective as to any loan "made, renewed, renegotiated, modified, or extended after December 31, 1986."[47] It can be expected that the Internal Revenue Service will apply the transition rules stringently. Thus, it would not be surprising for a post-1986 pledge of real estate in connection with a pre-1987 loan to be deemed "renegotiated" at the time of the pledge.

One additional area in which the TRA imposes restrictions beyond the conceptual limitations originally imposed on loans by TEFRA involves the loss of the interest deduction in connection with loan repayments. All employees with loans outstanding from qualified plans will be subject to the general phaseout of the interest deduction for consumer interest.[48] Given the administrative complexities of structuring plan loans to qualify as loans secured by the participant's residence, it is anticipated that relatively few borrowers from qualified plans will be able to base their interest deduction on any other grounds. Thus, one of the incentives for

---

[45]IRC Sec. 72(p)(2)(B)(ii).

[46]IRC Sec. 72(p)(2)(C).

[47]TRA Sec. 1134(e).

[48]IRC Sec. 163(h)(5); Sec. 163(d)(6).

borrowing from a qualified plan was diminished significantly starting in 1987 and vanished by 1991.

Persons who are key employees, as defined in Section 416(i), or who seek to secure their repayment obligation with an account balance in a Section 401(k) plan fare particularly poorly under the TRA. For these persons, no interest deduction is available. Interest for which no deduction is allowed does *not* create any basis in the participant's account.[49]

While plan loans still remain permissible, the combination of level amortization, the stricter limitation of loans to a five-year period, the offsets to the $50,000 loan ceiling, and the limited availability of the interest deduction act to curtail the attractiveness of such loans. This further limits preretirement access to qualified plan assets.

Hardship Withdrawals

Effective for plan years commencing after December 31, 1988, in-service withdrawals of amounts contributed pursuant to the participant's election to a qualified plan under Section 401(k) are curtailed. Combined with the new restrictions on loans from qualified plans, the restrictions on hardship withdrawals severely limit access to amounts held by Section 401(k) plans during employment.

Specifically, the TRA limits hardship withdrawals from a Section 401(k) plan to a participant's elective contributions plus pre-1989 earnings.[50] With post-1988 earnings on elective contributions excluded from withdrawal upon hardship, the utility of the cash or deferred plan as a device to accumulate capital for use during employment is further impaired, especially for long-term participants.

Although the rule is not entirely clear from the statute, it appears that qualified nonelective contributions and qualified matching contributions and earnings thereon that meet the Section 401(k) requirements of full vesting and nonwithdrawability prior to age 59½ are not withdrawable even in the event of hardship, if such contributions are used to satisfy the actual deferral percentage test of Section 401(k).[51]

---

[49]IRC Sec. 72(p)(3). See Conference Report, p. II–465.

[50]IRC Section 401(k)(2)(B)(i)(IV) made effective January 1, 1989, by TRA Section 1116(f)(1). See Conference Report, p. II–389; IRC Regulations Sec. 1.401(k)–1(d)(a)(ii).

[51]Conference Report, p. II–389; IRC Proposed Regulations Sec. 1.401(k)–1(d)(1)(iii)(6).

MINIMUM DISTRIBUTION REQUIREMENTS

The TRA refines the minimum distribution requirements initially applied to qualified plans by TEFRA. These requirements, along with the incidental death benefits rule, seek to ensure that qualified plans provide participants with retirement income, rather than serve merely to delay federal income tax or to transfer wealth upon death.[52] The refinements made by the TRA correct an administrative problem that hampered enforcement of the provision and create a sanction for noncompliance (apart from disqualification of the qualified plan) that participants can reasonably expect the Internal Revenue Service will impose when circumstances warrant. A sensible result of these refinements is that identical minimum distribution requirements will apply to all tax-favored retirement income vehicles (qualified plans, tax-sheltered annuities, IRAs, and Section 457 plans).[53]

Required Beginning Date

Prior to January 1, 1989, distributions from a qualified plan were required to begin by April 1 of the calendar year following the calendar year in which a participant (other than a 5 percent owner) attained age 70½ or retired, whichever was later. Distributions to a 5 percent owner had to begin after he or she attained age 70½, regardless of his or her continued employment.[54]

The Congress apparently believed that a required beginning date defined with reference to a participant's separation from service is unsatisfactory because a potential for abuse is inherent in such a standard. Thus, although the legislative history speaks of the administrative difficulty associated with determining whether a separation from service has occurred, the example used to illustrate this difficulty concerns a participant who postpones his required beginning date, even though ceasing regular employment, by continuing to perform work under a consulting

---

[52]H.R. Rept. No. 99–426, 99th Cong., 1st Sess., p. 726 (hereinafter cited as "House Report"); S. Report. No. 99–313, 99th Cong., 2d Sess., p. 605 (hereinafter cited as "Senate Report"); Joint Committee on Taxation, General Explanation of the Revenue Provisions of the Deficit Reduction Act of 1984, p. 868.

[53]TRA Sec. 1121(b); IRC Section 401(a)(9).

[54]IRC Section 401(a)(9)(C).

agreement.[55] Similarly, mention is made of an individual who is not a 5 percent owner, but nonetheless controls the employer and thus the date of her separation from service. Since this individual is said to be no different from the owner of an IRA, there is no reason for not requiring that her distribution begin after age 70½, regardless of her employment status.[56]

In response to those perceived abuses and in an effort to standardize to the extent possible the minimum distribution requirements applicable to tax-favored retirement income vehicles, the TRA provides that effective January 1, 1989, distributions from qualified plans must begin by the April 1 following the calendar year in which the participant attains age 70½.[57] Persons who attained age 70½ before January 1, 1988, are in general grandfathered so that they need not commence receiving distributions until their separation from service.[58] However, as under the pre-TRA rule, a person who is a 5 percent owner at any time during the five plan years beginning with the plan year that ends within the calendar year in which such person attains age 66½, or thereafter, must begin to receive distributions from a qualified plan no later than the April 1 following the

---

[55]House Report, p. 725.

[56]Senate Report, p. 604.

[57]IRC Sec. 401(a)(9)(C); TRA Sec. 1121(d)(1). The suspension of benefit rules generally permit a defined benefit plan to delay commencement of a normal retirement benefit until the participant ceases active employment without any actuarial increase to reflect delayed commencement. *See* 29 C.F.R. 2530.203-3. During the period when benefits are suspended, a participant's accrued benefit payable at normal retirement age must continue to increase along with his ongoing employment, unless a restriction unrelated to age limits additional accruals. As of the required beginning date, however, the minimum distribution requirement overrides the application of the suspension of benefits rules. Any benefit payments after normal retirement date, including minimum distribution payments, may be used to reduce additional increases in a participant's accrued benefit attributable to ongoing employment. The amount ultimately payable is calculated as of the participant's normal retirement age and no actuarial adjustment need be made to reflect the fact that all or a portion of the participant's accrued benefit went into pay status after such date. A defined benefit plan not using the suspension of benefit rules must actuarially increase a participant's benefit payable at normal retirement age to reflect its delayed commencement date, which cannot extend beyond the required beginning date. This actuarial increase may be used to reduce the additional accruals attributable to a participant's continued employment. IRC Sec. 411(b)(1)(H); IRC Proposed Regulations Sec. 1.411(b)-2(b)(4).

[58]TRA Sec. 1121(d)(4)(B)(i). An employee who has attained age 70½ in 1988 but has not retired by January 1, 1989, would be considered to have retired on January 1, 1989, and would be required to begin receiving distributions by April 1, 1990. Internal Revenue Service Advance Notice 89–42, I.R.B. 1989–15, p. 18.

calendar year in which he or she attains age 70½,[59] or the calendar year in which he or she becomes a 5 percent owner, if later.

Fifty Percent Excise Tax

Not only must distributions from qualified plans begin on time, but they must also proceed at a prescribed rate. Otherwise, the recipient (or nonrecipient in the case of nonpayment) will be subject to a nondeductible excise tax equal to 50 percent of the amount by which the minimum required distribution for the calendar year exceeds the amount actually distributed from the qualified plan.[60]

The minimum required distribution is not defined in the Code. Instead, the Secretary of the Treasury is granted authority to define the term in regulations.[61] According to proposed Treasury regulations,[62] the annual minimum required distribution for a participant who does not designate a beneficiary will be measured with reference to the payments that the participant would have received during a calendar year from the qualified plan if his benefit had been payable from the required beginning date in the form of a single life annuity for his life expectancy. A participant who has designated a beneficiary will also have an annual minimum required distribution measured with reference to a life annuity payable from the required beginning date for the joint lives of the participant and beneficiary. The annual amount payable from this annuity will be calculated on the assumption that the survivor benefit is not more than 100 percent of the periodic amount payable to the participant, or less to the extent necessary to satisfy the incidental death benefits rule.[63]

Although the excise tax provides the Internal Revenue Service with a sanction that can be imposed on the recipient of the offending distribution, the qualified plan must nevertheless be required to provide expressly that all distributions will satisfy the minimum distribution rules.[64] The excise tax is technically in addition to, not in lieu of, the

---

[59]TRA Sec. 1121(d)(4)(B)(ii).

[60]IRC Sec. 4974(a).

[61]IRC Sec. 4974(b).

[62]IRS Proposed Regulations Sec. 1.401(a)(9)–1, Q&A–f-3.

[63]Conference Report, p. II–451.

[64]House Report, pp. 726–27.

sanction of disqualification. However, it is likely that in all but the most abusive of situations the excise tax will be the only sanction. Nevertheless, nothing in the minimum distribution rules suggests that disqualification is no longer a sanction available to the Internal Revenue Service.[65] Conversely, approval of an improper form of distribution by the Internal Revenue Service in connection with the issuance of a favorable determination letter will not exempt such distribution from the excise tax.[66]

Most common forms of distribution allowed by qualified plans prior to 1989 comply with the new minimum distribution rules. The statute also gives the Internal Revenue Service discretionary authority to waive the excise tax due in case of reasonable error when corrective action is taken to rectify the shortfall.[67] Given the highly technical nature of these requirements, the Internal Revenue Service may exercise this discretionary authority to exempt distributions from the excise tax whenever a taxpayer can show that a good-faith attempt at compliance was made.

Section 242(b)(2) Elections

The TRA continues to except from the new rules any distributions made in accordance with a form of benefit designation made before January 1, 1984, under Section 242(b)(2) of TEFRA.[68] Proper designations made in accordance with this section will be given effect and will not be subject to the 50 percent excise tax.

RETIREMENT DISTRIBUTIONS

As part of the overall trend of the TRA to encourage the use of qualified plans as devices to provide retirement income, the favorable income averaging and capital gains treatment associated with the receipt of lump-

---

[65]Proposed regulations indicate that, for plan years beginning after 1988, a plan will not be disqualified merely because of "isolated instances when the minimum distribution requirements of Section 401(a)(9) are not satisfied in operation." IRS Proposed Regulations Sec. 1.401(a)(9)–1, Q&A–A-5.

[66]Conference Report, p. II–451.

[67]IRC Sec. 4974(d). Presumably, under some circumstances reliance on an Internal Revenue Service determination letter might prove to be a good-faith error. *See* text at fn. 66.

[68]TRA Sec. 1121(d)(4)(A).

sum distributions from qualified plans upon separation from service, disability, or death prior to attainment of age 59½ have been deleted from the Code[69] for distributions after December 31, 1986,[70] for all but a class of grandfathered taxpayers.[71] The legislative history points out that the Congress's policy of encouraging retirement income is better served by rollovers of amounts received in such circumstances to IRAs.[72] The continued availability of income averaging and capital gains treatment under these circumstances encouraged the preretirement use of amounts accumulated in tax-favored retirement vehicles.

Lump-Sum Distributions

The TRA did not change the Code's description of a lump-sum distribution.[73] The major change made by the TRA is to limit the availability of favorable income-averaging and capital gains treatment to lump-sum distributions made with respect to a participant who had attained age 59½.[74] Further, the TRA only permits one income-averaging and/or capital gain election to be made with respect to a participant.[75]

Income Averaging

Except to the extent modified indirectly by the new rate structure under the TRA, the income-averaging calculation will generally be carried out as under prior law, merely with the substitution of 5 years for 10 years.[76] Since the 10-year averaging period was originally selected because it was thought to approximate the life expectancy over which a person age 65 would have received the lump-sum distribution,[77] the switch to a 5-year

---

[69]IRC Sec. 402(e)(4)(B).

[70]TRA Sec. 1122(h)(1).

[71]TRA Sec. 1122(h)(3)(C).

[72]Senate Report, pp. 608, 609.

[73]IRC Sec. 402(e)(4)(A).

[74]IRC Sec. 402(e)(4)(B).

[75]Ibid.

[76]IRC Sec. 402(e)(1)(B). See IRS Form 4972 for 1990 for the IRS interpretation of the new income-averaging rules.

[77]H.R. Rept. No. 93–779, 93d Cong. 2d Sess. 148–49 (1974).

averaging period appears to be motivated by revenue concerns. In light of the new tax rates, however, 5-year averaging may not produce a greater tax than 10-year averaging under pre-TRA rules.

Although the new income-averaging provisions apply to distributions received after December 31, 1986, a grandfather rule covers any individual who attained age 50 before January 1, 1986.[78] Such an individual can elect to apply the 1986 rules for determining the eligibility of a lump-sum distribution for income-averaging treatment and the 1986 tax rates to any distribution received from a qualified plan.[79] This means that a person who attained age 50 in 1984, for example, could elect that a lump-sum distribution received from a qualified plan when he or she attained age 56 in 1990 be evaluated (for purposes of eligibility for income-averaging treatment) under the 1986 rules. If this distribution is received, for example, on account of separation from service, the fact that the individual had not attained age 59½ at the time of the distribution would not be enough to prevent the distribution from being a lump-sum distribution entitled to income-averaging treatment. Although no election is necessary to take advantage of the grandfather rule prior to the receipt of a distribution, an election under the grandfather rule will eliminate any further opportunity to elect five-year income averaging, even as to a participant who has not attained age 59½ at the time the grandfather rule becomes applicable to a distribution.[80]

The age-50 requirement of the grandfather rules relates to the age of the employee who receives the benefit.[81] Thus, an individual, trust, or estate that receives a postdeath lump-sum distribution on behalf of an employee who had attained age 50 on January 1, 1986, is permitted to make one election with respect to the employee to use income averaging on the lump-sum distribution. An individual who makes an income-averaging election on an amount he receives as a beneficiary does not lose his opportunity to make an income-averaging election with respect to a single lump-sum distribution made on his behalf.

---

[78]TRA Sec. 1122(h)(3).

[79]TRA Sec. 1122(h)(3)(A).

[80]TRA Sec. 1122(h)(3)(C) and (h)(5). Similarly, an election under the grandfather rule eliminates any further opportunity to elect grandfathering treatment with respect to any other distribution from a qualified plan.

[81]TRA Sec. 1122(h)(3)(C) as amended by TAMRA Sec. 1011A(b)(14).

Capital Gains

The long-term capital gains treatment available with respect to the portion of a lump-sum distribution attributable to pre-1974 participation is phased out by the TRA for distributions received after December 31, 1986, over a six-year period as described in this schedule:

Year	Percentage Treated as[82] Capital Gain
1987	100
1988	95
1989	75
1990	50
1991	25
1992	0

Although there was initially some confusion on this point, it is fairly clear that the percentage of a distribution characterized as a long-term capital gain is subject to a tax at the normal income-tax rates established by the TRA without applying the 60 percent long-term capital-gains deduction that was a feature of the pre-TRA Code. Thus, the advantage of the phaseout lies in the opportunity to offset pre-1987 capital losses against the post-1986 capital gains preserved by the phaseout.

Support for this reading comes from the TRA's silence about the applicable tax rate in the capital-gain phaseout rule and the failure to mention expressly the 60 percent long-term capital-gains deduction (especially because a specific tax rate is mentioned in connection with the grandfather rule discussed below), which is otherwise repealed by the TRA for tax years beginning after December 31, 1986. Additionally, applying the 60 percent long-term capital-gains deduction would produce the anomalous result of a lower tax rate for amounts subject to the phaseout (that is, 40 percent of 28 percent = 11.2 percent) than amounts subject to the grandfather rule discussed below.

---

[82]TRA Sec. 1122(h)(4).

Under the grandfather rule, individuals who attained age 50 before January 1, 1986, may elect to apply the 1986 rules for determining the eligibility of a lump-sum distribution for capital-gains treatment to a distribution from a qualified plan and to have the portion of a resulting lump-sum distribution attributable to pre-1974 participation taxed at a flat 20 percent rate.[83] This 20 percent rate, the maximum effective tax rate applicable to long-term capital gains under the pre-TRA Code, will apply even to an individual for whom capital gains in 1986 would have been taxed at an effective tax rate lower than 20 percent. As with the grandfather rule for income averaging, no election is necessary to take advantage of the grandfather rule prior to the receipt of a distribution, and an election under the grandfather rule will eliminate any further opportunity to elect five-year income averaging, even as to a participant who has not attained age 59½ at the time the grandfather rule becomes applicable to a distribution.[84]

Revised Treatment for Rollovers of Partial Distributions

As under prior law, an employee who takes advantage of the rule permitting a rollover of a partial distribution will forgo the right to report a subsequent distribution from the same plan (or any plan aggregated with such plan under Section 402(e)(4)(C)) on an income-averaging basis.[85] However, the TRA amends the Code to limit the opportunity to roll over a partial distribution to situations involving a separation from service, death, or disability.[86] Prior law permitted an in-service rollover of a partial distribution.[87] An IRA is still the only acceptable recipient of a partial rollover.[88]

Effective for distributions made after December 31, 1986, a partial distribution eligible to be rolled over without being included in current income is defined as a distribution

---

[83]TRA Sec. 1122(h)(3)(B)(ii).

[84]TRA Sec. 1122(h)(3)(C). Similarly, an election under the grandfather rule eliminates any further opportunity to elect grandfathering treatment with respect to any other distribution from a qualified plan.

[85]IRC Sec. 402(a)(5)(D)(iii).

[86]IRC Sec. 402(a)(5)(D)(i); IRC Sec. 402(e)(4)(A).

[87]Sec. 402(a)(5)(D)(i) of the Internal Revenue Code of 1954.

[88]IRC Sec. 402(a)(5)(D)(ii).

1. from a trust that is part of a qualified plan;
2. that is not one of a series of periodic payments and represents payment of at least 50 percent of the balance to the credit of the employee, without applying Section 402(e)(4)(C); and
3. that is payable on account of the employee's death, on account of the employee's separation from service, or after the employee has become disabled (within the meaning of Section 72(m)(7)).[89]

Only 50 percent (rather than 100 percent) of the balance to the credit of the employee must be distributed from the qualified plan. Whether or not the participant is a self-employed person or a common law employee, suffering a disability (within the meaning of Section 72(m)(7)) gives the right to roll over a partial distribution. The partial distribution cannot be rolled over merely because it is paid after age 59½.[90] Section 402(a)(5)(D) as originally amended by TRA provided that the aggregation rules of Section 402(e)(4)(C) were applicable to partial rollovers. However, a technical correction to TRA made by TAMRA removed this requirement.[91]

Net Unrealized Appreciation

Perhaps as part of the overall statutory structure, which favors the acquisition of employer securities by qualified plans, the rules with respect to unrealized appreciation in employer securities are left intact by the TRA. Thus, recognition of all unrealized appreciation in employer securities will be deferred if such securities are part of a lump-sum distribution.[92] There is no requirement that the lump-sum distribution be received after the recipient attains age 59½ or any limitation on the number of times a person can benefit from the rule applicable to unrealized appreciation of employer securities received as part of a lump-sum distribution.[93]

---

[89]Notice 87–13, Q&A–19. A distribution made by an ESOP to satisfy the diversification requirements of Section 401(a)(28) is treated as satisfying these requirements. IRC Sec. 402(a)(5)(D)(i), as amended by TAMRA Sec. 1011A(b)(4)(A)–(B).

[90]Ibid.

[91]TAMRA Sec. 1011A(b)(4)(A)–(B).

[92]IRC Sec. 402(e)(4)(J).

[93]IRC Sec. 402(e)(4)(J).

Unrealized appreciation in employer securities that are part of a lump-sum distribution received after December 31, 1986, may be recognized at the time of the distribution, however, if the taxpayer elects such recognition pursuant to regulations to be promulgated.[94] This TRA change probably results from the elimination of special treatment for capital gains so that a distributee in many instances may well be better off reporting the full market value of employer securities as part of a lump-sum distribution.

Potential Future Vesting

The TRA resolves a technical issue created by the fact that participants in qualified plans who receive distributions at separation from service when they are less than fully vested retain a contingent right to increase their vested interest upon subsequent reemployment. A question existed before the TRA about the impact, if any, of this future vesting on any income-averaging, capital gains, or rollover treatment obtained for the previous distribution. The TRA answers this question retroactive to the effective date of the Retirement Equity Act of 1984 provision being amended by the TRA, but the answer depends on how the previous distribution was taxed.[95]

If the previous distribution benefitted from income-averaging or capital-gains treatment, an increase in the recipient's vested interest in the benefit accrued prior to his or her separation from service because of reemployment will trigger a recapture of the tax benefit resulting from such treatment.[96] The amount of the recapture presumably will be the difference between the tax that would have been payable if the previous distribution had not benefitted from income-averaging or capital-gains treatment and the tax actually paid on such distribution. The details of the recapture are left to regulations. For purposes of determining whether an election of income averaging or capital-gains treatment has been made with respect to the employee, the election made for the previous distri-

---

[94]IRC Sec. 402(e)(4)(J). This election is to be made by attaching a signed statement to the tax return for the year in which the distribution was received or by including the net unrealized appreciation on Form 4972 or on line 16 of Form 1040 if no Form 4972 is filed. Notice 89–25, Q&A–1.

[95]IRC Sec. 402(e)(6).

[96]IRC Sec. 402(e)(6)(B).

bution is ignored when the tax benefit associated with that election is the subject of recapture.[97]

Qualified plans typically condition an employee's right to increase his vested interest in the benefit accrued prior to separation from service upon the employee repaying the full amount of the prior distribution to the qualified plan. Although not required by the Code, consideration should be given to notifying the employee that such a repayment could generate tax liability. With the TRA-accelerated vesting rules[98] and the five-year minimum participation period for lump-sum distributions, the issue of potential future vesting became less significant in 1989.

If the previous distribution has been the subject of a rollover, an increase in the person's vested interest in the benefit accrued prior to his or her separation from service because of reemployment will deprive the employee of the tax benefits associated with income-averaging treatment for any subsequent distribution from the qualified plan.[99] However, the employee can elect income-averaging treatment for a distribution received from another qualified plan, so long as that plan was not aggregated with the plan from which the original distribution was made, under Section 402(e)(4)(C). Further, if the rollover has been made in connection with a distribution received without the participant's consent ($3,500 or less), income-averaging treatment would be available for any subsequent distribution received from the qualified plan.[100]

Basis Recovery Rules

Under pre-TRA law, if under an annuity form of benefit the projected payments within the first three years after the annuity starting date were equal to or in excess of the employee's unrecovered basis in the qualified plan, payments in the form of an annuity would be nontaxable until an amount equal to the unrecovered basis was received by the employee.[101] The "three-year recovery rule," which was a popular way of receiving distributions under qualified plans that provided for after-tax contribu-

---

[97]Ibid.

[98]*See* IRC Sec. 411(a)(2).

[99]IRC Sec. 402(a)(6)(I).

[100]IRC Sec. 402(a)(6)(I)(ii).

[101]Internal Revenue Code of 1954, Sec. 72(d)(1).

tions, was repealed retroactively by the TRA with respect to any individual whose annuity starting date was after July 1, 1986.[102]

Since the three-year recovery rule has been repealed, each payment received in an annuity form will be at least partially taxable. The nontaxable portion of each payment will be determined with reference to the ratio of the employee's unrecovered basis in the qualified plan to the total expected payments the recipient is to receive from the qualified plan.[103] Correcting an apparent oversight under prior law, the TRA limits the nontaxable amount that can be recovered to the precise amount of the employee's unrecovered basis.[104] If annuity payments terminate, on the other hand, before the employee's unrecovered basis has been fully recovered (as a result of the death of the employee and any annuitant prior to the end of the anticipated payment period), the unrecovered basis is allowed as a deduction to the last surviving annuitant for the last year of her or his life.[105] When payments are made to a beneficiary or estate of the annuitant by the qualified plan in the form of a refund of consideration paid by the employee, the deduction is allowed to the beneficiary or estate.[106] Any deduction under these provisions is treated as if arising out of a trade or business conducted by the taxpayer for purposes of the net operating loss deduction under Section 172.[107]

RESTRICTIONS ON LARGE BENEFIT PAYMENTS

The TRA tightens the restrictions imposed by Section 415 on benefits payable from defined benefit plans and the annual additions allocable under defined contribution plans. Because the Section 415 restrictions can be avoided when an individual works for multiple employers and because Section 415 ignores amounts accumulated by the individual for retirement

---

[102]TRA Sec. 1122(c)(1); TRA Sec. 1122(h)(2)(A).

[103]IRC Sec. 72(b)(1). A simplified "safe harbor" rule that may be used to determine the taxable amount of each payment made to an individual whose annuity starting date was after July 1, 1986, is described in Internal Revenue Service Notice 88–118, I.R.B. No. 1988–47, p. 9.

[104]IRC Sec. 72(b)(2).

[105]IRC Sec. 72(b)(3)(A). The old law did "rough justice" by giving a break to recipients who outlived their life expectancies and overtaxing those who failed to survive their full life expectancies.

[106]IRC Sec. 72(b)(3)(B).

[107]IRC Sec. 72(b)(3)(C).

in other tax-favored retirement income vehicles, the TRA introduces the concept of a 15 percent excise tax on the individual for "excess retirement distributions" received during his lifetime[108] and on the individual's estate for "excess retirement accumulations" remaining in tax-favored retirement income vehicles at his death.[109] Distributions from or amounts accumulated under qualified plans subject to Section 401(a); annuity plans subject to Section 403(a); tax-deferred annuities, custodial accounts, or retirement-income accounts subject to Section 403(b); individual retirement arrangements under Section 408; or plans that once satisfied these qualification requirements are all subject to the excise tax provision.[110]

Excess Retirement Distributions

With the exception of a complicated grandfather clause, the mechanics of the penalty tax payable on excess retirement distributions are straightforward. All distributions, with certain stated exceptions, from the tax-favored retirement-income vehicles listed above received by or with respect to a taxpayer during a calendar year are aggregated by the taxpayer and subjected to the penalty tax to the extent in excess of a threshold.[111]

Certain distributions are excluded from consideration:

1. Any distribution received by a taxpayer with respect to a deceased person.
2. Any distribution made with respect to the taxpayer to an alternate payee pursuant to a qualified domestic relations order that is includable in the alternate payee's income.
3. The portion of any distribution to a taxpayer that represents a return of an employee's basis in the tax-favored retirement-income vehicle.
4. The portion of any distribution rolled over to another tax-favored retirement-income vehicle without tax.
5. Any distribution to a taxpayer of an annuity contract, the value of which is not taxable at the time of distribution.

---

[108]IRC Sec. 4980A(c). *See* House Report, p. 740.
[109]IRC Sec. 4980A(d). *See* House Report, p. 740.
[110]IRC Sec. 4980A(e).
[111]IRC Sec. 4980A(c)(1).

6. Any distribution to a taxpayer of excess deferrals under Section 402(g), excess contributions under Section 401(h)(8) or 408(d)(4), or excess aggregate contributions under Section 401(m)(6), and income allocable thereto.[112]

7. Any health coverage or distribution of medical benefits under Section 401(h) to the extent excludable under Section 104, 105, or 106.[113]

The general rule is that the 15 percent excise tax is imposed on distributions received by or made with respect to the taxpayer during the calendar year to the extent in excess of the greater of $150,000 or $112,500. The $112,500 figure is adjusted to reflect cost-of-living increases in the same manner and to the same extent as under Section 415(d).[114] Net unrealized appreciation in employer securities, even if not taxable, appears subject to the 15 percent excise tax.

A lump-sum distribution for which an income-averaging election is made under Section 402(e)(4)(B) (or an election to apply capital-gains treatment) is subject to a separately calculated excise tax to the extent in excess of a separate threshold; the tax will be imposed only to the extent the distribution exceeds five times the limitation applicable to other distributions.[115] Thus, the limitation for a lump-sum before the excise tax will apply is the greater of $750,000 (under the grandfather clause) or $562,500 adjusted. The amount of the excise tax due on excess distributions, whether or not qualifying for the special rule applicable to a lump-sum distribution for which an income-averaging election is made, is 15 percent.[116]

An individual can be liable for both the 10 percent penalty tax imposed on early distributions and the 15 percent excise tax imposed on excess retirement distributions. In these circumstances, however, the taxpayer is permitted to offset the 10 percent penalty tax against the 15 percent excise tax to the extent both taxes are assessed on the same distributions.[117]

---

[112]IRC Sec. 4980A(c)(2), as amended by TAMRA Sec. 1011A(g)(3)(A)–(B).

[113]Temporary Regulations Sec. 54.4981A–1T, Q&A–a–4.

[114]IRC Sec. 4980A(c)(1). The $112,500 figure was increased to $128,228 in 1990.

[115]IRC Sec. 4980A(c)(4).

[116]IRC Sec. 4980A(a).

[117]IRC Sec. 4980A(b).

A grandfather rule applies if the accrued benefit of an employee under the tax-favored retirement-income vehicles in which he participates exceeded $562,500 as of August 1, 1986.[118] If the employee elects grandfather treatment on his or her federal income tax ending before January 1, 1989, the 15 percent excise tax will be imposed on the amount by which the annual distributions exceed the greater of $112,500 adjusted as described above, or the amount deemed to be attributable to the grandfathered accrued benefit, as determined in accordance with regulations.[119] If the distribution qualified for income averaging under Section 402(e)(4)(B), the amount exempt from the excise tax will be the greater of $562,500, as adjusted, or the amount determined to be attributable to the grandfathered accrued benefit.[120]

In the case of tax-favored retirement-income vehicles that maintain separate accounts (that is, defined contribution plans), the accrued benefit as of August 1, 1986, will be equal to the account balance as of that date. Tax-favored retirement income-vehicles that provide a stated benefit for life commencing at some time in the future (that is, defined benefit plans) are to use the accrued benefit (presumably on a present-value basis) that would be payable if the employee separated from service on August 1, 1986.[121] Apparently the accrued benefit as of August 1, 1986, whether forfeitable or nonforfeitable, counts for purposes of determining an individual's eligibility for the grandfather rule.

Excess Retirement Accumulation

The mechanics of the 15 percent excise tax imposed on an estate on excess retirement accumulations are complex. Generally, the excise tax is imposed on the excess of the "value" of a decedent's interests (other than as a beneficiary) in tax-favored retirement-income vehicles over the present value of a single life annuity that provides for annual payments equal to the limitation in effect for excess retirement distributions in the year of death.[122] The respective values are to be measured either as of the

---

[118]IRC Sec. 4980A(f).

[119]IRC Sec. 4980A(f); IRS Temporary Regulations Sec. 54.4981A–IT, Q&A–b-4 and b-14.

[120]IRC Sec. 4980A(f); IRS Temporary Regulations Sec. 54.4981A–IT, Q&A–c-1.

[121]Conference Report, pp. II–477.

[122]IRS Temporary Regulations Sec. 54.4981A–IT, Q&A–d-7.

date of the decedent's death or the alternate valuation date under Section 2032,[123] using interest rate and other assumptions to be prescribed in regulations.[124]

The value of the decedent's interest in tax-favored retirement-income vehicles does not include the portion thereof that is subject to a qualified domestic relations order in favor of the decedent's spouse or former spouse, that represents the decedent's basis in the tax-favored retirement-income vehicles, that is attributable to the excess of any interests payable after death over the value of the interest before death, and that represents the decedent's interest in a tax-favored retirement-income vehicle by reason of the death of another individual.

If a decedent has made the grandfather election with respect to his annuity distribution, the excise tax on excess retirement accumulations is imposed on the excess of the "value" of the decedent's interest in the tax-favored retirement-income vehicles over the greater of the present value of a single life annuity as described above or the amount deemed to be the unrecovered portion of his grandfathered accrued benefit, as determined under regulations.[125]

An estate can be liable for the 15 percent excise tax, even if the estate will not otherwise pay an estate tax. Neither the unified credit[126] nor, since the tax is imposed without taking into account the amount of the taxable estate, the marital deduction or the charitable deduction can be used to reduce or eliminate the 15 percent excise tax. The penalty tax is payable by the estate regardless of who benefits from the excess retirement accumulation, and the estate has no separate right under Section 4980A of the Code to seek reimbursement of the tax from persons that the decedent has designated as the beneficiaries of the tax-favored retirement-income vehicles that gave rise to the excise tax. However, the decedent's will or the state apportionment law may provide that the estate is entitled to such reimbursement. Once amounts are subjected to the estate tax, subsequent payments received by beneficiaries are not again subject to the excise tax as received.[127]

---

[123]IRC Sec. 4980A(d)(3)(A).

[124]IRC Sec. 4980A(d)(3)(B).

[125]IRS Temporary Regulations Sec. 54.4981A–IT, Q&A–d-4.

[126]IRC Sec. 4980A(d)(2).

[127]Conference Report, p. II–471.

Effective Dates

The provisions relating to the penalty tax on excess retirement distributions are generally applicable with respect to distributions after December 31, 1986.[128] However, distributions after August 1, 1986, but before January 1, 1987, may reduce the grandfathered amount.[129]

The excise tax on excess retirement accumulations applies to the estates of individuals dying after December 31, 1986.[130]

Distributions from (and presumably accumulations under) qualified plans subject to Section 401(a), annuity plans subject to Section 403(a), and any tax-deferred annuity, custodial account or retirement-income account subject to Section 403(b) are exempted from the 15 percent excise tax if such arrangements were terminated before January 1, 1987, and distributions from such arrangements occurred before January 1, 1988.[131]

CONCLUSION

The changes made by the TRA to the Code to discourage the use of qualified plans as devices to accumulate capital rather than to provide retirement income radically alter the pre-TRA rules and, together with the grandfather rules, complicate tax planning for qualified plan distributions. This chapter can only present a preliminary picture of what these changes mean. The reader might keep in mind the statement of an attorney for the Joint Committee on Taxation to the effect that people "should not assume that a provision [of the TRA] intentionally gives the result you end up with."[132]

---

[128]TRA Sec. 1133(c)(1).

[129]Conference Report, p. II–477.

[130]TRA Sec. 1133(c)(2).

[131]TRA Sec. 1133(c)(3).

[132]*P–H Pension and Profit-Sharing Bulletin* 7 (January 28, 1987), p. 1, quoting Mary Levontin.

CHAPTER 50

THE FEDERAL TAX ENVIRONMENT FOR WELFARE BENEFIT PLANS*

Everett T. Allen, Jr.

Not too many years ago, welfare benefit plans were mostly free of significant regulation by federal authorities. Employer contributions for these benefits were tax deductible and, other than for group life insurance in excess of $50,000, were income tax free to employees. Benefits paid, for the most part, were also income tax free, the only notable exception being employer-provided disability-income benefits. Nondiscrimination requirements were generally nonexistent and, in addition, employers had much latitude in prefunding future plan liabilities.

The first major legislation relating to welfare benefit plans was the Employee Retirement Income Security Act of 1974 (ERISA), and even this law had limited application—the plans were subject only to its reporting, disclosure, and fiduciary requirements.

Legislative activity over the last ten years, however, along with regulatory interpretation, has brought these plans under an increasing amount of federal regulation. Age and sex discrimination laws and, in particular, the tax law now impose significant restraints on welfare plans and the benefits they provide.

This chapter presents an overview of the federal tax environment as it relates to the major employer-provided welfare plan benefits—group life insurance, health care, and disability income, as well as flexible

---

*Copyright Towers, Perrin, Foster & Crosby, Inc., 1990.

benefit plans. The first section discusses overall tax law provisions that apply to these plans with emphasis on nondiscrimination requirements. The discussion then moves to the taxation of contributions and benefits and how taxation varies when the nondiscrimination requirements are not met. Detailed coverage is beyond the scope of this chapter; additional information may be found in other chapters of the *Handbook* that deal with specific welfare and flexible benefit plans.

GENERAL TAX LAW REQUIREMENTS

Welfare benefit plans must comply with a number of tax law provisions in order to receive favorable tax treatment. Some of the major nondiscrimination requirements are found in Internal Revenue Code (IRC or Code) Section 79 (group life insurance), Section 105 (self-insured employer health plans), Section 125 (flexible benefit plans), Section 505 (voluntary employees' beneficiary associations, *VEBAs,* which utilize a tax-exempt trust), and Section 162 (the so-called Consolidated Omnibus Budget Reconciliation Act, *COBRA,* requirements for the continued availability of health care coverage in certain situations). The following subsections review the general concepts of these key provisions of the law.

Section 79—Group Life Insurance

Employee-pay-all group life insurance plans—in which all employees contribute, at all ages, either less or more than the imputed income rates published by the Internal Revenue Service (IRS), and in which there is no significant employer involvement—are not subject to Section 79 requirements. Employer-provided group life insurance benefits, however, must meet the nondiscrimination requirements of this section of the Code if key employees are to enjoy the tax advantages normally associated with these benefits.

In general, Section 79 requires that a group life insurance plan not discriminate in favor of key employees as to eligibility to participate and the type and amount of benefits available.

Eligibility Test
To satisfy the eligibility test, a group life insurance plan must meet *one* of four requirements: (1) the plan must cover at least 70 percent of all

employees; (2) at least 85 percent of the participants must not be key employees; (3) the employees covered must qualify under a classification set up by the employer and found by the Department of the Treasury (the Treasury) not to discriminate in favor of key employees; *or* (4) if the plan is part of a flexible benefit plan, it must meet the requirements of Section 125. Although this is called an *eligibility* test, it is in fact a coverage test.

Some employees may be excluded when applying the eligibility test. These are employees who: (1) have not completed three years of service, (2) are part-time or seasonal, and (3) are covered by a collective bargaining agreement.

Benefits Test

Assuming one of the four eligibility tests is met, it is also necessary that the plan meet a benefits test. This test is not met unless all benefits available to participants who are key employees are also available to all other participants. A plan will meet this test if the amount of coverage provided bears a uniform relationship to employee compensation. Also, the IRS has informally indicated that the use of reasonable compensation brackets in a benefit schedule will be acceptable. On the other hand, the IRS has indicated that coverage based upon job classifications will be acceptable only if it can be shown that their use does not discriminate in favor of key employees.

Section 79 Testing in General

The regulations require that all policies carried directly or indirectly by an employer that provide group life insurance to a common key employee are to be considered a plan (that is, aggregated) for purposes of these tests. The employer also has the option of treating two or more policies that do not provide coverage to a common key employee as a single plan. This allows an employer to treat a plan for key employees and a separate plan for non-key employees as one plan, thus increasing the likelihood that the tests will be met for the combined plan.

In all cases, coverage is tested separately for active and retired employees.

The regulations also provide that a plan will not be discriminatory as to the amount of coverage available if: (1) the coverage group consists of a key employee and all other participants who receive an amount of insurance, as a multiple of compensation, that is equal to or greater than the coverage of the key employee; and (2) the plan, if tested separately, will pass one of the four parts of the eligibility test. For example, assume that an employer has a total of 500 participants, 10 of whom are key employees. Assume further that 400 non-key employees have coverage equal to 100 percent of compensation and that the 10 key employees and 90 non-key employees have coverage equal to 200 percent of compensation. The plan will not be discriminatory because 90 percent (that is, more than 85 percent) of the participants in the group with 200 percent coverage are not key employees. In determining the groups that may be tested separately under this rule, allowances may be made for reasonable differences due to rounding, the use of compensation brackets, or other similar factors.

Section 79 uses the definition of "key" employee found in the pension-plan top-heavy rules (Section 416(i)). Under those rules, a "key" employee is one who, at any time during the plan year or any of the four preceding plan years, is (1) an officer with annual compensation in excess of 50 percent of the $90,000 (indexed) Section 415 limit for qualified defined benefit plans, (2) one of the ten employees with annual compensation greater than the $30,000 (indexed) Section 415 limit for qualified defined contribution plans and owning the largest interest in the employer, (3) a 5 percent owner, *or* (4) a 1 percent owner with annual compensation greater than $150,000. Section 79 adds retired employees to the Section 416(i) definition if any retiree was a key employee when he or she retired or separated from service.

There are certain qualifications as to who should be counted as a key employee. First, there is an overall limit on the number of employees who are considered officers. The limit is 50, or if fewer, the greater of three or 10 percent of the employees. This rule is particularly important for large employers, since it effectively caps the prohibited group at 50 employees. Also, the definition of *officer* is limited to executive officers; those with limited authority, such as bank loan officers, are not key employees under this rule. Certain other individuals are excluded as officers: (1) those who have not completed six months of service, (2) those who normally work less than 17½ hours per week or six months or less per year, (3) those who have not attained age 21, and (4) those who are covered by a collective bargaining agreement.

Section 105(h)—Self-Insured Employer Health Plans

Employer health plans that are insured are not subject to nondiscrimination standards. By contrast, self-insured employer health plans are subject to nondiscrimination rules under Section 105(h). The only exceptions to this distinction between *insured* and *self-insured* health plans involve plans that use a tax-exempt trust under Section 501(c)(9) of the IRC or plans that are subject to Section 125. Employer health plans provided through such a trust are subject to nondiscrimination rules even if the benefits are insured. Similarly, insured health plans are subject to the nondiscrimination rules of Section 125 if they are part of a flexible benefit plan.

To qualify as an insured plan and avoid discrimination testing, the regulations require a transfer of risk from the employer to an unrelated third party. The regulations also state that the tests apply to the self-insured portion of an employer's plan even if the plan is, in part, underwritten by insurance. Under these regulations, cost-plus arrangements without a meaningful limit would not qualify as being insured. The same is probably true for minimum premium arrangements. Administrative-services-only (ASO) plans obviously would be considered to be self-insured.

Self-insured health plans subject to nondiscrimination testing include medical, dental, vision, and health care spending accounts. Disability income, business travel accident, and accidental death and dismemberment (AD&D) plans are not subject to Section 105(h) nondiscrimination requirements.

Generally, amounts paid to employees under an employer's self-insured health plan are not included in their gross income. If such a plan discriminates in favor of "highly compensated individuals," however, some or all of the reimbursements those individuals receive may be taxable. The potential taxation of benefit payments under a self-insured plan is discussed in more detail later in this chapter.

The nondiscrimination standards of Section 105(h) require that the plan meet both an eligibility and a benefit test.

Eligibility Test

A self-insured plan does not meet the eligibility test unless it covers: (1) 70 percent or more of all employees, (2) 80 percent or more of all eligible employees if at least 70 percent of all employees are eligible, *or* (3) such employees as qualify under a classification set up by the employer and found by the Treasury not to discriminate in favor of highly compensated individuals. (The third alternative is often referred to as *the fair-cross-section test,* because this requirement is satisfied if the covered group represents a fair cross section of all employees.)

For all three alternatives, the eligibility test is based upon the *employees actually covered* by the plan, not just those who are eligible for coverage. Also, each individual plan of the employer must meet one of these alternative eligibility tests. As will be noted later, however, aggregation of plans is permitted for testing purposes.

In applying these eligibility tests, an employer is allowed to exclude the following employees: (1) those who have not completed three years of service, (2) those who have not attained age 25, (3) part-time or seasonal employees, (4) those covered by a collective bargaining agreement, and (5) nonresident aliens who receive no earned income from the employer that is income from sources within the United States.

Benefits Test
A self-insured plan does not meet the benefits test unless all benefits provided under the plan to highly compensated participants are provided to all other participants. This includes benefits provided to dependents as well as to employees.

In general, each individual plan of the employer must meet the benefits test although, as will be noted later, aggregation of plans is permitted for testing purposes. A plan that provides optional benefits will be treated as providing a single benefit as to the benefits covered by the option if: (1) all eligible participants may elect any of the benefits covered by the options, and (2) there are either no required employee contributions, or the required employee contributions are the same amount for all participants.

The benefits test is applied to the *benefits eligible for reimbursement* under the plan rather than to actual benefit payments, and all benefits are considered both as to the type of benefit and the amounts reimbursable.

An employer is not allowed to combine benefits available to highly compensated participants, determine the value of the combined benefits, and then compare that value with the value of benefits available to the other participants. Each benefit available under the plan must be considered separately.

If the difference in benefits is based upon different waiting periods for employees in different subsidiaries or divisions, the problem of providing different benefits may be avoided if separate plans are actually created for the different subsidiaries or divisions. Each separate plan would then have to pass the discrimination tests on its own, using all of the employees in the controlled group for the eligibility test and the covered employees for the benefits test.

A plan is permitted to integrate with benefits paid under another plan or with benefits paid under Medicare or other federal or state laws.

Section 105(h) Testing in General

Not only must a plan not discriminate on its face in providing benefits, it also must not discriminate in actual operation, based on the facts and circumstances of each case. A plan is not considered discriminatory, however, simply because highly compensated individuals utilize plan benefits to a greater extent than do the other employees.

The Section 105(h) regulations say that benefits provided to a retired employee who was a highly compensated individual will not be considered discriminatory if the type and dollar limitations of benefits provided to retired employees who were highly compensated individuals are the same as for all other retired participants. This rule could affect plans in which benefits differ by reason of employees' length of service—an approach that is becoming more popular as employers seek ways to limit their liability for postretirement health care coverage. Technically, each service bracket represents a plan, and that plan is nondiscriminatory only if it satisfies the fair-cross-section requirement.

Some additional matters under Section 105(h) requirements include the following.

• *Aggregation.* An employer may designate two or more self-insured plans as constituting a single plan for purposes of determining whether the nondiscrimination requirements are met. In the absence of comparability standards for aggregating plans, however, this rule is unclear. All employees under an aggregation of plans would probably not be eligible to receive the same benefits. If the combined plans fail the tests, the income of highly compensated individuals will be determined using the benefits paid under the combined plan.

• *Flexible-Benefit Plans.* If a self-insured health plan is included in a flexible benefit plan, Section 105(h) determines the status of the benefit as being discriminatory or nondiscriminatory—that is, as being taxable or nontaxable—and Section 125 determines whether an employee is taxed as though he or she elected taxable benefits.

• *Definition of Highly Compensated.* For purposes of Section 105(h), a highly compensated individual is (1) one of the five highest paid officers, (2) a 10 percent owner, or (3) an employee who is among the highest paid 25 percent of all employees (other than the 10 percent owners who are not participants).

• *Exception for Physical Exams.* The regulations provide an important exception from discrimination testing for reimbursements paid under a plan for "medical diagnostic procedures" for employees. Such procedures include routine medical examinations, blood tests, and X-rays. They do not include expenses incurred for the treatment, cure, or testing of a known illness or disability or for the treatment or testing for a physical injury, complaint, or specific symptom of a bodily malfunction. In addition, the procedures do not include any activities undertaken for exercise, fitness, nutrition, recreation, or the general improvement of health unless they are for medical care. The procedure may only be for employees, not dependents, and it must be performed at a facility that provides no services other than medical and ancillary services. An employee's annual physical examination conducted at the employee's personal physician's office under a self-insured health plan is not subject to the Section 105(h) nondiscrimination tests and may be excluded from the employee's income if the requirements of Section 105(h) are met. If the examination is conducted at a resort, however, it will be subject to the Section 105(h) nondiscrimination tests, with the taxation of the benefit being based upon whether the plan passes the tests.

Section 125—Flexible Benefit Plans

Under normal circumstances, an employee who has a choice of receiving an element of compensation either in the form of cash or as a nontaxable benefit would have to consider this element of compensation as currently taxable income even if she or he chose the nontaxable benefit. This "doctrine of constructive receipt" is waived, however, if the choice is made under a flexible benefit plan that meets the requirements of Section 125.

A *flexible benefit plan,* or *cafeteria plan,* is defined by Section 125 as one that permits such a choice. A plan that permits a choice between only two nontaxable benefits (for example, a choice between two medical expense plans or between group life insurance of less than $50,000 and disability income coverage) is not a "cafeteria" plan within the meaning of Section 125 and not subject to the requirements of this section or to the doctrine of constructive receipt.

A flexible benefit plan may involve full choice making, may be limited to a flexible spending account (FSA), or might simply involve an arrangement whereby employees contribute for nontaxable benefits on a before-tax basis by taking pay reductions. Even this latter arrangement constitutes a flexible benefit plan and must meet the requirements of Section 125.

Section 125 imposes three nondiscrimination tests on any flexible benefit plan: an eligibility test, a contributions and benefits test, and a concentration test.

Eligibility Test

The eligibility test requires that the plan be available to a nondiscriminatory classification of employees. The requirements for this test are generally the same as those that apply to qualified pension and profit-sharing plans. If the percentage of nonhighly compensated employees covered by the plan is at least 50 percent of the percentage of highly compensated employees covered, the test will be passed. On the other hand, if the percentage of nonhighly compensated employees covered is 40 percent or less of the percentage of highly compensated employees covered, the test will be failed. (Where the nonhighly compensated employees make up 60 percent or more of the total work force, both of these percentages are reduced.) If the coverage ratio is between these two levels, a subjective facts and circumstances standard will be applied to determine whether the test is met. Employees with less than three years of service may be disregarded for testing purposes.

Contributions and Benefits Test

The second test requires that contributions and benefits under the flexible benefit plan not favor highly compensated participants. No standard is prescribed for satisfying this test. However, a flexible benefit plan providing health benefits can elect to satisfy a "safe-harbor" provision if the contribution for all participants is either (1) the same as the cost of the health coverage chosen by the majority of highly compensated participants (similarly situated) or (2) at least 75 percent of the highest cost health coverage chosen by any similarly situated participant. Benefits or contributions in excess of these amounts must be uniformly proportional to compensation. Also, for these two tests a highly compensated employee is: (1) an officer of the employer, (2) a 5 percent owner, and (3) any employee who is "highly compensated."

Concentration Test

The third test, known as the concentration test, limits the benefits actually provided to "key" employees to no more than 25 percent of the aggregate benefits provided to all employees under the plan. For this test, "key" employees include: (1) 5 percent owners, (2) officer earning more than

$45,000 (indexed), (3) the 10 employees who own the largest interest in the employer and who earn more than $30,000 (indexed), and (4) 1 percent owners earning more than $150,000.

Additional Requirements

Other Section 125 requirements are the following.

• *Permissible Benefits*. Only *qualified* benefits, as defined in Section 125 and regulations, may be included in a flexible benefit arrangement. Permissible benefits include cash, Section 401(k) deferrals, medical expense benefits, dental expense benefits, employee group life insurance, disability income, time off, dependent care, and any other benefit permitted under regulations. Taxable benefits (for example, financial counseling) are considered to be the equivalent of cash and may be included in the flexible arrangement if such benefits are either purchased with after-tax employee contributions or are included in the gross income of the employees who elect the coverage.

• *Excluded Benefits*. Benefits that are not permissible include any other form of deferred compensation, educational assistance, statutory fringe benefits, scholarships, and fellowships.

• *Participant Elections*. A participant's choice must be made before the beginning of the plan year and must be irrevocable for the year unless the plan permits changes in the case of a "change in family status" such as marriage, separation, divorce, death, birth or adoption of a child, loss or commencement of employment by a spouse, change in job status of the employee or spouse, and any significant change in health care coverage of the employee or spouse by reason of change in employment. Any change must be consistent with the event that permits the change to be made. Change may also be made if a third party such as an insurer significantly changes the cost of the plan or if an insurer terminates or significantly cuts back benefits.

• *Spending Account Rules*. If a flexible spending account is maintained (for health care or dependent-day-care expenses), additional rules must be observed. A separate account must be maintained for each eligible benefit and there can be no commingling of assets, nor can there be a transfer of assets from one account to another. Amounts not utilized by the end of the plan year must be forfeited by employees, although they are permitted to share in a per capita reallocation of such forfeitures among all employees. Except for dependent day care, the full amount of coverage chosen must be available for reimbursement to the employees from the beginning of the plan year even though not yet contributed. Any claims against a spending account must be substantiated by a provider statement, and the employee must verify that the expense involved has not been otherwise reimbursed.

Section 505—Voluntary Employees' Beneficiary Associations

In order for a VEBA to retain its tax exemption under Section 501(c)(9), *any plan* of which it is a part must comply with the nondiscrimination provisions of Section 505. (An exception from this requirement exists for a VEBA that is part of a plan maintained pursuant to a collective bargaining agreement.)

A plan meets the requirements of Section 505 only if: (1) each class of benefits under the plan is provided for a classification of employees that is set forth in the plan and found by the Treasury not to be discriminatory in favor of highly compensated employees, *and* (2) no class of benefits discriminates in favor of highly compensated employees. The employer may elect to treat two or more plans as one plan for testing purposes.

In the case of any benefit that has its own statutory nondiscrimination rules, the above discrimination rules do not apply. The nondiscrimination requirements of the VEBA for such benefit will be treated as having been met only if the nondiscrimination rules applicable to that benefit are satisfied. Thus, for example, it will be necessary for Section 79 to be met with respect to group life insurance and for Section 105 to be met with respect to a self-insured medical reimbursement plan included in the VEBA if the VEBA is to enjoy a tax-exempt status.

An additional requirement is that a VEBA is discriminatory if any benefit provided through it (other than group life insurance) is based upon compensation in excess of $200,000 (indexed). As a result of this provision, many employers have elected to exclude long-term disability and AD&D coverage from their VEBAs.

The definition of *highly compensated employee* for Section 505 is the same as the one used for qualified pension and profit-sharing plans—that is, any employee who: (1) is a 5 percent owner, (2) receives annual compensation in excess of $75,000 (indexed), (3) receives annual compensation in excess of $50,000 (indexed) and is in the group consisting of the top 20 percent of employees when ranked by compensation, *or* (4) is an officer and receives compensation greater than 50 percent of the $90,000 (indexed) Section 415 limit for defined benefit plans.

The excludable employees for purposes of the Section 505 nondiscrimination rules are (1) employees who have not completed three years of service, (2) employees who have not attained age 21, (3) seasonal employees or less-than-half-time employees, (4) employees covered by a collective bargaining agreement, and (5) nonresident aliens with no earned income from the employer that is income from sources within the United States.

Section 162—COBRA Health Care Coverage Continuation

The Consolidated Omnibus Budget Reconciliation Act of 1985 amended the IRC and ERISA to require that health care coverage be available to employees (and their dependents) under employer-sponsored plans for a limited period of time after the coverage might otherwise terminate. Since then, these rules have been amended four times. These requirements generally apply to all employers with 20 or more employees.

In general, each "qualified beneficiary" who would otherwise lose health care coverage caused by a "qualifying event" must be given the opportunity to continue coverage during the applicable "continuation periods." A "qualified beneficiary" is the employee, the employee's spouse, and the employee's children if they were covered by the plan immediately prior to the qualifying event. A "qualifying event" is:

- The death of the employee.
- The employee's termination of employment (except for gross misconduct).
- A reduction in the employee's hours.
- The divorce or legal separation of the employee and his or her spouse.
- Eligibility for Medicare coverage.
- The cessation of a child's eligibility as a dependent.
- The reduction, loss, or subsequent elimination of retiree medical coverage one year before or after the beginning of an employer's bankruptcy proceeding.

The "continuation period" is 18 months if the qualifying event is termination of employment or reduction in hours; otherwise, it is 36 months. In addition, coverage must be available for up to 29 months for individuals determined by Social Security to be disabled at the time of the employee's termination of employment or reduction in hours.

The coverage provided must be identical to the coverage provided for active employees who have not had a qualifying event. The election period during which a qualified beneficiary may elect to continue coverage is the 60-day period following the day coverage is terminated or the day notification of eligibility is received, whichever is later. The beneficiary may be charged up to 102 percent of the cost of the coverage. This limit is raised to 150 percent of the cost for certain disabled individuals for months 19 through 29. A plan administrator who fails to give proper notice may be subject to a penalty of up to $100 a day for each day of the failure.

TAXATION OF CONTRIBUTIONS AND BENEFITS

In reviewing the federal tax law as it relates to the taxation of welfare plans, it is helpful to consider several aspects:

- The taxation of employer contributions.
- The taxation of benefit payments.
- The taxation of income on reserves held under the plan.
- The deductibility of employer contributions.
- The treatment of employee contributions.
- The imposition of excise taxes.

For most of these aspects it is also helpful to consider them in terms of the type of benefit, and this is the approach of the following discussion. It should be noted that for some aspects, the tax treatment depends upon whether the plan meets the qualification and/or nondiscrimination requirements of various IRC sections.

Taxation of Employer Contributions

The taxation of employer contributions for welfare plan benefits is quite favorable to employees. Employer contributions for health care coverage are not taxable to employees regardless of whether the plan is insured or self-insured, and in the case of a self-insured plan, regardless of whether it meets the nondiscrimination requirements of Section 105(h). Nor are employer contributions for disability income and accidental death and dismemberment coverage taxable to employees, even for plans that discriminate in favor of key or highly compensated employees.

The major exception is that employer contributions for group life insurance in excess of $50,000 are taxable to the employee (or retiree). The amount that is reportable as income is determined under Section 79 of the IRC and under a table prepared by the IRS (see Table 50–1), but the amount otherwise reportable is reduced by any after-tax employee contributions—including amounts the employee might have contributed for the first $50,000 of term coverage.

An exception to this is that an employee will not be taxed on employer contributions for group life insurance if the employee has named a tax-exempt charity as beneficiary.

If a group life insurance plan is discriminatory, all key employees lose the $50,000 exclusion and have imputed income for all employer-provided coverage. Further, this imputed income is determined using the "actual cost" of the coverage if it is higher than the Section 79 rates published by the IRS. Non-key employees, however, are not affected if a group life insurance plan is discriminatory. They continue to have the $50,000 exclusion, and any imputed income is determined under the IRS rates.

If a flexible benefit plan fails to meet the nondiscrimination requirement tests of Section 125, "highly compensated" or "key" employees,

TABLE 50–1
Reportable Income per $1,000 of Coverage Under Nondiscriminatory Group Life Insurance

Age Bracket	Reportable Income (monthly)
Under 30	$ .08
30–34	.09
35–39	.11
40–44	.17
45–49	.29
50–54	.48
55–59	.75
60–64	1.17
65–69	2.17
70 and above	3.76

as the case may be, will have to include as taxable income the value of all benefits they could have received in taxable form. No other employees, however, will be affected by a plan's failure to meet these tests. Also, if a flexible benefit plan fails to comply with the Section 125 requirements (other than the nondiscrimination rules), the doctrine of constructive receipt will apply, and *all* employees will have to include as taxable income the amounts they could have received in cash—even if their choices were for "nontaxable" benefits.

Taxation of Benefit Payments

Whether a group life insurance plan meets or fails to meet the nondiscrimination tests has no effect on how the actual benefits paid are taxed. Group life insurance proceeds that are received in a lump sum are free of income tax. If paid in installments, the portion of each payment representing interest paid by the insurer is taxable under the annuity rules of Section 72. Also, the proceeds are included in the employee's gross estate for federal estate tax purposes unless the employee assigned all incidents of ownership at least three years prior to death.

All insured health plan benefits are income tax free. The same is true for self-insured employer health plan benefits if the plan is nondiscriminatory. If a self-insured employer health plan is discriminatory, benefits received by nonhighly compensated individuals are income tax free, but some or all of the reimbursements received by highly compensated individuals may be included in their gross income. If the plan fails the eligibility test, the amount that is counted as income to a highly compensated employee is the amount he or she received under the plan that is attributable to employer contributions, multiplied by a fraction—the numerator of which is the total amount reimbursed during that plan year to all highly compensated participants, and the denominator of which is the total amount reimbursed during the plan year to all participants. If the plan fails the benefits test, all amounts received under the discriminatory features of the plan that are attributable to employer contributions are included in the income of highly compensated participants. In any event, benefits attributable to an employee's contributions are not included in the employee's income.

Employer-provided disability-income benefits are taxable as income. Benefits attributable to after-tax employee contributions are income tax free. It should be noted, however, that before-tax employee contributions—by way of salary reduction—are considered *employer* contributions and will result in the disability income benefit being taxable.

Taxation of Income on Plan Reserves

Some welfare plans hold assets or reserves to pay for future benefits. These reserves may be held for a number of purposes such as incurred but unreported claims, claims in process, and the like. Amounts so held are credited with investment income (either interest declared by an insurance company or actual income earned by assets held in trust). Provided that the reserves do not exceed a prescribed level and that certain other requirements are met, this investment income is generally free from income tax (to the employer or to the trust). Otherwise, it is taxed as unrelated business income.

Reserves that are actuarially reasonable are acceptable. An actuarial certification is required by the IRS if reserves exceed certain safe-harbor limits. In determining safe-harbor limits, reserves for benefits that exceed certain amounts are excluded even though the higher benefits may be included in the plan. The safe-harbor limits and the excluded benefits are shown in Table 50–2.

Additional amounts may be held for life insurance and medical expense benefits for retirees if additional requirements are met. These requirements are that separate accounts must be maintained for key employees, and that their benefits must be paid from such accounts.

TABLE 50–2
IRS Limitations on Welfare Plan Reserves

Type of Benefit	Reserve Limit	Excluded Benefit
Life insurance	To be determined by IRS under regulations	Taxable benefits (in excess of $50,000) for retirees
Disability income	Short-term plans: 17.5% of last year's claims; long-term plans: to be determined by IRS under regulations	Excess of the benefit over the lesser of 75% of highest three-year average pay or Section 415 limit for defined benefit plans
Medical	35% of last year's costs	None

Further, no amounts may be reserved in these accounts for discriminatory benefits or for group life insurance in excess of $50,000, and funding of these accounts must be on a level basis with no assumptions as to future increases in health-care costs. Finally, and most importantly, income on reserves held for postretirement health care (but not life insurance) is taxable to the employer or trust, even when the above requirements are met and the coverage is nondiscriminatory.

Deductibility of Employer Contributions

Employer contributions to a welfare plan generally are deductible if they do not result in the payment of unreasonable compensation. An exception is that contributions to a special reserve for life insurance or medical benefits for retirees are not deductible if the plan is discriminatory.

The general rule for deductibility is that contributions cannot exceed: (1) benefits actually paid *plus* (2) additions to a reserve within the limits previously described *minus* (3) after-tax income on plan assets, including employee contributions. Contributions within this limit are deductible in the tax year in which the contribution is made. Excess contributions are deductible in subsequent years.

Treatment of Employee Contributions

Employees may make contributions to welfare plans on an after-tax basis. As previously noted, such contributions for group life insurance reduce the amounts otherwise taxable under Section 79 and, in the case of disability income benefits, provide a benefit that is free of income tax.

If a flexible benefit plan meets the requirements of Section 125, employee contributions for group life insurance, medical-expense benefits, and disability income may also be made by way of pay reduction— that is, on a before-tax basis. This is particularly advantageous for medical-expense coverage since otherwise taxable income is converted into tax-exempt income, thus saving the employee an amount equal to his or her marginal tax rate on the amount involved.

Following are some additional comments concerning before-tax employee contributions.

• Unlike the pay reductions permitted for Section 401(k) savings plans, amounts contributed on a pay-reduction basis for welfare plan benefits are not subject to FICA taxes by the employee, nor are they taken into account when determining the employee's Social Security benefits. For most employees, however, the value of the tax savings will more than offset any loss of Social Security benefits.

• The employer also receives a tax advantage for such before-tax employee contributions in that it, too, does not pay FICA (or FUTA) taxes on the amount involved.

• Unless employee contribution rates are higher than the IRS rates published under Section 79, it rarely makes sense to make before-tax contributions for group life insurance in excess of $50,000.

• Disability income benefits attributable to after-tax employee contributions are free from income tax. If these contributions are made on a before-tax basis, the benefits are taxable.

• Even though an employee reduces his or her pay to make contributions under Section 125, other employee benefits may be based on gross compensation prior to the pay reduction. However, the employee's net pay, after the reduction, is used to determine contribution and benefit limitations for qualified pension and profit-sharing plans under Section 415 of the IRC.

Excise Taxes

A recent development in the field of employee benefits has been the imposition of excise taxes on employers (and sometimes employees) as a means of ensuring compliance with the tax law. Most of these excise taxes are associated with pension and profit-sharing plans qualified under Section 401 of the IRC. A few also apply to welfare benefit plans.

A 100 percent employer excise tax will be imposed on:

• The value of medical or life insurance benefits paid to a retired key employee unless paid from a separate account as required by law.

• The value of medical or life insurance benefits paid under a discriminatory plan funded through a welfare benefit fund such as a tax-exempt trust under Section 501(c)(9) of the IRC.

• Amounts reverting to the benefit of an employer from a welfare benefit fund.

A second area where an excise tax may be imposed on an employer concerns the COBRA requirements for the availability of continued medical expense coverage in certain situations. An employer may face an excise tax of $100 per day for each beneficiary for whom there is a failure to comply with this law. The maximum excise tax under this provision for a year is the lesser of (a) $50,000 or (b) 10 percent of the employer's group health plan expenses for the prior year.

A third area where an excise tax may be imposed involves employer plans that fail to pay their benefits (as primary payers), before Medicare pays, for certain active and disabled individuals who are also entitled to Medicare benefits. This tax is set at 25 percent of the employer's expenses for all group health plans to which the employer contributes.

THE FUTURE

Federal tax law regarding welfare plans is inconsistent and complex. No rational basis exists for having different nondiscrimination rules for each type of benefit, nor for the differing definitions of the ''key'' and ''highly compensated'' groups involved and the differing groups of employees that may be excluded when performing the various tests.

When the Tax Reform Act of 1986 was passed, it included a provision (Section 89) that would have adopted uniform testing provisions and requirements for all types of employee welfare plans. To that extent, Section 89 would have accomplished some good. Unfortunately, the approach encompassed by Section 89 was unworkable, and in response to public pressure, this section of the law was repealed. As a result, the pre-tax reform requirements, those described in this chapter, were reinstated. The notion of standard nondiscrimination requirements, however, is still alive, and it seems reasonable to expect that another attempt at unification will occur during the 1990s.

PART 10

EMPLOYEE BENEFIT PLAN ADMINISTRATION

An overview of the principles of administration of employee benefit plans is presented in the first chapter of this part. Chapter 51 provides a look at the types of administrators of group welfare plans with special attention to administrators under the Taft-Hartley Act and the Employee Retirement Income Security Act of 1974 (ERISA).

Chapter 52 deals with developing plan specifications after reevaluating a group insurance program. The steps in the process from determining whether a program should be rebid through the screening of new bidders is covered. The analysis of group insurance bids and the selection of an appropriate insurance carrier and/or service organization also are analyzed.

CHAPTER 51

PRINCIPLES OF EMPLOYEE BENEFIT PLAN ADMINISTRATION

Edward E. Mack, Jr.
Mary A. Carroll

To the average plan participant, complex issues of plan design, costing, and funding seem mysterious and perhaps irrelevant—problems for the decision makers in the executive suite or on the board of trustees to ponder. The participant's questions are more practical: Am I covered? How do I file a claim? How much of my claim will be paid? How long will I have to wait for payment? Just what does this plan do for me? Answering these questions—and establishing systems to ensure these questions *can* be answered promptly, accurately, efficiently, and in ways that help plan participants understand their benefits—is the central objective of benefit plan administration.

"Administration," as discussed in this chapter, is not necessarily performed by the person(s) defined by the Employee Retirement Income Security Act of 1974 (ERISA) as an "administrator":

   (i) the person specifically so designated by the terms of the instrument under which the plan is operated;

  (ii) if an administrator is not so designated, the plan sponsor; or

 (iii) in the case of a plan for which an administrator is not designated and a plan sponsor cannot be identified, such other person as the Secretary may by regulation prescribe (Section 3, 353(16)(A)).

The "administrator," under this definition, would typically hold discretionary authority and responsibility under the plan and serve in a fiduciary capacity. Throughout this chapter, however, "administration" is viewed as the *implementation* of decisions—on plan design, costing, funding, and any other discretionary issues—made by the plan sponsor or other plan fiduciaries.

Administration includes all the activities that translate elaborate proposals, complicated cash-flow analyses, and labyrinthine contract language into the daily operating reality that is the participants' only point of contact with the plan. Participants evaluate their benefit plans largely, if not entirely, on the basis of their satisfaction (or dissatisfaction) with the plans' day-to-day administration. Thus, it is essential that the plan sponsor pay as much attention to the *administration* of its benefit plans as to their structure and funding.

Administrative functions may be performed by employees of the plan sponsor (the personnel or benefits department of a corporation, for example, or the salaried administrator(s) of a jointly administered Taft-Hartley fund), or by firms specializing in this field (contract or third-party administrators, banks, benefit consultants, insurance brokers, or insurance companies). All administrative functions may be performed by a single entity, or these functions may be delegated to several different providers.

No matter what structure is selected, those who manage the administration of a benefit plan must be prepared to perform certain basic functions: to determine participants' eligibility for coverage; to communicate the nature and impact of plan provisions to participants and their families, plan advisers, and government agencies; to adjudicate claims for benefits; and to maintain the accounting and data processing systems that enable them to perform these functions.

The adoption of a flexible benefit plan adds an additional layer of administrative procedures to those just mentioned and can, in some cases, affect the administration of other employer plans even though they are not part of it. Flexible benefit plan administration is beyond the scope of this chapter and is discussed in Chapter 30 of the *Handbook*.

DETERMINATION OF ELIGIBILITY

Determining who is eligible for the plan and its benefits is the first requirement, and a number of plan provisions interact to affect eligibility. If a health plan, for example, does not require employee contributions, all employees within the eligible class(es) are covered; if employees contribute to the cost of coverage, their election of the benefit and payment of the required contribution must be verified. Health programs frequently delay the effective date of coverage until the employee is actively at work (or until a dependent ceases to be confined in a hospital or at home under the care of a doctor); if such a provision applies, eligibility cannot be verified without determining whether the individual has satisfied this requirement. Many employers impose an eligibility waiting period of 1 to 3 months (and may impose an even longer waiting period, such as 6 to 12 months, for certain benefits); the administrator must establish systems to ensure that new employees' protection becomes effective after the applicable waiting period. A retirement plan participant's ultimate benefit may rise or fall depending on the accuracy of the administrator's eligibility records.

Care must be taken when nonretirement coverage terminates—for an employee, a dependent, a class of employees, or the entire covered group—since claims incurred before termination are a liability of the plan, while those incurred after the termination date generally should be denied. Where eligibility for plan benefits continues *after* termination of employment—under COBRA or other federal or state mandates, or under a voluntary extension provided by the plan sponsor—the administrator's eligibility determination function becomes even more complex.

The plan administrator also generally is responsible for determining individuals' eligibility for special plan provisions, such as conversion privileges or waiver of premium. A pension or profit-sharing plan administrator generally is responsible for maintaining the records that permit determination of participants' years of service for vesting and benefit accrual purposes as well as the applicability of other plan provisions.

Special Problems

Employers frequently assign responsibility for eligibility verification to their personnel departments. Large firms with multiple locations may need one or more employees at each plant or office to maintain accurate eligibility records, together with a headquarters staff to coordinate the eligibility provisions of various plans and assist in resolving questions and disputes. Within a smaller company, eligibility determination may be only one of the several responsibilities of a personnel or administration department employee.

For most plans—and especially for multiple and multiemployer benefit plans—a second eligibility verification will be made by the insurance company or third-party administrator that handles claims for the plan. This function is particularly important in the administration of multiemployer plans in industries (like construction) where participants change employers frequently. If no *single* employer can certify that an individual has worked enough hours, days, or weeks to earn eligibility for plan benefits, it is vital that the administrative office maintain comprehensive and accurate data on participants' service with *all* contributing employers.

COMMUNICATIONS

Effective communication of plan benefits to participants and their families is essential if the plan is to achieve its objectives. In establishing a benefit program, most employers hope to attract and retain productive employees and to maintain good morale. If the program is poorly communicated, however, it is likely to be unappreciated and even ignored until a claim arises; plan provisions may lower, rather than improve, employee morale if claims must be denied or reduced. This *internal* need for benefit communication is matched by an *external* mandate: all benefit plans subject to ERISA must be communicated "in language calculated to be understood by the average plan participant." The passage of ERISA has stimulated a major investment in improved communication techniques by large employers, benefit consultants, brokers, and insurers; since 1974, benefit communications has been a "growth industry."

Communicating with Participants and Their Families

ERISA established minimum standards for benefit plan communications with participants in specific documents such as the summary plan description and summary annual report. Larger companies frequently supplement these plan documents with employee meetings, multimedia presentations, individual benefit statements, and other printed material designed to gain for benefit plans the visibility that their place in the expense budget demands; they feel employee understanding is essential to their plans' effective operation. (For a detailed discussion of benefit plan communications, see Chapters 53 and 54 of the *Handbook*.) While these formal modes of communication serve important legal and practical purposes, perhaps equally important to plan participants is their direct contact—on the telephone and through correspondence—with the people who administer the plan. The administrative office answers participants' questions about their eligibility and the plan's benefits, assists them in filing claims and appealing claim denials, and explains how specific payments were calculated. The skill and empathy of the administrative staff in handling these communications are essential to the participants' sense of security and satisfaction with their benefits.

Communicating with Health Care Providers

In underwriting coverage and processing claims, an administrator often needs to communicate directly with hospitals and other health care providers. The most frequent contact of this type undoubtedly is verification-of-benefits calls or letters from hospitals, which seek to ascertain what portion of the participant's charges will be paid by the plan. Accuracy in confirming benefits is particularly vital in parts of the country where carrier–provider agreements may require a plan to pay the promised benefits even when coverage is incorrectly confirmed.

In addition to benefit confirmations, an administrator's communications with providers frequently include requests for additional information about participants' medical histories and about specific charges, audits of large or complicated claims, and direct payment of assigned benefits. A plan sponsor's cost-containment or case-management program can produce a near-adversary relationship—for example, when a provider's recommendation is questioned. In all these areas, an administrative staff that thoroughly understands providers' operations and concerns is likely to provide more effective service to plan participants.

Communicating with Other Plan Advisers and Government Agencies

The administrator's control of plan data establishes an important information flow from the administrative office to the various professionals who provide services to the plan, as well as to the plan sponsor. Actuaries, brokers, and consultants need detailed information on participation, losses, expenses, and historical trends in order to evaluate the plan's status from time to time. As a surrogate for both the plan sponsor and, in insured plans, the insurance company, the administrator must provide sponsor and carrier with frequent reports comprehensive enough to convince these entities that the functions they have delegated are being performed properly. The administrator must provide the plan's (or employer's) attorney with details of any situation that may produce legal action against the plan or its sponsor and frequently works with counsel in analyzing the impact of federal and state legislation. Auditors, too, must depend upon the cooperation of the administrator in performing their examination of the plan's financial condition.

Finally, most benefit plans are required to file reports with a variety of government agencies. As statutory requirements change in such areas as nondiscrimination and vesting, for example, administrative systems must be revised to capture and summarize effectively the statistics needed to demonstrate the plan's compliance with the new standards.

Although most of the administrator's communications with the plan sponsor, professional advisers, and government agencies are invisible to participants, they are essential to effective functioning of the plan and are an important part of the administrator's overall responsibilities.

Special Problems

In controlling plan communication, the administrative office must also ensure plan privacy. Benefit plan records necessarily include information about individual participants that could be abused. Public concern about privacy has produced new standards to which administrators must conform. These laws, as well as the administrator's basic responsibility to plan participants, demand that potentially sensitive personal information about individuals be handled on a strict "need to know" basis.

Large employers can take advantage of economies of scale and centralization in developing sophisticated benefit communication programs; jointly administered plans frequently supplement required plan documents with articles in union publications and presentations at union meetings. Effective communications may be most difficult for multiple-employer plans—association-sponsored programs and multiple-employer trusts with minimal communications budgets and covering primarily small employers. For such plans particularly, the quality of participants' day-to-day contact with the administrative office is likely to be central to their satisfaction with the plan. And at the heart of that contact are participants' claims for benefits.

PROCESSING OF CLAIMS

Some types of employee benefit plans—for example, group term life insurance or a retirement program covering younger workers—can operate successfully for years without ever paying a claim. Their value lies in their *promise* to pay, and participants understand that there may be no current claims activity. Most employees judge their benefit program, however, by those portions that *pay* rather than promise to pay—by its handling of the medical, dental, and disability claims they submit from time to time. However effective an administrator's functioning in other areas may be, its claim processing must satisfy participants' expectations if the program is to achieve the sponsor's objectives.

In reviewing claims, the administrator has obligations to many masters. The demands of the plan sponsor, insurer, provider, and participant compete for the administrator's attention and may produce different treatment of specific claims. The administrator generally must rely on the plan document (and the insurance contract, if the plan is insured), together with any deviations adopted by the plan sponsor (and agreed upon with the carrier, where appropriate) in resolving doubtful situations. At the same time, the administrative staff must be diplomatic and empathetic in working with participants and health care providers. The administrator is a "middleman," balancing the desire of participants and providers for speedy, complete payment against the plan's requirement—of vital interest to the sponsor (and insurer)—that claims be investigated carefully and adjudicated in accordance with all relevant plan provisions. In the conflict between speed and accuracy, the administrative office must opt for accuracy, working hard meanwhile to help participants understand why investigative delay is necessary. An administrator who is able to handle effectively these multiple demands of claim processing has a head start toward success in other areas of administration as well.

Retirement Plans

In pension plans, payments generally are issued automatically once the administrator has reviewed the participant's eligibility for benefits and determined the benefit payable based on work history and plan provisions. Even here, however, it is essential that the administrative office establish checking procedures to prevent issuance of benefit payments to deceased or ineligible individuals. In addition, a defined benefit plan's sponsor may provide for an automatic or *ad hoc* adjustment in benefits for current retirees; when this occurs, the administrator must apply the adjustment accurately and consistently.

Health Protection

Medical claims probably are the most difficult to adjudicate because of the number of factors involved in determining the availability and amount of benefits for submitted charges. The administrative staff must determine whether the claimant is a covered individual, what benefits are in force, when the claimant's coverage became effective, and whether any special restrictions or exclusions apply. It must analyze the availability of other coverage—under government programs including Medicare, workers' compensation, and occupational disability laws as well as other insurance programs—and the effect, if any, of such duplicate coverage on the plan's liability for the charges submitted.

In reviewing specific charges, the administrator's claim specialists must make sure that the expenses themselves are eligible for payment under the plan and that they were incurred at a time when the relevant coverage was in force for the individual. The plan document must be reviewed for any exclusions or limitations that may apply; "preexisting condition" provisions require special care at this point in claim adjudication. Proper investigation of medical claims is complex and often time-consuming; the examiner must carefully compare the claim submitted to eligibility records and to the plan document and may seek additional required information from other administrative records, from providers, and from the claimant before a single calculation can be made. This attention to detail is essential, however, in order to ensure that only legitimate claims are paid under the plan.

Once an examiner has verified that the submitted expenses are *eligible* for benefits under the plan, he or she must apply all relevant plan provisions to determine the *amount* that should be paid. Unless first-dollar benefits are available for these charges, the file must be checked for possible satisfaction of the plan's deductible and coinsurance provisions. If the plan includes "first-dollar" coverage or internal limits for particular types of treatment, the applicability of these provisions to the submitted charges must be reviewed. If the plan's benefits are provided on a "usual, reasonable, and customary" basis, the administrative office must compare the charges submitted with the appropriate statistical data. Whether benefits are scheduled or unscheduled, the examiner should analyze each claim to see if the claimant's treatment, including the duration of any hospital confinement, is consistent with the diagnosis indicated, perhaps recommending an audit of the provider's billing if there appear to be serious discrepancies.

Life and Accidental Death and Dismemberment (AD&D) Coverage

In some respects, death claims would seem to be the least complicated claims to adjust, since the occurrence of the covered event can be
easily verified by reviewing certified death certificates, newspaper obit-
uaries, and other documents. Although life and accidental death plan
provisions may affect the availability of benefits for a particular claimant,
and the deceased participant's file must be reviewed to ascertain the
proper beneficiary, most death claims can be processed straightfor-
wardly. It is in this area of claim administration, however, that insurance
companies have been most reluctant to delegate responsibility, generally insisting that, even if an outside administrator reviews the submission and file and prepares the payment authorization, the draft itself
must be issued by the carrier. The relatively large dollar amounts payable for death claims, the complexity of probate law, and the special
legal problems involved in adjudicating AD&D claims are the major
reasons offered in support of maintaining insurer control of these claim
payments.

Loss-of-Income Protection

Disability-income claims also are frequently a source of concern for the
plan sponsor and/or insurer. The loss itself is difficult to prove (or
disprove), the plan's potential liability may be quite large, and the
combined disability benefits available under employment-related, Social
Security, and other plans may be sufficient to discourage claimants from
returning to work. Therefore, careful investigation is essential when a
claim is first submitted, recertification of disability by the claimant's
physician frequently is required, and carriers providing long-term disability benefits often review claims on a regular schedule, using service
bureau investigators or their own employees to confirm the continued
qualification of the claimant for plan benefits.

Special Problems

Self-administration of employee benefit plans may be attractive to large
employers because it appears to give the corporate staff more direct control
over plan costs and services. Other large employers prefer to retain an

outside third-party administrator (TPA) (or to have claims processed by insurance company employees) because of the experience and resources available to the plan through its carrier or TPA relationship. This approach also may direct employee dissatisfaction with claim denials away from the employer and toward a third party. Multiemployer plans frequently employ a staff of salaried administrators, including experienced claim examiners. Other jointly administered plans delegate claim administration to a TPA or an insurance carrier. In both corporate and Taft-Hartley plans, claim administration may sometimes be subject to internal pressures (from a key manager in a corporate plan or a trustee in a jointly administered plan) to handle some claims more favorably than would be justified by the plan's provisions. While the plan sponsor may intend for some provisions to be enforced less rigidly than others, the administrator must use extreme care in making exceptions to the provisions of the legal document that governs the plan's operations.

A significant problem in processing claims for multiple-employer plans (whose participants are, for the most part, employees of smaller employers) is that, with no one on the employer's staff who is really qualified to assist employees, many claims are incomplete or otherwise unacceptable when first submitted. Claim examiners for these plans must be especially patient in explaining to participants the reasons for various requirements. A similar problem may exist in the administration of some industrywide Taft-Hartley funds; here, too, participants may not have ready access to advice in submitting claims (although union trustees and business agents may be able to provide some assistance).

Because ERISA defines in considerable detail participants' rights when their claims are denied, controls are needed to ensure that the administrator's benefit explanations, response time, and appeals procedures meet or exceed the law's minimum standards.

ACCOUNTING FOR PLAN FUNDS

In essence, an employee benefit plan is simply a flow of funds: dollars flow in from the employer (and from the employees if the plan is contributory), earn interest while they are held, and then flow out to pay benefits to participants and providers and to cover the plan's expenses. To control this flow, the administrator must establish accounting systems adequate to ensure the plan's monies are being used properly.

Larger plans, particularly those funded through a trust, generally maintain accounting systems parallel to those of other economic entities. The plan sponsor and/or trustee(s) regularly review financial statements for the plan. The administrative office maintains the general and subsidiary ledgers that are the basis for these statements, controls accounts payable and receivable and cash receipts and disbursements, and may be involved in tax reporting for the plan, its participants, and providers to whom benefits have been paid. If the plan is insured, the insurance carrier frequently requires detailed premium breakdowns from the administrator, who is sometimes also involved in claim-accounting functions and in commission accounting on plans marketed through a network of insurance agents or brokers.

Special Problems

In some respects, administrative accounting systems for large corporate benefit plans are fairly simple, since plan funds generally come from a single source. Even here, however, benefit expenses are likely to be charged to the corporation's profit centers on some equitable basis, and accounting systems must be established to handle this allocation. More complicated systems are required to control the billing and collection process for the hundreds of smaller firms that participate in multiple-employer or multi-employer plans, or for companies that maintain a dozen or more *different* benefit plans for various classes of salaried and hourly employees.

DATA PROCESSING

There are few areas of plan administration that cannot benefit from the application of flexible, thoughtfully designed data-processing systems. While a very small benefit plan can perhaps be handled effectively with manual systems, most life, health, disability, and retirement plans can provide faster, more efficient service to participants and more accurate information for the plan sponsor, advisers, and insurers if the administrative office can rely on an appropriate level of computer support.

In designing data-processing systems for benefit-plan administration, administrative managers and systems analysts often work together to establish the system's parameters, define the database and reporting requirements and backup and retention criteria, and analyze methods of developing or converting data to build the system's master files. This approach has the advantage of matching the administrator's knowledge of the details of the plan's benefit provisions and limitations, rate structure, and other variables with the systems analyst's expertise in solving information-handling problems through computer hardware and software.

Special Problems

The objectives of the plan sponsor generally determine which aspect of the administrative operation will be automated first. In an industrywide Taft-Hartley welfare or pension plan, eligibility record keeping may be high on the list because of the errors and expense that result from manual tracking of participants' relatively frequent shifts from one employer to another. Large employers may be most interested in establishing a database that permits effective cost control and analysis of health-care-cost trends. Insurance carriers also are likely to be vitally concerned with information of this type. Because of the number of firms involved, multiple-employer plans generally require substantial computer support in the billing and collection process. The volume of paper generated in processing claims— and the impact of normal human error on benefit calculation—encourages administrators of all types of plans to develop or purchase software to allow computer adjudication of many types of claims.

For most employee benefit plans, more information and more efficient systems are almost always better. The only significant restriction on the value of more sophisticated reports and analyses and more automated operations is the investment required to produce them.

SUMMARY

Though employee benefit plans existed before World War II, they have had a significant impact on the American economy and the American public only during the past 50 years. Their administration—like their benefit structure, funding, and every other aspect—has changed substantially during this period, and the pattern seems likely to accelerate in the coming decade. No matter how much benefit plans may change, however, it seems clear that cost-efficient administration that meets employee needs and achieves the objectives of the plan sponsor will continue to be a vital element of effective plans.

CHAPTER 52

REVIEWING AND REBIDDING
GROUP INSURANCE PROGRAMS

David R. Klock
Sharon S. Graham
Joseph Casey

At different times and for a variety of reasons, an employer may wish to reevaluate its group insurance program and test the marketplace by obtaining bids on its benefit program. This process provides an opportunity to review how well the program meets benefit objectives. The reevaluation process typically consists of the following steps:

1. Determine if the program should be rebid.
2. Review plan design.
3. Select appropriate financing techniques.
4. Draft specifications for either negotiated placement or competitive bid.
5. Undertake prebid screening.
6. Analyze bids and select insurer or other provider.
7. Complete final negotiations with selected provider.
8. Implement new program.

WHY REBID?

Some employers (especially government units) believe that frequent bidding of their group insurance plans results in the lowest possible cost outlay. This contention generally is a misconception. Organizations that too often enter the employee benefits marketplace face the risk of being considered unstable or capricious consumers who frequently seek bids and/or change carriers. Insurers, knowing an account is unlikely to prove profitable unless it remains with the insurer for several years and thus allows the insurer to recover certain front-end costs associated with the installation of a group insurance plan, may shy away from an organization with this reputation. The organization soon discovers that the number of cost-competitive insurers or other service organizations willing to bid for its business declines dramatically.

This is not to imply that the rebidding of an employee benefits package is seldom advisable. There are several excellent reasons why organizations may wish to enter the reevaluation process. The following discussion covers the most important considerations in this decision.

Irreconcilable Management Dissatisfaction

The executives of a firm occasionally become disenchanted or frustrated with their insurance adviser and/or with their insurance company. The reasons for such dissatisfaction should be thoroughly investigated prior to any decision to rebid the coverage. Corrective actions and/or repair of poor communication lines may be a viable alternative. If, however, the credibility of the current insurer or adviser is beyond repair, rebidding will undoubtedly prove necessary.

Legal Requirements

Many government entities are required by law or by administrative resolution to rebid their insurance programs periodically. However, many experts believe a change in the regulations may be appropriate if rebidding is required more frequently than once every five to seven years. [1] The same guidelines apply to nongovernmental employers. Frequent rebidding should be avoided.

---

[1] Bernard M. Brown and Charles F. Moody, Jr., "Insurance Bidding and Specifications," *Risk Management Reports* 5, no. 5, p. 14.

Underwriting Cycle

Many insurance markets undergo underwriting cycles, in which periods of very restrained markets and conservative pricing/underwriting decisions follow more aggressive and very competitive pricing/underwriting decisions. Some employee benefit managers or risk managers try to take advantage of a perceived period of lower costs and/or expanded underwriting capacity by rebidding their insurance programs at that time.

Adviser Recommendations

Agents, brokers, and consultants all act as advisers to employers on their benefit plans. For simplicity, the term *adviser* is used in this chapter. The adviser is responsible for maintaining a high level of knowledge regarding the availability and relative competitiveness of alternative insurance carriers. When an organization has confidence in its adviser, his or her advice should be given serious consideration. If this confidence is lacking, a reevaluation of the relationship with the adviser is in order. The employer should, however, be both skeptical of and interested in the advice of *commissioned* advisers not currently handling the account, as these advisers have a potential financial interest in rebidding the coverage.

Substantial Change in the Organization

Mergers, acquisitions, or rapid growth may mean that the nature of the organization has changed dramatically since the current group coverage was obtained. Such changes often result in a need for changes in plan design and can necessitate a level of service or expertise unavailable from the current insurer or service organization. This problem will be especially evident if the employer has developed significant foreign operations with many overseas employees, because international employee benefits management often requires unique skills and products. See Chapter 62 for a detailed discussion of international benefits.

Nonrenewal or Significant Change in Conditions or Cost

An employer clearly has no choice but to rebid if its current plan is canceled. Alternatively, rebidding may be needed if the current insurer has given notice that renewed coverage will be altered significantly so that a serious diminution of benefits will occur, since this would almost certainly result in reduced employee morale. A renewal price increase that the employer perceives to greatly exceed general market costs likewise should trigger a rebidding of the program.

Inadequate Service

The most important reason for changing insurance carriers (or advisers) is proof of an inadequate level of service. The key areas of service are timeliness, quality and expertise in cost-reduction analysis, review of all financing alternatives, and claims handling.

Significant Time since Last Market Test

A periodic market test of the relative competitiveness of the current insurance program is recommended regardless of current service levels. As mentioned previously, experts seem to hold that an appropriate rebidding cycle is five to seven years.

Changes in Plan Design

Finally, an employer may wish to rebid its plan in conjunction with a change to a flexible benefit plan or a managed-care alternative such as a triple-option plan.

PREPARATION FOR REBIDDING

Reviewing the Plan Design

Prior to writing bid specifications, the organization and its adviser should review carefully the current plan design. Benefit programs often evolve in a piecemeal and haphazard fashion with little or no consistent input for personnel goals, long-term cash-flow constraints, and employee equity. The bidding process provides an excellent opportunity to seriously evaluate plan design in light of other critical and evolving corporate goals. A set of suggested questions to be answered would include:

1. What is the employer's attitude toward group insurance? For example, are group insurance benefits viewed as traditional compensation for work provided, an incentive to increase employee productivity, and/or a benevolent reward?
2. How should the responsibility for economic security be shared by the employer and individual employees?
3. What effect should seniority, salary, or position have on the level of benefits?
4. What is the firm's present cash flow available for employee benefits, and what are the probabilities of future cash flows at various levels?
5. How important is "income leveling"?
6. What are the quantity and quality of the corporate staff who will be responsible for handling the details of a group insurance program?
7. Should an agent, broker, or consultant be used?
8. Does the firm have subsidiaries with unique benefit planning problems?
9. Is company management concerned enough about unionization or about attracting key employees to affect employee benefit design by type of employee?
10. How should changes (increases) in employee benefits be ranked with other changes (increases) in the total employee compensation package?
11. Should flexibility be built into the program to recognize the differences in needs and desires among employees?
12. How much attention should be given to the attitudes of employees when making changes?
13. Is the proposed plan design consistent with cost-control standards concerning plan objectives, eligibility, preexisting conditions, utilization of outpatient and home health care, second opinions on surgery, out-of-pocket and co-pay provisions, and preventive care in lieu of larger claims stemming from neglect?
14. How will the contributions of the employee benefit plan to the employer's benefit plan objectives be measured? How often?[2]

---

[2]For further discussion of this topic, see David R. Klock and Bruce Palmer, "Group Insurance and the Role of the Professional Life Underwriter," *CLU Journal* 33, no. 3 (July 1979), pp. 44–53.

15. Does the plan meet nondiscrimination tests?
16. What competitive pressures exist from the industry and/or region?

In addition to addressing these questions, the benefit planners will also wish to review experience data carefully in order to detect any areas where changes in the current benefits package might result in significant cost reductions and/or benefit improvements with little or no additional premium outlay or compromise in personnel goals. This in-depth statistical analysis of plan experience may lead, for example, to changes in the existing plan deductibles and/or the addition of new deductibles. Effective use of deductibles may reduce excessive utilization of certain medical services by creating a financial disincentive. Redesign of plan deductibles based on actual plan experience could help create one source of funds to be used for the expansion of benefits in more critical areas of potential catastrophic loss.

The effectiveness of the foregoing plan design analysis is dependent on both the quality of the loss data provided in periodic claims reports and the level of technical service provided by the outside adviser or by the insurer. If a satisfactory level of data or statistical assistance is not currently provided, this poor service emphasizes the need to rebid the coverage. New bid specifications should clearly communicate a request for periodic loss data analysis.

Selecting Financing Techniques

During the past several decades, numerous alternatives to the traditional methods of financing group employee benefits have been developed. These alternatives to a pure insurance arrangement include experience-rated plans, monthly experience arrangements, retrospective-premium agreements, minimum-premium plans, administrative-services-only (ASO) programs, multi-option programs, and various types of self-administered and/or self-funded plans. See Chapter 47 for a detailed discussion of alternative insured funding arrangements for employee benefit plans.

Prior to developing its bidding strategy, the employer (with help from its adviser) must decide on the financing or cash-flow method most compatible with its circumstances. The selection of certain financing alternatives will significantly influence the type of information solicited from bidders.

Negotiated Placement or Competitive Bid?

There are at least three methods of entry into the employee benefits insurance marketplace:

1. Negotiated placement with a single insurer or service organization.
2. Competitive bidding, with a public announcement that all qualified insurance companies may obtain bid specifications and submit proposals.
3. Closed bidding, in which only invited insurers are allowed to submit bids.

Negotiated placement is appropriate if the employer, on advice from a qualified adviser, is convinced it has identified an insurer that is very competitive in the class of group business to be purchased. By developing and maintaining strong rapport and communication with a few highly competitive insurers in each line of group coverage, a firm can often obtain underwriting or pricing concessions that may not be possible in a more open bid process. Personal contacts and commitment can be very important in periods when the underwriting cycle is to the employer's disadvantage. However, it often is possible to obtain many of these financial gains through a multistaged bidding process that eliminates ''nonqualified'' bidders. The bidding process does not preclude personal contact and negotiations.

Open competitive bidding typically is used only when required by law. For example, many government entities advertise the bidding of group insurance. In theory, an open-competitive-bid system creates the widest possible market survey. It can, however, significantly increase the cost of the bidding process as a result of the added cost associated with reviewing very weak or poorly presented proposals. Without some prescreening, the employer or its consultant may be forced to analyze numerous noncompetitive bids. Furthermore, many qualified bidders will not play in an open field because of possible misunderstanding and/or communication failures.

With a *closed or limited bidding process,* the employer and/or the adviser prescreens potential bidders. Only ''qualified'' bidders are allowed to obtain detailed bid specifications and to submit a proposal. Since bids are received from only a limited number of insurers, the employer retains the flexibility to negotiate the final contract. If a change of coverage or financing techniques is desired by the employer, this can be accomplished in the final negotiation stage rather than in an expensive rebidding process. Most corporate employers and a growing number of public employers use some form of closed, negotiated bidding.

Negotiated Placement

The negotiated-placement method of purchasing group coverage is also referred to as the *interview* method. This is because it consists of a series of preliminary interviews during which the list of several potential service organizations is narrowed to one. That organization is provided with detailed census information and is the only insurer or other service organization to submit a price quotation. Negotiated placement typically consists of several steps.

1. After informing the current insurer of a decision to consider a plan change, the employer or its adviser prescreens several insurers (including the current one). These insurers should be recommended by the adviser and/or by such reliable sources of information as other risk managers or employee benefits managers. Prescreening considerations include the financial solvency of the insurer, its service facilities, its reputation regarding cost, and the quality of its sales, administrative, and claims staffs. Prescreening is described in more detail in a later section of this chapter.

2. The decision makers select a few insurers or service organizations (perhaps four to six) from those that have been prescreened and provide these organizations with general information about the employer, its current group insurance program, and any changes it would like to see in the new plan. Each of these companies should be requested to prepare a brief report on the general approach, philosophy, and structure of its proposed group insurance program. The purpose of this step is to determine if the risk management philosophy of the proposed insurer or other service organization is compatible with that of the employer and if the organization has the expertise and capacity to handle the employer's unique needs.

3. The suggestions of the alternative insurers will be evaluated to select the one company with which the final details of the group insurance plan will be negotiated. This company alone will be provided with detailed loss, financial, and employee data. Furthermore, only this one insurer or service organization will submit a detailed bid on the desired group plan.

4. After receiving this bid, the employer will negotiate any necessary changes with the help of its adviser. Success at this point depends heavily on the competence of the adviser. If an employer wishes to use the negotiated placement method but lacks confidence in the technical skills of its adviser, an obvious preliminary step would be the selection of a new adviser. This process is similar to that for selecting an insurer. Should an employer believe it is incapable of selecting a highly qualified adviser, it will have an additional reason to prefer the bidding procedure for selecting an insurer or service organization.

PREPARATION OF BID SPECIFICATIONS

Assuming an employer wishes to use a multiple-insurer bidding process (either open or closed), rather than a negotiated placement with one insurer or other service organization, specifications must be designed and distributed to all qualified bidders. The specifications must deal with the role of any adviser, the coverage desired, and the financing method to be used. Bid specifications also must provide detailed underwriting data (employee census, paid losses, and so on.)

The employer could provide several insurers with broad guidelines as to the type of coverage and then request proposals from these insurers. In fact, this is frequently what happens. The requests often are made verbally, and the specifications may be so broad that different insurers propose significantly different benefit designs. The resulting proposals seldom furnish detailed information on the fixed and variable retention charges and interest credits. *The solution to the potential problem of incomparable proposals is to write clear specifications and to include a format for the itemization of all cost factors.*

Specifications should consist of these parts:

1. Cover letter.
2. Plan experience data.
3. Description of desired coverage.
4. Census data.
5. Questionnaire and bid forms.

Cover Letter

A cover letter, which serves as an invitation to bid, should accompany the specifications. A primary purpose of this letter is to motivate the competitive insurers to bid. Responding to a bid request requires time and expenditure by an insurer. Each insurer needs some assurance that the process will be fair and that the employer requesting the bid is a desirable client. The major elements of the cover letter include:

1. Complete name, address, and telephone number. If the organization has operations in more than one location, a complete listing of all locations should be provided.

2. A description of the employer's principal operations.

3. Collective bargaining status. Indication should be made if any groups of employees will not be covered under the proposed plan.

4. Name of the employee or consultant to whom the proposal should be submitted. This person should be capable of answering technical and nontechnical questions. If a consultant has been retained and is available to answer questions, this fact should be indicated in the cover letter or the bid specifications.

5. Date and place for proposal submission. Insurers should be given at least 30 days to prepare their proposals.

6. Anticipated effective date of the new plan.

Plan Experience

Most competitive insurers are unlikely to prepare a bid unless a reasonable amount of plan experience information for at least the last three (preferably five) years is provided. These types of historical information should be furnished:

1. *A complete description of the benefits in effect during each period for which claims data are furnished.* This description is essential in helping the actuaries detect if changes in rates or claims resulted from a change in the benefit plan or from adverse experience. If copies of the plan document are unavailable, any booklets containing descriptions of pertinent benefits and plan provisions usually are adequate.

2. *Detailed information on all claims.* If the firm does not maintain its own computerized database on losses, an alternative source of information on claims charged to the account may be the current insurer's year-end financial accounting report to the group. This report should contain a breakdown of both paid claims and changes in claim reserves. Data on the following deductions from premiums also are desirable: (*a*) changes in reserves other than those for incurred-but-not-paid claims, (*b*) any losses carried forward from prior years, (*c*) pooling charges, (*d*) conversion charges on death-benefit coverage, (*e*) charges for waiver of premium claims, (*f*) retention charges for commissions, risk, and other expenses, and (*g*) balances in the various reserve accounts as of the end of the policy year. Any interest credited on the various categories of reserves and refunds should be clearly depicted.

3. *Pooling levels.* If insurers use different pooling levels, the bids will not be strictly comparable. A breakdown of claims experiences between employee and dependent claims also is desirable. While this report is not always furnished as a part of the insurer's annual financial statement, most carriers will make it available when requested by the group.

4. *Average number of persons insured during each period.* Premium statements for most insurers show the number of persons insured for the premium payment period. If the average number of persons insured cannot be obtained in this way, the information can be documented from employment records.

The organization is likely to have some unique characteristics that should be explained to the bidding insurers. For example, large claims that heavily influenced the claims experience for a particular year should be documented. A listing of each large claim (over $10,000 or $25,000) with a brief description of the nature of the claim should be provided in the loss data section of the bid specifications. A special rate-stabilization reserve allows an existing insurer to offer a lower premium for the next premium paying period than a new insurer could offer. The balance in this reserve should be obtained and furnished to all bidders. Currently disabled employees and other facts that might influence the rates quoted by an insurer should be furnished to all insurers.

Description of Desired Coverages

As noted earlier, specifications for desired coverages should be drawn up only after a very careful design of a plan that meets the objectives of the group. The design should reflect a compromise among employer needs, employee desires, and the need for cost controls.

Detailed descriptions of all desired coverages should be provided to each insurer from whom bids are requested. If any "special" benefits are desired, they should be requested as "alternatives" so that they will not discourage insurers from bidding.

Census Data

To prepare their bids, insurers need underwriting data about the people to be insured. This information typically is called an *employee census report* and includes distributions of employees by age, sex, geographical location, salary bracket, and dependent status. A listing by occupational class also may be helpful if many widely diverse occupations are represented and disability coverages are provided.

Census data ideally should be supplied in a grid format. While a printout of personnel data is acceptable to most insurers, its use does not encourage bidding because of the extra time the insurer must spend in organizing the personnel data.

Questionnaire and Bid Forms

Bids are easier to compare if the responding insurers are required to use the same format. The bid form should be designed to provide both an itemization of rates by type of coverage (life, employee health, dependent health, dental coverage, and any other benefits) and an exhibit detailing all the fixed and variable costs of the proposed retentions. The bid form also is an excellent tool to solicit insurer responses to questions about claims payment, services, facilities locations, interest rates on reserves, and similar concerns. These questions can be valuable if later disagreements arise between the insurer and group, since they provide a written record of the promises of the insurer.

PRESCREENING BIDDERS

To preclude the need to analyze proposals from insurers or other service organizations not qualified to serve the specific needs of an employer, a prescreening procedure often is advisable. This can be accomplished through the use of a prebid questionnaire and/or in a prebid conference.

Prebid Questionnaire

A prebid questionnaire is used to evaluate the qualifications of an insurer or adviser and allows an employer to gain the advantages of both an open and a closed bidding process. A notice to bid insurance can be provided to all interested purveyors of group insurance products. A government entity might even go one step further and issue a press release giving notice of a desire to rebid an insurance program. Any letter or public notice would indicate that all respondents would be provided not with bid specifications but with a prebid application or questionnaire. Only those purveyors who "pass" this initial evaluation would be provided with the detailed bid specifications and invited either to proceed directly with bid preparation or to first attend a prebid conference.

Prebid Conference

The prebid conference is designed to accomplish three important goals: (1) clarify any uncertainties about the specifications and the bidding forms, (2) motivate the selected insurance companies to submit bids, and (3) encourage creativity in bids.

Too frequently employers forget that in the bidding process they are marketing risks. Unless the insurance company representatives are convinced the potential new client will be profitable to them, they may decide not to bid. Thus, one goal of the prebid conference is to stimulate the enthusiasm of the adviser and/or insurer for the employer. The conference must be conducted in a very positive manner. As one expert says, "Present the package, 'warts' and all, in as appealing a manner as possible, but consistent with the facts."

It is important to encourage all bidders to be imaginative and creative, because an adviser or insurer can conceivably make suggestions that would significantly improve the quality of the group plan. Many group insurance purveyors have decades of experience that can be used to the employer's advantage. Submission of "creative" alternative bids in addition to the bid requested in the detailed specifications should be encouraged.

Finally, it is essential to assure all bidders confidentiality of their bids and to ask that they maintain confidentiality of all data provided in the bid specifications.

ANALYZING BIDS AND SELECTING A PROVIDER

The critical process of analyzing insurance bids and selecting an appropriate provider consists of the following steps on the part of the employer:[3]

1. Confirm that all bidders meet minimum requirements and eliminate any nonqualifiers.
2. Evaluate the financial implications of each bid (quantitative factors).
3. Review the policy specifications, claims-handling procedures, and loss control services provided by each bidding organization (qualitative factors).
4. Select the best provider(s) and negotiate the final details of the group insurance plan.
5. Present your findings and recommendations to the appropriate decision-making body (generally top management, executive committee, or board of directors).

Minimum Requirements

Employers seeking group insurance coverage often require that all bidders meet important minimum requirements, with no exceptions made for nonqualifiers. For example, the employer may require that bidding insurance companies have at least an "A" rating from Best's. Other minimum requirements may be that a qualified local agent or salaried representative is available on a regular basis at all employer locations to service the group and/or that the insurer maintain a full-time claims staff within a specified distance of the employer. Specified minimum requirements typically depend on the size and nature of the employer. For example, a very large corporate employer with a full-time risk-management and/or employee-benefits professional staff may not perceive the need for a local servicing agent, whereas a local or regional government employer may require all

---

[3]Depending on the employer's size, the person in charge of this process may be a risk manager, an employee benefits manager, or another middle-level manager. For purposes of simplicity the term *manager* is used in this chapter.

bidders to be domestic insurers and all servicing agents to maintain offices in the same community as the government seat.

Financial Implications

Assuming that bidders comply with the plan specifications, financial or cash-flow implications typically will be the critical variable in selecting a carrier. This analysis often is the subject of considerable confusion, because employers do not understand the mathematics and resulting cash-flow implications of group insurance proposals and because not all insurers use consistent terminology and methodology in presenting their proposed financial bids.

The confusion may easily result in the selection of an inappropriate bid by an employer who lacks a professional staff capable of fully understanding the financial implications of each bid. Accordingly, an employer without the appropriate internal staff generally is well advised to retain an experienced adviser to review the financial implications of the bids.

Financial analysis of proposed group insurance programs often is considerably more complex than one might initially suspect. If, for example, the proposal under review contemplates an experience- or retrospective-rated program, an analyst would be misled by a simple comparison of the standard premium paid at the beginning of the plan year (or monthly). Numerous other critical variables affect the ultimate cash-flow cost of such a plan.

The true cost of a group plan can be depicted as:

$$\text{Cost} = \text{Claims} + \text{Retention} - \text{Interest return}$$

Claims are further broken into paid claims and reserves for future payments. A thorough analysis of the retention exhibit should allow the manager or adviser to determine which bidders have presented the best financial proposal for the employer.

Analysis of Retention

Proposed retention factors are the major financial criteria that should be used to distinguish among bids. The term *retention* refers to that portion of the insurance premium kept by the insurer to cover expenses, pooling charges, risk charges, and/or profit. The part of the retention factor designed to realize a profit for the insurer typically is not an identifiable factor in the retention exhibit but is built into many of the other factors, especially the risk charge. Mutual insurance companies do not have a profit factor as such but include a contribution to surplus in their risk charges.

Careful analysis of the retention exhibit requires a comparison of the dollars that alternative insurance companies seek to "retain" for their own use through their various charges and those funds that they will credit to the employer in the form of reserves, refunds, and/or investment returns on any premiums paid in advance.

In reviewing alternative retention exhibits, the manager or adviser should determine if any inconsistencies are present in the claims expense factors. If all insurers use the assumed claims provided in the bid specifications, the claims expense factor in the various proposals should be comparable. If, on the other hand, insurers are left on their own to estimate incurred claims and claims adjustment costs, significant variations can be expected. Comparable retention illustrations demand that claims assumptions be as close as possible to the specified level, but experience has proven that some bidders use different claims assumptions than those provided in the bid specifications. If such is the case, the "nonconforming" bids must first be adjusted to a claims level consistent with all other bids. If this adjustment is not feasible, the employer may either return the bid to the insurer with a request to make the necessary adjustments or reject the bid from further consideration.

The manager or adviser should determine that all bidders have complied with specifications regarding premium quotations. Some insurers quote abnormally high premiums to produce unusually high dividends or refunds that can then be credited with interest. Such a practice can result in an understatement of the insurer's retention, because interest credited to a dividend or refund remains with the insurer and is used to reduce its retentions. If this potential distortion is suspected, the bidding insurer should be requested to separately specify the interest credited to dividends.

Bids must be checked to assure that insurers have consistently included expenses associated with claims processing in their retentions. Accounting practices relative to the treatment of claims payment expenses vary among insurers. Some insurers add these expenses to paid or incurred claims, while others combine claims payment expenses with the administrative expenses in the retention. The bid of an insurer that has assumed claims payment expenses to be part of the specified incurred claims will understate its retention. If such a problem is detected, the employer should request the insurer to provide the specific claims payment expense figures in order to adjust the retention illustration.

The manner in which bidding insurers have treated pooling charges should likewise be checked for consistency. Pooling charges are essentially a retention item, because none of the pooling charges will be returned to the employer in the form of either dividends or retrospective rate credits. If the request for bids does not specify that pooling charges be itemized, some bidding insurance companies may include these charges as a part of paid or incurred claims. The retentions of such an insurance carrier would thus be significantly understated.

Premium taxes are another item that should be illustrated on a common basis. Unless specific instructions were included in the request for bids, some insurers may depict premium taxes on the basis of gross premiums, while other underwriters may illustrate them as premiums minus anticipated dividends or other rate credits. These potential sources of retention-exhibit distortion require adjustments on a case-by-case basis.

In summary, consistent retention illustrations can form the basis for determining the premium dollars that will be returned to the organization and the amount that will remain with the insurance company. This analysis must review not simply the absolute dollar amounts, but the timing of the cash flows as well. Thus, it is very important that each bidder provide very specific information on the elements of fixed and variable costs in its bid.

Bid Cost Matrix

Table 52–1 provides an illustration of a quantitative analysis of group insurance bids. This type of analysis is commonly referred to as a *bid-cost matrix*. Section I of the matrix summarizes the basic assumptions the companies were requested to use in preparing their bids. Assumed claims levels were provided in the bid specifications in order to increase the likelihood that the cost figures provided by the various insurance companies can be determined on a consistent basis.

Section II outlines the monthly rates quoted by each of five bidders. Premium bids for each line of coverage are separated into pooled and nonpooled premiums. This information is needed to provide details for

TABLE 52–1
ABC & Associates Group Insurance Bid Comparison of Annual Cost

SECTION I

Life insurance in force	$37,500,000	
AD&D insurance in force	37,500,000	
Monthly covered payroll	2,083,333	
Employee health claims	$390,000	
Dependent health claims	350,000	
Employee life claims	10,000	
Total claims	$750,000	
Covered employees*	800	
Covered dependent units*	650	

SECTION II

	1 Longwood Life	2 Orlando Life	3 Sanford Life	4 Deland Life	5 Oviedo Life
Quote No.					
Company					
Monthly rates (as quoted by purveyors)					
Pooled premium					
Life rate†	$ .275	$ .56	$ .322	$ .28	$ .1995
AD&D rate †	.055	.062	.06	.0598	.07
LTD‡	.325	.581	.434	.55	.495
Employee health§	1.40	1.00	1.10	1.10	1.92
Dependent health§	2.05	2.00	1.95	1.65	1.92
Nonpooled premium (aggregate stop loss)					
Life rate	$ .28	$ 0‖	$ .44	$ .40	$ .39
Employee health	36.25	40.00	50.00	42.27	35.00
Dependent health	52.37	51.50	72.25	52.65	39.50

SECTION III

	1 Longwood Life	2 Orlando Life	3 Sanford Life	4 Deland Life	5 Oviedo Life
Retention based on					
Claims	.065	6.00	.055	.07	5.25
Employees					
Aggregate					

TABLE 52–1
ABC & Associates Group Insurance Bid Comparison of Annual Cost (concluded)

SECTION IV

Cost					
Pooled premium					
Life	$ 123,750	$ 252,000	$ 144,900	$ 126,000	$ 89,775
AD&D	24,750	27,900	27,000	26,910	31,500
LTD	81,250	145,250	108,500	137,500	123,750
Employee health	13,440	9,600	10,560	10,560	18,432
Dependent health	15,990	15,600	15,210	12,870	14,976
Total fixed cost	$ 259,180	$ 450,350	$ 306,170	$ 313,840	$ 278,433
Claims cost	$ 750,000	$ 740,000 ‖	$ 750,000	$ 750,000	$ 750,000
Retention	57,362	57,600	41,250	52,500	50,400
Total variable cost	$ 807,362	$ 797,600	$ 791,250	$ 802,500	$ 800,400
Total cost	$1,066,542	$1,236,050	$1,097,420	$1,116,340	$1,078,833
Claims/cost ratio	0.70	0.59	0.68	0.67	0.70

SECTION V

Cost at other claims levels					
70 percent	$ 841,542	$1,025,950	$ 872,420	$ 891,340	$ 853,833
80 percent	916,542	1,099,950	947,420	966,340	928,833
90 percent	991,542	1,173,950	1,022,420	1,041,340	1,003,833
110 percent	1,141,542	1,236,050	1,172,420	1,191,340	1,098,033
120 percent	1,141,666	1,236,050	1,247,420	1,266,340	1,098,033
130 percent	1,141,666	1,236,050	1,322,420	1,310,302	1,098,033
Maximum cost	$1,141,666	$1,236,050	$1,547,720	$1,310,302	$1,098,033

*Employee and dependent units eligible for Medicare supplements are excluded from consideration.
†Life and AD&D rates are quoted per $1,000 face amount.
‡LTD rates are quoted per $100 of monthly benefit.
§Employee and dependent health rates are quoted per unit.
‖Included in pooled premium.

the stop-loss provision. Section III provides both the retention factors quoted by each insurance company and the basis or method used by these bidders in calculating this factor.

Section IV gives the variable cost and the fixed cost for each bid based on the assumed claims and premium data appearing in Sections II and III. Most importantly, this section provides the critical "claims/cost ratio." Typically, the higher this ratio, the better the bid. On this basis, bids 1 and 5 appear to be the most attractive.

Section V responds to a question often asked by the ultimate decision-making body: "What if assumed claims vary from the levels assumed in Section I?" Based on claims ranging from 70 percent to 130 percent of those used in Section I, total costs are calculated for each bid. In addition to summarizing the range of possible costs, Section V also provides the manager with the maximum costs for each bid and the level of claims at which the maximum cost is obtained. If feasible, the manager is well advised to include this data in the cost matrix he or she provides to executive management.

Qualitative Factors

In the previous section, the detailed financial or cash-flow aspects of the premium bids provided by each insurance company were reviewed. While this analysis is extremely important, a satisfactory analysis of bids must include far more than a consideration of financial aspects for several reasons. Premiums and retention factors are guaranteed for only a short period of time (usually 12 to 18 months at most). Furthermore, as discussed previously, a change of companies after only one or two years generally is undesirable, although not always unconscionable. The employer and its adviser must carefully consider the most important qualitative factors associated with the alternative bids and choose an insurer that has a verified reputation for the desired quality of service. Selecting an insurer with a questionable service capability or contract specifications typically is a mistake. Minor differences in retention charges do not justify acceptance if day-to-day difficulties concerning administration and claims service are to be expected.

The first step in analyzing the qualitative aspects of the bids is to verify that all proposals have complied with the minimum coverage provisions outlined in the bid specifications. A valid bid comparison is possible only if all proposals are consistent for both the type of program proposed (such as a comprehensive major medical plan or a basic hospital-surgical plan with a supplementary major medical) and such basic coverage elements as limits on the maximum lifetime benefits, deductible levels, co-pay provisions, maximum employee out-of-pocket amounts, and scheduled versus "reasonable and customary" coverage of medical expenses.

When applicable, the question of the length of any rate guarantees must be addressed. Differences among the bids often arise on the issue of both initial and renewal guarantees of premiums and retention factors.

The manager or adviser should carefully review any descriptive literature provided with the bids. Listings of definitions, covered expenses, exclusions, and limitations may reveal significant benefit differences. Variations sometimes exist, for example, in the definitions of terms such as *hospital* and *physician*. Some plans may include coverage for second surgical opinions, home health care, ambulatory surgical facilities, nursing home care, hospitalization in a "progressive care unit," well-baby care, treatment of mental illness, and/or treatment of alcoholism and drug-related illnesses. Other plans may provide exceptional rehabilitation benefits. A review of the conversion provisions and of the provisions of any Medicare supplement included in the programs is also in order. For example, the analyst should know if a "carve out" or a "coordination" approach is being utilized in the Medicare supplement.

In reviewing the qualitative areas of plan coverage, the manager should attempt to minimize the aggregate inconvenience for employees and should be conscious that the demographics and financial needs of the employee group are important to the acceptance of any change in the group insurance plan. For example, if many of the employees reside in rural areas and receive their primary care from medical professionals other than M.D.s (that is, from D.O.s, chiropractors, and/or nurse practitioners), any restrictions on benefits for services provided by these medical professionals are likely to create significant employee discontent. The best analytical decisions concerning the cost of alternative bids can be in error if the decision process fails to consider the cost of extensive employee dissatisfaction with a proposed change.

The manager or adviser should attempt to predict whether the various insurance companies will render a satisfactory level of claims and administrative service. Questions that might be asked here include:

1. What is the projected average turnaround time for claims payments?

2. Are local claims facilities available? If not, will the insurer provide a toll-free telephone number or accept collect calls on claims inquiries?

3. What will be the extent of employer involvement in the verification or other processing of claims? Will this require the employer to hire or train additional staff?

4. What administrative and/or accounting procedures must the employer adopt to facilitate such matters as premium collections, enrollments, and terminations?

5. How satisfied with programs underwritten by the carrier in question are employers with similar demographic characteristics?

Finally, the manager or adviser will want to evaluate the potential flexibility with which the alternative insurers could respond to major changes in the employer organization and/or to employer desires to consider alternative financial arrangements at some point in the future. This analysis is particularly relevant if, for example, the employer's five-year goals include acquisitions, mergers, or a major plant relocation. Alternatively, the employer might have determined that an ASO contract or a self-insurance arrangement does not suit its current needs but it may wish to consider these alternatives in two to three years. The employer may place a high value on an ability to effectively respond to changes such as these without undergoing the potential disruption of a change in insurance carrier.

NEGOTIATING WITH THE CARRIER

Based on the analysis of the financial and qualitative implications of alternative bids, the manager charged with responsibility for group insurance will select that carrier most compatible with the needs of employer and employees alike. In many situations, the manager draws solely on his or her own skills and experience in making the selection, and guidance from outside the company is not sought. In other situations, the decision is aided by technical advice from a qualified adviser. Regardless of the manner in which this preliminary selection is reached, two final steps usually are required: (1) detailed negotiation with the selected underwriter and (2) presentation of the recommendations to the appropriate decision-making body, be it the CEO, an executive committee, or the board of directors (as is common in many smaller- or medium-sized companies). The sequence of these steps may vary. Some managers prefer to obtain a consensus on the selection of a particular insurance company prior to initiating final negotiations with the underwriter; others attempt to wrest all available concessions from the carrier before presenting their findings for a final decision.

This section deals with the final negotiation process, and the final discussion considers the critical ingredients of an effective presentation to the ultimate decision makers. The importance of the final negotiation process rests on two assumptions. First, the cost and provisions of a group insurance program are in fact negotiable. Armed with knowledge of the very complex technical aspects of a group program, a competent manager can win concessions from the insurance company that will benefit the employer and the employees. Second, specific areas in the bid of the selected insurer may not be as competitive as those found in other bids. If these discrepancies are pointed out to the underwriter, he or she may be willing to reevaluate and improve this particular portion of the bid. This process takes on added importance if the insurance company with the "lowest" bid is not the one selected by the manager and adviser. The "lowest" bidder may not be chosen for a variety of reasons relating to service considerations or to long-term costs not immediately evident in the bids. If this selection is going to "pass muster" with the CEO, the executive committee, or the board, all possible cost and coverage concessions must be obtained from this carrier.

The first step in the negotiating process is to select the proper "players." The decision as to whether the manager or the adviser will handle direct negotiations with the underwriter is often a difficult one. Allowing the adviser to take the lead in this area often proves more efficient. The adviser is usually more familiar with the behavioral aspects of negotiations with specific underwriters; he or she also may have more leverage with the insurance carrier. Should a decision be reached that the adviser will primarily handle the negotiations, the manager should clearly understand the areas to be negotiated and should be prepared to use his or her influence with the insurer when and if called on by the adviser.

Whomever is chosen, the negotiator must be familiar with the terminology used by the particular insurance company. Most home-office underwriters converse in terms that may be unique to their company. In fact, many of the common group insurance terms (like *retro*) have different meanings for different insurers. An ability to speak the appropriate lingo is crucial if one is seeking financial concessions from an insurer. This simple but important step can reduce significant confusion.

The negotiator(s) for the employer must develop a strategy for quickly directing the attention of home-office underwriters to the items where profit and/or excess interest may be hidden and thus where concessions may be obtained. This strategy often involves a list of very probing questions that go beyond such routine areas as reducing premium margins, releasing accumulated but not reported reserves, and negotiating commission levels.

Peter B. O'Brien, president of Johnson & Higgins of Colorado, has provided an excellent list of 10 very specific questions to use as the basis for final negotiations with a group insurance underwriter.[4]

1. Why should a conservation and review (C&R) charge be levied against our account when we have a 10-year service plaque hanging on the wall?

2. Why is your computer programmed to "load" our triangle chart when the results are supposed to represent our actual claims runout?

3. Why can't our "risk charge" be scaled based on our loss ratio, rather than on a flat percentage of our premium?

4. Why, after years of consistency in policy language for disability payments, is there a wide inconsistency in percentage of face-value claim charges?

5. Why can't we be presented with our state premium tax bill and eliminate the tax escrow account?

6. Why have you been lenient with customers whose premiums are delinquent by a few months, while charging us prevailing interest rates when late by only one month?

7. Why can't our pooling "point" and "factor" be adjusted to reflect our class of business and experience, rather than using overall company tables and rates that haven't been updated in years?

8. We hear lots of talk about severely escalating health-care trend factors, but where is the offsetting advance credit, life deflation factor?

---

[4]Peter B. O'Brien, "Negotiating Lower Costs for Group Insurance Plans," *Risk Management*, December 1978, pp. 34–38.

9. Why does a financial accounting have to occur every 12 months? Can't we have custom rates and retention factors to coincide with our collective bargaining periods?

10. Can't we define paid claims as money that has actually been withdrawn from your account, rather than amounts on claims forms?

The foregoing questions are illustrative only. Some of these questions obviously may not be relevant for some groups, while other questions of similar detail and nature may be more appropriate for other groups. The point is that the use of very specific questions significantly enhances the ability of negotiators for the employer to obtain all valid concessions. The underwriter should be allowed sufficient time (usually several weeks) to evaluate the case and to either agree to the requests or propose alternative adjustments. The impact of the underwriter's decisions must, of course, be evaluated prior to a presentation to the appropriate decision makers.

PRESENTATION TO DECISION MAKERS

The manager typically is required to make a presentation on the group insurance reevaluation process to a top-management decision maker or committee. This presentation has taken on increased importance in recent years as high-level executives have become more attentive to cost savings that can be realized in the employee benefits area. Rapid escalation of the costs of employee benefits (and especially of group insurance) means group insurance decisions are no longer relatively minor decisions. This phenomenon is compounded by increased volatility in the cost of money. Executives have become very conscious of the need to optimize the management of scarce and very costly cash flows. CEOs and other high-level executives have decided to periodically review and influence group insurance decisions in the hopes of more effectively managing required cash flows.

The following outline suggests the critical items that should be communicated during the presentation to top management:

1. State the objectives that dictated and influenced the decision to remarket the group insurance program. What financial and/or employee benefit goals were to be achieved by the rebidding process?

2. Identify any weaknesses in the current group insurance contract or carrier, and specify the steps in the bidding process that are aimed at avoiding these weaknesses in any new program or insurance company.

3. Identify any restrictions imposed by top management on the use of particular alternative financial arrangements with an insurance company (for example, self-insurance was or was not to be considered) and on the use of specific carriers, agents, or advisers.

4. Identify the markets (insurance companies or self-funding service organizations) that have been approached, the responses received, and the bids that were considered qualified and responsive to the needs of the employer. The decision makers will want to know that a thorough market test was conducted and that all qualified and competitive insurers had an opportunity to provide bids. If the decision makers perceive that the market test was less than complete, they may require a reexamination of other alternative providers.

5. Present the bid matrix (see Table 52–1), and outline the strengths and weaknesses of the individual bids.

6. Present the specific recommendation and the supporting logic.

7. Try to anticipate potential questions and deal with them in the presentation. For example, it was noted earlier that the decision makers are likely to ask why the bid specifications stipulate a specific level of claims be assumed in the preparation of the bids and how alternative loss assumptions would have affected the bid matrix.

CONCLUSION

The foregoing has presented a framework for reviewing and rebidding a group insurance program. This process may be undertaken for various reasons and at different times during the life of such a program. While the treatment here is not exhaustive, it provides a basis for understanding the process and enabling an employer to deal with it in an informed way.

PART 11

EMPLOYEE BENEFIT PLAN COMMUNICATIONS

Because of the complexity of employee benefits and regulatory requirements, the appropriate communication of all aspects of employee benefits
to various groups is an absolute mandate for employers. Chapter 53
reviews the fundamentals of employee benefit plan communications in
addition to basic communications theory. Chapter 54 continues the
discussion by giving examples of effective employee benefit communications approaches including the latest use of technology in such systems.

CHAPTER 53

FUNDAMENTALS OF EMPLOYEE BENEFIT PLAN COMMUNICATIONS

Thomas Martinez
Robert V. Nally

REASONS FOR BENEFITS COMMUNICATIONS

Communication and disclosure of employee benefits to plan participants and their beneficiaries is essential to the efficient operation of any benefit plan. The reasons for this can be categorized into two broad groupings: legal requirements and managerial requirements.

Legal Requirements

The Internal Revenue Code (IRC) has required from the very beginning of qualified pension or profit-sharing plans that such plans be in writing and be communicated by appropriate means to covered individuals. Thus, for such retirement plans to receive the desired favorable tax treatment, communication is essential. Moreover, the Employee Retirement Income Security Act (ERISA) and other federal enactments have specific reporting and disclosure requirements covering private employee pension and welfare plans. All types of qualified pension and profit-sharing plans are subject to these disclosure requirements regardless of the number of participants in the plan. Some nonqualified retirement plans also are subject to the reporting and disclosure requirements. Additionally, certain welfare plans providing such benefits as life insurance, medical expense, disability income, and other employee benefits are subject to reporting and disclosure requirements.

The reporting and disclosure regulations provide for three categories of information:

- Certain documents must be filed with the appropriate government agencies at required times and made available to employees.
- Certain information must be distributed automatically to plan participants and their dependents under each plan.
- Certain specified information must be given to plan participants on written request and/or made available for examination at the principal office of the plan administrator and at other locations convenient for participants.

These three categories of information cover five general groups of activities:

1. Annual plan maintenance.
2. Ongoing plan maintenance.
3. The installation of a new plan.
4. Revisions in an existing plan.
5. The termination of a plan.

Moreover, the requirements differ for the various types of employee benefit plans. Communication of these various forms of information and other topics discussed in a general way in this chapter are covered in greater detail in Chapter 54.

Managerial Requirements

Even if plans did not receive favorable tax treatment on meeting disclosure and other criteria, the managerial reasons for the communication of employee benefits still would exist. Modern management thinking fosters the use of employee benefits as an effective means of competing in labor markets for the attraction and retention of qualified personnel. Benefit plans also are viewed as tools for building and maintaining high morale within a work force and for meeting the social and ethical responsibilities of employers within the employment relationship. These managerial reasons for instituting employee benefit plans can be met only if the affected people are made aware of their existence. Benefit plans must be communicated and administered in a manner consistent with and supportive of the personnel policy goals that the benefits are designed to accomplish. Benefit plans cannot motivate a person if the individual does not know of the existence of the plans or how they affect him or her individually. An employee cannot be influenced to remain with a specific employer, to be more productive, or to view an employer in a favorable light by the presence of benefits that have not been communicated properly. Moreover, an employee cannot use a benefit plan as it is fully intended (for example, the cost-containment features of a medical plan or the use of a capital accumulation plan) if he or she is not acquainted with the nature and purposes of plan provisions. When viewed in this context, the communication of employee benefits is an essential factor in the whole array of activities commonly termed *good management practice*.

RESPONSIBILITY FOR COMMUNICATING BENEFITS

Realistically, the responsibility for communicating employee benefits is shared throughout the management hierarchy of an organization. Top management, the employee benefits manager, and line managers all have roles to play.

Top Management

Top management ultimately is responsible for employee benefit communications, since it has the basic authority for setting all organizational policies and plans. The term *top management* has different connotations depending on the size of an organization. In small organizations, there is usually little or no differentiation of top, middle, and first-line management people. There is just one level of management. However, as organizations grow in size, they tend to acquire several middle and upper levels of management, each with varying degrees and types of authority and responsibility. Moreover, the management positions are structured to function in a coordinated manner, with each contributing to the fulfillment of the total management process.

In large corporate organizations, the responsibility for recommending policies and establishing and implementing plans and procedures typically is delegated to upper-level division and department heads. In addition, all line and staff managers of an organization are expected to administer their departments in a manner consistent with and supportive of overall organizational policymaking and planning. For example, a vice president of marketing should run his or her division in a manner that accomplishes the marketing objectives of the firm and also includes appropriate consideration of the financial, production, personnel, and employee benefits policies established by top management. For employee benefits matters, the described planning and implementation responsibilities typically are placed with the person who serves as the vice president of personnel or as the employee benefits manager.

Employee Benefits Manager

An employee benefits manager engages in many activities in recommending and implementing employee benefits policies. The basic organizational responsibility for the communication of employee benefits to participants and their beneficiaries typically is vested in the individual who has this role or title in a firm. This situation exists regardless of whether a plan is self-funded and/or administered, insurance-funded and/or administered, or trusteed or structured under some other type of arrangement. Supporting services, including communications support activities and materials, often are provided to the sponsoring employer by a third-party administrator of a plan. However, the overall responsibilities of an employee benefits manager may not be diminished under such arrangements. Indeed, the presence of an insured or trusteed plan could increase the workload of the employee benefits manager, because the efforts of the third-party administrator must be monitored, evaluated, and coordinated with the firm's employee benefit program.

One of the employee benefits manager's major concerns is to make certain that the employees understand the coverages, operation, and value of the benefits package. Although many employees easily comprehend the nature of the benefits extended, others need to have these matters explained with greater care.

Attractive and readable posters, standard forms, pamphlets, brochures, and other written materials should be prepared. Perhaps the development of audio and visual materials might be necessary. The planning and conducting of meetings with groups of employees also may be required. Additionally, staff and line personnel must be trained to conduct meetings and deal with employees individually about employee benefits matters. The actual communication of employee benefits information to employees and others occurs in many ways at both specified and unspecified times. The efforts of the employee benefits manager, other personnel department people, and line people all are involved.

Line Management

Contemporary management theory emphasizes that the process of personnel management is spread throughout an organization. All managers are viewed as personnel managers because they are vitally connected with directing and motivating human resources. Their job effectiveness is dependent on the quality of the performance of the employees over whom they exercise authority.

Line managers of sales, manufacturing, and other departments usually play a substantial role in recruiting, selecting, evaluating, training, developing, and disciplining employees. Because of their close daily contact, line managers often are initially approached by employees with personal and employment-related problems and questions. In carrying out these activities, all managers can be viewed as employee benefits managers as well as personnel managers. Each of these activities involves a real or potential employee-benefit-communication event. Line managers must be equipped to give accurate employee benefit information. At a minimum, a line supervisor should be able to direct an inquiring employee to the office within the firm where assistance or advice can be obtained. Also, when a line manager makes a decision or takes any action involving an employee, the implications concerning a change in the benefits status of an employee should be considered. Disciplinary transfers, suspensions, layoffs, and terminations all typically involve employee changes with respect to the entitlement to or loss of benefits. Any such actions taken imprudently could be counterproductive.

Employee-Benefit-Communication Events

Many occasions exist in the working career of each employee that can be classified as employee-benefit-communication events. There also are such incidents in the life span of an organization. Several of these bear particular mention.

As part of the recruitment process, it is advisable to notify potential and active job applicants of the general nature of the firm's employee benefit package. Competition among employers for qualified people is an ever-present economic factor, and most prospective employees are quite aware of the important role of employee benefits in the total compensation package of a firm. The presence of a fine benefits program could be the ultimate factor in attracting superior job applicants and maintaining their interest in the firm. At the selection and placement stages more specific employee benefit information should be given to employment candidates. This will reinforce the commitment of the employer and help to increase positive attitudes in the candidates. The recruitment, selection, and placement processes typically are conducted through the interaction of personnel department staff and line people. Thus, both should be advised concerning their benefit communication functions and supplied with supporting brochures and other materials through the employee benefits office.

In the orientation process, new employees usually receive a tremendous quantity of information about their jobs, the products or services produced by the firm, and the organization itself. The employee benefits manager and his or her staff typically play the primary role in the orientation process of explaining the employee benefits program of the organization. Effective communications are essential at this point to aid in establishing lasting positive attitudes and keeping productive and mobile employees in the organization. Employees should understand the program fully from the very beginning of their employment.

An organization also should *schedule* employee-benefits-communication events, rather than merely reacting to or dealing with them as they occur. It is necessary to keep established employees informed of their benefits as a matter of legal and managerial responsibility. This can be accomplished by the employee benefits manager through the use of a continuous schedule for contacting employees at definitely set time intervals. Attractive and creative written communications can be sent to employees directly, placed in their pay envelopes, or displayed on bulletin boards. Meetings and seminars with groups of employees involving written and oral messages integrated with audio and visual materials often are useful.

Most employee-benefits-communication events are generated by employees themselves. Whenever an employee has some question or misunderstanding regarding benefit entitlements, has a claim processed, or meets some difficulty in the administration of a claim, this requires an immediate managerial response. The lines of communication between the employee benefits department and employees should be kept open continuously. This is essential in order to give proper attention to any benefits questions or problems that employees may have.

It has been noted that employee status changes. Events such as suspensions and layoffs have benefit effects that should be considered before making any decisions in these areas. As a corollary to this policy, the formal communications network of a firm should be geared to generate an awareness among employees of any loss, decrease, or freeze of benefits that accompanies a layoff, demotion, suspension, leave of absence, or termination. Likewise, increases or adjustments in benefits that take place in conjunction with transfers and promotions need to be understood. When an event involving a change in the employment status of an individual takes place, the person should be counseled specifically about the benefit aspects of the change. In connection with this, financial planning programs and preretirement counseling sessions can play significant roles.

The general operating posture of a firm may be revised periodically. For example, product lines are changed or broadened, geographic relocations or expansions occur, and other types of return-on-investment-oriented decisions are made. These actions sometimes are facilitated through modifications of the existing structure of a firm. This could mean a change in the basic method of departmentalization, an increased emphasis on centralization, the entire sale of a firm as a subsidiary to a competitor or a conglomerate, a merger arrangement, or a consolidation. These types of incidents typically cause concern among employees regarding their employment status and existing employee benefit programs. A firm should take steps at the time of such events to acquaint its employees with the nature and purpose of the organizational realignment and its impact on them personally. Whenever a merger or consolidation is carried out, some revisions of existing employee benefit plans invariably are necessary to dovetail existing plans with those of the new partner firm. Aside from the legal disclosure requirements that might apply in such circumstances, there is a need to acquaint employees with any benefit adjustments made. Moreover, sound management practice requires that existing benefits programs should not be downgraded or reduced at such times unless it is absolutely necessary.

THE COMMUNICATION PROCESS

Steps of the Communication Process

The communication process includes a sequence of seven steps, regardless of whether the form of communication is the spoken or written word or some other method. It begins with the formation of an idea and its placement into a message form. The message then is transmitted and received by the person or persons for whom it is intended. Understanding the content of the message and appropriate action by the receiver then follows. The final step consists of the transmission of feedback by the receiver to the sender of the message.

The complete sequence of steps is described here. Each of the steps—idea, message formation, transmission, receipt, understanding, action, and feedback—is discussed separately.

Idea

This step provides the content of a specific communication or message when the sender has an idea or chooses a fact to communicate. An individual must have some fact, feeling, or concept to convey before the communication process moves forward. The first step is crucial because further steps are superfluous without a solid content message. Moreover, a poor message cannot be improved by trimmings such as glossy paper or a bigger loudspeaker.

Message Formation

The sender organizes an idea into a series of symbols that transmit the idea to those with whom communication is desired. The selected symbols may be words, gestures, pictures, scientific formulas, graphs, and so on. After the message is organized for rationality and coherence, the medium appropriate to the message is selected. Therefore this step is related to the medium used as well as to the intended receivers. For example, a letter usually is worded differently than a brochure, and both are different from a face-to-face conversation. The medium selected must be capable of transmitting the message to the intended receivers. Thus, the written word usually is used for official employee benefit messages because of their nature and content, and face-to-face or telephone conversations are important between plan administrators and participants who have questions about their benefits or other aspects of the plan.

Transmission

The message is transmitted via the medium selected in the preceding step. A specific channel is chosen to perform this step, and appropriate timing also is important. For example, a channel may be used to bypass a particular group, or a message may be delayed because the sender feels it is not the best time to send it. The sender also tries to keep the communication channel free of interferences so that the message can reach the receiver and hold his or her attention. For example, in interviewing a plan participant regarding a complex claim, distraction is undesirable.

Receipt
In this step, the initiative in the communication process shifts to the receiver. He or she must be ready and able to receive the message. If it is oral, the receiver must be a good listener; if written, the receiver must be a good reader; if in some symbolic language, the receiver must be knowledgeable and observant in that particular area. If the receiver does not function well, the message is lost.

Understanding
The receiver takes meaning from the symbols used by the sender. An effective and cooperative receiver tries diligently to capture the meaning intended in the message by the sender. Nevertheless, the meaning the receiver takes will not be exactly the same as the one sent. This happens because the perceptions of the sender and receiver invariably differ to some extent. Thus, the sender of a message should be aware that some degree of distortion or lack of comprehension by the receiver is inevitable. This can be ultimately overcome by devoting careful attention to the formation of the message and through the use of repetition and message follow-up techniques.

Action
On the basis of the message, the receiver acts or responds in some way. For example, he or she may respond verbally to the sender by writing a memo to the sender requesting further information; the receiver may store the information contained in the message for the future or may engage in other activities in response to a request or command, such as forming a group to discuss the proposals at issue.

Feedback
It is desirable for the receiver to give feedback to the sender; this establishes two-way communication. (One-way communication processes unfortunately do not include this step.) The purpose of feedback is to provide the sender with information about his or her message that clarifies whether it was understood or put into effect. In some cases, the action step of the

process includes the element of feedback. For example, when the participants in an employee benefit plan are sent notices of claims procedure
changes, their degree of compliance in response to the message is an action
step that can be observed as a form of feedback.

Effective and Ineffective Communications

Effective communication occurs when a common understanding exists
between the sender and receiver of a message. However, as indicated, this
goal is not always achieved because of one or more interrelated factors.
Sometimes individuals transmit unintended messages, barriers can exist
within the communications process itself, and not all messages fully
reflect the thoughts of the senders. Additionally, the receiver can be an
impediment to an effective communication because of a low level of
literacy, a suspicious nature regarding management-sponsored benefits
programs, or general indifference.

Unintended messages are transmitted for innumerable reasons. For
example, the receiver of a message may delay in responding to a request
for information because of a heavy workload. The sender of the request
may interpret the delay as disinterest or hostility. Inadvertently, each
person has communicated a different message, when indeed only one was
intended. The same result can occur in oral communications because of
body language or voice inflections unconsciously used by the sender.

The communication process does not always function in a complementary environment. When this is the case, the existing barrier makes
effective communications difficult. Noise usually is the most annoying
barrier to effective communications because of its distracting characteristic. Organizational distance, another barrier, occurs when a message
must be transmitted through several people—a chain of command—
before ultimately reaching the receiver. The presence of message competition also stifles effective communication. This exists when the
receiver is bombarded by many related messages at the same time. If
there is little indication of the relative importance of each message, the
receiver may be confused.

A message should be constructed carefully in order to reflect the
thoughts of the sender. The language selected must be understood by the
receiver. For example, such terms as *coinsurance, deductible,* and
third-party payee are not universally understood and thus must be used
carefully. The language of a message also should not antagonize the
receiver. Words such as *minorities, unisex,* and *welfare* can produce

negative feelings that impede understanding. Slang, jargon, and buzz-words can be effective; however, such terms tend to be fashionable for brief periods of time and thus should be avoided in written communications that are intended for use over an extended period.

Messages can be too long and too brief. Excessively long messages lose reader interest and comprehension. Conversely, the receiver may make abstractions or inferences not intended by the sender if the message is too brief.

The sender and receiver of a message must be in tune for effective communications to take place. Unfortunately, the receiver sometimes presents a problem because his or her perceptions may differ from the sender's. For example, when the sender refers to "holding down costs," the receiver may interpret this as a directive to deny benefit claims that were accepted in the past. As another example, any message that involves a change of existing conditions such as changes in existing benefit policies, programs, or operating procedures could challenge the receiver to stiffly resist the message. Also, the status of the sender can be important to the receiver. Communications from the employee benefits manager of a large organization may carry greater impact than those of the support staff in the benefits department.

FORMS OF COMMUNICATION

Communications typically are classified as written, oral, or action messages. Written communications consist of many types, from handbooks, booklets, bulletins, memos, letters, and standard forms to posters, cartoons, films, prepared tapes, and pictures. Oral communications, on the other hand, generally consist of the spoken word in a speech, an order, a comment, or a discussion. Actions also are recognized as communication forms, regardless of whether the action exists independently or occurs in consort with a written or oral communication. Therefore, even laughter, a smile, a handshake, silence, and personal mannerisms significantly communicate some kind of message.

Written Communications

The primary focus in this chapter is on the written form of communication, because federal laws concerning employee benefits require the use of written communications in many specific instances. Moreover, the basic principles of effective writing also apply to the development and transmission of oral messages.

Written communications provide a permanent record of a transmitted message. Accordingly, written messages usually are constructed with greater care and have a higher degree of formality than oral messages. A written message can be read carefully and reread by the receiver to gain a fuller understanding of the content. Thus, when a message is lengthy or detailed, the written form often is used because oral communication would not be as effective. In addition, when a message must be transmitted through several people to the ultimate receiver, the written form is selected to avoid change or dilution of its content.

The federal regulations concerning the written communication of employee benefit matters provide that the required information must be written in a manner calculated to be understood by the average plan participant. Also, it must be sufficiently accurate and comprehensive to inform participants and beneficiaries of their rights and obligations under a plan. Generally, plan sponsors do not encounter any great difficulty in complying with these broadly stated legal guidelines. However, to obtain the improved morale and productivity that can flow from an effective employee benefits communication system, preparers of written communications must understand the nature and steps of the writing process and some basic writing principles.

The Writing Process

The first consideration in developing written materials is the nature of the readership. The technical, educational, and literacy levels of anyone who will receive the message must be ascertained, along with the language, social, and economic background of the reader. This is referred to as *knowing the audience.* As one should not write down to or patronize an audience, one should always consider how an idea can be best expressed in writing to all who will read the message. Clarity, the precision of the words chosen, is of paramount importance. Once this overall principle is accepted, the writing process can proceed through its four fundamental steps; namely, prewriting, writing or drafting, revising, and final editing and proofing.

Prewriting. Before writing the first word of the first draft, there are preliminary considerations. A writer must gather the necessary data, review it, and order it in a way that will be clear and logical for the readers. The writer then shapes the focus, reconsiders the audience at hand, and finally settles on the length of the communication. At this time the writer should reflect on what will be written and for whom.

Writing or Drafting.   The next step is to compose the initial, or "rough," draft. A writer need not be troubled with general correctness at this stage, because the central function is to elucidate the position being taken, express the ideas, and unravel what may seem to be ambiguous, sophisticated material. After this run-through to test the length of the communication, the accuracy of its concepts, and its clarity, the writer may return to the draft to check for its stylistic flow. This is the moment to work on those principles of style that add a sense of unity and fluidity to the thought. The essential reason for multiple drafts is to avoid rushing through the total composition process at one sitting. It is advisable to allow a first draft to rest—to "age," as it were—so that ideas have time to reassemble, solidify, and perhaps be reshuffled in order to include fresh points of view, more solidly supportive detail, and clarifying concepts that were not previously incorporated.

Revising.   The revision process is important because by this time writers have completed their thought processes, included most of their purposeful detail, and arrived at useful conclusions. Since writing is a recursive act—that is, throughout the writing process writers continually return to previous thoughts to review their logic, reread sentences to readjust their flow, or seek a fresher word to replace a stale one—some of this activity is an ongoing process as one pushes to complete a first draft. Yet this revision segment is reserved for writers to assess seriously how clearly and focused their ideas have been expressed, to check the logical arrangement of paragraphs and the transitions between them, to vary the length and pattern of sentences, and to judge the effectiveness of word choice. This, then, leads to what can be loosely called the *final draft*. However, in truth there may not be such a thing as a final draft, since a writer can always find a better word, delete wordiness that has crept in seemingly from nowhere, reposition a runaway sentence more precisely, or eliminate a detail that suddenly has become irrelevant.

Final Editing and Proofreading.   This last part of the writing process allows for *fixing* spelling, *ironing out* the typos, *correcting* punctuation and other mechanical gremlins, and *deleting* infelicitous phrases. Proofreading the final draft allows the writer to "catch" things that might reflect carelessness. When a memo or communication, no matter how trivial, is sent under someone's signature, that person is responsible for every thought, word, and structure. The more errors left undetected, the more that person's work will be considered careless. If a writer does not repair or trivializes obvious but easily corrected writing difficulties, how much can that person be depended on to *carefully* deliver or administer the material represented in the communication? Do not create a negative impression by not following through with a thorough proofreading of the final draft.

Finally, writers can relax when they realize that the act of composing is a continuous process, rather than an activity that stops completely with the distribution of the written communication. What has been overlooked or ungracefully expressed can be improved in the future. Also, the revising and subsequent editing or proofreading process allows writers the luxury of time to evaluate and correct both the real and imagined imperfections in their current drafts.

Overall Approach and Tone

Writers should take the middle road between high formality and low informality. An overly formal approach may be read as too pompous and officious, while an informal presentation may appear too casual, hurried, and ill-conceived. Both extremes produce negative responses from readers. The predominant impression sought should be one of care, honesty, and thoroughness, which will allow readers to judge the reasonableness of the communication's proposition.

Some Writing Principles

10-20-30. Some additional tips undoubtedly will lead to more effective communication. Among these is the "10-20-30 formula" for paragraphs, sentences, and word choice. Simply stated, the 10-20-30 formula is a rule of thumb that can aid a writer in sustaining reader interest. When the writer limits

Paragraphs to an average of 10 sentences,

Sentence length to 20 words, and

The number of polysyllabic words to 30 percent of the total words in the entire composition, reader interest does not diminish, and written communication is more effective.

The U-Shaped Curve.   It is most important not to lose the interest of readers or receivers of messages. Initially, within the first paragraph of a written communication, the reader's attention is high. We can say that it is at the top or the peak of a U-shaped curve. Unfortunately, this interest wavers as one reads other paragraphs, and it drops to the bottom part of the U—into the "valley of disinterest." Toward the conclusion of a communication, the typical pattern of attention moves upward to a second peak of the U, although this second peak is not as high as the first. Consequently, it follows that when written communications are received, readers are compelled to read the first paragraph. The reader is highly motivated at first, particularly when the message may have singular significance for him or her. Nevertheless, interest decreases as the message continues, especially when the receiver finds the message so common that it can be filed away for another day. However, curiosity could move that reader to push ahead to the concluding paragraphs to see if there may be some content more personally relevant than that contained in earlier paragraphs. Thus, a writer should shape a written communication so that the full body of the message is contained in the early paragraphs. The meat of the message must be present early and in a manner sufficiently viable to hold the reader's interest and not be casually dismissed.

Effort/Reward Ratio.   There also is an "effort/reward ratio" theory associated with the effectiveness of written communication. The reader typically asks, "How much reward is there for the effort I expend on this reading?" More selfishly stated, the reader asks, "What will this memo do for me?" or "What will it not do for me?" If the first paragraph does not elicit interest for the overall message, the reader quickly "slips into the valley of disinterest" and merely skims the rest of the material. The earlier a written message can relay a sense of importance to *and for* the reader, the longer it will be read and the less disinterest there will be. A writer must strive to keep the reader's interest; otherwise, ineffective communication may result.

The Three S's.   "The three S's" also can help writers. Writing should be *short, simple,* and *sincere.* Brevity induces recipients to read the entire message. Simplicity and clarity enable readers to understand the transmitted ideas, and sincerity is an intangible that might convince them to accept the content of a message. However, too little information may lead the reader to feel that the company is merely paying lip service to the idea of benefits, which could undermine the sincerity of effort behind the company's intentions.

Most people quickly tire of reading long, drawn-out communications. Conversely, they fully appreciate deriving the most information from the fewest words. Brevity is more than "the soul of wit"; it is an investment that pays dividends. A reader more frequently reads through something short and specific than something that is wordy and tedious. Too much in a paragraph tends to bore, confuse, or turn readers against the topic at hand.

Visual Appeal. Writing can be made visually appealing and immediately informative by headlining significant sections. Centering some major headings may make them even more inviting. This affords the reader with an opportunity to read a skeletal outline of a proposal and then return to each segment separately. Readers should not be compelled to scrutinize each paragraph to unearth the topic thought. Instead, they can scan the entire message, look for substantive matter, and be directed to what catches their eye or their interest.

Examples of Effective Written Communication

Three examples and accompanying explanations are included here to show applications of the principles just explained. The numbers in brackets after each sentence in each example represent, *first,* the number of words in the sentence, and *second,* the number of polysyllabic words in the sentence. This will help you to apply the 10-20-30 formula.

Example 1. This example consists of an introductory section of a memorandum regarding an employee benefit package.

TO: Current and Prospective Employees of XYZ Company

FROM: Employee Benefits Management Committee

SUBJECT: Employee Benefits Package

The management committee in charge of the Employee Benefit Package is presenting its plan to everyone currently employed and to all prospective employees [23 words, 11 polysyllabic words]. The introductory outline of the full package and the breakdown of each item should serve to acquaint you with the general provisions of each benefit [25, 8]. If you have any questions about the following, Mr. B _____ in the Personnel Office will gladly discuss specific areas of the plan with you [24, 7].

This memo clearly introduces its purpose. The approach is solicitous; the beginning suggests that there was a group meeting to discuss the welfare of the employees, and the remaining part opens the door for oral, personal communication if for some reason the written message is misunderstood. As for attention span, there would seem to be no time for disinterest, because by the time the reader might possibly begin to stray, the introductory pleasantries stop and the actual package is presented.

Example 2. This example consists of an outline of the benefits package made available by an employer. The outline is taken from the employee handbook of the sponsoring employer.

EMPLOYEE BENEFITS PACKAGE

Every employee with the XYZ Company at least six months is eligible for the benefits listed below: [16 words, 6 polysyllabic words]
A. Major Medical Insurance
B. Accident Insurance
C. Life Insurance
D. Disability Income
E. Supplemental Unemployment Benefits
F. Scholarship Services
G. Partial College Tuition Reimbursement
H. Prepaid Legal Services
Each of the above benefits is explained briefly in the following sections [12, 5].

Visually, this example engages the reader because there is no word clutter. If readers were turned off by the earlier introductory material, they can be brought to another peak of interest by looking through the benefits and focusing on those that are especially appealing. Therefore, the memo automatically directs readers to a high peak of interest and sustains that level as they locate the areas to investigate further. If sections A through H are kept relatively short, there should be no time to allow for a fall into that valley of disinterest. Note that the number of words per sentence and the number of polysyllabic words corresponds neatly to the 10-20-30 formula.

Example 3.   This example consists of a section in the employee handbook explaining the nature of one of the employee benefits provided.

MAJOR MEDICAL INSURANCE COVERAGE ELIGIBILITY

All employees with the company at least six months are eligible for medical benefits as outlined by the participating program the employee chooses [23, 10]. The company offers a choice of the following plans [9, 3]:
A. Blue Cross/Blue Shield, Plan B.
B. Great River Valley Health Plan.
C. The Priority Health Maintenance Plan.

Cost
The company will pay the cost of whatever plan an employee chooses, provided that employee meets the requirements of the plan [21, 8]. Dependent coverage is also available, but that cost must be paid by the employee [14, 4]. Although the costs of the plans may vary, the company will pay the employee's fee regardless of the difference [19, 6].

Exclusions
The only exclusions in medical coverage for employees and their families are those imposed by the medical plan itself [20, 9]. The company will not exclude any one of its employees from choosing one of its medical plans [17, 5].

This example demonstrates the principles previously outlined and the flexibility afforded management to list its medical offerings. Under "Eligibility," management may choose to introduce a brief summary of each plan or merely list the three. Each succinct paragraph forces readers to cover the central points of each plan as they glance quickly at the benefits that most interest them.

The longest section is the first, but the spacing serves a good purpose because readers can easily follow what is being offered. Since everything is spelled out clearly, there are no traps. The sentences are well within the 10-20-30 prescribed formula; although approximately 35 percent of the words are polysyllabic, any layperson can understand the language without resorting to a dictionary.

The sample is *short* and *simple,* but it is literate and erudite; nothing in the sample talks down or up to the reader. The tone is easy, direct, neither supercilious nor superior. The employer promotes its benefits honestly and adds *sincerity* by listing a number of alternatives, by informing an employee where specific material is available, and by insisting that the company excludes no one from its medical plans.

Oral Communications

Oral communications take place in many different ways. They involve face-to-face discussions or verbal orders between two or more people, telephone conversations, speeches, meetings, the use of public address systems, and other uses of the spoken word. Generally, oral communications are transmitted faster than written communications. Also, under some circumstances, oral communication can provide a greater basis for achieving common understanding by the participants than that allowable through written communication. This ability to gain a higher degree of common understanding varies with the form of oral communication used. For example, face-to-face communications between two people or within small groups typically have this quality to a greater extent than telephone conversations and speeches. Face-to-face communication gives each participant the immediate opportunity to observe the body language of the other, ask questions, and eliminate misunderstanding.

The seven-step communication process—idea, message formation, transmission, receipt, understanding, action, and feedback—applies to oral as well as written communications. Thus, the sender of an oral message should know him- or herself and the audience, understand the potential barriers to an effective communication, formulate the message in a thoughtful and articulate manner, and select and use an appropriate medium to transmit the message. The action and feedback steps then can be used to appraise the receipt and understanding of the message by the receiver or audience.

Oral communications also are subject to the same basic principles that guide written communications. That is, oral messages should be constructed in accordance with the 10-20-30 formula, the U-shaped-curve concept, the effect/reward ratio theory, and the three S's.

Some additional factors concerning oral communication should be noted. Oral communications are more effective when there is verbal interaction between the participants. A speaker can use gestures, facial expressions, and other types of body language to enhance the process. The level of the speaker's voice, the use of pauses, the rate of speaking, enunciation, and other vocal characteristics play an important role in speech communication. Moreover, as is the case with written communications, visual materials such as pamphlets, graphs, charts, diagrams, posters, and slides can improve the quality of oral communications immensely.

EVALUATING BENEFITS COMMUNICATIONS

Communications basically should be evaluated in terms of whether the intended message in fact has been received. Actually, this is incorporated within the communication process itself as the feedback step. In addition to confirming that the message has been received, there is another factor to be considered in the evaluation of employee benefits communications that focus on some action by the receiver. The evaluation of these types of communications includes some consideration of whether the desired action has taken place.

Employee-benefit-communication events frequently are action oriented, and they should be evaluated on the basis of two questions: Was the message received and understood? Has the desired action occurred?

When the desired results take place, generally, both questions are answered positively. For example, benefits claims typically are correctly completed and filed if the accompanying instructions are communicated in a clear manner that is understandable by the wide cross section of the audience. Also, there are fewer benefits-related questions and inquiries if the applicable employee handbook carefully covers most of the issues that tend to arise.

When the desired action does not follow a communication, it is because the message was not effectively communicated, or because it was fully communicated but not put into effect for some reason. Initially any analysis should focus on identifying the source or cause of the problem. Traditional problem-solving techniques are very useful for this identification stage, as well as for dealing with the problem itself, of course.

CHAPTER 54

EMPLOYEE BENEFIT COMMUNICATIONS IN OPERATION

Linda Grosso

As mentioned in Chapter 53, employee benefits have undergone many changes in recent years. Government legislation has increased the complexity of benefit plans; the cost of providing benefit coverages has risen dramatically;[1] and as Table 54–1 shows, benefits have come to be an important element in an organization's efforts to attract and maintain a qualified work force. All these factors have greatly increased the importance of benefit communications. This chapter reviews the role of communications in today's employee benefits environment. It then describes the categories of benefit communications and the process of developing, implementing, and evaluating benefit communications programs.

THE ROLE OF BENEFIT COMMUNICATIONS

Employers use benefit communications to educate and provide information to employees on their benefit coverages. In order to fulfill this function successfully, communications efforts need to address legislative

---

[1]According to the U.S. Chamber of Commerce, total benefit payments made by all U.S. employers rose from $743 billion in 1986 to $965 billion in 1989. Payments are expected to exceed $1 trillion in 1990.

TABLE 54-1
Importance of Employer-Sponsored Benefits in the Decision to Accept or Reject a Job Offer

Very Important	57%
Important	27%
Somewhat Important	10%
Not Important	4%
Do Not Know	1%

Source: Employee Benefit Research Institute and The Gallup Organization, Inc., 1990.

requirements, employee-relations issues, and the employer's administrative needs.

Legislative Requirements

The federal government has long required employers to communicate to employees on benefit issues. The Employee Retirement Income Security Act of 1974 (ERISA) is a landmark piece of legislation in that it contains specific employee benefit reporting and disclosure rules and imposes penalties on organizations that do not comply. Penalties for noncompliance can include fines and/or imprisonment for the sponsoring organization as well as a loss of special tax treatment for the benefit plan.[2] As a result, ERISA has been a major force in the growth of the employee benefit communications field.

ERISA defined three categories of communications materials for plan participants and beneficiaries on the basis of how they are to be provided:

- Materials that must be given automatically.
- Materials that must be given upon written request.
- Materials that must be made available for review at the plan administrator's office without the need for a written request.

ERISA requires plan sponsors to provide all participants with a written summary of each of their benefit plans. The regulations specify

---

[2]ERISA Sec. 501, 502(a), 502(c)(1) and (2) and IRC Sec. 6652(3).

that these documents, known as *summary plan descriptions* (SPDs), must be ''written in a manner calculated to be understood by the average plan participant.''[3]

SPDs are the primary reference source for an employee to find out how a plan works, what eligibility provisions exist, what benefits are available, and how to apply for those benefits. Under current law, summary plan descriptions must contain the information outlined in Table 54–2. The importance of SPDs should not be underestimated. Employers have lost court cases because an SPD implied an employee was entitled to a coverage for which the actual plan document did not provide.

Updated SPDs must be distributed to plan participants and beneficiaries receiving benefits under the plan every fifth year after the plan becomes subject to ERISA. If there have been no changes to the information contained in the SPD during that time, an updated SPD must be distributed every tenth year.[4]

In addition to summary plan descriptions, employees also must receive in writing:

- *Summary of material modifications,* which describes any significant changes made to the plan affecting the information contained in the SPD.
- *Summary annual reports,* which provide information about the financial status of defined benefit plans covered by ERISA.
- *Statement of accrued and vested pension benefit* upon termination of employment.
- *Explanation of any denied claims* and information on how to appeal the denial.
- *Notice of eligibility for the preretirement surviving spouse's death benefit* if this is an elective coverage (that is, not paid for by the employer). Employees must receive an explanation of the benefit, their right to waive coverage and the effect of doing so, the rights of their spouses, plus the employees' right to revoke their waiver and the effects of doing so.

---

[3]ERISA Sec. 102(a)(1). ERISA provides only general guidance on interpreting the term *written in a manner.* Employers are held accountable, nevertheless.

[4]ERISA Sec. 104(b)(1)(B).

TABLE 54-2
Legally-Mandated Information In Summary Plan Descriptions

Official plan name	Name/title/address of trustee(s)
Name/address of administrator	Description of relevant provisions of any applicable collective bargaining agreement
Name/address of persons(s) on whom legal process may be served	
	Source of financing for the plan
Whether records are kept on a calendar, policy, or fiscal year basis	Procedure for appealing a denied claim
Date of the end of the plan year	ERISA rights statement
Employer tax identification number	Name of any organization through which benefits are provided
Plan number	
Effect on participants of the termiation of the plan	Whether or not the plan is covered by the Pension Benefit Guaranty Corporation (PBGC)
Type of plan (defined benefit, defined contribution, or welfare plan)	

Source: ERISA Sec. 102.

- *Notice stating the sponsor has applied to the IRS for its plan to receive qualified status.* Employers can post this notice in the work site in lieu of distributing copies.
- *Plan termination notice.* Notification of intent to terminate single-employer pension plans.

Table 54-3 summarizes the reporting and disclosure requirements for all three categories of ERISA-mandated materials and tells when each item must be provided to employees.

Employee Relations Issues

Benefit communications programs can help employers maximize the return on their growing investment in employee benefits. These programs can promote employee understanding and appreciation of the total cost of their benefit coverages in addition to the details of the plans. At the same time, benefit communications can help employees to maintain the appropriate perspective when changes are made in their benefit plans.

For example, employees may not appreciate the benefits of an employee stock ownership plan (ESOP) or understand how an ESOP is

TABLE 54–3
Summary of Reporting and Disclosure Requirements for Benefit Communications Materials

	Required For			To Participants	To Government	
	Defined Contribution Plans	Defined Benefit Plans	Welfare Plans		Agency	When

A. Communication Materials Given Automatically

	Defined Contribution Plans	Defined Benefit Plans	Welfare Plans	To Participants	Agency	When
1. Summary Plan Description	Yes	Yes	Yes	Within 90 days after an employee becomes a participant; within 120 days after a plan becomes covered by ERISA.	DOL	Within 120 days after plan becomes covered by ERISA.
2. Updated Summary Plan Description	Yes	Yes	Yes	If amendments are made to a plan, every 5 years; if no amendments to plan, every 10 years.	DOL	If amendments made to plan, every 5 years; if no amendments to plan, every 10 years.
3. Summary of Material Modifications (SMM)	Yes	Yes	Yes	Within 210 days after the end of the plan year in which modifications or changes occur.	DOL	Within 210 days after the end of the plan year in which modifications or changes occur.
4. Summary Annual Report	Yes	Yes	Yes	Within 2 months after the deadline for filing the Annual Report.		
5. Statement of Benefits to Terminated Vested Participants	Yes	Yes	No	By the due date for the Form 5500 filed for the year following the termination. (See B2.)		
6. Statement of Reasons for Claim Denial	Yes	Yes	Yes	Within 90 days after denial of participant's claim for benefits (may be extended to within 180 days of such denial).		
7. Preretirement Surviving Spouse's Annuity Notice	No[1]	Yes[2]	No	Generally, to participants aged 32–35; within a reasonable period if participation occurs at a later age; earlier if participant separates prior to age 35.		
8. Notice of Intent to Terminate the Plan	No	Yes	No	At least 60 days before the proposed termination date.	PBGC	90 days after proposed termination date. (Form 500).
9. Notification to Interested Parties	Yes	Yes	No	Not less than 7 or more than 21 days prior to application if notice by posting or in person; not less than 10 or more than 24 days if by mail.		
10. Notice of Intent to Freeze or Significantly Reduce Benefit Accruals	No[3]	Yes	No	Within 15 days before proposed effective date.		

[1] Includes all money purchase plans; other plans are exempt if vested benefit is automatically payable to married participant's spouse upon death of participant.

[2] Notice not required where plan fully subsidizes cost of preretirement surviving spouse's annuity.

[3] Includes money purchase plans; other plans are exempt.

TABLE 54–3 (concluded)

| | Required For | | | To Participants | To Government | |
	Defined Contribution Plans	Defined Benefit Plans	Welfare Plans		Agency	When
B. Communication Materials Given to Participants on Written Request[4]						
1. Copies of Plan Documents	Yes	Yes	Yes	Within 30 days after request.		
2. Annual Report (Form 5500)	Yes	Yes	Yes	Within 30 days after request.	IRS	Last day of 7th month after end of plan year.[5]
3. Personal Pension Statement (Not more than once a year)[6]	Yes	Yes	No	60 days after receipt of written request (or 120 days after the end of the prior plan year).		
C. Communication Materials Made Available to Participants for Review						
1. Inspection of Plan Documents	Yes	Yes	Yes	At all times in the principal offices of the plan administrator and within 10 days after request at certain specified work locations.[7]		
2. Annual Report (Form 5500)	Yes	Yes	Yes	When the report is filed with the IRS.	IRS	Last day of 7th month after end of plan year.[5]
3. Application for Plan Qualification upon Adoption, Amendment, or Termination (Forms 5300 and 5310)	Yes	Yes	No	Upon request.	IRS	When a determination letter upon adoption, amendment, or termination is requested.

[4] A reasonable charge may be made for most requested materials.

[5] Extension available up to:
9½ months after end of plan year if extension for filing granted by IRS in response to filing of Form 5558, or
8½ months after end of tax year (but not later than the extended tax return due date) if plan year and tax year coincide and employer obtains an extension for filing tax return to later date.

A copy of the IRS extension must be attached to the annual report form (Form 5500 Series).

[6] Proposed regulation; no charge to participant for materials supplied.

[7] Locations specified in ERISA regulation 29 CFR 2520.104(b)1.

impacted by economic conditions unless it is properly communicated to them. Cost-containment programs are another area that can affect employee relations. Utilization monitoring, cost-sharing, and even benefit reductions are a few of the ways employers have tried to control rising health care costs. Employee reaction to such changes has ranged from a reluctant understanding and acceptance to—as NYNEX experienced in 1989—the staging of a strike.

Whenever an organization implements a benefit change—particularly one that could result in a negative employee reaction—a communications program is vital. Explaining the reasons for such change, putting the change in context with the economic state of the employer (and/or employer's industry), and telling employees why the employer chose this change over other alternatives help employees accept it as reasonable and necessary.

Administrative Needs

An effective benefit communications program can enhance productivity within an organization by reducing the amount of time it spends responding to routine or repetitive benefit questions from employees. In addition, recent communication innovations—such as the computer-based enrollment programs described later in this chapter—can help to reduce plan administration expenses.

TYPES OF EMPLOYEE BENEFIT COMMUNICATIONS

Benefit communications can be classified as either educational or personal.

Educational Programs

Educational programs include introductory, reference, and reinforcement communications. *Introductory* communications focus on explaining benefit programs to new hires who have little, if any, prior knowledge about the benefits available to them. *Reference* communications provide benefits information concentrating on ERISA-required materials such as summary plan descriptions, summary annual reports, and notices for preretirement surviving spouses' benefit coverages. *Reinforcement* communications are ongoing and are used to stimulate employee interest in their benefits and instill appreciation for the organization providing them.

Personal Communications

Personal communications include materials that provide employees with information about their specific benefits. This information may be the amount of money in their defined contribution plan account or the status of their accrued pension benefit. These communications show employees how a benefit program relates to their own specific circumstances.

THE BENEFIT COMMUNICATIONS PROGRAM

Developing a Strategy

Planning a benefit communications program is a multistep process. The first step is for the organization to identify the project's parameters. These include its budget, its goals, the messages to be communicated, and the audience.

Budget
The size of the budget influences the scope of a communications project and, therefore, has a direct impact on the communications tools used. For example, a typed memo duplicated in house costs much less than a four-page brochure printed in two colors on glossy paper. Therefore, it is sensible to specify a budget first. Otherwise, the communications effort may fail because it set unreachable goals given available finances.

Goals
The program's goals provide direction and define the scope of the project. For example, is the communications effort to introduce a new benefit plan, or to announce changes to an existing plan? Is the employer seeking to remind employees of their current coverages, or to increase participation in its savings plan? Minor changes to a benefit program, such as a new medical claim form, may require only the distribution of a memo describing the new form along with a copy of the form for

review. A major change, such as a new flexible benefits program, might require a more extensive, multimedia communications campaign including announcement letters, comprehensive brochures, and employee meetings.

If possible, goals should include a quantitative component to allow for evaluation of the project's effectiveness. Measurable goals might include:

- To obtain targeted levels of participation in certain benefit plans.
- To reduce the number of questions coming into the benefits department.
- To reduce the number of ballot errors during an enrollment.

Message

The nature of the communications program's message must be considered, too. It is an extremely important factor that is often overlooked. Not all messages are positive or simple to explain. For example, increasing the cost of participants' contributions to the health care plan is a sensitive issue, and the communications material should reflect this. Likewise, employees may have difficulty understanding how they will be affected by a switch from a defined benefit pension plan to a cash balance plan. A communications approach, including examples, might be considered in this situation, especially if employees can be shown how such a change would affect each of them personally.

Audience

The benefit communications program's audience also should be defined. Is this communications effort for employees in one location or several? Is it for active or retired employees? Consider the audience's knowledge and perceptions about their benefit coverages. This can be ascertained from the questions handled by the benefits department. In some instances, surveys or focus groups may be needed to obtain this information.

Know the demographics of the target audience. Today, organizations must develop communications programs to reach an increasingly diverse work force as measured by cultural background, level of education, lifestyle, and language(s) spoken. The communications tools and techniques utilized should reflect and respect this diversity. The growing use of bilingual communications is one example of how this diversity has impacted benefit communications programs.

Once an organization has defined the parameters for a benefit communications effort, it can select the appropriate tools to relay its messages to employees, develop an implementation schedule, and develop an evaluation process.

Traditional Tools and Techniques

As a rule, communications material should be organized logically (for example, explain participation requirements before describing how to apply for benefits) and should be personal in tone (for example, use the term *your spouse,* not *the employee's spouse*). Legal and technical jargon should be avoided whenever possible.

The current trend in benefit communications is to develop programs that offer the audience the opportunity to see and hear a benefits message. This approach acknowledges that individuals have different *learning styles.* Some people learn best by reading; others find it helpful to have a message explained orally to them; still others prefer a participatory approach, where they can ask questions and get personal information.[5]

As Table 54–4 indicates, employers rely heavily on print media. One reason for this is the large number of legal requirements for printed items, especially for employee benefit communications. However; a number of benefit communications tools are available that do not rely solely on the printed word, as the following subsections show.

Print Materials
Print materials used in employee benefit communications programs include:

• *Summary Plan Descriptions.* These are used mainly as a reference source. SPDs can be provided to employees as individual booklets or packaged together in a handbook that contains the SPDs for all employer-sponsored benefits (as well as other policies and practices related to human resources).

---

[5] Waynne B. James and Michael W. Galbraith, "Perceptual Learning Styles: Implications and Techniques for the Practitioner," *Lifelong Learning: An Omnibus of Practice and Research* 8 (January 1985), pp. 20–23.

TABLE 54-4
Media used by Employers to Communicate with Employees
(Asterisks indicate print media.)

Item	Utilization
*Employee publications (ongoing) for all employees	79%
*Newsletter/publications for management-level employees	26%
*Personnel handbook	76%
*Benefits—summary plan descriptions	87%
*Benefits—annual personalized statements	55%
*Benefits—highlights materials	45%
Benefits—interactive software	3%
Audiovisual presentations	41%
Group meetings	82%
One-on-one meetings with supervisors	56%
*Bulletin boards	84%
*Employee memos	78%

Source: *The Wyatt Communicator,* The Wyatt Company, 1989.

• *Announcement Letters, Memos, and/or Brochures.* These are used to explain changes in benefits or to introduce a new plan. In addition, they can serve as the ERISA-required summary of material modifications.

• *Highlight Brochures.* These materials can provide an overview of one plan or an entire benefits program. Highlight brochures are often given to employees to remind them of their benefits and are used to promote an organization's benefits program to new hires and prospective employees.

• *Promotional Materials.* These can include posters, payroll stuffers, "hot lines," and newsletters. Promotional materials can serve as advertisements, promote the value of the organization's benefits program, reinforce a message about major changes to a benefits program, or remind employees of deadlines for plan enrollments. Other promotional approaches include developing a benefits communications logo, theme, or "tag line" for use with all communications efforts.

Employee Surveys and Focus Groups
These tools provide employers with information useful in the development and evaluation of a communications effort. For example, when planning a communications strategy, employee surveys and focus groups can help identify current knowledge levels and perceptions of the targeted

audience. Employers then can use this information to tailor their communications messages appropriately.

Focus groups and surveys also can be used during the design phase of a project to pretest communications material. Although this step lengthens a project schedule, it offers the opportunity to "try out" new or different communication approaches as well as fine-tune material before it is put into production. As a result, pretesting can improve the effectiveness of the final product.

Another use of surveys and focus groups is to obtain employee feedback on the impact of a particular communications project. The "Evaluating the Results" section later in the chapter describes the use of these feedback techniques for assessment purposes.

Employee Meetings

Employee meetings offer the opportunity for a *two-way* exchange of information. Employees have the opportunity to ask questions—and get answers on the spot to most of them. Employee meetings also provide management with firsthand feedback regarding employee attitudes on the benefits program and the communications message(s).

Employee meetings can be formal or informal, and in group or individual settings. Formal meetings are those that are arranged specifically to discuss the benefits program. Informal ones include discussions arising from questions employees ask during staff meetings and in private conversations with supervisors.

Formal meetings require meeting leaders. These individuals can be members of the benefits department or company employees who have been trained for this purpose. Depending upon the circumstances, external personnel (such as benefit consultants) may fulfill this function.

Line supervisors and managers are more apt to play a role in informal meetings. Given their position in the organization and their daily contact with employees, supervisors and managers can influence employees' attitudes regarding their benefits. To assist supervisors and managers in this area, some employers have provided them with administrative guides covering frequently asked questions and early releases of benefit announcements.

Audiovisual and Audio Materials

Audiovisual materials include slide and/or video presentations and are used primarily in conjunction with employee meetings. They help ensure the consistency of the "spoken" message. This is a consideration when meeting leaders are not benefits professionals. Use of these materials also acknowledges employees' differing learning styles by giving employees the opportunity to both see and hear a benefits message. Audiovisual presentations can help announce benefit changes, introduce new plans, and provide an overview of the benefits program to new hires.

Audio materials, on the other hand, are designed for individual use. These materials include cassette recordings and are used primarily outside the workplace—for example, an employee might listen to a cassette tape while driving to work. Audio communications tools can also play an important role in getting benefits messages to employees who have visual problems, dyslexia, or difficulty comprehending written materials.

Personalized Communications Material

Personalized materials—or benefit statements—show how benefit programs affect employees' individual circumstances. They provide a written record of the benefit coverages a participant has with the employer as of a certain date. These statements often are oriented toward specific events, showing employees what benefits they are entitled to in the event they get sick or injured, become disabled, retire, or die. The statements can cover all benefits, the selections an employee made under a flexible benefits program, or an employee's accrued and projected pension plan benefits.

When personalized statements are used in conjunction with an enrollment process they can include the cost of optional coverages. This approach is common under flexible benefits programs. During the flexible benefit plan enrollment periods employers give a personalized statement to each employee detailing his or her current benefit selections as well as the cost for each of the benefit options available to him or her in the following year.

Another variation is the preretirement statement, which outlines all the employer-sponsored benefits an employee can look forward to after retirement. These statements also show Social Security benefits and the optional forms of payment possible under the pension plan.

Interactive Technology

Interactive technology is a relatively new force in employee benefit communications. Among its chief advantages are that it:

- Provides employees with 24-hour access to benefit information traditionally available only from benefits-department personnel.
- Reduces the number of repetitive questions currently handled by the employers' benefits departments.
- Automates the benefit transaction and enrollment process.

Current interactive communications programs fall into two technology categories:

- *Visual or PC-based programs.* These often include dedicated "user stations" with standard or customized computer equipment.
- *Audio- or voice-response programs.* These provide information over the telephone.

Both technologies have advantages and disadvantages. For example, whereas voice-response applications are as accessible as the nearest telephone, PC-based applications can present more detailed information because the user sees the information as opposed to just hearing it.

Uses of Interactive Communications

These technologies can be used to develop interactive communications applications that:

- Educate.
- Provide personal status information.
- Accept transactions.

Educational Programs.   These programs usually are PC-based. They can provide an overview of a benefit plan and explain how an employee's benefit coverage is affected by a change in status. This status change can be professional (such as a promotion, termination, layoff, leave of absence) or personal (such as marriage, divorce, birth of a child).

In addition, these programs can act as automated worksheets that enable employees to estimate:

- Repayment schedules for loans made through a defined contribution plan.
- The cost of benefit selections made through a flexible benefits program.

- The impact of 401(k) or Section 125 contributions on take-home pay.
- The growth of their contributions to a defined contribution plan over various time spans and at various contribution rates.

Educational programs can be the least expensive of all interactive approaches because they do not depend on outside data and require no specialized or dedicated hardware. These programs are self-service, and the employee enters all necessary salary and service-type information needed to do the calculations. For this reason, they are ideal for supporting communications efforts in locations without benefits representatives and in settings with round-the-clock operations.

Personal Status Programs.   These applications—which can be PC- or telephone-based—bring the user into the world of ongoing, *data-dependent* communications. They provide employees with personal information such as defined contribution plan account balances, flexible benefits coverages chosen, and accrued pension benefits. It also is common to include educational program features such as automated worksheets and plan highlights in personal status programs.

Table 54–5 depicts user statistics from one interactive, PC-based application. Note in the table that employee usage varies, although

TABLE 54–5
Interactive Communications Usage Statistics, 03/01/90 to 03/31/90
(population base of 24,000)

Name of Screen	Number of Times Used	Name of Screen	Number of Times Used
Savings plan balance	3,726	Flexible benefits plan coverages	204
Savings plan loans	1,031	Savings plan modeling	158
Savings plan withdrawals	799	Survivor benefits	88
Retirement benefits	721	Savings plan highlights	78
Vacation/holidays	351	Group life insurance	74
Employee spending account	287	Medical coverage	69
Investment projections	233	Disability benefits	43

Source: Metropolitan Life Insurance Company, 1990.

personal information for capital appreciation plans such as savings plans is used most frequently.

Since these programs use telephones, or PCs with touchscreens or modified keypads, they can be attractive to employees who are uncomfortable or unfamiliar with computers. In this regard, telephone-based systems offer the advantage of familiarity. All employees know how to use the telephone, and these systems can be reached by anyone with access to a Touch-Tone telephone in or out of a work setting.

Benefit Transaction Programs. The ability to use interactive technology to automate transactions has played the largest role in the growth of computer-based communications. Specifically, employees can use this technology to:

- *Enroll in plans.* Until now, the primary focus has been on flexible benefits and spending account enrollments. Several organizations, however, are beginning to pursue the automation of their defined contribution plan open enrollment process.

  Enrollments were the first benefit transactions to be automated.
- Automating an enrollment process has several advantages. An employer can reduce or eliminate the time needed to: check enrollment forms manually, input employee selections into the plan record-keeping or administration system, and correct paper enrollment forms not properly filled out when first submitted.
- *Make changes in their benefit coverages.* For defined contribution plans this can mean changing contribution rates and investment selections.
- *Request a loan or withdrawal* from a defined contribution plan.

Employers can use this technology to conduct surveys on benefits or other employee-relations issues. For example, they can solicit employees' opinions on current benefits or potential changes. This information is useful for benefit planning efforts as well as for measuring the effectiveness of communications programs.

Whatever the topic, the survey should be short if it is conducted through a dedicated user station or over a voice-response system. These interactive formats are geared toward short sessions and providing quick answers. The survey should not hinder the employees' ability to obtain the information *they* want. Three questions on a user station and two questions on a voice-response system are suggested limits.

Impact of Interactive Communications

Preliminary research on the impact of this technology on employers and employees is very positive. In 1989 the Metropolitan Life Insurance Company surveyed benefit administrators at 49 locations utilizing PC-based interactive programs. (These programs provided educational and personal benefit information to employees.) Table 54–6 shows the results to a question regarding the impact interactive communications had on the respondents' workload.

Future Trends in the Interactive Field

As interactive technology progresses, it will be used more frequently for bilingual applications, education-specific programs, and retiree communications, all three of which are growing concerns in the business world today. Employers can apply this technology in developing communications programs in languages other than English and in designing programs for specific educational needs. At the same time, with the graying of the population, communicating benefit information to retirees is very important for the 1990s. Retiree benefit programs offer casebook opportunities for voice-response systems.

Flexible benefits enrollment applications in English and Spanish are current examples of the use of bilingual software programs. As these programs evolve they will include educational and personalized communications in addition to benefit transaction capabilities.

Interactive preretirement or financial-planning programs represent a growing benefit communications area. They involve complex concepts (like diversification of investments, tax impact on postretirement income,

TABLE 54–6
Benefit Administrators' Survey

	Since your organization's interactive application was introduced, the number of:	
	Routine Questions	Complex Questions
Has increased	3%	13%
Has stayed the same	21%	48%
Has decreased	76%	39%
TOTAL	100%	100%

Source: Metropolitan Life Insurance Company, 1989.

and so on) and thus could benefit from education-specific as well as multi-lingual presentations.

Some organizations already use voice-response systems to communicate pension payment information to retirees. Potential future uses for interactive technology include enabling retirees to redirect where their pension checks are sent or confirm the status of a medical claim. This last application, reviewing the status of a medical claim, would be useful for active as well as retired employees.

Given the decision-making responsibilities current benefit programs place upon employees and the lack of staff available to conduct in-depth employee meetings, interactive technology offers employers a viable means of meeting the growing challenge of communicating ''in a manner calculated to be understood by the average plan participant.''

Developing a Schedule

Whether the project is a large, multimedia effort or just a newsletter article, it should have an implementation schedule. A schedule is insurance—particularly for a project requiring a team effort. It outlines to all parties involved what is required of them and when.

A schedule itemizes each phase of the project. This covers:

- *Drafting the materials.* Include print copy, audiovisual scripts, and, for computerized communications, an outline of any benefit calculations performed.
- *Reviewing and approving the drafts.* Identify areas—and individuals within these areas—that need to review draft copy (for example, benefits, legal, corporate communications) and determine who must approve the final copy before proceeding to the next step.
- *Producing materials.* Identify each component of the production process. For computerized communications this includes outlining when input data is needed and when software programs will be available for testing.
- *Training meeting leaders (if applicable).* Indicate if this can be accomplished at some point during the production stage, or if it must wait until later.
- *Distributing materials and (if applicable) conducting meetings.* Usually one meeting leader can conduct no more than four sessions during a standard work day.

Critical dates also should be identified on the schedule. These are dates that, if not met, jeopardize the deadline.

Evaluating the Results

Evaluations are an important part of the communications planning process. They enable an organization to determine if its goals for a project have been met, and they provide a benchmark for improving future communications efforts.

Audits

Given the rate at which benefit changes have occurred in recent years, employers should also conduct periodic assessments of their benefit communications programs. Usually called *audits,* these assessments should check current materials for legal compliance. In addition, they should evaluate whether these materials need to be modified to reflect changes in audience demographics, the employer's business focus, or economic conditions.

Surveys and Focus Groups

As stated earlier, surveys and focus groups are often used to obtain employee feedback. Typical questions to ask employees include:

• *How do you rate your employee benefits?* If ratings are low, is it because they don't understand how the plans work, because they feel the plans do not provide the coverages they want, or because they perceive the plans as inadequate in comparison with benefits offered by other employers in their geographic area or industry? Answers to questions such as these can determine whether the problem is a plan design or a communications issue.

• *How do you get answers to your benefit questions?* Is it through the "official" benefit communications channels, or do they look elsewhere for answers?

• *What do you like best/least about the benefit communications program and why?* Answers to these questions help point out what the communications program does well and where it needs improvement.

Surveys and focus groups must be conducted in an objective manner for the results to be valid. Questions with an implied "correct answer" are hard to avoid in surveys and more so in focus groups. Therefore, it is important to obtain the assistance of individuals with professional training in these research areas for employee feedback programs.

CONCLUSION

Benefits are intangible; employees cannot see or touch them. And, while employees will have firsthand experience with health care benefits during their working careers, they will not have the same level of experience with retirement, disability, and death benefits. For this reason, communications play a vital role in developing and maintaining employees' perceptions about their benefits.

PART 12

EMPLOYEE BENEFIT PLANS FOR SMALL BUSINESS

With most new jobs in the United States economy being accounted for by the growth of small businesses, benefit planning issues for such firms take on increasing importance. Many special problems and issues arise in designing, costing and funding plans for small business. Chapter 55 reviews the decisions involved in the choice among various qualified plans. Chapter 56 then evaluates the complex administrative and tax issues inherent in qualified plans for small businesses.

CHAPTER 55

QUALIFIED RETIREMENT PLANS FOR SMALL BUSINESS: CHOICE OF PLAN

Harry V. Lamon, Jr.
Joel R. Wells IV

Adoption of a qualified retirement plan yields one of the major tax benefits that may be obtained by a small-business organization. Such a plan permits current income tax deductions by the small business, a deferral of income tax until receipt by the participants, tax-exempt earnings during the existence of the trust, exemption of the trust from the claims of most creditors of both the participants and the small business, and the availability of favorable treatment under the income tax rules on the payment of benefits from the plan. Although most of these tax advantages may be obtained by the unincorporated business under what is commonly referred to as an H.R. 10 plan, several distinctions remain between corporate plans and H.R. 10 plans despite Congress's attempt in the Tax Equity and Fiscal Responsibility Act of 1982 (TEFRA) to achieve parity between corporate and H.R. 10 plans.

First, this chapter will review the various types of qualified plans that are available to, and generally used by, small businesses and will describe those factors that aid in choosing a particular type of qualified retirement plan. Second, the discussion will focus on the top-heavy plan concept that was inaugurated in TEFRA and on the concept's effect on plan choice. Finally, Section 401(k) cash or deferred arrangements will be discussed separately because of their large potential for use by small businesses. The specific TEFRA and Tax Reform Act of 1986 (TRA '86) changes that effect approximate parity between corporate plans and H.R. 10 plans are discussed in Chapter 56.

GENERAL CONSIDERATIONS IN PLAN CHOICE—TYPES OF PLAN

Once the decision to establish a qualified retirement plan is made by the small business, care should be taken to ensure that the plan is designed to meet its goals. The decisions regarding the type and design of the qualified retirement plan to be established are almost as crucial as the decision to adopt any plan at all.

Of course, a portion of the income received from any small business must be used to pay overhead (including rent, insurance, etc.), another portion must be used to provide direct compensation to the employees, and only the remainder may be used to provide fringe benefits and qualified retirement plan benefits. Thus, probably the most important aspect of choosing the appropriate qualified retirement plan is determining the amount of contributions that can be made on an annual, recurring basis to the plan. If the income of the small business is entirely exhausted through the payment of overhead expenses and the payment of direct compensation to the employees, funds will obviously not be available to make contributions to any plan. On the other hand, if the employer elects to reduce the amount of direct compensation or is able to economize in other ways, funds will be available for the qualified plan.

The choice of qualified retirement plans is probably easiest in a small business with one shareholder and probably most difficult in a small business with more than one but fewer than ten shareholders, particularly where there is wide divergence in the ages of the various shareholders. The authors' experience is that generally the older shareholders have seen the "handwriting on the wall" and desire to create as much in the form of retirement benefits as their income will allow, while the younger employee-shareholders may prefer to defer little or nothing.

The decade of the 1980s brought tremendous changes to the law governing qualified plans, many of which were specifically aimed at reducing what were perceived as abuses by small qualified plans. Examples of such changes discussed in this and the succeeding chapter include the top-heavy rules, the affiliated service group and employee leasing rules, the minimum participation rules, and the new exhaustive nondiscrimination rules. Moreover, small plans have been the target of new enforcement initiatives by the Department of Labor and the Internal Revenue Service. Finally, the economics of defined benefit plans, as well as increasingly stringent regulations that apply to them, have almost eliminated them as a viable option for all but a few larger small businesses with a substantial and completely reliable cash flow. Thus, in the absence of some compelling special needs, most small businesses in the decade to come will choose from an increasingly restricted set of fairly standard plan alternatives whose features have already been tested for compliance with the complex regulatory scheme.

The establishment of a qualified retirement plan should not proceed without the advice of attorneys, accountants, and consultants. Even if the shareholders desire to adopt one of the many available master or prototype plans, the assistance of an attorney and accountant should be sought prior to the adoption of the plan. After carefully reviewing the various needs and desires of the small business, in conjunction with the practical and legal ramifications of the various types of plans that are available, these advisers can greatly assist in designing the most appropriate plan for the small business.

The following discussion is not intended to provide exhaustive treatment of all aspects of qualified retirement plans; rather, the discussion merely focuses on those aspects that are particularly applicable to small business so that the owners of the small business and their advisers will not overlook them in designing the qualified retirement plan.

Regular Profit-Sharing Plans

A profit-sharing plan is typically the first type of qualified retirement plan that an employer should consider. Profit-sharing plans are among the many types of defined contribution plans. The common characteristic of all defined contribution plans is that they provide individual accounts for each participant, although all plan assets are normally commingled for investment purposes. A participant's retirement benefit under a defined contribution plan is based solely on the amount in the participant's account.[1] This arrangement provides a certain measure of security for the employer maintaining the plan because, unlike a defined benefit plan, a

---

[1] IRC 414 (i).

defined contribution plan does not promise any specific level of benefits; therefore, if the plan suffers poor investment experience, the employer will not be called on to underwrite the unanticipated shortfall in funds necessary to provide guaranteed benefits. A necessary corollary is that participants in a defined contribution plan bear the burden of poor investment experience and reap the benefit of favorable investment experience.

As the result of a change introduced by TRA '86, profit-sharing plan contributions no longer must be made using the current or accumulated profits of the small business. Since contributions may be totally discretionary on the part of the board of directors, partners, or proprietor, a profit-sharing plan is among the most flexible of tax-favored employee benefits. For example, a plan could require mandatory contributions equal to 5 percent of the participant's compensation but not in excess of current profits. For purposes of determining the amount of current or accumulated profits out of which such contribution is to be made, the plan could define profits in any manner desirable to the business owners. If a small business has profits as determined under generally accepted accounting principles, for example, contributions could be made even if there are no current or accumulated profits from a tax standpoint.[2]

Amounts that are contributed to a profit-sharing plan are allocated to each participant based on the percentage of the total compensation of all participants that his or her individual compensation represents. However, if the profit-sharing plan is integrated with Social Security, as discussed later in this chapter, then the allocation pertaining to the portion of a participant's compensation that exceeds the Social Security wage base may be increased (to account for the loss of Social Security coverage) in the allocation of employer contributions to the participant's individual account.

Amounts that are allocated to participant accounts are held by the trustee of the plan, and the earnings and losses arising from plan investments are allocated on an annual basis to the accounts of the participants. As noted, no guaranteed retirement benefit exists under a profit-sharing plan because a retiring participant is entitled to receive only the amount in his or her account, which may be more or less than the total of the contributions actually made to the account, depending on the investments made by the trustee.

A participant's account balance also may change due to forfeitures. A forfeiture is the unvested portion of a participant's account that is

---

[2]Rev. Rul. 80–252, 1980–2 C.B. 130; Rev. Rul. 66–174, 1966–1 C.B. 81.

forfeited by the participant on his or her early termination of employment. Forfeitures may be reallocated among the remaining participants, thus increasing the account balances of those participants who continue their employment with the small business.

The allocation of forfeitures usually is based on the current compensation levels of the remaining participants in the year in which forfeiture occurs. Allocation of forfeitures may be based on other factors, such as the account balances of all remaining participants; however, if this results in highly compensated employees receiving forfeitures that are a larger percentage of current compensation than is the case with rank-and-file employees, then the plan will lose its qualified status.[3] To prevent possible disqualification, forfeitures in profit-sharing plans should not be allocated on any basis other than current compensation.

Section 404(a)(3) of the Internal Revenue Code (IRC or Code) limits deductible contributions to a profit-sharing plan to 15 percent of the compensation of all plan participants. If a contribution of more than 15 percent is made during a given year, then the amount of the excess may be deducted in the next subsequent year(s) to the extent that the total profit-sharing deduction for any such subsequent year does not exceed 15 percent of the compensation of all plan participants for the given year.[4] A 10 percent excise tax will apply, however, as discussed in the succeeding chapter.

In addition to this annual aggregate contribution limitation, Section 415(c) of the Code limits annual additions to the account of each participant, a concept discussed further later in this chapter.

The authors feel that profit-sharing plans certainly should be considered by any small business, primarily because profit-sharing plans allow the amount of contributions to be based entirely on the profitability of the business and/or at the discretion of the owners. For example, profit-sharing plans may be very useful for owners of new small businesses who desire to implement some type of qualified retirement plan but are unsure of exactly how successful the small business will be. Many small businesses experience wide fluctuations in income from year to year. Although the

---

[3]Rev. Rul. 81–10, 1981–1 C.B. 172. For years beginning after 1988, the nondiscrimination rules, as set out in IRC 401(a)(4) and the regulations promulgated thereunder, prohibit discrimination in favor of "highly compensated employees" as defined in IRC 414(q). See below.

[4]In the case of an existing profit-sharing plan, where any pre-1987 contribution was less than 15 percent of the participant's compensation during the relevant period, the unused contribution amount may be carried forward so as to increase the deduction limit for years after 1986 up to a maximum deduction of 25 percent in any one year. IRC 404(a)(3).

contributions to a profit-sharing plan may be discretionary, employers should be aware that plan contributions must be substantial and recurring.[5] In order to meet this test, the general opinion is that contributions must be made at least once every three years. In any event, however, the failure to make contributions because of insufficient profits will not disqualify the plan.[6]

The allocation of unintegrated profit-sharing plan contributions for a small business with four employees where the contribution equals 15 percent of compensation is illustrated in the following chart:

Participant	Compensation	Contribution Allocation
Owner-employee	$175,900	$26,385
Staff employee	12,000	1,800
Staff employee	10,000	1,500
Staff employee	8,000	1,200
Total	$205,900	$30,885

As the chart illustrates, although the shareholder-employee receives the largest contribution, the contribution is based on the same percentage of compensation (15 percent) as that granted to the staff employees. As explained later in this chapter, however, TEFRA's top-heavy rules limit the flexible allocation of contributions in defined contribution plans such that a minimum contribution must be made on behalf of nonkey employees (generally nonowners and nonexecutive employees) equal to 3 percent of their compensation or, if lesser, the highest percentage contribution made on behalf of any key employee (generally an owner-employee, executive employee, or officer).

An employer may alter this pro rata allocation by integrating its contributions to a profit-sharing plan with the Social Security taxes that the corporation must pay. Generally, if a profit-sharing plan is integrated with Social Security benefits, contributions will be allocated first to those participants whose compensation is in excess of the Social Security wage base, in an amount up to 5.7 percent of such excess, with a

---

[5]Treas. Regs. 1.401–1(b)(2).
[6]See *Sherwood Swan & Co.*, 42 T. C. 299 (1964); Rev. Rul. 80–146, 1980–1 C.B. 90.

corresponding allocation to all participants so that 5.7 percent (or lesser excess allocation) is not greater than twice the contribution percentage with respect to compensation that is below the Social Security wage base; and second, to all participants as their compensation relates to total compensation. If the profit-sharing plan discussed above was integrated with Social Security benefits using, for example, the 1990 Social Security wage base of $51,300 and the same $30,885 contribution was made, then the maximum integration allocation would be as follows:

Participant	Compensation	Contribution Allocation
Owner-employee	$175,900.00	$27,419.81
Staff employee	12,000.00	1,386.08
Staff employee	10,000.00	1,155.06
Staff employee	8,000.00	924.05
Total	$205,900.00	$30,885.00

Obviously, an integrated profit-sharing plan provides a larger allocation for the shareholder-employee. The charts we have provided above, however, illustrate only how benefits being provided at an aggregate maximum of 15 percent of compensation could be reallocated under a regime of integration. If, instead, we examined a small business that wanted to maximize benefits under the profit-sharing plan for its highly compensated employees while contributing no more than 5 percent of compensation to nonhighly compensated employees, the power of integration becomes even more apparent.

The chart below shows the profit-sharing allocations to each employee in the small business discussed above under a straight 5 percent of compensation formula:

Participant	Compensation	Contribution Allocation
Owner-employee	$175,900	$ 8,795
Staff employee	12,000	600
Staff employee	10,000	500
Staff employee	8,000	400
Total	$205,900	$10,295

Suppose, then, that the owner-employee wanted to maximize his or her allocation under the profit-sharing plan without increasing the benefits of the other employees. By using integration, the owner-employee could double his or her profit-sharing allocation while keeping the profit-sharing allocations of the other employees constant. This would focus the profit-sharing contribution quite narrowly on the owner employee, as compared with the maximum 15 percent aggregate contribution shown above. Where the small business put the maximum 15 percent aggregate contribution into the profit-sharing plan, 88.7 percent of the contribution was allocated to the owner-employee. In contrast, where the small business keeps allocations below the integration level at 5 percent of compensation and then seeks to maximize the benefits of integration, 92.1 percent of the total profit-sharing contribution was allocated to the owner-employee. The chart below illustrates the results of maximizing the benefits of integration where allocations below the integration level are kept at 5 percent of compensation:

Participant	Compensation	Contribution Allocation
Owner-employee	$175,900	$17,590
Staff employee	12,000	600
Staff employee	10,000	500
Staff employee	8,000	400
Total	$205,900	$19,090

Integration can be a powerful tool, but it can also be a somewhat complicated one. The possibilities and flexibility of integration, though somewhat reduced from the early 1980s, remain substantial, and the small business should consult with its professional advisers about the applications that integration might have with respect to its particular qualified plans. Some additional features of integration are discussed later in this chapter, but a full-fledged discussion of integration is beyond the scope of this chapter.

One important factor, however, that an employer should consider before integrating a profit-sharing plan is that the integrated portion of an account may not be distributed prior to retirement, death, or other separation from service.[7] In contrast, a nonintegrated profit-sharing plan may provide for distributions to participants during their employment after a period of deferral of as little as two years, the attainment of a stated age, or the prior occurrence of some event demonstrating financial need. (However, a 10 percent excise tax may apply on an early distribution, as discussed in Chapter 56.) Finally, as discussed below, TEFRA severely restricts the integration of top-heavy profit-sharing plans, top-heavy plans being those plans in which a disproportionate amount of contributions are made on behalf of officers, owners, and executive employees.

Profit-Sharing Thrift Plans

Mandatory and/or voluntary employee contributions may be a feature of any profit-sharing plan. Aggregate voluntary employee contributions may not exceed 10 percent of the compensation paid to an employee during his or her participation in the plan.[8] As a general rule, for any year, mandatory employee contributions (the minimum contribution required as a prerequisite for participation or as a condition for increased employer contributions) may not exceed 6 percent of the amount of compensation paid to the employee for the year in question; however, the Internal Revenue Service refuses to treat the 6 percent rule as a "safe harbor" from a possible challenge of discrimination in operation.[9] Where employee contributions to a profit-sharing plan are required as a condition of participation, such a plan often is called a contributory plan. For example, a contributory plan might require employees to contribute 6 percent of their compensation before they are entitled to share in the employer contribution. Where the level of employer contributions is based on the amount or rate of employee contributions, such a plan is commonly referred to as a thrift or savings plan. An example of a thrift plan is where an employer matches 50 percent of an employee's contribution, up to a maximum of 5 percent of pay.

Voluntary and mandatory employee after-tax contributions must, when combined with any employer matching contributions, satisfy the average contribution percentage test set forth in IRC Section 401(m).

---

[7]Rev. Rul. 71–446, 15.03, 1971–2 C.B. 187.

[8]Rev. Rul. 80–350, 1980–2 C.B. 133.

[9]Rev. Rul. 80–307, 1980–2 C.B. 136.

Failure to satisfy this test would result in a violation of the nondiscrimination requirements of IRC Section 401(a)(4). The total of the employer matching contributions and employee after-tax contributions divided by total compensation is known as the average contribution percentage (ACP). IRC Section 401(m) requires that the ACP of all highly compensated employees not exceed the greater of

(1) 125 percent of the ACP of all other eligible employees, or
(2) The lesser of 200 percent of the ACP of all other eligible employees or such ACP plus 2 percent.

Contributions exceeding this ACP test must be distributed out of a thrift plan pursuant to instructions contained in the regulations in order to preserve the qualified status of the thrift plan. A distribution of such excess contributions must occur within 2½ months of the end of the plan year for which they were contributed in order to avoid a 10 percent excise tax.[10] If the 2½ month deadline is missed, the distribution must still occur by the end of the plan year following the plan year of contribution in order to avoid disqualification.[11]

These ACP requirements are quite similar to the actual deferral percentage (ADP) requirements that apply to pretax employee deferrals under a cash or deferred arrangement (CODA) subject to IRC Section 401(k). CODAs and the actual deferral percentage requirements that apply to them are discussed later in this chapter. As we will point out in that section, however, some of the contributions associated with the CODA portion of a qualified plan may be subject to the ACP requirements discussed above.

Thrift plans have several attractive features. First, employee contributions are normally made through payroll deductions, and an employee receives no company contributions unless he or she has authorized payroll deductions. Second, the company contribution is not tied to current profits; rather, the company usually contributes a fixed dollar amount for each dollar contributed by the employee. Historically, thrift plans have generally received an enthusiastic employee response, which is somewhat unusual since a regular profit-sharing plan normally provides the same type of benefits without the requirement of employee contributions.

---

[10]IRC Sec. 4979.
[11]IRC Sec. 401(m)(6).

As a general rule, thrift plans offer the same benefits as other profit-sharing plans to a small business. However, thrift plans serve an additional need in those small businesses in which shareholders have divergent retirement objectives, since the amount that is deferred is directly related to each shareholder's own voluntary contributions and may be adjusted annually. As a caveat, however, if a thrift plan is adopted and the compensation of those employees who do not contribute to the thrift plan is adjusted upward by the employer, then the plan may be a de facto CODA, as discussed later in this chapter, which is only qualified if certain additional requirements are met pursuant to Section 401(k) of the Code.

A disadvantage of thrift plans is that employee contributions that are matched by employer contributions are no longer eligible for treatment as deductible employee contributions.[12] One alternative that may be used to allow employees to make before-tax thrift contributions would be to convert a thrift plan to a CODA with the employer matching the amounts that employees elect to contribute to the plan under the cash or deferred provision.

Pension Plans

Pension plans, as opposed to profit-sharing plans, must provide definitely determinable benefits. Pension plan contributions are mandatory, irrespective of corporate profits, in an amount necessary to fund the benefits provided by the plan.[13] Further, in the case of defined benefit pension plans, forfeitures may not be used to increase the benefits of the individual participants but must reduce the annual employer contributions under such plans.[14]

Defined Benefit Pension Plans

The discussion below of defined benefit pension plans explores many of the traditional advantages and uses of defined benefit pension plans. Nevertheless, the authors now believe that defined benefit pension plans

---

[12]IRC 219(e).

[13]Though pension plan contributions are mandatory, the timing of the contributions necessary to fund the definitely determinable obligations of a defined benefit plan is fairly flexible, with a wide range of actuarial approaches to choose from.

[14]See Treas. Reg. 1.401–1(a)(2)(i) and 1.401-1(b)(1)(i); IRC 401(a)(8).

will only be appropriate for the largest and most vigorous of small businesses, and even then only when those businesses have a strong desire to
make a long-term commitment to a generous retirement program. Not only
are defined contribution plans cheaper, they also offer a kind of cost
predictability that defined benefit pension plans cannot. The rate of increase in pension insurance premiums to the Pension Benefit Guaranty
Corporation (PBGC), discussed below, continues to be dramatic. The
power of the PBGC to restore terminated defined benefit pension plans
under some circumstances also means that any small business that adopts
a defined benefit pension plan is, to some extent, signing on to underwrite
the defined benefit pension plans of other employers.[15] The new proposed
nondiscrimination rules discussed later in this chapter also impose much
stricter limits on flexibility in plan design, especially as that flexibility has
in the past been used to provide faster accruals to older employees. Finally,
the ability of the employer to terminate an overfunded defined benefit
pension plan and retrieve the excess amounts has been almost entirely
eliminated. The current 15 percent excise tax on reversions from defined
benefit pension plans has been increased to 50 percent under the Omnibus
Budget Reconciliation Act of 1990 (OBRA '90) unless the employer
effectively diverts between 20 percent and 25 percent of the reversion to
the benefit of the employees (in the manner prescribed under the new rules
contained in OBRA '90), in which case the reversion excise tax is increased to 20 percent.

As a general rule, defined benefit pension plans apply a greater share
of the employer contributions for the benefit of older employees than for
younger employees.[16] This result occurs because the defined benefit plan

---

[15]In *Pension Benefit Guaranty Corporation* v. *LTV Corporation*, 110 S. Ct. 2668 (1990), the
United States Supreme Court upheld a PBGC order restoring three defined benefit pension plans of
LTV Corporation that the PBGC had involuntarily terminated while LTV was in bankruptcy
reorganization, where LTV had adopted after the involuntary termination other employee benefit
plans providing benefits ''at the same level'' as under the terminated defined benefit pension plans.

[16]In Rev. Rul. 74–142, 1974–1 C.B. 95, a professional corporation established a pension plan
providing a retirement benefit of 60 percent of average compensation for each participant. There were
only two participants under the plan, a 60-year-old professional and a 52-year-old staff employee.
Because of the differences in ages and compensation, 90 percent of the contributions were applied
to fund the benefits for the older professional. Yet, the Service ruled that the plan was qualified and
did not discriminate in favor of the older professional. See also *Ryan School Retirement Trust*, 24
T. C. 127 (1955). The facts in this case would now be analyzed under the different principles
contained in the regulations under IRC 401(a)(4), discussed in detail below.

rules fix the amount of the retirement benefit, not the amount of the annual contribution that will produce the benefit. Where both individuals are to ultimately receive the same level of retirement benefit, the portion of each annual contribution that is required to fund the benefit of the older employee is larger than the amount required to fund the benefit of the younger employee, since there are fewer years in which to contribute the assets necessary to produce the older employee's benefit level. In contrast, the defined contribution plan rules fix the maximum amount of the annual contribution on behalf of each employee but do not limit the amount of the ultimate benefit. Thus, employers may produce a larger retirement benefit for younger employees than for older employees in a defined contribution plan because younger employees have more years in which to receive employer contributions before retirement and because the contributions can be held for a sufficient time for the compounding effects of tax-deferred earnings to have a tremendous impact. Thus, defined benefit pension plans are often very useful in a small business where older employees desire to defer a substantial amount of current income until retirement.

If an employee has not been a participant in the defined benefit plan for at least 10 years as of his or her date of retirement, then the maximum pension benefit that may be provided under Section 415(b) of the Code (the lesser of 100 percent of average annual compensation for the three highest-paid years or $90,000 per year adjusted for the cost of living in the same manner as Social Security benefits—$112,221 for 1992) must be reduced by 10 percent for each year of participation (in the case of the $90,000 limit) or service (in the case of the 100 percent of average annual compensation limit) less than 10.[17] A technique that is often available to increase the size of the maximum deductible pension plan contribution, particularly for senior employees, is to use a benefit formula that gives credit for service with the employer prior to the effective date of the plan; however, a limitation exists on the rate at which past service costs may be funded. If the unfunded cost of past and current service benefits attributable to any three individuals is more than 50 percent of the unfunded cost of past and current service benefits of all participants covered by the pension plan, then the cost attributable to such three individuals may not be funded over fewer than five

---

[17]IRC 415(b)(5).

years.[18] However, it is not necessary in such instances to have the benefits fully funded as of such individual's normal retirement date.

Although the ability to defer large amounts of compensation through deductible contributions to defined benefit pension plans may work well in some small businesses, it may create problems in others. For example, once the older employee has retired, the younger employees will be required to continue funding benefits under the existing plan or to terminate the plan. A problem is inherent if an older employee in a small business was credited with a sufficient amount of past service at the time the plan was established, and this past service credit is not fully funded by the date on which the older employee retires. In this case, the remaining younger employees will find their corporation making contributions to fund the pension of a person who no longer performs services for the corporation, and the temptation to terminate the plan may be overwhelming. Since a majority of the contributions of the employer to a defined benefit plan fund the retirement benefits of those employees closest to retirement, defined benefit pension plans work well in larger corporations where a sufficient number of employees exists at various age levels such that a level method of funding benefits over a number of years also exists. On the other hand, in a small corporation with one younger employee and one older employee, the majority of the employer contributions will be used to fund the benefit of the older employee, thus leaving the younger employee after the retirement of the older employee with a virtually unfunded benefit and many years of plan funding ahead. These aspects of defined benefit pension plans must be understood and must be carefully applied to a particular small-business setting as part of the initial plan design.

The annual contributions required under a defined benefit pension plan must be determined actuarially and based on factors such as the ages of the participants, the earnings of the trust fund, and inflation. Consequently, the administration of a defined benefit pension plan is normally more costly than that of a profit-sharing plan or a money purchase pension plan.

Except for those defined benefit plans that at no time cover more than 25 active professional participants and that are maintained by

---

[18]IRC 404(a)(1)(A)(ii). More rapid funding may be allowed under the minimum funding standard. IRC 404(a)(1)(A)(i).

employers whose principal businesses are providing services, defined benefit plans generally are subject to the Pension Benefit Guaranty Provisions of Title IV of the Employee Retirement Income Security Act (ERISA). The Pension Benefit Guaranty Corporation, which administers these provisions of Title IV, acts as an insurer of the pension benefits of plans that are not exempted from its protection.

One commonly used exception to PBGC coverage applies to professional service providers, including employers whose principal business is the performance of professional services and who are owned or controlled by physicians, dentists, chiropractors, osteopaths, optometrists, other licensed practitioners of the healing arts, attorneys, public accountants, public engineers, architects, drafters, actuaries, psychologists, social or physical scientists, and performing artists.[19] However, the PBGC, in a series of opinion letters, has taken the position that the professional service provider exception does not apply to opticians, food brokers, artists, designers, real estate brokers, individuals in advertising and public relations, foresters, and river-boat pilots.[20] The rationale of the PBGC in these opinion letters is that these occupational groups are outside the scope of the exception because the occupations involved do not require a prolonged course of specialized intellectual instruction and are not predominantly intellectual in character.

The PBGC exception is valuable to employers because pension plans that are subject to Title IV must pay annual premiums to the PBGC of $19 per participant per year.[21] For this purpose, the term *participant* includes all actual participants plus former participants or their beneficiaries who are currently receiving or who have a future right to receive plan benefits.

The 5717 limitations, which are contained in Treasury Regulations Section 1.401–4(c), restrict the benefits that may be paid to the 25 highest-paid employees at the time the plan is established or at the time that plan benefits are increased substantially. The 5717 limitations may

---

[19]ERISA Pub. L. No. 93–406, 4021(c)(2)(B), 818 Stat. 829 (1974).

[20]PBGC Opinion Letters 80–9 through 80–15.

[21]OBRA '90 increased this premium from $16 to $19 per participant. To the extent that a plan has unfunded vested benefits, there is an additional "variable rate premium" that should be calculated by the actuary for the plan. The variable rate premium is currently calculated at a rate of $6 per $1,000 of unfunded vested benefits, but OBRA '90 increased this rate to $9 per $1,000 of unfunded vested benefits. Moreover, OBRA '90 also increased the participant cap on this variable rate premium from $34 to $53.

have a substantial impact on pension plans of a small business; they generally are effective if a lump-sum distribution is payable with respect to certain highly compensated participants within 10 years after the plan either is established or amended to increase benefits substantially or if the plan either is terminated within its first 10 years or within 10 years of an amendment that substantially increases benefits. Further, if the plan is underfunded within the first 10 years, these limitations may apply beyond 10 years.

The new nondiscrimination rules discussed later in this chapter, however, have superseded the 5717 limitations for plan years beginning after January 1, 1993.[22]

The following is a discussion of the several types of defined benefit plans that are available.

Fixed Benefit Plans

Fixed benefit plans generally define a participant's ultimate retirement benefit in terms of a specified percentage of a participant's average monthly compensation for the 3 or 5 highest paid consecutive years of service during the participant's last 10 years of service. However, the participant's entitlement to the benefit generally is phased in over a period of time. For example, if a participant has completed 15 or more years of service by retirement age, then the participant might be entitled at normal retirement age to an annuity for life equal to 25 percent of his or her average monthly compensation for the highest 5 consecutive years of service out of his or her last 10 years of service. If the participant has completed fewer than 15 years of service by normal retirement age, the annuity determined under the immediately preceding sentence might be reduced by one fifteenth for each year of service less than 15 that the participant has then completed. As a caveat, however, to the extent that a plan is top-heavy, as discussed later in this chapter, the nonkey employees (nonowners and nonexecutives) must accrue a benefit at least equal to 2 percent of their compensation for each year of service.[23] Thus, top-heavy fixed benefit plans may be unable to offer this advantageous phase-in period.

---

[22]See Treas. Reg. 1.401(a)(4)–5(c).
[23]IRC 416(c)(1).

A fixed benefit plan can be particularly advantageous in a small business where a limited number of employees are in their mid-to-late forties or early fifties and intend to work at least 10 more years. For example, assume that a company has the following employees:

Employee	Age	Years of Service	Salary
Older shareholder	55	20	$100,000
Younger shareholder	30	5	30,000
Staff employee	30	5	10,000

Assume further that the normal retirement benefit formula is 25 percent of a participant's average monthly compensation for the highest 5 consecutive years of service during the participant's last 10 years of service. Finally, ignoring interest considerations, salary increases, and the top-heavy rules (which are discussed later in this chapter), assume that a total of $500,000 will be needed to fund the older shareholder's benefit at age 65, $150,000 will be needed to fund the younger shareholder's benefit at age 65, and $50,000 ultimately will be needed to fund the staff employee's benefit at age 65. Based on these assumptions, $500,000 must be funded over 10 years for the older shareholder; hence, the contribution on behalf of that employee must be $50,000 or 50 percent of his or her annual compensation during each of his or her final 10 years. In contrast, $50,000 must be funded over 35 years for the staff employee, producing an annual contribution of under $1,500, or less than 15 percent of the staff employee's annual compensation.

If an interest assumption is added to this example, the disparity in the contribution levels, expressed as a percentage of compensation, required to fund the older versus the younger shareholder's benefit becomes even more pronounced, since the contributions made on behalf of the younger shareholder will have a much longer period of time to compound interest; hence, even smaller contributions would be needed to fund the younger shareholder's benefit. To illustrate, a dollar invested at an 8 percent return for 10 years will be worth $2.16, while a dollar invested at an 8 percent return for 35 years will be worth $14.79. Admittedly, this example does not conform to accepted actuarial practice;

however, it illustrates that a fixed benefit plan will be allocated to the older shareholder who is approaching normal retirement date.

The example above attempts to illustrate generally the ways in which fixed benefit plans have been able to provide dramatically faster accruals for older employees. The nondiscrimination regulations discussed later in this chapter, however, place much stricter limits on such faster accruals. The authors recommend that any employer with a defined benefit pension plan ensure that this plan fits within one of the regulatory safe harbors. To fit within a safe harbor, however, a fixed benefit plan such as the one described above could not permit accrual of the maximum benefit over a period of less than 25 years unless it could be shown that the average of the normal accrual rates for all nonhighly compensated employees under the plan were at least 70 percent of the average of the normal accrual rates of all highly compensated employees under the plan.

Unit Benefit Plans

Unit benefit plans usually define a participant's pension amount by reference to an annually adjusted formula that takes into account both years of service and compensation. As before, top-heavy plans subject to the minimum benefit rules for nonkey employees will face greater restrictions than the following discussion indicates.

1. Career Average Unit Benefit Plans. Under this type of plan, each participant is credited with a benefit for each year of service based on the participant's compensation for that particular year of service. Tying the unit benefit accruals to compensation in the year of accrual has the effect of basing benefits on the average of an employee's compensation over the course of his or her career. For example, assume that a participant who is 55 when first employed is entitled to a benefit equal to 1 percent of his or her compensation for each year of service. If such a participant earns the compensation shown in the first column of the table on the next page, his or her annual benefit accrual and annual pension benefit will be as listed in the second column.

2. Final Average Unit Benefit Plans. Under this type of plan, each participant is credited with benefits for each year of service, and these benefits are based on a participant's average compensation for a particular period of time, generally the highest 5 consecutive years out of the last 10 years. For example, assume that a benefit formula provides 1 percent for each year of service multiplied by a participant's highest 5 consecutive

Year	Compensation	Benefit
1	$ 50,000	$ 500
2	55,000	550
3	60,000	600
4	65,000	650
5	70,000	700
6	80,000	800
7	85,000	850
8	90,000	900
9	95,000	950
10	100,000	1,000
Annual pension equals:		$7,500

years of service out of the last 10 years. Assume further that the participant was 55 when initially employed and worked 10 years and that his or her compensation is as shown in the career average unit benefit plan example above. The average compensation for the highest 5 consecutive years of service out of the last 10 years of service is $90,000. Since this employee has completed 10 years of service he or she will be entitled to an annual pension of 10 percent of $90,000, or $9,000.

A unit benefit plan will principally be advantageous when the shareholders either have or are expected to have many years of service. A career average unit benefit plan, as opposed to a final average benefit plan, will serve to avoid both a large unfunded liability and accelerated funding during later years in the event of substantial salary increases, since benefits under a career average plan are determined each year based on each year's income. Of course, as a result, the benefits under a career average unit benefit plan are not likely to keep pace with inflation.

Again, the discussion of the nondiscrimination and integration rules later in this chapter should be consulted with respect to the limits these rules impose as well as the opportunities they provide for unit credit defined benefit pension plans.

3. Flat Benefit Plans. Benefits under a flat benefit plan are not dependent on a participant's compensation. Under a pure flat benefit plan, the participant will be entitled to a flat monthly pension at normal retirement, such as $200, irrespective of his or her length of service or compensation. Alternatively, the monthly pension at normal retirement may be defined in terms of a specified dollar amount per year of service, for example, $20 multiplied by the participant's years of service. Flat benefit plans usually are adopted only in collectively bargained plans between labor and management.

Choosing between Defined Benefit Pension Plans

In the small-business setting, a fixed benefit plan with a final average formula is usually considered to be the most appropriate type of defined benefit plan. Normally, after careful consideration of personal savings, investments, and anticipated Social Security benefits, an employer will be able to determine the percentage of the employee's income that must be continued after retirement through qualified plan benefits in order to provide adequate retirement security. Since the objective of the small-business owner is the continuation during retirement of that standard of living attained immediately prior to retirement, a final average pay formula usually will be selected. The plan's actuary will make assumptions regarding the anticipated impact of inflation on salaries and, using these assumptions, calculate the level of funding necessary to provide a benefit that anticipates future salary levels. Of course, if several share holders or owners are involved, a collective decision must be made regarding the benefit level as a percentage of income.

Usually a flat benefit plan approach is completely out of the question for a small-business employer, since it fails to take compensation levels into account. A unit benefit plan is a plausible alternative; however, in many cases the owners or controlling shareholders will be uncertain as to how long they will remain in service with the small business, and, in many cases, age differences among the shareholders will result in a wide divergence of opinions as to the ideal level of benefits based on a percentage of salary if this approach is used. For example, older share-holders with shorter periods of total service will want higher unit benefit levels (i.e., 7 to 10 percent per year of service) so as to accrue higher levels of benefits. Younger shareholders, however, who expect to retire with higher total years of service can obtain high levels of benefits using more moderate unit benefit levels (i.e., 2 to 3 percent per year of service).

As previously discussed, defined benefit plans and, in particular, fixed benefit plans that require only a 10- to 15-year minimum period of service for full benefits create a greater funding obligation for the older participants. Acknowledging this fact, the compensation package of older and younger employees may be adjusted equitably after adoption of the qualified pension plan so that the current compensation of younger employees will be reduced as a result of the plan to a lesser extent than the compensation of the older employees. This kind of adjustment can be responsive to the financial realities and the desires of the employees, since the younger employees generally want almost all their compensation paid currently while older employees are more cognizant of their retirement needs and, therefore, are more willing to relinquish current compensation to provide for retirement security. In addition, the younger employees often are faced with the personal expenses associated with starting a home and family that the older employees have already experienced. If the younger employees desire to shelter more current compensation than the amount required to fund their defined benefits, adopting a defined contribution plan in addition to the defined benefit plan should be considered. Furthermore, the defined contribution plan may be drafted in such a manner that the older employees are excluded from participation.[24]

Target Benefit Pension Plans

A target benefit plan is technically a defined contribution plan but functionally it operates as a hybrid of a defined contribution plan and a defined benefit plan.[25] Under a target benefit plan, benefits are defined by using formulas similar to those that are incorporated in defined benefit plans. As in the case of defined benefit plans, employer contributions are determined actuarially. However, as with defined contribution plans, the contributions and the earnings and losses thereon are allocated to the individual accounts of the plan participants, and actual pensions are based on the amounts in the respective individual accounts as of retirement. Thus, a target-benefit plan is simply a pension plan that sets a "target" benefit that ultimately may or may not be funded by the amount in an individual participant's account. The employer only has an obligation to make the contribution required by the plan formula; the employer has no obligation to make sufficient contributions to produce the actual benefit targeted. The targeted benefit provided under the plan is not a promise to the participant of a fixed benefit since the ultimate benefit that will be paid is simply that amount that is actually in the participant's account.

---

[24]See *James E. Thompson, Jr.,* 74 T. C. 873 (1980).
[25]Rev. Rul. 76–464, 1976–2 C.B. 115.

Four factors should be considered before a small employer adopts a target benefit plan: (1) the PBGC provisions of Title IV of ERISA do not apply to target benefit plans; (2) the 5717 limitations do not apply to target benefit plans; (3) all target benefit plans should attempt to fit within a specialized safe harbor now provided under the new nondiscrimination regulations;[26] and (4) the annual addition limitations that apply to target benefit plans are those that apply to defined contribution plans, a significant consideration since the dollar-amount limitations were reduced drastically by TEFRA, as noted later in this chapter, and may be significantly less than the contribution that could otherwise be made in a regular defined benefit plan.

Money Purchase Pension Plans

A money purchase pension plan contains a formula that determines the amount of employer contributions to the plan. The amount of contributions is not subject to the employer's discretion and may not be made a function of profits. Amounts contributed to the plan are allocated to participant accounts, and no guaranteed benefits exist. Consequently, on retirement, the participant will be entitled only to the benefit that can be purchased with the "money" in his or her account; hence, the term *money purchase*.

Money purchase pension plans typically provide for a contribution based on a stated percentage of a participant's annual compensation. The contribution required under such plans may be integrated with Social Security benefits, subject, of course, to the top-heavy limitations, if applicable. Under the integration formula generally permissible in money purchase pension plans, the differential between the contribution percentage above the wage base and the contribution percentage below the wage base may not exceed the lesser of (1) 5.7 percent or (2) the contribution percentage below the wage base. For example, the employer may contribute 2.85 percent of a participant's compensation below the wage base

---

[26]Treas. Reg. Sec. 1.401 (a)(4)–8(b)(3). A description of this very specialized safe harbor is beyond the scope of this chapter, but any small employer planning to use a target benefit plan should consult with a professional adviser to ensure that the benefit formula satisfies the safe-harbor requirements.

and 5.7 percent of compensation above the wage base (differential [5.7 − 2.85 = 2.85] does not exceed contribution percentage below wage base [2.85], which is less than 5.7 percent); or 5.7 percent of compensation below the wage base and 11.4 percent of compensation above the wage base (differential [11.4 − 5.7 = 5.7] does not exceed the contribution percentage below the wage base [5.7] or 5.7 percent); or 7 percent of compensation below the wage base and 12.7 percent above the wage base (differential [12.7 − 7 = 5.7] does not exceed 5.7 percent, which is less than the contribution percentage below the wage base [7]). The following table illustrates a fully integrated money purchase pension plan that has a contribution formula of 5.7 percent of compensation up to the Social Security wage base of $51,300 for 1990 plus 11.4 percent of all compensation in excess of that wage base. This table should be compared with the table illustrating the integrated profit-sharing plan presented earlier in this chapter in the "Regular Profit-Sharing Plan" section.

Participant	Compensation	Contribution Allocation
Owner-employee	$175,900.00	$17,193.94
Staff employee	12,000.00	684.00
Staff employee	10,000.00	570.00
Staff employee	8,000.00	456.00
Total	$205,900.00	$18,903.94

The comparison reveals that the shareholder-employee who is more highly compensated receives 89 percent of the total contribution to the integrated profit-sharing plan, yet receives 91 percent of the total contribution to the integrated money purchase plan. The staff employee having the least amount of compensation, on the other hand, receives 2.9 percent of the total contribution to the integrated profit-sharing plan, yet only 2.4 percent of the total contribution to the integrated money purchase plan. This differential is not inherent in the comparison of the two types of plans. Rather, it shows that the effect of integration decreases slightly as the size of the total contribution increases.

In considering the adoption of a money purchase pension plan, the employer should note four facts. First, contributions to a money purchase plan are mandatory and are in proportion to compensation. The allocation is similar to the allocation under a profit-sharing plan and stands in contrast to the possibility of disproportionately higher contributions on behalf of higher-paid employees under fixed-benefit plans, unit-benefit plans, and target-benefit plans. Second, neither the PBGC provisions of Title IV of ERISA nor the 5717 limitations apply.[27] Third, a money purchase pension plan is a defined contribution plan for purposes of the annual addition limitation under Section 415 of the Code. Finally, unlike a defined benefit plan for which forfeitures must be applied to reduce future employer contributions, after TRA '86, money purchase forfeitures may be allocated to the accounts of participants.

COMBINATIONS OF PLANS

Defined Contribution Plans

As noted, target-benefit plans, money purchase pension plans, and profit-sharing plans are all classified as defined contribution plans because benefits are determined by the participant's individual account balance. Under Section 415 of the Code, the annual additions that are made to all such plans maintained by one employer on behalf of any participant must be aggregated. The aggregate maximum annual addition must not exceed the lesser of (1) 25 percent of the participant's compensation for the year or (2) $30,000 or, if greater, one quarter of the dollar limitation for defined benefit plans, as discussed later in this chapter.

A combination of defined contribution plans, each requiring contributions of less than the Section 415 limit, often provides an excellent method of maximizing benefits while also maximizing flexibility. For example, if only a profit-sharing plan is maintained, the maximum deductible contribution is limited to 15 percent of compensation paid during the year. Therefore, while the profit-sharing plan provides flexibility, the contribution ceiling under Code Section 415 cannot be fully utilized. On the other hand, an employer could adopt only a money purchase plan having a contribution formula that itself requires the maximum contribution allowed by Section 415; however, the full contribution to the plan will always be required, even in "lean" years, since

---

[27]ERISA, 4021(b)(1).

money purchase plan contributions are mandatory. If, in a given year, the small business experiences cash flow problems and is unable to make the required contribution, a nondeductible excise tax equal to 10 percent of the deficiency will be imposed under Section 4971 of the Code. Moreover, if a timely correction of the deficiency is not made, an additional nondeductible excise tax equal to 100 percent of the deficiency will be imposed. However, exemptions to the funding requirements may be granted by the IRS in situations involving unforeseen business hardships.

To escape these restrictions on single plans, a small business may adopt a money purchase plan requiring the contribution of that part of the total benefit that the employer feels reasonably certain could be paid even in cash-lean years, in tandem with a totally discretionary profit-sharing plan. This combination ameliorates the inflexible funding requirement created by exclusive use of a money purchase plan, yet it avoids the bar on making a full "25 percent of compensation" employer contribution that arises with the exclusive use of a profit-sharing plan. Also, in this scheme, the money purchase plan may be fully integrated so that the employer always will receive the full benefit of integration even for those years in which substantial contributions are not made to the profit-sharing plan.

Defined Benefit and Defined Contribution Plans

If a small-business employer wants to defer more than the 25 percent of compensation or the $30,000 limit applicable to defined contribution plans, then the only alternative is to adopt either a defined benefit plan or a combination of plans that includes both a defined benefit plan and a defined contribution plan.

Any combination of defined benefit and defined contribution plans is subject to a complex mathematical limitation imposed by Code Section 415(e). Basically, an employer is prevented by this subsection from adopting both (1) a defined contribution plan or plans providing the maximum contribution, that is, the lesser of 25 percent of compensation or $30,000 (or one quarter of the defined benefit plan limitation, if greater), and (2) a defined benefit plan or plans providing the maximum benefit, that is, $90,000 (indexed in the manner described previously in this chapter) or 100 percent of the participant's average compensation for his or her high three years.[28] Instead, as the percentage of the defined

---

[28]IRC 415(b), 415(c).

contribution maximum that is provided by the defined contribution plans increases, the percentage of the defined benefit maximum that may be provided by the defined benefit plans decreases. Prior to TEFRA, this liquidation was embodied in the so-called 1.4 Rule; after TEFRA, this limitation is embodied in a "1.0 Rule."[29]

The calculation of these rules is complex; however, the following example illustrates the old 1.4 Rule and the new 1.0 Rule.

Step 1. Assume Employee A is in his first year of service. He earns $60,000; participates in defined benefit and defined contribution plans; prefers to defer $7,500 of income, or 12.5 percent of his compensation, using the defined contribution plan; and wants to defer the maximum amount allowed under a defined benefit plan.

Step 2: Under the Old 1.4 Rule. The old and new rules are based on defined benefit and defined contribution fractions. One of the two fractions is computed first, using certain assumptions about the amount of contributions to that type of plan; thereafter, application of the appropriate "rule" produces the other fraction, from which the permitted amount of contribution to the other type of plan may be calculated. Given the assumptions above, the defined contribution fraction in this case is

$$\frac{\$7{,}500 \text{ (contribution to defined contribution plan)}}{\$15{,}000 \text{ (maximum according to } 415(c)(1) \text{ as amended)}} = 0.50$$

The 1.4 test: $1.4 - 0.5 = 0.90$

The defined benefit fraction can equal 0.90.

The calculation of the fraction is:

$$\frac{\$x \text{ (anticipated benefit that employee may fund)}}{\$60{,}000 \text{ (maximum anticipated benefit if employer maintains only a defined benefit plan)}} = 0.90$$

$$x = \$60{,}000 \times 0.9 = \$54{,}000$$

Step 3: Conclusion under 1.4 Rule. The employee can fund an anticipated benefit of $54,000 per year using the defined benefit plan.

Step 4. Under the New 1.0 Rule. The defined contribution fraction denominator is the lesser of

a. 1.25 (assuming the plan is not top-heavy) multiplied by $30,000 (the IRC 415(c)(1)(A) limitation for the year) or $37,500; or

---

[29]IRC 415(e), 416(h).

b. 1.4 multiplied by $15,000 (the IRC 415(c)(1)(B) limitation) or $21,000.[30]

The fraction is thus:

$$\frac{\$7,500 \text{ (amount of contribution to plan)}}{\$21,000 \text{ (the maximum amount according to new Section 415(c))}} = 0.643$$

The 1.0 test: $1.0 - 0.357 = 0.643$.

The defined benefit fraction can equal 0.643. The defined benefit fraction denominator is the lesser of

a. 1.25 (since not a top-heavy plan) multiplied by $90,000 (the dollar limitation in effect for the year for defined benefit plans) or $112,500; or

b. 1.4 multiplied by $60,000 (the IRC 415(c)(1)(B) limitation) or $84,000.

The calculation of the fraction is thus:

$$\frac{\$x \text{ (anticipated benefit that employee may fund)}}{\$84,000 \text{ (maximum anticipated benefit if employer maintains only a defined benefit plan}} = 0.643$$

$$x = 0.643 \times \$84,000 = \$54,000$$

Step 5: Conclusion under New 1.0 Rule. The employee can fund an anticipated benefit of $54,000 per year using the defined benefit plan.

Clearly, the new 1.0 Rule imposed by TEFRA produces no change from the old 1.4 Rule in the amount of compensation that an employee who earns $60,000 per year may defer. However, the small-business owner's income may be far in excess of $60,000, in which case a substantial difference exists between the old 1.4 Rule and the new 1.0 Rule. Algebraic examination reveals that the new rule severely restricts the ability of an employee or owner/employee earning more than $80,357.14 to defer income using a combination of defined benefit and

---

[30]For the sake of simplicity, this example involves a participant with one year of service. Importantly, the defined contribution fraction actually utilizes cumulative figures over the course of the participant's participation. The numerator of the fraction is the sum of all annual additions to a participant's account as of the end of a plan year, whereas the denominator is the sum of the figures determined in accordance with the formula stated in the text for all previous years and the current year.

defined contribution plans. Moreover, as explained later in this chapter, certain top-heavy plans are subject to a more restrictive version of the 1.0 Rule, and employees and owner/employees who participate in those plans will be adversely affected if they individually earn more than $64,285.71.

Notwithstanding the 1.0 Rule, if a combination involves a defined benefit plan and one or more money purchase or profit-sharing plans, TRA '86 imposes a further limitation for tax years commencing after 1986. The deductible contributions under the combined plans may not exceed the greater of (1) 25 percent of the compensation paid to the plan participants during the year, or (2) the employer contributions required to satisfy the minimum funding standards that are applicable to the defined benefit plan alone. Hence, if a defined benefit plan and a defined contribution plan are maintained by an employer, and if the annual contribution required under the defined benefit plan is equal to 20 percent of the compensation paid to the participants during the year, the deductible contribution for the defined contribution plan will be limited to only 5 percent of the compensation paid to the participants during the year, regardless of such plan's contribution formula. However, any contribution that is not deductible for a given year as the result of this rule may be carried forward and deducted in a subsequent year to the extent that the total contribution deducted in such subsequent period does not exceed 25 percent of participant compensation for that year. However, a 10 percent excise tax will apply each year until the excess contribution has been removed or "used up."

Simplified Pension Plans

The Revenue Act of 1978 established the simplified employee pension (SEP) for years beginning after 1978. Effectively, a SEP is not a qualified plan; rather, it is a plan for contributing to a group of individual retirement accounts (SEP-IRAs).[31] The primary advantage of a SEP is simplicity; it is not subject to most of the government reporting and disclosure requirements that apply to other qualified retirement plans. Generally, SEP administration consists only of filing a single form, Form 5305-SEP, with the IRS annually.

---

[31]IRC 408(k).

A SEP generally must cover every employee who is at least age 21, has performed any service for the employer maintaining the plan during at least three of the immediately preceding five calendar years, and has received at least $300 in compensation from the employer for the year. Contributions must be fully vested when made. Only the first $200,000 of a given employee's compensation may be taken into account under the plan, and employer contributions to the SEPs must bear a uniform relationship to the total compensation of each participant. Further, if compensation in excess of $100,000 is taken into account, all eligible SEP participants must receive contributions of not less than 7.5 percent of their compensation.

The maximum amount that may be contributed to a participant's SEP account for any year is $30,000, and the maximum SEP contribution that an employer may deduct is 15 percent of the compensation of its employees.

Effective for tax years beginning after 1986, TRA '86 allows employers with 25 or fewer employees to establish SEPs on a salary reduction basis. Under such an approach, an employee may elect to have the employer make payments to the SEP on his or her behalf (not currently taxable) or to pay such amounts to them in cash (taxable as current income). A salary reduction SEP will be qualified only if at least 50 percent of employees elect to have SEP contributions and the "deferral percentage" for each highly compensated employee does not exceed 125 percent of the average "deferral percentage" for employees who are not highly compensated employees. (The terms *deferral percentage* and *highly compensated employees* are defined in the next two sections of this chapter.)

The SEP offers an inexpensive, prepackaged employee benefit plan that will suit the needs of many small employers.

SPECIFIC QUALIFICATION ASPECTS RELEVANT TO SMALL-BUSINESS EMPLOYERS

Eligibility and Minimum Participation Standards

Section 410 of the Code sets forth the minimum participation standards imposed on all qualified retirement plans. In order to obtain qualified status, a plan may not as a condition of participation require that an employee complete a period of service extending beyond the later of reaching age 21 and completing one year of service. Part-time employees working fewer than 1,000 hours during any given year may be indefinitely excluded, even if they are older than 21, but they will have to be covered if they ever have a year in which they earn 1,000 hours of service. Where a plan provides immediate full vesting for all participants, employees may be excluded until they have completed two years of service. (CODAs may only require one year of service.)

A plan must provide that an employee who has satisfied the age and service requirements will participate in the plan no later than the earlier of (1) the first day of the first plan year beginning after the date on which the employee satisfied the requirements, or (2) the date six months after the date on which the employee satisfied the requirements.[32] However, in the interest of simplicity, qualified retirement plans adopted by a small business should provide that participation begins after the completion of one year of service and attainment of age 21 and that participation is retroactive to the first day of the first plan year in which the later of these two requirements is met. No maximum age exclusion is permitted regardless of plan type.[33]

Code Section 410(b), which specifies minimum eligibility standards for qualified plans, requires that, to be qualified, a plan must satisfy one of the following tests:[34]

1. Seventy percent of employees who are not highly compensated employees must be covered by the plan (percentage test).[35]
2. The percentage of employees who are not highly compensated employees covered by the plan must be at least 70 percent of the percentage of highly compensated employees who are covered (ratio test).
3. The plan must have an eligibility classification that does not discriminate in favor of highly compensated employees, and the

---

[32]IRC 410(a)(4).

[33]IRC 410(a)(2).

[34]In applying these tests, certain employees may be treated as though they were not employees. Examples include employees who have not met statutorily acceptable minimum age or service requirements, nonresident aliens, and, in most cases, employees covered by a collective bargaining agreement. See IRC Sec. 410(b)(3) and (4).

[35]The reader will note that, while this test still exists in the statute, it can be ignored, because it will never be met without also meeting one of the other two tests.

average benefit (expressed as a percentage of pay) provided to
employees other than highly compensated employees must equal
at least 70 percent of the average benefit provided to highly
compensated employees.

The term *highly compensated employees* includes employees who, during
the year in question or the preceding year, (1) were 5 percent owners of
the business; (2) earned more than $75,000 (indexed to $93,518 in 1992)
or more than $50,000 (indexed to $62,345 in 1992) and were among
the top 20 percent of employees by pay; or (3) were officers of the
corporation receiving compensation greater than $45,000 per year (in-
dexed to $56,110 in 1992).

The minimum coverage requirements usually do not present a
problem for a small business unless groups of related or affiliated small
businesses are involved. If there are several such small businesses
involved, then an insufficient number of employees may be eligible to
participate in each business plan or plans, since Code Sections 414(b),
414(c), and 414(m) provide that all employees of all corporations and
partnerships that are members of a controlled or affiliated group are
treated as if employed by a single employer.

A major problem in the controlled-group context is posed by the
definition of a "brother-sister controlled group of corporations" that is
contained in Code Section 1563. Section 414 incorporates this definition
for certain qualified plan purposes. The term *brother-sister controlled
group of corporations* generally means two or more organizations
conducting trades or businesses if (1) the same five or fewer persons own,
singularly or in combination, a controlling interest in each organization;
and if (2), taking into account the ownership of each such person only
to the extent such ownership is identical with respect to each such
organization, such persons are in effective control of each corporation.
The term *controlling interest* means ownership of 80 percent of the total
combined voting power of all classes of stock entitled to vote or at least
80 percent of the total value of shares of all classes of stock. The term
effective control means ownership of stock possessing more than 50
percent of the total combined voting power of all classes of stock entitled
to vote or 50 percent of the total value of shares of all classes of stock of
such corporation.

In *U.S.* v. *Vogel Fertilizer Co.* [455 U.S. 16, 70 L. Ed. 2d 792, 102
S Ct. 821 (1982)], the U.S. Supreme Court held that for purposes of
computing the 80 percent controlling interest, only persons who owned

an interest in each tested corporation should be taken into account—a holding that vastly restricts the Service's ability to amalgamate employees of several corporate employers for eligibility-test purposes. The following two examples illustrate the interaction of the 50 percent test and the 80 percent test and the restrictive effect of *Vogel*.

Example 1. Mr. A. owns 90 percent of corporation X and 55 percent of corporation Y. Ms. B., who is unrelated to Mr. A, owns 10 percent of corporation X and 45 percent of corporation Y.

80 Percent Controlling-Interest Test		*50 Percent Identical-Ownership Test*	
Corporation X	*Corporation Y*	*Corporation X*	*Corporation Y*
Mr. A.: 90	55	55	55
Ms. B.: 10	45	10	10
100	100	65	65

In example 1, Mr. A. and Ms. B. together own 100 percent of both corporations; therefore, the 80 percent controlling-interest test is satisfied. Mr. A.'s identical-ownership interest in corporations X and Y is 55 percent, since he owns at least 55 percent of each corporation. Ms. B.'s identical-ownership of corporations X and Y is 10 percent, since she owns at least 10 percent of each corporation. Since the sum of the identical-ownership of Mr. A. and Ms. B. exceeds 50 percent, the 50 percent identical-ownership test is met. Since both tests are met, corporations X and Y are brother-sister controlled corporations.

Example 2. Assume the same facts as in example 1 except that Mr. A. owns 100 percent of corporation X.

80 Percent Controlling-Interest Test		*50 Percent Identical-Ownership Test*	
Corporation X	*Corporation Y*	*Corporation X*	*Corporation Y*
Mr. A.: 100	55	55	55
Ms. B.: 00	45	0	45
100	100	55	100

At first blush it might appear that both the 80 percent controlling-interest test and the 50 percent identical-ownership test are satisfied; however, under *Vogel*, Ms. B. cannot be taken into account for purposes of applying the 80 percent controlling-interest test, because she does not have an interest in each corporation that is being tested under the 80 percent test. As a result, the 80 percent controlling-interest test is not satisfied in example 2 and the two corporations are not part of a brother-sister controlled group.

If two or more entities constitute either a controlled group of corporations or trades or businesses under common control, as defined in Code Section 414(b) and (c), respectively, then the rules of Section 401 (qualification standards), Section 410 (participation), Section 411 (vesting), and Section 415 (limitations on benefits and contributions) are applied to all members of the controlled group as if all of the employees worked for the employer adopting the plan. (For purposes of Section 415 limits, the 80 percent ownership requirement for a controlled group is reduced to 50 percent.) The rules under Section 404 (deductions) and Section 412 (funding) generally are applied only with respect to members of the controlled group who adopt the same plan.[36]

As noted, special rules exist under Section 414(m) of the Code that relate to affiliated groups of service corporations; however, these are discussed in Chapter 56.

Nondiscrimination Under 401(a)(4)

In the spring of 1990, the Internal Revenue Service introduced a monster package (more than 300 single-spaced pages) of proposed regulations centering on IRC Section 401(a)(4), which prohibits contributions and benefits provided under a plan from discriminating in favor of highly compensated employees. A complex package of final regulations was released in September of 1991. At the time this chapter was written, it appears that most provisions of the nondiscrimination rules will be effective beginning with the 1993 plan year. These important regulations impose a new and complex regulatory gloss on a rather brief statutory section. The qualified plans of small businesses will probably be the hardest-

---

[36]G.C.M. 39208, Dec. 28, 1983.

hit by the new regulations. Whether by design or by default, these new regulations will substantially reduce plan design flexibility and substantially increase the incentive to choose a standard or generic plan design.

The regulations break discrimination into roughly three classes: discrimination in amounts of contributions or benefits (quantitative), discrimination in availability of benefits, rights, and features (qualitative), and discrimination in special circumstances. Of these three, by far the most important and threatening is the first. Nevertheless, each class has important implications that cannot be ignored.

Discrimination in Amount of Contributions or Benefits

The regulations take a "carrot and stick" approach to discrimination in amount of contributions and benefits. The carrot takes the form of attractive safe harbors, some of which are purely "design-based" (that is, a plan can come within the safe harbor purely by design, without reference to the demographic impact of this design). The stick takes the form of a strict general test that many plans, especially small-business plans with more limited ability to restructure, will find difficult to satisfy.

The general test on the basis of benefits typically requires that plans test both the normal and most valuable accrual rate under the plan. (The most valuable accrual rate is determined by measuring the value of each year's accrual under the plan until the participant's normal retirement date and then normalizing each year's accrual to determine which accrual rate is actuarially the most valuable.) However, if additional uniformity requirements are met, the testing may be limited exclusively to the most valuable accrual rates. Employers are given the discretion of testing on any of the following bases:

- The value of the accrual earned during a single testing year
- The average amount accrued each year for all prior years of service including the current year
- The average amount the employee will accrue each year over the employee's projected years of service under the plan.

Employees are then grouped by bands of accrual rates (for example, 4.95 to 5.05 percent of compensation) and then combined into a set of rate groups based on the number of highly compensated employees in the plan. Each rate group consists of one of the highly compensated employees and every other employee (highly compensated or nonhighly compensated) with both a normal and most valuable accrual rate equal to or greater than the rates of the specific highly compensated employee defining the group. Each rate group then must pass either the ratio test, or a modified version of the average benefit percentage test. The actual benefit accrual rate can be adjusted to reflect the maximum accrual rate that could have been used in a defined benefit excess benefit formula under the permitted disparity rules.

The general test on the basis of contributions is somewhat simpler in that only one allocation rate is tested. The regulations allow a plan to calculate allocation rates as either a percentage of compensation or a dollar amount. To meet the general test, each rate group must meet the minimum coverage tests. For purposes of this test, a rate group is defined as the highly compensated employee and every other employee (highly compensated or nonhighly compensated) with an accrual rate equal to or greater than the rates of the specific highly compensated employee defining the group.

The regulations also provide a method for converting contributions to benefits and vice versa to enable so-called cross-testing, that is, testing of defined contribution plans on the basis of benefits and testing of defined benefit plans on the basis of contributions.

Not only will the general test be difficult for many qualified plans to pass, it will also be expensive to administer on an annual basis. This is why many small businesses will find it so important to ensure that their qualified plans fit within a safe harbor.

There are two defined contribution plan safe harbors: a single uniform allocation formula safe harbor, and an age- or service-weighted uniform allocation formula. Admission to the first safe harbor is based purely on plan design. A plan fits within this safe harbor if it allocates the same percentage of compensation or the same flat sum to each participant.

Both plan design and a simplified and liberalized form of testing determine whether a plan fits within the second safe harbor. Because it is not purely design-based, this safe harbor has been described as a "hybrid" safe harbor. The plan must be designed so as to allocate a uniform percentage of compensation or flat sum to each participant of the same age with the same amount of service and plan participation. If the plan's design satisfies this requirement, the plan in operation must satisfy a liberalized nondiscrimination test in which the average allocation rate of highly compensated employees cannot be higher than the average allocation rate of nonhighly compensated employees.

As is usually the case, things are a little more complicated for defined benefit plans. There are four safe harbors for defined benefit plans: a unit credit safe harbor, a fractional-unit credit safe harbor, a design-based flat benefit safe harbor, and a "hybrid" safe harbor for flat benefit plans.

A unit credit plan provides for accruals of specific benefits for each year of service. If the unit credit accrual formula is uniform and the plan satisfies the 133⅓ percent accrual rule, the defined benefit plan will fit within the unit credit safe harbor. An accrual formula is uniform if it provides that the same dollar amount or the same percentage of compensation will accrue for each plan year for all employees with equal years of service.

Some unit credit plans calculate benefit accruals on the basis of a fractional method under which the unit that accrues is not based solely on years of service, but also on age, so that the total accrued benefit for any particular year will equal the total projected retirement benefit (based on an assumption of service until retirement) multiplied by the ratio (or fraction) of actual service to projected total service (to normal retirement age). A defined benefit plan calculating benefit accruals based on a fractional unit credit method fits within the safe harbor, disregarding those with a projected total service of more than 40 years, if no employee can accrue in any given year more than 133⅓ percent of the accrual of any other employee for such year or any other plan year. This effectively discourages large, concentrated benefit accruals for older employees who are close to normal retirement age, where such benefit accruals are denied to younger employees.

Flat benefit plans provide flat benefits to employees at retirement that are not dependent on years of service. These plans can be used to provide accelerated accruals for older employees who are closer to retirement. The design-based safe harbor for flat benefit plans generally requires that the maximum benefit accrue over a period of at least 25 years. This safe harbor also requires that certain other requirements with respect to grants of past service credit, the definition of compensation, a uniform normal retirement age, subsidized early-retirement benefits, and subsidized joint and survivor annuities be met.

Flat benefit plans that meet the other requirements of the design-based flat benefit safe harbor but fail to satisfy the 25-year minimum for accrual of the maximum benefit can still fit within the "hybrid" safe harbor by conducting an operational nondiscrimination test. This test requires that the average of the normal accrual rates of all nonhighly compensated employees meet or exceed 70 percent of the comparable average for highly compensated employees.

It would be difficult to overstate the importance for qualified plans of small businesses of these new rules on nondiscrimination in amount of contributions or benefits. They place much more severe restrictions on plan design than under the prior view of IRC Section 401(a)(4). The feature of the new rules that mitigates their harshness for large plans—that is, restructuring—will not usually be a viable option for small plans.

Aggregation and Restructuring

Testing qualified plans under the nondiscrimination rules can require an almost metaphysical inquiry into the nature of a "plan," approaching, in its obscurity, medieval scholasticism. Actual, existing plans may have to be combined and then broken down into myriad hypothetical plans in order to steer safely into a safe harbor or through the dangerous straits formed by the general nondiscrimination test.

The starting point is the definition of "plan" contained in IRC Section 414(l), which generally provides that the limits of a plan are defined by availability of all plan assets to pay benefits to covered employees. The nondiscrimination regulations also build on the IRC Section 410(b) regulations by requiring aggregation or disaggregation where such is required by, or in order to pass, the IRC Section 410(b) regulations. This is an important basic principle: for any plan, including a so-called component plan discussed below, to be testable for purposes of the nondiscrimination regulations, it must pass the IRC Section 410(b) coverage tests.

The first step, then, is to identify the "plan" initially derived through the application of IRC Sections 414(l) and 410(b). Once this plan has been identified, it must be tested under the nondiscrimination rules. If the plan fails to pass in its initial form, it is still possible that the plan could pass in a restructured form. Restructuring is the process of dividing a plan that fails to either fit within a safe harbor or pass the general nondiscrimination test into "components" (which must satisfy IRC Section 410(b)) that either fit within a safe harbor or pass the general nondiscrimination test.

Employers may allocate employees to component plans using whatever criteria they choose, but may allocate an employee to only one component plan.

A final note of some importance is that the restructured component plans will not only have to satisfy the requirements with respect to nondiscrimination in amount of contributions and benefits, but also the other nondiscrimination requirements discussed below.

Nondiscriminatory Availability of Benefits, Rights, and Features

Benefits, rights, and features under a plan (or component) must be available on a nondiscriminatory basis. Benefits include optional forms of benefit and ancillary benefits. An optional form of benefit is a distribution alternative, an early retirement benefit, or some other subsidy. An ancillary benefit includes such things as Social Security supplements, insurance-like benefits (life, health, and disability), preretirement death benefits, and shutdown benefits. Other rights and features are a kind of catch-all category including any right or feature with significant value to employees, such as loan provisions or the power to direct investments.

Benefits, rights, and features must be both "currently" and "effectively" available to a nondiscriminatory classification of employees. Current availability is determined without regard to age or service requirements. Effective availability takes into account the effect of age and service requirements on actual availability.

The requirement that benefits, rights, and features be available to a nondiscriminatory classification of employees imposes a kind of coverage requirement, but this coverage requirement is much more liberal than that of IRC Section 410(b). In fact, it is tied to the first half of the average-benefits test under that Code Section. The average-benefits percentage test prong need not be applied in testing availability, which represents a considerable lessening of the stringency of the current and effective availability requirements.

Nondiscrimination in Special Circumstances

The regulations contain some specific rules on three types of special circumstances: plan amendments, grant of past service credit, and lump-sum payments from a pension plan to the 25 most highly compensated employees. Plan amendments must be nondiscriminatory. Whether a plan amendment is nondiscriminatory is determined on the basis of all the relevant facts and circumstances. "Relevant facts and circumstances" include certain demographic facts about the makeup of the plan's participant pool (for example, differences between highly and nonhighly compensated employees as to employee turnover or length of service), the impact of the amendment on the relative accrued benefits of the highly and nonhighly compensated employees, and even additional benefits provided to nonhighly compensated employees under other employer plans.

The breadth and vagueness of a facts-and-circumstances test will make the permissibility of plan amendments much more difficult to evaluate. It will remain difficult to evaluate the requirement that plan amendments be nondiscriminatory until the Service's approach to enforcement of this requirement becomes more clear.

Grants of past service credit are prohibited from discriminating significantly in favor of highly compensated employees. The following are all grants of past service credit subject to the nondiscrimination requirement: (*a*) credit for service with the same employer prior to the effectiveness of a new plan, (*b*) credit for service with another employer, and (*c*) a plan amendment that has the effect of increasing benefit accruals on the basis of service prior to the amendment. The regulations provide a safe harbor, however, for any reasonably uniform grant of past service credit that does not exceed five years.

Finally, current restrictions on lump-sum distributions from defined benefit plans to the 25 most highly compensated employees will no longer apply if two conditions are met: (*a*) the value of plan assets immediately after the distribution equals or exceeds 110 percent of current liabilities and (*b*) the distribution represents less than 1 percent of the current liabilities.

Vesting and Benefits Accrual

Subject to Section 416 of the Code, which, as discussed later in this chapter, establishes special rules for so-called top-heavy plans, Section 411 of ERISA provides the minimum vesting standards. Prior to 1989, when the vesting rules of TRA '86 became effective, these sections generally authorized the adoption of three types of vesting schedules, two of which have been widely used. The first was so-called 10-year cliff vesting. A cliff-vesting schedule required full vesting for a participant with at least 10 years of service, but no vesting for a participant with fewer than 10 years of service. The second common pre-TRA '86 statutory vesting schedule was the so-called 5–15-year vesting schedule. A 5–15-year vesting schedule called for at least 25 percent vesting after 5 years of service, an additional 5 percent for each of the next 5 years, and 10 percent every year thereafter so that the participant would be 100 percent vested after 15 years of service. The third pre-TRA '86 statutory vesting schedule, known as the rule of 45, generally required 50 percent vesting when a participant completed at least 5 years of service and the sum of his or her age and service equaled or exceeded 45, with an additional 10 percent for each year thereafter until 100 percent vested.

Notwithstanding these statutory vesting schedules, the Service formerly required that professional corporations use the so-called 4-40 vesting schedule unless it could be shown that the turnover rate of highly paid employees was not appreciably lower than the turnover rate among the rank-and-file employees.[37] The 4-40 vesting schedule called for vesting as described below:

Years of Service	Nonforfeitable Percentage
1	0
2	0
3	0
4	40
5	45
6	50
7	60
8	70
9	80
10	90
11	100

During 1980, the Service made a concerted attempt to enforce vesting schedules that were significantly more restrictive than the 4-40 schedule. Specifically, it tried to enforce a three-year vesting schedule for closely held and professional corporations where the owners typically do not terminate their employment. There was, however, specific authority in the legislative history of ERISA that vesting at a rate more rapid than the 4-40 rate is not required, notwithstanding a substantial turnover rate

---

[37]See Rev. Proc. 75–49, 1975–2 C.B. 584, as modified by Rev. Proc. 76–11, 1976–1 C.B. 550. The Internal Revenue Service has withdrawn Rev. Proc. 75–49 for post-1988 plan years by stating that, absent a pattern of abuse, use of one of the new TRA '86 vesting schedules or a top-heavy vesting schedule will warrant issuance of a determination letter. Rev. Proc. 89–29, 1989–1 C.B. 893.

among staff employees, unless there was actual misuse in operation of vesting to deny participants' accrued benefits.[38]

Effective for plan years commencing after 1988, TRA '86 replaced the three statutory vesting schedules just described (10-year cliff vesting, 5–15 vesting, and rule of 45) with two more-restrictive schedules. The first of these, five-year cliff vesting, requires that a participant be 100 percent vested on his or her completion of five years of service. The second schedule is 3–7-year graded vesting. The 3–7-year graded schedule requires that participants be 20 percent vested after completing three years of service and receive an additional 20 percent for each year of service thereafter until 100 percent vested after seven years of service. IRC 411(a)(2).

The vesting schedule is obviously an inducement to employees to continue employment until they are fully vested. If a participant's employment is terminated before he or she is fully vested, benefits that are forfeited either will be allocated to the advantage of the other participants under the plan (an option available only in defined contribution plans) or will serve to reduce the employer contributions. Forfeitures may be substantial if the employee turnover rate is high.

Assuming that the accelerated vesting schedules applicable to top-heavy plans are not applicable, the authors feel that the 5-year cliff vesting schedule should be the vesting schedule of choice for many small businesses, because it keeps the cost of providing employee benefits lower by focusing those benefits on loyal employees who remain with the company for a substantial period of time. As leanness and competitiveness become the watchwords of the '90s, as the cost of providing health benefits continues to escalate, and as the supply of qualified personnel begins to shrink, small businesses will need to use every tool at their disposal to hold onto qualified employees and reduce the cost of providing retirement benefits to those employees.

Past Service

Past service with former employers may be used for determining eligibility to participate in a qualified retirement plan, for benefit accrual, and for vesting of benefits. At one time, the Service maintained that past

---

[38]House Committee on Ways and Means, Brief Summary of the Provisions of H.R. 12481, 93 Cong., 2d sess. 3 (February 5, 1974).

service as a self-employed individual (partner or sole proprietor) could not be counted for purposes of a plan adopted by a corporate successor of the unincorporated business. The Service was unsuccessful with this position in litigation,[39] and it now acknowledges that a corporate qualified plan may include service with a prior partnership or as a sole proprietor for purposes of participation, vesting, and benefit accrual.[40] Until 1980, the Service had maintained that, if past service credit was given for purposes of benefit accrual in a defined benefit plan, then the plan provisions giving past service credit had to prohibit "duplication of benefits," the crediting of benefits under two plans simultaneously.[41] In Revenue Ruling 80–349,[42] the Service reversed its position on prevention of "duplication of benefits"; however, the ruling implies that where duplication of benefits does exist it may result in discrimination, thereby disqualifying the plan.

The Service also takes the position that the use of prior service for purposes of eligibility, vesting, and benefit accrual is subject to the nondiscrimination rules. Using prior service may disqualify a plan where no staff employees received past service credit for their service with a former employer, or possibly where none of the existing staff employees were employed with the former employer.[43] Consequently, the authors generally do not recommend that past service credit be granted for service with predecessor employers unless there are also staff employees who were employed by the predecessor organization. Any grant of past-service credit should attempt to fit within the safe harbor described above with respect to the new proposed nondiscrimination regulations.

Integration with Social Security Benefits

In computing contributions to a qualified retirement plan, the Service generally permits an employer in a non-top-heavy plan to take into consideration its contributions to the Social Security system. For example, in 1992 an employer will pay a Social Security tax equal to 7.65 percent of the first $55,500 of compensation paid for each employee.

---

[39] *Farley Funeral Home*, 62 T.C. 150 (1974).

[40] Tech. Advice Memo. 7742003.

[41] See Rev. Rul. 62–139, 1962–2 C.B. 123, Rev. Rul. 72–531, 1972–2 C.B. 221.

[42] 1980–2 C.B. 132.

[43] See Rev. Rul. 69–409, 1969–2 C.B. 98.

Since Social Security taxes theoretically are used to fund an employee's government-sponsored retirement benefit, a somewhat lower contribution or benefit may be provided under a qualified plan with respect to a participant's compensation below the Social Security wage base. This concept of taking into account Social Security taxes when computing contributions or benefits under a qualified plan is known as "integration." Although TRA '86 reduces the cost-saving effect of integration, the authors feel that small businesses should always consider adopting integrated plans and should not hesitate to do so where a desirable cost savings can be achieved.[44]

The rules governing Social Security integration are provided under Code Sections 401(a)(5) and 401(l), the nondiscrimination regulations under 401(a)(4) and 401(l), and Revenue Ruling 71–446.[45] Profit-sharing plans and money purchase pension plans are generally integrated with the Social Security wage base using an integration factor equal to the Old-Age, Survivors, and Disability Insurance (OASDI) contribution rate, which is 5.7 percent for 1990. Thus, in both a money purchase pension plan and in a profit-sharing plan, the account of each participant may be credited with a contribution equal to 5.7 percent of the compensation earned by the participant during the plan year that was in excess of the Social Security wage base. Any contribution in excess of the amount allocated under the preceding sentence is then allocated to the accounts of all participants in an amount equal to a uniform percentage of all compensation earned.

Effective for plan years beginning after 1988, TRA '86 adds another requirement to integrated money purchase and profit-sharing plans. Such plans are now only integrated properly where, in addition to the rule described above, the contribution rate below the wage base is at least 50 percent of the contribution rate above the wage base.[46]

A defined benefit pension plan is properly integrated with Social Security if the benefits provided by the plan, when added to the benefits provided by the employer-financed portion of Social Security, result in a combined benefit that is a uniform percentage of the compensation paid by the employer to each participant in the plan. Basically, there are

---

[44]For a complete discussion of integration, see para. 19,056 et seq. of Prentice-Hall *Federal Taxes*.
[45]1971–2 C.B. 187.
[46]IRC 401(l) as amended by TRA '86 1111.

two types of integrated defined benefit plans: step rate excess plans and offset plans.

Step Rate Excess Plans

A step rate excess plan pays an additional benefit based solely on an employee's compensation in excess of a certain amount, referred to as the plan's integration level. The plan provides proportionately greater benefits to higher-paid participants since a greater proportion of their compensation will exceed the integration level. For example, if participant A's compensation is $10,000 and participant B's compensation is $20,000, a nonintegrated defined benefit plan could provide a benefit to B that is no greater than twice the benefit provided to A. However, if the plan is integrated at an integration level of $10,000, then none of A's compensation and $10,000 of B's compensation is taken into account in computing the additional benefits, and, therefore, the plan can provide a benefit to B that is up to 3 times greater than the benefit provided to A.

The first step in integrating a step rate excess plan is choosing an integration level. This can be a somewhat complicated process, and it should only be undertaken with the assistance of the professional advisers of the small-business employer.[47] The least-complicated rule relating to integration levels in defined benefit plans allows a plan to adopt an integration level that does not exceed the greater of $10,000 or one half of the covered compensation of an individual who attains the Social Security retirement age in the current year. Any integration level not meeting these criteria will require that other tests be satisfied or that the excess benefit percentage be reduced.

Once a permissible integration level has been determined, the second critical variable to be determined is the excess benefit percentage. The excess benefit percentage is the retirement benefit provided by the plan, expressed as a percentage of compensation, that is in excess of the integration level. The excess benefit percentage cannot yield a benefit

---

[47]The rules concerning permissible integration levels are far too complex to be covered in any detail here. The reader should note, however, that there is a complex set of rules governing the process of determining a permissible integration level, and the integration level chosen can under some circumstances affect the maximum permissible integration rate.

above the integration level that exceeds the benefit below the integration level by more than the lesser of: (a) the benefit provided below the integration level, or (b) 0.75 percent multiplied by the participant's years of service (up to 35 years). This means that, assuming that the excess benefit is not more than twice the benefit below the integration level, the maximum excess benefit (at 35 years of service or more) cannot exceed the benefit below the integration level by more than 26.25 percent.

Distribution alternatives other than an immediate, nondecreasing single-life annuity for the life of the participant must also satisfy the limits on excess benefits. Whether such optional distribution forms satisfy the limits on excess benefits is determined by converting the distribution form into an immediate, nondecreasing single-life annuity for the life of the participant.

A participant's compensation with respect to which a fixed benefit plan's integrated benefit is determined normally must be averaged over a period of at least three consecutive years. This is to prevent the creation of a large integrated benefit based on only one or two years' compensation.[48]

Offset Plans

An offset plan establishes a defined benefit under which no participant and no part of a participant's compensation is excluded because of a minimum compensation level. However, the benefit so determined is then reduced or "offset" by a percentage of the participant's Social Security benefit. If this type of offset method is chosen, care must be taken by the professional advisers of the small business to ensure that the offset satisfies the general nondiscrimination test set forth in the proposed nondiscrimination rules, because the IRS has refused to provide a safe harbor for this type of offset. For example, a fixed benefit offset plan could provide a benefit equal to (1) 25 percent of a participant's final five years' average pay minus (2) one half of the participant's OASDI pension.

Effective for plan years beginning after 1988, TRA '86 further restricts the degree to which defined benefits may be offset by Social Security benefits. Generally, Social Security offsets may not reduce a benefit by more than 50 percent of the amount of the benefit that would

---

[48]IRC 401(a)(5)(D).

have otherwise accrued under the plan. Further, the maximum offset allowance percentage may not exceed 0.75 percent of the participant's covered compensation multiplied by the participant's years of service taken into account under the plan, up to 35 years.

Payment of Benefits

Benefits normally become payable under qualified retirement plans on retirement, the termination of employment prior to retirement, disability, or death. The vesting schedule established under the plan generally will apply only to benefits payable on termination of employment prior to the normal retirement dates. On death, disability, or attainment of normal retirement age, participants must be fully vested. In drafting qualified retirement plans for a small business, questions often arise with regard to when benefits should be paid to employees who terminate employment prior to reaching normal retirement age. Some retirement plans provide, and some advisers recommend, that qualified retirement plans actually be retirement plans and that benefits should be postponed as a matter of plan policy (as opposed to participant choice) until actual retirement. Under this arrangement, an employee who terminates participation at age 30 must wait until either the normal or early retirement date established under the plan before benefits are received. Those employers who utilize this approach maintain that it prevents employees who leave the business from immediately receiving their benefits and using them to fund a competing business. However, the cost of maintaining records for terminated participants and locating them at normal retirement is also a major problem.

Although providing retirement benefits for participants and prohibiting competition by departing employees are important, the authors feel that benefit payments usually should be made to terminating participants as soon after termination as possible. If the payment of benefits is held until retirement age, terminated employees will remain participants under the plan and must be furnished with annual reports and other documents required under the reporting and disclosure regulations. Paying vested benefits to terminated participants also should eliminate the proliferation of partially vested participants that will normally occur over the years as turnover occurs in a small business.

Following the passage of ERISA in 1974, various rules have been enacted with regard to providing survivorship annuities to married participants under qualified retirement plans so as to protect them from premature loss of retirement benefits due to death. The most recent of such rules were included in the Retirement Equity Act of 1984 (REA). Generally, a pension plan will only be qualified if it provides married participants with both (1) a qualified joint and survivor annuity, as the normal form of retirement benefit, and (2) a qualified preretirement survivor annuity, in the event of the participant's death prior to benefit commencement. However, these rules do not generally apply to profit-sharing plans and stock bonus plans if the participants thereunder cannot elect benefits in the form of a life annuity and if the participant's spouse, if any, must be the participant's 100 percent beneficiary in the absence of such spouse's consent to a different beneficiary designation.

A life annuity means an annuity that requires the survival of an annuitant thereunder as one of the conditions for payment. For example, an annuity that makes payments for the duration of the participant's life and an annuity that makes payments until the earlier of 10 payments or the participant's death both constitute life annuities and would invoke the qualified joint and survivor annuity and qualified preretirement survivor annuity requirements in a profit-sharing plan. However, an annuity for a period of 30 years certain is not a life annuity and would not cause the joint and survivor provisions to apply to the plan.[49]

While the annuity rules provide protection to participants and their spouses, they can be very burdensome on plan administrators. Since, in practice, the authors have found that most small businesses have overlooked the notice and election requirements of the joint and survivor annuity regulations, they generally recommend that profit-sharing plans of small business not include an annuity option. While this approach avoids the qualified annuity requirements, the authors feel that employees will not be prejudiced since they are still in a position to obtain an annuity, if one is desired, by rolling over a lump-sum distribution of their account into an individual retirement account or an individual retirement annuity as permitted under Section 402(a)(5) of the Code. If a rollover is made, the participant will not be taxed on the initial distribution of funds from the plan prior to the rollover but, instead, will only be taxed on subsequent distributions from the individual retirement account or annuity.

---

[49]IRC 401(a)(1) and Treas. Reg. 1.401(a)(11).

Code Section 417(b) defines a qualified joint and survivor annuity as an annuity that is the actuarial equivalent of a single life annuity for the participant, makes payments for the participant's life, and also pays a survivor's benefit for the life of the spouse (if the spouse survives the participant) that is at least 50 percent of the primary annuity payment. Where required, a qualified joint and survivor annuity must be the normal form of benefit paid under a plan unless both the participant and the participant's spouse elect otherwise in writing.

A qualified preretirement survivor annuity is designed to protect the surviving spouse of a participant who dies prior to retiring. Upon the preretirement death of a participant, the surviving spouse must receive lifetime annuity payments that are at least equal to the survivor benefits that he or she would have received had the participant commenced the receipt of plan benefits in the form of a qualified joint and survivor annuity one day prior to dying. As with the qualified joint and survivor annuity, a qualified preretirement survivor annuity must be provided unless the participant and the spouse elect otherwise in writing.

TOP-HEAVY RULES

One of the most radical changes to pension law that was invoked by TEFRA was the creation of the top-heavy plan concept. TEFRA Section 240 added Section 416 to the Code, effective for years beginning after December 31, 1983. Code Section 416(a) states that a trust is not a qualified trust if it is a part of a top-heavy plan unless the plan meets certain additional requirements, as discussed below. Before the top-heavy rules can be understood, however, several key terms that are applicable to top-heavy plans must be defined.

Top-Heavy Terminology

Key Employee
Key employee means a plan participant who at any time during a current plan year or the last four immediately preceding plan years was: (1) an officer with compensation in excess of $45,000, (2) one of the 10 employees holding the largest ownership interest in the employer, (3) a 5 percent owner of the employer, or (4) a 1 percent owner of the employer receiving annual compensation of more than $150,000 from the em-

ployer.[50] Unlike the $45,000 level for officers, the $150,000 compensation figure for 1 percent owners is not adjusted for cost-of-living increases.[51] Treasury Regulations issued under Section 416 also provide that, for example, if 20 people have equal ownership of all of a corporation's stock, then all 20 are key employees because all are holders of the "largest interest in the employer."[52]

Employees
Not surprisingly, self-employed individuals, as defined in Code Section 401(c)(1), are treated as employees—an implicit "price" for the establishment of parity between corporate and noncorporate plans—and the earned income of self-employed individuals constitutes their "compensation" for purposes of computing their status as key employees.[53] Moreover, the terms employee and key employee include the beneficiaries of such persons.[54]

Officers
The number of employees who are treated as officers is limited to the lesser of: (1) 50 or (2) the greater of 3 employees or 10 percent of all employees.[55] The Conference Report on TEFRA states that if an employer has more officers than are required to be counted as key employees, then only those officers with the highest compensation are to be considered in applying the top-heavy rules.[56] The Conference Report relies on prior authority to define officer.[57] Thus, although all of the facts and circumstances are to be considered in determining whether a particular employee is an officer, several key facts that must be considered are the source of the employee's authority; the term of service; the nature and extent of his or her duties; and whether the employee is characterized

---

[50]IRC 416(i)(1)(A).

[51]Ibid.

[52]Treas. Reg. 1.416–1, T–12.

[53]IRC 416(i)(3).

[54]IRC 416(i)(5); Treas. Reg. 1.416–1, T–12.

[55]IRC 416(i)(1).

[56]S. REP. NO. 530, 97th Cong., 2nd sess. 626 (1982). See Treas. Reg. 1.416–1, T–14.

[57]S. REP. NO. 530, 97th Cong., 2nd Sess. 626, n. 1 (1982) (Citing Rev. Rul. 80–314, 1980–2 C.B. 152).

fairly as an administrative executive engaged in regular and continued service.[58] For years beginning after February 28, 1985, noncorporate business organizations may have officers.[59]

Ownership

Ownership, for purposes of Code Section 416, is defined specifically and in a complex fashion. If the employer is a corporation, *ownership,* for purposes of the 1 percent owner and 5 percent owner rules, means (1) ownership of either 1 percent or 5 percent of the stock of the corporation or (2) ownership of stock possessing more than 1 percent or 5 percent of the total combined voting power of all stock of the corporation. If the employer is not a corporation, ownership means possession of 1 percent or 5 percent of the capital or profits interest of the employer.[60] The constructive ownership rules of Code Section 318 generally apply in determining the ownership percentage of corporate employees. The "from entity" rules of Section 318 are altered, however, such that if 5 percent of a corporation's stock is owned by a potential key employee (instead of 50 percent as usual) then the proportionate share of the corporation's holdings of the plan employer's stock is attributed to the employer.[61] The Conference Report and Code require the Secretary of the Treasury to issue regulations that define constructive ownership as it pertains to noncorporate employers, and that are based on principles similar to the Code Section 318 Regulations.[62] While Code Section 318 rules are used in determining ownership by employees, the Section 414 aggregation rules are not used in calculating ownership.[63]

Determination Date

Determination date means the last day of the preceding plan year or the last day of the first plan year.[64]

---

[58]Treas. Reg. 1.416–1, T–13.

[59]Treas. Reg. 1.416–1, T–15.

[60]IRC 416(i)(1)(B).

[61]IRC 416(i)(1)(B)(iii)(I).

[62]IRC 416(i)(1)(B)(iii)(II); S. REP. NO. 530, 97th Cong., 2nd Sess. 626 (1982).

[63]IRC 416(i)(1)(C).

[64]IRC 416(g)(4)(C).

What is a Top-Heavy Plan?

A defined benefit plan is top-heavy if "the present value of the cumulative accrued benefits under the plan for key employees exceeds 60 percent of the present value of the cumulative accrued benefits under the plan for all employees" on the determination date.[65] The "present value" aspect of the calculation means that the benefits are treated as if they were accrued in a defined contribution plan.[66] A defined contribution plan is a top-heavy plan if "the aggregate of the accounts of key employees under the plan exceeds 60 percent of the aggregate of the accounts of all employees under such plan" on the determination date.[67] Treasury regulations state that only accrued benefits attributable to deductible employee contributions are excluded from the computation of accrued benefits.[68]

A plan is also top-heavy if it is part of a top-heavy group. First, the proper grouping of plans must be determined. Two types of plans must be aggregated (mandatory aggregation): plans in which any of the employer's key employees participate and plans that are grouped by the employer to meet the coverage and discrimination tests of Code Sections 401(a)(4) and 410(b).[69] As discussed in Chapter 56, the Conference Report states that the top-heavy group rule applies to affiliated service groups, as well as the other Section 414 groups of related employees that were discussed earlier.[70]

The employer also may aggregate plans with a top-heavy group (permissive aggregation) in an attempt to destroy the top-heavy group classification as long as the new aggregated group satisfies the coverage and nondiscrimination requirements.[71] A group of plans is a top-heavy group if the sum of "the present value of the cumulative accrued benefits for key employees under all defined benefit plans included in such group"

---

[65]IRC 416(g)(1)(A)(ii).

[66]See Treas. Reg. 1.416–1, T–25 for a discussion of how the present value of accrued benefits is determined for a defined benefit plan.

[67]IRC 416(g)(1)(A)(ii). See Treas. Reg. 1.416–1, T–24, for a discussion of how the present value of accrued benefits is determined for a defined contribution plan.

[68]Treas. Reg. 1.416–1, T–28.

[69]IRC 416(g)(2)(A)(i); Treas. Reg. 1.416–1, T–1, T–6.

[70]S. REP. NO. 530, 97th Cong., 2nd Sess. 625 (1982).

[71]IRC 416(g)(2)(A)(ii); S. REP. NO. 530, 97th Cong., 2nd Sess. 625 (1982); Treas. Reg. 1.416–1, T–7.

and "the aggregate of the accounts of key employees under all defined contribution plans included in such group" exceeds 60 percent of the same sum computed for all employees.[72]

Impact of Top-Heavy Rules

The consequences of being a top-heavy plan are severe. Aside from the 1.0 Rule discussed earlier, several restrictions exist on top-heavy plans.

First, a top-heavy plan must vest accrued benefits derived from employer contributions according to one of two vesting schedules:[73]

1. Three-year cliff vesting, in which the benefits of an employee with three years of service are 100 percent vested.
2. Six-year graded vesting according to the following chart:

Years of Service	Nonforfeitable Percent
2	20
3	40
4	60
5	80
6 or more	100

Again, however, the accelerated vesting schedules that TRA '86 imposes for plan years commencing after 1988 make this top-heavy rule of dubious significance for most plans.

Second, a top-heavy defined benefit plan must provide an annual retirement benefit derived from employer contributions to nonkey employees that at least equals the lesser of (1) 2 percent of the participant's average compensation per year of service or (2) 20 percent, multiplied by the employee's average annual compensation during his or her highest consecutive five years.[74] Social Security benefits originating from an

---

[72]IRC 416(g)(2)(B).

[73]See IRC 416(b).

[74]IRC 416(c)(1); Treas. Regs. 1.416–1, M–2 through M–6.

employer's contribution to the Social Security system cannot be integrated to reduce the minimum benefit.[75]

For defined contribution plans, the employer must contribute on behalf of nonkey employees at least the smaller of (1) 3 percent of the employee's compensation or (2) the highest percentage contribution made on behalf of any key employee.[76] As before, Social Security benefits arising from employer contributions to the Social Security system cannot be used to reduce the minimum contribution.[77]

The rule that allows minimum contributions on behalf of nonkey employees merely to equal the highest percentage contribution on behalf of any key employee (instead of requiring such contributions to equal at least 3 percent) obviously creates the potential for abuse in the case of employers sponsoring two or more plans. To prevent this abuse, Code Section 416 requires use of the 3 percent rule if the defined contribution plan enables a defined benefit plan that is required to be included in a top-heavy group to meet the coverage and nondiscrimination rules of Code Sections 401(a)(4) and 410. Moreover, all defined contribution plans that are required to be included in a top-heavy group are treated as one plan.[78]

If an employer provides both a defined benefit and defined contribution plan to an employee, then the employee is not entitled to both minimum benefits.[79]

Finally, as noted earlier, if a small business maintains a defined contribution plan and a defined benefit plan, the new 1.0 Rule is applicable.[80] The required mathematical changes in the 1.0 Rule formula generally mean that the maximum contribution and benefits for employees earning over $64,285.71 annually are severely reduced.

Depending on the circumstances, the consequences of having a plan characterized as top-heavy may be harsh and quite expensive. Accordingly, care must be taken to avoid top-heavy status whenever possible and, when not possible, to react in the most advantageous manner.

---

[75]IRC 416(e); Treas. Regs. 1.416–1, M–11.

[76]IRC 416(c)(2); Treas. Regs. 1.416–1, M–7 through M–10.

[77]IRC 416(e); Treas. Regs. 1.416–1, M–11.

[78]IRC 416(c)(2)(B)(ii).

[79]Treas. Regs. 1.416–1, M–8.

[80]IRC 416(h)(i).

SECTION 401(k) CASH-DEFERRED/SALARY REDUCTION PLANS

IRC 401(k) plans have become very popular as employers have scaled back benefit programs to increase their competitiveness. These plans are sanctioned by Section 401(k) of the Internal Revenue Code as interpreted by several regulations. Any employer who is considering adopting a Section 401(k) plan should understand the basic elements of such a plan and the restrictions on employer and employee contributions to such a plan.

Basic Elements of a Cash-Deferred/Salary Reduction Plan

A Section 401(k) plan is distinguished by a cash or deferred option, usually in the form of a salary reduction agreement between an eligible employee and the employer. Under a salary reduction agreement plan, a contribution is made by the employer to the employee's account only if the employee elects to reduce his or her compensation or to forgo an increase in his or her compensation equal to the contribution.[81] A salary reduction agreement plan may provide for contributions by the employer and the employee other than those subject to the salary reduction agreement.

The regulations limit the cash or deferred option to profit-sharing or stock bonus plans.[82] Of course, the plan and the trust that implements the plan must meet the general requirements of the Code for tax-favored treatment under Sections 401(a) and 501(a) of the Code.

Withdrawal Restrictions

IRC Section 401(k) imposes special distribution or withdrawal restrictions on deferrals pursuant to any qualified cash or deferred arrangement. Of course, any deferral or other contribution taken into account for purposes of the actual deferral percentage test discussed below is fully vested immediately. Such deferrals and such other contributions, how-

---

[81]Treas. Regs. 1.401(k)–1(a).
[82]Treas. Regs. 1.401(k)–1(a)(1).

ever, may not be distributed sooner than the earliest of the following events: retirement, death, disability, separation from service, attainment of age 59½, or the occurrence of a hardship.[83]

Discrimination Restrictions on Contributions to Cash-Deferred/Salary Reduction Plans

The Code generally discourages discrimination between lower-paid employees and other employees by imposing several coverage and discrimination requirements on all qualified retirement plans. In addition to the minimum coverage and nondiscrimination requirements imposed by Code Section 410(b)(1) and Code Section 401(a)(4), special nondiscrimination restrictions apply to cash or deferred arrangements. The annual amount of a participant's elective contribution (which is also referred to as an "elective deferral") cannot exceed $7,000, as adjusted for the cost of living ($8,728 for 1992). Moreover, elective deferrals are subject to a special nondiscrimination test set forth in IRC Section 401(k)(3) and known as the actual deferral percentage (ADP) test, which we discuss below. After-tax employee contributions, matching contributions, and certain nonelective contributions known as "qualified nonelective contributions" are also subject to the average contribution percentage test, which has already been discussed in this chapter. Deferrals will be deemed nondiscriminatory in amount under the nondiscrimination regulations pursuant to IRC Section 401(a)(4) as long as they satisfy the ADP test. Matching contributions will be deemed nondiscriminatory in amount as long as they satisfy the ACP test. The portion of the plan not subject to IRC Section 401(k) or (m), however, must be tested under the nondiscrimination regulations to determine whether the contributions thereto are nondiscriminatory in amount. The nonelective contributions that make up this portion of the plan must satisfy this nondiscriminatory amount test both with and without any qualified nonelective contributions an employer chooses to utilize with respect to the ADP or ACP test. Nonelective contributions are those that are not subject to the cash or deferred election.

---

[83]Unfortunately, a detailed description of the conditions constituting a "hardship" and the restrictive rules that apply in administering hardship distributions is beyond the scope of this chapter.

The General Coverage Requirement of Section 410(b)(1)

As noted earlier, this section provides that a plan will qualify for favorable tax treatment only if one of the percentage tests specified therein is met. Also noted above, TRA '86 has imposed new, more rigorous tests that came into effect in 1989.

The Nondiscrimination Requirement of Section 401(a)(4)

The special 401(k) nondiscrimination regulations discussed later in this chapter generally provide that satisfaction of the nondiscrimination requirements specific to IRC 401(k) is satisfaction of the nondiscriminatory amount requirements of IRC 401(a)(4) (though the cash or deferred arrangement must still satisfy the other nondiscrimination requirements imposed by this Code section).[84]

Special Cash or Deferred Discrimination Rules

In a cash-deferred/salary-reduction plan, special discrimination rules apply. However, before these rules can be understood, the following term must be defined:

> *Actual deferral percentage.* The actual deferral percentage of any employee is the amount of employer contributions paid under the plan on behalf of that employee during a plan year divided by the employee's compensation for such period. The actual deferral percentage for either the group of highly compensated employees (as defined on p. 33) or for a group of other employees is the average of those separately determined ratios.[85]

There are two actual deferral percentage tests under Code Section 401(k), one of which must be met for a cash or deferred plan to meet the special nondiscrimination rules.

1. The actual deferral percentage for the group of highly compensated employees is not more than the actual deferred percentage for all other eligible employees multiplied by 1.25.

---

[84]Treas. Reg. 1.401(a)(4)–2(d)(1).
[85]IRC 401(k)(3)(B).

2. The actual deferral percentage for the group of highly compensated employees is not more than the actual deferred percentage for all other eligible employees multiplied by 2.0 and does not exceed such other actual deferred percentage by more than 2 percentage points.[86]

If the cash or deferred plan does not meet either test for a given year, the plan will be disqualified unless the excess contributions for the highly compensated employees are distributed prior to the close of the following plan year or are treated as nondeductible employee contributions.[87]

A final factor that limits contributions to a cash-deferred plan is the general limitation on employer contributions to profit-sharing plans imposed by Code Section 404. As noted, that Section provides that an employer may not deduct employer contributions to a stock bonus or profit-sharing plan that are in excess of 15 percent of the participant's total compensation. Obviously, few employers will allow employees to direct employer contributions to profit-sharing plans that the employer cannot deduct.

A cash-deferred/salary reduction plan offers an attractive alternative for those employers who are considering the adoption of new retirement plans or the revision of existing profit-sharing or stock bonus plans. At the same time, all cash or deferred arrangements are restricted by Code Section 401(k) and the proposed regulations; therefore, a cash or deferred arrangement should only be adopted after careful thought and study and after analysis by a knowledgeable retirement consultant or attorney specializing in such plans.

---

[86]IRC 401(k)(3)(A)(ii).
[87]IRC 401(k)(8).

CHAPTER 56

QUALIFIED RETIREMENT PLANS FOR SMALL BUSINESS: ADMINISTRATIVE AND TAX ISSUES

Harry V. Lamon, Jr.
Joel R. Wells IV

GENERAL ADMINISTRATION OF THE PLAN

Employees are often too busy to handle their own personal financial affairs, and, as a result, the administrative aspects of the qualified retirement plans adopted by small businesses are often overlooked. It is important that qualified retirement plans be administered properly because, if they are not, such plans may become "discriminatory in operation" and be disqualified by the Internal Revenue Service.

Once a qualified retirement plan is established, someone should be assigned the responsibility of dealing with the attorney, the accountant, the trustee, and the investment manager (if all of these exist). Also, when the plan is established, some consideration should be given to who will perform the technical administrative functions of the plan, such as filing annual reports and making annual allocations. Under defined benefit pension plans, these functions are almost always performed by the actuary, since an actuarial analysis is necessary to compute the accrued benefit annually. The normal fees for actuaries for most small businesses' defined benefit plans range from $1,500 to $3,000 per year, depending on the number of employees and the complexity of the plan.

Most problems arise, however, under defined contribution plans, for which it is not necessary to have an actuary. In many such cases, the plan trustee is a local bank that will offer administrative services. However, not all banks seek out small-business plans, because such plans often have total assets that are not within the scope of the bank's overall employee benefit market. Moreover, not all plan sponsors and participants desire to have a bank act as trustee and invest plan assets, because of the generally conservative nature of most banks. Many brokerage houses, life insurance companies, and retirement plan consulting firms offer administrative services for defined contribution plans. Further, some accounting firms will assist a small business with its annual administrative functions; but most accounting firms will do so only if there are fewer than 10 employees, because of the complexity of the allocations when more than 10 employees are involved. The administrative services for defined contribution plans sponsored by small businesses should normally run between $500 and $1,500 per year per plan, depending on the number of participants and the activity in the plan.

The fees for administering qualified retirement plans on an annual basis may be paid either by the trust or by the employer. The authors generally recommend that such fees be paid by the employer, as they are deductible by the employer. Further, payment of such fees by the plans reduces the funds that will eventually be available to pay retirement benefits.

The authors also generally recommend that the employer, and not one of the shareholders or employees, be designated as the plan administrator. To designate an individual as the plan administrator requires obtaining a separate employer identification number (EIN) from the Internal Revenue Service for the individual and formally changing plan administrators if the individual leaves the employer. In addition, an individual who serves as plan administrator may be subject to suits by disgruntled participants.

ADOPTION OF PLANS AND ADOPTION OF AMENDMENTS

A qualified retirement plan may be established or amended at any time prior to the close of the employer's taxable year, with such plan or plan amendment effective retroactive to the first day of the employer's taxable year. For example, assume a calendar-year employer adopted a qualified defined benefit plan on December 31, 1990, with an effective date of January 1, 1990. The employer could contribute and deduct for 1990 the amount necessary to pay the normal cost for the entire 1990 plan year plus an amount necessary to amortize the cost of past service credit (if any) provided for in the plan. The contribution could be made and the appropriate deduction taken at any time prior to the date for filing the 1990 tax returns, including extensions.

An employer who adopts or amends a qualified plan is permitted to file a request that the Service make a determination that the provisions of the plan as adopted or as amended satisfy the requirements of the Internal Revenue Code for qualification; such a request is allowed during the "remedial amendment period." The significance of filing the determination request during the remedial amendment period is that if a request is filed during that period and the Service determines that changes are necessary to cause the plan to be qualified, then the necessary changes may be adopted retroactively to the effective date of the plan (or the effective date of a plan amendment) so that the plan will be qualified from its initial effective date (or the effective date of an amendment).[1] If a request for a determination is filed after the close of the remedial amendment period and the Service discovers deficiencies in the plan, retroactive cure of the deficiencies may not be possible. Where the plan year corresponds to the employer's taxable year, the remedial amendment period for initial qualification or for a plan amendment will extend until the date for filing the employer's tax return (including extensions) for the first taxable year of the employer in which the plan or the amendment is effective. The remedial amendment period may be extended at the discretion of the Service, but the Service does not extend the period where failure to file a timely determination letter request was due merely to oversight.

It should be remembered that the period for adopting a qualified retirement plan by an employer ends with the last day of the first taxable year of the employer for which the plan is effective. Although contributions may be made after the end of the employer's taxable year and may be deducted for the year to which they apply, the plan itself may not be adopted retroactive to a taxable year that ended prior to the date of

---

[1]Treas. Regs. 1.401(b)-1.

adoption. In *Engineered Timber Sales,*[2] the Tax Court held that no deductions would be permitted for the first taxable year for which a plan was made effective where the employer had adopted a trust agreement and the employer's board of directors had passed a resolution to adopt the plan prior to the expiration of the employer's first taxable year for which the plan was to be effective, but no enforceable plan was drafted until the following taxable year of the employer.

A plan that satisfies all the requirements of the Code for qualification and that receives a favorable determination letter is not assured of permanent qualification. Two distinct classes of events that would disqualify the plan could occur. First, the plan might become disqualified in operation. As an example, the plan administrator might improperly exclude some rank-and-file employees, despite the plan's express eligibility requirements, and thereby cause the plan to discriminate.[3] Another example might be a "demographic" change, such as a change in the percentage of highly compensated employees or a change in deferrals by nonhighly compensated employees, that causes a violation of nondiscrimination rules and triggers disqualification of the plan in operation. Second, the legal requirements applicable to qualified plans might change, for example, by issuance of new or modified Treasury Regulations, by enactment of a new law, or by promulgation of a new revenue ruling.[4] Generally, when there is a change in applicable law, a plan will remain qualified if the plan is amended not later than the close of the plan year following the plan year in which the change in law occurred, and if the amendment is made effective as of the first day of the plan year following the plan year in which the change in law occurred. It is therefore critical that plan administrators, or their counsel, keep abreast of changes in the laws applicable to qualified plans so that timely plan amendments may be adopted.

Finally, any employer planning to amend a qualified plan should be mindful of, and consider with the advice of its legal counsel, the new requirement that a plan amendment be nondiscriminatory under IRC

---

[2]74 T.C. 808 (1980).

[3]*Myron* v. *U.S.*, 550 F.2d 1145 (9th Cir. 1977).

[4]*Wisconsin Nipple & Fabricating Co.* v. *Commissioner,* 67 T.C. 490 (1976), aff'd 581 F.2d 1235 (7th Cir. 1978).

401(a)(4). This aspect of the new regulations under that statute is discussed in the previous chapter.

ENFORCEMENT

The topic of enforcement will be an important one in the 1990s for small employers with qualified plans. Thus, small employers should be aware of the kinds of issues they may be facing as the Service and the Department of Labor begin committing more resources to auditing plans under the tax and ERISA rules they are responsible for enforcing.

The topic of enforcement is far too broad to be covered in any great detail in this chapter. This section will highlight, however, some of the important enforcement issues for qualified plans and some of the developments that can be expected in the future.

Small employers should be aware that small qualified plans are the likeliest target of any new governmental enforcement initiatives. The consensus among officials of the Labor and Treasury departments appears to be that the majority of abuses occur in small, rather than large, qualified plans. Thus, small employers should be prepared to bear the brunt of the impact of increased enforcement activity.

Small Defined Benefit Plan Audit Program

The Service has provided a kind of preview of the new emphasis on enforcement in the form of an audit program targeting small defined benefit plans. This audit program is challenging the reasonableness of the actuarial assumptions used by many small defined benefit plans. The Service has asserted that unreasonable actuarial assumptions have been used by many small defined benefit plans to generate excessive contributions.

There are two actuarial assumptions in particular that the Service believes have been used to inflate contributions: the assumption about the interest that plan investments will earn (the less the interest rate, the more that will have to be funded with contributions) and the assumption about the date employees can be expected to retire (the earlier the retirement, the greater the contributions will need to be in order to fund the retirement benefit). The Service has stated that its ''guideposts'' for reasonable assumptions are an 8 percent interest-rate assumption and a retirement-age assumption of 65. Although falling short of these guideposts will not result in automatic disallowance, it has resulted in disallowance in a number of cases.

The Service has recovered a great deal already through its audit program. At the time of this writing, the proposed adjustments have averaged about $150,000 per plan.

The pivotal case testing the issues addressed in this audit program is the case of *Jerome Mirza & Associates, Ltd.* v. *United States,*[5] which the Service won on appeal to the Seventh Circuit Court of Appeals in 1989. In that case, the court agreed with the Service that an 8 percent interest rate assumption was reasonable and that a 5 percent interest rate assumption was unreasonable.

Reporting and Disclosure

The following are some of the important reporting and disclosure requirements for qualified retirement plans.[6]

Summary Plan Description (SPD). A summary plan description, prepared in a manner calculated to be understood by the average plan participant, must be provided to participants and beneficiaries within 120 days after the plan is adopted. A copy must also be filed with the Department of Labor within that 120-day period. Further, a summary description of material modifications to the plan must be furnished to participants and beneficiaries within 210 days after the end of the plan year in which such modifications occur. The summary plan description must be provided to new employees within 90 days after they become participants.

An administrator who fails to provide a participant with a summary plan description within 30 days of the participant's request for a summary plan description may be personally liable to the participant in an amount up to $100 per day from the date of such failure (ERISA Sec. 502(c)(1).) The administrator may provide the participant with the summary plan description by mailing it to the participant's last known

---

[5]629 F.Supp. 918 (C.D.Ill. 1988), affirmed, 882 F.2d 229 (7th Cir. 1989), rehearing denied (1989), cert. denied (May 14, 1990).

[6]A detailed treatment of the reporting and disclosure requirements of ERISA is beyond the scope of this chapter. Only the highlights can be discussed here. Any small employer should expect to encounter additional reporting and disclosure requirements (e.g., the notice of rollover eligibility that must be provided in connection with certain distributions) in the administration of its qualified plans.

mailing address. It is always wise to use Registered or Certified Mail when mailing a summary plan description in order to be able to prove the date of mailing and delivery.

The required contents of the summary plan description are described in Labor Regulations 2520.102-3 and include a general statement of the benefits provided under the plan and the manner in which the plan operates.

Participant's Benefit Statements on Request. On the written request of a participant or beneficiary, the plan administrator must supply, without charge to the participant or beneficiary, a statement based on the latest available information of his or her total accrued benefit, and either the percentage of accrued benefits that are nonforfeitable or the date on which benefits will become nonforfeitable.[7] The plan administrator is not required to provide more than one such benefit statement during any 12-month period.[8]

Furnishing Other Documents Relating to the Plan. The plan administrator must make available for inspection by participants and beneficiaries copies of the plan document and trust agreement, copies of any collective bargaining agreement or contract under which the plan was established or is maintained, a copy of the latest annual report filed with the Service, and a copy of the latest summary plan description.[9] No charge may be made for exercising the right to inspect these documents. If the participant or beneficiary requests copies of these documents, copies must be provided. A reasonable charge not in excess of the actual cost of reproducing the documents may be required, but no charge may be made for the postage or handling involved in providing requested documents.[10] Not later than nine months after the close of a plan year, the plan administrator must furnish each participant and each beneficiary receiving benefits with a "summary annual report" that summarizes the annual report that was sent to the Service on Form 5500 series. The format for this report is prescribed in Labor Regulations 2520.104b-10. Notably, the Department of Labor may impose a penalty of up to $1,000 per day for the failure to timely file a *correct* annual report or summary annual report with the Department of Labor.[11]

---

[7]ERISA 105(a).

[8]ERISA 105(b).

[9]ERISA 104(b)(2).

[10]Labor Regulations 2520.104b-30.

[11]ERISA 502(c)(2).

Fiduciary Duties and Penalties

The small employer itself, and potentially some of the key employees who exercise authority or control with respect to the employer's qualified plans, may be "fiduciaries" under ERISA. A fiduciary is basically someone who exercises discretionary authority or responsibility in the administration or management of the plan, or who exercises any authority or control with respect to the management of plan assets.[12] A fiduciary has special responsibilities to act for the benefit of the plan and its participants. ERISA imposes a number of special legal duties and restrictions on fiduciaries, and the penalties for the breach of any of these duties could be severe.

The most basic of a fiduciary's duties is the duty of loyalty. A fiduciary must discharge his or her duties solely in the interest of participants and beneficiaries. Thus, a fiduciary's actions with respect to a plan must be for the exclusive purpose of providing benefits under the plan or defraying the reasonable administrative expenses of the plan.[13] In other words, an action taken primarily to serve outside interests, such as the use of plan assets to assist the employer in a takeover, may violate the duty of loyalty even if the plan is not harmed by the action.[14] The best examples of violations of the duty of loyalty are prohibited transactions, a topic discussed below.

The second major fiduciary duty is the duty of prudence. A fiduciary must act with the care, skill, prudence, and diligence of a reasonable person who is familiar with such matters under like circumstances.[15] This duty is especially important when a fiduciary is making a decision about the investment of plan assets. The duty of prudence requires that the fiduciary's actual decision not only be a reasonable one, but also that the decision-making process be thorough and diligent.

There are other fiduciary duties, as well. A fiduciary is required to diversify plan assets unless it is clearly prudent not to do so.[16] In addition, a fiduciary must act in accordance with the plan documents.[17]

---

[12]ERISA 3(21)(A). This chapter will not discuss the problems of investment advisers as fiduciaries.

[13]ERISA 404(a)(1)(A).

[14]*Leigh* v. *Engle*, 727 F.2d 113 (7th Cir. 1984).

[15]ERISA 404(a)(1)(B).

[16]ERISA 404(a)(1)(C).

[17]ERISA 404(a)(1)(D). See *Tilley* v. *Mead Corp.*, 927 F.2d 756 (4th Cir. 1991); *In re Gulf Pension Litigation*, 1991 WL 92,963 (S.D.Tex., Civ. Action No. 86-4365, April 10, 1991).

While it has always been important for small employers to understand the special responsibilities they assume when they establish a qualified plan, this consideration has recently become even more important because of new enforcement initiatives and because a powerful new weapon has been added to the arsenal of the Department of Labor: the mandatory 20 percent penalty.[18] The mandatory 20 percent penalty created by the Omnibus Budget Reconciliation Act of 1989 (OBRA '89) is imposed any time the Department of Labor is involved in obtaining a recovery for a breach of a fiduciary duty either through a court judgment or through an out of court settlement. The penalty, in the amount of 20 percent of the recovery, is in addition to any recovery. The penalty may be imposed not only on fiduciaries, but even on nonfiduciaries who knowingly participate in a fiduciary breach.

The mandatory 20 percent penalty gives the Department of Labor substantial additional leverage in negotiations over an allegation of fiduciary breach, especially because the Department of Labor has the authority to waive or reduce the penalty under certain conditions. Moreover, even the threat of Department of Labor involvement can provide additional leverage for private litigants.

The effective date of the mandatory penalty is December 19, 1989, but this could be misleading. Many fiduciary violations are deemed to continue and renew at the beginning of each year until corrected. Thus, any fiduciary breach that occurred prior to the effective date could still trigger the mandatory 20 percent penalty if not corrected prior to the effective date.

Prohibited Transactions

Section 406 of ERISA and parallel provisions of Section 4975 of the Code prohibit employee benefit plans from engaging in certain types of transactions. The provisions of Section 4975 of the Code only apply to qualified retirement plans, while the provisions of Section 406 of ERISA apply to both retirement plans (whether or not "qualified" under the Code) and welfare plans (such as medical, accident, or layoff benefit plans). Violations of the prohibited-transaction provisions of the Code can result in the imposition of a nondeductible excise tax equal to 5 percent of the "amount involved" in the transaction for each year that the transaction

---

[18]ERISA 502(l).

continues. An additional excise tax of 100 percent of the amount involved is imposed if correction is not made upon receipt of notice from the Service. A fiduciary who permits a prohibited transaction to which Section 406 of ERISA applies may be held personally liable under Section 409 of ERISA for any loss to the plan resulting from the transaction.

Transactions that constitute prohibited transactions are absolutely forbidden, regardless of the financial or economic soundness of the transaction and regardless of whether the transaction offers the plan a more attractive financial opportunity than is available elsewhere. Generally, the defenses of good faith, innocence, and reasonable lack of knowledge that a transaction is prohibited will not prevent imposition of the excise tax under Code Section 4975; however, violation of Section 406 of ERISA can sometimes be avoided with these defenses.

The specific transactions prohibited are certain transactions between plans and "parties in interest." ERISA Section 3(14) enumerates a rather broad class of persons who constitute parties in interest with respect to a plan. Parties in interest include all plan fiduciaries, including the plan administrator, trustee, or custodian of plan assets, any person who provides services to a plan, the employer whose employees are covered by the plan, a relative (spouse, ancestor, lineal descendant, or spouse of a lineal descendant) of any of the foregoing individuals, and any employee, officer, director, or 10 percent (direct or indirect) shareholder of the employer who maintains the plan.

A prohibited transaction will occur if there is a direct or indirect instance of the following:

1. Sale, exchange, or leasing of any property between a plan and a party in interest.
2. Lending of money or other extension of credit between a plan and a party in interest.
3. Furnishing of any goods, services, or facilities between a plan and a party in interest.
4. Transfer of any plan assets to or use of any plan assets by or for the benefit of a party in interest.
5. Acquisition of securities of the employer under certain circumstances or in excess of certain maximum amounts.

In addition, certain dealings by fiduciaries will constitute prohibited transactions. Specifically, a fiduciary if prohibited from dealing with assets of the plan for his or her own personal gain, representing any person in a transaction involving the plan in which the party represented has interests adverse to the plan, and receiving a kickback from any person in connection with a transaction involving assets of the plan.

Section 4975 of the Code and Section 408(b) of ERISA contain a number of "statutory exemptions" from the prohibited-transaction provisions. For example, the statutory exemption dealing with loans to participants has been discussed. Other statutory exemptions include the following:

1. To provide reasonable services necessary to establish or operate the plan.
2. To permit bank trustees to invest plan assets in savings accounts and pooled investment accounts of the bank and to provide ancillary banking services to the plan.
3. To permit fiduciaries to receive reasonable compensation for services (unless they are full-time employees of the employer).
4. To permit fiduciaries who are plan participants to receive plan benefits as they become payable.

In addition to the statutory exemptions, Section 408(a) of ERISA and Section 4975(c)(2) of the Code permit administrative exemptions from the prohibited transaction rules to be granted. Administrative exemptions may be granted in favor of a particular transaction (an individual exemption) or a class of transactions (class exemptions). Individual exemptions apply only to the specific transaction for which the exemption was granted and will not authorize an identical transaction engaged in by different parties. Class exemptions generally exempt any past, present, or future transaction that satisfies the requirements of the exemption.

Requests for prohibited-transaction exemptions are filed with the Department of Labor. It normally takes from four to six months for an exemption request to be finally resolved, and nearly 90 percent of the requests for exemptions are denied. In order to obtain an administrative exemption, a plan must complete a rather tedious application in which it must be demonstrated that the exemption, if granted, would be (1) administratively feasible, (2) in the interest of the plan, its participants and beneficiaries, and (3) protective of the rights of participants and beneficiaries of the plan. Chances for approval are increased if the applicant can show that, due to the independent safeguards, the transaction provides a "no lose" opportunity for larger financial benefit to the plan than other available investment alternatives.

Conclusion: A Glimpse at Some Possible Future Developments

Small employers should be prepared for more enforcement initiatives during the coming decade. The Department of Labor, for instance, is beginning a program of hiring additional enforcement staff.[19] In addition, a series of proposals from the Department of Labor, if enacted into law, would create, among other things, a mandatory award of legal costs (including legal and expert fees) to successful plaintiffs in fiduciary breach cases and a "bounty" proposal in which the Department of Labor could award up to 10 percent of the amount collected under the mandatory 20 percent penalty to any person who brought information to the attention of the Department of Labor leading to the institution of a lawsuit.

Small employers should consult closely with their professional advisers in making important decisions with respect to their qualified plans, especially decisions with respect to the investment of plan assets. Preventing problems from occurring is the best way to avoid fiduciary or other enforcement problems. If allegations of a fiduciary breach are made, or if the small employer suddenly finds itself the target of a Department of Labor investigation, the small employer should immediately contact its legal counsel, and possibly retain specialized ERISA counsel, before responding in any way.

LOANS TO PARTICIPANTS

A loan from a qualified retirement plan to a participant of that plan is a prohibited transaction under Section 406(a)(1)(B) of the Employee Retirement Income Security Act and Section 4975(c)(1)(B) of the Code. However, Section 408(b)(1) of ERISA and Section 4975(d)(1) of the Code provide an exemption from the prohibited transaction rules where the following requirements (further explained in DOL Reg. 2530.408-1(b)(1)) are met:

1. Loans are made to all participants and beneficiaries on a reasonably equivalent basis. While the Department of Labor first took the position that this requirement meant that loans must be made to former

---

[19]See, e.g., "Ball Says Congress Has Not Seen the Last of ERISA Enforcement Proposal," 49 Tax Notes 1072 (December 3, 1990).

employees with account balances in the plan, it subsequently reversed itself as a practical matter by allowing plans to deny loans to participants who are not "parties in interest."[20] For a discussion of "parties in interest," see section on prohibited transactions below. No irrelevant or improper factors such as race, color, religion, sex, age, or national origin should be considered. The loans should be made on the basis of the legitimate financial criteria a commercial lender would consider. The new regulations provide a safe-harbor minimum loan amount of $1,000 that will not violate the reasonably equivalent basis requirement.

   2. Loans are not made available to highly compensated employees, officers, or shareholders in an amount greater than the amount made available to other employees. In addition to the requirement that loans be available on a reasonably equivalent basis, the new regulations prohibit a loan requirement excluding large numbers of participants from qualifying for loans. This requirement will not be violated merely because the plan permits all plan participants to borrow the same percentage of their vested accrued benefits even though officers, shareholders, and highly compensated employees may, as a group, have larger vested accrued benefits than rank and file employees.

   3. Loans are made in accordance with specific provisions regarding such loans set forth in the plan. After January 1, 1990, the plan or a document forming a part of the plan must set forth the following information concerning the loan program:

   a. The person or persons authorized to administer the loan program.
   b. The application process.
   c. The basis for approving or denying loans.
   d. Loan limits.
   e. A formula for determining a reasonable rate of interest.
   f. Events triggering default.
   g. The plan's response to a default, which must be aimed at preserving plan assets.

   4. Loans bear a reasonable rate of interest. A "reasonable" rate is one "commensurate with the interest rates charged by persons in the business of lending money for loans which would be made in similar circumstances."[21] The Department of Labor appears to have approved

---

[20]DOL ERISA Advisory Opinion 89-30A (October 2, 1989).
[21]DOL Reg. 2550.408b-1(e).

national rates, thus avoiding the burdensome necessity of individualized rates. If state usury laws set an unreasonably low ceiling on the rate of interest, the Department of Labor has warned that adhering to such laws could violate ERISA fiduciary principles. To the extent that state usury laws conflict with ERISA, they would be preempted.[22]

5. Loans are adequately secured. Under the new regulations, no more than 50 percent of the present value of the vested portion of a participant's account may serve as security for a loan. Because of this limit, most plans will be designed to limit the amount of any loan to 50 percent of the present value of the vested portion of a participant's account, even though a larger amount is permissible in some circumstances under Section 72(p) (discussed below).

A caveat: while Congress purported to establish parity between corporate and noncorporate plans in the Tax Equity and Fiscal Responsibility Act (TEFRA), loans to owner-employees of proprietorships and partnerships continue to be prohibited transactions after TEFRA, and no loan can be made without first obtaining a specific exemption from the Department of Labor.

Further, a direct or indirect loan from any qualified plan to a participant or beneficiary is treated as a distribution and, thereby, is taxable unless the loan falls within an exception specified in Code Section 72(p). A loan falls within the exception and is not treated as a distribution only if it meets all three of the following requirements:

1. The loan must be repaid within five years.
2. The aggregate balance of all loans from the plan made to the borrower-participant does not exceed the lesser of (*a*) $50,000 reduced by the highest outstanding balance of such loans during the preceding one-year period or (*b*) one half of the present value of the nonforfeitable accrued benefit of the employee in the plan (but not less than $10,000).
3. The loan requires substantially level amortization (with payments made at least quarterly) over its term.

The five-year limitation does not apply if the loan is applied toward acquiring any house, apartment, condominium, or mobile home (not used

---

[22]As the United States Supreme Court has pointed out quite recently, a state law may be preempted even if it is not designed to affect, or affects only indirectly, such ERISA employee benefit plans. *Ingersoll-Rand Company* v. *McClendon*, 59 USLW 4033, 4035 (December 3, 1990).

on a transient basis) that is used or is to be used within a reasonable time as the principal residence of the participant.

This provision severely restricts the availability of plan loans to participants and their beneficiaries; however, plan loans remain a valuable advantage of qualified retirement plans. Fortunately, while a loan that is not repaid on a timely basis is treated as a taxable distribution, it will not disqualify the plan.

As the funds in an existing qualified retirement plan accumulate, the participants often desire to borrow those funds so that they can, in effect, "pay interest to themselves." Thus, availability of loans from qualified retirement plans is useful in times of inflation. Although plan loan interest is no longer deductible by the participant after the Tax Reform Act of 1986 (TRA '86), the authors believe that, as long as the loans are made within the exemption provided in Section 408(b)(1) of ERISA, they can still serve as an attractive source of financing or emergency funds to plan participants. Loans cannot, however, be made either directly or indirectly to the plan sponsor's business without obtaining a specific exemption from the Department of Labor.

The authors feel that the following are essential components of any loan program:

1. The loan must be represented by a bona fide promissory note.

2. Because of the limitations imposed by the Department of Labor regulations discussed above, loans should generally be made only to the extent of 50 percent of the vested account balance or accrued benefit of the participant, with the vested account balance acting as security. If loans in excess of 50 percent of the vested account balance of the participant are made, the plan must obtain sufficient additional collateral security, such as listed stocks, bonds, or a second mortgage. Any security taken by the plan should be segregated from the assets of the participant and held by the trustee as collateral security.

3. Loans should be made in a consistent, businesslike manner, and loan applications should be completed by the participant desiring to borrow.

4. Loans made by a participant can be earmarked as investments of that particular participant's account so that, if that participant does default on the loan, only that participant and not the other participants will suffer a loss.

A rather subtle problem may arise in the case of loans from a pension plan (defined benefit or money purchase plan). One of the characteristics of qualified pension plans is that such plans may not make distributions to participants prior to separation from service or attainment of normal retirement age. A loan from a pension plan does not violate this distribution limitation, because bona fide loans are not plan distributions. A problem may arise, however, if the security for a loan from a pension plan is the vested accrued benefit of the participant. If the participant defaults on the plan loan and the only assets out of which collection may be made is the participant's vested accrued benefit, the satisfaction of the loan by reduction of the participant's accrued benefit could constitute a premature distribution that would disqualify the plan. A similar problem could arise in the case of loans from integrated profit-sharing plans, since distributions from integrated profit-sharing plans are proscribed prior to separation from service or attainment of normal retirement age. To avoid the premature distribution problem, pension and integrated profit-sharing plans that provide for loans to participants could require adequate security for such loans other than the participant's accrued benefit. A foreclosure of any loan from a cash or deferred arrangement by resort to the funds in an account may constitute an in-service distribution to a participant and, if the participant is under 59½, could thereby disqualify the plan under Section 401(k).[23] The authors recommend the use of payroll deduction for repayment of plan loans, as that method of repayment greatly reduces the risk of default as long as the employee continues in the employer's service. Furthermore, a 401(k) plan should not foreclose on a participant's plan account until such participant separates from employment with the plan sponsor.

BONDING REQUIREMENTS OF ERISA

Section 412 of ERISA requires that every fiduciary and every person who handles funds or other property of a qualified retirement plan must be bonded and that the bond shall be not less than 10 percent of the amount of the funds handled. While such bonds (ERISA bonds) are inexpensive and can be obtained as a rider to the general fidelity insurance of the business, they are often overlooked. Further, questions arise with regard

---

[23] IRC 401(k)(2)(B)(i) and Treas. Reg. 1.401(k)-1(d)(4).

to who "handles" funds and what are the "funds" handled. For these reasons, it is prudent to require that all trustees or members of a plan administrative committee be bonded and that the bond be in the amount of 10 percent of the funds in the plan.

Investments

ERISA does not require any specific type of investment to be maintained by any type of qualified retirement plan. However, Section 404 of ERISA requires that fiduciaries exercise the care, skill, prudence, and diligence that a "prudent man acting in a like capacity and familiar with such matters" would use and also requires that fiduciaries diversify investments unless it is clearly prudent not to do so. These standards can normally be met by investments that are generally available, such as listed stocks and bonds. However, since a qualified trust is tax-exempt, the authors feel that an effort should be made to maximize the annual income under the trust in order to take advantage of the compounding effect that the tax-exempt status provides without forgetting the value of a good equity mix. Obviously, tax shelters and other investments with tax-favored status provide very little benefit to a tax-exempt trust, and as such, they should generally be avoided.

Often, employers desire to leverage the ability of their qualified retirement plans to purchase various assets such as real estate. Where the assets are purchased within a qualified retirement plan, and either funds are borrowed to acquire those assets or the assets are purchased through the use of purchase money indebtedness, the gains generated from the sale of those assets will be partially taxable to the trust as if it were a regular taxable entity. This rule also applies to margin accounts.[24] There are, however, certain exceptions with regard to the debt-financed purchase or improvement of real estate by a qualified plan if a number of very specific conditions set forth in the Code are met.[25]

---

[24]*Elliot Knitwear Profit Sharing Plan,* 614 F.2d 347 (3rd Cir. 1980) affirming 71 T.C. 765 (1970); IRC 511-514; investment in partnerships (even as a limited partner) may also generate unrelated business taxable income. See Rev. Rul. 79-222, 1979-2 C.B. 236, Treas. Regs. 1.514(c)-1(a)(2) example (4).

[25]IRC 514(c)(9). One recent pronouncement from the Service that may provide some assistance where the qualified plan's interest in the debt-financed real estate takes the form of an interest in a limited partnership having nonexempt partners is Advance Notice 90-41, 1990-26 I.R.B. 7 (June 1, 1990).

Many qualified retirement plans of small businesses will have assets of less than $500,000. Such plans may be unable to obtain the services of a registered investment adviser to handle investments. Consequently, the management of fund assets will fall to the trustee, be it a bank or the employers themselves. Qualified retirement plan assets held by a bank as trustee will have the benefit of professional asset management. If employers are the trustees of the plan, they should take steps to ensure that all assets held by the plan are segregated from their personal assets and from the assets of the business. Also, as trustees, the employers will be responsible for the investments of the plan.

Since most employers either do not have the time or are not adept at investing large sums of money, the investment of assets of a qualified retirement plan of many small businesses falls to a stock broker or to an investment adviser. If a local stock broker is employed, it should be recognized that he or she will generally not be considered a fiduciary unless he or she exercises discretionary control or authority over the fund or renders investment advice for a fee. Most stock brokers have disclaimers that eliminate them from the fiduciary responsibility rules of ERISA. Further, many qualified retirement plans of small businesses are invested in "guaranteed investment contracts" with insurance companies. While these contracts appear to offer a good annual return, employers should be fully aware of the implications of investing in such contracts, since they usually involve some type of termination discount or some type of extended payout on termination. Also, several large insurance companies have been downgraded by Standard & Poor's and Moody's because of the fact that their general accounts contain large positions in real estate and junk bonds.[26]

Very often, the investment approach of the participants will differ from the recommendations of the investment adviser or the plan trustee. It is possible to provide in a qualified retirement plan that the participants will have the ability to earmark (direct the investment of) their accounts. Under an earmarking arrangement, the participant will have the authority to direct the trustee with regard to the vested balance of his or her account.

---

[26]See, e.g., "Ominous Signs: Equitable's Troubles Show Mounting Risks Facing Life Insurers," *The Wall Street Journal,* Page A1, Column 6 (November 30, 1990); "Hard Times Not Likely to Sink Insurers," *USA Today,* Page B1 (December 17, 1990).

There are limitations on earmarking. First, earmarking exists only in defined contribution plans and is not available with respect to defined benefit plan assets derived from employee contributions, although defined benefit plans that permit voluntary employee contributions may permit employees to earmark their voluntary employee contribution accounts. Further, if a participant does earmark the investment of his or her account, the fiduciary may be relieved of liability for a loss by reason of the participant's control.[27]

Finally, it should be recognized that participants may not direct the investment of their accounts into items that are held for personal use, since such use would constitute a prohibited transaction and would result in the imposition of excise taxes under Section 4975 of the Code. Furthermore, Code Section 408(m) provides that the acquisition by an individually directed account under a qualified pension or profit-sharing plan of any collectible will be treated as a distribution from the account in an amount equal to the cost of the collectible. Collectibles are defined to mean any work of art, any rug or antique, any metal or gem, any stamp or coin, any alcoholic beverage, or any other tangible personal property specified by the Secretary of the Treasury. This provision "grandfathers" collectibles that were already held by accounts as of December 31, 1981 and does not apply to collectibles acquired by the plan's trustee as plan assets not earmarked to the account of any participant. In addition, it may be possible to use after-tax voluntary employee contributions to make earmarked investments in collectibles, since the "deemed distribution" of an employee contribution does not give rise to gross income. TRA '86 amended this rule with respect to IRAs and now allows investment of IRA assets in certain United States coins.[28] This exception does not, however, appear to apply to individually directed accounts under a qualified plan.

---

[27]ERISA 404(c). But see, e.g., Letter to John Welch and Randall Bassett from Robert A. G. Monks, Administrator, Office of Pension and Welfare Benefit Programs, dated April 30, 1984, 11 BNA Pens. Rep. 633 (1984), in which the Department of Labor made a controversial assertion it has echoed often since then: that under certain circumstances a trustee cannot simply rely on the directions of participants, but must rather make an independent determination of what its fiduciary obligations require it to do.

[28]P.L. 99-514, 1144(a). See also P.L. 100-647, 6057(a), amending this exception to include coins issued under the laws of any state.

Investment managers disagree about how the type of plan involved should affect the type of investment a plan makes. Some believe a defined benefit pension plan with a definite fixed benefit that must be reached should be invested in GICs, high-grade bonds, preferred stocks, and blue-chip stocks. On the other hand, they feel that since there is no defined benefit provided under profit-sharing and money purchase plans, funds of such plans may be invested in higher-risk assets. Others believe (in what may be the majority opinion) exactly the opposite, namely, that higher-risk investments are appropriate in defined benefit plans where the employer bears the risk but inappropriate in defined contribution plans where employees bear the risk. While the character of investments may vary from defined benefit to defined contribution plans, security of principal is an essential element to any investment strategy under any qualified retirement plan.

Following ERISA, it was felt that corporate trustees should be employed in order to minimize the risk of a suit against the individual employer acting as trustee. Using a corporate trustee will certainly help to shield shareholder-employees from lawsuits, but the controlling shareholders of many small employers still choose to serve as trustees of their qualified plans without necessarily exposing themselves to inordinately high risks. Moreover, the absence of a fiduciary title will not necessarily preclude a shareholder-employee from being deemed a fiduciary (with all the concomitant fiduciary duties) under ERISA. A shareholder-employee serving as a fiduciary must take precautions that disinterested fiduciaries might not have to take when dealing with plan assets. If shareholder-employees do choose to serve as trustees, to serve as plan administrators, or to perform other services for the plan, they normally must do so without pay other than reimbursement of expenses properly and actually incurred, since Section 408(c)(2) of ERISA prohibits persons who already receive full-time pay from an employer from receiving compensation from the plan other than expense reimbursement. Care should be taken to assure that the investment of the plan's assets, particularly the amounts credited to the accounts of the staff employees, be done in a conservative manner. In other words, the shareholder-employee who wishes to serve as an ERISA fiduciary with respect to the employer's qualified plan should be wary of the additional constraints imposed by virtue of the dual roles and should make every effort to consult frequently with professional advisers who understand these constraints. For example, the Department of Labor is making new law by pushing the concept that the attorney-client privilege is lost if the same attorney represents both the plan and the employer.[29]

Whether an employee of the business or a professional fiduciary acts as trustee, the rights and duties of the trustee must be prescribed either in the plan itself or in a separate trust document. Although many plans and trust agreements are unified in a single document, the authors recommend establishing both a plan and a separate trust agreement. In this manner, the plan need only be executed by the corporation, whereas the trust agreement must be executed by the corporation and the trustee. Consequently if the corporation decides to amend the plan, it need only pass a board resolution and sign the amendment; the signature of the trustee is not necessary. Trustees are becoming increasingly aware of this important distinction and are requesting this approach.

MASTER PLANS VERSUS INDIVIDUALLY DESIGNED PLANS

A number of banks, brokerage houses, insurance companies, mutual funds, and consulting firms offer preapproved master or prototype plans that can be adopted by a small business. These plans have received a master determination letter and can be adopted by the small business with either a limited or no requirement to seek further service approval (depending on whether the plan is standardized or nonstandardized and on the particular circumstances of the business). Such plans are typically adopted by the completion of an adoption agreement under which a number of alternatives can be selected, such as participation rules and vesting schedules.

Master plans appear to offer an attractive alternative to very small employers (under 25 employees) because they can require considerable initial assistance from the attorney and accountant of the master plan sponsor. They will normally be kept up to date by the sponsoring entity. Of course, most master plans are customarily offered by entities that are selling a service or a product. Banks, mutual funds, brokerage houses, and insurance companies all sell investment products and/or services and may charge administrative fees. Moreover, master plans are less flexible

---

[29]See *In re Gulf Pension Litigation,* supra.

than individually designed plans and are not always adequately tailored to the particular situation of the small business. Nevertheless, the authors believe that a carefully selected master or prototype plan may be the best choice for many small employers. The difficulty and cost of continuous compliance with frequent changes in the laws governing qualified plans can no longer be adequately borne by many small employers. Moreover, the flexibility offered by individually designed plans has been greatly reduced by trends in the law, such as the nondiscrimination regulations under IRC 401(a)(4) discussed in the previous chapter. At the time of this writing, the IRS and the Department of Labor are pushing the prototype concept in legislation pending in Congress.[30]

Employers should realize that some organizations offer plans that appear to be master or prototype plans but are, in fact, individually designed plans. The authors are aware of a number of insurance companies that engage in this practice and, in fact, draft individually designed retirement plans for small businesses. Employers encountering this arrangement should carefully assess the potential problems that may arise in adopting an individually designed plan drafted by someone other than the employer's attorney or an ERISA attorney retained for this specific work. There is a greater possibility that problems will arise under such a plan than under a master or prototype plan. Further, drafting such plans and the accompanying trust agreements is generally considered by the American Bar Association to be unauthorized practicing of law.[31]

CONTRIBUTIONS

The determination of the deductibility of contributions to a qualified retirement plan is generally made pursuant to Section 404 of the Code. The amounts that may be deducted as contributions to a qualified pension

---

[30]*See Sec. 203 of "The Pension Access and Simplification Act of 1991" (HR 2730), sponsored by Rep. Rostenkowski and the "POWER" proposal put forth by the Department of Labor.*

[31]"Final Opinion on Employee Benefit Planning" issued by the Committee on Unauthorized Practice of Law dated October 17, 1977. But see *The Florida Bar Re: Advisory Opinion—Nonlawyer Preparation of Pension Plans,* 17 BNA Pens. Rep. 2031 (November 29, 1990) (in which the Florida Supreme Court rejected a proposed advisory opinion from the Florida State Bar that would have categorized as the unauthorized practice of law "certain nonlawyer involvement in the area of designing and preparing pension plans and advising clients concerning such plans").

plan (defined benefit or money purchase) are determined under Section 404(a)(1).

An employer may deduct its contribution to a pension plan (defined benefit or money purchase) to the extent the contribution was necessary to pay the normal cost of plan benefits plus any amount necessary to amortize past service liabilities. The normal cost of a defined benefit plan must be calculated by the plan's actuary. The normal cost of a money purchase plan is determined by the plan's contribution formula; for example, 10 percent of participants' compensation. Generally, past service liabilities are created by plan amendments that increase the rate at which benefits accrue for prior service and by plan provisions that grant past service benefits on establishment of the plan. Past service liabilities attributable to all participants may be amortized over as many as 30 years or as few as 10 years. Alternatively, past service liabilities may be amortized over the remaining future service of each employee; but, if over 50 percent of plan costs are attributable to three or fewer individuals, past service liabilities attributable to those three or fewer individuals may not be amortized over fewer than five years.

Effective for tax years beginning after 1986, TRA '86 imposed an overall limit on the total amount of the annual deduction that may be taken for contributions made to a combination of defined benefit and defined contribution plans. Generally, the total deductible amount may not exceed 25 percent of the plan participants' annual compensation. However, if the defined benefit plan contribution required by the minimum funding standards exceeds such 25 percent, the greater amount may be deducted.[32]

The deductibility of contributions to profit-sharing plans is determined under Section 404(a)(3), which sets a basic deduction limit for profit-sharing contributions of 15 percent of the compensation otherwise paid or accrued during the taxable year to all participants under the plan. If an employer contributes an amount in excess of the deduction limits for a particular year, the excess payment is deductible in succeeding years. However, effective for taxable years beginning after 1986, nondeductible contributions (to pension plans, as well as profit-sharing plans) are subject to an annual 10 percent excise tax until the excess is eliminated. If a pre-1987 contribution made to a profit-sharing plan was less than 15

---

[32]IRC 404(a)(7).

percent of the annual total compensation for the period the contribution is made, the difference between the amount actually contributed and the 15 percent limitation may be carried forward so as to increase the deductible amount in a succeeding taxable year to the extent that the total deduction in any later year does not exceed 25 percent of compensation.[33]

If amounts are deductible under both pension plans and profit-sharing plans, the employer may first deduct the entire amount deductible with respect to the pension plans. If the amount deductible on account of the pension plans is less than 25 percent of the participants' compensation for the plan year, the employer can make up the difference by making additional contributions to profit-sharing plans. If the employer's contribution to the pension plans equals or exceeds 25 percent of the participants' compensation for the plan year, then obviously no amount may be deducted for the profit-sharing plans. Contributions must also satisfy the applicable contribution and benefit limitations of Section 415 of the Code.

Corporate contributions to qualified retirement plans are considered general business expenses. Consequently, in order for an employer to obtain a deduction for such expenses under Section 404, the expenses must be ordinary and necessary under Section 162 of the Code. In determining whether deductions to qualified retirement plans are ordinary and necessary, the question of reasonable compensation must be considered. When reasonable compensation for an employee is determined, all benefits are taken into account, including contributions under qualified retirement plans. Consequently, if the reasonableness of the compensation to the employer is challenged, a challenge may also be made to the deductibility of that portion of the contribution to the qualified retirement plan. If the compensation is found to be unreasonable, a portion of the deduction for contributions may be disallowed or the Service may attempt to disqualify the plan. If discrimination results from contributions attributable to unreasonable compensation, a defined contribution plan may avoid disqualification by permitting the reallocation to other employees of any contribution determined to be unreasonable.[34] The reasonable-

---

[33]IRC 404(a)(3)(A). In one case, however, where the employer made "advance contributions" to a profit-sharing plan to enable the plan to make an investment, the Tax Court found the advance to constitute a loan, and the plan was held to have debt-financed, unrelated business income as a result of the investment. *Marprowear Profit Sharing Trust* v. *Commissioner,* 74 T.C. 1086 (1980).

[34]Rev. Rul. 67-341, 1967-2 C.B. 156.

compensation requirement may be a particular problem where the first year of the small business is a short fiscal year during which large contributions are made. This may be especially true if large amounts of income are held over from the pre-incorporation period and paid during the first year of incorporation in order to permit large contributions to the qualified plans.[35]

Under Section 404 of the Code, deductions are generally allowed for the tax year in which they are made. However, Section 404(a)(6) of the Code permits a deduction for a particular year to be taken where the contribution for that year is made on or before the filing deadline of the federal income tax return (plus extensions thereof). In order to obtain a deduction under Section 404(a)(6) of the Code, the contribution for a year must be (1) paid to the plan on or before the due date for filing the federal income tax return (plus extensions, if any), (2) allocated on the books of the plan in the same manner as it would have been allocated if it had been actually contributed on the last day of the plan year, and (3) deducted on the federal income tax return.[36] The requirement as to the timing of the contribution is strictly enforced. Even where the amounts to be contributed had been segregated in a separate corporate account, the Tax Court has held that a contribution could not be credited for purposes of IRC 404(a)(6) where the taxpayer inadvertently failed to have the segregated amounts contributed.[37]

The initial contributions to a qualified retirement plan may also be made during the grace period. That is, although it is absolutely necessary to adopt the plan prior to the end of the fiscal year of the employer, no contribution to that plan need be made (even though the trust may be a "dry trust" under local law) until the time for filing the corporation's federal income tax return (plus extensions).[38] However, the authors recommend that, on the establishment of a qualified plan, the trust of that plan be funded with a $100 contribution even though the remainder of the contribution will be made at a later date.[39]

---

[35]*Angelo J. Bianchi,* 66 T.C. 324 (1976), aff'd 553 F.2d 93 (2d Cir. 1977). *Anthony LaMaestro,* 72 T.C. 377 (1979), *Robert A. Young,* 650 F.2d 1085 (9th Cir. 1981).

[36]Rev. Rul. 76-28, 1976-1 C.B. 106.

[37]*D. J. Lee, M.D., Inc.* v. *Commissioner,* 92 T.C. 291 (1989, appeal pending (6th Cir.)).

[38]Rev. Rul. 57-419, 1957-2 C.B. 264.

[39]For important recent IRS guidance on the issue of frozen and wasting trusts, see Rev. Rul. 89-87, 1989-2 C.B. 81.

Nondeductible Voluntary Employee Contributions

Qualified retirement plans may permit nondeductible voluntary employee contributions of up to 10 percent of an employee's compensation.[40] This 10 percent limit is a maximum limitation for all plans, so that if 10 percent is contributed under a profit-sharing plan, nothing may be contributed under a money purchase pension plan.[41] However, the 10 percent voluntary contribution is cumulative, so that the contribution may be made equal to 10 percent of the employee's aggregate compensation for all years that he or she has been a participant.[42] Furthermore, the 10 percent limitation is not reduced or affected by amounts rolled over or directly transferred from another qualified plan if the employer's plan permits such rollovers.

Nondeductible voluntary employee contributions are also subject to the annual addition limitations under Section 415 of the Code. Thus, if the employer contribution for a given year places an employee near or at his or her Section 415 limit, little or no amount may be contributed as a voluntary employee contribution, regardless of the 10 percent rule.

Nondeductible voluntary employee contributions, like nondeductible mandatory employee contributions, are also subject to the nondiscrimination rules contained in IRC Section 401(m), discussed in Chapter 55. The ability of an employee to make voluntary employee contributions to a qualified retirement plan is an excellent benefit that creates for the employee the ability to defer income taxes on the earnings in the voluntary account. Although voluntary employee contributions must be made with after-tax dollars, the earnings on the amounts contributed voluntarily by the employee remain tax-exempt until withdrawn. Consequently, the employee may take advantage of the compounding effect of tax-exempt earnings through the use of voluntary employee contributions. Voluntary employee contributions are particularly useful for deferring income until later years when it will be needed for expenses such as college education for children. Savings or thrift plans that allow voluntary nondeductible contributions are generally found in large-employer plans and not in small plans, because of the administrative cost of monitoring and accounting for these additional accounts.

---

[40]Rev. Rul. 80-350, 1980-2 C.B. 133; Rev. Rul. 59-185, 1959-1 C.B. 86.

[41]Rev. Rul. 69-627, 1969-2 C.B. 92.

[42]Rev. Rul. 69-217, 1969-1 C.B. 115, as clarified by Rev. Rul. 74-385, 1974-2 C.B. 130.

ANNUAL ADDITION LIMITATION

Section 415 of the Code provides limitations on the annual benefits that may be provided under qualified retirement plans. Under Section 415(b)(1), the employer may not fund a defined benefit plan benefit that is greater than the lesser of $90,000 or 100 percent of the participant's average compensation for his or her highest three consecutive calendar years.

With respect to defined contribution plans, the annual addition made on behalf of a participant may not exceed the lesser of $30,000 or 25 percent of the participant's compensation. For purposes of determining the annual addition, the following allocations are considered: (1) the employer contributions, (2) the employee contributions (voluntary and mandatory), and (3) any forfeitures allocated to the participant's account.

QUALIFYING PLANS WITH THE INTERNAL REVENUE SERVICE

Although obtaining a favorable determination letter with regard to a retirement plan is not a prerequisite for having a "qualified" plan, obtaining a favorable determination letter does permit the sponsoring employer to receive advance determination of the qualified status of the plan. For this reason, the authors feel that all plans that are intended to be qualified plans should be filed with the district director of the local Service office for qualification by the EP/EO Key District to which that district is assigned. If plans are filed for determination during the remedial amendment period discussed above and qualified status is not received, either the plans may be amended retroactively to permit qualified status or the contributions may be returned to the employer. Further, the authors believe that all amendments to a plan or trust document, other than ministerial amendments like the change of the trustee or the change in the name of the plan, should be filed with the Service for continued qualification for historical reasons even if the filing requirement is not mandatory.

The receipt of a favorable determination letter from the district director does not, however, give carte blanche as to a plan's qualified status. The favorable determination letter merely states that, on the facts and law that exist as of the date of the letter's issuance, the plan in that form meets the qualification rules. Further changes in the facts relating to the employer and the employees and changes in the rules and regulations of the Service may later disqualify the plan. In *Wisconsin Nipple & Fabricating Corporation* v. *Commissioner,*[43] the court upheld the Commissioner's retroactive revocation of favorable determination letters (issued in 1960 and 1962) where a later revenue ruling (issued in 1971) indicated on similar facts that the plan discriminated in favor of a prohibited group. In arriving at this result, the Seventh Circuit clearly placed responsibility on the taxpayer for "keeping abreast of current developments in the law to be assured that the plan is still in compliance." For this reason, the authors feel that sponsoring employers should continue to monitor the status of their retirement plans with their professional advisers to ensure that they remain qualified and keep copies of all such filings, because the Service has had a tendency to lose a great many filings since the implementation of the User Fee Program established by TRA '86.

Rev. Proc. 80-30, Section 2.15, states that "a favorable determination letter on the qualification of a pension, annuity, profit-sharing, stock bonus, or bond purchase plan, and the exempt status of a related trust, if any, is not required as a condition for obtaining the benefits pertaining to the plan or trust."[44]

DISCRIMINATION IN OPERATION

Obviously, qualified retirement plans may be disqualified if they fail to meet the specific statutory requirements provided under Section 401, et seq., of the Code, such as the eligibility rules, vesting rules, and rules relating to contributions and benefits. However, it is possible for qualified retirement plans to be disqualified because of the manner in which they have been operated, even though favorable determination letters have been issued with respect to those plans.

In addition to the specific statutory requirements for qualified plans, Section 401 also contains several rather vague prohibitions. For example, under Section 401(a)(2), a plan must be used for the "exclusive benefit" of participants and their beneficiaries. Further, under Section 401(a)(4),

---

[43]67 T.C. 490 (1976), affirmed 581 F.2d 1235 (7th Cir. 1978).

[44]1980-1 C.B. 685.

a plan may not discriminate in favor of highly compensated employees (the new regulations under this provision are discussed in Chapter 55). Treasury Regulation 1.401-1(b)(3) provides a general overview of what may constitute impermissible discrimination:

> The plan must benefit the employees in general, although it need not provide benefits for all of the employees. Among the employees to be benefitted may be persons who are officers and shareholders. However, a plan is not for the exclusive benefit of employees in general if, by any device whatever, it discriminates either in eligibility requirements, contributions, or benefits in favor of employees who are officers, shareholders, or highly compensated employees.

Those situations in which a qualified retirement plan is diverted to the use of the highly compensated employees of the small business are often apparent from the plan's terms (for example, a plan that permits loans of plan funds only to such highly compensated employees). However, even if the terms of a plan in form comply with the statutory requirements, it is possible that in operation the benefits and contributions provisions may discriminate in favor of highly compensated employees, even though there is no intention that they do so. The proposed nondiscrimination regulations discussed in the previous chapter contain the principles under which most discrimination issues must now be analyzed. Nevertheless, the following are a few examples of operational discrimination that may still be relevant after the new nondiscrimination regulations.

Erroneous Administration of Plan Provisions

In several cases, the participation provisions of qualified retirement plans were inadvertently not followed, leading to disqualification of the plans due to discrimination in operation. In *Myron* v. *U.S.*,[45] five eligible employees were excluded from coverage for two consecutive years, and the company's contributions were allocated only to the account of the corporation's sole shareholder. The lower court found that the exclusion was inadvertent but, nevertheless, concluded this innocent error justified disqualification. In affirming, the Seventh Circuit Court of Appeals

---

[45]550 F.2d 1145 (9th Cir. 1977).

agreed that even an inadvertent failure in coverage could be a proper basis for denying qualification.[46]

Several cases of erroneous administration of plan provisions specifically involve small businesses. In *Allen Ludden,*[47] a pre-ERISA case, Allen Ludden and Betty White, the famous actor and actress, formed a corporation, Albets, that adopted a money purchase pension plan and a profit-sharing plan for the benefit of the corporation's employees. The plans, as written, met the requirements for qualification, and determination letters were issued by the Service. Through a bookkeeping error, the only staff employee of Albets, a production secretary, was inadvertently excluded from participation in the plan even though she met the plan's participation requirements. The Service argued, and the court held, that the exclusion of the production secretary constituted discrimination in favor of highly compensated officers in violation of (pre-1986 Code) Sections 401(a)(3)(B) and 401(a)(4) of the Code and meant that the plan had failed to meet the minimum coverage provisions of (pre-1986 Code) Section 401(a)(3)(A).

In *Forsyth Emergency Services, P.A.,*[48] a professional corporation was engaged in emergency medical services and operated the emergency room facilities at Forsyth Memorial Hospital in Winston-Salem, North Carolina. The corporation was owned by three physicians who adopted a money purchase pension plan. They received a determination letter from the Service. During 1972 and 1973, certain nonprofessional employees of the corporation were inadvertently omitted from coverage under the retirement plan. However, in August of 1975, after this fact was brought to the corporation's attention by the Service, additional contributions were made so that retroactive allocations could be made for these nonprofessional employees for the years in which they were excluded. The exclusion of the nonprofessional employees resulted from a misreading of the plan by the professional adviser to the corporation.

The court held that the plan did not meet the eligibility requirements for coverage and that the plan discriminated in operation. The court further held that discrimination in operation could not be cured by retroactively funding contributions accrued but unallocated to the non-

---

[46]See also *Ma-Tran Corp.,* 70 T.C. 158 (1978).

[47]68 T.C. 826 (1977), affirming 620 F.2d 700 (9th Cir. 1980).

[48]68 T.C. 881 (1977).

professional employees, even if such retroactive allocation was made voluntarily by the corporation. The court noted that, because the plan covered primarily professional employees, the plan did not cover a cross-section of all employees. In examining the question of whether a retroactive cure for discrimination was available, the court stated that it found no support in the Code, the Regulations, or case law that would permit retroactive correction.

Cases like *Ludden* and *Forsyth* are dramatic examples of the problems that can occur as a result of the inadvertent errors of employers, even where they seek the advice of their professional advisers. The Service has, in some situations, relented from its position in *Ludden* and *Forsyth*. In Private Letter Ruling No. 7949001 a corporation was permitted to reallocate contributions to its money purchase pension plan and profit-sharing plan so that the plans would qualify under Section 401 of the Code. The corporation adopted a prototype plan in 1973 and made contributions in 1973, 1974, and 1975. On audit, the Service held that the eligibility requirements of the plan were not followed and that one part-time employee was erroneously included while three full-time employees were excluded from coverage. The Service ruled that the entity sponsoring the prototype plan was in error, not the corporation. Since the mistake was one of fact and not one of law, and since no distributions had been made from the plan, the corporation would be allowed to restructure the plan to meet the coverage requirements.

In 1980, the Service promulgated Document 6651, "IRS Employee Plans Restoration Guidelines." Under these guidelines, retroactive relief is available for a variety of plan deficiencies. In the case of plans that are discriminatory, restoration may be accomplished by increasing benefits to defined benefit plans or making supplemental contributions to defined contribution plans. Such corrections will reinstate the qualified status of the plan but will not restore qualified plan status treatment of employer contributions made during the plan's discriminatory period. As a result, contributions to defined benefit plans during open tax years in which there was discrimination will normally be disallowed, and contributions to defined-contribution plans during open years in which there was discrimination will be deductible only when an amount attributable to the contribution is includable in the gross income of participants.[49]

---

[49]IRC 404(a)(5).

Improper Exclusion of Employees

If the plan sponsor expressly attempts to categorize employees as independent contractors or employees of third-party organizations, the plan may discriminate in favor of the highly compensated employees by denying participation to staff employees.

Withdrawals from Qualified Plans

A profit-sharing plan may permit participants to withdraw all or part of their vested benefits provided that the underlying contributions have been allocated to their accounts for at least two years.[50] However, if withdrawals are subject to the approval of a plan administrative committee and withdrawals are permitted only by highly compensated employees, then the plan discriminates in favor of the prohibited group and will be disqualified.[51]

Voluntary Waivers of Participation

Because of the often divergent needs of employees, some employers consider placing a provision in qualified retirement plans that permits employees to "opt out" of the plan. Any such opt-out right must be carefully structured and administered. First, persons who voluntarily waive their participation are taken into account under the minimum participation tests. Therefore, if the number of persons opting out is substantial, such a provision may create coverage problems. Second, any opt-out provision should be disclosed in the summary plan description.

Third, if lower-paid employees opt out of the plan, the plan may be found to discriminate against them.[52] Moreover, if only highly paid

---

[50]Rev. Rul. 71-295, 1971-2 C.B. 184.

[51]Rev. Rul. 57-587, 1957-2 C.B. 270.

[52]Rev. Rul. 80-351, 1980-2 C.B. 152, Rev. Rul. 73-340, 1973-2 C.B. 134. Also in *Richard F. Olmo*, 38 T.C.M. 112 (1979), pension and profit-sharing plans established by a professional corporation wholly owned by two dentists failed to qualify. The plan discriminated in favor of the prohibited group because, for the years in issue, the only participants in the plan were the two dentists. Of the two other employees who met the plan's minimum service requirements, one did not meet the minimum age requirement and the other had voluntarily waived her right to participate pursuant to the provisions of the plan.

employees have the right to opt out, this would violate the nondiscrimi-nation provisions of IRC Section 401(a)(4). The ability to opt out of a plan is a right or feature that must be currently and effectively available to a nondiscriminatory classification of employees under the proposed nondiscrimination regulations discussed in the previous chapter. Fifth, and finally, the opt-out right could only be offered as a one-time irrevoc-able election when the employee first has the opportunity to enter the plan. If the employee were permitted to opt out after beginning partici-pation or to opt back in after declining participation, this would constitute a cash or deferred election, disqualifying the plan unless it complied with the strict requirements of IRC Section 401(k).

Defining Compensation

Although most qualified retirement plans provide benefits based on the compensation contained in the employee's W-2 (the basic compensation), the term compensation would normally include both contractual and voluntary bonuses paid to the employees. Such a definition normally should not cause problems. In most cases, however, small employers should adopt a definition of compensation that fits within certain safe harbors provided in IRS regulations under IRC 414(s). By adopting a safe-harbor definition of compensation, the employer can avoid having to test to see whether the definition of compensation is discriminatory.[53]

Employee Turnover

During the pendency of a qualified retirement plan, if the staff employees of the corporation regularly terminate their service or are fired prior to their benefits becoming vested, the plan may be considered to have a discrim-inatory vesting schedule. Prior to TRA '86, this result was more likely where the schedule was less favorable than the 4-40 schedule.[54] Arguably, however, employee turnover poses less of a threat to plan qualification since 1988 when the accelerated vesting schedules of TRA '86 took effect.

Further, the use of so-called last-day rules in qualified retirement plans may prove discriminatory if, because of the turnover statistics of the

---

[53]*Treas. Regs. 1.414(s)*.
[54]Rev. Proc. 76-11, 1976-1, C.B. 550.

employer, they generally have been applied only against staff personnel. Last-day rules provide that an employee will not be entitled to receive employer contributions for the particular plan year of a defined contribution plan unless he or she is employed at the end of that plan year. Since it is generally staff personnel and not highly compensated employees who terminate during a plan year, the rules, in operation, may only apply to staff personnel. Last-day rules should be eliminated from plans established by small businesses in order to avoid this potential discrimination in operation.[55]

The risk of a discriminatory impact of vesting schedules and last-day rules can be dramatically reduced (other than in the case of a plan amendment) by fitting within a safe harbor under the nondiscrimination regulations.

Tax Consequences of Disqualification

If a plan is disqualified because it discriminates in operation, the following tax consequences will occur:

1. The trust will lose its tax-exempt status under Section 501(a), making the trust income taxable to the trust.

2. Section 402(b) will govern the taxability of employer contributions to the beneficiaries of the trust. Generally, contributions will be included in the employees' income under Section 83 to the extent they have a vested right to such benefits. Employer contributions that are taxable to the employee are considered part of current compensation; thus, the withholding of taxes by the employer is required.

3. The contributions of the employer will be deductible only to the extent that such amounts are includable in the participant's income and only if separate accounts are maintained to record the interest of each participant.[56] As a result, deduction of employer contributions to nonqualified defined contribution plans will be delayed for the period of years necessary for employer contributions to vest, and employer contributions to nonqualified defined benefit plans will simply not be deductible. Because of the possible loss of the deduction, the authors recommend that plans incorporate provisions requiring employer contributions to revert to

---

[55]Ibid.

[56]IRC 404(a)(5).

the employer within one year of the disallowance of a deduction under Code Section 404.[57]

In some cases, however, these disastrous consequences can be avoided through retroactive corrective action. For example, even though a failure to meet the IRC Section 410(b) minimum coverage requirements is a disqualifying event, it is possible under the proposed regulations to avoid disqualification by taking corrective action after the close of the plan year in which the failure to meet the minimum requirements occurred. Treas. Reg. Sec. 1.401(a)(4)-11(g)(1). Moreover, under its new closing-agreement pilot program, the IRS has announced that qualified plans will, under certain conditions, be allowed to avoid the sanction of disqualification for nonrecurring and minor ''disqualifying'' errors if the errors are corrected retroactively and prospectively and if a penalty is paid.

INSURANCE

Qualified retirement plans may insure the lives of the participants. There are a number of advantages in maintaining life insurance in a qualified plan.

1. First, the possibility of an immediate and substantial benefit is secured without the necessity of relying on plan investments.
2. Second, life insurance purchased by a qualified retirement plan is purchased with tax-deductible dollars.
3. Finally, the ''at risk'' portion of the proceeds of the life insurance policy are received income tax-free by the trust or other designated beneficiary. The ''at risk'' portion of the proceeds is the excess of the face value of the policy over its cash-surrender value immediately prior to death.

There are also disadvantages in maintaining insurance in a qualified plan.

1. First, whole life insurance historically provides a low-yield investment for the trust. However, with the development in recent years of new insurance products such as universal life that

---

[57]ERISA 403(c)(2)(C) permitting this type of reversion if the plan so provides.

pay close to market rates on the investment component, this problem has been ameliorated.

2. Second, adequate death benefits may be provided outside a qualified retirement plan through the use of other types of insurance such as split-dollar arrangements and group term life insurance.

3. Third, the payment of life insurance premiums by the trust will reduce the amount of cash available for other more suitable retirement fund investments.

4. Finally, the cost of term life insurance protection (the P.S. 58 cost) is currently taxed to the employee.

Since the purpose of a qualified retirement plan is to provide retirement benefits, life insurance protection may be provided only if it is "incidental."[58] As a result, specific limitations are placed on the amount of life insurance that may be maintained in each type of qualified plan, unless the proceeds of such insurance are payable into the general assets of the qualified retirement plan. See the discussion of key-man life insurance below.

Profit-Sharing Plans

A profit-sharing plan is a plan that is primarily established to provide deferred distribution of profits to participants.[59] As previously mentioned, profit-sharing plan funds may generally be distributed only after the funds have been accumulated for a fixed number of years, which is at least two years.[60] A distribution of funds before that time may cause a profit-sharing plan to lose its qualified status.

Applying this general rule to the purchase of life insurance, premiums for life insurance in a profit-sharing plan may be paid using funds that have been accumulated for two or more years without causing disqualification of the plan.[61] On the other hand, insurance premiums that are paid out of funds that have not been accumulated for at least two years

---

[58]Treas. Regs. 1.401-1(b).

[59]Ibid.

[60]Rev. Rul. 54-231, 1954-1 C.B. 150.

[61]Ibid.

normally are considered to be distributions to the employee. An exception exists if the purchase of insurance with funds that have not been accumulated for two years is incidental to the plan's primary purpose of providing deferred benefits. The purchase will be deemed incidental if certain requirements are met.

1. Where ordinary (whole life) insurance is purchased, the aggregate life insurance premiums for each participant must be less than one half the aggregate contributions allocated to that participant at any particular time, without regard to trust earnings and capital gains and losses. Moreover, the plan must require the trustee either to convert the entire value of the life insurance policy at or before the employee's retirement into cash, or to provide periodic income so that no portion of such value may be used to continue life insurance protection beyond retirement.[62]

2. In the case of term insurance, the aggregate life insurance premiums for each participant must not exceed 25 percent of the total amount of funds allocated to the participant's account.[63] The limitations on the purchase of life insurance protection do not apply to voluntary employee contributions.[64]

Notwithstanding that it is permissible for qualified profit-sharing plans to maintain life insurance on the lives of the employees, the authors generally recommend that profit-sharing plans not be used as life insurance vehicles. It is possible that in certain years a profit-sharing plan may not be funded, because there are no profits and thus the plan may not have sufficient funds to pay the premiums without causing the incidental limits to be exceeded.

Defined Benefit Pension Plans

A defined benefit pension plan funded with life insurance will be deemed to provide an incidental (and hence permissible) preretirement death benefit if either of two sets of requirements is met.

1. The purchase of insurance will be incidental if less than 50 percent of the employer contributions credited to each participant's account

---

[62]Rev. Rul. 73-501, 1973-2 C.B. 127; Rev. Rul. 69-421, 1969-2 C.B. 59; Rev. Rul. 54-51, 1954-1 C.B. 147, as amplified by Rev. Rul. 57-213, 1957-1 C.B. 157, and Rev. Rul. 60-84, 1960-1 C.B. 159.

[63]Rev. Rul. 61-164, 1961-2 C.B. 99; Rev. Rul. 66-143, 1966-1 C.B. 79; Rev. Rul. 70-611, 1970-2 C.B. 89, as modified by Rev. Rul. 85-15, 1985-1 C.B. 132; and Rev. Rul. 73-510, 1973-2 C.B. 386.

[64]Rev. Rul. 69-408, 1969-2 C.B. 58.

is used to purchase ordinary life insurance policies on the participant's life, even if the death benefit consists of both the face amount of the policies and the amount of other contributions credited to the participant's accrued benefit under the plan.

2. The purchase will also be incidental if the death benefit funded by ordinary life insurance provides no more than the greater of 100 times a participant's anticipated monthly normal retirement benefit or the accumulated reserve, and if the preretirement death benefit (in a pension with an auxiliary fund) that does not exceed the greater of: (*a*) 100 times the anticipated monthly normal retirement benefit or (*b*) 100 times the reserve under the life insurance policy plus the participant's account in the auxiliary fund.[65]

A defined benefit pension plan will not qualify if all of the employer's contributions are used for the purchase of ordinary life insurance policies on the lives of the participants.[66]

A postretirement death benefit is considered incidental if it does not exceed 50 percent of the base salary in the year before retirement and it costs less than 10 percent of the total cost of funding other pension plan benefits.[67]

Money Purchase Pension Plans

A money purchase pension plan may provide incidental preretirement death benefits that meet either the tests for profit-sharing plans or defined benefit pension plans.[68]

Tax Treatment

Employer contributions made to a qualified retirement plan that are used to pay insurance premiums are deductible to the employer, as are other contributions. However, the cost of the insurance provided under a qualified plan is treated as a current distribution to the participant and must be included in the participant's income for the year in which the premium is paid to the extent of the P.S. 58 cost defined below. The result is the

---

[65]Rev. Rul. 74-307, 1974-2 C.B. 126, clarifying Rev. Rul. 68-453, 1968-2 C.B. 163 and Rev. Rul. 73-501, 1973-2 C.B. 127.

[66]Rev. Rul. 61-164, 1961-2 C.B. 99, and Rev. Rul. 54-67, 1954-1 C.B. 149.

[67]Rev. Rul. 60-59, 1960-1 C.B. 154.

[68]Rev. Rul. 74-307, 1974-2 C.B. 126, and Rev. Rul. 69-421, 1969-2 C.B. 59.

same without regard to the type of policy purchased. The employee is taxed on the cost of the insurance protection if either the proceeds are payable to his or her estate or his or her designated beneficiary, or if the proceeds are payable to the trustee of the plan where the trustee is required by the terms of the plan to pay all proceeds over to the beneficiary of the participant. A participant is not taxed on the purchase of "key man" insurance by a qualified retirement plan where the proceeds of the insurance are payable into the general assets of the plan.

The amount of current taxable income to the participant is measured by the pure insurance protection under Treas. Regs. 1.72-16. The rates to be used are the one-year term rates established under Rev. Rul. 55-747 or the so-called P.S. 58 rates.[69] However, if the insurance company's rates for individual one-year term policies available to all standard-risk customers are lower than the P.S. 58 rates, the lower rates may be used.[70] Where group term life insurance is provided under a qualified retirement plan, the cost of the entire amount of protection is taxable to the employee and no part is exempt.[71] It is important to note that the P.S. 58 cost that has been taxed to the employee for life insurance protection may be recovered tax-free from the benefits received under the policy.[72] Tax-free recovery of the P.S. 58 cost will be available only if the benefits are ultimately received from the insurance contract with respect to which the P.S. 58 cost was included in gross income. If, however, the life insurance policy is surrendered and the proceeds are used to purchase an annuity or the proceeds are distributed in cash, tax-free recovery of the P.S. 58 basis will be forfeited.[73]

OTHER ISSUES

One significant result of the passage of TEFRA was the establishment of approximate parity between corporate plans and noncorporate or H.R. 10 plans. Prior to TEFRA, qualified plans maintained by

[69]1955-2 C.B. 228.

[70]Rev. Rul. 66-110, 1966-1 C.B. 12.

[71]IRC 72 and 79(b)(3).

[72]Treas. Regs. 1.72-1(b).

[73]Private Letter Rulings 780082 and 7902083, and Rev. Rul. 67-336, 1967-2 C.B. 66.

corporations offered significant advantages over qualified plans maintained by partnerships and proprietorships. These advantages were so great that many practitioners advised small businesses to incorporate in order to obtain the more favorable tax treatment afforded to corporate plans. TEFRA largely eliminated the advantages of corporate plans such that a small business might not desire to incorporate if the only advantage of incorporation is the availability of a qualified corporate plan.

Nevertheless, several important differences between corporate and noncorporate plans remain. First, the aggregation rules applicable to entities controlled by an owner-employee (a significant partner or a sole proprietor) are more inclusive than the aggregation rules applicable to related corporations.[74] Second, no deductions are allowed for qualified plan contributions on behalf of self-employed individuals to the extent that the contributions are allocable to the purchase of life, accident, health, or other insurance.[75] Third, self-employed participants may not elect forward averaging for distributions "on account of" separation from service except when the separation from service is caused by disability.[76] Fourth, a Treasury Regulation issued under pre-TEFRA law, which may or may not be rescinded, prohibits forfeitures in defined contribution plans from being allocated to the accounts of self-employed individuals.[77] While these differences are not the only differences between qualified corporate and noncorporate plans, they illustrate the relatively minor nature of the current discrimination against noncorporate plans. Assuming, however, that the small business owner wishes to incorporate, whether for the purpose of obtaining these advantages or for other purposes, such as limited liability, the small employer's existing H.R. 10 plan or plans must be dealt with in some fashion. The authors also point out the fact that the top corporate tax rate, rather than the normal graduated rate schedule, applies to all of the taxable income of "qualified personal service corporations" (as defined in IRC 448(d)(2)).[78]

---

[74]IRC 401(d)(1)(2).

[75]IRC 404(a)(8)(C).

[76]IRC 402(e)(4)(A).

[77]Treas. Regs. 1.401-11(b)(3).

[78]IRC 11(b)(2).

DISPOSITION OF H.R. 10 PLANS ON INCORPORATION

Freezing the H.R. 10 Plan

Many tax advisers recommend that, upon an employer's incorporation, its existing H.R. 10 plan be "frozen"; that is, no further contributions will be made to the plan, and benefits of participants are either distributed in a lump sum or held for distribution under the normal distribution provisions of the plan. As a caveat, Code Section 72(t), as enacted by TRA '86, imposes a 10 percent penalty tax on certain distributions to employees who are under age 59½. The distribution method may be elected by participants in a one-time irrevocable election offered for an election period that expires prior to the date on which distributions may be made under the election. Earnings on amounts that are not distributed will continue to compound tax-free, and the frozen plan will simply constitute another deferred compensation benefit that will be payable at a later date.

Termination of Plans and Distribution to Participants

If the H.R. 10 plan participant is over 59½, he or she may generally receive a distribution of funds on plan termination without incurring a penalty. However, if the employee is under age 59½ and a distribution is made, the 10 percent penalty tax on the premature distribution will generally be assessed under Section 72(t)(5) of the Code unless the distribution, reduced by any amounts contributed by the employee, is rolled over within 60 days into an individual retirement account or individual retirement annuity.

A termination distribution that is rolled over will not be subject to the 10 percent excise tax imposed as a result of a premature distribution, since Section 72(t)(5) of the Code only imposes the tax on amounts that are included in gross income. Given a rollover of the entire H.R. 10 distribution less employee contributions, no amount is included in gross income. Formerly, a distribution from an H.R. 10 plan on behalf of a participant who is a 5 percent owner could not be rolled over into another H.R. 10 plan or corporate qualified plan either directly[79] or through a

---

[79]Former IRC 402(a)(5)(F)(ii).

conduit IRA.[80] These limitations on rollovers of termination distributions from an H.R. 10 plan were eliminated by TRA '86 and TAMRA '88 for tax years beginning after 1986.[81] The IRS has also approved a direct transfer from the trustee of one H.R. 10 plan to the trustee of another H.R. 10 plan or to the trustee of a corporate plan.[82] Of course, a Form 5310 must be filed with the Service at least 30 days before any trustee-to-trustee transfer by both the ''sending'' and ''receiving'' trustees, and the subject plans must permit such transfers.

Termination of Plan and Transfer of H.R. 10 Funds to Qualified Retirement Plans of the New Small Business

The assets of an existing H.R. 10 plan may be transferred from the trustee of the H.R. 10 plan directly to the trustee of the successor corporate qualified retirement plan without creating a premature distribution, as long as the special requirements of H.R. 10 plans for the owner-employees are observed and as long as the assets do not pass through the hands of participants. In Rev. Rul. 71-541,[83] the Service approved the transfer of H.R. 10 plan assets to a profit-sharing plan of a successor corporation, since the profit-sharing plan provided that (1) the trustee would always be a bank; (2) separate accounts would be maintained for funds transferred on behalf of each owner-employee; (3) no payment of benefits would be made from the separate accounts on or before the owner-employee reached age 59½ or became disabled; and (4) distribution from the owner-employee's account had to begin prior to the end of the taxable year in which he or she attained age 70½. As noted, however, TEFRA and TRA '86 eliminated many of the distinctions between H.R. 10 plans and corporate plans, some of which are the provisions of Rev. Rul. 71-541. Thus, while Rev. Rul. 71-541 has not been withdrawn or rescinded, it is hoped that these restrictions will no longer apply to plan-to-plan transfers.

---

[80]Former IRC 408(d)(3)(A).

[81]P.L. 99-514, 1121(c)(1) and (2). See also P.L. 100-647, 1011A(a)(2)(A).

[82]See Private Letter Ruling 7733009.

[83]1971-2 C.B. 209.

INCOME AND ESTATE TAX CONSEQUENCES OF DISTRIBUTIONS ON TERMINATION

Qualified retirement plans are normally established because of the tax advantages that they offer at the time they are adopted: the corporation is able to deduct contributions currently, and participants can defer inclusion of the contributions in their gross incomes until amounts are distributed or made available under the plan. However, the employer should not overlook the important and unique tax opportunities that are available on the ultimate distribution of benefits. This section will deal with the unique tax aspects of benefits received on termination of participation in a qualified retirement plan. The tax treatment of certain preretirement benefits, such as life insurance, preretirement profit-sharing plan distributions, and loan provisions has been dealt with previously and will not be repeated here.

Plan provisions govern the various forms in which plan benefits may be paid to participants and beneficiaries. In an individually designed plan, the employer may assure that the benefit provisions are drafted in such a manner as to be consistent with the tax planning and business needs of the company. For example, while certain valuable tax advantages are available only if a participant's accrued benefit is paid as a lump-sum distribution, employers often decide to limit the circumstances under which lump sums are paid so as to prevent a departing employee from using a lump-sum payment as a financial springboard for setting up a competing business.

The initial step in determining which forms of benefit distribution are to be included in a plan is to consider the various benefit options that are theoretically available. If the participant's vested accrued benefit (i.e., the vested amount in the participant's profit-sharing or money purchase account, or the present value of the participant's vested retirement annuity) does not exceed $3,500, the plan may be drafted so as to give the plan administrator the option to "cash out" the participant involuntarily on his or her termination by paying the participant the lump-sum value of the vested accrued benefit.[84]

In most situations, the retiring employee will have a choice that includes (1) receiving the benefit as a lump-sum distribution, (2) re-

---

[84]IRC 411(a)(7)(B)(i).

ceiving payments for a fixed number of years certain, or (3) receiving payments in the form of an annuity measured by the participant's expected lifetime (a life annuity) or the combined lifetime of the participant and some other person such as the spouse or designated beneficiary of the participant (a joint and survivor annuity). It is quite common for profit-sharing plans and stock bonus plans to eliminate the life-annuity option so that the plan will be able to avoid compliance with the burdensome joint and survivor-annuity rules. However, all plans that are subject to the minimum funding standards of Code Section 412 (money purchase and defined benefit plans) must make a qualified joint and survivor annuity the normal form of benefit.

Once the employee determines the options that are available, he or she should consider the following issues as they apply to each alternative:

1. What are the immediate income tax consequences of this form of distribution?
2. What are the long-term income tax consequences of this form of distribution?
3. What are the estate tax consequences of this form of distribution?
4. Is this form of distribution coordinated with the employee's personal retirement, financial, and estate planning?

Consequences of Lump-Sum Distributions

A lump-sum distribution, in general terms, is a distribution of the balance of a participant's account under a plan (and in certain cases several plans maintained by an employer must be aggregated) within one recipient taxable year, which distribution is made as a result of the participant's death, disability, or separation from service or after the employee attains age 59½. Complexities and potential pitfalls for the unwary abound in the area of lump-sum distributions, and professional advice should normally be sought in advance if this alternative is considered. If a lump sum is received, the employee is faced with the critical decision of determining whether to "roll the distribution over" into an individual retirement account (IRA) or to retain the distribution and elect to have it taxed under the special five-year averaging rule of Section 402(e) of the Code or grandfathered ten-year averaging under TRA '86 if the participant was age 50 before January 1, 1986, as pointed out below and also in Chapter 55. The five-year and grandfathered ten-year averaging rules are slated for repeal in legislation pending in Congress at the time of this writing.[85]

Tax Consequences of Five-Year Averaging

A recipient of a lump-sum distribution will be taxed under five-year averaging only if this method of taxation is elected.[86] An election to use five-year averaging is made by filing Form 4972 with the recipient's income tax return for the year in which the lump sum is received.[87] This election can be made or revoked at any time during the period in which the income tax return for the year of receipt of the distribution can be amended; that is, within three years of the filing deadline. Five-year averaging may be elected only once with respect to a participant and may only be elected if the participant whose accrued benefit is distributed was an active participant in the plan, including certain predecessor plans, for at least five years.[88]

In general, the amount of tax imposed on a lump-sum distribution will be five times the amount of tax that would be imposed under Section 1(c) of the Code if an unmarried individual received one fifth of the lump sum as his or her only income during the taxable year and such individual could not utilize any personal exemptions or deductions.[89] The tax may be further reduced by a minimum distribution allowance under Section 402(e)(1)(c) of the Code. (See Chapter 55 for a discussion of the grandfather provisions of TRA '86 that may make 10-year averaging and/or capital gains treatment available, as under pre-1987 tax law, to certain electing recipients of lump-sum distributions.)

Table 56–1 indicates the amount of tax that would be imposed in 1990 on a lump-sum distribution of various amounts, as well as the percentage of the distribution that would be paid to satisfy the tax imposed:

---

[85]See The Employee Benefits Simplification and Expansion Act of 1991 (S 1364) and the Pension Access and Simplification Act of 1991 (HR 2730).

[86]IRC 402(e)(4)(B).

[87]An election to use five-year averaging is not available if the recipient of a lump-sum distribution is younger than 59½ at the time of receipt. IRC Sec. 402(e)(4)(B).

[88]IRC 402(e)(4)(H) and Private Letter Rulings 8002078 and 8027025, with respect to using service in a predecessor plan to satisfy the five-year requirement.

[89]IRC 402(e)(1)(B).

TABLE 56–1
Tax Imposed on Lump-Sum Distributions, 1990

Amount of Lump Sum	Tax Imposed	Percentage of Distribution Required to Pay Income Taxes
$ 20,000	$ 1,500	7.50%
100,000	16,398	16.40
250,000	60,110	24.04
500,000	140,000	28.00
1,000,000	280,000	28.00

Table 56–1 indicates that, if the amount of the distribution is small, the five-year averaging election will create a very attractive tax rate. On the other hand, as the size of the lump sum increases, the advantage of continued deferral of tax by way of a rollover to an individual retirement account will in many cases outweigh the benefit of an immediate "reduced" tax under the five-year averaging formula. Persons contemplating the use of five-year averaging should consider not only the immediate tax impact but also the long-term tax consequences. First, once the distribution is received, earnings generated by the distribution are exposed to immediate taxation. Also, where made on account of a participant's death, a lump sum is included in the individual's gross estate for estate tax purposes. Finally, lump-sum recipients might be tempted to increase current expenditures for unneeded or luxury items, so that a large portion of the lump sum might not be available to provide for future retirement security. The authors predict that lump-sum distributions will probably be required by Congress to be rolled over in the not-too-distant future, eliminating the five-year averaging rules. Congress is likely to pass the same law for private pension plans as it did for Civil Service Plans in 1990.[90] The excise tax on large distributions, which we discuss below, is applied without regard to five-year averaging rules.

Rollover of Lump Sums

The alternative to electing five-year averaging of a lump-sum distribution is rolling over all or any part of the lump sum into an individual

---

[90]See 7101, et seq. of the Omnibus Budget Reconciliation Act of 1990.

retirement account or individual retirement annuity. An amount may be rolled over no later than 60 days after receipt of a lump-sum distribution.[91] Although this may sound like a simple requirement, the Service enforces it in a manner that allows little margin for error, even if it is clerical in nature.[92] Therefore, one should plan in advance and identify the specific vehicle to be used for the rollover prior to receipt of the distribution. A recipient who changed his or her mind after completing a rollover used to be able to revoke the rollover with a minimum financial penalty if action to revoke was taken prior to the time for filing an income tax return, including extensions, for the taxable year in which the lump sum was received.[93] Unfortunately, it is no longer possible to revoke an election to roll over.[94]

Rollover of a lump sum is available even if the participant whose accrued benefit is distributed was not an active participant in the plan for five years or any other minimum period. Furthermore, a rollover may be accomplished even if the recipient has previously elected five-year averaging after age 59½. The entire amount received in a lump-sum distribution need not be rolled over,[95] and any amounts not rolled over will be subject to tax at ordinary income tax rates. A recipient cannot elect five-year averaging with respect to a portion of a lump sum that is not rolled over.

The amount of a lump sum that represents employee contributions may not be rolled over but will be retained by the recipient tax-free.[96]

---

[91]IRC 402(a)(5)(C).

[92]In the case of *Wood* v. *Commissioner*, 93 T.C. 114 (1989), a client of Merrill Lynch received a part-cash, part-stock distribution, which he delivered to Merrill Lynch within 60 days of receipt. Merrill Lynch, however, through a bookkeeping error failed to record the transfer of stock to the IRA within the 60-day period. The court ruled against the Service and in favor of the taxpayer, holding that the contribution had actually been completed within the 60-day period. Both before and after the *Wood* case, the Service has maintained that there is no authority in the Code for any waiver of any violation of the 60-day requirement. See, e.g., PLR 8548073 (revoking earlier letter ruling and insisting that the 60-day requirement was not met where the taxpayer did everything in his power to effectuate the rollover in a timely fashion, but was stymied by an account executive who erroneously deposited the funds into a personal savings account); PLR 864703 (60-day requirement not met because the taxpayer's instructions to designate money market account as IRA were not followed); and PLR 9013078 (60-day requirement violated where taxpayer's instructions for amounts to be transferred from one IRA to another were bungled, causing the amounts to be transferred to non-IRA accounts). You just cannot be too careful with respect to IRA rollovers.

[93]IRC 408(d)(4) and Private Letter Rulings 8044031 and 8045026.

[94]Temp. Regs. 1.402(a)(5)-1T, Q&A-3 and -4.

[95]IRC 402(a)(5)(A)(ii).

[96]IRC 402(a)(5)(B).

Income attributable to employee contributions may, however, be rolled over.[97] If the distribution includes property other than cash, the recipient either must roll over the identical property distributed, or he or she must sell the property distributed during the period of up to 60 days between receipt of a lump sum and its rollover, and then, roll over the proceeds of sale.[98] No gain or loss will be recognized on such sales to the extent the proceeds are rolled over. A rollover is available not only to a participant who receives a lump sum, but also to the spouse of a participant who receives a lump sum on account of the participant's death.[99]

The immediate tax consequence of a rollover is that taxation of benefits is deferred with respect to the amount rolled over until such amount is actually received from the IRA. Distributions from the IRA may begin at any time after the year in which the owner of the IRA reaches age 59½. An earlier distribution would result in a 10 percent excise tax under Section 72(t) of the Code. Once age 59½ is attained and prior to reaching age 70½, distributions from the IRA are up to the discretion of the owner. Furthermore, there is no "constructive receipt" from an IRA. Thus, the owner can have the ability to demand all or any part of the IRA at any time without fear of being taxed before the money is actually received.[100] Amounts actually distributed from an IRA are taxed as ordinary income. One cannot receive a lump sum from an IRA and elect five-year averaging on the amount received; therefore, in most cases the decision to use an IRA will foreclose use of five-year averaging.

Once age 70½ is attained, or beginning with the year of the rollover if in that year the owner is older than 70½,[101] the owner of an IRA must have an amount distributed from the IRA that is a certain fraction of the balance in the IRA at the beginning of the year. Failure to receive the minimum required distribution results in an excise tax under Section 4974 of the Code equal to 50 percent of the amount by which the required distribution exceeds the actual distribution. The fraction of the beginning year's balance in the IRA that must be distributed has a numerator equal to one and a denominator equal to the life expectancy of the owner, or

---

[97]Private Letter Ruling 8037034.

[98]IRC 402(a)(5)(A)(ii) and 402(a)(6)(D).

[99]IRC 402(a)(7).

[100]Private Letter Rulings 8008170, 8015093, and 8038101.

[101]Private Letter Ruling 8044059.

combined life expectancies of the owner and his or her spouse, as of the owner's 70th birthday minus the number of calendar years that have commenced after the owner attained age 70½.[102] The single life expectancy of a man aged 70 is currently 12.1 years, and that of a woman aged 70 is 15 years. The joint life expectancy of a husband and wife who are both aged 70 is 18.3 years.[103] Rather than receiving payments for a period certain, an annuity for the life of the participants or joint lives of a participant and his or her spouse may be purchased at age 70½. This option might be attractive to an individual who is relying on a rollover IRA as the principal source of retirement income.

TEFRA added a new level of complexity to the use of rollover IRAs. Specifically, effective for individuals dying after December 31, 1983, an individual's entire interest in an IRA must be distributed within five years of his or her death or, if applicable, the death of his or her surviving spouse, if distributions over a term certain have not commenced before the death of the individual for whose benefit the account was maintained.[104]

Summarizing the key characteristics of using a rollover IRA, this alternative will create no initial income taxation, since neither the rollover nor the return of employee contributions is subject to tax. In the long term, the IRA alternative may be used to defer taxation of benefits distributed from a qualified plan; however, since voluntary employee contributions cannot be rolled over, use of the IRA rollover forecloses further deferral of income earned on voluntary employee contributions. The use of a rollover IRA will undoubtedly increase the likelihood that the participant will retain his or her plan benefits to provide retirement income, rather than use the distribution for current expenditures, as might be the case where five-year averaging is utilized with a lump-sum distribution. A rollover IRA can provide tremendous advantages, especially where the amount of the rollover is large, in terms of flexibility in timing of distributions and in terms of estate planning and minimizing the excise tax on excess distributions discussed below.

---

[102]Treas. Regs. 1.408-2(b)(6).

[103]A deferred payment over 18.3 years may be very attractive because, under the formula of Treas. Regs. 1.408-2(b)(6), the required annual distribution during the first 10 years will normally not even be equal to the interest earned on the IRA. This permits continued deferral of all the principal and some of the interest until future years.

[104]IRC 401(a)(9).

Receipt of Periodic Retirement Benefits from the Qualified Corporate Plan

Rather than receiving a lump-sum distribution, a participant could elect to receive a distribution over a fixed number of years from the qualified corporate plan. One advantage of this alternative is that payments may commence prior to age 59½ without giving rise to the 10 percent penalty on early distributions. However, the manner of distribution elected by a participant must provide for the payment of his or her entire interest under the plan over his or her life, or over the joint life expectancies of the participant and his or her designated beneficiary. As discussed below, failure to receive periodic payments that meet this requirement can give rise to a 50 percent penalty.

Receipt of installment benefits directly from the corporate plan provides greater flexibility in the timing of payments than receipt from an IRA. Also, the doctrine of "constructive receipt" does not apply to qualified retirement plans. Therefore, a participant will not be subject to income tax on amounts made available to him or her until such amounts are actually distributed.

Distributions from a qualified corporate plan after the death of the participant, including amounts attributable to employee contributions, are included in the participant's gross estate. However, where the participant's spouse is the designated beneficiary, or receives the proceeds through the participant's estate, the distribution will qualify for the unlimited marital deduction under Code Section 2056(a). Also, to reduce the income tax payable on the death benefit, the spouse could elect five-year averaging on a lump-sum distribution. Alternatively, the spouse of the participant may be given a lump-sum distribution that could be rolled over into an IRA by the spouse.[105]

In summary, a participant may prefer receiving deferred benefits directly from a corporate plan, particularly if the participant has a large amount of voluntary employee contributions. This alternative permits continued deferral of income taxation of accrued benefits and of earnings on accrued benefits including earnings on employee contributions. This alternative might be best suited for a corporation that has only one shareholder because, after the shareholder participant retires, the plan could be

---

[105]IRC 402(a)(7).

frozen. Freezing the plan would minimize the opportunity for later events to disqualify the plan, alter the investment strategy, or modify the administration in a manner that would be to the detriment of the retired shareholder.

Minimum Payout Rules

As alluded to above, effective for years beginning after 1988, TRA '86 imposes minimum distribution rules on all qualified plans including IRAs and annuity plans. Generally, the rules require that distribution of a participant's benefit must commence by the April 1 of the year following the year in which the participant attains age 70½, even if the participant is still employed by the employer.[106]

The minimum distribution amount is generally the participant's entire interest in the plan. However, where distribution is in the form of periodic payments, the minimum periodic payment amount must be sufficient to distribute the participant's entire interest under the plan over his or her life expectancy or the joint life expectancies of the participant and his or her designated beneficiary.[107] Where the amount distributed during a year is less than the maximum periodic payment, the recipient is liable for an excise tax equal to 50 percent of the amount by which the minimum required payout exceeds the amount actually distributed.[108]

TRA '86 provides a transitional rule that excludes certain participants from the minimum distribution requirements. To be so exempted, a participant must not be a 5 percent owner and must have attained age 70½ by January 1, 1988. Such individuals may defer the commencement of benefits until they actually retire under the plan.[109]

Excise Tax on Large Benefits

TRA '86 also imposes a 15 percent excise tax on benefits that exceed certain distribution limits. Generally, the annual limit is equal to $150,000 or $112,500 (indexed for inflation to $140,276 for 1992) and includes distributions from all plans in which an individual participates, including IRAs. The recipient of an excess distribution is liable for the

---

[106]IRC 401(a)(9)(c).
[107]IRC 4974(b).
[108]IRC 4974(a).
[109]TRA '86 1121(d)(4).

excise tax.[110] Where a distribution qualifies as a lump-sum distribution, the limit is increased to $750,000 or $562,500 (indexed for inflation).

For purposes of determining whether a distribution exceeds the limits, amounts that are attributable to employee contributions or rollovers are not taken into account. Further, TRA '86 offers transitional relief with respect to benefits that were in amounts exceeding $562,500 accrued prior to August 1, 1986. Note, however, that an election had to be made on the individual's tax return for the 1988 tax year in order to qualify for this transitional relief.

AFFILIATED SERVICE GROUPS, EMPLOYEE LEASING, AND RELATED ISSUES

The Code contains several provisions designed to prohibit employers, especially small employers, from evading or circumventing various non-discrimination requirements (such as the minimum participation rules, the minimum coverage rules, and the general nondiscrimination rules of IRC 401(a)(4)) by breaking down what is functionally one business into several different entities. IRC 414(m) deals with arrangements involving "service organizations" having some ownership linkages (though not to the point of being a "controlled group"). IRC 414(n), on the other hand, is designed to inhibit the practice of leasing individuals who are functionally "employees" from another entity to avoid having to treat them as employees for purposes of certain qualified plan requirements. Under IRC 414(o), the Service has been given the authority to prohibit similar attempts to evade employee benefit requirements through the use of multiple organizations, employee leasing, or other arrangements.

Proposed regulations that have been issued under these three statutory subsections have been roundly criticized and are, at the time of this writing, undergoing extensive revisions. The Service has acknowledged that current proposed regulations cast far too wide a net and has committed to curing the problem of overbreadth. Particularly for small business, however, the rules concerning affiliated service groups and employee leasing continue to create tremendous risks and to yield far too few solutions. Moreover, the prospect that future regulations will provide substantial relief from burdensome requirements are not bright, since

---

[110]IRC 4980A.

small business has, from the beginning, been the main target of the affiliated service group and employee leasing rules.

IRC 414(m): Affiliated Service Groups

Section 414(m) of the Code requires that related entities that constitute an "affiliated service group" must be treated as a single employer for purposes of determining whether a qualified retirement plan maintained by any member of the affiliated service group satisfies a number of the qualification requirements, including the nondiscrimination provisions, minimum participation rules, vesting rules, and IRC 415 limitations. The applicability of IRC 414(m) is specifically limited to "service organizations"—entities that have as their principal business the performance of services—and to other entities that regularly perform services for or in connection with service organizations. Because the focus of IRC 414(m) is service organizations, the principal target of IRC 414(m) is professional corporations. Therefore, the discussion that follows will examine the impact of IRC 414(m) in the context of professional corporations, although it should be kept in mind that any "service organization" is within the purview of IRC 414(m).

Under IRC 414(m), partnerships of professional or other service corporations may not discriminate in favor of the shareholder/professionals in providing qualified retirement plans. To enable the reader to better understand the reasoning behind the complex affiliated service group rules, attached to this chapter as an appendix is an examination of the state of the relevant law prior to the enactment of the affiliated service group rules in 1980.

Section 414(m), which was enacted in 1980, provides rules for the aggregation of employees of certain separate organizations for purposes of applying qualification tests to various employee benefit plans. It is an emphatic response to the absurd results that have received judicial approval in the *Kiddie* and *Garland* cases, but applies only to service organizations.[111]

---

[111]*Thomas Kiddie, M.D., Inc.*, 69 T.C. 1055 (1978) (Tax Court holding that employees of professional partnership do not have to be allowed to participate in professional corporation's qualified plan unless the professional corporation owns more than 50 percent of the professional partnership); *Lloyd M. Garland, M.D., F.A.C.S., P.A.*, 73 T.C. 5 (1979) (Tax Court holding that Sections 414(b) and (c) are the exclusive means for determining whether the employees of affiliated entities should be aggregated for purposes of applying the nondiscrimination provisions).

For purposes of determining the qualified status of a member's pension plan under Section 414(m), all employees of members of an "affiliated service group" are treated as employed by a single employer. An affiliated service group consists of a service organization and one or more other organizations, service or otherwise, that are related in their ownership. The broad definition of organization includes a corporation, partnership, or "other organization." Section 414(m)(2) defines an affiliated service group as follows:

> (2) AFFILIATED SERVICE GROUP—For purposes of this subsection, the term "affiliated service group" means a group consisting of a service organization (hereinafter in this paragraph referred to as the "first organization") and one or more of the following:
>
> (A) any service organization which
>
> (i) is a shareholder or partner in the first organization, and (ii) regularly performs services for the first organization or is regularly associated with the first organization in performing services for third persons, and
>
> (B) any other organization if
>
> (i) a significant portion of the business of such organization is the performance of services (for the first organization, for organizations described in subparagraph (A), or for both) of a type historically performed in such service field by employees, and (ii) 10 percent or more of the interests in such organization is held by persons who are highly compensated employees, (within the meaning of section 414(q)) of the first organization described in subparagraph (A).

In Rev. Rul. 81-105,[112] the Service provided an explanation of Section 414(m) and illustrated the application of the affiliated service group classification by way of three examples. Rev. Rul. 81-105 ruled that it obsoletes Rev. Rul. 68-370, so that entities that must be treated as a single employer under Section 414(m) may not satisfy the minimum coverage and nondiscrimination requirements by providing a full benefit to one entity of the affiliated service group and providing a partial benefit to the rank-and-file employees in affiliated entities.

In Rev. Proc. 81-12,[113] the Service provided a procedure under which plan sponsors could request a ruling from the national office of the

---

[112]1981-1 C.B. 256.
[113]1981-1 C.B. 652.

IRS as to whether two or more entities are part of an affiliated service group, and could request a determination letter from the key district director as to whether plans maintained by members of an affiliated service group satisfy the qualification requirements. The Service withdrew its offer to rule on the question of whether two or more entities constitute an affiliated service group in Rev. Proc. 85-43, 1985-2 C.B. 501. The Service has revised Forms 5300 and 5301 to permit plan sponsors to indicate whether they are, or believe they are, a part of an affiliated service group.

In the typical affiliated service group situation, a corporate partner that is a member of a partnership of professional corporations establishes a plan covering only the individual who is the sole shareholder and sole employee of the professional corporation. As a result of the required aggregation of Section 414(m), the plan, when considered alone, fails to satisfy the minimum participation and nondiscrimination requirements for qualification.

Prior to TRA '86, it was necessary for the partnership including corporations to establish a qualified plan that benefitted the staff employees employed by the partnership, in order that the professional corporations could establish retirement plans that were "comparable" to the partnership's plan. This determination was made under Rev. Rul. 81-202,[114] in which the Service provided a comprehensive set of rules for testing the comparability of contributions and benefits provided by qualified pension and profit-sharing plans. These rules permitted plans that were required to be aggregated under Sections 414(b), (c), or (m) to provide either comparable contributions or comparable benefits and thereby satisfy the nondiscrimination tests of Section 401(a)(4) and the minimum participation tests of Section 410(b)(1). As is explained below, effective on or after January 1, 1991, "comparability" is tested under the new regulations under IRC 401(a)(4). See Chapter 55 for a discussion of the regulations under IRC 401(a)(4) and 410(b).

Commencing after 1988, the new minimum participation rules under Section 401(a)(26), which were introduced by TRA '86, have required the termination of most one-person professional corporation plans in this "affiliated service group" context. As an affiliated service group will be treated as a single employer for purposes of Section 401(a)(26), the

---

[114] 1981-2 C.B. 93.

requirement that each plan include the lesser of (*a*) 50 employees of the employer, or (*b*) 40 percent of the employees of the employer, will effectively force small affiliated service groups to adopt single plans covering all members.

To the extent that the minimum participation requirement does not rule out separate plans for the separate employers in an affiliated service group, the minimum coverage requirements of IRC 410(b) will still have to be met. In most cases, aggregation will be required to meet these requirements. Where plans are aggregated for 410(b) purposes, they must be tested as one plan under the nondiscrimination regulations discussed in the previous chapter. The regulations that provide the new rules under which "comparability" will be determined are discussed in more detail in Chapter 55.

IRC 414(n): Employee Leasing

IRC 414(n) deems certain "leased employees" to be employees for purposes of the satisfaction of many qualification requirements by the qualified plans of the lessee employer (known as the "recipient").[115] Anyone performing services rfor the recipient as an employee of a third party under an agreement between the recipient and the third party is a leased employee if such person has been performing such services (of a type historically performed by common-law employees in the recipient's field of business) on a substantially full-time basis for a period of at least 12 months.[116]

One of the major complaints leveled against the employee-leasing rules relates to one of the central components of the test for separating garden-variety contracts for the provision of services from contracts to lease employees: whether the services performed are of a type historically performed by common-law employees. Not only is this so-called historically performed test vague and overbroad, but it also fails to distinguish between legitimate structural changes deriving from economic evolution and tax-motivated reshuffling of formal entities without any functional

---

[115]Although beyond the scope of this discussion, the employee leasing rules apply not only for purposes of the rules governing qualified plans, but also for the purposes of other sets of rules governing, for instance, some welfare plans. IRC 414(n)(3)(C).

[116]IRC 414(n)(2).

significance. Conceding that there are serious problems with the "historically performed" test, the Service has promised that the final regulations under this statutory subsection will replace this test with one focusing on "control."

Small businesses should examine their utilization of services provided under service contracts with third parties to determine whether any of these arrangements will cause them to be treated as leasing employees under IRC 414(n). If so, the recipient must determine the consequences of treating the leased employees as though they were employees for purposes of many employee benefit requirements.[117] The recipient will first have to determine what its qualified plans provide with respect to leased employees. A qualified plan must, as a condition of qualification, specifically state whether leased employees will be allowed to participate in the plan.[118]

If the recipient covers the leased employees, then particular care should be taken if the leased employees are also covered by a qualified plan of the leasing organization. The recipient's qualified plan in that case would be deemed to provide not only the actual benefits provided under its plan but also the benefits provided under the plan of the leasing organization.[119]

If the recipient's plans do not cover the leased employees, then those plans will be tested (under the minimum participation and minimum coverage rules, for instance) as though the leased employees were regular, common-law employees. The contributions and benefits provided for leased employees under the leasing organization's qualified plans are deemed to be provided under a hypothetical, separate qualified plan of the recipient. If one or more of the recipient's qualified plans fail to satisfy the minimum coverage requirements of IRC 410(b) because of the inclusion of leased employees as employees, the recipient may, for testing purposes, aggregate its *actual* qualified plans (except for any 401(k) plan) with the *hypothetical* plan it is deemed to maintain. If these plans are aggregated for purposes of IRC 410(b), however, they will also have to

---

[117]A representative sampling of these employee benefit requirements includes the minimum participation requirements of IRC 401(a)(26), the minimum coverage requirements of IRC 410(b), the nondiscrimination requirements of IRC 401(a)(4), and the annual addition limitations under IRC 415.

[118]Prop. Regs. 1.414(n)-2(a)(1)(i).

[119]Prop. Regs. 1.414(n)-2(b)(3)(iv).

be aggregated for nondiscrimination testing under IRC 401(a)(4). In other words, if aggregation is necessary for minimum coverage purposes, then the plans will have to be "comparable" for nondiscrimination purposes.

If leased employees constitute less than 20 percent of the recipient's nonhighly compensated work force, the leased employees will not be deemed common-law employees for employee benefit purposes if the leasing organization maintains a so-called safe-harbor plan.[120] A safe-harbor plan is a money purchase pension plan with (1) a nonintegrated contribution rate of at least 10 percent of compensation, (2) full and immediate vesting, and (3) immediate vesting for each employee of the leasing organization (other than those who perform substantially all of their services for the leasing organizations).[121]

It should be remembered that this safe harbor is only available where leased employees make up less than 20 percent of the recipient's nonhighly compensated work force. Small business owners should be particularly careful of leasing organizations that claim to provide a qualified plan that always solves any leased-employee problem. First, these plans are not always safe-harbor plans. Some are plans that the leasing organization believes will be comparable for nondiscrimination purposes to most other qualified plans maintained by any small business. Such plans cannot, however, solve a minimum participation problem for the recipient's qualified plans, if such a problem exists. Moreover, certain types of plans (e.g., a 401(k) plan) cannot be aggregated with the hypothetical plan for leased employees in order to solve a serious minimum coverage problem.[122] Thus, a 401(k) plan, common in many small businesses, may present an almost insurmountable problem (unless the safe harbor is available). Second, even if a leasing organization maintains a safe-harbor plan, the safe harbor will not be available if the small business leases too many nonhighly compensated employees.

The leased-employee rules of IRC 414(n) thus may pose a problem for some small businesses. The owner or manager of a small business who believes the business may be leasing employees should immediately consult the business's attorney or an ERISA attorney called in to examine

---

[120]IRC 414(n)(5)(B).

[121]IRC 414(n)(5)(B).

[122]Prop. Regs. 1.410(b)-7(c)(2). A 401(k) plan is aggregated under IRC 410(b) with an employer's other qualified plans for the limited purpose of applying the second prong of one of the available minimum coverage tests (the average benefits test).

the issue. Leased employees can pose a hidden risk to the qualification of a retirement plan.

IRC 414(o): The Catchall Provision

If the reader finds the affiliated service group and employee-leasing rules broad, the reader will find the proposed regulations under IRC 414(o) even broader. IRC 414(o) is a catchall provision based on the premise the affiliated service group and employee-leasing rules do not cast a wide enough net. On the theory that inventive professionals in the employee benefits field will devise methods to avoid even the long arm of the affiliated service group and employee-leasing rules, Congress granted the Service authority under IRC 414(o) to prohibit evasive techniques involving functional economic units broken into several entities.

The Service has issued proposed regulations under IRC 414(o). Until the Service revises these proposed regulations, the authors believe that small employers should understand something of the complexity and chilling overbreadth of the proposed regulations. The following is a good example of such overbreadth.

In addition to providing special rules for "leased owners," "shared employees," "5 percent owners," and "inside corporate directors," the proposed regulations create a special category known of leased employees known as "leased managers." Leased managers are removed from the ambit of the leased-employee rules in order to be brought under a special set of rules. The effect of these special rules is, *inter alia,* to subject the qualified plans of the leasing organization to special requirements. Ordinarily, the qualification of a leasing organization benefit plan is not in any way affected by the leased-employee rules. Under the leased-manager rules, however, the leasing organization's qualified plans are put at risk.

If more than 50 percent of the management functions of an organization are performed by leased managers, then the rules create an imaginary plan for these leased managers. Any benefits actually provided to the leased managers (attributable to services performed for the recipient) are treated as though they were provided under a qualified plan of the recipient.[123] This imaginary plan has to satisfy all the important

---

[123]Prop. Regs. 1.414(o)-1(c)(1).

employee benefit requirements (e.g., minimum coverage and nondiscrimination). Depending on the circumstances and the types of plans involved, aggregation with one or more of the recipient's qualified plans may be possible, but once again no aggregation will be possible to satisfy minimum participation standards, and 401(k) plans cannot be aggregated with non-401(k) plans for minimum coverage purposes. Thus, an organization that leases managers to other organizations runs a risk of disqualifying its plans.

Conclusion

The whole area of affiliated service groups, employee leasing, and related issues is likely to remain unsettled for some time to come. The Service is currently working on a major overhaul of the proposed regulations in this area. Until this overhaul is complete, employers will have to be aware of the problems in this area and, in conjunction with their professional advisers, to act with caution and within the parameters of the proposed regulations (to the extent that these parameters can be identified).

PART 13

EMPLOYEE BENEFIT PLAN ISSUES

The final part of *the Handbook* is devoted to issues of special interest in employee benefit planning and begins with Chapter 57 on the topic of ERISA Fiduciary Liability Issues. In Chapter 58, Plan Termination Insurance, recent crucial changes in the pension plan termination insurance program are analyzed both from the perspective of the plan sponsor and the employee. Just about every employer must consider issues concerning welfare benefits for retirees. The Financial Accounting Standards Board (FASB) recent pronouncements on accounting for welfare benefits after retirement are discussed in Chapter 59 along with many other relevant issues.

Chapter 60, Multiemployer Plans, compares the major components and issues relating to such plans as contrasted with single employer plans. Chapter 61, Public Employee Pension Plans, examines the characteristics, magnitude, and differences involved in pension plans for public employees.

In an increasingly global economy, international employee benefit planning assumes a much greater role in corporate planning. This topic is explored in Chapter 62.

The final Chapter in *the Handbook* takes a visionary look at the future of employee benefits.

CHAPTER 57

FIDUCIARY LIABILITY ISSUES UNDER ERISA

Alan P. Cleveland

An appreciation of the legal duties and responsibilities of a fiduciary to the participants and beneficiaries of a trusteed employee benefit plan is both fundamentally simple and exceptionally difficult. Legal definitions and statements of basic principles that seem straightforward in concept often prove elusive when applied in real situations. A plan fiduciary in the discharge of his or her duties under the Employee Retirement Income Security Act of 1974 (ERISA) is well-advised to err on the side of caution, to resolve doubt in favor of a liberal interpretation of plan benefits, to be well-informed at all times of the duties and responsibilities of all the fiduciaries of the plan, and to act uniformly and in strict accordance with the plan document but with a broad reading given to the fiduciary responsibilities and standards of the Act.

FIDUCIARY DUTIES UNDER THE COMMON LAW OF TRUSTS

In the employee benefits area, fiduciary relationships are fundamental to the administration and investment of employee benefit trusts. When does a fiduciary relationship exist? Under the common law of trusts, it is said that a person is in a fiduciary relationship with another if the person who receives certain powers or property does so on the condition that with such receipt is the corollary duty to utilize that conferred power or property for the benefit of that other. A trust is recognized as a formal fiduciary relationship concerning property and imposing on the person (the trustee) who holds title to that property (trust assets) certain fiduciary duties to deal with that property for the benefit of another (the beneficiary). When a person as trustee accepts ownership of such property "in trust" for a beneficiary, the trustee at the same time accepts the fiduciary responsibility and duty to use the power over trust assets for the benefit of the beneficiary of that trust.

Under the common law of trusts, a trustee has several basic fiduciary duties to the beneficiaries of the trust: a duty to see that the property of the trust is legally designated as trust property; a duty not to delegate to others trustee powers over trust property; a duty of undivided loyalty to the beneficiaries of the trust; and a duty to invest prudently by maximizing return on and ensuring the safety of trust assets. Primary among these trustee responsibilities are the duties of loyalty and prudence.

Duty of Loyalty

A trustee's duty of loyalty is the duty to act in the interest of the trust as if the trustee had no other competing interests to protect, especially his or her own. The trustee must resolve all conflicts between his or her personal or other interests and those of the trust and its beneficiaries in favor of the trust beneficiaries. This duty of loyalty is a component of all fiduciary relationships, but is particularly important in the case of a trust created to provide economic support or benefits for a specific beneficiary. A much-cited court opinion by Justice Benjamin Cardozo articulates this high standard of loyalty, and warrants quoting at length:

> Many forms of conduct permissible in a workaday world for those acting at arm's length, are forbidden to those bound by fiduciary ties. A trustee is held to something stricter than the morals of the market place. Not honesty alone, but the punctilio of an honor the most sensitive, is then the standard of behavior. As to this there has developed a tradition that is unbending and inveterate. Uncompromising rigidity has been the attitude of courts of equity when petitioned to undermine the rule of undivided loyalty by the "disintegrating erosion" of particular exceptions. Only thus has the level of conduct for fiduciaries been kept at a level higher than that trodden by the crowd.[1]

This extreme expression of singular loyalty under the common law of trusts sets out that strict prohibition against fiduciary conflicts of interest which

---

[1]*Meinhard* v. *Salmon*, 294 N.Y. 458, 464, 164 N.E. 545, 546 (1928).

has been the hallmark of subsequent legislation and judicial law under ERISA in regulating the fiduciary management of employee benefit plans.

Duty of Prudence: The Prudent Man Rule

In addition to the duty of undivided loyalty to the beneficiaries of a trust, a trustee under the common law of trusts has the duty of prudence in managing trust assets. This duty of prudence established a standard of performance in managing trust assets measured as equivalent to that care exercised by a person of ordinary prudence in dealing with the fiduciary's own personal property. The standard of skill and care established under traditional American trust law—that of a person of ordinary prudence, or the Prudent Man Rule—is largely derived from a decision of the Supreme Judicial Court of Massachusetts in 1830, the case of *Harvard College* v. *Amory,* 26 Mass. (9 Pick.) 446, 461, which held:

> All that can be required of a trustee to invest, is that he shall conduct himself faithfully and exercise a sound discretion. He is to observe how men of prudence, discretion and intelligence manage their own affairs, not in regard to speculation, but in regard to the permanent disposition of their funds, considering the probable income, as well as the probable safety of the capital to be invested.

This flexible standard under the common law later proved so vague that trustees, including the fiduciaries of employee pension plans, found little comfort in making individual investment choices on behalf of the trust. Likewise, beneficiaries who were disappointed in the investment of a trust often found it difficult to maintain a legal action in proving a fiduciary's lack of prudence and breach of trust. The Prudent Man Rule also was applied on an investment-by-investment basis rather than looking to the overall performance of the trust's portfolio of assets as a whole. All in all, the common law of trusts ultimately proved a poorly stocked tool box in meeting the special requirements of employee pension plans.

EXCLUSIVE BENEFIT RULE UNDER THE INTERNAL REVENUE CODE

As a precondition for the substantial tax advantages afforded contributing employer sponsors and the participants and beneficiaries of qualified pension plans as tax-exempt organizations, Congress had long included in the Internal Revenue Code (Code) certain limitations and safeguards analogous to those provided under the common law of trusts. The Code provisions were intended to ensure that a pension plan in fact was operated for the exclusive benefit of its members. This intent is codified as the Exclusive Benefit Rule. A key provision under Section 401(a) of the Internal Revenue Code, which enumerates the general qualification requirements for a pension plan's tax-exempt status, mandates that a trust created by an employer as part of a pension or profit-sharing plan must be "for the exclusive benefit" of the plan's covered employees and their beneficiaries, and that it must be "impossible . . . for any part of the corpus or income . . . to be . . . used for or diverted to, purposes other than for the exclusive benefit" of the employees or their beneficiaries. The duty of loyalty of the trustee of a pension plan qualified under Code Section 401(a) is, therefore, threefold:

- To be qualified as tax-exempt, a plan must be established for the "exclusive benefit" of the covered employees and their beneficiaries.
- All contributions received by the plan must be "for the purpose of distributing to such employees or their beneficiaries the corpus and income of the fund accumulated by the trust."
- And, under the express terms of the trust, it must be impossible for trust assets to be diverted to purposes "other than for the exclusive benefit of [the] employees or their beneficiaries" prior to the satisfaction of benefits due under the plan.

Failure of an employee benefit pension plan to operate in accordance with the Exclusive Benefit Rule would cause it to lose its tax-exempt status under the Code, further resulting in a loss of deductibility of employer contributions to the plan as well as loss of the tax-preferred treatment enjoyed by the plan's participants and beneficiaries.

FIDUCIARY STANDARDS UNDER ERISA

Immediately prior to the passage of ERISA, it was estimated that more than 35 million employees were dependent for their retirement benefits on a private pension system whose noninsured trust assets then exceeded $130 billion. Congress determined that the rapid and substantial growth in size and scope of hundreds of thousands of pension plans had such economic impact on the continued well-being and security of their millions of covered employees that it was in the national public interest to establish under ERISA adequate safeguards to ensure the adequacy of funds to pay the retirement benefits promised under those pension plans. Toward these ends, ERISA mandated national standards of conduct, responsibility, and obligation for the fiduciaries of employee benefit plans, and further provided appropriate remedies, sanctions, and access to the Federal courts for the enforcement of such fiduciary standards.

Before ERISA, pension plan fiduciaries were largely subject to the common law of trusts, the principles of which were developed and refined primarily during the 19th century to order personal trust relationships between private parties. Unfortunately, traditional trust law proved inapposite to the special purposes of pension plans, which had evolved to such a massive scale in the postindustrial period. The only real sanction under federal law before ERISA for fiduciary breaches involving an employee pension plan was revocation of the plan's tax-exempt status for violation of the Exclusive Benefit Rule under the Internal Revenue Code, but it was realized early that the adverse consequences of withdrawal of a plan's tax preferences would bear most heavily on innocent employees as the plan's beneficiaries, and the sanction was rarely applied in practice.

Under ERISA, Congress intended to establish a comprehensive federal regulatory scheme for the operation of pension and other employee benefit plans based on new and unwavering principles of fiduciary duty to be enforced with uncompromised rigidity. This new federal law of employee benefit trusts had four main objectives:

• A uniform legal culture of fiduciary duties would be developed incrementally by the federal courts to define further the statutory standards of ERISA on a case-by-case basis that would supersede the traditional common law of trusts unevenly applied and interpreted under the individual laws of each state.

• Those fiduciary standards developed under ERISA would be clarified and modified purposely to accommodate the special needs and purposes of pension funds.

• Employee pension plan beneficiaries would have liberal access to the federal courts in enforcing the fiduciary standards of ERISA, and those plan fiduciaries found to have breached their duties could be held personally liable for resulting plan losses.

• Fiduciaries of employee benefit plans not utilizing the trust form as a funding vehicle would still be subject to the fiduciary standards of the Act.

ERISA in a number of important respects went beyond the common law of trusts in establishing or extending new legal standards of conduct for plan fiduciaries.

• By combining the Exclusive Benefit Rule under the Internal Revenue Code with the "sole benefit standard" as stated under the Labor Management Relations Act, ERISA now required plan fiduciaries to act *solely in the interest* of the plan's participants and beneficiaries for the *exclusive purpose* of providing plan benefits or defraying the reasonable administrative expenses of the plan. This established the *Sole Benefit Standard* of fiduciary conduct under ERISA.

• For the future, a plan fiduciary could take little comfort in acting for a plan with only the ordinary prudence required under the traditional Prudent Man Rule. Instead, a fiduciary needed to act under ERISA with the care, skill, prudence, and diligence under the circumstances then prevailing that a prudent man *acting in a like capacity and familiar with such matters* would use in the conduct of an *enterprise of a like character and with like aims*. This established the *Prudent Expert Rule* of ERISA.

• A fiduciary was still required to diversify the investments of a plan portfolio so as to minimize the risk of large losses unless under the circumstances it was clearly prudent not to do so. This closely resembled the fiduciary principle well known under the common law of trusts as the *Diversification Rule*.

• A fiduciary needed to follow strictly the terms of the written plan document (unless otherwise in violation of ERISA) and to administer the plan in a fair, uniform, and nondiscriminatory manner. This principle has come to be called the *Plan Document Rule*.

• Unless otherwise exempted, a fiduciary could not allow the plan to engage directly or indirectly in transactions prohibited under ERISA, a caveat known as the *Prohibited Transactions Rule*.

The Sole Benefit Standard

The Sole Benefit Standard of ERISA borrows from the previously discussed Exclusive Benefit Rule of Section 401(a) of the Internal Revenue Code and also in large part from Section 302(c)(5) of the Labor Management Relations Act (LMRA). The LMRA had long required that a collectively bargained employee benefit trust fund be maintained "for the sole and exclusive benefit of the employees . . . and their families and dependents."

The United States Supreme Court in *NLRB* v. *Amax Coal Company,* 453 U.S. 322, 335 (1981), stressed the legislative intent of ERISA as designed to prevent a fiduciary "from being put into a position where he has dual loyalties, and, therefore, he cannot act exclusively for the benefit of a plan's participants and beneficiaries." The federal courts have continued to strengthen this fiduciary duty of unwavering loyalty under ERISA to require a fiduciary to act with an "eye single to the interests of the participants and beneficiaries" and to impose liability against plan fiduciaries "at the slightest suggestion that any action taken was with other than the beneficiaries in mind." At this point in the evolution of the national fiduciary law of pension trusts under ERISA, the Sole Benefit Standard should be understood as imposing on the fiduciary a rigid, complete, and undivided loyalty to act for the beneficiaries of the employee benefit trust devoid of any other motivating considerations by the fiduciary.

The Prudent Expert Rule

In an effort to draw attention to the distinction between the standard of ordinary prudence under the common law of trusts and the prudent-expert standard contemplated under ERISA as particular to pension plans, the U.S. Department of Labor promulgated prudency regulations in 1979 that introduced the new ERISA standard as one "built upon, but that should and does depart from, traditional trust law in certain respects." For example, unlike traditional trust law, the degree of riskiness of a specific investment would not render that investment per se prudent or imprudent. Rather, the prudence of the investment decision would be judged under ERISA in the context of the plan's overall portfolio. The prudent-expert standard of ERISA differs from the traditional prudent-man standard under the common law of trusts in three important respects. First, the plan fiduciary under ERISA must invest plan assets not in the same way as he or she would handle his or her personal estate but must look to how similar pension plans under similar circumstances are being invested. Second, it is not enough for an ERISA fiduciary to be merely "prudent," but he or she additionally must exercise the skill of a prudent person especially knowledgeable and experienced—that is, an expert—in the management of pension plans. Third, the focus is not to be on the performance of the individual plan investment but on how the investment contributes to the net performance of the pension portfolio as a whole, which assumes the conceptual framework of modern portfolio theory in its broadest terms. In investing a pension plan portfolio under the prudent-expert rule, the fiduciary should weigh the risk of loss against the opportunity for gain, taking into consideration the following elements: (1) the liquidity and current return of the portfolio relative to the liquidity requirements of the plan; (2) the projected return of the portfolio relative to the funding objectives of the plan; and (3) the composition of the portfolio with regard to diversification.

The Diversification Rule

Consistent with the traditional common law of trusts, an ERISA fiduciary is required to diversify plan investments "so as to minimize the risk of large losses, unless under the circumstances it is clearly prudent not to do so." The legislative history of ERISA suggests those elements a fiduciary should consider in diversifying a plan's portfolio as including the purposes of the plan, the amount of plan assets, the overall financial and industrial conditions of the economy, the special characteristics of the particular type of investment (such as mortgages, bonds, and shares of stock), distribution as to geographical location, distribution as to industries, and dates of maturity. There are, unfortunately, no clear-cut tests under the statute as to what would constitute a plan's lack of diversity or undue concentration in any particular investment.

During the legislative hearings leading to the enactment of ERISA, Congress heard testimony that under the common law of trusts, fiduciaries had rarely been held liable for investment losses unless trust holdings in a single investment exceeded 50 percent. Also under the pre-ERISA common law of trusts, a plan's concentration of investments of 25 percent or less of portfolio assets in an individual security or geographic locale did not ordinarily result in sanctions by the courts. However, since passage of ERISA, fiduciary liability has been imposed by the courts in a case where 23 percent of a plan's assets were invested in a single real estate loan. In a separate case, the investment of 85 percent of a profit-sharing plan's assets in long-term government bonds without the fiduciary having first adequately investigated the plan's liquidity needs was found to be a breach of the fiduciary duty to diversify plan assets.

The Plan Document Rule

Plan fiduciaries are required to act in strict accordance with the documents and instruments governing the plan insofar as such documentation is consistent with the provisions of ERISA. As a corollary to this statutory mandate, and in part a derivative of the Sole Benefit Standard, the federal courts are now developing a growing body of fiduciary law under ERISA relating specifically to fiduciary conduct in the administration of plans, especially concerning the role of the plan administrator in the disposition of benefit claims. Plan fiduciaries are required in all cases to uniformly follow the express, written terms of the plan's documents. A plan administrator's decisions on benefits claims are normally accorded deference by the courts *unless* there is a substantive issue raised as to whether (1) the relevant terms of the plan are overly vague or ambiguous, (2) the plan document fails to expressly include a provision that the courts should defer to the administrative decisions of the plan's fiduciaries, or (3) there is an apparent conflict of interest and the fiduciary would be personally or institutionally affected by the benefit decision. A recent holding of the United States Supreme Court in *Firestone* v. *Bruch,* 109 S. Ct. 948 (1989), is significant for its apparent rejection of the judicial deference normally accorded administrative benefit decisions under case law decided under the Labor Management Relations Act and, instead, has substituted those governing principles developed under the law of trusts in cases involving abusive discretion by plan fiduciaries in deciding benefit claims.

Prohibited Transactions Rule

Arising from yet going well beyond the common trust law duty of loyalty, ERISA prohibits a fiduciary from causing a plan to directly or indirectly enter into transactions with certain persons defined as "parties-in-interest." This group is similar to but more narrowly defined than the class of "disqualified persons" identified under companion provisions of the Internal Revenue Code. A fiduciary may not cause the plan to directly or indirectly engage in a transaction with a party-in-interest, as either buyer or seller, that would constitute a (1) sale or exchange, or leasing, of any property between the plan and a party-in-interest; (2) lending of money or other extension of credit between the plan and a party-in-interest; (3) furnishing of goods, services, or facilities between the plan and a party-in-interest; (4) transfer to or use by or for the benefit of a party-in-interest of any assets of the plan; or (5) the acquisition, on behalf of the plan, of any employer security or employer real property not otherwise specifically exempted by law or regulation.

Congress recognized the great potential for abuse in self-dealing with plan assets and so made fiduciaries liable for any losses sustained by a plan resulting from a prohibited transaction. Under ERISA, the fiduciary has a duty to make a thorough investigation of any party's relationship to the plan to determine if that person is a party-in-interest with respect to the plan. The term "party-in-interest" is broadly defined as including nearly everyone who has a direct or indirect association with a plan and specifically includes, but is not limited to, the following persons listed under Section 3(14) of ERISA:

1. A plan fiduciary (such as an administrator, officer, trustee, or custodian of the plan).
2. The legal counsel or employee of the plan.
3. Any other person providing services to the plan.
4. An employer whose employees are covered by the plan.
5. An employee organization (such as a union) any of whose members are covered by the plan.
6. A direct or indirect 50 percent or more owner of an employer sponsor of the plan.
7. Certain relatives of the foregoing persons.
8. The employees, officers, directors, and 10 percent shareholders of certain other parties-in-interest.
9. Certain persons having a statutorily defined direct or indirect relationship with other parties-in-interest.

Even as the prohibited-transaction provisions of ERISA precisely codify what would in many instances be considered only a possible conflict of interest under the common law of trusts, the ERISA rules in this area are less tolerant and more strictly applied than those of the traditional law of trusts. For example, a plan's engaging in a prohibited transaction would still result in a fiduciary breach even if the plan profited by the prohibited transaction. Upon application to the Secretary of Labor, however, a plan fiduciary may request an exemption to prospectively enter into what otherwise would be deemed a prohibited transaction upon the secretary's finding that granting such an exemption would be administratively feasible, demonstrably in the interests of the plan and of its participants and beneficiaries, and otherwise protective of the rights of the plan's participants and beneficiaries. Administrative exemptions may be granted for specific transactions on an individual plan basis or as a class exemption for certain categories of transactions typical of the industry for a substantial number of unrelated plans.

The comprehensive definitional scope of what would constitute a "prohibited transaction" as defined under ERISA, the involved attribution rules identifying persons as "parties-in-interest" (many of whom may themselves have no personal knowledge of the plan), the broad regulatory definition as to what property constitutes "assets" of the plan for purposes of applying the prohibited transaction rules, and the severe sanctions and excise taxes assessed for such prohibited transactions dictate that a fiduciary should approach this area with great caution, be well counseled, and seek an administrative exemption in questionable cases *before* causing the plan to enter into the transaction.

WHO IS A FIDUCIARY?

ERISA defines a plan fiduciary as any person who (1) exercises any discretionary authority or control over the management of a plan, (2) exercises any authority or control concerning the management or disposition of its assets, or (3) has any discretionary authority or responsibility in the administration of the plan. Fiduciary status extends not only to those persons named in the plan documents as having express authority and responsibility in the plan's investment or management but also covers those persons who undertake to exercise any discretion or control over the plan regardless of their formal title. Fiduciary status under ERISA depends on a person's function, authority, and responsibility and does not rest merely on title or label. To illustrate: A person who exercises discretion in the administration of a plan by making the final decision on a participant's appeal of a denial of a benefit claim would be considered a plan fiduciary under ERISA, even if the plan document makes no express provision authorizing such person's discretionary responsibility. However, those persons simply performing ministerial functions for a plan under administrative procedures established by others would not be considered fiduciaries. Professional service providers to a plan, such as attorneys, accountants, actuaries, and consultants, acting strictly within their professional roles and not exercising discretionary authority or control over the plan or providing investment advice for fees or other compensation, are unlikely to be considered fiduciaries of the plan. Plan trustees and administrators, on the other hand, by the very nature of their functions and authority would be considered fiduciaries.

A written plan document is required to provide for "named fiduciaries" having authority to control and manage the plan so that employees may know who is responsible for its operation. A named fiduciary may in fact manage or control the plan, or merely be identified in the document by name or office as the person authorized to appoint those fiduciaries who actually will exercise discretion and control in administering the plan or investing its assets. Only the named fiduciary may appoint a plan's investment manager and allocate investment responsibility to such manager as to make him a plan fiduciary. ERISA forbids persons convicted of any of a wide variety of specified felonies from serving as a fiduciary, adviser, consultant, or employee of a plan for a period the later of five years after conviction or five years after the end of imprisonment for such crime. A fine of up to $10,000 or imprisonment for not more than one year may be imposed against the named fiduciary and others for an intentional violation of this prohibition.

LIABILITY FOR FIDUCIARY BREACHES UNDER ERISA

A plan fiduciary breaching the fiduciary requirements of ERISA is to be held personally liable for any losses sustained by the plan resulting from the breach. The fiduciary is further liable to restore to the plan any profits realized by the fiduciary through the improper use of the plan assets. Additionally, the fiduciary is subject to a broad panoply of other equitable relief, including removal, as may be ordered by the courts. If found to have engaged in a prohibited transaction with a plan, a fiduciary as a party-in-interest would be subject to an excise tax payable to the U.S. Treasury equal to 5 percent of the amount involved in the transaction, for each year the prohibited transaction was outstanding, plus interest and penalties on this excise tax. This excise tax increases to 100 percent of the amount involved upon failure to remedy the transaction upon notification.

Co-Fiduciary Liability

A plan fiduciary moreover is liable for the fiduciary breaches of other fiduciaries for the same plan if such fiduciary participates knowingly in or knowingly undertakes to conceal an act or omission of a co-fiduciary knowing such action constitutes a breach, imprudently fails to discharge his or her own fiduciary duties under the plan (and thereby enables the co-fiduciary to commit the breach), or has knowledge of the co-fiduciary's breach and makes no reasonable effort under the circumstances to remedy the breach.

Enforcement

Enforcement of the fiduciary provisions of ERISA may be by civil action brought in federal or state court by a plan participant or beneficiary (individually, or on behalf of a class of plan participants and beneficiaries), by the Secretary of Labor, or by another plan fiduciary.

Exculpatory Provisions

Exculpatory provisions written into a plan document or other instrument to relieve a fiduciary from liability for fiduciary breaches against the plan are void and to be given no effect under ERISA. A plan may purchase liability insurance for itself and for its fiduciaries to cover losses resulting from their acts or omissions if the insurance policy permits recourse by the insurer against the fiduciaries in case of a breach of fiduciary responsibility.

Bonding and Fiduciary Insurance

Every fiduciary of an employee benefit plan and every other person who handles plan funds or property is required to be bonded, naming the plan as the insured, in an amount fixed at the beginning of each plan year as not less than 10 percent of the amount of funds handled but in no event less than $1,000. Certain insurance companies, banks, and other financial institutions handling plan assets may be relieved of the bonding requirement if such institutions meet certain capital and other regulatory criteria established by the Secretary of Labor.

Further Sanctions for Breaches of Fiduciary Responsibility

In addition to a fiduciary's personal liability to restore losses sustained by the plan as a result of a breach of the fiduciary's responsibilities, the fiduciary also may be liable for (1) court-ordered attorneys' fees and costs incurred to remedy the breach, (2) punitive damages awarded by a court against the fiduciary, (3) special damages in an amount equal to the profits received by a fiduciary resulting from the wrongful use of plan assets, and (4) mandatory assessment of a civil penalty equal to 20 percent of the amount recovered by the Secretary of Labor on account of a fiduciary breach.

Attorneys' Fees. A court in its discretion may award attorneys' fees to a prevailing plaintiff under ERISA against a plan fiduciary by taking into account certain factors, including the degree of the fiduciary's culpability or bad faith, the offending party's ability to satisfy the award of attorneys' fees, whether its award would deter other fiduciaries from acting similarly under like circumstances, the relative merits of the parties' positions in the litigation, and whether the action conferred a common benefit on the plan's participants and beneficiaries.

Punitive Damages. The courts have broad discretion under ERISA to award punitive damages to a plan for fiduciary breaches in cases where it is found a fiduciary acted with malice or wanton indifference. On awarding such damages, a court would take into consideration (1) the trust and pension laws as developed by the state and federal courts in a particular jurisdiction, (2) whether the allowance of such relief would conflict with other public-policy objectives under ERISA, and (3) whether granting such relief would best effectuate the underlying purposes of ERISA.

Restitution for Wrongful Profits. Where a fiduciary has personally profited by wrongfully using plan assets for the fiduciary's own account, even where the plan itself has sustained no direct loss and may actually have gained by the transaction, the fiduciary likely will be required by the courts to disgorge to the plan the full amount of those personally realized profits. And if there is any commingling of plan assets with the fiduciary's personal property, all issues of apportionment of the wrongful profit will be resolved against the fiduciary and in favor of the plan. The purpose of this disgorgement requirement is to remove any incentive for the fiduciary to misuse plan assets whether or not the plan sustains a loss by the fiduciary breach. As a matter of equity, the fiduciary will not be permitted to gain by his or her wrongful acts.

Twenty Percent Civil Penalty. Added by the Omnibus Budget Reconciliation Act of 1989 (OBRA '89), ERISA was amended to require the Secretary of Labor to assess a civil penalty against fiduciaries who breach their fiduciary responsibilities under ERISA and also to make such assessments against any nonfiduciary who knowingly participates in such breach. The amount of civil penalty is equal to 20 percent of the amount of applicable recovery obtained pursuant to any settlement agreement with the Secretary of Labor or ordered by a court to be paid in a judicial proceeding instituted by the Department of Labor. The 20 percent civil penalty assessment is to be reduced by the amount of any excise tax payable to the U.S. Treasury on account of a prohibited transaction. In the Secretary of Labor's sole discretion, the civil penalty may be waived or reduced if the secretary determines in writing that the fiduciary or other person so assessed acted reasonably and in good faith, or that it is reasonable to expect that as a consequence of the penalty's assessment it would not be possible to restore all losses to the plan without severe financial hardship unless the waiver or reduction were granted.

ALLOCATION OF FIDUCIARY RESPONSIBILITIES

Plan documents may provide that specific duties may be allocated by agreement among the fiduciaries provided those duties are specifically delineated in writing, the procedures for such allocations are sufficiently detailed, and the fiduciaries act prudently in implementing the established allocation procedure. If fiduciary responsibilities are allocated in accordance with the plan documentation, the fiduciary would not be held liable for any plan loss arising from the acts or omissions of those other fiduciaries to whom such responsibilities had been properly delegated. Regardless, a plan fiduciary will remain fiduciarily responsible if he or she does not act in general accordance with the prudency requirements of ERISA in making the delegation or if the fiduciary had knowledge of another's fiduciary breach and yet failed to make reasonable efforts to remedy the breach.

Only the named fiduciary of a plan may allocate or delegate duties involving the management and control of plan assets. In duly appointing an investment manager in writing and in accordance with the procedural requirements of ERISA, the fiduciary responsibility of investing or otherwise managing the assets of the plan may be transferred to the manager within the terms of the delegation. Yet, the named fiduciary would still be held liable for imprudently selecting or retaining the manager or for permitting, concealing, or failing to remedy a known breach of that fiduciary's responsibility to the plan.

A fiduciary also must demonstrate procedural prudence in the management of the plan's affairs and must be able to show that the fiduciary's reliance on the plan's advisers and other fiduciaries was reasonable and informed. As fiduciary status is functionally determined, so too is prudency measured by conduct no less than result. The court in a lead ERISA case, *Donovan* v. *Cunningham*, 716 F.2d 1455, 1467 (5th Cir. 1983), aptly summarized the fiduciary obligation of affirmative vigilance in holding that "a pure heart and an empty head are not enough" to avoid liability for a breach of fiduciary responsibility under the Act.

SUMMARY

This brief survey has reviewed the changing course of the fiduciary standards of *employee pension plans* from their traditional meaning under the common law of trusts to the passage of the broad statutory standards set out under ERISA. The national fiduciary law of pension trusts was continuously shifted by the decisions of the federal courts and by administrative rule-making. This chapter merely touches the surface of the deep, swift-running, and ever wandering stream that plan fiduciaries must negotiate. Knowing its ways and understanding their own roles, fiduciaries may guide the plan and its beneficiaries to their intended destination in trust without upset or misadventure.

CHAPTER 58

PLAN TERMINATION INSURANCE FOR SINGLE-EMPLOYER PENSION PLANS*

Jack L. VanDerhei

The Pension Benefit Guaranty Corporation (PBGC) is a federal government agency created under Title IV of the Employee Retirement Income Security Act (ERISA). In general, the purposes of the PBGC are to encourage the continuation and maintenance of voluntary private pension plans for the benefit of their participants, provide for the timely and uninterrupted payment of pension benefits to the participants and beneficiaries under all insured plans, and minimize over the long run the premiums charged for the insurance coverage. The PBGC administers two insurance programs: one for single-employer and one for multi-employer pension plans. This chapter deals exclusively with single-employer plans.[1]

In 1974, ERISA established a plan termination insurance program for the majority of defined benefit pension plans in the United States to ensure that pensioners' benefit rights would be protected (up to a maximum amount per month) in the event of a pension plan terminating

---

*Parts of this chapter are based on material that appears in Everett T. Allen, Jr., Joseph J. Melone, Jerry S. Rosenbloom, and Jack L. VanDerhei, *Pension Planning*, 7th ed. (Homewood, Ill.: Richard D. Irwin, 1992).

[1]ERISA, and more significantly, the Multiemployer Pension Plan Amendments Act (MEPPAA) of 1980, had major effects on the PBGC jurisdiction over multiemployer plans, employer liabilities, and the administrative practices of trustees. The MEPPAA has many implications for almost all aspects of multiemployer plans, especially concerning plan termination insurance and employer liabilities.

with unfunded liabilities. In 1986, one of the major defects associated with the original design was corrected when the Single Employer Pension Plan Amendments Act (SEPPAA) changed the insured event from that of, in essence, any plan termination to a termination accompanied by a specified event for the plan sponsor.

This change effectively limited the insurable event to an insufficient termination due to bankruptcy by the sponsor, thereby virtually eliminating the opportunity for an ongoing sponsor to exchange the unfunded vested liabilities of the plan for 30 percent of its net worth (an option existing under the original provisions of ERISA). However, it did nothing to change the premium structure from a flat dollar amount per participant. Congress redressed this shortcoming in part by enacting a *variable-rate premium* structure in 1987 that relates the sponsor's annual premium to the plan's underfunding (as measured on a termination basis). Although this change factors the plan's potential severity into the determination of the annual premium, it falls short of a *risk-related premium* structure that would characterize the insurance if it were written in the private sector. Such a structure would base annual premiums not only on the potential severity but also the probability of an insured event taking place (that is, bankruptcy of a sponsor with an underfunded plan). The new premium system also differs from a free market approach in that it specifies a maximum charge per participant.

PLANS COVERED

The PBGC's single-employer plan termination insurance provisions apply to virtually all defined benefit pension plans. The following material examines the specific plans covered and then describes the type of pension benefits protected by the PBGC's insurance program.

Subject to specific exceptions, ERISA Section 4021(a) requires mandatory coverage of employee pension benefit plans that either affect interstate commerce (and in the case of nonqualified plans, have for five years met the standards for qualified plans) or that are qualified under the Internal Revenue Code (IRC). The following plans are specifically *excluded* from coverage:

1. Individual account plans (for example, money purchase pension plans, profit-sharing plans, thrift and savings plans, and stock bonus plans).

2. Government plans.

3. Certain church plans other than those that have voluntarily opted for coverage.

4. Certain plans established by fraternal societies to which no employer contributions are made.

5. Plans that do not provide for employer contributions after September 2, 1974.

6. Nonqualified deferred compensation plans established for select groups of management or highly compensated employees.

7. Plans established outside of the United States for nonresident aliens.

8. So-called excess benefit plans established and maintained primarily to pay benefits or accrue contributions for a limited group of highly paid employees in excess of the Section 415 limits (described in Chapter 55).

9. Plans established and maintained exclusively for "substantial owners," meaning proprietors, partners with a greater than 10 percent interest in the capital profits of a partnership, or shareholders of a corporation owning, directly or indirectly, more than 10 percent in value of either the voting stock or of all the stock of the corporation.

10. Plans of international organizations exempt from tax under the International Organization Immunities Act.

11. Plans maintained only to comply with workers' compensation, unemployment compensation, or disability insurance laws.

12. Plans established and maintained by labor organizations as described in Section 501(c)(5) of the IRC that do not provide for employer contributions after September 2, 1974.

13. Plans that are defined benefit plans to the extent that they are treated as individual account plans.[2]

14. Any plan established and maintained by professional service employers, provided that there are not, at any time after September 2, 1974, more than 25 active participants in the plan.

---

[2]However, if the assets under a terminating cash balance plan (see Chapter 36) are insufficient to meet the benefit obligation under the plan, the PBGC will assume the unfunded benefits on the same terms as those applicable to traditional defined benefit plans.

For purposes of the last category, a professional service employer means any proprietorship, partnership, corporation, or other association or organization owned or controlled by professional individuals or by executors or administrators of professional individuals, the principal business of which is the performance of professional services.

PLAN TERMINATION DEFINED

The termination of a pension plan should be a clearly identifiable event. Otherwise, it may be difficult to assess if a termination has occurred and, if so, when. Establishing the exact date of termination is important to all parties concerned—the plan sponsor, the plan participants, their beneficiaries, and the PBGC. A plan termination can be voluntary or involuntary. However, the PBGC will not proceed with a voluntary termination of a plan if it would violate the terms and conditions of an existing collective bargaining agreement.[3]

During the first 10 years of PBGC coverage, the insured event for single-employer plan termination insurance was simply the termination of the defined benefit pension plan. Because this event generally is within the control of the sponsor, coupled with the fact that the sponsor's liability to the PBGC was at that time limited to 30 percent of its net worth, several underfunded plans were terminated even though the sponsors continued in existence and in some cases even attempted to establish new pension plans immediately after the original plans were terminated. As the financial condition of the PBGC continued to deteriorate in the first half of the 1980s, several attempts were made to amend legislatively the definition of the insured event. The SEPPAA radically changed these provisions in an attempt to preserve the financial integrity of the system. The following section describes the new circumstances under which the single-employer plan termination insurance applies.

Voluntary Plan Termination

A single-employer plan may be terminated voluntarily only in a standard termination or a distress termination. Disclosure of the appropriate infor-

---

[3]It should be noted that this does not limit the PBGC's authority to proceed with an involuntary termination as described later in this chapter.

mation is provided through a series of PBGC forms known as the Standard Termination Filing and Distress Termination Filing.

Standard Termination

A single-employer plan may terminate under a standard termination if, among other things, the plan is sufficiently funded for benefit liabilities (determined as of the termination date) when the final distribution of assets occurs.

Provided the PBGC has not issued a notice of noncompliance and the plan's assets are sufficient for benefit liabilities when the final distribution occurs, the plan administrator must distribute the plan's assets in accordance with the requirements for allocation of assets under ERISA Section 4044 (described below).

Distress Termination

After receiving the appropriate information, the PBGC must determine whether the necessary distress criteria have been satisfied. Basically, these criteria are met if each person who is a contributing sponsor or a member of the sponsor's controlled group meets the requirements of any of the following:

1. Liquidation in bankruptcy or insolvency proceedings.
2. Reorganization in bankruptcy or insolvency proceedings.[4]
3. Termination required to enable payment of debts while staying in business or to avoid unreasonably burdensome pension costs caused by a declining work force.

If the PBGC determines that the requirements for a distress termination are met, it will determine either that (1) the plan is sufficient for guaranteed benefits or it is unable to make a determination on the basis of the available information, or (2) the plan is sufficient for benefit liabilities or it is unable to make a determination on the basis of the available information. The plan administrator will be notified of the decision, and one of the following types of terminations will be carried out[5]:

---

[4]For this requirement to be met, a bankruptcy court must determine that unless the plan is terminated the sponsor will be unable to pay all its debts pursuant to a plan of reorganization and will be unable to continue in business outside the Chapter 11 reorganization process.

[5]ERISA Sec. 4041(c)(3).

1. In any case in which the PBGC determines that the plan is sufficient for benefit liabilities, the plan administrator must distribute the plan's assets in the same manner as described for a standard termination.
2. In any case in which the PBGC determines that the plan is sufficient for guaranteed benefits, but is unable to determine that the plan is sufficient for benefit liabilities, the plan administrator must distribute the plan's assets in the same manner as described for a standard termination.
3. In any case in which the PBGC determines that it is unable to determine that the plan is sufficient for guaranteed benefits, the PBGC will commence proceedings as though an involuntary termination (described below) were taking place.

The plan administrator must meet certain requirements during the interim period from the time the PBGC is notified to the time a sufficiency determination is made. Essentially, the administrator must

1. Refrain from distributing assets or taking any other actions to carry out the proposed termination.
2. Pay benefits attributable to employer contributions, other than death benefits, only in the form of an annuity.
3. Not use plan assets to purchase from an insurer irrevocable commitments to provide benefits.
4. Continue to pay all benefit liabilities under the plan, but, commencing on the proposed termination date, limit the payment of benefits under the plan to those benefits guaranteed by the PBGC or to which the assets are required to be allocated under ERISA Section 4044 (described below).

When two organizations merge, the resulting single plan does not result in a termination if the new, merged organization assumes responsibility for the plan. Also, under ERISA, a pension plan may not be merged or consolidated with another pension plan, or have its assets transferred to another plan, unless each participant in the prior plan is credited in the successor plan with a benefit at least as great as that which he or she would have received had the old plan terminated.[6]

---

[6]IRC Sec. 401(a)(12).

Involuntary Plan Termination

The PBGC may institute termination proceedings in a U.S. district court in the jurisdiction where the employer does business if it finds that *(a)* the plan does not comply with the minimum funding standards of the IRC; *(b)* the plan is unable to pay benefits when due; *(c)* within the preceding 24 months, and for a reason other than death, a distribution of $10,000 or more has been made to a participant who is the substantial owner of the sponsoring firm and following the distribution there are unfunded liabilities; or *(d)* the eventual loss to the PBGC for the plan may be expected to increase unreasonably if the plan is not terminated. Moreover, the PBGC is required to institute proceedings to terminate a single-employer plan whenever it determines that the plan does not have assets available to pay benefits currently due under the terms of the plan. The PBGC may decide not to seek involuntary termination, even if one of the conditions for such action has occurred, if it deems that it would be in the best interests of those involved not to force termination of the plan.

Reportable Events

The administrator of any covered pension plan is required to report to the PBGC certain events that may indicate possible termination of a pension plan. These reportable events are

1. Inability of the plan to pay benefits when due.
2. A failure to meet the minimum funding standards.
3. Determination that a complete or partial plan termination for tax purposes has occurred.
4. A merger or consolidation of the plan with another plan.
5. Loss of qualified status under the IRC.
6. A plan amendment that decreases the benefits of the participants.
7. If the unfunded vested benefit is at least $250,000, a decrease in active participants of more than 20 percent of the number at the beginning of the plan year, or 25 percent of the number at the beginning of the previous plan year.
8. A distribution of $10,000 or more within a 24-month period to a substantial owner, for reasons other than death, that creates or increases unfunded vested liabilities.

9. Whenever the Department of Labor determines a plan has failed to meet any of the requirements contained in ERISA Title I.

10. If the Department of Labor prescribes an alternative method of compliance for a particular plan or a specific limited group of plans.

11. When a contributing sponsor in a controlled group files for bankruptcy, becomes insolvent, or is in the process of complete liquidation or dissolution.

12. Whenever, as a result of a transfer of assets, a new contributing sponsor emerges which is not a member of the controlled group of the previous contributing sponsor, the contributing sponsor leaves the controlled group, or the contributing sponsor becomes a member of a different controlled group.

13. Any other event the PBGC designates as reportable.[7]

Date of Termination

For purposes of Title IV of ERISA, the termination date of a single-employer plan is one of the following:

1. In the case of a plan terminated in a standard termination, the termination date proposed in the notice of intent to terminate.

2. In the case of a plan terminated in a distress termination, the date established by the plan administrator and agreed to by the PBGC.

3. In the case of an involuntary termination, the date established by the PBGC and agreed to by the plan administrator.

4. In the case of distress or involuntary termination in any case in which no agreement is reached between the plan administrator and the PBGC, the date established by the court.

The date on which the termination of a plan becomes effective is significant for a number of reasons. It not only establishes the date the PBGC assumes legal obligation for the plan's benefits, but also establishes the date for the determination of the employer's possible contingent liability for unfunded benefits (described below). The effective termination date also is important to the participant. It fixes the date on which

---

[7] ERISA Sec. 4043 and PBGC regulations [29 CFP Part 2615].

benefit accruals cease, vesting schedule position is determined, and the phase-in of insurance coverage stops.

Restoration of Plan

If it appears that the pension plan could be continued even though plan termination proceedings have begun, the PBGC may halt the proceedings and take whatever action is necessary to restore the plan.[8]

BENEFITS GUARANTEED

Even though a plan is covered by the PBGC's single-employer plan termination insurance, there is no assurance that all a participant's accrued pension benefit will be paid after the plan's termination. The individual participant (or beneficiary) must first meet three prerequisites before the benefit is guaranteed by the PBGC, and even if the prerequisites are met, the individual may still be subject to specific limitations on the amount of the benefit covered.

Prerequisites for PBGC Guarantees

Subject to the various limits described below, the PBGC guarantees the payment of all nonforfeitable benefits that qualify as a pension benefit other than those accelerated by plan termination. A benefit that becomes nonforfeitable solely because of plan termination is not subject to ERISA benefit guarantees; however, a benefit won't fail to satisfy the PBGC requirement merely because a participant is required to submit a written application, retire, or complete a mandatory waiting period as a condition for receiving pension payments.

There are two additional exceptions to the general rule on forfeitability. First, guaranteed benefits paid to survivor beneficiaries are not deemed to be forfeitable for purposes of the PBGC guarantee merely because the plan provides for termination of benefit payments should the beneficiary remarry or attain a specific age. Second, disability benefits are not deemed forfeitable solely because they end on a participant's recovery.

---

[8]ERISA Sec. 4047.

For a payment to qualify as a pension benefit, it must be payable as an annuity or as one or more payments related to an annuity. Further, the benefit must be payable either to a participant who permanently leaves or has left covered employment or to a surviving beneficiary. It also is necessary that the pension benefit payment provide a substantially level income to the recipient, although the leveling could be accomplished in conjunction with Social Security payments. Under certain circumstances, the PBGC also guarantees annuities payable for total disability[9] and benefits payable in a single installment.[10]

The final requirement for protection under the PBGC guarantee is that the participant or beneficiary be *entitled* to the benefit. This prerequisite is met if any of the following is satisfied:

1. The benefit was in pay status on the date of plan termination.
2. The benefit payable at normal retirement age is an optional benefit under the plan, and the participant elected the optional form of payment before the plan termination date.
3. The participant is actually eligible to receive benefits and could have received them before the plan terminated.
4. The benefit would be payable on the participant's retirement absent a contrary election.
5. The PBGC determines the participant is entitled to the benefit based on the particular circumstances.

Limitation on Amount of Monthly Benefits

There is a limit on the amount of monthly guaranteed benefits insured by the PBGC. The amount is adjusted annually to reflect changes in the Social Security taxable wage base. The original limit was $750 per month, but for plans terminated in 1991 the limit increased to $2,250 per month. The limit is in terms of a single-life annuity commencing at age 65 and without a refund feature. If the benefit is payable at a lower age, it is reduced by actuarial factors denoted by the PBGC. The benefit is not actuarially increased when the participant retires at an age later than 65.

---

[9]PBGC Regulation Sec. 2613.7.

[10]The benefit will not be paid in a single installment, but the PBGC will guarantee the alternative benefit, if any, in the plan that provides for the payment of equal periodic installments for the life of the recipient. PBGC Regulation Sec. 2613.8.

The guaranteed monthly benefit of a participant cannot be greater than his or her average gross monthly income during the five consecutive years of highest earnings (or, if the period is shorter, the time during which he or she was an active participant in the plan).

New or Amended Plans and Benefits

To prevent possible abuses, the insurance covers guaranteed benefits provided those benefits have been in effect under the provisions of the plan for 60 months or longer at the time of plan termination.[11] If benefits are attributable to a plan amendment or to a new plan adopted, the benefits attributable to that amendment or new plan are guaranteed only to the extent of the greater of 20 percent of the amount of such increased or new benefit multiplied by the number of years (up to five) that the plan or amendment has been in effect, or $20 per month multiplied by the number of years (up to five) that the plan or amendment has been in effect.

Payments in Excess of Unfunded Guaranteed Benefits

Participants, beneficiaries, and alternate payees under qualified domestic relations orders (QDROs) under a single-employer plan will be paid a percentage of the plan's unfunded benefit liabilities in excess of PBGC-guaranteed benefits equal to a percentage recovered by the PBGC on the total claim.[12] Amounts will be allocated to participants in accordance with the ERISA Section 4044 asset allocation rules. Generally, the recovery percentage will be determined from past PBGC experience. In the case of large amounts (that is, unfunded benefit liabilities in excess of guaranteed benefits of at least $20 million), data from the particular termination will be used in determining the recovery percentage.

Specifically, the amount is determined by multiplying (1) the "outstanding amount of benefit liabilities" by (2) the applicable "recovery ratio." The "outstanding amount of benefit liabilities" is (1) the value of the benefit liabilities under the plan less (2) the value of the benefit liabilities that would be so determined by only taking into account

---

[11]ERISA Sec. 4022(b)(8).
[12]ERISA Sec. 4022(c).

benefits which are guaranteed or to which assets of the plan are allocated under ERISA Sec. 4044.[13]

In the case of a terminated plan in which the outstanding amount of benefit liabilities is less than $20 million, the "recovery ratio" is the average ratio, with respect to "prior plan terminations" under the plan sponsor liability rules, of the following[14]:

$$\frac{\text{The value of the recovery of the PBGC under the plan sponsor liability rules for the prior plan terminations}}{\text{The amount of unfunded benefit liabilities under the plan as of the termination date of the prior plan terminations}}$$

In the case of a terminated plan for which the outstanding benefit liabilities exceed $20 million, the "recovery ratio" is

$$\frac{\text{The value of the recoveries of the PBGC under the plan sponsor liability rules for the terminated plan}}{\text{The amount of unfunded benefit liabilities under the plan as of the termination date}}$$

For purposes of the above ratios, the "amount of unfunded benefit liabilities" is (1) the value of benefit liabilities under the plan less (2) the current value of the assets of the plan.

Determinations under these rules are to be made by the PBGC. A determination will be binding unless shown by clear and convincing evidence to be unreasonable.

ALLOCATION OF ASSETS ON PLAN TERMINATION

Priority Categories

Plan assets must be allocated to the benefit categories applicable on plan termination under ERISA Sec. 4044. This prevents employers from

---

[13]ERISA Sec. 4001(a).

[14]A "prior plan termination" is a termination of which (1) the PBGC has determined the value of recoveries under the plan sponsor liability rules and (2) notices of intent to terminate were provided after December 31, 1987, and within the five fiscal years of the federal government ending before the year in which the date of the notice of intent to terminate the plan of which the recovery ratio is being determined was provided.

establishing new benefit levels, terminating plans, and allocating existing plan assets to such benefits resulting in the subordination of insured to uninsured benefits. On termination, the assets of a plan must be allocated in the following order of priorities[15]:

1. Employees' voluntary contributions.
2. Employees' mandatory contributions.
3. Annuity payments in pay status at least three years before the termination of the plan (including annuity payments that would have been in pay status for at least three years if the employee had retired then) based on the provisions of the plan in effect during the five years before termination of the plan under which the benefit would be the least.
4. All other insured benefits. This includes benefits that would be insured except for the special limitation with respect to a "substantial owner"; also, the aggregate benefit limitation for individuals does not apply.
5. All other vested, but uninsured, benefits.
6. All other benefits under the plan.

An allocation within a priority category that cannot be covered in full is settled on a pro rata basis, except that subpriorities within a priority category may be provided for by the plan. If there are any assets remaining after satisfaction of all liabilities for accrued benefits, they may be paid to the employer if provided for by the plan provisions.

Reversion of Residual Assets to the Employer

In general, the funds in a qualified pension plan may not be used for purposes other than the exclusive benefit of employees or their beneficiaries prior to the termination of the plan and the satisfaction of all liabilities. However, with the exception of pension plan assets attributable to employee contributions, employers may recapture any residual assets of a terminated single-employer defined benefit pension plan if the following conditions are satisfied:

---

[15]ERISA Sec. 4044.

1. All liabilities of the plan to participants and their beneficiaries have been satisfied.

2. The distribution does not contravene any provision of law.

3. The plan provides for such a distribution in these circumstances.

Residual assets are equal to the plan funds remaining after satisfaction of all liabilities.[16]

The PBGC, Treasury Department, and Department of Labor have issued the following joint implementation guidelines on asset reversions:

1. An employer may not recover any surplus assets until it has fully vested all participants' benefits and has purchased and distributed annuity contracts.

2. If employees are offered lump-sum payments in lieu of future pensions, the amount of the lump-sum distribution must fairly reflect the value of the pension to the individual.

3. An employer that terminates a sufficiently funded defined benefit pension plan may establish a new defined benefit plan covering the same group of employees, granting past-service credit for the period during which an employee was covered by the terminated plan. This is known as a termination/reestablishment, and the successor plan is exempt from the five-year phase-in of benefit guarantees that applies to newly established plans.

4. Spinoff/terminations[17] will not be recognized, and any attempt to recover surplus assets will be treated as a diversion of assets for a purpose other than the exclusive benefit of employees and beneficiaries unless the employees receive timely notice of the event and the following conditions are satisfied:

a. The benefits of all employees must be fully vested and nonforfeitable as of the date of the termination. This also applies to the benefits covered by the ongoing plan.

---

[16]Restrictions on reversions from recently amended plans are specified in ERISA Section 4044(d)(2). The allocation of residual assets attributable to employee contributions is described in ERISA Section 4044(d)(3).

[17]Under a spinoff/termination, the active participants (and their liabilities) are spun off from the original defined benefit plan. Assets are then transferred from the original plan to the new plan in an amount at least equal to the active participants' liabilities. The original plan, which at this point covers only retired and terminated employees, is then terminated, and annuities are used to satisfy the plan's obligations.

b. All accrued benefits must be provided for by the purchase of annuity contracts.

5. In the case of a spinoff/termination and a termination/reestablishment, attempts to recover surplus assets will be treated as a diversion of assets for a purpose other than the exclusive benefit of employees and beneficiaries unless the funding method for the ongoing plans is to be changed by modifying the amortization bases.[18]

6. An employer may not engage in either a termination/reestablishment or spinoff/termination transaction, involving reversion of assets, any earlier than 15 years following any such transaction.

Amounts recovered under a reversion are subject to a 50 percent excise tax.[19] This penalty is reduced to 20 percent if (1) 25 percent of the otherwise recoverable reversion is transferred to another qualified retirement plan that covers at least 95 percent of the active participants of the terminated plan, (2) 20 percent of the otherwise recoverable reversion is used to provide pro rata increases in the benefits accrued by participants under the terminated plan, or (3) the employer is in Chapter 7 bankruptcy liquidation.

If the employer adopts a plan amendment increasing terminated defined benefit plan benefits, the 25 percent cushion is reduced dollar for dollar by the present value of the increase. These benefit increases must satisfy the generally applicable qualification requirements, such as the nondiscrimination rules described in Chapter 55.

Compliance with the 20 percent pro rata increase option requires that increased benefits must be provided to all qualified participants. This includes active participants, participants and beneficiaries receiving benefits on the termination date, and other participants who retain rights under the plan and who terminate employment (or plan eligibility) during a period starting three years before the termination date and ending on the final asset distribution date.[20] Beneficiaries of this last group also are eligible if they have a vested plan benefit. Employees who stop working

---

[18]The modification must be in accordance with IRC Section 412(b)(4). Details of the modification are provided in PBGC News Release 84-23.

[19]Prior to the Omnibus Budget Reconciliation Act of 1990, the tax rate had been 15 percent. In addition to the increased penalty, this legislation allowed employers to use surplus pension assets to prefund retiree health plans through 401(h) accounts. See Chapter 59 for more details.

[20]The assets allocated to increase the benefit of nonactive participants cannot exceed 40 percent of the total.

before the plan termination date and receive a lump-sum distribution are not entitled to benefit increases.

LIABILITIES ON PLAN TERMINATION

Distributee Liability-Recapture

When a plan terminates, the termination trustee is authorized to recover for the benefit of the pension plan certain payments received by a participant within the three-year period prior to plan termination. The "recoverable amount" is the sum of all payments made to the participant in excess of $10,000 made during any consecutive 12-month period within three years before termination or, if less, the amount he or she would have received as a monthly benefit under a single-life annuity commencing at age 65.[21] Payments to a disabled participant and payments made after or on account of the death of a participant are not subject to recovery. The PBGC can totally or partially waive any amount otherwise entitled to be recaptured whenever recapture would result in substantial economic hardship to a participant or his or her beneficiaries.

Employer Liability

During the legislative process leading up to the enactment of ERISA, concern was expressed that in the absence of appropriate safeguards under an insurance system, an employer might establish or amend a plan to provide substantial benefits with the realization that its funding might be inadequate to pay the benefits called for. Such an employer might, it was argued, rely on the insurance as a backup enabling it to be more generous in promised pension benefits to meet labor demands than would be the case if it knew that the benefit would have to be paid for entirely out of the assets of the employer. On the other hand, it was clear that the imposition of heavy obligations on employers would discourage provisions for adequate pension plans.

To deal with these competing considerations, the decision was made to impose on the employer a limited liability to reimburse the insurance

---

[21]ERISA Sec. 4045.

system for a portion of the payment that must be made by the PBGC in satisfaction of its obligation if the employer plan fails. Unfortunately, the limited liability was much smaller than the amount of unfunded benefit for many sponsors, and several plans in this category were terminated to take advantage of this so-called pension put.

The SEPPAA substantially modified the computation of the sponsor's liability on termination, and the Omnibus Budget Reconciliation Act of 1987 made further modifications the following year. Currently, in any case in which a single-employer plan is terminated in a distress termination, or an involuntary termination is instituted by the PBGC, any person who is, on the termination date, a contributing sponsor of the plan or a member of such a contributing sponsor's controlled group will incur a liability under Sec. 4062 of ERISA. This liability consists of two components:

1. The liability to the PBGC.
2. The liability to the Sec. 4042 trustee (described below).

Although special rules pertain to a case in which it is discovered that the plan is unable to pay guaranteed benefits after the authorized commencement of termination,[22] the following section defines the rules generally applying to the two components of the sponsor's liability and the required means of payment.

Liability to the PBGC

The liability to the PBGC consists of the total amount of the unfunded benefit liabilities[23] (as of the termination date) to all participants and beneficiaries under the plan, together with interest (at a reasonable rate) calculated from the termination date in accordance with regulations prescribed by the PBGC.

The total amount of the liability is paid to the PBGC, which, as described in the "Payments in Excess of Unfunded Guaranteed Benefits" section of this chapter, pays out a portion of unfunded benefit liabilities in excess of the unfunded guaranteed benefits based on the total value of the PBGC's recovery with respect to the total liability of the employer.

---

[22]ERISA Sec. 4062(b)(1)(B).

[23]Benefit liabilities are defined in the "Standard Termination" section of this chapter.

Amounts paid to participants are allocated in accordance with Sec. 4044 as described in the "Priority Categories" section of this chapter.

The liability to the PBGC is generally due as of the termination date. The PBGC and any person liable for payment may also agree to alternative arrangements for the satisfaction of the liability.

Liability to the Section 4042 Trustee

The liability to a Sec. 4042 trustee for the sponsoring employer and each member of its controlled group consists of the outstanding balance (accumulated with interest from the termination date) of the following:

1. The accumulated funding deficiency of the plan, modified to include the amount of any increase that would result if all pending applications for waivers of the minimum funding standard and for extensions of the amortization period were denied and if no additional contributions were made.
2. The amount of waived funding deficiencies.
3. The amount of decreases in the minimum funding standard account.

Determination of Net Worth

In general, the collective net worth for purposes of determining the liability to the PBGC consists of the sum of the individual net worths of all persons who have individual net worths greater than zero and who are contributing sponsors of the terminated plan or members of their controlled groups. The net worth of a person is determined on whatever basis best reflects, in the determination of the PBGC, the current status of the person's operations and prospects at the time chosen for determining the net worth of the person. The net worth is increased by the amount of any transfers of assets made by the pension that are determined by the PBGC to be improper under the circumstance. Determinations of net worth are made as of a day chosen by the PBGC during the 120-day period ending with the termination date. Net worth is computed without regard to termination liabilities.

Liability of Substantial and Multiple Employers

A liability applies to all employers, other than multiemployer plans terminating after April 29, 1980, who maintain a plan under which more than one employer makes contributions. The liability also attaches to all employers who, at any time within the five plan years preceding the date of plan termination, made contributions under the plan. The liability is allocated among the employers in the ratio of their required contributions for the last five years prior to termination.

If the withdrawing employer prefers, a bond may be furnished to the PBGC in an amount not exceeding 150 percent of its liability. The bond must be issued by a corporate surety acceptable on federal bonds under the authority granted by the Secretary of the Treasury.

PBGC Lien for Employer Liability
To the extent an employer liability is not satisfied and the amount does not exceed 30 percent of the collective net worth of the sponsor and its controlled group, the amount of the liability (including interest) is a lien in favor of the PBGC upon all property and rights to property, whether real or personal, belonging to the employer. The lien is in the nature of a tax lien that supersedes the liens of other creditors of the corporation.

PREMIUMS

Although Congress corrected several of the major design flaws in the single-employer plan termination insurance system with the passage of SEPPAA, there were still lingering doubts concerning the equity of a premium structure based solely on a flat-rate premium per participant. Therefore, Congress mandated that the PBGC prepare a study on several issues relating to the premium structure. On the basis of their findings, the PBGC proposed a variable-rate premium structure that added an additional premium charge based on the difference between the plan liabilities and the plan assets. This basic concept was incorporated into the Omnibus Budget Reconciliation Act of 1987 and later modified by the Omnibus Budget Reconciliation Act of 1990.

For plan years beginning after 1990, the single-employer flat-rate per-participant premium is $19. An additional premium of $9 per $1,000 of unfunded vested benefits, with a maximum per-participant additional premium of $53, is also required of underfunded plans.[24] The contribut-

---

[24]For purposes of determining the value of vested benefits, the interest rate is equal to 80 percent of the yield per annum on 30-year Treasury securities for the month preceding the month in which the plan year begins.

ing sponsor or plan administrator must pay the premiums imposed by the PBGC. If the contributing sponsor of any plan is a member of a controlled group, each member is jointly and severally liable for any premiums.

SECURITY RULES FOR UNDERFUNDED PLANS

If a single-employer defined benefit plan adopts an amendment that increases current liability under the plan, and if the funded current liability percentage of the plan in the year in which the amendment takes effect is less than 60 percent (including the amount of the unfunded current liability[25] under the plan attributable to the plan amendment), the contributing sponsor and members of the controlled group must provide security (e.g., a bond) to the plan. The amount of the security required is the excess over $10 million of the lesser of:

1. The amount of additional plan assets that would be necessary to increase the funded current liability percentage under the plan to 60 percent, including the amount of the unfunded current liability under the plan attributable to the plan amendment.
2. The amount of the increase in current liability under the plan attributable to the plan amendment.

---

[25]In computing unfunded current liability, the unamortized portion of the unfunded old liability amount as of the close of the plan year is not taken into account.

CHAPTER 59

WELFARE BENEFITS FOR RETIREES

Richard Ostuw

Almost all large companies provide life insurance and health care benefits for their retired employees. Because most of the U.S. work force is employed by small- to medium-sized companies, however, only a minority of workers is currently eligible for postretirement welfare benefits.

Many employers began providing postretirement benefits when their retiree populations were small and their costs were low. Costs have grown tremendously since then. As a result, companies are paying close attention to their retiree benefit programs and are attempting to ensure that they meet specific objectives, including the following:

- Protecting retirees against the cost of unbudgetable medical expenses and providing a modest life insurance benefit to cover burial expenses.
- Promoting cost-effective use of medical care and discouraging the use of unnecessary care.
- Ensuring that employer contributions make the program competitive with that of other employers and that the employee contributions are affordable.

In the following pages we will review current practice with respect to retiree benefits, focusing primarily on medical benefits.

CURRENT TRENDS AND ISSUES

Employers have begun to reexamine their retiree welfare benefit programs. Many will redefine their commitments to reduce the cost to an affordable level. This activity has been generally prompted by benefit cost increases while companies are trying to become more cost efficient. The study of the Financial Accounting Standards Board (FASB) of possible changes in accounting rules has accelerated this review. The new rules were published in December 1990 as Financial Accounting Standard No. 106 (FAS 106). Many more employers will modify these benefits in the next few years. Companies will attempt to strike the optimum balance between satisfying the needs of employees and controlling the company's costs. The specific steps will vary from employer to employer but may include

- Revisions in the definition of covered expenses.
- Increases in employee contribution, especially for short-service retirees and for dependent coverage.
- Limits on the dollar amount of employer contribution.
- Greater use of managed-care techniques.

Employers will have to address the following issues in their decision to retain or modify their current plans:

- Should we offer a plan to retirees?
- What benefits provisions should the plan include? Should the medical plan, for example, have a low deductible and high co-insurance or vice versa?
- How should the premium cost be shared between the company and employees?
- How should retiree welfare benefits be integrated with other components of the retirement program?
- What special grandfather or transition rules, if any, should apply?
- What are the appropriate elements of the expensing policy?
- How should the plan cost be funded?

LIFE INSURANCE

In general, retirees' death benefit needs are less than those of active employees and are met to some extent by survivor-income benefits under the pension plan and Social Security or by significant savings or profit-sharing balances at retirement. Many employers also provide some form of retiree life insurance, and some provide a modest death benefit through the pension plan.

Benefit Design

Life insurance for active employees typically takes the form of a basic employer-paid benefit amount that can be supplemented with optional employee-paid insurance. For retirees, the life insurance benefit is usually a flat dollar amount—generally in the range of $3,000 to $20,000—that the employer may update from time to time for new retirees. Ad hoc increases for current retirees are unusual. Another common approach, particularly for salaried employees, is to express the postretirement life insurance schedule as a percentage of the employee's final preretirement life insurance amount or final preretirement salary. Some employers reduce the benefit amount during retirement. They might, for example, reduce life insurance of two times salary for active employees by 20 percent per year during retirement to an ultimate level of 20 percent of the preretirement benefit—i.e., 40 percent of final pay. Such a benefit may also have a modest postretirement coverage maximum of perhaps $20,000.

Group universal life programs (GULP) have become more common. They provide a flexible vehicle for employees to tailor the amount of insurance to their needs, reflect changes in their needs over time, and prefund postretirement costs as desired. For a detailed discussion of group universal life programs, see Chapter 9 of the *Handbook.*

Cost

Growth in the size of the retiree population—exacerbated in many companies by downsizing—has increased the cost of postretirement benefits substantially. Nearly all employers provided coverage on a pay-as-you-go basis, but FAS 106 requires that they recognize the cost of these benefits on a pension-style expensing basis.

On such an advance-expensing basis, the cost of postretirement life insurance is typically about 0.5 percent or less of the active employee payroll. In those companies that provide significant postretirement life insurance (such as two times pay without reduction), however, the advance-expensing cost can approach 2 percent of payroll.

HEALTH BENEFITS

Few employers provided medical coverage to retirees before 1965 because the cost of doing so was prohibitive. When Medicare became effective in 1966, however, companies realized they could supplement Medicare coverage for their retirees at a modest cost. Over the years, the share of medical expenses covered by Medicare has diminished— although Medicare is still the primary payer for retirees—and the benefits provided by these employers have become more and more liberal. Thus, what was once low-cost postretirement medical coverage has become enormously expensive.

Benefit Design

Retirees usually receive the same medical benefits as active employees until they reach age 65 and become eligible for Medicare. At that point, their employer-provided benefits are coordinated with Medicare in one of two ways:

- The employer plan continues to provide the same benefits structure, but those benefits are offset by Medicare payments.
- Plan coverage is limited to expenses that are not paid by Medicare. This Medicare fill-in approach often is called MediGap or MediFill coverage.

Under the Medicare fill-in approach, the employer plan might pay all or part of the following hospital expenses for its retirees:

- The first level of expenses for each hospital admission, i.e., the Medicare Part A deductible ($652 in 1992).
- The Medicare copayment amounts beginning on the 61st day of hospitalization ($163 in 1992).
- Copayment amounts during the lifetime reserve days ($326 in 1992).
- The cost of hospital care extending beyond the period covered by Medicare.

Similarly, the employer plan may pay all or part of the expenses for physician and other nonhospital services not reimbursed by Medicare Part

B. It also may cover all or part of the expenses commonly excluded by both parts of Medicare, such as prescription drugs and private nursing. Few plans cover custodial care in a nursing home.

We can use the Medicare Part A deductible to illustrate two methods of updating retiree medical coverage. Under one approach, the employer plan defines covered expense as the Medicare Part A deductible. When the Part A deductible amount increases, the employer plan automatically fills the gap. Under the other approach, the employer specifies a coverage amount (such as $500) and increases that amount only by plan amendment. The latter approach gives the employer the ability to control the impact of inflation and Medicare changes on its plan and its costs.

Liberal Medicare fill-in plans virtually eliminate out-of-pocket medical expenses for retirees; more restrictive plans may provide only modest benefits. For example, some plans do not cover hospital stays beyond the Medicare limit, physicians' fees not fully covered by Medicare, prescription drugs, and nursing care.

By its terms, Medicare appears to reimburse 80 percent of physician's fees after a modest deductible ($100 in 1992). In actual practice, however, the reimbursement level has been much lower—as low as 50 percent—because of Medicare's low level of allowed charges. Most employer plans define "reasonable and customary" physician fees as those charged by about 90 percent of physicians in the area—the 90th percentile. Medicare's reasonable and customary fees were set at a lower level and are increased on the basis of general price increases (the overall Consumer Price Index). Because physicians' fees have risen significantly faster than overall prices; Medicare fee limits have fallen further and further behind actual doctors' fees. The change in Medicare fees to the Resource Based Relative Value Scale (RBRVS) and lower balance billing limits significantly reduce the retiree's share of the cost and, therefore, the cost under the employer's medical plan.

Eligibility

In the typical retiree benefit program, eligibility rules for postretirement health care and life insurance benefits follow the employer's pension plan definition of retirement. The most common such definition is termination of employment after attainment of age 55 and 10 years of active service. An employee hired at age 40, for example, first becomes eligible for retirement at age 55; a person hired at age 50 becomes eligible at age 60.

Some plans impose no minimum service requirement for employees who terminate employment at or after age 65.

Employees may also be eligible for retirement after 30 years of service regardless of age, or upon attaining a specified number of years of age plus service. The "Rule of 80," for example, would be satisfied by any combination of age and service that equals or exceeds 80. This approach is common for both unionized and salaried employees in industries with a strong union presence.

These eligibility rules are very liberal, considering the value of lifetime medical benefits and the potentially short working careers of some covered retirees. Few employers impose more restrictive eligibility requirements, however. For one thing, they are concerned about meeting employee needs. For another, many of them are only beginning to recognize the true cost of providing these benefits.

Nearly all retiree medical plans extend coverage to the spouses and children of retirees as those relationships are defined in the active employee plan. Some plans are more restrictive, however, and may, for example, exclude the spouses of marriages that occur after employees retire.

Employee Contributions

According to TPF&C's Employee Benefit Information Center, the prevalence of contributory plans for retiree medical coverage among large employers is approximately as follows:

	Percentage of Plans Requiring Employee Contributions	
	Until Age 65	*Age 65 and Later*
Employee coverage	70%	60%
Dependent coverage	80	65

In general, it is more common for employers to require contributions from retirees than from active employees. Post–age-65 retiree contributions cover a greater portion of total plan cost than do contributions by pre-65 retirees or active employees. Employee-pay-all coverage is rare for active employees, for example, but not for retirees over 65.

Employee contributions may represent a percentage of plan cost or a flat dollar amount as summarized below:

Percentage of Cost

Under this approach, often used for post-65 coverage, retirees are required to contribute a specified percentage of the expected plan cost for the coming year—usually 20 percent to 33 percent but sometimes as much as 100 percent. If a plan required a 25 percent employee contribution and plan costs were expected to be $80 per month per covered person, for example, retirees would have to contribute $20 per month.

Dollar Amounts

It is more usual for employers to require specified dollar contributions. Although such an approach may reflect a cost-sharing policy, the underlying percentage of plan cost generally is not disclosed to employees or retirees. Employers using this approach usually update dollar amounts every three to five years. Nonetheless, updates generally have failed to keep pace with increases in plan costs. Employers often procrastinate in making changes that employees will view as benefit reductions. Further, planning for and implementing such updates is very time-consuming.

The percentage approach is becoming more popular because it allows employers to update contribution amounts without creating the perception of a benefit take-away. This is especially important in view of recent court decisions limiting employers' ability to reduce retiree benefits.

Employee contributions generally are payable by deduction from the employee's pension check, although in some companies retirees send a monthly check to the employer. Coverage is terminated if payment is not made on a timely basis.

Medical Plan Design Elements

Medical plan design elements are the same for retirees and active employees. There are key differences between the two groups, however. For example:

• Age differences make retiree medical costs substantially higher than those of active employees. The average annual cost per person for retirees under age 65 commonly is about two times the average cost for active employees. Both the frequency and intensity of health care increase with age.

• Certain health conditions are more common among the elderly, such as hearing impairments and the need for various prostheses.

• Elderly individuals require more time to recover from serious medical conditions and therefore are much more likely to need institutional care after a hospital discharge. Depending on the situation, that care may include extensive medical attention or may be largely custodial.

• Medicare assumes the bulk of the cost of hospital and physician services after age 65. The relative share of employer plan costs by type of expense for retirees over 65 thus differs from the cost share for active employees.

Covered Services

As with active-employee plans, retiree medical plans generally cover a wide rage of care and treatment, including hospital care, surgery, doctors' visits, therapy, and prescription drugs. Typically excluded form coverage are routine physical examinations, hearing and vision care, cosmetic surgery, and experimental procedures.

New developments in technology will have a substantial impact on medical costs for retirees. How the plan defines experimental procedures and how the administrator updates the rules will have significant consequences.

Benefit Levels

During the 1980s, many employers changed from "basic plus major medical" programs to comprehensive plans for both active employees and retirees. The two types of coverage are summarized below:

Basic Plus Major Medical. Basic benefits provide 100 percent reimbursement of covered expenses for certain types of services. Examples might include:

• Hospital inpatient services for up to 180 days.
• Surgery.
• Diagnostic X-ray and laboratory procedures.
• Emergency treatment for an accident.

The major medical component supplements basic benefits but reimburses less than the full expense—usually 80 percent of the expense in excess of an annual deductible of between $100 and $200 per person.

Comprehensive.   The typical plan pays 80 percent of expenses for all services, with an annual deductible of perhaps $200 per person, until the individual incurs out-of-pocket expenses of a specified amount— perhaps $1,000 in a year (taking into account the 20 percent coinsurance and the deductible). The plan pays 100 percent of expenses thereafter.

Employers have shifted to comprehensive programs for a number of reasons, including the following:

• Medical costs almost doubled between 1982 and 1984 for many employers. Many companies that were unable or unwilling to absorb the full increase changed to a comprehensive program to reduce plan costs.

• Basic/major medical programs provide no financial incentives for patients to avoid costly in-hospital treatment and, in fact, often provide an incentive to use inpatient care rather than less expensive outpatient care. The change to a comprehensive plan redefines the reimbursement basis to establish financial incentives for using medical care more efficiently.

• Relatively low-cost services such as laboratory work and treatment for accidents add up to a significant portion of basic/major medical plan costs. Comprehensive plans shift this budgetable cost to the employee through application of the annual deductible.

The following table illustrates the cost impact of a switch from a basic/major medical plan to a comprehensive medical plan for the active-employee group and for retirees under age 65.

Annual Plan Cost for Employee Coverage	Active Employees	Retirees Under 65
Basic/major medical	$1,500	$3,000
Comprehensive	1,200	2,550
Cost reduction		
Amount	$ 300	$ 450
Percentage	20%	15%

Although the dollar amount of savings is larger for the retiree group, the reduction represents a smaller percentage of plan costs. The difference is due largely to the greater frequency of high-cost cases among retirees. The following examples show how the reimbursement percentage varies by level of expense for a plan with a $100 deductible, 80 percent reimbursement, and a $1,000 out-of-pocket limit:

	Expense A	Expense B	Expense C
Charge	$100	$1,000	$10,000
Benefit	0	720	9,000
Reimbursement	0%	72%	90%

Utilization Review

In addition to or in lieu of the change to comprehensive coverage, many employers have established utilization review programs or incentive arrangements to minimize the use of unneeded medical care. Such provisions can be summarized as follows:

• *Reimbursement differences.* The plan pays a higher level of reimbursement (such as 100 percent instead of 80 percent) for types or locations of services presumed to be more cost-efficient, including preadmission testing and outpatient surgery. The benefit differential may apply only in certain circumstances—for specific surgical procedures identified by the employer, for example.

• *Review requirements.* The plan pays a higher reimbursement when there is a pretreatment review such as a second surgical opinion or hospital preadmission review.

The goal of these incentives is to reduce the use—and cost—of unnecessary care or to substitute less costly forms of care. To achieve these savings, a plan will incur some added cost in the form of administration expenses and more liberal benefits for selected services. For active employees and retirees who are not eligible for Medicare, the employer will experience a net cost reduction. There may be a net cost increase to the employer for retirees covered by Medicare. This is because the employer pays administration expenses and the cost of benefit increases while

Medicare enjoys most of the savings from reduced in-hospital care or surgery.

Defined Dollar Benefit Approach

Under a traditional retiree medical plan, the employer ''promises'' to provide a stated level of benefits (with the possibility of changes in the benefit provisions). The key element is the *benefits level*. Under a new approach, the key element is the *dollar amount* the employer will pay toward the cost of the benefits. The employer contribution is the defined dollar benefit (DDB). Here is an illustration of how the DDB approach might work:

- The employer offers a medical plan with benefit features comparable to those offered to active employees.
- The employer contributes up to $100 per month per person for coverage until age 65 and $50 per month thereafter. The retiree must pay the balance of the plan cost. The employer contribution is available only as a subsidy toward the cost of the medical plan.
- The employer updates benefit features from time to time and will consider ad hoc increases in the defined dollar benefit.

The defined dollar benefit approach has these advantages:

- The employer has full control over future increases in its benefit costs because it determines the amount and timing of any increases in its contributions. (Employee concern about benefit adequacy and competition may create pressure for ad hoc increases, however.)
- Benefit features can be updated more easily than in traditional programs. This is because the employer's promise involves its contribution—not the benefits themselves—and any reduction in the benefit level will directly reduce employee contributions.
- Because benefit costs are communicated, employees will better understand the substantial value of the benefits they receive.
- The approach facilitates service-related benefit coverage, which is discussed below. In the above illustration, for example, the $100 and $50 employer contribution amounts could be prorated for service of less than 25 years.
- Retirees can be offered choices in how to apply their defined dollar benefit.

Service Recognition

The cost of retiree medical benefits is prompting more and more employers to tie employee contributions to service. Employee contributions might vary with service as follows:

Years of Service	Retiree Contribution As Percentage of Plan Cost
10–14	70%
15–19	55
20–24	40
25–29	25
30+	10

In this example, the employer contribution is approximately 3 percent of the plan cost for each year of employee service.

It is also possible to vary the benefit level by length of service, although this approach is generally more difficult to administer than one that uses variable employee contributions.

FINANCING

The three key considerations in financing retiree benefits are expense recognition, level of cost, and the funding vehicle.

Expense Recognition

Nearly all employers have recognized the cost of retiree welfare benefits on a pay-as-you-go basis. In a sense, this is a historical accident. When employers began providing these benefits, they believed they were making a year-by-year commitment rather than a lifetime promise. They did not consider postretirement benefits to be a form of deferred compensation earned during an employee's working career. This was in sharp contrast to prevailing views applicable to postretirement income benefits, i.e., pension plans. Court decisions (discussed below) and changes in accounting rules have now prompted many employers to change their views.

The Financial Accounting Standards Board (FASB) has been considering the issue of how retiree welfare benefits should be expensed for a number of years. The key question is this: Should companies be required to recognize the expense of postretirement welfare benefits during the working careers of employees and charge such amounts against current earnings? As a first step, FASB Statement 81 required the disclosure of the amount expensed for these benefits and the basis for expensing. Pay-as-you-go cost recognition still was permitted.

The FASB has published new accounting rules (FAS 106) that require a pension-type expensing approach for medical benefits on the ground that such benefits represent a form of deferred compensation whose cost should be charged against earnings during the period when employees are productive. The effective date of the new rules is for fiscal years beginning after December 15, 1992. Under FAS 106, companies must recognize the accruing cost of postretirement coverage during the working years of employees and must disclose specific information about the plan, the aggregate value of accrued benefits, and the actuarial assumptions used to calculate the results.

Cost

On a pay-as-you-go basis, retiree medical plan costs typically are about $2,500 per year per person until age 65 and $850 per year thereafter. Overall, the average cost per retiree (including dependents) commonly is about $1,500 per year. (The cost for individual employers may be significantly higher or lower.) The present value of these costs depends on employee age at retirement and, of course, on the assumptions for the interest discount rate, mortality rates, and inflation. Representative amounts are as follows:

Age at Retirement	Present Value of Medical Benefits (per retiree)	
	Single Coverage	Family Coverage
55	$55,000	$110,000
60	$35,000	70,000
65	$20,000	40,000

Roughly 60 percent of the cost is attributable to retired employees and 40 percent to their dependents. By comparison, the cost commonly is split 50–50 between active employees and their dependents, reflecting the larger average family size of these employees. Relatively few retirees have children who are still eligible under the medical plan.

Pay-as-you-go costs will rise in the future as a result of

- Price increases measured by the Consumer Price Index (CPI).
- The introduction of new medical technology and new procedures.
- Changes in the frequency or utilization of health care or in the mix of services.

The health care share of the gross national product (GNP) is now more than 12 percent, compared with 9.1 percent in 1980 and 7.3 percent in 1970. Continued growth of national medical care costs at the pace we have witnessed in the last 20 years would result in an unaffordable level of costs. It is not likely that society will not allow the health care share of the GNP to reach 25 percent.

Expensing annual retiree benefit costs on a pension-type basis during the working years of employees under FAS 106 has these results for representative groups of employees:

	Cost as Percent of Payroll
Normal cost	2 – 3%
Amortization of unrecognized past service liability	2 – 3
Interest on past service liability	3 – 5
Total Expense	7 – 11

Funding

Several funding alternatives are available to employers who want to recognize the cost of retiree benefits on a pension-type basis. These include the following:

- *Book reserve.* The employer accrues the cost on its financial statement and retains the assets within the organization.

• *Voluntary Employees' Beneficiary Association (VEBA)* under Section 501(c)(9) of the Internal Revenue Code. The employer contributes funds to an independent trust from which benefits subsequently are paid. The Deficit Reduction Act of 1984 (DEFRA) severely restricts the use of VEBAs for retiree health plans by limiting the amount of tax-deductible contributions to such trusts and subjecting the investment income to the Unrelated Business Income Tax. Neither of these problems applies to prefunding of retiree life insurance or to the welfare plans of a not-for-profit organization.

• *Pension plans.* A special account for medical benefits may be maintained as part of a pension plan under Section 401(h) of the Internal Revenue Code. Within limits, contributions to the account are deductible when made and investment income is exempt from tax even after DEFRA. Under certain circumstances, it may be possible to establish such an account under a profit-sharing plan.

• *Insurance contracts.* Insurance contracts can be used in either of two ways to prefund retiree welfare benefits. Assets can be accumulated in an insurance continuation fund for subsequent payment of pay-as-you-go costs. Paid-up insurance also may be used. Under the latter approach, a one-time premium is paid to fund benefits for the lifetime of the retirees. These insurance approaches may be used for either life or medical insurance but are much more common for the former.

• *Union funds.* Under many multiple-employer union-negotiated plans, contributions are made to a Taft-Hartley fund. The fund is responsible for the benefits to retirees.

Legal Issues

Employee communication materials often describe current postretirement welfare benefits and include a statement reserving the employer's right to modify or terminate the overall benefit plan. Many employers, however, fail to communicate their right to reduce benefits or fail to reserve this right consistently, omitting it in certain editions of the summary plan description or in such ancillary vehicles as employee newsletters or preretirement counseling materials.

Employer attempts to reduce or eliminate medical benefits for current retirees have resulted in significant litigation. (It is interesting to note that no case has involved the issue of whether such actions improperly infringed on the rights of active employees.) Following is a summary of several representative cases:

• In *U.A.W.* v. *Yardman,* the employer attempted to terminate medical coverage for retirees. A federal appeals court held that the employer was obligated to continue the benefits because it had promised coverage to retirees. Once an individual achieved the *status* of retiree, the benefits could be discontinued only if the individual no longer held that status. Thus, the employer was obligated to continue lifetime coverage for retirees.

• In *Eardman* v. *Bethlehem Steel,* the employer attempted to reduce the level of benefits and increase the level of required contributions by retirees. A federal district court ruled that, in effect, the employer had given up its right to make such changes by omitting the required language in written communications and by making oral promises to retirees at exit interviews. The company and its retirees subsequently reached a compromise whereby benefit reductions and increased contributions were implemented but the company promised not to attempt such changes again.

• In the case of *In Re White Farm Equipment,* a federal district court went further than the above cases. It concluded that benefits were vested and could not be reduced or eliminated regardless of any statements by the employer. On appeal, however, this reasoning was not accepted and the case was returned to the lower court for review on its merits.

In another situation, LTV terminated its retiree welfare benefits when it filed for protection under Chapter 11 of the bankruptcy laws. It restored the benefits under great pressure from Congress and others. Congress then legislated a mandatory continuation of coverage under certain situations for companies in Chapter 11.

These cases have been widely reported and have received a great deal of attention. Many other employers have made changes in their medical benefits for current retirees, usually concurrent with and similar to changes in their active-employee plans, but these actions have not been reported by the press because there has been no litigation.

At this time, neither the employer's ability to modify retiree benefits nor the employee's rights under the plans are fully defined. Further litigation—and perhaps legislation—probably will help clarify the situation.

CHAPTER 60

MULTIEMPLOYER PLANS

Cynthia J. Drinkwater

Multiemployer plans provide benefits to employees in unionized industries such as the apparel trades, professional and consumer services, entertainment industry, transportation, and construction. Often these employees are highly mobile, working for several employers a year. If it were not for multiemployer plans, which are arranged by industry (or related industries) on a local, regional, or national level, such employees would be forced to switch plans as often as they do employment. Benefit coverage would be haphazard and incomplete.

Within the structure of a multiemployer plan, employers contribute to one trust fund from which benefits are paid to all eligible employees. Staff of a separate, centralized office perform administrative functions such as determination of eligibility, maintenance of participant records, claim processing, and payment of benefits. Contributing employers thus avoid the details of administering and delivering benefits. To some extent, contributing employers also enjoy economies of scale inherent in the maintenance of a common plan versus numerous separate ones. This accounts for multiemployer plans maintained even by employers with relatively more permanent work forces, such as those in the retail trade industry.

As with collectively bargained single-employer plans, employer contributions to (or, less frequently, benefits of) multiemployer plans are negotiated between the respective employees and employers and formalized contractually in collective bargaining agreements. Unlike single-employer collectively bargained plans, which are likely to be administered unilaterally by the employer, multiemployer plan responsibility falls upon a board of trustees consisting of an equal number of labor and management representatives. The board of trustees is charged with making plan decisions in the interests of plan participants and beneficiaries without regard to the labor or management constituency that designates the board.

It is not always logical or feasible to apply benefit knowledge appropriate for a benefit plan designed, funded, and administered by one employer to a multiemployer plan. In some areas, such as withdrawal liability, plan termination, and plan insolvency, special multiemployer plan rules have been established. In other areas, such as plan qualification, most requirements apply to multiemployer plans as well as single-employer plans, but sometimes multiemployer plan practice is more liberal than what is specified in the requirements, or the requirements are at odds with the multiemployer plan structure. And at times, employee benefits law has been modified to fit the multiemployer plan framework as well as that of the single employer plan, as evidenced by amendments to the Consolidated Omnibus Budget Reconciliation Act of 1985 (COBRA).

The unique features of a multiemployer plan—mobile employees, numerous contributing employers, a common trust fund with centralized administration, collectively bargained benefits and a joint board of trustees— have the potential to complicate the responsibilities of trustees, plan administrators, and professionals who carry out the day-to-day tasks of running a plan. Yet, advantages of multiemployer plans to both employees and employers is evidenced by their continued presence in the United States for nearly 45 years. Multiemployer pension plans in 1985 alone numbered approximately 3,000 plans, with about 6,500,000 active participants.[1] Multiemployer plans have been and will remain an important part of the employee benefits environment.

MULTIEMPLOYER PLAN DEFINED

Two characteristics of an employee benefit plan make it multiemployer in nature: the number of contributing employers and a collective bargaining origin. As indicated by its name, more than one employer contributes to

---

[1]U.S. Department of Labor, Pension and Welfare Benefits Administration, *Trends in Benefits,* ed. John A. Turner and Daniel J. Beller, 1989, Table 4.1, 53. The number of plans includes both multiemployer and multiple-employer collectively bargained plans, which elected not to be treated as multiemployer plans under the Multiemployer Pension Plan Amendments Act of 1980, as well as both defined contribution and defined benefit plans.

a multiemployer plan. Employers contribute to the plan pursuant to a collective bargaining agreement (or agreements) with one or more employee organizations. Typically, these employee organizations are unions.

Employer contributions to multiemployer plans are negotiated through the collective bargaining process and fixed in the collective bargaining agreement—usually on a cents-per-hour, unit-of-production, or percentage-of-compensation basis. A distinguishing feature of a multiemployer defined benefit plan is that it actually resembles both a defined benefit and a defined contribution plan—although employer contributions are fixed, participants' benefits are based on a formula. Since contributions to multiemployer plans are calculated on some basis of work performed, a multiemployer plan's income is dependent on the level of economic activity in participants' industries. Contributions and/or benefits, therefore, are adjusted periodically to reflect the actual experience of the plan.

The description "multiple employer" plan is sometimes incorrectly interchanged with "multiemployer" plan. A multiple employer plan has only the first feature of a multiemployer plan—more than one employer contributes. There are no collective bargaining agreements requiring contributions in a multiple-employer plan. Moreover, *multiple-employer plan* generally refers to an arrangement that provides health benefits whereas *multiemployer* characterizes a plan that provides health, welfare, or pension benefits.

THE TAFT-HARTLEY CONNECTION

"Taft-Hartley" plan, too, often is used synonymously with "multiemployer" plan. It is not the number of contributing employers, however, that distinguishes a Taft-Hartley plan but its joint, labor-management administration. Under Section 302(c) of the Taft-Hartley Act of 1947 (also referred to as the Labor-Management Relations Act), it is a criminal act for an employer to give money or anything else of value to employee representatives or a union, including contributions to an employee benefit plan administered solely by the union. An employer is permitted, though, to contribute to a jointly administered employee benefit trust fund for the "sole and exclusive benefit" of employees, their families, and dependents.[2]

---

[2]LMRA Sec. 302(c)(5). Trust funds established before January 1, 1946, that are unilaterally administered by a union are valid.

Joint labor-management employee benefit plan administration required by the Taft-Hartley Act can be found in either a multiemployer or single employer plan. Single-employer Taft-Hartley plans, in which an individual employer enters into a collective bargaining agreement with union employees and administers a benefit plan jointly with the union, are not common. Multiemployer plans always are jointly administered.

Contributions to a jointly administered trust fund are legal under the Taft-Hartley Act only if (1) payments are in accordance with a written agreement with the employer, (2) the agreement provides for employers and employees to agree upon an impartial umpire for disputes (if no neutral persons are authorized to break deadlocks), (3) the trust fund is audited annually, and (4) the employer and employees are represented equally in fund administration. Furthermore, Taft-Hartley plans may be established only to fund certain types of employee benefits. The types of benefits have expanded over the years, generally from just medical/hospital care; pensions; occupational illnesses/injuries; unemployment; life, disability/ sickness, or accident insurance to vacation, holiday, or severance benefits; apprenticeship and training programs; educational scholarships; child care centers; and legal services. In 1990, Congress added financial assistance for employee housing to the list of valid purposes for establishment of a Taft-Hartley trust fund.

Purposes of Taft-Hartley Funds

Medical/hospital care	Pooled vacation/holiday/severance benefits
Pensions	Apprenticeship/training programs
Occupational illness/injury	Educational scholarships
Unemployment benefits	Child care centers
Life insurance	Legal services
Disability/sickness insurance	Financial assistance for housing
Accident insurance	

"BUILT IN" PORTABILITY OF BENEFITS

One of a multiemployer plan's greatest advantages for a mobile work force is its built-in portability. Portability refers to the ability to transfer benefits from one employer's plan to another. Although they might work for numerous employers over the course of their work lives, employees covered under collective bargaining agreements that require employer contributions to multiemployer plans usually do not have to be concerned with losing benefits from or transferring benefits among employers' plans. In multiemployer pension plans, for example, employees will be credited years of service for vesting and participation purposes as long as they work for a contributing employer in covered service or in contiguous noncovered service with the same employer. (Contiguous noncovered service is nonbargaining unit service, such as supervisory work, preceding or following covered service.[3])

In addition to built-in portability, some multiemployer plans enter into reciprocal agreements with other multiemployer plans—both pension and health and welfare. Not only, then, are benefits portable from one employer to another through the multiemployer plan, but benefits of employers contributing to different multiemployer plans also are portable among multiemployer plans.

In multiemployer pension plans, reciprocity agreements are arranged in two ways. Among some funds, pension contributions "follow the man." Contributions on behalf of a "traveler" to a local fund are paid to the traveler's home fund, which distributes the entire benefit to the participant based on its own formula. In other reciprocity agreements, no contributions are transferred. Instead, years of service among funds are combined for purposes of plan participation and vesting. Each fund pays benefits based only on its own years of service, or a pro rata share. In health and welfare plans, reciprocity agreements are arranged similarly and used to avoid a period of noncoverage while an employee waits to satisfy another multiemployer plan's eligibility requirements.

First developed in the mid-1960s, reciprocal agreements are most common among the building and construction trades. In 1987, almost one half of all multiemployer funds were party to reciprocity agreements.[4] In some instances, these agreements extend portability among multiemployer plans to a national level.

Since participants of multiemployer pension plans enjoy the plans' portability features as well as those of reciprocal agreements among plans, the impact of a 10-year cliff minimum vesting standard for bargaining unit employees participating in multiemployer plans is minimal. The Tax Reform Act of 1986 retained the 10-year cliff-vesting standard for

---

[3]29 CFR Sec. 2530.210(c). For benefit accrual purposes, covered service with any employer maintaining the plan will be taken into account.

[4]"Reciprocity and Multiemployer Funds: A Model of Portability," *Employee Benefit Notes,* February 1987, p. 5, contributed by the Martin E. Segal Company.

bargaining-unit employees covered by multiemployer plans while accelerating the minimum vesting standards for participants of single employer plans to the alternative of five-year cliff vesting or three- to seven-year graded vesting. Nonbargaining unit employees covered by multiemployer plans *are* subject to the five-year cliff or three- to seven-year graded minimum vesting schedules.[5]

JOINT BOARD OF TRUSTEES

A unique feature of multiemployer plans is equal representation of employers and employees in plan administration. Unlike a unilaterally administered, single-employer plan where the employer directly administers the plan without employee participation, a multiemployer plan is administered by a joint board of trustees. The board of trustees is the "plan sponsor" of a multiemployer plan (the equivalent of an employer in a single-employer plan) as well as the plan's "named fiduciary" and has exclusive authority and discretion to manage the assets of the plan.

Multiemployer plan trustees are designated by labor and management and do not necessarily have a background in employee benefits or any specific aspects of plan administration, although professional trustees do exist. How, then, can a politically and economically divided board of trustees administer a plan solely in the interests of plan participants and beneficiaries? Moreover, how can multiemployer plan trustees prudently administer a plan without appropriate skills and experience? The answer lies in the trustees' awareness of and dedication to fulfilling fiduciary duties to plan participants and the trustees' ability to delegate, within limitations, plan responsibilities to experts.

Multiemployer plan trustees, unlike trustees of unilaterally administered single-employer plans who have been selected by management, inevitably face conflicts of interest given their labor or management backgrounds. Often, multiemployer trustees also are officers or agents of either a contributing employer or a union and therefore have loyalties both to employee benefit plan participants and to the bargaining party they represent.

---

[5]ERISA Sec. 203(a)(2)(C); IRC Sec. 411(a)(2)(C).

Described by many as the "two-hat dilemma," multiemployer plan trustees are inevitably faced with making decisions that promote the interests of plan participants and beneficiaries but conflict with positions they would take if they were not plan trustees. Advising legal action for the collection of delinquent employer contributions, for example, is an area of potential conflict of interest, particularly for management trustees. Despite union or employer selection, the multiemployer plan trustee's labor or management "hat" comes off when administering the plan. "[A]n employee benefit fund trustee is a fiduciary whose duty to the trust beneficiaries must overcome any loyalty to the interest of the party that appointed him," the Supreme Court has declared in an oft-repeated statement.[6]

As with all employee benefit plan fiduciaries, multiemployer plan trustees are charged with administering a plan with the care, skill, prudence, and diligence that a prudent person acting in a similar capacity and familiar with such matters would use. Most labor and management trustees have full-time jobs outside of their plan responsibilities, are not paid for their efforts (except for reasonable expenses), and are not necessarily skilled or experienced in employee benefit plan operation. Fiduciary, trustee, and other responsibilities of multiemployer plan trustees, therefore, frequently are delegated to other individuals. This delegation of responsibility is proper as long as it is authorized and prudent.

Under the overview of the joint board of trustees, plan administrators and professionals such as attorneys, accountants, actuaries, consultants, and investment managers handle the daily functions of multiemployer plans. Some multiemployer plan administrators are salaried, working solely for the fund in an employee status. Other plan administrators work under contract for several benefit plans (sometimes both single and multiemployer) at one time. The administrators of most Taft-Hartley funds are salaried.[7]

Through education of multiemployer plan trustees about the two-hat dilemma and prudent delegation of plan responsibilities, potential weaknesses of multiemployer plans can turn into strong points. As a well-

---

[6]*NLRB* v. *Amax Coal Co.*, 453 U.S. 322, 323 (1981).

[7]Bernard Handel, "Forms and Functions of Administration," chap. in *Trustees Handbook*, 4th ed., ed. Marc Gertner (Brookfield, Wisc.: International Foundation of Employee Benefit Plans, 1990), p. 255.

known employee benefits attorney has said about the contribution of lay labor and management trustees to multiemployer plan operation, "The greatest strength that the trustee brings to the Taft Hartley trustee table is his or her knowledge and feeling for the industry and the people in it."[8] The interests of plan participants, when trustees separate labor and management duties from plan duties and prudently delegate responsibilities to other persons better equipped to perform them, are well-served by the multiemployer plan.

WITHDRAWAL LIABILITY

In addition to joint labor-management administration and the unique characteristic of built-in portability, the multiemployer plan is notable for a somewhat perpetual existence independent of individual contributing employers. Since other employers participate in a multiemployer plan, an individual employer's withdrawal does not cause the plan to terminate.

This structural aspect of multiemployer plans, specifically of multiemployer pension plans funded for benefits payable far in the future and not on a pay-as-you-go basis, is potentially hazardous to participants. Without some sort of safeguard, employers remaining in a multiemployer defined benefit plan could owe vested benefits earned by employees of employers opting out of the plan. Given this disincentive to remain in a multiemployer plan, particularly one covering employees in a declining industry, many employers would want to withdraw and the plan would be unable to pay participants the retirement benefits they had been promised.

The Employee Retirement Income Security Act of 1974 (ERISA) originally addressed this problem, but did not go far enough in discouraging employers from withdrawing from a financially weak multiemployer defined benefit plan. Employers faced liability for unfunded vested benefits only if they contributed to a multiemployer plan within five years of the plan's termination. Moreover, liability was limited to 30 percent of the employer's net worth.

In 1980, Congress recognized the precarious financial condition the multiemployer defined benefit plan structure placed on both employers and the Pension Benefit Guaranty Corporation (PBGC) and passed the

---

[8]Marc Gertner, "Basic Concepts of Trusteeship," chap. in *Trustees Handbook,* p. 21.

Multiemployer Pension Plan Amendments Act (MPPAA). The MPPAA amended ERISA's withdrawal liability rules, making withdrawal liability harsher for withdrawing employers but fairer for those remaining in the plan. Under the MPPAA, any employer withdrawing from a multiemployer defined benefit plan that has unfunded, vested benefits is liable for its proportionate share of the benefits—whether the plan terminates or not. Hence, remaining employers no longer shoulder the full burden of the plan's unfunded vested benefits.

PLAN TERMINATION AND INSOLVENCY

Although an employer's withdrawal from a multiemployer plan does not terminate the plan, a mass withdrawal (all employers withdrawing) will. Also, a multiemployer plan terminates if a plan amendment is adopted to either freeze service credits or change a defined benefit plan to a defined contribution plan. When a multiemployer plan does terminate, no reversion of residual assets to a contributing employer is allowed. In contrast, a single-employer sponsor may recover surplus plan assets upon plan termination (but also will encounter an excise tax of up to 50 percent of the reversion).

Unlike the guarantee of nonforfeitable benefits under a single-employer plan upon plan termination, the PBGC guarantees the nonforfeitable benefits of participants of a multiemployer defined benefit plan only upon plan insolvency—not plan termination. When the available resources of a multiemployer plan are not sufficient to pay benefits for a plan year, the PBGC provides the insolvent plan with a loan.

The PBGC's insolvency insurance program for multiemployer plans is funded and maintained separately from its termination insurance program for single-employer plans. The multiemployer program covers about 8.3 million participants in about 2,300 plans; the single-employer program covers about 31 million participants in about 100,000 plans.[9] The PBGC insolvency insurance premium for multiemployer plans, unlike the termination insurance premium for single-employer plans, is not risk-related. The annual premium for each participant of a multiemployer plan is $2.60. In comparison, the annual PBGC premium for

---

[9]Pension Benefit Guaranty Corporation, *1989 Annual Report,* (Washington, D.C.), pp. 11, 14.

single-employer plans is $19 per participant, plus $9 per participant for every $1,000 of unfunded vested benefits up to a cap of $53 per participant. More simply put, the single-employer premium ranges from $19 to $72, depending on the funded status of the plan.[10]

With the more stringent withdrawal liability provisions MPPAA introduced in 1980, the majority of multiemployer plans are now fully funded and chances of plan insolvency have decreased. From 1980 to 1989, in fact, the proportion of all multiemployer plans that were fully funded jumped from 50 percent to 75 percent. Only 2 percent of all multiemployer plans are funded at less than 50 percent of vested benefits.[11]

PLAN QUALIFICATION

Unlike withdrawal liability and PBGC insolvency insurance, which are areas distinct to multiemployer plans, Internal Revenue Code (IRC) plan qualification provisions generally apply to single-employer and multiemployer plans alike. These qualification provisions, such as the minimum participation, minimum coverage, and minimum and full-funding rules, permit tax advantages to pension plans that meet them. As with single-employer plans, if a multiemployer plan is "qualified," contributions are tax deductible for contributing employers, and benefits (including investment income) are tax-deferred for employees until distribution.

In some instances, bargaining-unit employees in multiemployer plans are excluded from or easily meet plan qualification rules. For example, a plan of which a qualified trust is a part must benefit the lesser of 50 employees or 40 percent of the employees of an employer. This minimum participation standard does not apply to employees in a multiemployer plan who are covered by collective bargaining agreements.[12]

Plan qualification provisions designed to prevent discrimination in favor of highly compensated employees similarly call for a disaggregation

---

[10]ERISA Sec. 4006(a)(3), as amended by the Omnibus Budget Reconciliation Act of 1990, Sec. 12021, effective for plan years beginning after December 31, 1990.

[11]*1989 Annual Report*, p. 15. The proportion of single-employer plans that were fully funded increased from 53 percent to an estimated 81 percent over the same time period.

[12]IRC Sec. 401(a)(26)(E). A special testing rule for nonbargaining-unit employees allows the plan to meet the minimum participation standard if 50 employees, including those covered by a collectively bargained agreement, benefit from the plan.

of a multiemployer plan into a plan covering the bargaining-unit employees and plans covering nonbargaining-unit employees. In the case of the minimum coverage requirements, bargaining-unit employees are excluded from the testing of that portion of the plan covering nonbargaining-unit employees if retirement benefits were the subject of good-faith bargaining. Tested separately and as employees of one employer, the collectively bargained portion of a multiemployer plan should automatically pass the minimum coverage test because all other employees are excluded (i.e., 100 percent of the nonhighly compensated and 100 percent of the highly compensated employees in the bargaining unit will be covered).[13]

In nondiscrimination tests that compare the benefits actually provided to highly and nonhighly compensated employees rather than the coverage, such as the 401(k) actual deferral percentage and actual contribution percentage tests, plan qualification requirements become more difficult for multiemployer plans. Bargaining-unit employees, again, are similarly treated as employees of one employer and tested as a separate plan. However, multiemployer plan administrators have to rely on contributing employers for identification of highly compensated employees, and it is unclear whether an employer's failure to do so will disqualify the plan. As with other nondiscrimination testing, each employer's nonbargaining-unit employees probably are properly treated as a separate plan.[14]

As mentioned earlier, sometimes multiemployer plan practice is more liberal than the plan qualification rules under the IRC, and sometimes plan qualification rules are more liberal for multiemployer plans than for single-employer plans. To constitute a qualified trust, for example, the plan of which it is a part generally cannot require an employee to complete a period of service longer than the later of one year or age 21. Since most collective bargaining agreements require contributions for individuals within a bargaining unit or classification—regardless of age—multiemployer plans seldom have an age prerequisite for participation.[15] And, as noted previously, although single-employer plans had to shorten their vesting schedules to an alternative five-year cliff or three- to seven-year graded schedule, multiemployer plans were permitted to retain 10-year cliff vesting.

---

[13]Prop. Treas. Reg. Sec. 1.410(b)-6(e)(1), 54 Fed. Reg. 21437 (1989).

[14]See Gerald E. Cole, Jr., and Gregory A. Delamarter, "401(k) for Negotiated Plans," *Employee Benefits Digest,* March 1990, pp. 6, 7.

[15]Daniel F. McGinn, "Minimum Participation and Vesting," chap. in *Trustees Handbook,* p. 192.

Compliance with qualification requirements either intended for single-employer plans or incognizant of multiemployer plans, is, at times, difficult for multiemployer plan trustees and administrators. Compliance with the full funding limitation changes of the Omnibus Budget Reconciliation Act of 1987 (OBRA '87) was particularly problematical. OBRA '87 placed a cap of 150 percent of current liabilities over plan assets on the deductible contributions an employer may make to a pension plan. This full-funding limitation modification was intended to prevent the loss of tax revenue through the overfunding of pension plans for liabilities not yet incurred—particularly the overfunding of single-employer plans targeted for recovery of surplus assets upon termination.

Since most multiemployer plans are fully funded, and employer contributions are negotiated over a fixed number of years, contributing employers were concerned about their possible inability to deduct obligatory, negotiated contributions that exceeded the full funding limitation (as well as the related 10 percent excise tax on nondeductible contributions). Options to counter OBRA '87's effects, such as increasing benefits or reopening bargaining, were either impractical or potentially harmful to multiemployer plans. Even more frustrating was the fact that neither unions nor employers had much incentive to overfund a multiemployer plan.[16]

The sometimes arduous application of plan qualification rules and other benefit laws and regulations to multiemployer plans is one contributing factor to a comparatively slow appearance of employee benefit trends such as flexible benefit plans and 401(k) plans among multiemployer plans. It is understandable that employers contributing to multiemployer plans for employees who often change jobs with seasons, business cycles, or construction projects are somewhat reluctant to handle administrative matters that must be taken care of at the employer level. Salary deferrals to a multiemployer 401(k) plan, for example, have to be withheld from payroll by each employer and forwarded to the plan administrator. Inherent multiemployer plan differences also somewhat impede experimentation with health and welfare benefit plan designs. The extent of employee assistance and wellness programs among multiemployer plans, although increasing, lingers well behind that found among single-employer plans.

---

[16]"Relentless Pursuit of Fair Funding Treatment: Making Sense of Pension Funding Limitations," *NCCMP Update*, Spring 1989, p. 7.

COBRA

Multiemployer employee benefit plan regulation by ERISA, the Internal Revenue Code, and other benefits-related law, outside of the plan qualification rules, also sometimes is incongruous with the structure and operation of multiemployer plans. COBRA is an excellent example of a federal statute that, while originally enacted with little acknowledgment of multiemployer plans, has since been interpreted through proposed regulations and amended to clarify and ease the compliance process for multiemployer plans and contributing employers.

One of the first questions COBRA posed for those connected with the administration of multiemployer health plans was its application to contributing employers with fewer than 20 employees. Proposed Treasury regulations, issued in 1987, confirmed the worse: each of the employers maintaining a multiemployer health plan must have fewer than 20 employees during the preceding calendar year for the plan to be excluded from COBRA. Employers maintaining multiple-employer welfare plans, conversely, are treated as maintaining separate plans and therefore are excluded from COBRA if they have fewer than 20 employees.[17]

Even the intent of COBRA—to allow qualified beneficiaries who lose employer-sponsored group health plan coverage to elect continued coverage at their own expense—was not as relevant in the multiemployer plan context because most multiemployer plans already had continued health coverage options in place. Historically, multiemployer health plans provide an extended period of eligibility to participants during times of temporary unemployment, often based on an hours bank or through a series of self-payments.

Because many multiemployer health plan participants do continue their eligibility for health benefits for a time period despite a reduction in hours or termination (many times without even accessing their hours bank), there often is no loss of coverage upon these events as there is for participants in single-employer plans. Accordingly, employers contri-

---

[17]Prop. Treas. Reg. Sec. 1.162-26, Q&A 9(a), 10(d), 52 Fed. Reg. 22716 (1987). The confusion over the characteristics of a "small employer plan" persists in applying other group health plan statutes to multiemployer plans. For example, the Medicare secondary-payer provisions for group health plans that cover the working aged also, like COBRA, apply to employers with 20 or more employees. But, in the case of the Medicare secondary payer provisions, employers contributing to multiemployer or multiple-employer plans that have less than 20 employees can elect out if the plan so provides, leaving Medicare as primary payer for employees (and spouses) 65 and older.

buting to multiemployer plans, who are required under COBRA to notify a plan administrator of certain qualifying events, are not always aware whether an employee's reduction in hours or termination has resulted in a loss of coverage, i.e., whether a qualifying event has taken place. Advised to err on the side of caution, employers were likely to notify the plan administrator of every reduction in hours and every termination. The plan administrator, in turn, was obliged to notify qualified beneficiaries if continued coverage could not be verified within COBRA's 14-day notification period.

COBRA has since been amended to introduce alternative means of notification for reductions in hours and terminations of employees covered by multiemployer plans, and also longer notification periods for employers contributing to and administrators of multiemployer plans. If a multiemployer plan so provides, the determination of a reduction in hours or termination as a qualifying event may be made by the plan administrator instead of the contributing employer. Also, if the plan so provides, contributing employers may take longer than 30 days to notify the plan administrator of qualifying events, and the plan administrator may take longer than 14 days to notify qualified beneficiaries of their rights. Finally, for any group health plan, notice by the employer to the plan administrator and extension of coverage may begin with the loss of coverage instead of the qualifying event.[18]

COBRA also has been amended since its passage in 1985 to change the entity directly liable for the noncompliance tax burden as well as the form of the sanction. Somewhat atypically placed, the tax penalty for COBRA violations (generally, a $100 excise tax for each day of noncompliance per qualified beneficiary up to a maximum of the lesser of 10 percent paid for medical care or $500,000) now falls upon the multiemployer plan, not contributing employers.[19] Prior to amendment by the Technical and Miscellaneous Revenue Act of 1988 (TAMRA), the failure of one contributing employer to comply with COBRA caused all contributing employers to lose their respective tax deductions for contributions to any multiemployer group health plans they maintained and

---

[18]ERISA Sec. 606; IRC Sec. 4980B(f)(6), as amended by the Omnibus Budget Reconciliation Act of 1989, Sec. 7891(d), effective for plan years beginning on or after January 1, 1990.

[19]IRC Sec. 4980B(e). Other persons who are responsible for administering or providing benefits under the plan, such as contributing employers, can also be liable for the excise tax if they cause a COBRA failure.

highly compensated employees of all employers to be denied an income exclusion for employer group health coverage.

CONCLUSION

A multiemployer plan has five basic features: (1) numerous employers contribute to the plan; (2) employees frequently change jobs without loss of benefits (or benefit eligibility); (3) a joint, labor-management board of trustees, not contributing employers, manages the plan and its assets, which (4) are placed in a trust fund; and (5) the plan is maintained under a collective bargaining agreement or agreements. These features have led to separate legislation for multiemployer plans in some instances, such as withdrawal liability and plan insolvency insurance. In other employee benefit areas, such as certain plan qualification rules and the continued health care coverage requirements of COBRA, multiemployer plans either have had to adapt to a framework set up for single-employer plans or modify the framework.

In a number of aspects of employee benefit plan design, funding, and administration too numerous to mention in this chapter, application to multiemployer plans differs. In areas even as basic as investment policy, where multiemployer plans historically are more conservative than single- employer plans, multiemployer plans are something of a wrinkle in an otherwise smooth spread of employee benefits. Yet, significantly, multiemployer plans are the only way to provide meaningful benefits to skilled, frequently mobile employees at a cost and level of responsibility acceptable to the industry employers who employ them.

CHAPTER 61

PUBLIC EMPLOYEE
PENSION PLANS*

Dan M. McGill

Pension plans operated for the employees of state and local governments are distinctive and diverse. As a group, they antedate the plans adopted by business firms to provide for the orderly and humane retirement of their employees. The first public employee retirement system was established in 1857, covering the police force of New York City. During the next half century, many other municipal employee retirement systems were brought into existence, including several whose coverage was confined to teachers. In 1911, Massachusetts established the first retirement system at the state level, the system covering the general employees of the state. Since then plans at all levels of government have proliferated until today the vast majority of all state and local government employees participate in a staff retirement system of some kind.

State and local government retirement systems function in an environment that has been well described by Thomas Bleakney in the prologue to his book *Retirement Systems for Public Employees*.[1] This environment gives rise to some unique problems and renders less tractable other problems commonly encountered by pension plans generally. Creatures of the political process, public employee retirement systems do not lend themselves well to the traditional constraints and disciplines that

---

*This material first appeared in Howard E. Winklevoss and Dan M. McGill, *Public Pension Plans* (Homewood, Ill.: Dow Jones-Irwin, 1979). It is reproduced herein with written permission of the publisher.

[1]Thomas P. Bleakney, *Retirement Systems for Public Employees* (Homewood, Ill.: Richard D. Irwin, 1972), pp. 1–9.

shape the structure and reinforce the foundation of pension plans in the private sector. They present challenges in plan design, funding, and financial disclosure.

The boundaries of the public retirement system universe have not been firmly established. A massive survey undertaken several years ago by the Pension Task Force of the House of Representatives Subcommittee on Labor Standards identified nearly 7,000 pension plans of state and local government subdivisions and estimated that there may be 10 to 15 percent more unaccounted for, presumably small in size. More than 1,400 plans have been located in the Commonwealth of Pennsylvania alone. About 75 percent of the total universe of plans are found in 10 states, including in descending order Pennsylvania, Minnesota, Illinois, Oklahoma, and Colorado. The systems range in size from the New York State Employees' Retirement System, with more than 400,000 participants, to arrangements at the township or borough level covering fewer than five employees. Nearly 75 percent of the plans have fewer than 100 active members. At the other extreme, there are 131 known plans with 10,000 or more active members, and these plans are believed to account for approximately 85 percent of the total active membership of all state and local government pension plans.

State and local government retirement systems cover about 15 million full-time and part-time employees, 40 percent of the coverage of plans in the private sector. Employer and employee contributions to the plan amount to about $38 billion per year, with benefit disbursements running around $20 billion annually. The plans hold assets of more than $500 billion, as compared with roughly $1.5 trillion held by private sector plans.

A profile of the retirement systems operated by states, municipalities, counties, townships, boroughs, school districts, and other public authorities is presented in this chapter. The systems or plans are examined from the standpoint of several pertinent characteristics: (1) classes of employees covered, (2) level of plan administration, (3) legal form, (4) exposure to collective bargaining, (5) legal commitment of the plan sponsor, (6) Social Security coverage, and (7) source of contributions.

CLASSES OF EMPLOYEES COVERED

Some plans cover all types of employees of the jurisdictions involved, sometimes with different benefit formulas and other pertinent plan provisions. In the great majority of jurisdictions, however, there are separate plans for different categories of employees, reflecting varying conditions of employment, jockeying for preferential pension treatment, political clout, and other indigenous influences.

Public school teachers frequently have their own pension plan, especially when the plan operates at the state level and covers all teachers in the state. There is a variety of arrangements for the faculty and staff of institutions of higher learning. They may have their own plan, they may participate in the plan for elementary and secondary school teachers, or they may be members of a general retirement system for all employees. The faculty and staff of many state colleges and universities participate in the individual annuity contract agreement made available by the Teachers Insurance and Annuity Association (TIAA) and its sister institution, College Retirement Equities Fund (CREF), both chartered under special laws of the New York State Legislature.

In almost every jurisdiction, police and firefighters have their own plans, usually one for police officers and another for firefighters. In a few instances, these two classes of employees are combined for pension purposes and placed in their own distinctive plan. These plans are characterized by relatively generous age and service requirements for retirement, as well as other attractive features. They typically permit retirement with one half of final average salary at age 50 or 55 after 20 or 30 years of service. Some provide half-pay after 20 or 25 years of service, irrespective of attained age. Such favorable retirement terms have been justified as necessary to maintain an energetic force to carry out the hazardous and physically demanding duties of these two occupations.

Other groups that often have their own pension plans are judges and legislators. Even when they do not have their own plan, they are almost certain to receive preferential treatment under the general plan in which they participate. It is common for judges to receive a pension of two thirds to three fourths of their salary at retirement with only 10 to 15 years of service. Retirement with such a benefit may be permitted as early as age 60 or at any age after 20 to 30 years of service. Under some plans for the judiciary, benefits for retired individuals are linked to the compensation of active members, being expressed as a percentage of the salary currently associated with the position occupied by the pensioner before his or her retirement. This practice, called recomputation, was used in the federal military retirement system until 1958 and is still found in many plans for police and firefighters. It not only protects the purchasing power of the pension benefits but gives retired persons a share in the productivity gains of the economy (as reflected in the salaries of their successors). With

Social Security, most judges receive greater after-tax income in retirement than they enjoyed while on the bench. They also generally contribute to their retirement systems at a higher rate than other employees. It has been considered sound public policy to place members of the judiciary in a position where they have no concern over their future economic security, freeing their minds for their judicial duties and minimizing their susceptibility to bribery and other forms of improper financial rewards.

Legislators are less likely than judges to have their own pension plan, but they are almost certain to receive preferential treatment. This preferential treatment may take the form of higher annual benefit accruals, a lower retirement age, shorter required period of service, earlier vesting, or all of these. In one state, legislators, who are also covered by Social Security, accrue a pension benefit equal to 7.5 percent of their final average salary for each year of service and may retire at age 50 with full, unreduced benefits. At the expense of an actuarial reduction, they may begin receiving their pension at any age after only six years of legislative service. Legislators who have voted more generous benefits to themselves than to rank-and-file employees have generally defended their action on the grounds that they are underpaid and are entitled to higher pensions to redress the inequity. It is less obtrusive to increase their pensions than to increase their pay. It is generally agreed that earlier vesting is justified for legislators (and members of city councils) because of their uncertain and frequently short tenure.

Perhaps the most common type of public employee retirement system is that for the general employees of the governmental unit—all employees other than teachers, police, firefighters, and other special groups who have their own plan. This plan is frequently known by the acronym PERS (Public Employment Retirement System). It tends to be the largest retirement system for a given governmental subdivision, especially if it includes the public school teachers, as it may. In many jurisdictions the teacher retirement system and the retirement system for general employees are about the same size.

LEVEL OF PLAN ADMINISTRATION

As might be expected, the great majority (80 percent according to the findings of the Pension Task Force) of public employee retirement systems are administered at the city, county, or township level. This is due in large part to the fact that plans for police or firefighters account for two thirds of the entire universe of public plans, and these tend to be local in character and sponsorship.

All states operate retirement systems for their own employees, and some operate them for employees of their political subdivisions. Most states operate at least two plans, one for public school teachers and another for all other state employees. There may be separate plans for the judiciary, state police, guards at correctional institutions, and other special groups. Some states permit the employees of their political subdivisions to participate in the appropriate state plans. In some cases, participation by local government employees is voluntary (in the sense that the local government entities elect to have their employees participate in a statewide plan rather than operating their own plans), whereas in other cases participation is mandatory. Some states operate statewide plans for employees of their political subdivisions in which local government employees are not commingled with state employees. Participation by the local units may be either voluntary or mandatory. It is worthy of noting that in 21 states teachers, who are typically local employees, participate in a statewide retirement system covering state employees as well as teachers. In other states, public school teachers participate in a statewide plan for teachers only. Except for large cities, public school teachers tend to participate in statewide plans of some sort. In Hawaii, all state employees and all employees of the state's political subdivisions participate in a single retirement system operated by the state. This is the only state in which all public employees are covered by a consolidated system. Massachusetts has a single pension law for all new employees (since 1945) that provides a uniform set of benefits and retirement conditions for all state and local government employees, with the exception of security personnel and others in hazardous occupations, but the law is administered through 101 separate systems.

There is a trend toward merging the plans of numerous and frequently small political subdivisions into statewide plans, either on a voluntary or mandatory basis. There are many advantages to consolidation: (1) administrative economies; (2) the potential for better investment performance through greater diversification, improved cash flow, and employment of more sophisticated investment managers; (3) pooling of mortality risk; (4) elimination of competition among systems for plan improvements; (5) protection of benefit accruals of employees who move from one locality to another; (6) sounder benefit design because of the legislature's freedom to concentrate its attention on fewer systems; and (7) improved services to plan members and their beneficiaries because of a larger and more professional staff.[2]

There are some potential disadvantages in consolidation. There is clearly some loss of flexibility: a uniform plan may not accommodate local circumstances and needs. There is also the possibility that, in an effort to make the consolidated plan attractive to all groups, the plan designers will make the benefits and other substantive features too generous. There may be a tendency to build in the most appealing features of all the plans to be merged into the statewide plan. Unless safeguards are applied, the consolidated system may attract only those groups whose benefit expectations have a greater actuarial value than their anticipated contributions. This threat can be dealt with through making participation mandatory or by adapting contributions to the population characteristics of the participating units. A final disadvantage is diminished ability to experiment and to seek answers from a diversity of approaches to problems.

Bleakney concludes that the biggest obstacle to consolidation is political, the reluctance of local authorities to relinquish any of their influence and the resistance of the administrative staffs of existing systems. "Combining two or more systems into one results in fewer titles, fewer boards, and fewer persons bearing the trappings of office, minimal as they may be."[3] There may also be opposition from the local employee groups unless the consolidated plan holds out the promise of more generous benefits and other features.

LEGAL FORM

One of the distinctive features of state and local government retirement systems is that their terms and provisions are promulgated in the form of a legislative enactment of some type. The terms of a retirement system for state employees are invariably contained in a law enacted by the state legislature and, of course, approved by the governor. States that provide a state-administered system for the employees of local government units,

---

[2]Bleakney, *Retirement Systems,* p. 20.
[3]Ibid., p. 23.

on an optional or mandatory basis, also embody the terms of such a plan in a conventionally enacted law. The plan, as contained in the law, may permit some discretion by the local jurisdictions as to benefit levels, normal retirement age, employee contribution rate, and other critical features. The legislated plan would be duly adopted by the city council, county commission, or other legislative body of the local unit, with whatever variations might be desired and permitted. In a sense, this arrangement permits separate "plans" within a central or consolidated "system."

States that do not operate a central system or systems for local government employees still have something to say about the types of pension plans that may be adopted by their subdivisions, except for municipalities that have been granted home rule. A state with this policy enacts a law that outlines the essential features of a pension plan that can legally be adopted by municipalities and other local subdivisions, the provisions being keyed to the size of the unit. Again, the law may permit variations within prescribed limits. In these states, the pension plan actually adopted by the local unit may be contained in an ordinance or other legislative document. Retirement systems instituted by municipalities with home-rule charters will be evidenced by duly adopted ordinances.

Several of the largest cities established municipal pension plans before the state in which they are located established retirement systems for its own employees or enacted broad pension guidelines for its political subdivisions. Some of these pioneer systems continue to function under the exclusive authority of the sponsoring municipality, especially when the latter has a home-rule charter. In many jurisdictions these plans have been brought under the control of the state legislature in one way or the other. Several of the New York City pension plans predate the statewide plans established by the legislature. Despite this and the fact that New York City has home rule in a broad sense, the state legislature reserves to itself the right to make changes in the New York City retirement systems, with two limited exceptions. However, the state constitution requires the city to consent to changes in three of its major pension plans, unless the legislature acts by general law applicable to a broad class of municipalities.

In 22 states there are pension commissions or oversight committees that evaluate all proposals for amending retirement systems subject to the state legislature and make recommendations to the legislature. These bodies vary greatly as to their structure, the scope of their functions, their authority, their independence, and overall effectiveness.[4]

EXPOSURE TO COLLECTIVE BARGAINING

The Inland Steel decision of 1949[5] declared pensions to be a bargainable issue, and since that time bargaining over pension has become standard (indeed, required) practice in those segments of the private economy subject to collective bargaining. Many states have recognized the right of public employees to bargain collectively, and in those states they bargain vigorously over wages and other conditions of employment. Yet it is the exception for public employee unions to bargain over pensions.

The explanation of this anomaly is the statutory foundation of public employee retirement systems. There is an inherent conflict over the right of the legislature to legislate and the right of organized employees to bargain collectively.

A municipality with home rule could presumably negotiate pension demands to a definitive conclusion, assuming that its negotiator has the authority to commit the municipality's legislative body. Moreover, a public authority might have enough autonomy to negotiate its own pension arrangements. In all other cases, however, it would be necessary for the legislature to approve any pension bargain that might be negotiated between a political subdivision and a public employee union. In practical effect, the pension pact would be nothing more than a recommendation to the legislature that it amend the pension law or laws in a particular manner. If the legislature refused to do so, the bargain would be of no effect. The only recourse of the union would be to take its case to the legislature and the governor. In the light of this political reality, most collective bargaining units have apparently concluded that they might as well go to the legislature in the first place, where in the past they have had considerable success.

---

[4]See Robert Tilove, *Public Employee Pensions Funds* (New York: Columbia University Press, 1976), pp. 257–59, and Suzanne Taylor, *Public Employee Retirement Systems* (ILR Press, New York School of Industrial and Labor Relations 1986), pp. 72–74, for a critique of pension commissions.

[5]*Inland Steel Company* v. *National Labor Relations Board*, 170 F. 2d 247, 251 (1949). Certiorari denied by the Supreme Court, 336 U.S. 960 (1949).

The conflict between New York City and the New York state legislature in the early 1970s over negotiated pension increases, which for fiscal reasons the legislature refused to approve, led to strikes and ultimately to the amending of the Taylor Law on public employee collective bargaining to eliminate pensions as an item of bargaining. The Permanent Pension Commission was directed to develop some form of "coalition bargaining" by the various unions involved as a substitute for conventional bargaining and in an effort to avoid conflicting union demands.

Given the statutory foundation of public employee pension plans, the only way that collective bargaining over pensions could be meaningful would be for the state, through its constitution or appropriate legislation, to commit itself to implement any pension agreements reached by the collective bargaining parties. The Commonwealth of Pennsylvania has come close to making such a commitment. Since 1966 its constitution has authorized the General Assembly to enact laws that would make it mandatory for the General Assembly to take such legislative action as might be necessary to implement a collective bargaining agreement between police and firefighters and their public employers. Pursuant to this constitutional authority, the General Assembly enacted a law that states that if the appropriate law-making body does not approve a collective bargaining agreement (on any subject) negotiated by police and firefighters or if the bargaining reaches an impasse, the issues are to be submitted to a three-member board of arbitration. The decision of the arbitration boards is final and binding, with no recourse to the courts. Moreover, if the issue involves legislation, the decision constitutes a mandate to the appropriate lawmaking body (of the commonwealth or a political subdivision) to enact the required legislation. In a separate law, the General Assembly has provided that for public employees generally a binding arbitration decision that would have to be implemented through legislative, as opposed to administrative, action shall be considered advisory only. The disparity in treatment of general employees and uniformed employees is another example of the political influence wielded by the latter group.

Collective bargaining over pensions could be made effective, of course, by removing the statutory foundation of public employee retirement systems. This would leave the parties free to arrive at their own pension arrangements, just as they do for wages and salaries and other conditions of employment. This would open up the possibility of plan changes with each new labor contract and more "leapfrogging" (seeking benefits superior to other groups) of pension benefits than has occurred heretofore. The various state legislatures have thus far shown no disposition to relinquish their control over the retirement systems of their political subdivisions. In view of the fiscal plight of many municipalities and the growing realization, hastened by the New York City experience, of the threat to municipal solvency posed by unwise pension expansion, it is doubtful that state legislators in the near future will be willing to grant autonomy to local government units over their retirement systems.

There is a broader question of whether pension benefits in the public sector should be subject to collective bargaining, or even subject to state legislature surveillance. A pension plan is a highly technical arrangement, the terms of which with their actuarial overtones do not lend themselves well to the pressure and compromises of collective bargaining. More important, pension promises are deferred obligations that need not be funded immediately. In a budget crisis (or at any other time) it is all too easy for the incumbent public officials to relieve the pressure for higher salaries by granting pension increases that will become a charge against future budgets, the responsibility of subsequent administrations. To harried public officials it looks like a painless way to win points with public employees and their families. Unfortunately, the costs have to be met eventually, but a different generation of taxpayers will have to pay them.

It should be recognized, of course, that the same pressures and forces are at work whether or not the public employees engage in formal collective bargaining. Employees will always be seeking plan liberalizations, and public officials, who themselves may be participants in the same plan, will always be tempted to substitute deferred obligations for current ones. Public employees are adept at lobbying for their objectives at all levels of authority and can be expected to continue to pursue what they consider to be legitimate goals.

LEGAL COMMITMENT OF THE PLAN SPONSOR

There are two aspects to the question of the plan sponsor's obligations. The first is whether the sponsoring governmental unit undertakes to provide a stipulated set of benefits, as articulated in a benefit formula, to employees who meet certain age and service requirements, or whether it merely undertakes to contribute to the retirement system on behalf of each participating employee on a scale specified in the governing law or document. Plans set up under the first concept are known as *defined benefit* plans. Plans operated under the second concept are referred to as *defined contribution* plans. While many of the early plans were established on the defined contribution basis, with the sponsoring agency and the participating employees contributing at the same rate (a specified percentage of the employee's salary), the overwhelming majority of plans today observe the defined benefit principle.

The second type of commitment is concerned with the right of the sponsoring agency to change the terms of the pension bargain. It is well settled for private sector plans that, except for termination of employment before the vesting requirements have been satisfied, pension benefit rights *already accrued* cannot be rescinded, altered, or diminished without the consent of the individuals involved. This is in accordance with the concept that an accrued pension right is legally enforceable under the principles of contract law, in contrast to the older view that pensions, especially those granted by a public body, were gratuities and not enforceable at law. Unfortunately, the contract theory of benefit entitlement is not as firmly anchored in the public sector as in the private sector. In fact, the case law of the majority of states and the federal government continues to apply the gratuity theory to public sector pension plans. This theory holds that the benefits of a public pension plan are gifts of the governmental sponsor, which entity is free to confer, modify, or deny as long as it avoids arbitrary action.[6] For the participants this is an unfortunate state of affairs that should be remedied as promptly as possible by legislation if necessary. For the purpose at hand, however, the primary legal question is whether the term of a pension plan can be changed in such a manner as to adversely affect the accrual of pension benefits *in the future* by persons already in the plan.

By statute, judicial decision, or constitutional provision, a number of states have declared that pension rights under a public employee retirement system are contractual obligations of the system that cannot be diminished or impaired in respect of present members *now or in the future*. New York, Florida, and Illinois have constitutional provisions to that effect. For example, Article 5, Section 7 of the New York State Constitution provides that ''membership in any pension or retirement

---

[6]For a comprehensive analysis of participants' rights under public employee retirement systems, see Robert W. Kalman and Michael T. Leibig, *The Public Pension Crisis: Myth, Reality, Reform* (Washington, D.C.: American Federation of State, County, and Municipal Employees, 1979), chap. 5.

system of the state or of a civil division thereof shall be a contractual relationship, the benefits of which shall not be diminished or impaired.'' This provision was adopted by the Constitutional Convention of 1938 out of concern fostered by the recent Great Depression that benefits might be cut as an economy measure. It has been construed to mean that for each individual participant the benefits in a system's law at the time that he or she first becomes a member may not in any way be diminished, not only in regard to benefit accruals based on past years of service but also with respect to future years of service. In practice the guarantee of nondiminution has the same effect as if the permanent provisions of the retirement plans were embodied in the Constitution itself.

Massachusetts has stated in its retirement statute that the rights created thereunder are contractual obligations, not subject to reduction. The courts in several states have held that pension expectations are implicit contractual obligations, the terms of which cannot be changed with respect to present members. The Supreme Court of California has ruled that the terms of a retirement plan cannot be changed with respect to present members unless the change is necessary to preserve the integrity of the system or is accompanied by comparable new advantages to the members. Pennsylvania permits an adverse change only when it bears ''some reasonable relation to enhancing the actuarial soundness of the retirement system.'' On the other hand, a 1969 survey found that in 35 states benefit accruals based on prospective service could be legally reduced, even for present members.[7] Even without constitutional, statutory, or judicial constraints, however, state legislatures and local councils have been extremely reluctant to reduce benefits promised to persons already in the system.[8]

SOCIAL SECURITY COVERAGE

In the beginning, employees of state and local governments were excluded from Social Security coverage because of concern that the taxation of state and local government entities by the federal government might be

---

[7]Report of the Governor's Committee to Study the State Employees' Retirement System, New York State, Albany, 1969.

[8]For a more detailed discussion of contractual guarantees, see Tilove, *Public Employee Pension Funds*, pp. 253–56 and 304–7.

unconstitutional. In 1950 the Social Security Act was amended to permit states to elect Social Security coverage for such of their employees as were not already under a retirement system, and, at the option of the employing unit, the employees of all their subdivisions, thus waiving their immunity from federal taxation in their capacity as employer. In 1954 the act was further amended to permit election of coverage for employees already participating in a staff retirement system, but such an election was to be effective only if a majority of the members voted in favor of the coverage. Coverage was to be automatic for all public employees not holding membership in a retirement system on the effective date of the election and for those entering an existing retirement system thereafter. Except in specified states, members of a police retirement system do not have the privilege of electing Social Security coverage. This restriction was sought by police and the persons who administer their retirement systems.

About 70 percent of all full-time employees of state and local governments are covered by Social Security, and 70 percent of this group are also participating in an employer-sponsored staff retirement system. About 93 percent of all public school teachers are covered by Social Security.

The section of the Social Security Act that permitted states and their political subdivisions to elect coverage under the act also permitted them to revoke their election and terminate coverage of their employees. After five years of participation in the Social Security system, a state or local government unit could terminate its affiliation by giving notice to the Social Security Administration of its intention two years in advance of the effective date.[9] No referendum of the affected employees was required.

Under this authority, a number of governmental units, mostly small and concentrated in the states of California, Texas, and Louisiana, withdrew from the Social Security system in a desire to avoid Social Security employer payroll taxes and in the belief that Social Security benefits could be duplicated at less cost through a staff retirement system.[10] New York City filed a notice of intent to withdraw from the

---

[9]A local government unit can terminate its affiliation only with the approval of its own state authorities.

[10]On this latter point, the interested reader should consult Actuarial Note No. 95, published by the Social Security Administration in April 1978. This study shows that, except for unusual circumstances, the present value of Social Security benefits to be "gained" in the future exceed the present value of the combined employer and employee payroll taxes to be paid in the future. The results of this comparison are highly sensitive to the underlying assumptions, especially the interest assumption.

system but revoked it before the proposed date of withdrawal. After revoking one notice of intention to withdraw from the Social Security system, the state of Alaska filed another notice and eventually withdrew, its action being binding on all governmental units in the state. Recognizing that employees of disaffiliated agencies continue to be entitled to some protection and some benefits under the Social Security program and desiring to protect the program against further loss of much-needed revenue from disaffiliations, Congress included a provision in the Social Security Amendments Act of 1983 removing the right of state and local government units to withdraw from the system thereafter and permitting those that had already withdrawn to reenter the system. The provision was made applicable to governmental agencies that had already filed a notice of intention to withdraw. The applicability of the provision to pending withdrawals has been upheld in several judicial challenges.

In the Budget Reconciliation Act of 1986, Congress amended the Social Security Act to require all persons thereafter becoming an employee of a state or local government agency not participating in Social Security, whether by original choice or withdrawal, to be covered under the HI segment of the program and to be subject to the employer and employee payroll taxes allocable to that portion of the overall program. Legislation in 1990 made participation in all components of the Social Security program mandatory, as of July 2, 1991, for all state and local government employees not covered by a retirement system.

By their collective choice, policemen continue to be excluded from all portions of the Social Security program.

SOURCE OF CONTRIBUTION

State and local retirement systems have traditionally been supported by contributions from both the employing agencies and the participating employees. Employee contributions have been required to provide a steady source of income to the plan, independent of the whims of the legislature or other financing agency and the state of the public coffers, and to dampen employee demands for plan liberalizations.

The Pension Task Force found that about 75 percent of the plans that it surveyed require employee contributions. A substantial number of other plans permit voluntary contributions by employees. In the aggregate and for all the state and local government plans surveyed, employee contributions accounted for about one third of total contributions. Contributions of the employing agencies generally come out of general revenues. In some jurisdictions they are drawn from special earmarked taxes or levies.[11] Some small plans are financed on a pay-as-you-go basis through public subscriptions from an annual appeal.

[11]For example, in one state the plan for firefighters is financed out of taxes levied on fire insurance premiums paid to out-of-state companies.

CHAPTER 62

INTERNATIONAL EMPLOYEE BENEFITS

Mark S. Allen

Around the world, the rationale for employee benefits is much the same as in the United States. They generally are provided in order to protect employees in the event of retirement, death, disability, and illness. But for most countries, this is where the similarities end. The framework in which these benefits are provided varies significantly from country to country, ranging from comprehensive government programs (''cradle to grave'' coverage provided by the government) to partnership arrangements (combinations of employer, employee, and government benefits with many options from which to choose).

In the past, many U.S. multinational corporations left the management of these benefits up to the local operations with little or no supervision or direction as to the level or type of benefits to be provided. The prevailing attitude was that the management of the local operations knows what is best—both for the employees and the company—and U.S. managers were unwilling or unable to intervene. This is changing, although not to the extent that U.S. managers are beginning to dictate what type of benefit programs should be provided for local employees. Instead, what is changing is that U.S. managers are becoming more aware of the cost and internal equity issues related to the benefits provided locally—whether they are for local nationals or expatriates—and are making a greater commitment to understanding and managing these issues.

For most managers, this process involves gaining an understanding of the local environment; establishing global benefit objectives and designing local plans; and assisting, to the extent required, in the administration and management of local plans.

BACKGROUND CONSIDERATIONS

Benefits for individuals in international operations often are affected by where they were hired and the location of their assignment. For clarification, the main situations are described below.

• *U.S. Expatriates.* These are citizens and resident aliens ("green card" holders) originally employed in the United States and working and residing overseas. U.S. expatriates normally are paid a U.S. base salary and generally are entitled to U.S. benefits.

• *Local Nationals.* This group comprises individuals employed, working, and residing in the country of which they are citizens. Compensation and benefits programs usually are based on local practices.

• *Third Country Nationals* (TCNs). TCNs normally are individuals working for a foreign company on assignment outside of their home country. "True" TCNs will serve in at least two, but usually more, countries during their career. They can be employees of the corporate office, the subsidiary at which they were hired, or the subsidiary where they are working. Consequently, pay and benefits might be provided on a home country, a host country, or some special basis designed to suit operational needs. Usually, the duration and number of foreign assignments are key considerations when establishing benefit packages for TCNs.

UNDERSTANDING THE LOCAL ENVIRONMENT

The local issues which need to be understood are

1. Statutory and government-provided benefits.
2. Regulatory environment and taxation of employee benefits.
3. Economic and labor environment.

Statutory and Government-Provided Benefits

These benefits generally include retirement, disability, severance, and medical plans, and the amount and type of coverage will vary significantly from country to country. Some countries, like Italy and France, have fairly comprehensive systems that mitigate to some extent the need for supplemental plans. Other countries, like Australia and Hong Kong, have minimal benefits, while others—usually impoverished or developing countries—have none. The way in which these benefits are financed also will differ, but most are financed by employer and employee taxes on pay, while some provide the benefits from general revenues. Almost all countries fund the benefits on a "pay-as-you-go" basis.

Retirement and Old Age Benefits

With respect to retirement, most social security systems provide an income benefit for the life of the individual with reduced benefits to survivors. Benefit formulas range from final pay plans (USSR, People's Republic of China, Sudan, Pakistan) to career average plans (Germany, Belgium, USA—although Germany and Belgium adjust career-average pay for inflation). Some countries, like Australia and Hong Kong, provide flat rate benefits. The most common plan is a final average pay plan with the averaging period ranging from one to ten years. Table 62–1 provides an example of the approximate level of final pay replaced by some countries in Europe, Latin America, and the Pacific region for an employee earning the equivalent of $25,000, $50,000, and $75,000 after 30 years of coverage. As the table indicates, the level of pay replacement by social security is very high in some countries, while in others social

TABLE 62–1
Social Security Pay Replacement

Country	Approximate Percentage of Final Pay Replaced for Employees Earning the Equivalent of:		
	$25,000	$50,000	$75,000
Belgium (Married)	56%	32%	21%
Canada	35	19	12
Germany	50	41	27
Italy	80	78	68
Japan	47	34	27
Mexico	28	14	9
Netherlands	33	18	12
Spain	86	60	39
Taiwan	13	7	5
United Kingdom (Contracted In)	28	16	10

Note: Exchange rates effective as of November 30, 1990.

security provides only a limited benefit leaving sufficient scope for supplemental or private retirement plans.

Social security benefit levels correlate closely to the level of contribution. Table 62–2 shows a comparison of the employee and employer contribution rates and applicable contribution ceilings for the retirement portion of social security for each of these countries. Total contributions range from a high of almost 29 percent in Spain (which provides a generous benefit) to none in Canada (where benefit levels are not as competitive).

Some social security systems provide a two-tier benefit, where the first part is a flat benefit for all eligible employees and the second piece is an earnings-related benefit, which is provided in addition to the flat benefit. The United Kingdom and Japan are two countries that have this type of benefit. In both these countries, companies can ''contract out'' of the earnings-related portion of social security if a private plan is provided

TABLE 62–2
Social Security Contribution Levels

	Maximum Employee and Employer Contribution Rates for Old Age and Survivor Benefits				
Country	Employee	Employer	Local Currency	Earnings Ceiling Local Currency	Earnings Ceiling U.S. Dollars
Belgium (Married)	7.50%	8.86%	BF	None	None
Canada	None	None	C$	None	None
			Financed Through General Revenues		
Germany	9.35%	9.35%	DM	75,000	$50,000
Italy	6.10%	17.00%	Lit	51,727,000	$45,736
Japan (Contracted In)					
Males	7.15%	7.15%	Yen	6,360,000	$47,964
Females	6.90%	6.90%	Yen	6,360,000	$47,964
Mexico	1.50%	4.20%	Ps	36,792,000	$12,544
Netherlands	15.55%	0.00%	f	42,123	$24,778
Spain	4.80%	24.00%	Pt	3,498,480	$36,826
Taiwan	1.40%	5.60%	NT	241,200	$ 9,017
United Kingdom (Contracted In)	28.28/wk	10.45%	£	18,200 (None for Employer)	$35,000

Note: Exchange rates effective as of November 30, 1990.

to all employees that produces equal or greater benefits. "Contracting out" simply means that companies can divert the contributions earmarked for that part of the social security system to a private plan if certain conditions are met.

In some countries social security retirement benefits are provided in the form of a defined contribution plan. This is most common in Asian and African countries. Singapore, Malaysia, India, Indonesia, Egypt, and Nigeria all have a defined contribution arrangement, usually called "provident funds," from which benefits generally are paid out in a lump sum. One exception to this is France, which has a complicated system of social security and mandatory complementary plans funded on a quasi-defined contribution basis—similar to cash balance plans in the United States. However, in France, benefits are paid out in the form of an annuity.

Eligibility conditions for qualifying for and receiving benefits also will vary from country to country. In some countries residency is the only requirement, whereas in others 10 years or more of coverage is needed in order to qualify for benefit payments. The age at which these benefits commence generally is different for men and women, but there is a gradual worldwide trend to equalize the retirement age. This trend is perhaps more apparent in Europe than in other parts of the world. Table 62–3 shows the age at which normal retirement benefits can commence for men and women in several countries, with a brief description of the plan type.

Disability Benefits
Salary continuation, workers' compensation, and long-term disability benefits commonly are mandated by most countries, although the amount of benefit and the length of payment vary considerably. Long-term disability benefits often are related to the retirement benefits provided through social security.

Medical
Some form of national health insurance for all ages is provided by most countries. Argentina, Brazil, Canada, Mexico, Australia, Japan, Hong Kong, Germany, and the United Kingdom are some examples of countries providing comprehensive coverage. Although this would appear to eliminate the need for supplemental medical plans, these plans are common practice in many countries with national health insurance programs. The

TABLE 62–3

Social Security Normal Retirement Age, Required Service or Years of Contributions, and Plan Type

Country	Normal Retirement Ages For: Men	Women	Service or Contribution Requirement For Full Benefit	Plan Type
Argentina	65	60	30 Years	Highest 3 of last 5 years
Australia	65	60	10 Years and Means Tested	Fixed Amount
Belgium	65	60	None	Adjusted Career Average
Colombia	60	55	10 years	Final 3-Year Average
Egypt	60	60	10 years	Final 2-Year Average
France	60	60	37.5 Years or Age 65	Adjusted 10-Year Average
Germany	65	65	5 Years	Adjusted Career Average
Greece	65	60	13.5 Years	Final 2-Year Average
Hong Kong	65	65	Residency	Fixed Amount
Ireland	65	65	3 Years	Fixed Amount
Italy	60	55	15 Years	Final 5-Year Average
Japan	65	65	25 Years	Adj. Career Avg. Plus Flat Amount
Korea	60	60	20 Years	Career Average Plus Flat Amount
Mexico	65	65	10 Years	Final 5-Year Average
Netherlands	65	65	None	Fixed Amount
New Zealand	60	60	Residency	Fixed Amount
Norway	66	66	3 Years	20-Year Average Plus Flat Amount
Pakistan	55	50	15 Years	Final Pay
Peru	60	55	15 Years	Final Pay
Portugal	65	62	10 Years	Highest 5 of last 10 years
Saudi Arabia	60	60	15 Years	Final 2-Year Average
United Kingdom	65	60	None	Adj. Career Avg. Plus Flat Amount

Note: Data effective January 1990.

reasons range from necessity—the poor quality of service from national health providers—to executive compensation—(perquisites given to executives but not other employees).

Severance Benefits

In some countries, statutory severance benefits were originally designed to force employers to provide some form of retirement benefit. In these countries, the amounts can be significant and are an important factor in supplemental plan design. As an example, in some Latin American countries, the statutory severance benefit can exceed two months' pay times years of service where the definition of pay includes all components of compensation, including benefits-in-kind such as company cars, ancillary benefits, nonaccountable cash payments and expense accounts (representation allowances), and the like. For some positions, particularly in those countries where there is a confiscatory tax environment, the value of the benefits-in-kind can exceed 50 percent or more of base salary.

Bilateral Social Security Treaties—for Expatriates and TCNs

Many countries have bilateral social security agreements that enable expatriates, including TCNs, to avoid making simultaneous contributions to both their native and host countries' social security systems. They also permit employees to combine periods of coverage under foreign systems for the purposes determining eligibility in their home-country programs (totalization). Currently, the United States has agreements with the following 12 countries:

Belgium	Germany	Norway	Sweden
Canada	Italy	Portugal	Switzerland
France	Netherlands	Spain	United Kingdom

The specific provisions regarding coverage and totalization of benefits will vary among the individual agreements. For U.S. expatriates, most agreements provide that work performed abroad on a permanent basis be covered under the system in the country in which the employee is working. For temporary assignments, generally less than five years, it usually is possible to remain in the U.S. system and not make duplicate contributions.

The European Community (EC) has a special totalization agreement created by the Treaty of Rome. It has three main features:

1. It allows nationals of EC countries to combine their years of participation under the social security systems of all EC countries in order to establish eligibility for benefits. Each country then pays proportionate benefits for the years of coverage under its own system.

2. It allows employees on temporary assignment to another EC country to remain in their home-country system for pension

benefits and to participate in the host-country system for other benefits. "Temporary" is defined as 12 months with the possibility of one 12-month extension.

3. It provides for equal, nondiscriminatory treatment of all EC nationals under the systems of member countries.

REGULATORY ENVIRONMENT

Taxation of Benefit Plans

In most countries, employer and employee contributions and pension plan assets receive some form of tax relief. Benefits normally are taxed as ordinary income, although some countries tax either lump-sum or income benefits on a more advantageous basis. The requirements for this tax relief will differ from country to country, but generally they include provisions similar to those in the United States. However, while similar, the requirements usually are not as comprehensive, and they typically permit discrimination in one form or another.

Not all countries offer complete tax relief on pension plans. In Australia employer contributions (and certain employee contributions) to approved plans are partially taxed, as are the plan assets. In New Zealand pension plans are tax neutral. Here, employer and employee contributions to pension plans and the assets are fully taxed, but benefit payments generally are tax free.

In many countries, discrimination is not as significant a concern as it is in the United States. In those countries where it is not, benefit programs often can discriminate by using different

Retirement ages for males and females.

Required levels of employee contributions.

Eligibility requirements.

Benefit formulas for classes of employees.

There are many other ways in which employers may discriminate. What is permitted will depend on the country, and for some countries the ability to discriminate is beginning to disappear. In 1990, in the case of *Barber* v. *the Guardian Royal Exchange,* the European Court of Justice ruled that occupational pension schemes are considered as pay, and therefore must be equal between the sexes. It cited the nondiscrimination clause of the Treaty of Rome as the basis for its decision. This case has implications for all companies with operations in the European Community.

Financing and Funding Restrictions

Often the requirements for an approved plan will include restrictions on the funding of the plan or on where the plan assets may be invested. In Japan for example, plans with fewer than 100 employees cannot utilize trust banks—they must insure the benefits with an insurance company or a portion (40 percent) may be book-reserved. Those plans that can use trust banks also can invest the assets with foreign investment managers— a relatively new phenomenon in Japan—provided that

1. The fund is at least eight years old.
2. The amounts allocated to the foreign managers are from cash flow—not from existing assets.
3. The maximum amount allocated is not greater than one third of the existing assets.
4. The minimum amount to be managed is greater than 1 billion yen.
5. A minimum of 50 percent must be invested in bonds.

There are approximately 1,400 plans in Japan that can use trust banks, but only 300 or so can qualify to use foreign investment managers. Similarly, in Germany, employers have several choices for the funding of retirement plans that include a form of trust fund (support fund), book reserves, and direct insurance, but only plans that are book-reserved are free from restriction. Tax-free contributions to direct insurance and support funds are limited.

Many other countries have restrictions. Currently, in Brazil funds can invest only in certificates of deposit offered by the Brazilian government. In Switzerland the restrictions are less onerous, but still are there and include limitations on the amounts that can be invested outside of Switzerland and in certain asset classes like real estate and equities.

Other Issues
There are numerous other regulatory issues particular to each country that need to be understood. The principal ones include mandatory indexation

of benefits, Works Councils and employee representation, and accounting and reporting requirements.

Mandatory Indexation. Typically, most countries do not require that pension payments be indexed to inflation (although it may be customary practice to provide such protection to pensioners)—but this may be changing. Inflation is a worldwide concern, and its effect on the erosion of pension benefits is being addressed by some countries. Recently in the United Kingdom legislation was enacted (the 1990 Social Security Bill) that mandates limited indexation of pensions in payment. Similar legislation is pending in the Netherlands and Canada.

Works Councils and Employee Representation. Many countries, particularly those in Europe, require that employees have a say in the management of a company's activities, and this generally includes issues relating to pay systems (which includes employee benefits), dismissals, recruitment, and working hours. The form that this role takes varies, but most common are Works Councils. The degree of authority and control will be different for each country, but they almost always cover employee benefit plans. The table below indicates the minimum number of employees in a company before a Works Council is required in five European countries.

	Number of Employees in Company
Belgium	100
Denmark	50
France	50
Germany	5
Netherlands	35

Employee representation may take other forms, such as direct representation on pension committees or boards. As an example, in Spain there has been recent legislation permitting pension funds on a tax-advantaged basis. However, one of the requirements for achieving the tax-qualified status is that each company must establish a committee to oversee the plan and fund management, and employees must represent a majority of that committee.

Accounting and Reporting Requirements. U.S. multinationals must be concerned with both local and U.S. reporting requirements. Local accounting and reporting requirements usually are not as onerous as the requirements in the United States for domestic plans, but they still exist. In the United States most of the requirements for foreign plans relate to Financial Accounting Standards Board (FASB) Statement 87 (FAS 87), published in December 1985. FAS 87 requires U.S. companies to calculate and report pension costs using explicit assumptions and also requires expanded disclosure in financial statements. Most non-U.S. plans must be included on a basis similar to U.S. plans. Similar rules exist in the United Kingdom in the form of Statement of Standard Accounting Practice 24 (SSAP24), which details how pension costs should be represented in financial statements. Germany and Australia also have rules that deal with accounting and reporting requirements, and it is likely that many more countries will follow with their own set of guidelines.

Economic and Labor Environment

Prevailing economic conditions can be an influencing factor in the design of international benefit plans, but rarely will they dictate the final plan design. They will, however, have a significant impact on plan costs. The more important factors are inflation and interest rates, but exchange-rate manipulation or currency controls also can have an impact—particularly in the countries with high inflation. Normally, currencies appreciate or depreciate in line with inflation, but some countries (Mexico and Brazil, for example) have previously manipulated exchange rates to further other economic goals. In these instances, costs in U.S. dollar terms can be impacted. Table 62–4 shows inflation and growth rates, and also indicates if there are any currency or exchange controls.

With respect to labor, it is important to have an understanding of the following:

1. The prevalence and types of labor unions—whether they are local or national in scope.
2. The depth of the labor movement—does it encompass management as well as hourly employees?
3. The local supply and demand of labor.

The make-up of the labor movement will vary significantly in each country. In some, most of the work force may not be unionized, and those

TABLE 62–4
Inflation, Interest Rates, and Currency/Exchange Control

Country	1990 Est. Inflation	10-Year Govt. Interest Rates (or Proxy)	Potential for Currency or Exchange Controls
Argentina	600.0%	—	Yes
Australia	7.0%	13.6%	No
Belgium	3.3%	9.8%	No
Colombia	30.0%	—	Yes
Egypt	45.0%	—	Yes
France	3.5%	10.2%	No
Germany	2.8%	8.9%	No
Greece	24.0%	21.0%	Yes
Hong Kong	9.8%	—	No
Ireland	3.5%	9.2%	No
Italy	6.2%	11.8%	No
Japan	3.0%	6.9%	No
Korea	9.0%	11.0%	No
Mexico	27.0%	—	Yes
Netherlands	2.5%	9.2%	No
New Zealand	5.0%	12.5%	No
Norway	4.9%	10.8%	No
Pakistan	9.2%	—	Yes
Peru	5250.0%	—	Yes
Portugal	12.8%	16.0%	No
Saudi Arabia	2.3%	—	No
United Kingdom	9.6%	10.5%	No

Note: Data effective January 1990.

workers that are generally are concentrated in small, loosely organized local unions. In others, most of the country may belong to one union or another, as in Belgium, where over 80 percent of the work force is unionized—including white-collar or management employees. Unions may operate at the local or national level. In Italy, management employees, or *dirigenti,* generally belong to one of three trade unions, which negotiate on their behalf on a national basis.

Obviously, the supply and demand of labor also can affect the design and costs of benefit plans. As an example, countries with younger populations generally might find defined contribution plans more acceptable than defined benefit plans. Similarly, older populations probably would prefer the security of a defined benefit plan. Around the industrialized world there is a trend, as there is in the United States, for governments to shift a greater burden of their benefit costs to the private sector. As in the United States, the population in these countries is growing older, and there are fewer workers to contribute to programs like social security. Table 62–5 shows the population of people under age 15 and over age 64 as a percentage of the population between ages 15 and 64 in 7 industrialized countries. It shows that the number of older people is steadily increasing while the number of young people entering the work force is declining.

But, this is not the case in every country. Many Latin American countries, as well as some of the developing countries, are enjoying a "baby boom" period, and the number of eligible workers far outnumbers older workers and retired employees. For example, in Mexico over 56 percent of the population is under age 20, which contrasts with 29 percent

TABLE 62–5
Population Growth—Industrial Countries

Country	Population Under 15 as a Percentage of Population 15–64						
				Projections			
	1965	*1975*	*1985*	*1995*	*2005*	*2015*	*2025*
United States	51	39	33	34	29	29	30
Japan	38	36	32	25	28	28	27
Germany	35	34	22	23	22	19	23
France	41	38	32	31	28	26	28
Italy	—	—	—	25	25	22	24
United Kingdom	36	37	29	31	31	31	31
Canada	57	41	32	30	27	25	28

Country	Population 65 and Over as a Percentage of Population 15–64						
				Projections			
	1965	*1975*	*1985*	*1995*	*2005*	*2015*	*2025*
United States	16	16	18	19	18	21	29
Japan	9	12	15	19	26	33	32
Germany	18	23	21	24	29	31	37
France	19	22	20	22	24	27	33
Italy	—	—	—	22	25	28	32
United Kingdom	19	22	23	23	22	24	28
Canada	13	13	15	18	19	25	34

Source: IMF, Staff Papers.

in Japan and 28 percent in Italy. However, the problem in some of these countries may not be the quantity of labor, but the quality.

INTERNATIONAL GLOBAL BENEFIT OBJECTIVES AND PLAN DESIGN

Most employers recognize the importance of rewarding their employees for their contributions to growth and profits without regard to whether they are domestic or international employees. One of the ways in which employers balance the need for employee reward and business objectives is to develop a statement of policy and objectives that acts as a guide to the establishment, modification, and administration of benefit plans. Usually this statement is an expression of the employer's preferences as opposed to rigid instructions. While most U.S. employers have something similar for their U.S. employees, they generally do not for their foreign operations. Yet, local plans require equal discipline.

Establishing international benefit programs takes place at two levels— determining global objectives and designing plans for local nationals, expatriates, and TCNs that meet these objectives.

Global Benefit Objectives

Global policy statements and objectives generally state the company's philosophy and overall attitude for employee benefits. They also include broad policy statements on total remuneration; definition of competitive practice; uniformity of treatment and internal equity; mergers and acquisitions; costs; and employee communications.

Global objectives rarely get into specifics on the type of benefits for each country, because the variations are likely to be too great. The following is a synopsis of the elements in a global policy.

Total Remuneration
This part of the policy encompasses the overall level of competitiveness for each element of pay, including employee benefits. The total package (base pay, regular bonus, incentive bonus, perquisites, allowances, and employee benefits) as well as each individual component of pay usually is addressed. Items such as tax effectiveness and the state of the business

(for example, start-up situations require different rewards than mature, stable operations) also are covered.

Preferences for specific levels and types of benefits are included. For example, a policy for retirement plans might state the following:

Defined contribution plans are preferred to defined benefit plans.

For defined benefit plans, career average formulas are preferred to final pay plans.

Where possible, employees should share in the cost of funding the plans.

Benefits should be at the 60th percentile of comparable companies for management employees, and the 50th percentile for all other employees.

Plans should be integrated with social security wherever possible.

Trust arrangements are preferred to insurance.

Insurance contracts should be experience-rated where possible by using a multinational pooling arrangement (discussed in detail later in the chapter).

Actuarial valuations should be performed for defined benefit plans no less frequently than every three years.

Similar information should be recorded for each benefit area—retirement, death, disability, and medical.

Definition of Competitive Practice

While actual competitive practice is likely to differ from country to country, it is helpful to have some broad guidelines for each local operation to follow. In some countries it may be appropriate to limit the definition to only those companies that are direct competitors in a specific industry. In other countries it may make sense to expand to other industries. Much will depend on the state of the business in a particular country—for example, a manufacturer may not want to limit the definition to only those companies in its industry when the competition operates principally sales and distribution facilities and does no or little manufacturing. Similarly, a start-up operation in a mature market environment will want to include relatively stable and long-standing companies in their definition. The definition does not have to be limited to industry alone, nor does one standard have to apply for all groups of employees. Many companies expand it to include geographic location (city, suburb, or country location), ownership (U.S. multinationals, foreign multinational, indigenous), type of activity (sales or manufacturing), and size, and also will have different definitions for different groups of employees. Figure 62–1 is a useful guideline for determining appropriate comparator groups and companies for different categories of employee.

Uniformity of Treatment
In many countries it is permissible to differentiate between groups of employees—senior management and other employees for example—although this differential treatment may not be considered appropriate by U.S. management whether it is permissible or not. This section of the policy usually deals with these issues, and it generally is expanded to include matters concerning internal equity, particularly those that involve cross-border comparisons. Cross-border evaluations are difficult because many factors, such as exchange-rate fluctuations, local taxes, social security, and living standards are involved.

Mergers and Acquisitions
Typically companies have three choices for dealing with mergers and acquisitions issues: (1) integrating immediately with corporate benefit programs and policies, (2) maintaining current arrangements without change, or (3) a gradual integration into corporate programs. To the extent a company's preference is articulated in a global policy statement, local managers will be better equipped to handle mergers and acquisitions situations. Many companies simply follow established U.S. company policy in these instances.

Costs
A global statement will outline how costs are to be budgeted and reported and also indicate the preferred level of employee cost sharing.

Employee Communications
This section might indicate the information that employees are entitled to have on existing programs and the frequency to which it should be provided to the employees. It also may specify how the information might be made available to employees.

FIGURE 62–1
Guidelines to Identification of Comparison Companies

Comparison Factor	Category of Employees				
	Production	Clerical and Administrative	Professional and Technical Staff	Salespersons and Middle Managers	Senior Managers
Geographical Location	City and Country				
Industry	Type of Industry(ies)				
Ownership of Company	Locally Owned, Multinational Companies, U.S. Owned Subsidiaries				
Type of Activity	Manufacturing, Marketing, Sales and Distribution				
Company Size (Sales)	Comparable, Smaller, Larger Than Operations				
Competitive Level	Percentile Ranking--1st, Median, 3rd, Other				

Local Benefit Plan Design

Local benefits should be determined for each country within the framework of the global policy, but this is not always possible. The employer must try to balance corporate policy against the local realities, which include the following:

Legislative restrictions.

Tax implications.

Other liabilities, such as termination indemnities that are really retirement plans.

Different actuarial practices.

Smaller, more volatile local investment markets.

Cultural differences or preferences.

The local programs can be designed by a corporate benefits manager, but more often they are developed locally for approval by the head office. Generally it makes sense to involve local management in the decision-making process wherever possible.

Plan Design—U.S. Expatriates

The objective of the vast majority of U.S. employers with respect to benefit plans for expatriates is to keep the employee in the U.S. programs—but this is not always possible. Much will depend on whether the employee is working for a branch or foreign subsidiary of the U.S. company.

Employees working in a foreign branch of a U.S. corporation are automatically covered by their employer's U.S. qualified plan unless specifically excluded. IRC Section 410(b)(3)(c) and Section 4(b) of the Employee Retirement Income Security Act (ERISA) allow a U.S. qualified plan to exclude nonresident aliens from plan coverage in cases where they do not receive any U.S. source income. This permits companies to cover only those employees of a foreign branch who are U.S. citizens or resident aliens.

Any company considering this approach should note the following:

The exclusion of nonresident aliens must be specifically written into the plan document.

The law in some foreign jurisdictions may treat the accrual of benefits under a U.S. plan as a taxable event.

The law in some countries may not allow a deduction, for foreign income tax purposes, to the foreign branch; a U.S. tax deduction is allowed, however.

Individuals working in a foreign subsidiary, unlike employees in a branch, are not employees of the U.S. corporation. As such, these employees are not legally entitled to participate in qualified plans maintained in the United States unless specific steps are taken. IRC Section 406 allows such employees to be deemed employees of the U.S. parent company, but in order to qualify, companies must elect, under Section 3121(1), to provide U.S. Social Security coverage for all U.S. citizens and resident alien employees of the foreign subsidiary. This election can be made separately for each subsidiary and is irrevocable. The election is made by filing Form 2032 with the Internal Revenue Service.

Plan Design—Third Country Nationals

By definition, TCNs are expatriate employees, but for benefit purposes they are often treated differently. Few companies will try to maintain a TCN in his or her home-country benefit plan unless the assignment is temporary. If the transfer abroad is clearly denoted as temporary and if the employees can be classified as "on loan" to the foreign office, then it usually is possible to continue home-country coverage for periods up to two or three years. If this is not possible, then the employee is typically "made whole" on his return to the home country.

Other TCNs can be either permanent or mobile ("True TCNs"). Permanent TCNs normally are included in the host-country plan and usually are not a problem. True TCNs, on the other hand, do create problems because they rarely are in one country long enough to accrue any meaningful service for retirement benefits. For this reason, many companies design international retirement plans that cover this specific category of employee. These plans may provide a benefit based on home- or host-country programs, U.S. levels, or a special benefit formula designed for the TCNs. These plans generally are either book-reserved or funded offshore in order to minimize the tax implications. Many of these plans are umbrella plans, in which case the actual benefit provided by the plan generally is offset by other retirement benefits accrued during the employee's career.

ADMINISTRATION AND FINANCIAL MANAGEMENT OF INTERNATIONAL BENEFIT PLANS

The administration and management of international plans, from the corporate perspective, typically involves two key areas—design and financial considerations. But before these can be examined, there probably will be a need to get information concerning the benefit programs at each foreign location.

Most companies conduct periodic audits of their international benefit plans. Generally this process involves designing a questionnaire, getting the local operations to complete the questionnaire, and analyzing the results. Figure 62–2 provides a list of the items that typically are included on a questionnaire.

FIGURE 62–2
Data Collection Items For International Audit

Retirement Plans	Medical	Long-Term Disability
Type of Plan	Type of Plan	Type of Plan
Eligibility Requirements	Eligibility	Eligibility
Definition of Covered Earnings	Hospital Room & Board	Benefit Amount
Benefit Formula	Hospital Miscellaneous	Integration
Normal Retirement	Surgical	Duration of Benefit
Early Retirement	Attending Physician	Lump-Sum Benefits
Integration	In-Hospital	Employee Contributions
Benefit Payment Form	Outpatient	
Disability Benefits	Major Medical	
Vesting	Deductible	
Employee Contributions	Coinsurance	Severance
Company Contributions/Cost	Maximum	
Financing Medium	Employee Contributions	Amount of Payment
	Dental	Conditions of Payment
	Vision/Hearing	Notice Period
	Maternity	
	Prescription Drugs	
	Psychiatric	

Salary Continuation	Preretirement Death Benefits	Perquisites
Type of Plan	Eligibility	Company Cars
Eligibility	Lump-Sum Amount	Driver
Benefit Amount	AD&D	Club Memberships
Integration	Business Travel	Annual Physicals
Duration of Benefit	Survivor Income	Subsidized Meals
Lump-Sum Benefits	Employee Contributions	Free Telephone
Employee Contributions		Long-Term Incentives

Once the data have been collected, it will be possible to determine the potential cost savings with respect to design considerations by evaluating the following:

1. The relative competitive position.
2. Whether the plans are properly integrated with statutory benefits.
3. Whether the program specifications, such as normal retirement age and employee contribution levels, are consistent with the global objectives.
4. The administration of the plans to see if there are more cost-effective methods.

The financial considerations include funding, investment management, and risk management. With respect to funding and investment management, corporate managers need to focus on issues in each country similar to those for their U.S. plans. These include funding costs at each location with respect to acceptable U.S. expense levels; appropriate funding media; whether the plan should be funded at all—or book-reserved; the actuarial process—reporting, methodology, and assumptions; and investment management.

The investment-management process probably has the most scope for controlling or reducing benefit costs. It has been estimated that a 1 percent per-year improvement in return on plan assets can reduce costs by 10 percent or more per year. In the United States this area gets considerable attention, but this is not so overseas, where the plans generally are smaller and encumbered with different types of legislation. However, in countries such as Australia, New Zealand, Canada, Japan, and the United Kingdom, where trusts are common or at least an acceptable alternative for pension investing, the same scope exists for managing the investment process and generally the same principles used in the United States can be exported overseas.

The risk-management aspect of international benefit plans generally revolves around the concept of multinational pooling.

MULTINATIONAL POOLING

Insured employee benefits in a multinational company generally are undertaken through separate arrangements in each country. Thus, employees in each country will be covered for benefits such as life insurance, medical/dental coverage, disability, and retirement benefits through a local insurance company or financial organization in accordance with local conditions and practices. In the absence of multinational pooling, local insurance arrangements would not enjoy any economies of scale based on the worldwide size of the international group.

Using group life insurance as an example, the insurance contract in each country involves a premium payment to the local insurance company in return for the agreed coverage. Dividends may be paid out of the insurer's overall profits (if any) at the end of the contract year. A variation on this, known as "experience rating," involves the linking of either the dividend or the premium to the actual claims experience of the local subsidiary.

Experience rating is an advantage when claims are lower than the "average," since the cost of insurance is based partly on the company's own claims rather than on the average level of claims. Experience rating also can reduce insurance costs by reducing the "risk charge" made by the insurer. In return, the company incurs an additional risk of loss when claims are high. This generally is more practical if the company has a large number of employees insured under the contract, since there is likely to be greater stability of total annual claim payments.

Multinational pooling enables the principles of experience rating to be applied to the worldwide insurance arrangements of a multinational company. If the subsidiary companies use insurers associated with an insurance "network," then a "multinational dividend" can be paid based on the actual combined experience of those subsidiaries. Thus, the group will benefit from favorable experience and also bear some of the risk of bad experience.

The multinational pooling arrangement consists of a contract between the parent company and the coordinating insurer of the network. It is thus independent of local practice governing payment of dividends on local contracts. In fact, the existence of the multinational contract has no effect on the premiums, dividends, and claim payments under the local contracts.

A multinational pooling arrangement operates on two levels. First, an employer contracts with an insurance network to share the profits and losses of the network's business with the subsidiaries of the parent company. Second, individual contracts are negotiated between the subsidiary and the local-network insurer. These contracts conform with local laws, competitive practice, dividend payments, and the like. A multinational dividend is paid based on the sum total of experience under each of the individual contracts. In essence, this is the meaning of multinational pooling.

Advantages of Multinational Pooling

The primary objective of multinational pooling is a reduction in overall insurance costs, resulting from the receipt of multinational dividends. These dividends arise in years when experience is favorable. If experience is unfavorable, however, the worst that can happen is the cancellation of the dividend, perhaps for several years.

In a sense, an insurance network can afford to give "something for nothing." Multinational dividends arise from the following factors:

If a company has low claims, the experience-rating approach enables that company to share in the savings.

In many countries, local regulations or gentlemen's agreements exist that limit the freedom of the insurers to compete on premiums and dividends. Pooling arrangements may provide a legal means of returning some of the profits resulting from these restrictions.

Pooling reduces the risk faced by the local insurers, since heavy claims in one country can be met out of the multinational dividend earned from favorable experience in other countries. This can result in reduced "risk charges" by the local insurers.

Membership in a multinational network offers competitive advantages to a local insurer. Therefore, an insurer may be willing to offer favorable terms to users of a network in order to become the network's associate insurer in the local country.

Reduced insurance costs are the main advantage of multinational pooling. However, there are a number of other benefits to be gained:

Annual accounting on a centralized basis. More information is available on a company's group insurance costs around the globe and on how those costs are determined.

Centralized communication. In dealing with one "group" office, rather than individual local insurance companies or branches in each country, a company can reduce administrative time and expense.

Relaxed underwriting limits. Because insurance companies wish to protect themselves against high risks, group life and disability coverage for executives typically are subject to satisfactory medical examinations. By pooling lives in a number of locations, the risk of adverse experience is reduced substantially, and the insurance company is more willing to raise or eliminate the limits at which medical evidence is required.

The Multinational Pooling Account

The multinational pooling account sometimes is known as a "second stage account" because it is drawn up after all payments under the local contracts (e.g., premiums, claims, and dividends) have been made. Its principal advantage is that it provides financial information, normally not available from the local insurers, on the foreign benefit programs for each operation in the pooling program.

Although the actual format of a multinational pooling account (or experience statement) will vary from one carrier to the next, it normally will contain the following items:

Credits
    Premiums paid by the company.
    Investment earnings on company-paid premiums.

Debits
    Claims.
    Risk charges.
    Insurer expenses.
    Commissions.
    Local dividend payments.

Funds Retained
    Additions to reserves (most often for pensions but also occasionally for some risk benefits).

Balance
    Multinational dividend.

The multinational dividend is the balance of the account, and the anticipated result of a pooling program. Positive balances arising in countries where experience has been favorable are used to offset negative balances in countries where experience has been poor. Any remaining balance is paid by the network as a dividend to the multinational parent company. In some companies, this dividend is then distributed to the subsidiary companies.

Where Multinational Pooling May Not Work

Over recent years, many companies have established multinational pooling contracts for their overseas employee benefit coverage, and more can be expected to do so. However, pooling is not necessarily appropriate for every multinational organization or every situation. Examples of situations in which multinational pooling may not work include the following:

> Not enough employees are located overseas. Typically, an employer should have at least 500 employees in at least two countries outside the United States or Canada who are covered by group insurance.
>
> In some countries, the network's local insurer may not be competitive or the network may not have a local representative insurer.
>
> In countries with blocked currencies, some networks may experience difficulty in pooling or in paying dividends outside the country.
>
> Local management may refuse to change carriers. This could occur for a number of reasons, including excellent service from the existing carrier, long-standing personal relationships, or national pride.
>
> In some countries, such as the United Kingdom or Australia, premium rates are extremely low. This means that the insurer's profit margin is low and the risk of adverse claims experience might outweigh the expected additional multinational dividend.
>
> The employer's business is in an industry with above-average claims experience.

SUMMARY

There have been a number of recent events that are spurring on the globalization of many U.S. companies. These include the formation of a common market in Europe by the end of 1992, the Canadian/U.S. Free Trade Agreement, which might be expanded to include Mexico, the rapid development of the Pacific Rim economies, and the democratization of many countries in Eastern Europe. Companies are trying to position themselves competitively, either in anticipation of or in reaction to these events, to take advantage of the opportunities that will arise.

The challenge for employee benefit managers is to assist their companies in developing and maintaining their competitive edge while at the same time keeping an eye on issues such as internal equity and cost. In order to accomplish these tasks on a global basis, managers must have a thorough understanding of the employee benefits and related environments in the countries in which they operate.

CHAPTER 63

THE FUTURE OF EMPLOYEE BENEFIT PLANS

Dallas L. Salisbury

Predicting the future is a game of chance in which the normal laws of probability do not hold. The passage of time allows numerous unexpected events to intervene, and this has been the rule rather than the exception with employee benefits.

The field of employee benefits will be increasingly dynamic and challenging during the '90s. The greatest rewards will go to those who carefully anticipate and plan. This chapter attempts to lay a base for that purpose.

PRE-ERISA PREDICTIONS ABOUT EMPLOYEE BENEFIT PLANS (1970)

In 1970 experts made predictions concerning the future of employee benefits. The predictions were based upon specific beliefs regarding *(a)* the economy of the 1970s and *(b)* expected population change.

The economy of the '70s was expected to be strong. Median incomes were expected to rise substantially; they did. Inflation was expected to drop from the abnormally high rate of 4 percent: it didn't. The makeup of the work force (male–female) was expected to remain fairly constant: it didn't. The population over age 65 was expected to approach 23 million: it did. The average workweek was expected to move to 35 hours per week or less: it didn't.

Based upon these economic and population predictions the seers specified future benefit trends. They predicted:

- The '70s would see dramatic increases in income replacement, reaching an average of 75 percent of final earnings (for many it did, and it's moving this way).
- The '70s would see a movement towards encouraging early retirement with the average moving to age 55 (it moved down to the 61–62 range for all individuals; to 58 for large employers).
- The '70s would see plans move toward shorter vesting periods and earlier participation (it happened).
- The '70s would see dramatic growth of, and pressure for, survivor benefits (it happened).
- The '70s would see liberalization of eligibility rules for disability benefits (it happened).
- The '70s would mark the beginning of active and competitive portfolio management (it happened).

The seers of 1970 were surprisingly accurate.

Many things are known now about the '70s and '80s. Inflation reached its highest historical point for the United States and then came back down. Median income rose dramatically, but then slowed. The over-65 population continued to grow, and the proportion of women in the work force grew dramatically.

These economic and population trends of the '70s and '80s are still with us. They will help to shape what occurs in the '90s as they did in the '70s and '80s. They are relevant to a number of factors that will determine the future of benefit programs:

• *Families are changing.* Just over one third of first marriages now remain intact for life. Fewer than one in eight families now consists of a married couple with children in which the mother does not work outside the home. Today, more than half of all women with a child under age 6 are in the paid labor force. More than 6 million households with young children are headed by a single parent, and this number could increase to 7.5 million by 2000 under current trends. Time constraints, competing pressures, and marital dissolution are undercutting the family's ability to perform its role as the mainstay of assistance to dependent family members.

- *Life expectancy has increased and more people are surviving to older ages.* In 1935, when the Social Security Act was passed, life expectancy in the United States was just below 62 years. Now, it hovers around 75 years and shows signs of continued improvement. By 2030, one in five Americans will be age 65 or older, compared with just one in eight today. And the number of people aged 85 or older is expected to triple by 2030, accounting for more than 8.6 million people. Nearly half of today's 20-year-olds can expect to reach 80, compared with less than one in four in the 1930s. The increasing number of older Americans will put a significant strain on the nation's health care services and retirement-income programs in the years ahead.

- *Racial and ethnic diversity is increasing.* Birth rates of the non-Hispanic white population have been at or below replacement level for the past 25 years. Meanwhile, immigration from abroad and higher fertility rates among blacks and some Asian and Hispanic groups are creating greater racial and ethnic diversity in the population. While people of color currently account for 20 percent of the U.S. population, this proportion is expected to grow to over 30 percent by 2030. As minorities become a larger share of the population and the labor force, their special needs and problems will begin to impact more directly on the support systems and economic structures of U.S. society. Minorities today are more likely than their white counterparts to have lower levels of education, to have fewer job skills, and to be poor. If these patterns persist, it could affect not only the number of people in need of assistance but also the productivity and future economic competitiveness of the nation.

- *The income gap between the rich and the poor is widening.* In 1969, families in the top 20 percent of the nation's income distribution accounted for 41 percent of all income; by 1989, they held 45 percent. Meanwhile, the families at the bottom 20 percent of the income scale lost ground, their share declining from 5.6 percent to 4.6 percent. Middle-income families also held a smaller share of national income by 1989. One fifth of the nation's children currently live below the U.S. poverty line, and 8.8 million young adults (ages 18 to 34) are in poverty, a 50 percent increase over 1977 levels. Economic polarization is affecting the number and composition of people who are poor and raising questions about the vitality of America's middle class as well as social and economic prospects for our youth. And, the ability of those people to afford employee benefits with heavy cost-sharing could undermine the fabric of economic security.

• *State and regional differences affect our ability to design employee benefit programs*. During the 1960s, '70s and '80s, the U.S. population shifted from the Northeast and Midwest to the South and West. Growth in the Sunbelt states was also spurred by the influx of immigrants. Over 40 percent of new immigrants during the 1980s settled in just three states—California, Texas, and Florida. While most central cities in the Northeast and Midwest lost population during the 1980s, the surrounding outer suburbs appeared to grow exponentially. New and growing residential areas often are selective of young adults who are well-educated and have high earnings potential. Left behind are some of the neediest and most vulnerable population groups. Such patterns only widen the breach between those who need supportive services and the community's capacity to pay for and staff them; and limit the ability to meet needs through employment-based programs.

Taken together, these economic and population trends will challenge the employee benefit system in the '90s and beyond, threatening continued erosion of health and retirement security.

SOCIAL SECURITY

In 1980, on the 45th anniversary of Social Security, William Driver, then commissioner of the Social Security Administration, made bold predictions about its future. "Social Security will not go bankrupt," he said. "Its benefits will continue to be the basic source of retirement income upon which people rely." The Social Security Act Amendments of 1983 brought renewed stability to the retirement portion of the program.

Predicting the future of Social Security or the stability of the entire employee benefit system has never been an easy task, but Social Security was in severe financial trouble. The Medicare portion still faces the potential of bankruptcy by the year 2000.

For the plan sponsor, the participant, and the taxpayer, the stability of Social Security has far-reaching implications. The prospects for stability are affected by numerous factors, but the level of inflation, the size and makeup of the work force, and the selected age for retirement are particularly important.

There is no easy solution to Social Security's long-term financial problems. The importance of Social Security to all elements of benefit programs and current employee compensation cannot be overstated. Should Social Security continue to absorb an ever-growing share of our nation's resources, it *will* limit the expansion of other benefit programs and take-home pay. Incremental change is likely to remain the rule. This will cause the cost of the program to go steadily upward and the resources available for other benefits to shrink.

THE EMPLOYEE'S DECISION TO RETIRE

The retirement decision is crucial for retirement income programs: it determines the amount of money required by the programs. The difference between paying benefits for 20 years versus 10 years is much greater than a doubling. Future trends, therefore, are extremely important.

What motivates a person to leave a job? What are the factors considered by an individual who has worked for 30 or 40 years and has the opportunity to decide whether to continue working or to retire? The worker must examine all sources of income, from Social Security, savings, and pensions. To the extent that the income from these sources promises to be inadequate, the worker is likely to delay retirement.

During the '90s actions are likely to be taken that will encourage later retirement. Such changes for Social Security might include relaxing the earnings test, raising the age of eligibility for initial benefits to 68 or 70, and adjusting the level of indexing.

Private-plan changes are also possible. Changes in the tax status of benefit program contributions and benefits could alter the future pattern of benefit receipt. Government could require private plans to raise the normal retirement age (with mandatory retirement eliminated, workers may want to work longer) to match Social Security.

But what are the effects of a mandatory retirement age change? Studies indicate that few older workers previously subject to mandatory retirement chose to remain on the job just because the mandatory age had been lifted to 70. The effects on firms if the worker *does* remain past the previous age limit will in large part determine whether the outlawing of mandatory retirement will encourage later retirement. This unknown will have large work force implications in the '90s and beyond.

High inflation does seem to cause persons to delay retirement. The worker may anticipate that wages will rise with prices, especially if the older worker expects several years of inflation. The worker can also anticipate that higher wages will result in higher pension benefits, so that a delay in retirement will pay off. A return of high inflation would affect retirement patterns.

Other factors affecting retirement trends are health, education, personnel policies, and changes in negotiating employee benefit plans. On the whole, health has improved, and further improvements could increase the proportion of older workers in the labor force. Were the result to increase the length of retirement rather than work, the implications for plan financing would be extremely adverse.

Older workers may desire to reduce their hours of work gradually or shift to less arduous tasks while remaining employed. Whether or not unions continue to press for subsidized early retirement features will have an effect on future retirement patterns.

The consequences of retirement age are great for all benefit programs in terms of the period of coverage, the cost of coverage, and the mix of programs. Benefit professionals should watch developing trends carefully.

DEMOGRAPHIC CHANGE

The makeup of both the retired and working populations affects all public and private benefit programs. The '70s saw the World War II Baby Boom entering the work force for the first time. The '80s saw this group in its 40s and possibly focusing for the first time on long-term security issues.

While the Social Security program is sound today, we must consider the prospects for the years beyond 2010 when this group will begin to retire. Payroll tax rates could rise to between 25 percent and 64 percent to finance the present program, dependent upon economic performance and population behavior. Should rates go this high, numerous other benefit programs could find themselves crowded out.

The '90s will be the period during which the nation begins to seriously focus upon the implications of the Baby Boom. The implications, however, go well beyond the age mix of the population.

• Due to longer life expectancies the cost of providing health care and retirement income support to current retirees is higher than expected and rising. This will continue to be the case for future retiree groups. The need for long-term care financing will gain recognition throughout the '90s.

• Changing family relationships are having, and will continue to have, a major effect on the stability and future development of benefit programs. The number of families headed by a woman is increasing, as is women's labor force participation. Child care and eldercare will both command increased attention during the '90s, as will coordination of benefits for two-earner households.

These changes will lead to greater flexibility in benefit design. The traditional model—working husband, housewife, children—around which benefit programs have been designed in the past, now applies to less than 15 percent of households. The challenge of the '90s will be designing programs that match worker desires while still providing economic security in the event of unavoidable problems (health) or poor economic planning (retirement security).

The productive work force will continue to shrink as a proportion of the total population, increasing the proportion of each worker's income that will be needed to support the young, the old, and the infirm. As the consequences of this change become more clearly understood, decision makers will be forced to make policy changes. While this began in the '80s, it is not likely to have its full effect until the '90s. Employers and the government will both continue the trend of reducing benefit promises, increasing the financial involvement of participants and beneficiaries, and focusing on catastrophic protection.

ECONOMIC CHANGE

The strength of the economy during the '90s will be a principal determinant of the future of employee benefits. A low-growth, high-unemployment, high-inflation economy like that of the '70s would carry with it very negative consequences. A brief look at those years allows one to understand why.

Inflation was a persistent problem during the '70s, averaging 7.4 percent per year and topping 14 percent in 1979. Social Security and many other public benefit programs are indexed to inflation. The 14.3 percent July 1980 adjustment, attributable to 1979 inflation, increased

Social Security costs by over 16 billion dollars per year. The July 1981 increase added approximately 17 billion dollars to annual program costs. The nation would have difficulty affording such a trend should it continue.

For private pension plans a fixed pension would lose 66 percent of its value over 10 years, and 90 percent over 20 years, at 12 percent inflation—a rate that was exceeded in the 1979–80 period.

The only real solution for retirees is the end of inflation. The same is true for active workers. Renewed inflation would jeopardize Social Security, Medicare, and both private pensions and private medical insurance. The fact that one system is indexed and the other is not does not represent a statement of success and failure. Over the long term society cannot afford the luxury of full indexing if initial benefit levels are maintained.

During the '90s, we are likely to see an acceleration of government and employer deemphasis of retirement income programs to pay for cut-back, but increasingly expensive, health programs.

GOVERNMENT REGULATION

The '70s and '80s saw a marked increase in the scope of government regulation of employee benefits—both pension and welfare programs. The movement in this area was part of a broad general expansion of the government's role in numerous areas of the economy. Many of the changes adopted were not preceded by detailed analysis of costs, benefits, or secondary consequences. Experience with the changes indicates that many carried undesired and unexpected results.

Regulatory thrusts that never succeeded were also prominent. Such was the case of government-run national health insurance and comprehensive health care cost containment.

During the '90s it is unlikely that these initiatives will be enacted into law. In addition, it is likely that regulation imposed by ERISA will be adjusted and in some cases removed.

• Reporting and disclosure requirements are likely to be reduced in cases where no apparent gain resulted from the requirement.

• Adjustments to the program of the Pension Benefit Guaranty Corporation are likely to continue as more experience with the program is gathered and excesses of the '80s lead to bankruptcies that drop pensioners at the door of the PBGC. The PBGC also is likely to be required to guarantee purchased annuities, causing higher PBGC premiums.

• Emphasis is likely to be given to making all benefit components work better together—including emphasis on integration of retirement benefit programs, disability benefit programs, and health benefit programs. For active workers and retirees this will be essential.

• Greater equity is likely to be sought for various benefit programs in terms of tax treatment, particularly retirement programs. This is likely to include maximizing flexibility of program design so that the maximum number of people are accommodated while introducing portability and limiting consumption of preretirement distributions.

• Continued attention will be given to improving the quality and cost effectiveness of health care, with special emphasis on provision for the needy and assuring that retirement, health, and income promises are kept, once made.

• Welfare reform will continue to be discussed, with reforms likely to place increased emphasis on state and local governments. In addition, the Supplemental Security Income program is likely to be expanded as a vehicle for income delivery, and Medicaid as a guarantor of health protection for poor Americans.

While the overall role of government as direct provider is not likely to *expand* significantly in the '90s, it will, however, continue to be a very active actor and will continue to impose new requirements. Knowledge of the regulatory environment will become no less necessary, the '90s will provide an excellent opportunity for study, review, and refinement, with the public and private sectors increasingly working together as partners rather than adversaries.

EMPLOYEE BENEFIT TRENDS

The period ahead will be one of challenge and change for employee benefits. Their major role in the total compensation package will be recognized, even if the characterization of ''fringe benefits'' persists. The combined effects of economic, political, and population changes will not and cannot be ignored. The dynamics of change are already in progress, with much of the '90s likely to be reinforcing.

The continued success of employment-based benefits will rest, however, on whether employers continue to focus on why they originally provided retirement and health protection—to assure economic security. During the '80s we increasingly redesigned benefits to provide employees instant gratification at the expense of long-term economic security. This trend must be reversed in the '90s if the results we seek are risk protection, economic security, worker wellness, and the ability for people to retire with dignity.

During the late 1970s a number of study groups were appointed to look at the future of components of the employee benefits world including the National Commission on Social Security (NCSS), the President's Commission on Pension Policy (PCPP), the National Commission for an Agenda for the '80s, the Minimum Wage Study Commission (MWSC), and the White House Conference On the Aging.

These groups produced well over 100 recommendations on how to "improve" employee benefit programs. The recommendations most likely to be adopted relate to incentives to encourage retirement income savings and capital formation: they deal with recognized economic problems. The keystone recommendation of the PCPP was for creation of a mandatory private pension system. Along with mandated health benefits we can expect a move toward mandatory savings to ease pressure on Social Security.

The private sector also exhibited increasing concern in the late 1970s with creation of organizations such as the Employee Benefit Research Institute (EBRI) in Washington, D.C., and development of programs such as Certified Employee Benefit Specialist (CEBS) training. Both give recognition to the growing importance of employee benefits to national and organizational policy and management.

There are already trends for the 1990s taking form that are likely to reinforce the concern noted above. They include the following:

• The management of employee benefits is increasingly recognized as an important and vital business function. As such, the function will be given increasing prominence within organizations and increasing responsibility. Employee benefits will become more of a career area, rather than a stop along the management training schedule. This should lead to increasingly responsible management of benefit programs to the advantage of employers and employees.

• Efficiency in the financing of benefit programs will be increasingly emphasized. Cost management will be the watchword. Some of these changes may be the result of legislative activity. Cutbacks in federal government expenditures will lead to "cost shifting" to other levels of government and employers, and to greater consumer choice and the development of classes of medical care. (In addition, emphasis on better health and wellness is likely to increase.)

• Efficiency in benefit design will be increasingly emphasized in an effort to eliminate and prevent overlap and to provide participants with the particular benefits they need. Depending on economic developments, this could include benefit cutbacks during the '90s. Flexible compensation and benefits will expand as cost pressures close in and as the makeup of the work force continues to change. A continuing emphasis on employee productivity will speed this trend. The challenge will be to provide flexibility while still providing economic security.

• Relatively new employee benefits, such as long-term care insurance, will be offered on an employee-pay-all basis, and preretirement counseling and financial counseling will expand as employee benefits.

• The trend toward providing supplemental defined contribution plans will continue among large employers. Small employers will continue to shift to *primary* defined contribution plans. Such plans provide a means of better accommodating relatively short-service workers. Defined benefit plans will continue to provide the base level of retirement income above Social Security for large employers' retirees. It will become increasingly important, as lump sums become more common, that those who receive lump-sum distributions preserve them or purchase annuities.

• Advances in computers and their voice simulation capabilities will lead to more understanding of programs by participants, will enhance communications, and make flexible compensation an option for the smallest employers.

• Part-time or contract employment of annuitants will be more and more common. These changes will be a natural addition to a growing emphasis on preretirement counseling and the effects of the Age Discrimination in Employment Act. Employers have increasing incentives to make retirement attractive. Retirees have now been recognized as both a growing market and as a growing political force. Both their relative numbers and life expectancies are increasing, and the market is beginning to respond.

• Employers will recognize the liability associated with retiree health benefits and move to (1) prefund them and (2) redesign them with cost-management and cost-shifting in mind. Fewer future retirees will receive retiree medical protection, beyond Medicare, paid for by a former employer.

Beyond these developments we are likely to see increasing recognition of the advantages of private-sector benefit provisions. The most striking advantage of providing benefits through the private sector is flexibility: the ability to adjust quickly to changing work-force needs. Flexible benefit programs, whether formally structured or not, are likely to become more common during the '90s to accommodate changes in the work force and employer desires to shift costs explicitly to the worker and retiree.

The public and private sectors will see increasing advantages in cooperation, coordination, and nonduplication. Regulatory and legislative initiatives are likely to be consistent with such recognition.

CONCLUSION

The vast majority of public- and private-sector workers now enjoy protection for health care. Through government programs such protection is available to nonworkers as well. And, means will develop to ensure access to protection for all individuals. The public/private mix is likely to change in the '90s, however, with more and more responsibility being placed on the individual.

Social Security now promises a floor of income protection to most workers, while nonworkers have access to Supplemental Security Income, in-kind benefits, unemployment compensation, workers' compensation, disability income, and other programs.

Supplementing these programs is an array of private income security programs. Private pensions, for example, are now participated in by over 70 percent of all steady full-time workers over age 21. Over 85 percent of those working for large employers have pensions. A quarter of present retirees now receive private pension income, and the percentage continues to grow. Public pensions provide coverage and benefits to many more workers.

Employers are also providing a wide array of additional programs discussed in this book. They help to meet the needs of tens of millions of persons. They help to maintain morale, ensure family security, and maintain employee health.

Taken together, employee benefit programs provide a blanket of protection against numerous risks. For the most part they deliver with reliability, effectiveness, and efficiency. They are an integral part of our social structure, and with prudent employer action in the '90s they will continue to be.

INDEX

Boldface numbers refer to pages in Volume I.

A

AAPPO. *See* American Association of Preferred Provider Organizations (AAPPO)

AARP. *See* American Association of Retired Persons (AARP)

ABO. *See* Accumulated benefit obligation (ABO)

Abortion, **228–29**

Abuse, alcohol and drug, **247**. *See also* Mental health/chemical dependency (MH/CD)

Accidental death and dismemberment (AD&D) insurance, **165**, 261

Accidental loss, **52**

Accident expense benefits, supplemental, **234–35**

Accidents, occupational, **252**

Accounting, 1–2, 3–42, 43–74
 accounting records, 45–46
 and administration, 262–63
 amortization of prior service cost, 16–19
 auditor's report, 59–61, 67–74
 balance sheet recognition, 20–21
 business combinations, 37–38
 and cafeteria plans, **640–41**
 commingled and master trust funds, 49
 for costs, 118–21
 defined benefit pension plans, 11–22
 defined benefit plans, 54–56
 defined contribution pension plans, 22–24, 26
 defined contribution plans, 56–58
 disclosure, 25–27
 of employee benefit plans, 1–2, 3–42, 43–74
 employers' accounting for pension costs, 3–42

and ESOP, **834–40**
 and executive retirement benefit plans, **906–14**
 extended plan year accounting, 172
 financial statement requirements, 44–45
 funding related to, 121
 GAAP. *See* Generally accepted accounting principle (GAAP)
 GASB. *See* Government Accounting Standards Board (GASB)
 glossary of terms, 7–10
 government contracts, 41–42
 for health and welfare benefit plans, 75–82
 health and welfare plans, 58–59
 historical background, 4–10
 for liabilities, 118–21
 multiemployer pension plans, 24–25, 26
 rate-regulated enterprises, 38–40
 and reporting, 43–74
 and Section 457 plans, **946**
 and self-funding, 196–99
 for settlements and curtailments, 29–37
 state and local governemnts, 40–41
 for termination benefits, 29–37
 "Accounting for ESOP Transactions," **839**

Accounting Research Bulletin, 4

Accrual, and small business, 373–75

Accrued benefit cost method, 103–4

Accrued benefits method, 102

Accrued liability, 99

Accumulated benefit obligation (ABO), 7

Accumulation, **30**, **548**, 229–30

Achievement awards, **590**

ACP. *See* Average contribution percentage (ACP)